Applied Economics and Policy Studies

Series Editors

Xuezheng Qin⬤, *School of Economics, Peking University, Beijing, China*
Chunhui Yuan, *School of Economics and Management, Beijing University of Posts and Telecommunications, Beijing, China*
Xiaolong Li, *Department of Postal Management, Beijing University of Posts and Telecommunications, Beijing, China*

The Applied Economics and Policy Studies present latest theoretical and methodological discussions to bear on the scholarly works covering economic theories, econometric analyses, as well as multifaceted issues arising out of emerging concerns from different industries and debates surrounding latest policies. Situated at the forefront of the interdisciplinary fields of applied economics and policy studies, this book series seeks to bring together the scholarly insights centering on economic development, infrastructure development, macroeconomic policy, governance of welfare policy, policies and governance of emerging markets, and relevant subfields that trace to the discipline of applied economics, public policy, policy studies, and combined fields of the aforementioned. The book series of Applied Economics and Policy Studies is dedicated to the gathering of intellectual views by scholars and poli-cymakers. The publications included are relevant for scholars, policymakers, and students of economics, policy studies, and otherwise interdisciplinary programs.

Xiaolong Li · Chunhui Yuan · John Kent
Editors

Proceedings of the 7th International Conference on Economic Management and Green Development

Set 2

Springer

Editors
Xiaolong Li
Department of Postal Management
Beijing University of Posts
and Telecommunications
Beijing, China

Chunhui Yuan
School of Economics and Management
Beijing University of Posts
and Telecommunications
Beijing, China

John Kent
Supply Chain Management
University of Arkansas
Fayetteville, NC, USA

ISSN 2731-4006　　　　　　ISSN 2731-4014 (electronic)
Applied Economics and Policy Studies
ISBN 978-981-97-0522-1　　　ISBN 978-981-97-0523-8 (eBook)
https://doi.org/10.1007/978-981-97-0523-8

© The Editor(s) (if applicable) and The Author(s), under exclusive license
to Springer Nature Singapore Pte Ltd. 2024

This work is subject to copyright. All rights are solely and exclusively licensed by the Publisher, whether the whole or part of the material is concerned, specifically the rights of translation, reprinting, reuse of illustrations, recitation, broadcasting, reproduction on microfilms or in any other physical way, and transmission or information storage and retrieval, electronic adaptation, computer software, or by similar or dissimilar methodology now known or hereafter developed.
The use of general descriptive names, registered names, trademarks, service marks, etc. in this publication does not imply, even in the absence of a specific statement, that such names are exempt from the relevant protective laws and regulations and therefore free for general use.
The publisher, the authors, and the editors are safe to assume that the advice and information in this book are believed to be true and accurate at the date of publication. Neither the publisher nor the authors or the editors give a warranty, expressed or implied, with respect to the material contained herein or for any errors or omissions that may have been made. The publisher remains neutral with regard to jurisdictional claims in published maps and institutional affiliations.

This Springer imprint is published by the registered company Springer Nature Singapore Pte Ltd.
The registered company address is: 152 Beach Road, #21-01/04 Gateway East, Singapore 189721, Singapore

Paper in this product is recyclable.

Contents

International NGO Issues on Female Migrant Workers 1
   Yinwei Li

Time Lagged Effects of ESG Scores and Investor Attention on Stock
Returns 9
   Jiaqi Liu

Analyzing Reasons for the Selection of Investment Objects Based
on the Construction of Enterprise Ecological Value Network 18
   Caixiaoyang Ge

Analysis of the Motivation and Performance of Merger
and Reorganization of Companies Under Performance
Commitment--Based on the Dual Case Study of DF Company's
Acquisition of Pride and Fosber 27
   Liu Yu

Monetary Policy Regulation and Macroeconomic
Fluctuations—Empirical Research Based on VAR Model 41
   Xiaochen Liu

Recession Risk Prediction with Machine Learning and Big Panel Data 63
   Yunhao Yang

Investigate the Relationship Between Financial Risk and Financial
Performance: An Insight of China Life Insurance Company 88
   Shikang Wang

Model Innovation and Value Creation in E-commerce Platform
Ecosystems: A Case Study of Douyin 98
   Jiahang Hu and Yiming Zhong

An Investigation into the Relationship Between Transportation Network
and Economic Agglomeration 108
   Chenhao Zheng

A Study of the Dual Carbon Target and Green Finance Development
in Jiangxi Province 119
   Liwen Dai

Dynamic Correlation, Volatility Spillover Inside UK Capital Markets 129
  Mingze Yuan and Ziqi Guo

Challenges and Opportunities of Digital Construction of Chinese
Grassroots Government in the Information Age – Taking
the Construction of "Four Platforms" in Zhejiang Province as an Example 137
  Zhuofan Zong

Research on the Impact of Digitalization on Individual Investors'
Behavior from the Perspective of Behavioral Finance 146
  Zhihan Zhao

A Review of ESG Research in China: From the Perspective of Chinese
Enterprises 155
  Daoer Wang

PIC Planning Model and Geographic Information System Applied
on the Old District Renovation Using Intelligent Data Analysis 168
  Junyuan Li, Zihao Ma, and Xiyuan Zhang

Agriculture Trade Competitiveness, and Influencing Economic Factors:
A Study on China's Agricultural Trade 180
  Benjamin Kofi Tawiah Edjah

Financial Cloud Drives Digital Transformation of Enterprises:
——Taking Hisense's Application of Kingdee Financial Cloud
as an Example 188
  BoYong Chen and Zhuohao Zhang

Study on the Influence of Rural Revitalization on Regional Tourism
Development: An Empirical Analysis Based on the Data of 16
Prefectures in Yunnan Province 199
  Qing Wang

The Discussion of the Impact on the Stock Price After the Comments
or Recommendations from Stock Analysts–The Case Study on EV Stocks 214
  Jiaxi Zhang

The Effects of Transforming the CDMO Strategy on the Business
Performance of Porton Based on Financial Statement Analysis 224
  Lei Zhang

Economic Policy Uncertainty, ESG, and Corporate Performance 235
  Fumian Huang

Identification and Analysis of Risk Spillover Effect of Commercial
Banks in China 247
    Moran Wang

Case Analysis of Kingfisher PLC's Operational Quality Based
on the Perspective of Financial Report 253
    Xinyi Song

Comedic Violence Advertisement and Limiting Factors 262
    Yuting Tong

The Impacts of Goal Setting on Enterprises from a Corporate Social
Responsibility Perspective 273
    Yu Chen

Behavioral Economics and Macroeconomics: Relationship Identification
by Case of Economy Crisis in 2008 280
    Haocheng Yan

The Impact of Endogenous Sentiment on US Stock Market Trading
Volume 291
    Lvqin Huang

The Factors Affecting Electric Vehicle Adoption in the United States,
2016–2021 299
    Qing Hou, Shuai Zhou, and Guangqing Chi

Assessing Endowment Effect in Different Cooperative Settings 307
    Fengyi Zhang

The Primary Performance Trait of Corporations with High Managerial
Short-Termism 314
    Yuping Wang

Research on the Factors Affecting Inequality – Evidence from China ... 321
    Gengqiang Xiao

Accounting Measurement and Recognition of Digital Cryptocurrencies:
Challenges, Practices, and Recommendations 328
    Jiajun Ma

Study on the Spillover Effect of Shanghai Crude Oil Futures Price
Fluctuations on New Energy Stock Prices 338
    Zhang Xinyu

Exploring the Impact of Social Economic Status on Migrant Workers'
Sense of Social Equity from the Economic Sociology Perspective 350
   Hu Xinrui

Microeconomic Study of the Digital Economy's Importance
on Manufacturers' Management 365
   Yuyan Wang

Fintech Development and Corporate Innovation 373
   Chen Huan

Analysts' Characteristics and Forecast ability–An Empirical Study
from China's A-Share Market 382
   Mengyan Lei

Is There Salary Discrimination by Race and Nationality in the NBA?
A New Approach 391
   JiaYou Liang, ShuaiJie Zhao, and HaoYuan Zhu

Choice Overload Paradox in Online Shopping Environment 400
   Jiaxin Wang, Fang Han, Manting Ding, and Jia Zhang

The Influence of Endowment Effect on the Investment Decisions
in Hybrid Funds 414
   Huiqi Zhang

Research on Empowering Huawei's Financial Transformation
by Financial Shared Service Center 421
   Yiru Su

A Study on the Relevance of Corporate Solvency – A Case Study
of Procter & Gamble 431
   Huangzhiyi Zhang

ESG Performance Under Economic Policy Uncertainty: An Empirical
Study of Chinese Corporations 443
   Song Qiuge

Relationship Between Macroeconomy and Stock Market in the United
States 456
   Lixiang Zheng

Research on the Activated Utilization and Digital Innovation
Development of Cultural Heritage Under the Concept of Sustainable
Development 466
 Yuting Yu

Analysis of the Reasons for the Development of the New Energy
Vehicle Industry and Prospects —Taking BYD as an Example 478
 Boyu Liu

Challenges of Stock Prediction Based on LSTM Neural Network 490
 Rufeng Chen

Explore the Impact of Natural Factors on the Use of Shared Bicycles 500
 Liu Jiamei

Economic Dynamics Analysis of Higher Education Development 511
 Tian Mo

The Impact of Fintech on Enterprise Innovation: Take Companies
that Issue Fintech Concept Stocks as an Example 521
 Yuyao Sun

Resilience Assessment of the South-to-North Water Diversion Central
Route Project by Using Urban Futures Method 534
 Qiaozhi Zhang

Research on Factors Influencing the Rewarding Behavior of Virtual
Anchors' Fans 544
 Xinran Zhao

Analyzing the Reasons of BYD's Low-Profit Margin Through Financial
Data 555
 Tianqi Ma

Analysis and Forecast of USD/EUR Exchange Rate Based on ARIMA
and GARCH Models 566
 Jiatong Li, Jiawen Yin, and Rui Zhang

Forecasts on Euro-to-USD Exchange Rate Based on the ARIMA Model 576
 Qiaoyu Xie

Analysis and Forecasting of Exchange Rate Between Yuan and Dollar 588
 Sitian Yi

Forecast of China's Real Estate Industry Development Situation Based
on ARIMA Model: Taking Vanke as an Example 598
    Xiangyu Li

US Trade Balance Analysis on Imports and Exports Based on ETS
and ARIMA Models 611
    Shiqi Fan

Research on the Factors Affecting Mobility Rate Across States
in the United States 626
    Xinyu Shi

Exploring the Risks of Blockchain to the Financial Market and Its
Countermeasures 633
    Yujiang Duan, Fengfan Ge, and Zhixing Wen

To a Decentralized Future: Benefits that Blockchain Could Endow
the Financing World 642
    Yiping Li, Yuqing Liu, Ruixuan Sun, and Zihui Xu

Relevance Between ESG Scores and Annual Turnover: Evidence
from 453 Industrial Hong Kong Stocks 652
    Nanqi Liu, Changyou Qi, and Junjie Zhuge

How Does Years Since Immigration to the U.S.A. Affect Hourly Wage? 662
    Shizhe Lyu

A Controversy in Sustainable Development: How Does Gender
Diversity Affect the ESG Disclosure? 669
    Bolin Fu, Keqing Wang, and Tianxin Zhou

Controlling Shareholders' Equity Pledges, Environmental Regulations
and Corporate Green Performance—Based on Data from Listed
Companies in Highly Polluting Industries 679
    Mingfei Chen

ESG Performance's Effect on the Firm Performance the Evidence
from Chinese A-share Market 690
    Liqi Dong

The Factors Influence Purchase Intentions from the Consumer's
Perspective and the Characteristics of Green Buyers 702
    Ziyao Yang

A Study on the Motivation and Financial Performance of Haidilao's
Equity Crave-Out 716
   Tingxuan Dong

Study on the Reasons for the Failure of the Audit of Luckin Coffee
and Suggestions for Countermeasures 729
   Yufan Li

Baidu's Financial Competitiveness Research Based on DuPont Analysis
Method 738
   Yuqing Zhang

The Impact of COVID-19 on the Aviation Industry: Event Study on U.S.
Passenger Airline Stocks 752
   Yuxin Chen and Ziqing Gong

Predicting Customer Churn in a Telecommunications Company Using
Machine Learning 771
   Yinming Wu

Research on Real Estate Price Index Forecasting Based on ARIMA
Model: Taking Los Angeles as an Example 784
   Xiao Han

Research on the Reasons for Abnormal Changes in the Operation Status
of Domino's Pizza 796
   Yining Feng, Yunong Li, Jingyu Qin, and Yuankai Tao

Detect the Change Points in the Growth Rate of US Real Export Data
Based on Mean and Variance 804
   Yiwei Zhang

Forecasting the Stock Market Index with Dynamic ARIMA Model
and LSTM Model 815
   Siyuan Zhu

Public Goods Game Based on the Combination Model of Reputation
and Punishment 828
   Qing Liu

The Stylized Facts of Income Inequality in Mainland China, Korea
and Taiwan: Development and Comparison 836
   Yanshu Wang

Factors Influence Loan Default–A Credit Risk Analysis 849
Xianya Qi

An Empirical Analysis of the Causal Relationship Between Equity
Incentives and Idiosyncratic Volatility in Chinese A-Share Listed
Companies 863
Zhaoxuan Gan

An Empirical Analysis of the Relationship Between Chinese GDP
and Deposit Savings 873
Yichuan Bai

FinTech Promotes the Development of Green Finance 885
Heqing Huang and Qijie Yang

Comprehensive Analysis of China's Local Government Financing
Vehicle Debt 893
Zihao Tang

The Relationship Between ESG Ratings and Financial Performance
of Coal Firms — the Case of China Shenhua and China Coal Energy 903
Aimiao Zhang

Research on the Impact of Regulatory Inquiries Related to Information
Disclosure of Listed Companies – A Case Study of ANDON HEALTH 915
Miaoxuan Ma

Research on Financial Competitiveness of a Listed Company Based
on DuPont Analysis Method 925
Yile Kong and Xitong Zhu

Time Series Analysis in Pfizer Stock Prices in the Pre-
and Post-COVID-19 Scenarios 937
Rixin Su

Stacking-Based Model for House Price Prediction 947
Yiqian Zhou

A Dynamic Game Study on the "Big Data Discriminatory Pricing"
Behavior of E-commerce Platforms Under Government Regulation 959
Zhuang Yao

Analysis on Marketing Strategy of Chinese Online Music Platform–QQ
Music 969
Jiayi Hong

The Causality Between Executive Compensation, Equity Concentration,
and Corporate Performance: A Multiple Regression Analysis 977
  Xiao Rao

Exploring the Interplay Between Inflation, Energy Prices,
and COVID-19 Amidst the Ukraine Conflict 986
  Zeyao Li

An Empirical Analysis of Asset Pricing Models 998
  Ziqi Chen, Zhenwu Sun, and Xiaoyu Wang

The Empirical Analysis of Asset Pricing Models in the Asia-Pacific
Stock Market Under COVID-19 1008
  Hui Wang

The Impact of Technological Change on Labour Market Outcomes
and Income Inequality in China: An Empirical Analysis 1018
  Xueyao Tong

The "Strong" Development of RMB 1025
  Shengran Huang

Research on Business Value Assessment Model for New Generation Star 1035
  Ziyi Xing

Fiduciary Duty Regime of Private Fund Managers: Insights from the US
Regulatory Experience 1043
  Jia Cheng

The Impact of Capital Globalization on Green Innovation:
A Cross-Country Empirical Analysis 1054
  Yuyang Yuan

Financing Constraints, Local Government Debt, and Corporate Stock
Returns: An Empirical Analysis 1064
  Yike Lu

Sustainable Supply Chains: A Comprehensive Analyse of Drivers
and Practices 1075
  Qichao Gong, Yuxi Wang, and Yuli Zhu

Innovating Online Operational Models for Independent Hotels:
Assessing the Feasibility of a "Regional Independent Hotel Network
Alliance" in Yunnan 1083
  Qijing Li

Supply Chain Management in the Era of "Internet+": Case Analysis
of Agricultural Product Supply Chain 1094
   Huimin Liu, Yangmeng Liu, and Siyan Yi

An Empirical Study on the Causes of Default of US Dollar Debt
in the China's Property Based on Z-score Model 1102
   Yijing Wang

The Influence of Key Opinion Leaders on High-End Beauty Brands
in the Age of Self-media 1112
   Xilin Liu, Haonan Qian, and Haoyun Wen

Supply Chain Risk Management Process: Case Study of the Chinese
Aviation Industry in COVID-19 1120
   Jiangjia Xu

The Marketing Value of User-Generated Content in the Mobile Industry 1130
   Le Han, Zhuoer Wei, and Shuyan Zhang

Direct Carbon Emissions, Indirect Carbon Emissions, and International
Trade: An Analysis of OECD Member Countries 1143
   Yirong Xi

To What Extent Can We Use Google Trends to Predict Inflation
Statistically? 1156
   Minrui Huang and David Tai Li

A Literature Review on the Model of EGARCH-MIDAS, LMM, GBM
for Stock Market Prediction 1175
   Yingtong Wang

The Impact of Changes in Sales Prices of Non-durable Goods
on Consumers' Purchase Intentions When Using Online Shopping
Platforms 1185
   Zehao Xu

Analyzing Problems and Strategies of International Organizations
in Global Governance and Cooperation – Taking UNDP as an Example 1197
   Haosen Xu

Implementation of Monte-Carlo Simulations in Economy and Finance 1206
   Jintian Zhang

InstaCart Analysis: Use PCA with K-Means to Segment Grocery
Customers 1218
   Chenyu Lang

Research on the Influencing Factors of Housing Prices Based
on Multiple Regression: Taking Chongqing as an Example 1231
   Yijia Qi

Game Analysis of Cross-Border Entry of Enterprises into New Markets:
Case Study of Bytedance 1242
   Feiyue Lei and Lu Meng

Research on the Effectiveness of Clarifying Rumors by Listed
Companies in the Pharmaceutical Industry – Taking the Market
Reaction of Ling Pharmaceutical as an Example 1252
   Chuhan Wang, Beining Xu, and Qianwen Zhang

The Relationship Between ESG Performance and Financial Constraints
and Its Impact on Firm Value 1265
   Shengyang Qu

A Study on the Relationship Between ESG Performance and Stock
Returns – Take A-share Listed Company Stocks as the Example 1274
   Liqi Dong, Shifeng Deng, and Qian Gao

Digital Transformation in the New Energy Industry for Sustainable
Development: A Grounded Theory Analysis 1285
   Ming Liu

Causality Between Board Features and Corporate Innovation Level:
Empirical Evidence from Listed Companies in China 1295
   Zicheng Bu

Analysis of the Impact of Digital Inclusive Finance on Farmers' Income
Growth - An Empirical Analysis Based on 31 Provinces in China 1303
   Yuhan Sun

The Energy Consumption and Economic Growth 1315
   Yiguo Huang, Yizhen Zhang, and Heyu Cai

Research on the Merger and Acquisition Performance and Brand
Management of Cross-Border LBO—Take Qumei Home's Acquisition
of Norwegian Ekornes Company as an Example 1327
   Runbang Liu

The Impact of Investor Sentiment on Stock Returns 1361
    Xinran Fu

The Impact of Digitisation Degree on Agricultural Science
and Technology Innovation: Based on Panel Data of 31 Provinces
in China 1371
    Lanjie Huang

An Empirical Study on the Impact of Behavioural Bias on Investment
Decision-Making 1382
    Chutian Li

Matrix Factorization Model in Collaborative Filtering Algorithms
Based on Feedback Datasets 1405
    Yuqing Hu

Research on the Mall Customers Segmentation Based on K-means
and DBSCAN 1413
    Yifan Wang

Valuation and Analysis of the Canadian Banking Sector During
the COVID-19 Pandemic 1426
    Bo He

ChatGPT Concept Industry Valuation Analysis: Evidence from iFlytek
and Kunlun 1437
    Yajing Chen

Optimizing Trading Recommendations in Portfolio Trading: A Bilateral
Matching Theory Approach 1445
    Wenzheng Liu

The Impact of "Three Arrows" Policies on China's Real Estate Market:
An Event Study 1455
    Zixuan Wang, Yangjie Jin, and Jianuo Su

Corporate Social Responsibility Disclosure Quality and Stock Price
Crash Risk: Evidence from China 1474
    Minxing Zhu

An Analysis of the Effect of Social Medical Insurance on Family
Consumption 1491
    Siyun Yuan

The Influence of Impulsive Purchase on the Consumption Behaviour in Social Media 1503
   Sirui Wang

Analysis of the Reasons of HNA Group's Bankruptcy and Future Prevention Measures for Enterprises 1513
   Jiaheng Zhang

Cognitive Biases in Second-Hand and Pre-sale Real Estate Prices in Nanjing 1522
   Bing Shen

How Targeted Poverty Alleviation Policy Program and Other Possible Factors Affect the Wellbeing of Chinese Seniors 1530
   Xinru Fang

Investor Sentiment, Idiosyncratic Risk, and Stock Returns: Evidence from Australia 1548
   Aiqi Li

Sovereign CDS Spreads and Covid-19 Pandemic 1559
   Ying Xi

Portfolio Optimization for Major Industries in American Capital Market 1570
   Xinyi Liu

The Impact of Investor Sentiment on Stock Returns Based on Machine Learning and Deep Learning Methods 1577
   Xiangjun Chen

An Empirical Research on the Impact of ESG Performance on Chinese Stock Market 1597
   Jiayun Yin

Research on the Application of Artificial Intelligence Technology in Risk Management of Commercial Banks 1606
   Wensi Huang, Yiling Shi, and Wenjie Zhou

Exploring the Development Rule of GDP Based on Time-series Moran's Index 1616
   Zhengjie Zang

An Empirical Study of U.S. Stock Market Forecasts and Trend Trading Strategies Based on ARIMA Model 1630
   Siying Wang

Impact of 5G Commercial License Issuance on Stock Prices of Related
Listed Companies: Using Difference-in-Differences Model 1641
    Xi Zhou

Socio-Economic Determinants of National Saving in Pakistan 1649
    Munir Ahmad and Asghar Ali

Research on the Influence Mechanism of Experiential Interaction
on Consumers' Impulsive Buying 1664
    Liang Chen

A Qualitative Study on How the Covid-19 Pandemic Has Helped
in the Enablement of Entrepreneurial Ambitions Among Chinese
Entrepreneurs 1675
    Xiaodan Wang

The Application of Price-Earnings Ratio in Hong Kong Hang Seng
Index Futures Trading Strategy 1684
    Yishan Hou, Yifei Xu, and Shuye Zhou

The Effect of Governance Dimension of ESG on Corporate Performance 1694
    Huijia Zhang and Keyou Pang

Impact of Green Financing and Public Policies Towards Investment
Yield: Evidence from European and Asian Economies 1705
    Mirza Nasir Jahan Mehdi and Syed Ali Raza Hamid

The Long and Short Term Impact of COVID-19 on E-Commerce
and Retail Industries for US 1720
    Zixuan Li, Chenwen Song, and Tianrui Xiao

An Exploration of Bank Failure in Silicon Valley and the Interaction
of Failure Factors - Empirical Analysis Based on VAR Model 1746
    Tianqi Peng

Prediction of Lending Club Loan Defaulters 1765
    Xueyan Wang

Research on the CRE of China's Carbon Trading Pilot Policy 1778
    Jiayue Jiang, Meixin Wang, Mengzhen Xiao, Yuwei Yang, and Dan Wei

IEEE-CIS Fraud Detection Based on XGB 1785
    Zhijia Xiao

Unraveling the Link Between Federal Reserve Interest Rate Hikes
and the Chinese Stock Market 1797
   Jialin Li

Stock Market Volatility During and After the Covid-19 Pandemic:
Academic Perspectives 1809
   Yining Yang

Unveiling the Effects of the China-US Trade Conflict: A Comparative
Study of Stock Market Behaviors in the United States and China 1818
   Shuying Chen

Financial Analysis and Strategic Forecast of Tesla, Inc. 1831
   Xiaoke Wang

Mechanisms and Strategies of Smart Governance for Improving Urban
Resilience 1842
   Jianhang Du, Yongheng Hu, and Longzheng Du

The Impact of Low Carbon Economic Development on the Income
Gap Between Urban and Rural Residents - An Empirical Study Based
on Inter-provincial Panel Data in China 1848
   Yang Chengye

Addressing Credit Fraud Threat: Detected Through Supervised Machine
Learning Model 1863
   Yihan Yang

The Impact Caused by the COVID-19 Pandemic Re-opening on Catering
Industry in China: A Short-Term Perspective 1873
   Shiqi Pan

The Impact of the Russia-Ukraine War on Tesla: Evidence from ARIMA
Model 1882
   Jintian He

Research on the Link Between RMB Exchange Rate and Tesla's Stock
Price: A Long-Term Perspective 1893
   Jinhao Yu

Dynamic Impact of the Covid-19 on Cryptocurrency and Investment
Suggestion 1903
   Haozhe Hong

Research on the Relationship Between Chinese and American Stock
Markets: Spillover Effects of Returns and Volatility 1914
    Lin Liu

Research on the Impact of China's Industrial Structure Upgrading
on the Balance of Payments Structure 1924
    Yimeng Wang

The Impact of Digital Economy on Industrial Agglomeration 1933
    Yuting Huang and Kaixvan Ma

Analysis of Influencing Factors of Housing Affordability Crisis
in Vancouver 1949
    Jiaxuan Chen

Analysis of the Impact of Female Executives on Corporate Financial
Leverage 1960
    XiangLin Cheng

Corporate Social Responsibility and Financial Performance: Evidence
from Listed Firms in China 1971
    Jiali Wang

The External Shock of the Epidemic on Employees' Turnover Intention
in Central-Dominated China: The Mediating Effect of Automation
and Teleworking 1987
    Xinyu Chen

Research on the Mechanism of Farmers' Interest Linkage in Agricultural
Technology Transformation 2001
    Yuanyuan Chen

Analysis of Spatio-Temporal Evolution Patterns in the Green
Development of Cluster-Type Cities: A Case Study of Zibo City in China 2010
    Minne Liu

Correlation Between Chinese Outbound Tourism Numbers and Chinese
Outward Foreign Direct Investment Study 2021
    Peili Yu

Volatility Analysis Using High-Frequency Financial Data 2031
    Junchi Wang

Can Environmental, Social and Governance Performance Alleviate
Financial Dilemma? 2043
    Junyi Wang

Reinforcement Learning for E-Commerce Dynamic Pricing 2051
    Hongxi Liu

Impact of ESG Performance on Firm Value and Its Transmission
Mechanism: Research Based on Industry Heterogeneity 2061
    Xingzhuo Liu

Author Index 2071

ESG Performance's Effect on the Firm Performance the Evidence from Chinese A-share Market

Liqi Dong(✉)

The University of Melbourne, Grattan Street Parkville, Melbourne, VIC 3010, Australia
liqid@student.unimelb.edu.au

Abstract. Global agreement has emerged on the need to create a green finance system to promote sustainable development. The concept of ESG (Environmental, social and governance) is accepted by the bulk of companies and investors. However, the effect of ESG performance on the firm performance is still not clear. This paper studies this effect with the historical data of 286 Chinese enterprises with A-share listings from 2011 to 2021. The result shows that improving of the company's ESG performance will lead to higher enterprise performance, especially on the increasing of Tobin's Q. In addition, the individual Social and Governance score both have a significant impact on the enterprise performance. Through further analysis, in the ESG requirements sensitive industries, for example, the high carbon industry, the ESG performance has a greater influence on the firm performance than that of ESG requirements non-sensitive industries. Therefore, especially for the company within the sensitive industry, the firm can improve its firm performance through improve its ESG performance.

Keywords: ESG performance · Firm performance · China's A-share market

1 Introduction

Global climate, environment, and energy crises have recently brought challenges to the stability of the whole economic system. Global agreement has emerged on the need to create a green finance system to promote sustainable development. Environmental, social, and corporate governance (ESG), a crucial element of the green financing system, is the evaluation of an organization's internal corporate governance, social responsibility, and environmental protection, based on information that has been made publicly available by the organization.

Specifically, good ESG performance will contribute to environmental improvement, better corporate governance, and maintaining societal stability and development, reflecting the relevance of businesses actively engaging in social responsibility. As a result, the creation and management of such businesses adhere to the idea of sustainable development and are appropriate for long-term value investments [1].

Nonetheless, there is conflicting data linking ESG practices to financial performance [2]. Investors still need to have a clear grasp of how to utilize ESG data responsibly [3].

Despite the fact that several studies have demonstrated that good ESG performance has a positive influence on a company's performance [4], some have also shown negative or minor impacts [5].

This study seeks to accomplish two goals. The study will first assess how ESG performance affects business performance. Second, this study will compare how much the performance of ESG factors in ESG requirement sensitive and non-sensitive sectors affects business performance.

This study's key contribution is to offer proof of the influence of ESG on business performance in Chinese A-share listed market and to further investigate the influence of ESG performance on business performance in sensitive and non-sensitive industries.

2 Literature Review and Hypothesis

The fundamental explanation for why corporations publish their ESG initiatives is the stakeholder theory. As a result of their status as a vital component of society, businesses now place a greater emphasis on serving all stakeholders' interests rather than just maximizing shareholder wealth [6]. According to the stakeholder hypothesis, businesses gain competitive advantages by maintaining positive connections with their stakeholders [7]. Its significance has also been emphasized by the crises that have occurred over the last few decades and, most recently, the COVID-19 epidemic. Due to the problems, ESG has been more widely accepted as a method of conducting business and have expanded internationally [5].

In this sense, managers prioritize ESG practice disclosure since it generates value for multiple stakeholders by limiting the future risk of the firm. Moreover, improved ESG disclosure creates a competitive advantage and increases stakeholder trust by presenting a favorable picture of corporate accountability [8].

The influence of ESG performance on financial performance of enterprises has been the subject of several research. Businesses may experience improvements, competitive advantages, and improved reputations if they disclose more information about ESG issues, invest more in CSR, and actually implement sustainable business practices. For instance, efficient resource usage and employee happiness may boost effectiveness, which in turn spurs innovation [9]. Also, it can save pointless expenditures and provide greater earnings, which improves financial performance.

The majority of the empirical research examining how ESG affects company performance is conducted in industrialized nations, particularly in the United States. An analysis of listed businesses from EU members revealed a positive correlation between ESG performance and corporate performance [10]. Similar outcomes were found by Sidhoum and Serra [11], which implies that improving working conditions, environmentally friendly initiatives, and balancing stakeholder interests are the key factors in boosting enterprise value. Similar to this, the findings of Ferrat et al. [12] analysis of company portfolios in the United States point to the possibility for businesses to increase both long- and short-term profitability by enhancing ESG behavior. The study also demonstrates the beneficial impacts of the S and G dimensions on company performance in terms of specific ESG components, however, the governance element takes longer to manifest its effects than the social aspect.

Another empirical study by Cupertino et al. [13] in the context of U.S. manufacturing enterprises found that high E and S ratings and strong ESG scores had a beneficial impact on firms' investment, which mitigating the detrimental effects of financialization on the accumulation of the capital and encourages long-term value-adding activity.

Contrary to the supportive research, however, ESG performance is discovered to be adversely related to financial performance [14].

According to literatures, the majority of researchers discovered that ESG performance had a favorable effect on company performance in established and emerging markets. However there haven't been many studies done in China. In order to evaluate ESG performance's effect on business performance with a sample of enterprises listed in China's A-share, the following research hypothesis is developed in this study:

H1. ESG performance and enterprise performance are positively correlated.

H2. Components of ESG performance and enterprise performance are positively correlated.

Despite the fact that a vast body of empirical data indicates that ESG performance has a beneficial influence on firm success, there is a dearth of study on the extent of the effect of ESG performance on enterprise performance in different industries. Hence, in this investigation, the following hypothesis is put out.

H3. In comparison to non-sensitive sectors, ESG performance has a stronger influence on business performance in sensitive industries.

This paper divides industries into sensitive and non-sensitive industries according to their different sensitivities to ESG requirements [15]. Sensitive industries are those that use a lot of natural resources in production and have an adverse effect on ecosystem viability. The activities of these industries also have environmental and social-economic sustainability impacts.

3 Methodology

3.1 DataSample and Source

The sample examined in the study is the historical data of 286 Chinese A-share listed enterprises from 2011 to 2021.

The ESG score is provided by Wind database, which is updated once a year and covers 100% A-share listed companies. The scoring system contains 3 primary indexes, 16 secondary indexes, over 40 tertiary indexes and above 300 bottom indicators. The main categories are Environment, Social and Governance. The Environment category considers climate change, resource utilization and other environmental performance of the firm to evaluate the degree of environmentally friendly of the firm. The Social category involves human capital, product liability and other indicators related with the society to evaluate the society contribution of the firm. The Governance category includes governance structure, disclosure quality and other governance quality indexes to measure the governance level of the firm. All individual category score ranges from 0 to 100. The weighted average score of the three categories serves as the foundation for the ESG score.

The accounting data is provided by CSMAR database, which is annual.

3.2 Measurement of Variables

As this research tries to assess the effect of firm's ESG performance on its performance, the response variable is the firm performance. ROA, ROE and Tobin's q are the performance metrics of the business employed in this study [16]. Specifically, ROA and ROE are accounting-based metrics. Tobin's q is market-based measurement. The combining of two types of measure can give a relatively comprehensive evaluation of the firm performance.

ROA is computed as the net income of the enterprise divided by its total assets, which measures the profitability of the firm. A higher ROA suggests the firm uses its total assets to create profitability more efficiently. Thus, the firm is better for long-term investment. ROE measures the level of return on owner's equity of a firm, which is computed by dividing the equity by the net income.

Tobin's q is determined by the market value of assets divided by their book value. The calculation of the market value is a relatively complex process; therefore, this study uses the sum of asset book value and the discrepancy between the market value and book value of common stocks [17]. A higher Tobin's q suggests that the firm manages its resources and capabilities more efficiently and asset values are greater than their replacement costs.

According to the literature examining the link between ESG and enterprise performance, specific variables will be involved in the model as the control variables [5, 8]. This study selects the size, debt ratio, age, capital expenditure situation and sales growth rate of the firm. Specifically, the natural logarithm of the company's total assets is used to calculate its size. The large-scale company is more likely to have a better financial performance. Total debt divided by total assets is calculated as the debt ratio. A lower debt ratio implies that the company is steady and suitable for long-term investment. The age is calculated by the observation year minus the incorporated year of the firm. The older a company is, the more likely it has a better and steady firm performance. The capital expenditure situation is the operating cash flow to the capital expenditure of the firm. It evaluates the ability of the firm to utilize its cash flow and measure the enterprise's capacity to operate for the long term. The higher of the indicator suggests the steadier of the firm. The sales growth rate is calculated by (Salest-Salest-1)/Salest-1 * 100%. A higher sales growth rate will imply that the firm has a better investment prospect (see Table 1).

3.3 Model

The effect of ESG performance on enterprise performance will be tested within three master models as followings:

$$Model\ 1\ ROA_t = \beta_0 + \beta_1 ESG_{t-1} + \beta_2 SIZE_t + \beta_3 DEBT_t + \beta_4 AGE_t + \beta_5 Capex_t + \beta_6 SG_t + \varepsilon_t$$

$$Model\ 2\ ROE_t = \beta_0 + \beta_1 ESG_{t-1} + \beta_2 SIZE_t + \beta_3 DEBT_t + \beta_4 AGE_t + \beta_5 Capex_t + \beta_6 SG_t + \varepsilon_t$$

Table 1. Variable explanation.

	Variable	Measure
Explained variable	ROA	Net income/Total assets
	ROE	Net income/Equity
	Tobin's q	(The book value of assets + the market value of common stocks - the book value of common stocks)/book value of assets
Explanatory variable	ESG	The ESG score of the firm. The weighted average score for each individual environment, social and governance factors, between 0 and 100
	ENV	Individual Environment score, ranging from 0 to 100
	SOC	Individual Social score, ranging from 0 to 100
	GOV	Individual Governance score, ranging from 0 to 100
Control variable	SIZE	Log (total assets)
	DEBT	Total debt/Total assets
	AGE	The observation year – the incorporated year of the firm
	Capex	Operating cash flow/Capital expenditure
	SG	(Salest-Salest-1)/Salest-1 * 100%

$$Model\ 3\ Tobin'sq_t = \beta_0 + \beta_1 ESG_{t-1} + \beta_2 SIZE_t + \beta_3 DEBT_t + \beta_4 AGE_t + \beta_5 Capex_t + \beta_6 SG_t + \varepsilon_t$$

where the ESG score is lagged one period to diminish the endogenous [18].

Each master model has three secondary models to evaluate the correlation between three individual score, namely Environment, Social and Governance score, and the firm performance.

$$Model\ 1.1\ ROA_t = \beta_0 + \beta_1 ENV_{t-1} + \beta_2 SIZE_t + \beta_3 DEBT_t + \beta_4 AGE_t + \beta_5 Capex_t + \beta_6 SG_t + \varepsilon_t$$

$$Model\ 1.2\ ROA_t = \beta_0 + \beta_1 SOC_{t-1} + \beta_2 SIZE_t + \beta_3 DEBT_t + \beta_4 AGE_t + \beta_5 Capex_t + \beta_6 SG_t + \varepsilon_t$$

$$Model\ 1.3\ ROA_t = \beta_0 + \beta_1 GOV_{t-1} + \beta_2 SIZE_t + \beta_3 DEBT_t + \beta_4 AGE_t + \beta_5 Capex_t + \beta_6 SG_t + \varepsilon_t$$

$$Model\ 2.1\ ROE_t = \beta_0 + \beta_1 ENV_{t-1} + \beta_2 SIZE_t + \beta_3 DEBT_t + \beta_4 AGE_t + \beta_5 Capex_t + \beta_6 SG_t + \varepsilon_t$$

Model 2.2 $ROE_t = \beta_0 + \beta_1 SOC_{t-1} + \beta_2 SIZE_t + \beta_3 DEBT_t + \beta_4 AGE_t + \beta_5 Capex_t + \beta_6 SG_t + \varepsilon_t$

Model 2.3 $ROE_t = \beta_0 + \beta_1 GOV_{t-1} + \beta_2 SIZE_t + \beta_3 DEBT_t + \beta_4 AGE_t + \beta_5 Capex_t + \beta_6 SG_t + \varepsilon_t$

Model 3.1 $Tobin'sq_t = \beta_0 + \beta_1 ENV_{t-1} + \beta_2 SIZE_t + \beta_3 DEBT_t + \beta_4 AGE_t + \beta_5 Capex_t + \beta_6 SG_t + \varepsilon_t$

Model 3.2 $Tobin'sq_t = \beta_0 + \beta_1 SOC_{t-1} + \beta_2 SIZE_t + \beta_3 DEBT_t + \beta_4 AGE_t + \beta_5 Capex_t + \beta_6 SG_t + \varepsilon_t$

Model 3.3 $Tobin'sq_t = \beta_0 + \beta_1 GOV_{t-1} + \beta_2 SIZE_t + \beta_3 DEBT_t + \beta_4 AGE_t + \beta_5 Capex_t + \beta_6 SG_t + \varepsilon_t$

4 Results

4.1 Descriptive Data Analysis

The descriptive statistics for each variable utilized in this investigation are shown in Table 2, with the number of observations, mean, standard deviation, minimum and maximum values for each variable. According to Table 2, the average ESG score for 286 businesses in the 11-year period is 74.5230. Meanwhile, the minimum ESG score is 47.4100 and the maximum ESG score is 90.1500, which implies that ESG performance varies relatively greatly among firms.

4.2 Correlation Test

The association indices between different factors are shown in Table 3. As the result suggest, the correlation coefficient of ROA or ROE is correlated with ESG score. However, the correlation coefficient of Tobin's q is uncorrelated with ESG score. The coefficient of ROA or ROE or Tobin's q is not correlated with Environmental or Social score respectively. Furthermore, the result of correlations suggests that there is no multicollinearity as none of correlations is above 0.9; according to Al-Jalahma et al. [19], a correlation below 0.9 will not harm the regression result.

4.3 Analysis of Regression

The regression result of Model 1 is listed in Table 4. Specifically, the column (1) shows the relationship between ESG score and ROA; the column (2) – (4) summarize the relationship between the individual score of E, S, G and ROA respectively. The adjusted

Table 2. Summary statistics.

Variables	ROA	ROE	Tobin's q	ESG	ENV	SOC
N	3146	3146	3146	3146	3146	3146
Mean	0.0458	0.0644	1.9320	74.5230	62.4778	76.1127
Std. Dev	0.0632	0.3349	1.5027	5.6316	8.2394	10.5644
Min	−0.5247	−10.6484	0.7236	47.4100	37.1100	4.8800
Max	0.5262	0.8466	26.8177	90.1500	92.2100	100.0000
Variables	GOV	SIZE	DEBT	AGE	Capex	SG
N	3146	3146	3146	3146	3146	3146
Mean	79.7732	23.1304	0.4723	19.8217	0.0506	0.3396
Std. Dev.	7.3871	1.3369	0.2126	5.9893	0.0503	1.5664
Min	38.4400	19.8743	0.0075	1.0000	0.0000	−1.7000
Max	96.1300	29.2246	0.9801	46.0000	0.6419	60.2172

Table 3. Correlations between Variables.

	ROA	ROE	Tobin's q	ESG	ENV	SOC	GOV	SIZE	DEBT	AGE	Capex
ROE	0.5280										
Tobin's q	0.2670	0.0607									
ESG	0.2509	0.1789	0.0334								
ENV	−0.0143	0.0111	−0.0675	0.4690							
SOC	0.0655	0.0690	0.0107	0.4547	0.2669						
GOV	0.2637	0.1793	0.0689	0.4714	0.1512	0.0467					
SIZE	−0.1264	0.0235	−0.3487	0.1711	0.2285	0.1053	0.0115				
DEBT	−0.4575	−0.1666	−0.3803	−0.0855	0.1130	0.0413	−0.2537	0.6013			
AGE	−0.1363	−0.0414	−0.0300	0.0067	0.0902	0.1065	−0.1326	0.2827	0.1964		
Capex	0.1015	0.0501	0.0394	0.0299	0.0024	−0.0441	0.1467	−0.1362	−0.0974	−0.1498	
SG	−0.0057	0.0246	0.0014	0.0018	−0.0234	0.0120	−0.0106	0.0281	0.0751	−0.0222	−0.0658

R2 are 0.2817, 0.2558, 0.2614 and 0.2650 separately, which is at an acceptable level considering other homogeneous studies [19].

The coefficient of ESG score suggests that one point of score increase of ESG will associate with a 0.19% increase in ROA of the firm. Individual S and G score coefficients are both significant at 1% level. However, individual E score coefficient is not statistically significant. One point of score increases in individual score of S and G will lead to 0.04% and 0.09% higher ROA of the firm. Overall, the higher the ESG score or individual score, the better performance of the firm indicated by ROA.

The regression result of Model 2 is tabulated in Table 5. Similar as the regression result of Model 1, the ESG score, and three individual score all have positive correlation with ROE separately. The coefficient of individual E score is neither statistically significant. A one-point rise in ESG score, S and G score will associate with a 0.77%, 0.21%

Table 4. Regression result (Model 1).

Column	(1)	(2)	(3)	(4)
Variables	ROA	ROA	ROA	ROA
ESG	0.0019***			
ENV		0.0000		
SOC			0.0004***	
GOV				0.0009***
SIZE	0.0096***	0.0124***	0.0121***	0.0110***
DEBT	−0.1623***	−0.1770***	−0.1761***	−0.1647***
AGE	−0.0008***	−0.0009***	−0.0009***	−0.0007***
Capex	0.0770**	0.0869***	0.0889***	0.0698***
SG	0.0013***	0.0014**	0.0013**	0.0013**
Constant	−0.2276***	−0.1464***	−0.1712***	−0.1898***
Observation	3146	3146	3146	3146
Adjusted R2	0.2817	0.2558	0.2614	0.2650

*** denotes 1% level significance, ** denotes 5% level significance, * denotes 10% level significance

Table 5. Regression result (Model 2).

Column	(1)	(2)	(3)	(4)
Variables	ROE	ROE	ROE	ROE
ESG	0.0077***			
ENV		0.0000		
SOC			0.0021***	
GOV				0.0049***
SIZE	0.0410***	0.0527***	0.0510***	0.0444***
DEBT	−0.3882***	−0.4479***	−0.4438***	−0.3792***
AGE	−0.0018*	−0.0021**	−0.0024**	−0.0013
Capex	0.2812**	0.3217***	0.3306***	0.2260*
SG	0.0086**	0.0091**	0.0089**	0.0087**
Constant	−1.2513***	−0.9202***	−1.0362***	−1.1639***
Observation	3146	3146	3146	3146
Adjusted R2	0.0706	0.0555	0.0597	0.0656

*** denotes 1% level significance, ** denotes 5% level significance, * denotes 10% level significance

and 0.49% increase of ROE. However, the adjusted R-squared are 0.0706, 0.0555, 0.0597 and 0.0656 separately, indicating that these models have weak explanatory power.

Table 6. Regression result (Model 3).

Column	(1)	(2)	(3)	(4)
Variables	Tobin's q	Tobin's q	Tobin's q	Tobin's q
ESG	0.0132***			
ENV		0.0008		
SOC			0.0050**	
GOV				0.0032
SIZE	−0.2549***	−0.2359***	−0.2387***	−0.2400***
DEBT	−1.8299***	−1.9319***	−1.9231***	−1.8885***
AGE	0.0213***	0.0208***	0.0201***	0.0213***
Capex	−0.1082	−0.0433	−0.0165	−0.1004
SG	0.0276*	0.0285*	0.0280*	0.0281*
Constant	7.2801***	7.8291***	7.5718***	7.6936***
Observation	3146	3146	3146	3146
Adjusted R2	0.1749	0.1727	0.1739	0.1729

*** denotes 1% level significance, ** denotes 5% level significance, * denotes 10% level significance

Table 6 displays the Model 3 regression outcome. All of the adjusted R-squared values are higher than 0.17, which is a common explanatory power in previous homogenous investigations [19]. At 1% and 5% level, the coefficients of ESG score and individual S score are significant. The coefficient of individual E and G score are statistically insignificant. Furthermore, the correlation relationship of ESG score and individual S score with Tobin's q are both positive relatively. One point increase in the ESG score and individual S score is related to 1.32% and 0.50% higher Tobin's q of the firm separately.

4.4 Test of Robustness

In this paper, the robustness test is conducted by replacing the index. Ln (market capitalization) is commonly used to measure the performance of a company. Therefore, this paper uses this indicator to replace the explained variable to carry out the robustness test of the replacement indicator. Table 7 displays specific outcomes. The results show that the significance level of the regression coefficient of ESG is basically consistent with the results of the master models which is shown in Table 4, 5 and 6, indicating that the research results have good robustness.

4.5 Heterogeneity Test

Based on the classification method of Naeem et al. [15], 286 firms are classified into ESG requirement sensitive and non-sensitive sectors. According to Table 8, the correlation

Table 7. Robustness test

Variable	Ln (Market capitalization)
ESG	0.0067***
SIZE	0.8777***
DEBT	−0.6730***
AGE	0.0024***
Capex	0.0160***
SG	0.0070
Constant	3.1015

*** denotes 1% level significance, ** denotes 5% level significance, * denotes 10% level significance

Table 8. Heterogeneity test

Variable	Sensitive Industry			Non-Sensitive Industry		
	ROA	ROE	Tobin's q	ROA	ROE	Tobin's q
ESG	0.0019***	0.0081***	0.0123***	0.0016***	0.0040***	0.0041
SIZE	0.0135***	0.0581***	−0.1790***	0.0012	0.0081**	−0.3877***
DEBT	−0.1726***	−0.5277***	−1.1553***	−0.1379***	−0.1098***	−3.0056***
AGE	−0.0012***	−0.0031**	−0.0030	−0.0006*	−0.0011	0.0553***
Capex	0.0623***	0.2543*	0.0775	0.1263***	0.2906***	−0.0738
SG	0.0014**	0.0098**	0.0088	−0.0054	0.0049	0.3249**
Constant	−0.3099***	−1.5925***	5.5974***	−0.0212	−0.3425***	11.1835***

*** denotes 1% level significance, ** denotes 5% level significance, * denotes 10% level significance

between ROA, ROE of the enterprise and ESG is greater in sensitive industries than it is in non-sensitive industries.

This indicates that the improvement of ESG performance of companies in sensitive industries will significantly leads to more increase of the ROA and ROE of companies within sensitive industries than that of non-sensitive industries. This shows that the ROA and ROE of enterprises in sensitive sectors will grow much more than those in non-sensitive industries when ESG performance improves. This paper argues that the main reason for this difference is that the nature of listed companies in sensitive industries determines that they need to be more in line with political requirements and fulfill more environment and social responsibilities. Therefore, a better ESG performance is in line with the company and shareholder benefit.

5 Conclusion

This study evaluates the influence of ESG performance on financial performance of enterprises operating in ESG requirements sensitive industries. The findings demonstrate a positive and substantial association between ROA, ROE, Tobin's q and overall ESG performance, suggesting that profitability benefits from improved ESG performance. Companies in sensitive sectors' ESG performance has a greater impact on their profitability than those in non-sensitive industries. This shows that, compared to the non-sensitive industries, in sensitive industries, increasing and investing in ESG operations and activities may have a more positive financial impact while preserving social and environmental sustainability.

By concentrating on the effect of ESG performance on enterprise performance with the historical data of Chinese A-share listed businesses, this study adds to the existing literature. Especially, the examination of the impact of ESG performance on Chinese sensitive-sector enterprises performance is a significant addition that highlights the disparities in how ESG performance has an influence on various types of industries. Researchers will be able to better understand the link between ESG performance and company success across industries with various ESG sensitivity levels according to the findings of this study. This comparative research will assist regulators and investors in understanding the effect of ESG performance on the enterprise performance in various industries and in making critical investment decisions.

References

1. Habib, A.M., Mourad, N.: The influence of environmental, social, and governance (ESG) practices on US firms' performance: evidence from the coronavirus crisis. J. Knowl. Econ. 1–22 (2023)
2. Nollet, J., Filis, G., Mitrokostas, E.: Corporate social responsibility and financial performance: a non-linear and disaggregated approach. Econ. Model. **52**, 400–407 (2016)
3. Bang, J., Ryu, D., Yu, J.: ESG controversies and investor trading behavior in the Korean market. Finance Res. Lett. **54**, 103750 (2023)
4. Bissoondoyal-Bheenick, E., Brooks, R., Do, H.X.: ESG and firm performance: the role of size and media channels. Econ. Model. **121**, 106203 (2023)
5. Ruan, L., Liu, H.: Environmental, social, governance activities and firm performance: evidence from China. Sustainability **13**(2), 1–16 (2021)
6. Jones, T.M., Harrison, J.S., Felps, W.: How applying instrumental stakeholder theory can provide sustainable competitive advantage. Acad. Manag. Rev. **43**(3), 371–391 (2018)
7. Freeman, R.E., Wicks, A.C., Parmar, B.: Stakeholder theory and the corporate objective revisited. Organ. Sci. **15**(3), 364–369 (2004)
8. Alsayegh, M.F., Rahman, R.A., Homayoun, S.: Corporate economic, environmental, and social sustainability performance transformation through ESG disclosure. Sustainability **12**(9), 1–20 (2020)
9. Jin, M., Kim, B.: The effects of ESG activity recognition of corporate employees on job performance: the case of South Korea. J. Risk Financ. Manag. **15**(7), 316 (2022)
10. Chiaramonte, L., Dreassi, A., Girardone, C., Pisera, S.: Do ESG strategies enhance bank stability during financial turmoil? Evidence from Europe. Eur. J. Finance **28**(12), 1173–1211 (2021)

11. Sidhoum, A.A., Serra, T.: Corporate social responsibility and dimensions of performance: an application to US electric utilities. Utilities Policy **48**, 1–11 (2017)
12. Ferrat, Y., Daty, F., Burlacu, R.: Short- and long-term effects of responsible investment growth on equity returns. J. Risk Finance **23**(1), 1–13 (2022)
13. Cupertino, S., Consolandi, C., Vercelli, A.: Corporate social performance, financialization, and real investment in US manufacturing firms. Sustainability **11**(7), 1–15 (2019)
14. Masulis, R., Reza, S.W.: Agency problem of corporate philanthropy. Rev. Financ. Stud. **28**(2), 592–636 (2015)
15. Naeem, N., Cankaya, S., Bildik, R.: Does ESG performance affect the financial performance of environmentally sensitive industries? A comparison between emerging and developed markets. Borsa Istanbul Rev. **22**, S128–S140 (2022)
16. Minutolo, M.C., Kristjanpoller, W.D., Stakeley, J.: Exploring environmental, social, and governance disclosure effects on the S&P 500 financial performance. Bus. Strategy Environ. **28**(6), 1083–1095 (2019)
17. Lee, S.-P., Isa, M.: Environmental, social and governance (ESG) practices and financial performance of Shariah-compliant companies in Malaysia. J. Islamic Account. Bus. Res. **14**(2), 295–314 (2023)
18. Ni, Y., Sun, Y.: Environmental, social, and governance premium in Chinese stock markets. Glob. Finance J. **55**, 100811 (2023)
19. Al-Jalahma, A., Al-Fadhel, H., Al-Muhanadi, M., Al-Zaimoor, N.: Environmental, social, and governance (ESG) disclosure and firm performance: evidence from GCC banking sector. In: 2020 International Conference on Decision Aid Sciences and Application (DASA), Decision Aid Sciences and Application (DASA), pp. 54–58 (2020)

The Factors Influence Purchase Intentions from the Consumer's Perspective and the Characteristics of Green Buyers

Ziyao Yang[✉]

Bachelor of Science (Hons), King's College London, London, UK
18954113333@163.com

Abstract. This paper discusses the influence of factors on consumers' propensity to purchase electric vehicles (EVs): finances, education, commute distance, and top speed. EVs are viewed as a solution to reduce the environmental impact of transportation. Despite this, their market share remains constrained due to consumer preferences. Due to the energy efficiency paradox and consumer trade-off considerations, the article suggests that pollution may have a positive effect on EV choice. Surprisingly, the study found that price had no significant effect on consumer choice, indicating that automobile ownership is not solely based on utilitarianism. The analysis demonstrates that vehicle speed has a significant impact on consumer preference, while the neglect of the pollution index in favour of car size and personal factors may have an effect on the adoption rates of electric vehicles.

Keywords: Electric Vehicles · Energy Upgrades · Consumer Studies

1 Introduction

In recent years, electric vehicles (EVs), as an alternative to conventional fuel vehicles, have been seen as the optimal solution to reduce the transport sector's impact on environmental degradation [1–6]. Electric empowerment avoids the traditional internal combustion engine's dependence on fossil fuel dependence, greenhouse gas emissions and other environmentally unfriendly issues and effectively improves energy efficiency [1–3, 5–7]. The electric vehicle contains different technologies, including the widely recognized battery electric vehicles (BEVs), plug-in hybrid electric vehicles (PHEVs) and hybrid electric vehicles (HEVs) [3, 7, 8]. In this paper, EVs refer to vehicles that derive all or part of their energy from the grid for power operation [9]. Even with these advantages, apparently EVs have a minimal market share worldwide [2–4, 10–13]. The choice of independent consumers largely determines the promotion rate of this EV [9, 14, 15]. Studies have shown that people receive four main factors when choosing an EV, technology, infrastructure, cost and personal factors [3]. Therefore, in this article, we will use a different analysis to identify how finance, education, commuting distance and maximum driving speed affect consumers' willingness to purchase an EV.

© The Author(s), under exclusive license to Springer Nature Singapore Pte Ltd. 2024
X. Li et al. (Eds.): ICEMGD 2023, AEPS, pp. 702–715, 2024.
https://doi.org/10.1007/978-981-97-0523-8_67

2 Hypothesis Development

2.1 Financial Factors

The impact of financial factors on consumer vehicle preferences is widely accepted in numerous studies. Existing research identifies the higher purchase price of EVs compared to conventional fuel vehicles as the main reason for the slow penetration of the EV market [4, 7–9, 13]. Electric vehicle production technology is still at the cutting edge. For example, the lithium batteries currently used in mainstream manufacturing have a non-negligible cost, and the higher selling price leads to financial barriers [4, 7]. Secondly, in terms of operating costs, EVs have meager operating costs compared to conventional energy sources, similar to those of gasoline, natural gas and diesel [4, 16, 17]. However, Larson et al. and Michael et al. find that consumers overlook future fuel and lifetime operating costs [9].

Due to the expensive attribute of EVs from the consumer perspective, the following hypotheses are inferred.

A1, the difference in price makes a significant difference in consumer choice of EVs.
A2, lower prices have no positive effect on EV acceptance.

2.2 Educational Factors

Proponents argue that higher education has a positive impact on EV acceptance. Michael et al. presents that consumers with higher education are more likely to adopt EVs as a response to societal expectations. This can be interpreted as consumers gaining a sense of self or social identity by reducing their greenhouse gas emissions [9, 18]. Also, having a higher educational background would theoretically enhance consumers' understanding of EVs [19]. Consumers who are relatively more knowledgeable about EVs have higher purchase intentions and are willing to pay a higher premium for their environmental attributes [9]. Surprisingly, according to Zhang et al., higher education is associated with negative purchase intentions. The researchers speculate that this may be since more knowledge about EVs allowed respondents to learn more about the disadvantages of EVs.

In order to explore the effect of higher education on EV purchase intentions, the following hypotheses were inferred.

B1, there is a significant difference between university education on EV acceptance.
B2, there is no positive effect of having a university degree on the acceptance of EVs.

2.3 Commuting Distance Factor

Limited commuting distance is also a barrier to widespread EV acceptance by the general public.

Firstly, range anxiety is a reason for some drivers to reject EVs. This is mainly caused by the inability to predict the approximate distance that can be covered by the remaining battery power when driving for long periods [4, 7, 13, 20]. The mileage indicated by EVs is obtained in a relatively ideal training ground. However, in consumers' daily driving, the driving environment could be in a better state, so it is difficult to determine the range of the vehicle by mileage limited and undetermined [21]. Secondly, consumer concerns about commuting distances may stem from the long charging times of electric vehicles due to the nature of the battery resulting in a higher recharge time than traditional internal combustion engines [20]. Finally, limited charging facilities also contribute to the barrier. Except for a few economically developed areas, the coverage of EV charging services is minimal [22]. Meanwhile, the lack of charging services tends to prevent some drivers from relying on it [4, 13].

To summarise, consumers' concerns about commuting distance may prevent consumers with higher commuting distances from rejecting EVs, thus assuming that.

C1, the difference in commuting distance significantly affects EV choice.
C2, there is no positive effect of smaller commuting distances on the acceptance of EVs.

2.4 Maximum Speed Factor

The maximum speed attainable by a vehicle is also an important factor for consumers to consider when purchasing transport [8, 16]. The effect of speed on consumer EV purchase propensity is currently seen to be relatively blank. In this paper, the following assumptions are made.

D1, there is a significant effect of achievable top speed on the choice of EV.
D2, higher maximum speed has no positive effect on EV acceptance.

3 Experimental Design

An experimental model from a previous study, an experiment from California, was used for the experimental design to select six alternatives from 120 possible profiles, differentiated by four fuels, five sizes and six body types. 23 The dataset used for this study had 300 respondents, and the data originated from TAYLOR (2019), with a collection period from 2016 ending in 2018.

3.1 Descriptive Analysis

From the Table 1 above, it can be seen that in terms of college, more than 60% of the sample is "1.0," which means that the respondent has received a college education. Regarding the distribution of hsg2, the majority of the sample is "0.0", with 212.0 or 70.67%, meaning that the respondent's family size is greater than or equal to 2. For com15, the highest percentage of "0.0" is 58.00%, meaning the commute is greater than five kilometers. The other 1.0 sample is 42.00%, meaning the proportion of people who commute less than five kilometers. For fuel, "gasoline" was the most popular choice at 34.67%. Price is the ratio of the price of the car to the respondent's income, and the majority of the sample was "3.5329841", with 14.0 or 4.67%. The proportion of the sample choosing "85.0" for the highest achievable speed was 28.00%. For size, the highest percentage of "3.0" was 59.00%.

Table 1. Descriptive analysis result.

Name	Option	frequency	percentage(%)
college	0.0	108	36.000
	1.0	192	64.000
hsg2	0.0	212	70.667
	1.0	88	29.333
coml5	0.0	174	58.000
	1.0	126	42.000
type	regcar	178	59.333
	sportcar	7	2.333
	sportuv	15	5.000
	stwagon	10	3.333
	truck	42	14.000
	van	48	16.000
speed	55.0	15	5.000
	65.0	8	2.667
	85.0	84	28.000
	95.0	57	19.000
	100.0	12	4.000
	110.0	72	24.000
	140.0	52	17.333
pollution	0.0	51	17.000
	0.1	17	5.667
	0.25	46	15.333
	0.4	49	16.333
	0.5	29	9.667
	0.6	36	12.000
	0.75	49	16.333
	1.0	23	7.667
size	0.0	3	1.000
	1.0	30	10.000
	2.0	90	30.000
	3.0	177	59.000
total		300	100.0

Table 2. Correlation analysis result.

	choice	college	hsg2	coml5	type	fuel	price	speed	pollution	size
choice	1									
college	−0.011	1								
hsg2	0.011	−0.157**	1							
coml5	0.000	−0.051	−0.074	1						
type	0.002	−0.104	0.261***	−0.126*	1					
fuel	0.022	−0.011	−0.014	0.040	−0.070	1				
price	−0.076	−0.010	−0.058	−0.004	−0.119*	0.035	1			
speed	0.232***	0.066	−0.070	−0.035	−0.034	−0.411***	−0.079	1		
pollution	0.640***	0.095	−0.027	−0.141*	−0.042	−0.195***	−0.057	0.346***	1	
size	0.012	0.007	0.119*	0.045	0.042	0.027	−0.055	0.012	0.228***	1

3.2 Correlation Analysis

The Table 2 above shows when the Pearson correlation coefficient exceeds 0.7, generally consider the two variables to be strongly connected; when it drops between 0.3 and 0.7, generally consider it to be moderately correlated; and when it falls below 0.3, we consider them to be weakly correlated. The criterion must be met: the significance threshold is less than 0.01 or 0.05, and we consider the correlation between the two variables to be significant and statistically significant. Using the Pearson correlation coefficients, the table illustrates the degree of correlation between the two variables. Choice and speed and choice and pollution have a significant association, with correlation coefficients of 0.232 and 0.640, respectively. All are more than 0, indicating a positive correlation between choice and speed and pollution.

3.3 Analysis of Variance (Anova)

Table 3. College anova result.

	College (Mean ± Standard deviation)		F	p
	0.0(n = 108)	1.0(n = 192)		
choice	3.611 ± 1.728	3.573 ± 1.593	0.037	0.847

*$p < 0.05$ ** $p < 0.01$ *** $p < 0.001$

From the Table 3 above, it can be seen that the different college samples do not show the significance for all of the choices ($p > 0.05$), which means that the different college samples show consistency for all of the choices, and there is no difference.

The Table 4 above shows that the different hsg2 samples do not show the significance for all of the choices ($p > 0.05$), which means that the different hsg2 samples show consistency for all of the choices, and there is no difference.

Table 4. hsg2 for choice anova result.

	hsg2 (Mean ± Standard deviation)		F	p
	0.0(n = 212)	1.0(n = 88)		
choice	3.575 ± 1.661	3.614 ± 1.601	0.034	0.855

*$p < 0.05$ ** $p < 0.01$ *** $p < 0.001$

Table 5. com15 for choice anova result.

	com15(Mean ± Standard deviation)		F	p
	0.0(n = 174)	1.0(n = 126)		
choice	3.586 ± 1.704	3.587 ± 1.556	0.000	0.995

*$p < 0.05$ ** $p < 0.01$ *** $p < 0.001$

As can be seen from the Table 5 above: the different com15 samples do not show the significance for all of the choices ($p > 0.05$), meaning that the different com15 samples show consistency for all of the choices, and there is no difference.

Table 6. Type for choice anova result.

	Type (Mean ± Standard deviation)						F	p
	Regcar (n = 178)	Sportcar (n = 7)	Sportuv (n = 15)	Stwagon (n = 10)	Truck (n = 42)	van (n = 48)		
choice	3.584 ± 1.659	3.143 ± 1.676	3.333 ± 1.589	4.900 ± 1.792	3.524 ± 1.700	3.521 ± 1.444	1.496	0.191

*$p < 0.05$ ** $p < 0.01$ *** $p < 0.001$

From the Table 6 above, it can be seen that the different type samples do not show significance ($p > 0.05$) for all of the choices, meaning that the different type samples show consistency for all choices, and there is no difference.

Table 7. Fuel for choice anova result.

	Fuel (Mean ± Standard deviation)				F	p
	cng (n = 63)	electric (n = 82)	gasoline (n = 104)	methanol (n = 51)		
choice	2.349 ± 1.034	3.927 ± 0.927	5.192 ± 0.396	1.294 ± 0.460	389.597	0.000***

*$p < 0.05$ ** $p < 0.01$ *** $p < 0.001$

From the above Table 7, it can be seen that: all of the different fuel samples show significance for choice ($p < 0.05$), which means that the different fuel samples have different choices. Specifically, fuel showed a 0.01 level of significance for choice (F = 389.597, p = 0.000), and the mean scores of the groups with significant differences were "electric > cng; gasoline > cng; cng > methanol; gasoline > methanol; cng > methanol. Methanol;gasoline > electric;electric > methanol;gasoline > methanol".

Table 8. Speed for choice anova result.

	Speed (Mean ± Standard deviation)							F	p
	55.0 (n = 15)	65.0 (n = 8)	85.0 (n = 84)	95.0 (n = 57)	100.0 (n = 12)	110.0 (n = 72)	140.0 (n = 52)		
choice	1.133 ± 0.352	1.250 ± 0.463	3.714 ± 1.662	4.000 ± 1.439	1.333 ± 0.492	4.236 ± 1.261	3.615 ± 1.430	20.313	0.000***

* $p < 0.05$ ** $p < 0.01$ *** $p < 0.001$

From the above Table 8, it can be seen that: all of the different speed samples showed significance (p < 0.05) for choice, implying that the different speed samples have variability for choice. The specific analysis shows that speed is significant for choice at the 0.01 level (F = 20.313, p = 0.000), and the specific comparisons show that the mean scores of the groups with significant differences are "85.0 > 55.0; 95.0 > 55.0; 110.0 > 55.0; 140.0 > 55.0; 85.0 > 65.0; 95.0 > 65.0; 110.0 > 65.0; 140.0 > 65.0; 85.0 > 100.0; 110.0 > 85.0; 95.0 > 100.0; 110.0 > 100.0; 140.0 > 100.0; 110.0 > 140.0".

Table 9. Pollution for choice anova result.

	Pollution (Mean ± Standard deviation)								F	p
	0.0 (n = 51)	0.1 (n = 17)	0.25 (n = 46)	0.4 (n = 49)	0.5 (n = 29)	0.6 (n = 36)	0.75 (n = 49)	1.0 (n = 23)		
choice	1.294 ± 0.460	2.118 ± 1.111	4.174 ± 1.371	3.408 ± 1.135	5.069 ± 0.258	3.250 ± 1.296	4.755 ± 1.051	5.130 ± 0.344	72.826	0.000***

* $p < 0.05$ ** $p < 0.01$ *** $p < 0.001$

From the above Table 9, it can be seen that: all of the different POLLUTION samples showed significance (p < 0.05) for CHOICE, implying that the different POLLUTION samples have variability for CHOICE. The specific analysis shows that pollution is significant for choice at the 0.01 level (F = 72.826, p = 0.000), and the specific comparison of differences shows that the group means scores with significant differences are "0.1 > 0.0; 0.25 > 0.0; 0.4 > 0.0; 0.5 > 0.0; 0.6 > 0.0". 0.0;0.6 > 0.0;0.75 > 0.0;1.0 > 0.0;0.25 > 0.1;0.4 > 0.1;0.5 > 0.1;0.6 > 0.1;0.75 > 0.1;1.0 > 0.1;0.25 > 0.4;0.5 > 0.25;0.25 > 0.6;0.75 > 0.25;1.0 > 0.25;0.5 > 0.4; 0.75 > 0.4; 1.0 > 0.4; 0.5 > 0.6; 0.75 > 0.6; 1.0 > 0.6".

Table 10. Choice for price anova result.

	choice (Mean ± Standard deviation)						F	p
	choice1 (n = 57)	choice2 (n = 19)	choice3 (n = 68)	choice4 (n = 26)	choice5 (n = 107)	choice6 (n = 23)		
price	4.629 ± 2.323	3.552 ± 1.223	4.091 ± 1.875	4.101 ± 2.309	4.239 ± 1.655	3.541 ± 1.963	1.613	0.156

* $p < 0.05$ ** $p < 0.01$ *** $p < 0.001$

From the above Table 10, we can see that using ANOVA to investigate the variability of CHOICE for price total 1, from the above table, we can see that: different CHOICE samples for price all do not show significance ($p > 0.05$), meaning that different CHOICE samples for price all show consistency and there is no variability.

3.4 Logistic Regression

The dependent variable in this paper is the willingness to buy, and the independent variables are college, hsg2, com15, type, fuel, price, speed, pollution, and size. Therefore, a multiple logistic regression model is used as the purpose of regression is to use specific mathematical expressions to describe the variables of a particular probability distribution. This study does so use spss software. The general logistic regression equation is

$$y = \frac{1}{1+e^{-z}}$$

This function has the domain of definition $(-\infty, +\infty)$ and the domain of values $[0, 1]$, and its derivative expressions are as follows:

$$y'(z) = y(z)(1-y(z))$$

In conclusion, logistic regression consists of the sigmoid function and a regression model. Given the independent variable x, we already know the output y, and estimating the model's parameters is necessary. Excellent likelihood estimation can then be utilized for parameter estimation. Let P represent the statistical probability that an event will occur. These yields:

$$logit(p) = ln(p/(1-p))$$

Let there be k factors x1, x2,....xk affecting the value of y, then state that

$$ln\left(\frac{p}{1}-p\right) = \beta_0 + \beta_1 x_{1+}...+\beta_k x_k$$

where are model parameters.

$$p = \frac{exp(\beta_0 + \beta_1 x_{1+}...+\beta_k x_k)}{1+exp(\beta_0 + \beta_1 x_{1+}...+\beta_k x_k)}$$

The regression coefficient Table 11 for com15 was 2.479 and had a significance level of 0.01 ($z = 4.080$, $p = 0.0000.01$), indicating that com15 would have a considerable

Table 11. Logistic regression result.

choice2	Regression coefficient	Standard error	z value	Wald χ^2	p value	OR value	OR value 95% CI
college	1.119	0.702	1.594	2.541	0.111	3.061	0.774 ~ 12.112
hsg2	0.990	0.670	1.477	2.182	0.140	2.691	0.724 ~ 10.005
coml5	0.301	0.685	0.439	0.192	0.661	1.351	0.353 ~ 5.173
type	0.467	0.155	3.006	9.036	0.003	1.595	1.176 ~ 2.162
fuel	0.281	0.457	0.615	0.378	0.539	1.325	0.540 ~ 3.247
price	−0.390	0.210	−1.856	3.445	0.063	0.677	0.448 ~ 1.022
speed	0.007	0.018	0.362	0.131	0.717	1.007	0.971 ~ 1.043
pollution	−0.579	3.275	−0.177	0.031	0.860	0.560	0.001 ~ 343.716
size	0.024	0.495	0.048	0.002	0.962	1.024	0.388 ~ 2.702
intercept	−3.603	3.180	−1.133	1.284	0.257	0.027	0.000 ~ 13.875
Choice3	Regression coefficient	Standard error	z value	Wald χ^2	p value	OR value	OR value 95% CI
college	0.604	0.541	1.116	1.246	0.264	1.829	0.634 ~ 5.279
hsg2	0.688	0.610	1.128	1.272	0.259	1.990	0.602 ~ 6.576
coml5	2.479	0.608	4.080	16.643	0.000	11.926	3.625 ~ 39.234
type	0.172	0.142	1.213	1.472	0.225	1.187	0.900 ~ 1.567
fuel	−1.148	0.381	−3.011	9.064	0.003	0.317	0.150 ~ 0.670
price	−0.129	0.153	−0.841	0.707	0.400	0.879	0.651 ~ 1.187
speed	0.030	0.014	2.090	4.370	0.037	1.031	1.002 ~ 1.060
pollution	14.012	2.226	6.296	39.638	0.000	1217091.804	15520.409 ~ 95442873.071
size	−1.235	0.400	−3.088	9.538	0.002	0.291	0.133 ~ 0.637
intercept	−3.327	2.313	−1.438	2.069	0.150	0.036	0.000 ~ 3.341
Choice4	Regression coefficient	Standard error	z value	Wald χ^2	p value	OR value	OR value 95% CI
college	0.292	0.664	0.440	0.193	0.660	1.339	0.365 ~ 4.917
hsg2	−0.039	0.720	−0.054	0.003	0.957	0.962	0.235 ~ 3.945
coml5	1.776	0.745	2.385	5.687	0.017	5.908	1.372 ~ 25.438
type	0.689	0.169	4.068	16.548	0.000	1.992	1.429 ~ 2.776
fuel	−0.334	0.438	−0.763	0.582	0.445	0.716	0.304 ~ 1.689
price	−0.154	0.179	−0.859	0.738	0.390	0.857	0.603 ~ 1.218
speed	0.025	0.017	1.480	2.192	0.139	1.026	0.992 ~ 1.060
pollution	14.503	2.515	5.766	33.248	0.000	1988117.142	14372.145 ~ 275018784.371

(*continued*)

Table 11. (*continued*)

Choice4	Regression coefficient	Standard error	z value	Wald χ^2	p value	OR value	OR value 95% CI
size	−1.273	0.499	−2.553	6.519	0.011	0.280	0.105 ~ 0.744
intercept	−6.230	2.741	−2.273	5.166	0.023	0.002	0.000 ~ 0.424
Choice5	Regression coefficient	Standard error	z value	Wald χ^2	p value	OR value	OR value 95% CI
college	−0.293	0.558	−0.525	0.276	0.599	0.746	0.250 ~ 2.225
hsg2	0.019	0.629	0.030	0.001	0.976	1.019	0.297 ~ 3.498
com15	2.133	0.605	3.524	12.417	0.000	8.441	2.577 ~ 27.650
type	0.020	0.144	0.139	0.019	0.889	1.020	0.769 ~ 1.353
fuel	1.907	0.399	4.784	22.886	0.000	6.734	3.083 ~ 14.709
price	−0.178	0.147	−1.217	1.481	0.224	0.837	0.628 ~ 1.115
speed	−0.001	0.016	−0.045	0.002	0.964	0.999	0.968 ~ 1.031
pollution	18.276	2.343	7.799	60.818	0.000	86490868.128	875430.488 ~ 8545133364.293
size	−1.433	0.376	−3.812	14.532	0.000	0.239	0.114 ~ 0.499
intercept	−6.521	2.525	−2.583	6.670	0.010	0.001	0.000 ~ 0.208
Choice6	Regression coefficient	Standard error	z value	Wald χ^2	p value	OR value	OR value 95% CI
college	0.160	0.721	0.221	0.049	0.825	1.173	0.285 ~ 4.821
hsg2	0.755	0.778	0.971	0.942	0.332	2.128	0.463 ~ 9.773
com15	1.910	0.771	2.479	6.146	0.013	6.755	1.492 ~ 30.590
type	0.465	0.175	2.656	7.052	0.008	1.591	1.129 ~ 2.242
fuel	2.296	0.597	3.847	14.796	0.000	9.932	3.083 ~ 31.992
price	−0.350	0.199	−1.757	3.088	0.079	0.705	0.477 ~ 1.041
speed	0.014	0.020	0.696	0.485	0.486	1.014	0.975 ~ 1.055
pollution	18.942	2.500	7.577	57.412	0.000	168363223.6625	4201.370 ~ 22600976014.623
size	−1.735	0.502	−3.455	11.939	0.001	0.176	0.066 ~ 0.472
intercept	−11.345	3.359	−3.377	11.405	0.001	0.000	0.000 ~ 0.009
McFadden *R* Square:0.454							
Cox & Snell *R* Square:0.767							
Nagelkerke *R* Square:0.799							

positive influence on option. And a dominance ratio (OR value) of 11.926, indicating that a one-unit increase in com15 results in an 11.926-fold change; the regression coefficient value for speed is 0.030 and demonstrates a 0.05 level of significance (z = 2.090, p = 0.0370.05), indicating that speed will have a significant favorable influence relationship. And a dominance ratio (OR value) of 1.031, indicating a change (increase) of 1.031 times for a one unit increase in speed; the regression coefficient value for com15 was

1.776 and showed significance at the 0.05 level (z = 2.385, p = 0.0170.05), indicating that com15 would have a significant favorable influence on the option relationship. And a dominance ratio (OR value) of 5.908, indicating a change of 5.908 times when com15 increases by one unit; the regression coefficient value for pollution was 14.503 and showed significance at the 0.01 level (z = 5.766, p = 0.0000.01), indicating that pollution would have a significant favorable influence on selection produce a significant positive effect relationship. And the dominance ratio (OR value) is 1988117.142, indicating that a one unit increase in pollution results in a change (increase) that is 1988117.142 times greater; the regression coefficient value for fuel is 1.907 and demonstrates significance at the 0.01 level (z = 4.784, p = 0.0000.01), indicating that fuel will have a significant favorable influence on a significant positive effect relationship between option Moreover, a dominance ratio (OR value) of 1.591, indicating a 1.591-fold change (increase) when type is increased by one unit; the regression coefficient value for size was -1.73 and showed significance at the 0.01 level (z = -3.455, p = 0.0010.01), indicating that size would have a significant adverse effect on the choice relationship. a dominance ratio (OR value) of 0.176, indicating a 0.176-fold change (reduction) when size is raised by one unit.

4 Conclusions and Discussion

1) The positive impact of increased pollution on choice may result from the energy efficiency paradox and the consumer trade-off. Perhaps this can be explained by the 'energy efficiency paradox' [24]. Specifically, consumers' expectations of energy-efficient products are lowered because of the financial savings in operating costs associated with their purchase. This phenomenon can be explained by various reasons, for instance, information asymmetry, differences in private social discount rates, the short-sightedness of individual consumers seeking to maximize short-term benefits, or by placing greater importance on the certainty of costs than on the direction of future cash flows [25]. Secondly, consumers' disregard for vehicle pollution indices may stem from the pursuit of vehicle size. According to Lane and Banks, once consumers have chosen a segment regarding vehicle size, they have less incentive to look for fuel-efficient models. This behavior may be because they overlook the possibility of looking for environmentally friendly vehicles in the segment. According to the analysis, the attributes of vehicle speed can have a significant impact on consumer choice. Finally, individual buyers may perceive the eco-friendly choice as representing a sacrifice of economy and comfort and thus reject EVs [26].
2) Surprisingly, the different choice samples do not show the significance for all the prices—the original hypothesis A is rejected because car ownership is not necessarily utilitarian [27]. Therefore, the effect of choice price is reduced. When purchasing a car, consumers become identified with the product they are buying, and at the same time, ownership becomes part of the consumer's display of self [28]. It also gives consumers greater security [29].
3) COLLEGE and CHOICE show consistency in line with previous research. On the one hand, a better educational background makes it easier for consumers to gain a sense of self and social identity by choosing a more environmentally friendly vehicle.

On the other hand, higher education also makes car consumers more aware of the current limitations of EVs. For example, learning about the scope for improvement in EV technology reduces the desire to buy.

4) In the ANOVA, commuting distance also proved to have a significant influence on consumer choice. When implying a one-unit increase in commuting distance, the change in choice was 5.908 times greater, reflecting that most commuters care a lot about car choice [30].

5) speed shows a weak correlation with choice. Speed has a regression coefficient value of 0.030 and shows a 0.05 level of significance ($z = 2.090$, $p = 0.037 < 0.05$), implying that speed has a significant positive effect on choice. The different speed samples all show the significance of choice.

The effect of maximum reachable speed on consumer choice is confirmed, while an increase in the maximum reachable speed of the vehicle has a POSITIVE effect on consumers' purchase intentions. The effect was explained as different hypothetical motives would lead to different target driving speeds, with drivers tending to increase their driving speed when they desire higher driving pleasure [31]. It is worth mentioning that according to risk homeostasis theory, drivers would decide and maintain their driving speed based on the target risk level rather than the highest attainable speed [32].

References

1. Helmers, E., Marx, P.: Electric cars: technical characteristics and environmental impacts. Environ. Sci. Europe **24**(1), 1–15 (2012). https://doi.org/10.1186/2190-4715-24-14
2. Rasouli, S., Timmermans, H.: Influence of social networks on latent choice of electric cars: a mixed logit specification using experimental design data. Netw. Spat. Econ. **16**(1), 99–130 (2013). https://doi.org/10.1007/S11067-013-9194-6
3. Rezvani, Z., Jansson, J., Bodin, J.: Advances in consumer electric vehicle adoption research: a review and research agenda. Transp. Res. Part D Transp. Environ. **34**(1), 122–136 (2015). https://doi.org/10.1016/J.Trd.2014.10.010
4. She, Z.-Y., Sun, Q., Ma, J.-J., Xie, B.-C.: What are the barriers to widespread adoption of battery electric vehicles? A survey of public perception in Tianjin. China. Transp. Policy **56**, 29–40 (2017). https://doi.org/10.1016/J.Tranpol.2017.03.001
5. Holmberg, K., Erdemir, A.: The impact of tribology on energy use and co2 emission globally and in combustion engine and electric cars. Tribol. Int. **135**, 389–396 (2019). https://doi.org/10.1016/J.Triboint.2019.03.024
6. Secinaro, S., Brescia, V., Calandra, D., Biancone, P.: Employing bibliometric analysis to identify suitable business models for electric cars. J. Clean. Prod. **264**, 121503 (2020). https://doi.org/10.1016/J.Jclepro.2020.121503
7. Kv, S., Michael, L.K., Hungund, S.S., Fernandes, M.: Factors influencing adoption of electric vehicles–a case in India. Cogent Eng. **9**(1), 2085375 (2022)
8. Chowdhury, M., Salam, K., Tay, R.: Consumer preferences and policy implications for the green car market. Mark. Intell. Plan. **34**(6), 810–827 (2016). https://doi.org/10.1108/Mip-08-2015-0167
9. Larson, P.D., Viáfara, J., Parsons, R.V., Elias, A.: Consumer attitudes about electric cars: pricing analysis and policy implications. Transp. Res. Part A: Policy Pract. **69**, 299–314 (2014). https://doi.org/10.1016/J.Tra.2014.09.002

10. Liao, F., Molin, E., Van Wee, B.: Consumer preferences for electric vehicles: a literature review. Transp. Rev. **37**(3), 252–275 (2016). https://www.tandfonline.com/doi/full/10.1080/01441647.2016.1230794
11. Hackbarth, A., Madlener, R.: Willingness-to-pay for alternative fuel vehicle characteristics: a stated choice study for Germany. Transp. Res. Part A: Policy Pract. **85**, 89–111 (2016). https://doi.org/10.1016/J.Tra.2015.12.005
12. Orlov, A., Kallbekken, S.: The impact of consumer attitudes towards energy efficiency on car choice: survey results from Norway. J. Clean. Prod. **214**, 816–822 (2019). https://doi.org/10.1016/J.Jclepro.2018.12.326
13. Ortar, N., Ryghaug, M.: Should all cars be electric by 2025? The electric car debate in Europe. Sustainability **11**(7), 1868 (2019). https://doi.org/10.3390/Su11071868
14. Schuitema, G., Anable, J., Skippon, S., Kinnear, N.: The role of instrumental, hedonic and symbolic attributes in the intention to adopt electric vehicles. Transp. Res. Part A: Policy Pract. **48**, 39–49 (2013). https://doi.org/10.1016/J.Tra.2012.10.004
15. Kang, M.J., Park, H.: Impact of experience on government policy toward acceptance of hydrogen fuel cell vehicles in Korea. Energy Policy **39**(6), 3465–3475 (2011). https://doi.org/10.1016/J.Enpol.2011.03.045
16. Caulfield, B., Farrell, S., Mcmahon, B.: Examining individuals preferences for hybrid electric and alternatively fuelled vehicles. Transp. Policy **17**(6), 381–387 (2010). https://doi.org/10.1016/J.Tranpol.2010.04.005
17. Wang, X., González, J.A.: Assessing feasibility of electric buses in small and medium-sized communities. Int. J. Sustain. Transp. **7**(6), 431–448 (2013). https://doi.org/10.1080/15568318.2012.667864
18. Taylor, S.: Stated Preferences for Car Choice. www.kaggle.com (2019). https://www.kaggle.com/datasets/steventaylor11/stated-preferences-for-car-choice. Accessed 14 Mar 2023
19. Zhang, Y., Yu, Y., Zou, B.: Analyzing public awareness and acceptance of alternative fuel vehicles in china: the case of Ev. Energy Policy **39**(11), 7015–7024 (2011). https://doi.org/10.1016/J.Enpol.2011.07.055
20. Lane, B., Banks, N.: "Lowc Car Buyer Survey": webcache.googleusercontent.com (2010). https://webcache.googleusercontent.com/search?q=cache:hz3l_7kjsvaj:https://www.zemo.org.uk/assets/reports/lowcvp-car-buyer-survey-2010-final-report-03-06-10-vfinal.pdf&cd=1&hl=zh-cn&ct=clnk&gl=uk&client=safari. Accessed 18 Mar 2023
21. (Jason) Zhu, J.: Analysis of New Zealand Specific Electric Vehicle Adoption Barriers and Government Policy. researcharchive.vuw.ac.nz (2016). Accessed 14 Mar 2023. http://researcharchive.vuw.ac.nz/handle/10063/6190
22. Huang, Y., Qian, L.: Consumer preferences for electric vehicles in lower tier cities of china: evidences from south Jiangsu region. Transp. Res. Part D: Transp. Environ. **63**, 482–497 (2018). https://doi.org/10.1016/J.Trd.2018.06.017
23. Mcfadden, D., Train, K.: Mixed MNL models for discrete response. J. Appl. Econom. **15**(5), 447–470 (2000). https://doi.org/10.1002/1099-1255(200009/10)15:5%3c447::Aid-Jae570%3e3.0.Co;2-1
24. Jaffe, A.B., Stavins, R.N.: The energy-efficiency gap what does it mean? Energy Policy **22**(10), 804–810 (1994). https://doi.org/10.1016/0301-4215(94)90138-4
25. Anderson, R.C., et al.: The Americas And Oceania: Assessing Sustainability. Berkshire Publishing Group (2012). https://books.google.co.uk/books?hl=zh-cn&lr=&id=4p29dwaaqbaj&oi=fnd&pg=pp1&dq=+the+americas+and+oceania:+assessing+sustainability&ots=lhz5gtolzt&sig=s8nrpgw9ce3u4rtzt4gwtcbep6g&redir_esc=y#v=onepage&q=the%20americas%20and%20oceania%3a%20assessing%20sustainability&f=false. Accessed 18 Mar 2023

26. Van Rijnsoever, F., Farla, J., Dijst, M.J.: Consumer car preferences and information search channels. Transp. Res. Part D: Transp. Environ. **14**(5), 334–342 (2009). https://doi.org/10.1016/J.Trd.2009.03.006
27. Belk, R.: Sharing. J. Consum. Res. **36**(5), 715–734 (2010). https://doi.org/10.1086/612649
28. Belk, R.W.: Possessions and the extended self. J. Consum. Res. **15**(2), 139–168 (1988). https://doi.org/10.1086/209154
29. Cheshire, L., Walters, P., Rosenblatt, T.: The politics of housing consumption: renters as flawed consumers on a master planned estate. Urban Stud. **47**(12), 2597–2614 (2010). https://doi.org/10.1177/0042098009359028
30. Curtis, C., Headicar, P.: Targeting travel awareness campaigns. Transp. Policy **4**(1), 57–65 (1997). https://doi.org/10.1016/S0967-070x(96)00034-0
31. Shinar, D.: Traffic Safety and Human Behavior. Emerald Publishing, Bingley (2017)
32. Wilde, G.J.S.: The theory of risk homeostasis: implications for safety and health. Risk Anal. **2**(4), 209–225 (1982). https://doi.org/10.1111/J.1539-6924.1982.Tb01384.X

A Study on the Motivation and Financial Performance of Haidilao's Equity Crave-Out

Tingxuan Dong[✉]

Faculty of Business, Macao Polytechnic University, Macao 999078, China
p2010287@mpu.edu.mo

Abstract. Since the 1980s, many European and American companies have chosen the means of equity carve-out for more diversified development, and this method is also popular and perfected in the European and American capital markets while the Chinese market started late with equity carve-out, many companies are also favorable to this means. China's restaurant industry is highly competitive, but it is difficult to go public due to the lack of financial transparency and imperfect systems. Haidilao, the leading restaurant industry in China, spun off its spice business subsidiary Yihai International to go public with a representative approach and path. This article analyzes the motivation for the listing of Haidilao Group and analyzes the performance of its subsidiaries after the carve-out by selecting financial indicators before and after the listing and concludes that the carve-out can improve the financial performance to a certain extent. Other restaurant brands can learn from the successful experience of Haidilao to achieve the effect of disguised IPO, but enterprises should plan reasonably according to their strategic development.

Keywords: Equity Carve-out · Motivation · Financial Performance

1 Introduction

In the face of fierce competition in the capital market, European and American companies have tried to carve out to make breakthroughs since the 1980s and have had many successful cases. Compared with the well-established equity carve-out system and cases in Europe and America, not many companies have completed in China due to the late start of the market and the strict policies. The fresh power and capital dividends that carve-out can bring are very attractive, and many Chinese companies naturally want to gain more competitiveness by doing so. The restaurant industry in China is very competitive and chain brands want to gain a competitive advantage by going public. However, due to the characteristics of the industry, there are many reasons such as opaque financial situation, imperfect system, and strict institutional supervision, restaurant companies generally face the dilemma of going public. This paper selects the leading Chinese catering company Haidilao as a case study and concludes that the main reasons for Haidilao to go public are: to pilot the listing of its parent company and to obtain some advantages that listed companies can obtain to help the group's development, such as to broaden financing channels. Also, the reasons are to cooperate with corporate development and to reduce information asymmetry. In addition, this paper also analyzes the financial indicators of the subsidiary Yihai International in terms of financing, earnings, growth, and company value, and finds that the spin-off has a positive performance on the company's financial situation, and its financial situation is developing in a good direction.

The listing of Yihai International, a subsidiary of Haidilao's compound seasoning business, was very successful and Haidilao subsequently completed the listing of its parent company, which is a reference for other restaurant brands with the same problems and motivations to go public. Other F&B companies can also draw on Haidilao's successful case to designate a capital market development path that is in line with their strategies, according to their actual situation.

2 Literature Review

2.1 Studies on the Concepts Related to Equity Carve-Out

Concept Studies. Equity carve-out first originated in the United States in the 1980s and became prevalent in Europe and the U.S. Schipper and Smith are the first to conduct research on equity carve-outs, defining them as a parent company splitting up a subsidiary or part of it that it fully controls and then going public to raise capital [1]. In 1999, Vijh has proposed a similar definition: an equity carve-out is the sale of part or all of a wholly owned subsidiary by the parent company to the public [2]. Both emphasize that the subsidiary is fully owned by the parent company. Since then, Power has broadened the definition of ECOs by not focusing on the size of the parent company's ownership of the subsidiary [3].

In China, equity carve-outs started late and the capital market is still in the development stage compared to foreign countries. In 2010, Guo H. X., and Wan D. F. have combined a lot of foreign theoretical and empirical studies and proposed that a carve-out is an initial public offering of a subsidiary to the public, where the parent company has absolute control over the subsidiary but the parent company can profit from the change in shareholding after the listing depending on the subsidiary [4]. In addition, Chen X. and Chen D. also divided the definition of equity carve-out into broad and narrow-based on whether the parent company is listed or not [5, 6].

Concept Definition. The equity carve-outs studied in this article are in a broad sense and do not require the parent company to be a public company. The parent company spins off its subsidiaries to be listed for the operation to raise capital for the enterprise to synergize the group's development.

2.2 Studies Related to Motivations

The motivation for companies to choose to go through an equity carve-out after weighing the pros and cons is generally multifaceted. According to domestic and foreign scholars, the main motivations include financing needs, information symmetry issues, the concentration of corporate business, and management incentives.

In 1998, Allen and McConnell have proposed the financing hypothesis that the parent company, which often has financial problems in the process of business operation, obtains financing by carve-out and giving up part of the control of the subsidiary, while the parent company can still maintain the controlling position because it is an IPO to the public [7]. For the parent company, the independent listing of the subsidiary can broaden the financing channels to alleviate the financing constraints.

Nanda has argued that equity carve-outs are made because the subsidiaries are undervalued and are split up in order for outside investors to know the true value of the subsidiaries [8]. The information asymmetry between the two parties is caused by the fact that the company has internal access to complete information about its business status while external investors do not, and the disclosure of information in the IPO can correct this information asymmetry and allow investors to redefine the value of the firm.

The motivation for the concentration of a company's business is from the company's strategic perspective, Comment and Jarrell have found in their study of U.S. listed companies that the more concentrated a listed company's business is, the greater the wealth of the company's shareholders [9]. The theory suggests that concentrating resources on core areas can lead to greater market value for the firm. Li Y. S. has suggested that the carve-out of listed companies facilitates the optimal reorganization of resources and promotes the rapid development of the unit business of subsidiaries [10]. Li X. Z. has suggested that after a company grows to a certain size, the business structure is complex, and negative synergy effects are difficult to avoid, so a carve-out can introduce the negative systemic effects of the parent company and the subsidiary, focus on their respective core businesses, and enhance the effectiveness of both parties [11].

Based on Aron and Holmstrom, Tirole, the management incentive hypothesis was proposed that equity carve-outs are the result of internal incentives [12, 13]. In 1993, Holmstrom and Tirole have found that the closer management and employee earnings are to the value of the company's stock after an equity carve-out, the more effective it is to improve the level of internal incentives [13]. Guo H. X., and Wan D. F. proposed that parent companies use equity carve-out as a tool to enhance the incentive level of department managers while allowing employees to purchase company stock in the secondary market, which ties managers' and employees' earnings to the company, can effectively improve the internal incentive level and solve the problem of insufficient internal incentive that is common in some companies [4]. In addition, Chen D. in 2021 suggested that the equity carve-out can make the results of operating results of the division to which it belongs more clear and the performance more visually presented, which helps to provide motivation to the person in charge [6].

2.3 Studies of the Financial Effect

Short-Term Financial Effects. Schipper and Smith were the first to focus on the performance of carve-outs and found that carve-outs were associated with an average excess return of 1.83% on the parent company's stock price after selecting companies that underwent equity carve-out from 1963 to 1984 for their study and analysis [1]. Allen and McConnell have studied 188 objects from 1978 to 1998 and found that the parent company's cumulative excess return over the announcement period was 2.12% [7]. These two studies suggest that equity carve-outs can lead to excess short-term returns.

However, a 1977 study by Hand and Skantz has found negative 5-day stock price performance returns for the parent company after the announcement of the carve-out of the subsidiary [12]. The short-term financial effect is questionable.

The situation is similar in the Chinese market. In 2003, Wang H. C. and Wang X. K. have studied Tongrentang and found that the carve-out brought a positive premium effect to the parent company [13]. In 2004, Li Q. Y. and Wang Y. H. have found that Tongrentang achieved positive cumulative returns but negative cumulative excess returns for comparable firms in the same industry in all three announcement periods, concluding that the carve-out brought short-term wealth benefits [14]. By studying the case of Kangenbei, Zhang S. H. found negative cumulative excess returns for three announcement periods, contradicting the conclusion of positive short-term wealth effects [15]. In 2023, after studying 93 companies from 2018 to 2021 in terms of investor expectations and firm specialization, Lv L. J. et al. have concluded that a carve-out would generate a relatively significant positive abnormal return near the event date [16].

Long-Term Financial Effects. In 1999, Vijh has studied a sample of 628 between 1981 and 1995 and found that the performance of subsidiaries did not fall below the corresponding benchmark within three years after the carve-out [2]. However, Madura and Nixon studied 88 public companies that were spun off from 1988 to 1993 and came to a contradictory conclusion by finding that carve-out reduces the long-term performance of both parent and subsidiary companies [17]. Dasilas and Leventis empirically analyzed European firms and found that the parent company's long-term market value rises and then falls [18].

In 2016, Tu H. X. and Zhou Q. have studied the case of Tongrentang and found that spin-offs can have a positive value effect on firms [19]. In 2022, Xu Z. Y. et al. have studied companies that underwent carve-out in Shanghai and Shenzhen from 2000 to 2018 and concluded that equity carve-out can positively affect firm value [20].

2.4 Research Review

The above-mentioned literature demonstrates the continuous exploration and research of domestic and international scholars on the motivation and financial effects of equity carve-out. The motives of equity carve-out can be broadly categorized into the financing hypothesis, information asymmetry hypothesis, centralization strategy hypothesis, and management incentive hypothesis. On the whole, the core motive of equity carve-out is to enhance the value of the company and improve corporate governance. In the exploration of the financial effects, domestic and international research findings are divergent in terms of both the long-term and short-term benefits. For short-term financial benefits, most of the findings focus on the positive short-term financial benefits of a carve-out. In the long run, however, the companies investigated have different profiles and findings, and existing studies do not yield consistent conclusions. The financial effects of a carve-out need to be analyzed on a case-by-case basis as each company differs in terms of corporate management strategy, investment situation, operation, and industry in which it operates. Lv, L. J. et al. have argued that the degree of information disclosure and the consistency of the industry of the parent company of the subsidiary are factors that can influence the financial effect of the company [16]. This paper studies the motivation and financial performance of the carve-out of a subsidiary in the manufacturing industry by the parent company of the restaurant industry to provide a reference for equity carve-out in the restaurant industry, but since each company's specific situation is different, companies should not follow the trend blindly according to the actual situation.

3 Haidilao Equity Carve-Out Case Study

3.1 Introduction of Haidilao

The Haidilao brand was founded in 1994 in Jianyang, Sichuan Province, China. After more than 20 years of development, as of June 30, 2022, Haidilao has a total of 1,435 directly operated restaurants, of which 1,310 are located in mainland China, 22 stores are located in Hong Kong, China, Macau, China, and Taiwan, China, and 103 are located in 11 other countries. The total number of employees exceeds 100,000. Haidilao is not only the leader in China's hot pot restaurant industry but is also growing into an internationally renowned restaurant company as it continues to develop and go global. On September 26, 2018, Haidilao was successfully listed on the Hong Kong Stock Exchange.

The concept of "service first, customer first" has always been upheld by Haidilao. By providing special and personalized services, the brand differentiates itself from other traditional restaurant brands. The "Haidilao" style service has also become synonymous with excellent service quality. In addition to the traditional dine-in service at the front-end stores, Haidilao also sells hot pot bases, dipping sauces, and marinated dishes separately, and sells self-heating hotpots as derivative products in supermarkets and online e-commerce platforms. In addition, the company grows, raises, transports, and packages raw materials in-house, eschewing outsourcing and procurement. As a result, the Haidilao Group has developed a robust supply chain, which has powered Haidilao to become the top-ranked Chinese restaurant brand in terms of revenue worldwide. In 2022, Haidilao's brand value reaches US$3.427 billion and the total market value reaches HK$121 billion.

Haidilao, a leading company in the restaurant industry, had tried to go public earlier but ended up in failure. The dilemma of listing in the catering industry has always existed, and choosing the path of spin-off listing can circumvent the problems and gain listing advantages for the group, which has demonstrated significance for other catering enterprises.

3.2 Introduction of Yihai International

Yihai International is a wholly-owned subsidiary of Haihailao, established in 2005. Its main business is the production and sale of hot pot bases, dips, and other Haihailao-derived products such as self-heating hotpot and self-heating rice. Yihai International is the exclusive supplier of hot pot bases to Haidilao and its subsidiaries and also supplies and sells products to major commercial supermarkets while using e-commerce platforms to further expand its sales reach. It is a leading manufacturer of compound condiments in China. In 2016, Yihai International was successfully listed on the Hong Kong Stock

Exchange on July 6, 2016. Yihai International currently has over 2,500 employees and assets totaling HK$5.75 billion. It generated revenue of $5.943 billion in 2021 and $2.688 billion in the first half of 2022, up 2.2% compared to the same period last year.

3.3 Motivation Analysis

Piloting and Driving the Parent Company to go Public. Since 2011, there had been numerous reports about the listing of Haidilao, and the founder Zhang Yong also clearly expressed his good wishes for the listing of Haidilao in 2011, but it has not been realized. In 2016, the catering industry has entered the maturity period, the turnover has grown in a big way year by year, and the competition in the industry was fierce. At the same time, with the rise of take-out platforms, the traditional catering industry suffered some impact. Because Haidilao needed to sustain its development and continue to expand its market share, it needed to continuously invest and make the market see the market value of Haidilao. Listing is undoubtedly a good way to combat the risks in the industry and gain more investor recognition.

However, there are many difficulties for the restaurant industry to go public. First, most of the raw materials in the catering industry are time-sensitive, for example, the ingredients of the hot pot of Haidilao need to ensure freshness. Cost loss is difficult to measure, and financial management is difficult to standardize and transparent. Secondly, the growth and success of chain stores are difficult to replicate. The business conditions of stores in different locations can be very different. There is also the impact of food safety issues and the difficulty of managing standards. At the same time, the regulatory authorities have a very high threshold for restaurant companies to be listed. All of these factors hinder successful IPOs in the restaurant industry.

The listing of Yihai International is much easier. Yihai International belongs to the category of manufacturing industry, the production and sales process is more standardized, the revenue and cost industry is easier to measure, and the regulatory agencies are more convenient to supervise, so it is easier to go public.

The listing of the subsidiary can obtain more social shareholder support, enhance the group's risk resistance, and facilitate the subsequent development and promote the listing of the parent company. At the same time, enterprise-related information, such as shareholding structure, financial situation, and business mechanism, is disclosed, and the market and investors can more clearly evaluate Yihaihai Group and understand its market potential for future listing works. In addition, the listing of the subsidiary can also test investors' attitudes and confidence in the Haidilao Group and facilitate the parent company's strategic adjustment.

Broaden Financing Channels. The restaurant industry was highly competitive, and the industry is nearly saturated. If Haidilao Group wanted to survive and develop in such a market environment, it needed huge financial support. At that time, Haidilao had been expanding and rapidly opening stores to seize the market, all these strategic initiatives needed a lot of capital investment. However, the group has trouble with the listing, Haidilao chose the method of equity crave-out to go list, taking its subsidiaries public to obtain capital to support development, and the listing could help Haidilao to obtain a lot of funds to continue to invest.

The Need for a Centralized Strategy. Haidilao has been seizing the market through rapid expansion, and also rapidly and gradually expanding overseas, laying out around the world and building an international restaurant brand. After the listing, with more capital support, Haidilao would have more energy to expand outward to the international market.

Haidilao has a complete supply chain system, forming a "Haidilao" ecology that has a synergistic effect on the development of the Haidilao Group. When an enterprise has limited energy and resources, the distribution is inevitably uneven, and there are multiple industrial chains, the management efficiency may have a side synergy effect, and the value of each industry cannot be maximized. Separating Yihai International from the Haidilao Group would allow Yihai International to focus more on the research and development and sales of its own hot pot base business and refine its business while driving the parent company's development through the IPO. The parent company can also focus more on improving the competitiveness of its core business, gaining greater recognition from customers and the market, and ultimately maximizing its overall corporate value and competitiveness.

Improving Information Asymmetry. One of the reasons why it is difficult for restaurant companies to go public is the lack of transparent financial information. After the subsidiary crave-out, the company's operation and financial data will have to be disclosed to the public promptly and be monitored by more new shareholders, the market, and the government, and the transparency of information will be improved. At the same time, the attention of investors for the parent company due to the listing of the subsidiary can also enable the parent company to obtain a more reasonable market value assessment and promote the value of the whole Seabed Group. Therefore, improving information asymmetry is also one of the motivations for the crave-out.

3.4 Crave-Out Process

Yihai International was established in 2005, formerly as the Chengdu branch of the Haidilao Group. To optimize the company's structure for future development and access to international capital markets, the Group optimized and restructured the company's business so that Yihai could focus more on its core business of seasonings and facilitate its listing. The core path of Haidilao's carve-out of Yihai International was to build a red-chip structure outside of China.

The first step was an offshore restructuring. In 2013, YIHAI was incorporated in the Cayman Islands as an exempted company with limited liability, then established as a BIV company, and on October 29, YIHAI LTD, a wholly owned subsidiary, was established in the British Virgin Islands. Next, YIHAI International established a wholly-owned subsidiary in Hong Kong.

The second step was to conduct a domestic restructuring. First, on April 28, 2014, a wholly-owned subsidiary, Zhengzhou Shuhai, was established as Chengdu Yue Yihai LLC. This company then replaced the other four branches of Haidilao and took over all sales of compound seasonings together with the Beijing sales branch. on November 24, the Haidilao Beijing sales branch changed its system to become a limited liability company and changed its name to Yihai Beijing, and in December of the same year, became a wholly-owned subsidiary of Zhengzhou Shuhai. on December 1, Yihai (China) established Yihai Shanghai, a foreign-invested enterprise. In 2015, Yihai Shanghai established Yihai Bazhou. In addition, Seabed Chengdu transferred all its facilities and inventory for the production of seasonings to Chengdu Yue Yihai. The production of compound seasonings was then handled by Chengdu Yueyihai and Yihai Bazhou, while the sales were handled by Chengdu Yueyihai and Yihai Beijing. At this point, the production and sales of all the seasonings under Haidilao were handled by Yihai International's subsidiaries, and the domestic reorganization was completed. The specific restructuring chronology is shown in Fig. 1 below.

After the restructuring and integration, Yihai International was successfully listed on the Hong Kong Stock Exchange in June 2016.

Crave-out process timeline

Formation (Cayman Islands)	Registration of YIHAI LTD	Establishment of Yihai China (HK)	Establishment of Chengdu Yue Yihai	Beijing branch restructured Yihai Beijing affiliated with Zhengzhou Shuhai	Established Yihai Shanghai and acquired Zhengzhou Shuhai	Establishment of Yihai Bazhou	Haidilao Chengdu Branch Transferred Assets to Chengdu Yuet Yihai
2013 10.18	10.29	12.9	2014 4.28	11.24	12.1	2015 6.11	12.20

Fig. 1. Crave-out process timeline.

4 Financial Effects Study

4.1 Financing Capability

The financing efficiency of Yihai International has been significantly improved after the crave-out. As shown in Fig. 2 below, Yihai International's gearing ratio had been maintained at around 80% for three years before the IPO, which was a very high and dangerous level. After the crave-out in 2016, Yihai International's gearing ratio dropped rapidly to 11.06% and has been maintained steadily at below 20%, since then, with a significant increase in the proportion of assets. Before the IPO, Yihai International's current ratio had been low, and after the IPO in 2016, the current ratio increased significantly, reaching 7.99, and has been steadily and slowly declining since then, with a current ratio of 3.27 in the data disclosed in the 2021 annual report. From these data, Yihai International's short-term solvency has improved a lot after the crave-out and its assets are highly liquid. If the asset liquidity is too large it may have a side effect on the operating profitability, but after Yihai International went public, the funds obtained from the financing were partially invested in production and construction, and the current ratio slowly decreased, which shows that Yihai's asset liquidity is developing to a healthier situation. Therefore, overall, Yihai International's current ratio has become more reasonable and healthier.

In conclusion, the crave-out has significantly improved the solvency and financing ability of Yihai, reduced financial risk, and made the related financial position healthier and more reasonable.

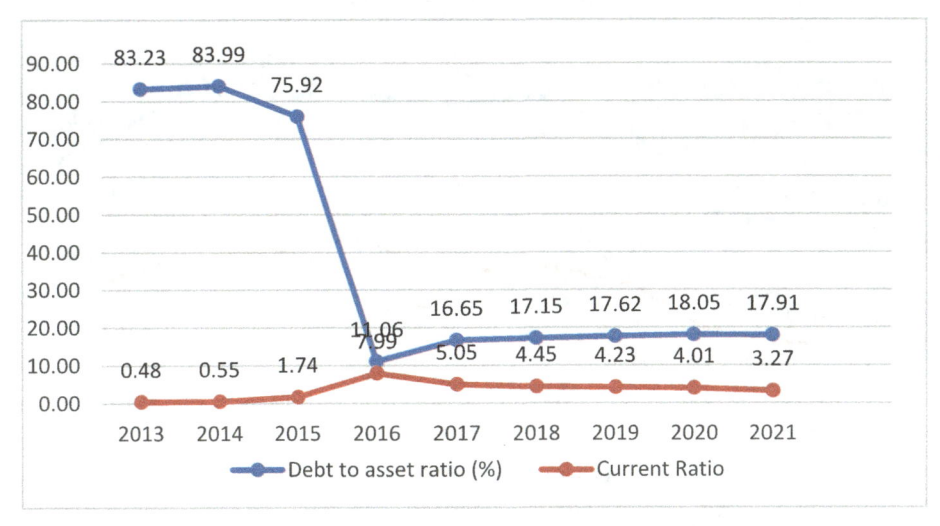

Fig. 2. Financial liquidity indicators trend chart.

4.2 Profitability

The profitability of a company has been an important indicator of its business condition. As shown in Fig. 3 below, Yihai International's gross profit margin has been high and stable. The gross profit margin had a large increase in 2015 because the number of Haidilao stores increased significantly in 2015, driving the sales of Yihai International as the exclusive supplier, while Yihai International made improvements in the production process to reduce costs. After the listing, the gross margin has no particularly significant impact and change, and the gross margin remains stable. The net profit margin is similar to the gross profit margin, which has been improved and stabilized after the IPO, indicating that Yihai International's profitability is not very volatile and is stable, which is a very good sign for investors who tend to be conservative.

Return on Total Assets As can be seen by the trend of the dashboard in graph 4, Yihai International has a stable return on total assets. This indicates that Yihai International has been having relatively good asset utilization efficiency, and the profitability of the enterprise is relatively stable and long-lasting. In addition, Yihai International has been steadily expanding its business, and the overall operation and profitability are developing in a good way, and the enterprise is facing low risk. In turn, the change in the ROE curve is relatively intense, with a sharp decline at the listing node in 2016, which is due to the low net assets of Yihai International before the listing, and after the listing, the enterprise issued shares and the net assets increased significantly, after which the net income rate was also stable and improving.

Earnings per share (EPS) is the net profit received by the company's common shareholders for each share held and is an important indicator of the company's profitability. As shown in Fig. 4, the trend of EPS of Yihao International has been on the rise without huge fluctuations, which indicates that the profitability of the company is steadily improving, especially after the IPO, EPS has been growing steadily and rapidly, although there may be a small drop in 2021 due to the impact of the epidemic, which is also an

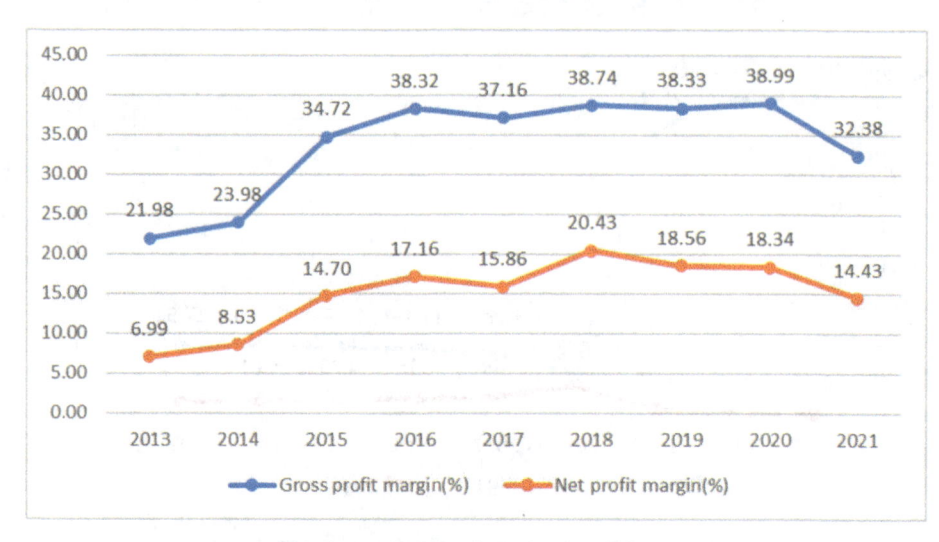

Fig. 3. Profitability indicator trend chart.

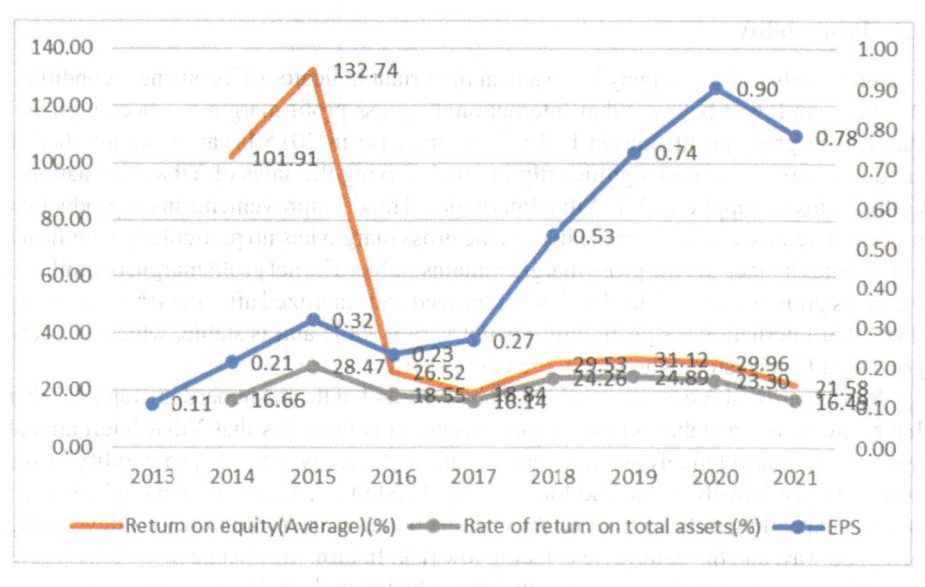

Fig. 4. Returns trend chart.

indication of the stable good and long-lasting profitability of the company, without huge fluctuations even under huge external shocks.

4.3 Growth Capability

The company's growth capacity reflects the company's future development prospects, this article analyzes Yihai International's growth capacity after listing from three indicators. The details are shown in Fig. 6. Yihai International's revenue growth rate reached the highest in 2015 before the IPO, which was due to the rapid expansion of Haidilao in 2015 to drive Yihai's revenue, and the growth rate slowed down after the IPO, with a small and steady decrease. The profit growth rate follows a similar trend to revenue, continuing downward after plummeting in 2015 but falling below 0 in 2021. With revenues still growing and profits falling, companies need to be concerned about cost control. As can be seen from the graph, after the IPO, revenue and profit growth slowed down and are still basically growing, but companies still need to plan for the long term and not rely too much on the parent company to change the current increasingly weak growth rate, improve the continued decline and enhance the ability to sustain growth.

For the total asset growth rate, this indicator responds to the change in the total asset scale of the enterprise. As can be found from Fig. 5, the violent trend of Yihai International's asset growth disappeared after the IPO, but the asset scale is still growing steadily, and the surface enterprise asset development is relatively reasonable and the development prospect is promising.

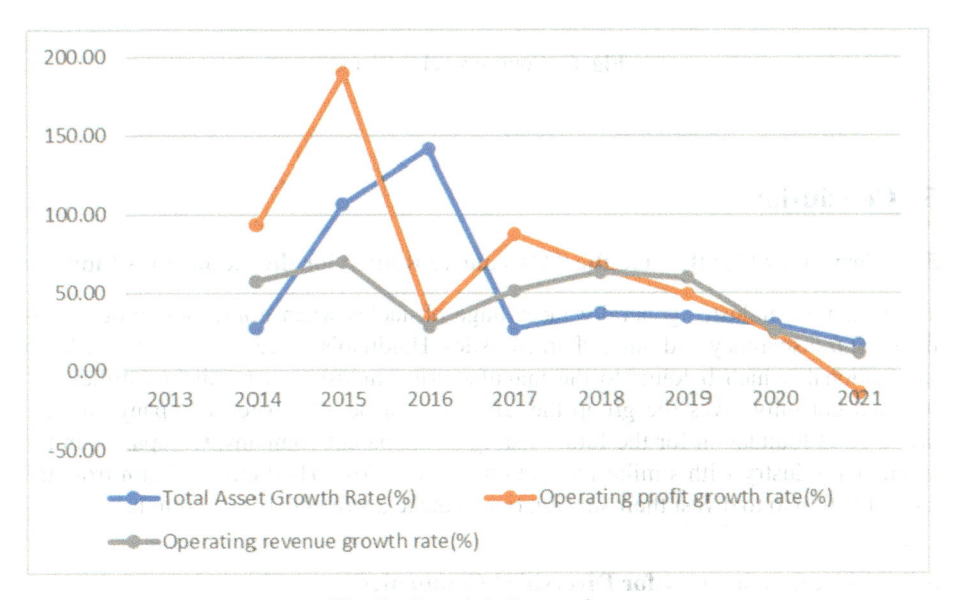

Fig. 5. Growth indicator chart.

4.4 Company Value

As can be seen from Graph 6, the market value of Yihai International has grown rapidly since its listing, reaching its peak in 2020 and becoming the second company in the compound seasoning industry with a market value of over 100 billion, which is growing rapidly. Although the market capitalization has fallen in recent years, Yihai International is in the leading position in the industry, in addition, the Chinese compound seasoning industry is still in the growth period, so it can still be optimistic about the future value of Yihai International.

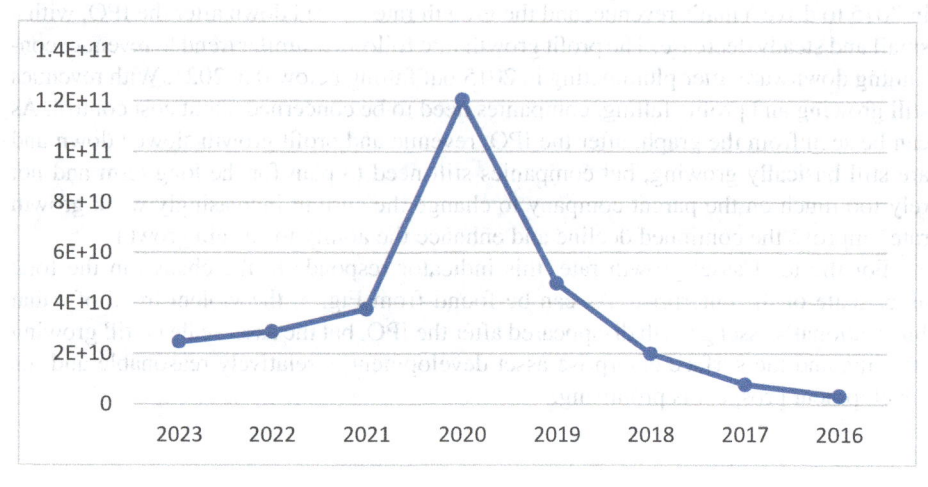

Fig. 6. Company value Chart.

5 Conclusion

5.1 Carve-Out Has Become the "Alternative Route" for the Restaurant Industry

The restaurant industry generally faces huge obstacles when going public due to its financial transparency and other characteristics. Haidilao's successful spin-off of Yihai International, which belongs to the manufacturing industry, is much less difficult to list, and not only gives the group the advantage of being a listed company but also lays a good foundation for the future listing of the parent company. Companies in the restaurant industry with similar motivation to divest from Haidilao can learn from the case of Haidilao to divest their subsidiaries to make a strategic breakthrough.

5.2 Nucleation Strategy for Diversified Companies

Companies are often faced with negative synergy effects of multiple industry chains due to uneven distribution of resources while diversifying their business, and a spin-off can improve this situation in a more friendly way. Yihai International can focus more on its core business after the spin-off and can find good financial results and improved operational efficiency. Therefore, diversified companies can also focus on business enhancement, improve core competitiveness and maximize the value of each industry through carve-out.

5.3 Formulate Long-Term Strategic Planning and Focus on the Future

The equity carve-out of Yihai International has not only improved the company's financial position but also the successful listing of the parent company afterward, which depends on the long-term planning of the group's strategy. However, after the IPO, the subsidiary also needs to develop its strategic plan, not to rely too much on the parent company, to prevent all losses, to make full use of the advantages of being a listed company, and to enhance the ability to develop independently and sustainably.

References

1. Schipper, K., Smith, A.: A comparison of equity carveouts and seasoned equity offerings: share price effects and corporate restructuring. J. Financ. Econ. **15**(1/2), 153–186 (1986)
2. Vijh, A.M.: Long-term returns from equity carveouts. J. Financ. Econ. **51**, 273–308 (1999)
3. Powers, E.A.: Deciphering the motives for equity carve-outs. J. Financ. Res. **26**(1), 31 (2003)
4. Guo, H.X., Wan, D.F.: A review of research related to equity carve-outs. Secur. Mark. Her. **211**(02), 61–67 (2010)
5. Chen, X.: Motivation and impact of corporate equity carve-out. Bus. Cult. (Acad. Ed.) **08**, 125–126 (2010)
6. Chen, D.: Motivations of listed companies' carve-outs and their impact on company development. China Manag. Inf. Technol. **24**(05), 49–50 (2021)
7. Allen, M.: Equity carveouts and managerial discretion. J. Finance **53**(2), 163–186 (1998)
8. Nanda, V.: On the good news in equity carve-outs. Finance **46**(5), 1717–1737 (1991)
9. Comment, J.: Corporate focus and stock returns. J. Financ. Econ. **37**, 67–87 (1995)
10. Li, Y.S.: Institutional construction leads capital market reform. China Finance **920**(02), 27–29 (2020)
11. Li, X.Z.: The article behind listed companies' eagerness to equity carve-out. China Bus. **362**(01), 134–136 (2023)
12. Hand, S.: The bad news in equity carveouts. Working paper (1997)
13. Wang, H.C., Cheng, X.K.: An empirical analysis of "Tongrentang" equity carve-out subsidiary listing. Manage. World **04**, 112–121 (2003)
14. Li, Q.Y., Wang, Y.H., Han, H.: The case of "Tongrentang": a reanalysis of the equity carve-out and shareholder value creation. Econ. Manag. **08**, 51–59 (2004)
15. Zhang, S.H.: Study on the economic consequences of equity carve-out of listed companies: a case study of Zoli Pharmaceuticals. J. Finance Account. **593**(09), 23–26 (2013)
16. Lv, J.L., Liu, Y.Z., Huang, Z., et al.: Exploring the share price effect of equity carve-out of listed companies. Finance Econ. **547**(02), 25–40 (2023)
17. Madura, N.: The long-term performance of parent and units following equity carve-outs. Appl. Financ. Econ. **12**, 171–181 (2002)
18. Dasilas, A., Leventis, S.: The performance of European equity carve-out. J. Financ. Stab. **34**, 121–135 (2018)
19. Tu, H.X., Zhou, Q.: Research on the value effect of contraction-based capital operation: the case of "Tongrentang" equity carve-out. Bus. Account. **23**, 50–53 (2016)
20. Xu, Z.Y., Sun, M., Liu, Y.S., et al.: The impact of equity carve-out listing on the value of corporate groups. East China Econ. Manag. **36**(03), 106–118 (2022)

Study on the Reasons for the Failure of the Audit of Luckin Coffee and Suggestions for Countermeasures

Yufan Li(✉)

Lee Shau Kee School of Business and Administration, Hong Kong Metropolitan University, Hong Kong 999077, China
s1280678@live.hkmu.edu.hk

Abstract. With the rapid development of China, auditing is essential to developing and managing every company. Strict auditing procedures and professional auditors can ensure the authenticity of corporate accounting information and prevent incidents detrimental to the company's rights and interests. This paper examines the Luckin Coffee audit failure and provides insight into the countermeasures and recommendations for audit failure. The paper introduces the whole incident and the companies involved to reveal the means of financial fraud and the reasons for audit failure. Finally, it proposes countermeasures and recommendations for audit failure and calls on companies to strengthen their management to avoid similar incidents.

Keywords: Luckin Coffee · Audit · Financial Fraud · Financial Fraud

1 Introduction

Since the spread of the new coronavirus, the country's economic situation has been on a gradual downward trend, with it, a shift in consumer habits. There is a greater tendency to shop online without leaving home, and the penetration of online shopping has increased by more than 40% during the epidemic (2020). The term "home economy", as the name suggests, describes this phenomenon. The food and beverage industry has also been hit hard, with a loss of RMB 99.5 billion in 2020 compared to the Chinese New Year 2019 food and beverage economy. Luckin Coffee opened a new business model in response to this shift in consumer habits: online + offline, attracting many customers and going public with flying colors. Just as it took off, the Luckin Coffee: Fraud + Fundamentally Broken Business (2020) report released by Muddy Waters in the US exposed Luckin Coffee's financial fraud, which has since fallen from grace. Many scholars have studied the causes of audit failures and the solutions but are still determining the difficulty of implementing these initiatives. Auditing is not just a matter between two companies but for society, the state, and everyone. National policies, social orientation, and personalities can influence auditing quality, so studying how to put measures to reduce audit failure rates into practice is essential.

Based on the failed audit of Luckin Coffee, this study analyzes the causes from three aspects: the accounting firm, the CPA, and the auditing industry. It reviews the whole incident, sorts out the entire fraud process, and describes the reasons for the success of the fraud in four aspects: inflated sales, inflated costs, transfer of assets by related party transactions, and cash out by major shareholders, to put forward corresponding implementable countermeasure suggestions.

2 Literature Review

2.1 Relevant Foreign Studies

Some foreign scholars have analyzed the factors influencing audit quality in terms of personality, social trust, and the professional qualification of auditors.

Personality Affects Audit Quality. Jere R. Francis (2023) argues that the partners and managers of the firm have personal consideration skills and initiating structure skills so that their behavior can improve the effectiveness of the audit. Also, if the firm wants auditors with diverse personalities, then the firm can re-examine the performance evaluation system to avoid bias [1].

António Samagaio and Teresa Felício (2022) argue that it is vital for auditing firms to improve the fit between personality traits and the quality of audits they expect. Because personality is a complex and dynamic definition that changes with many factors, audit firms should not focus on one trait but on the overall trait when selecting, developing, and managing [2].

Social Trust Reduces the Demand for Audit Quality. Kuo et al. (2022) argue that social trust works by building networks of trustworthy norms and relationships, thereby alleviating agency problems. These demonstrate that social trust is negatively related to the need for audit quality [3].

Professionally Qualified Human Capital is Associated with Audit Quality. Albert L. Nagy, Matthew G. Sherwood, and Aleksandra B. Zimmerman (2022) argue that this phenomenon is more pronounced in peak season audits. Audit firm leaders and investors can assess the quality of an audit by assessing the professionalism of the auditor team's human capital [4].

2.2 Relevant Domestic Studies

Domestic research focuses on audit independence, model, process, management responsibility, professional ethics, and regulators to reduce audit failure rates.

Maintaining Audit Independence Can Improve Audit Success. Xu Qianqian (2023) argues that financial independence should exist between the auditor, the auditor, and the audited entity during their work. Independent monitoring and information transfer systems are needed to supervise and control the independent audit system when constructed [5].

Audit Quality is Related to the Audit Model. Yang Baoxue (2023) argues that the traditional audit model affects audit independence, as seen in previous examples. The disaggregation of our audit firms would better prevent the current corporate diversification from affecting audit quality, meaning that CPAs would be better off withdrawing from non-audit engagements [6].

Greater Management Accountability Helps to Reduce the Rate of Audit Failure. Wang Hongtai (2022) argues that the financial fraud at Luckin Coffee was committed and known only by the directors and that some company executives were motivated by profit to take the risk of falsification, which shows tacit approval by management. Above shows that the internal controls of Luckin Coffee are very loose, and there are no strict procedures to identify fraudulent behavior [7].

The Design and Implementation of Appropriate Audit Procedures Can Also Reduce the Audit Failure Rate. According to Shen Yanyin and Zheng Zhu (2022), appropriate audit procedures are designed and implemented for different audited institutions. Setting audit procedures by assessing the company's risks can lead to more reliable audit results [8].

Strengthening the Professional Ethics of Cpas Can Prevent Audit Failures. Hu Mingxia and Dou Haocheng (2021) argue that for financial colleges, majors, and those preparing for financial-related certificates, professional CPAs and regulators should be asked to provide training on cases of violations and ethics. Those who have become CPAs conduct professional and ethical assessments to make them quantifiable [9].

The Relevant Regulatory Authorities are Strict about the Quality of the Audit. Ye, Chen-Gang Wang, and Yun-Han (2020) argue that some accounting firms undertake audits that exceed the scope of their business capacity for the sake of reputation, resulting in frequent audit errors. The SFC should assess the size of different accounting firms and the competence of CPAs and limit the amount of work that the firms can undertake [10].

2.3 Research Review

The above literature points to different aspects of improving audit quality and reducing audit failure rates, which is a big challenge for the audit profession. However, some of the measures can be difficult to implement as it takes a long time to change the habitual behavior of society as a whole. This paper hopes to raise society's awareness of the importance of auditing, which is relevant to everyone's life, through the audit failure of Luckin Coffee.

3 The Luckin Coffee Audit Failure

3.1 About Luckin Coffee

Luckin Coffee opened its first shop in 2017, and by the end of 2018 had opened more than 2,000 shops in 22 cities across China before continuing to enter more cities at a rapid pace, eventually surpassing Starbucks, the industry's most powerful competitor, in terms of the number of shops and stealing a large portion of customers from Starbucks at a low price. 2019, Luckin Coffee successfully listed on the US NASDAQ exchange and raised US$560 million. It became the much-anticipated company with the shortest time from inception to IPO. Luckin Coffee mainly operates a coffee drink-making service and sells pastries and bakery items. Its household name online + offline business model creates an entirely cashier-free in-store environment for customers through a mobile app and shop network, making the buying process efficient and convenient and giving customers a great customer experience. This new business model is all due to advanced technology. Lackin Coffee uses data analytics and artificial intelligence to conduct extensive data analysis on customers, shop operations, and supply chain management to improve the accuracy of analysis to pinpoint customer preferences, cost control, and future forecasting.

In recent years, although the love of coffee among workers in China has been on the rise, it is still smaller than the coffee intake of people in Western countries. The "new retail" model adopted by Luckin Coffee is well suited to the pace of national life in China, attracting national consumption with affordable coffee beverages and setting off a new retail coffee boom in China, resulting in the emergence of businesses like Cudi Coffee imitating the new retail business model. Nevertheless, these imitations have never been surpassed. It was cheap, high quality, and had great offers compared to Starbucks. When many professionals predicted that Luckin Coffee must not be profitable, its financial information was breathtaking. It then managed to list on the NASDAQ exchange in the US at a rapid pace, an unprecedented achievement for a Chinese company. It was also because of its astonishing speed of rise and the specificity of its industry model that American Muddy Waters began to employ many people to squat and investigate the foul play. Soon the fraudulent practices of Luckin Coffee surfaced and have since fallen from grace. Table 1 shows that while cash from operating activities was negative in the three quarters of 2019, most corporate cash came from financing activities, and the total amount of financing gradually increased. The above analysis shows that to let shareholders and potential investors see the development and opportunities of the enterprise, Luckin Coffee has already started to fake step by step to gain the trust of all investors. The Luckin Coffee case is over, but its internal audit flaws represent some of the common fraud problems in the audit industry today and are worth exploring and studying.

3.2 Audit Firm Introduction

Ernst & Young is one of the Big Four accounting firms focusing on assurance, tax, transactional and advisory services, with a mission to "build a better business world", making it a household name today.

Currently, the primary services provided by Ernst & Young are advisory, audit, and tax services; advisory services focus on performance improvement, risk, IT, and financial services support; Ernst & Young's audit professionals, numbering over 85,000 (2023) worldwide, deliver high-quality audit services using three leading technology platforms unique to Ernst & Young: EY Canva, a global online audit platform, EY Helix, a global suite of analytical tools, and EY Atlas, a global cloud knowledge platform; tax services include domestic and international tax services, transactional tax services, and indirect tax services, and so on. Tax professionals provide the most comprehensive services following ever-changing laws and policies.

Ernst & Young has clients in 150 countries in various industries, including resources, financial services, government, healthcare, media, retail, and high technology. Three hundred thousand people use their expertise and knowledge to help clients manage risk, seize opportunities and respond to crises with quality. The Management Board includes its global leadership and governance, and EY's three business regions, divided into 28 territories: the Americas; EMEA; and Asia Pacific, make up EY's organizational structure. Furthermore, Ernst & Young in Asia Pacific China is responsible for the audit of Luckin Coffee from 2016 to 2018.

3.3 The Luckin Coffee Incident

Since the exposure of the financial fraud, the whole incident has been fermenting at a breakneck pace, and Luckin Coffee has experienced a series of significant changes such as delisting, fines, and personnel changes, encountering the biggest Waterloo since its listing (Fig. 1).

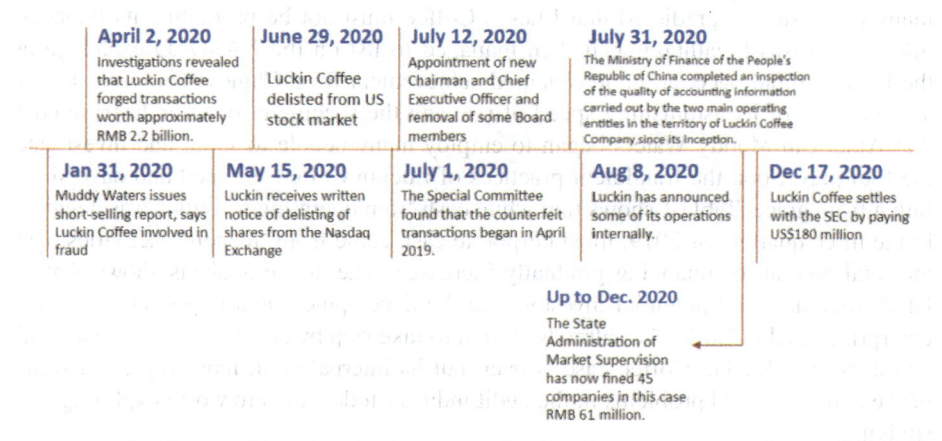

April 2, 2020	June 29, 2020	July 12, 2020	July 31, 2020
Investigations revealed that Luckin Coffee forged transactions worth approximately RMB 2.2 billion.	Luckin Coffee delisted from US stock market	Appointment of new Chairman and Chief Executive Officer and removal of some Board members	The Ministry of Finance of the People's Republic of China completed an inspection of the quality of accounting information carried out by the two main operating entities in the territory of Luckin Coffee Company since its inception.

Jan 31, 2020	May 15, 2020	July 1, 2020	Aug 8, 2020	Dec 17, 2020
Muddy Waters issues short-selling report, says Luckin Coffee involved in fraud	Luckin receives written notice of delisting of shares from the Nasdaq Exchange	The Special Committee found that the counterfeit transactions began in April 2019.	Luckin has announced some of its operations internally.	Luckin Coffee settles with the SEC by paying US$180 million

Up to Dec. 2020
The State Administration of Market Supervision has now fined 45 companies in this case RMB 61 million.

Fig. 1. Time combing chart for details after Luckin Coffee was exposed as a fake.

4 Luckin Coffee Fraudulent Means

4.1 Inflated Sales

Luckin Coffee first used number skipping to make it impossible to know the daily sales and guest traffic from direct order numbers, thereby inflating sales. Muddy Waters hired a large number of employees to monitor and record daily shop traffic, ultimately suggesting in the short-selling report that each shop inflated daily by at least 69% in Q3 2019 and by at least 88% in Q4 and that the actual selling price was 46% of the list price rather than the 55% previously claimed by management. The amount of falsification is to be considered, giving people and investors the illusion that Coffee's turnover is significant. In order to avoid being caught by the audit, Luckin Coffee claimed that the order flow was not available to the auditors due to technical reasons, exploiting the audit loophole. Secondly, Luckin Coffee recorded the free coffee delivered in the sales revenue section of the financial report, which not only maintained the goodwill of customers but also filled the gap in revenue from operating activities.

4.2 Overstatement of Costs and Expenses

The overstatement can be achieved by the illusion of high revenue growth, mainly in the advertising expenses of Luckin Coffee for Focus Media, which was reported to be inflated by more than 150% in the third quarter of 2019. However, the analysis found that Luckin's inflated shop operating profit in Q3 2019 was almost identical to the difference between its reported advertising expenses and the actual expenses of Focus Media tracked by CTR, which was approximately RMB 336 million, leading Muddy Waters to believe that Luckin Coffee had included shop operating costs in its advertising expenses so that operating costs were no longer harmful. Filling this gap is critical to the growth in the cash flow statement for revenue from financing activities. The company successfully avoided being audited by shifting advertising costs through an outsourcing company.

4.3 Transfer of Assets in Related Party Transactions

Wang Bai, a classmate of Chairman Lu Zhengyao, made a profit of $137 million on acquiring BaoWo Auto for $3.97 billion in January 2019 and sold it to Shenzhou YouChi for $4.11 billion later in February. It has been confirmed that Lu Zhengyao is the de facto controller of Shenzhou Youzhi. Wang Baiin opened a shop next to Luckin Coffee to sell coffee machines, coffee beans, and other supply chain products that Luckin Coffee needs to buy. Luckin would transfer assets from affiliated companies at prices well above the market price.

4.4 Significant Shareholders Were Cashing Out

The core management of Luckin and ShenZhou rent cars is the same people. They manipulated ShenZhou to rent a car when nine months after the listing began to cash out, a total of 1.6 billion, causing the share price to plummet and investors' interests to be damaged. This is the largest source of income for Luckin Coffee, other than financing, used to cover revenue and provide investors with an illusion of very high sales (Fig. 2).

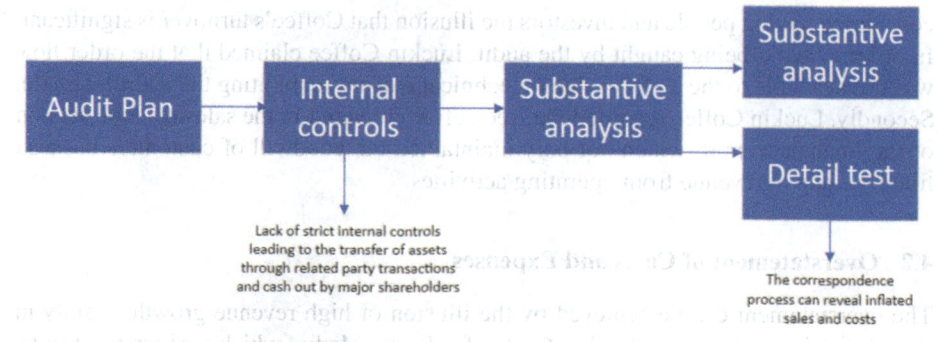

Fig. 2. Analysis of the causes of fraud through audit flow charts.

5 Analysis of Reasons for Audit Failure

5.1 Accountancy Firm Perspective

As an accounting firm responsible for auditing large listed companies, Ernst & Young did not promptly point out the problems with the 2019 financial report of RuiYing Coffee but only gave the corresponding explanation after Muddy Waters released its shorting report. From the perspective of Ernst & Young, the auditor cannot go to each shop to conduct the investigation in the standard audit procedure as Muddy Waters did, which directly led to the audit news lagging and causing information omission.

5.2 CPA Perspective

Internal Audit. The role of internal auditors is to detect and stop financial fraud. On the one hand, their sense of responsibility and morality was shallow, and they were profit-oriented, which led to a loss of authenticity in the company's financial situation; on the other hand, they did not have a good understanding of their internal audit position and did not have a comprehensive understanding of the laws and regulations involved in auditing. The company needed more education, which led to unclear ideological propositions and gave opportunities to people who wanted to take advantage of them. It is essential that internal auditors are not subject to strict rules and regulations and that no reward and punishment system is more appropriate to their work and life. Some internal auditors with weak ethics will gamble for immediate personal gain, and the prosecution will not investigate them. The stricter the rules and regulations, the fewer internal audit department mistakes.

External Audit. The income statement and balance sheet combination show that revenues and expenses are up significantly, which should increase sales. Still, inventories were down in the third quarter, and Luckin Coffee needed to be on time in releasing its fourth quarter financial statements, from which the accountant needed to be more sensitive to capture the fishy. The external CPA needed to understand the economic business activities and accounting information process of Luckin Coffee, perhaps because of complex accounting procedures which lead to many related party transactions or the complexity of economic operations, and so on. This resulted in the auditors being insensitive to some hints of fraud and having to be led by the nose of the audited company.

Audit Industry. There needs to be more supervision and guidance in the profession. The mixed status of the auditing profession is becoming increasingly evident, with some auditors exploiting the system for their profit and getting away with it. At the same time, some of those who want to stand firm in their positions and ethics are still forced to take advantage and are helpless to follow malicious commands. Only if the entire profession is vigilant and all auditors are twisted into one rope can the unscrupulous be left with no way out.

6 Conclusion

The following improvement measures and countermeasures can be concluded from the study of the failed audit case of Luckin Coffee from accounting firms, CPAs, and the auditing profession aspects.

6.1 Accountancy Firm-Level Response

Accounting Firms Should Always Be Alert and Sensitive to the Company Being Audited. While Ernst & Young, as an accounting firm, cannot do the same kind of hired workforce round-the-clock supervision that does not meet audit standards as Muddy Waters, it still has the opportunity to identify falsification even after performing detailed analysis of extensive data audit procedures. Moreover, this can be seen in the previous quarterly earnings reports and the delay in releasing the fourth quarter financial statements of Luckin Coffee. According to a statement issued by Ernst & Young, fraudulent elements were found during the audit of the 2019 annual report of Luckin Coffee. Still, there is no way to verify the statement's veracity, as the report was issued later than the report by Muddy Waters. This shows that improving the efficiency and accuracy of the review and making it public as soon as possible after confirming the problem can preserve the credibility of the accounting firm.

Familiarise Cpas with the Business Model of Luckin Coffee. Different business models for selling coffee brands will also have different ways of financial representation. The accounting firm can improve the accuracy of the audit by combining financial analysis and annual reports with the new business model to gain a deeper understanding of the audited company's daily income and expenditure, bookkeeping methods, and others.

Conducting Phased Audits. Changing the previous annual audits to quarterly audits is more accurate than annual audits and less labor-intensive than monthly audits. The company's financial signs can be tracked more closely, and the first signs of financial fraud can be detected and stopped in time.

6.2 CPA Level Response

Internal Auditors. Maintain a healthy and positive working atmosphere by doing careful background checks when recruiting new staff and prohibiting those with previous financial convictions from joining. Provide training to every auditor who joins the company and reinforces education on the law and staying sober in the face of temptation. Set up an internal reward and punishment system and set reasonable and legal criteria for rewards and punishments to increase the motivation of internal auditors.

External Auditors. Change audit firms regularly because once both companies become familiar with each other, some interest disputes may arise, leading to cover-up fraud. It is necessary to change the audit firm or the audit team of the same company to maintain the interests of both companies and the image of social fairness.

6.3 Audit Industry-Level Responses

There needs to be more supervision and guidance from society, leading to lawless elements not obeying or fearing the law. Using information technology, digital networks, and blockchain technology to see real-time data uploads from audited units through big data is also possible. It makes it easier to bring unruly elements to justice.

References

1. Francis, J.R.: Going big, going small: a perspective on strategies for researching audit quality. Br. Account. Rev. 101167 (2022)
2. Samagaio, A., Felício, T.: The influence of the auditor's personality in audit quality. J. Bus. Res. **141** (2022)
3. Kuo, N.T., Li, S., Jin, Z.: Social trust and the demand for audit quality. Res. Int. Bus. Financ. 101931 (2023)
4. Nagy, A.L., Sherwood, M.G., Zimmerman, A.B.: CPAs and big 4 office audit quality. J. Account. Public Policy 107018 (2022)
5. Xu, Q.: A study of ways to strengthen audit quality control in general. China Coll. Econ. (06), 28–31 (2023)
6. Yang, B.: Reflections on some issues of comprehensive audit quality control. China Coll. Econ. (06), 144–147 (2023)
7. Wong, H.: A case study of corporate internal audit failure - the case of Luckin coffee. Old Brand Mark. (21), 147–149 (2022)
8. Shen, Y., Zheng, Z.: Study on preventing audit failure in accounting firms: the case of ruihua certified public accountants. J. Hubei Univ. Sci. Technol. **42**(04), 47–54+73 (2022)
9. Hu, M., Dou, H.: Causes of audit failure and governance in China's accounting firms. Financ. Account. Monthly (15), 101–106 (2021)
10. Ye, C., Wang, Y.: A study on audit failure of accounting firms. Friends Account. (20), 36–42 (2020)

Baidu's Financial Competitiveness Research Based on DuPont Analysis Method

Yuqing Zhang(✉)

School of Social Audit, Nanjing Audit University, Nanjing 211518, China
202021028@stu.nau.edu.cn

Abstract. With the attention of enterprise management, financial competitiveness has gradually become an important component of the company's comprehensive competitiveness, and one of the evaluation methods is DuPont analysis. With the rapid development of the Internet economy and the rapid rise of artificial intelligence, China's Internet industry is facing opportunities and challenges. As one of the three giants of the Internet, Baidu's research on this enterprise is conducive to the development of China's Internet industry. To understand the relationship between DuPont analysis and financial competitiveness, this paper takes Baidu as an example to analyze Baidu's financial report data by using the DuPont analysis method, obtains Baidu's financial advantages and shortcomings, and then proposes methods to improve financial competitiveness.

Keywords: DuPont analysis · Baidu · Financial Competitiveness

1 Introduction

Due to the rapid development of productivity and the emergence of agency theory, the importance of management for enterprises continues to increase, and people gradually pay attention to the impact of financial level on the competitiveness of companies. As a result, many methods of analyzing financial competitiveness have emerged, one of which is DuPont analysis. With the development of economic globalization and the deepening of reform and opening up, China's economy is increasingly connected with the world, and Chinese enterprises are facing the challenges of transformation and upgrading. As one of China's Internet leaders, Baidu plays a pivotal role in the development of China's Internet industry. In the face of the trend of economic and social development, Baidu's active adjustment strategy has achieved certain results, but while exploring new development paths, some drawbacks have emerged. To better understand the connotation of financial indicators and the role of DuPont analysis in real life, and explore why Baidu has achieved Baidu as well as why Baidu's momentum has declined compared with Internet companies in the same period, this paper uses DuPont analysis to disassemble financial ratios, analyzes Baidu's financial data with horizontal and vertical directions, combines Baidu's actual actions and financial report changes to find the reasons for the data, finds problems accordingly, and finally makes appropriate suggestions. Based on the domestic and international economic situation, this study is convenient to learn

© The Author(s), under exclusive license to Springer Nature Singapore Pte Ltd. 2024
X. Li et al. (Eds.): ICEMGD 2023, AEPS, pp. 738–751, 2024.
https://doi.org/10.1007/978-981-97-0523-8_70

lessons for other similar types of enterprises, help the development of China's Internet industry, and ultimately serve China's modernization construction.

2 Literature Review

2.1 Definition of the Concept of "Financial Competitiveness"

In the face of fierce market competition, enterprises cannot ignore financial management if they want to achieve long-term development. Financial competitiveness is an important component of the core competitiveness of enterprises, which draws on the concept of enterprise competitiveness and uses management economics to understand the financial situation of enterprises. Regarding the concept of financial competitiveness, experts and scholars have conducted many studies on it, but its connotation has not been clear.

Yanhui Wang and Xiaoming Guo (2005) believe that financial competitiveness can be defined as a proprietary, excellent, and dynamically developing corporate financial knowledge with knowledge and innovation as the basic core and rooted in the financial capability system of enterprises [1].

Chenglin Hao (2006) believes that financial competitiveness is the ability to create value for customers by investing capital in income activities and the financial relationships generated by the capital investment of value chain or supply chain business cluster, taking market competition as the driving force, and focusing on obtaining competitive advantages of enterprises [2].

Wenlei Yu and Ying He (2018) believe that financial competitiveness is rooted in the financial resources and financial management activities of enterprises, and is based on the comprehensive strength of value-oriented growth management, profit management, and risk management [3].

Enterprise competitiveness is the survival and development ability of enterprises in market competition, and financial performance is one of the indicators to measure the comprehensive ability of enterprises. Through good financial management, enterprises can rationally use resources to implement corporate strategies, and business operations are reflected by financial indicators. The research of this paper analyzes the basic survival and development potential of enterprises based on three indicators reflecting profitability, asset use efficiency, and solvency, and analyzes the existing operation of enterprises with the help of financial data and explores their competitive advantages. Therefore, after fully understanding the research of experts and scholars and combining their research, this paper believes that financial competitiveness is the ability to reflect the level of corporate finance and sustainable operation with statement analysis as the main means and daily business behavior as the basis to enhance the core competitiveness of enterprises.

2.2 DuPont Analysis

DuPont analysis is a method of analyzing business performance from a financial perspective, named after the first application of DuPont in the United States. The idea of the traditional DuPont analysis method is to take the return on equity as the core indicator, decompose it into three ratios: net profit margin on sales, total asset turnover rate, and equity multiplier, and look for the intrinsic relationship between them, to find out the advantages and disadvantages of evaluating the operation of the enterprise. This approach is based on the goal of maximizing shareholder wealth and considers the return on capital to be the most critical analysis point, mainly looking at corporate profitability. The ratios it divides can find the factors that affect the return on capital, identify which sector is wrong and infer the corresponding improvement. Using the DuPont analysis method to build a ratio system can make the ratio analysis more organized and hierarchical, which is convenient for analysts to comprehensively understand the financial status of the enterprise.

2.3 Literature Review

Research on Financial Competitiveness

(a) Research Abroad. Dimitriu M (2009) believed that improving financial competitiveness should be a long-term process of building investment structure and innovation, taking into account the relationship between macro environment and micro policies as well as the costs caused by loopholes [4].

Herciu M and Ogrean C (2017) argued that there is a correlation between ROE and leverage ratios, but this correlation varies with different scenarios. At the same time, they believed that capital structure affects corporate profitability and that each company must determine the best capital structure to improve its profitability by fusing financing sources [5].

(b) Domestic Research. Xiao Zhu (2007) used factor analysis to construct an evaluation system for financial competitiveness and believed that financial competitiveness can be divided into financial viability, financial development, and financial potential [6].

Wenlei Yu and Ying He (2018) believed that the competition of Internet enterprises is essentially the competition of business models, and the strength of financial competitiveness could be measured and evaluated based on the perspectives of cash flow, comprehensive performance, and economic added value.

Zheyuan Chen (2022) analyzed the information technology industry and concluded that the financial competitiveness of this industry can be improved by improving innovation capabilities, increasing added value, optimizing capital structure, and building a talent introduction and training system [7].

Research on the Application of Dupont Analysis

(a) Research Abroad. Mihaela Herciu et al. (2010) studied the relationship between corporate profits and investment attractiveness, arguing that the financial objectives of profitable firms focus primarily on debt and demand capital from external suppliers of equity, but the correlation between high profits and high profitability ratios is weak [8].

Chatzimanolis G and Georgios K (2011) analyzed the profitability of Lekki Bank before and after the acquisition, showing that the return on equity of the new bank after the acquisition was lower than that of the original company, and that profitability needs to be improved to reduce the lasting impact of the financial crisis [9].

(b) Domestic Research. Ying Han (2013) selected China's listed commercial banks as DuPont analysis case enterprises, believing that the factors of the difference in the profitability of Chinese commercial banks mainly include system, the interest-bearing capacity of unit assets, intermediate business, and management expenses [10].

Zhixiao Hu (2020) used DuPont analysis to analyze the profitability of Q Group, and found the deep reasons behind the decline in Q Group's performance, believing that China's time-honored restaurants can rejuvenate consumption through high-end and rejuvenation of brands, adherence to quality, service improvement, and diversification of sales channels [11].

Yan You (2023) believed that the DuPont analysis system is a relatively complete comprehensive proportional analysis method, which systematically analyzed the overall operating conditions and economic returns of enterprises, analyzed WZ enterprises through the DuPont analysis method, and concluded that enterprises should pay equal attention to accounting development planning and overall strategic grasp to achieve overall profit targets [12].

A Review of the Study. At present, the research on financial competitiveness at home and abroad covers a wide range of industries, and various methods such as factor analysis, EVA model, and Harvard analysis framework are used to provide a methodological reference for this study. The analysis of the Internet and related industries facilitates this study to understand the differences between Internet financial competitiveness analysis and traditional industries. In addition, these studies construct more reasonable evaluation methods for different industries and can propose enterprise improvement strategies, which is helpful for this paper to understand the connotation of financial competitiveness and clarify the analysis direction of financial competitiveness.

Compared with foreign countries, many domestic studies based on the DuPont analysis method introduce case enterprises, calculate financial indicators to derive financial advantages and shortcomings, and put forward development suggestions. These studies provide inspiration and analytical ideas for applying DuPont analysis to practical cases. However, there are still certain problems in the current research on the DuPont analysis method, such as the current use of the DuPont analysis method to analyze specific enterprises mostly concentrated in sales, finance, and other industries. They lack of analysis of Internet enterprises and the combination of new economic trends. In the selection of case enterprises, there are not many studies that choose Baidu, biased towards a specific event, and the time is relatively old, which cannot more accurately reflect the new situation of Baidu after strategic adjustment. Therefore, this article chooses Baidu, a special enterprise, hoping to fit the background of the times, find ideas on how to develop enterprises under the new situation and promote the international development of Internet enterprises by analyzing Baidu's data in the past five years and comparing international leaders.

3 Case Business Profile

3.1 Case Enterprise Introduction

Baidu Online Network Technology Co., Ltd. (hereinafter referred to as Baidu), founded in 2000, was listed on the NASDAQ global market and the Hong Kong Stock Exchange in 2005 and 2021 respectively. Today, Baidu has established branches in many countries around the world, has more than 30,000 employees, and has been listed as one of the "Top 10 World-class Brands in China" by the Financial Times. Its Baidu search engine has become the world's largest Chinese search engine website, with more than 1 billion users. In addition to search engines, Baidu has also actively expanded into artificial intelligence, autonomous driving, chip research, and other fields, and established a diversified product and service portfolio.

In 2022, Baidu released its unaudited financial report for the fourth quarter and full year, which showed that Baidu's revenue in 2022 was 123.675 billion yuan, and its net profit (non-GAAP) was 20.68 billion yuan, a year-on-year increase of 10%. Fourth-quarter revenue of 33.077 billion yuan and net profit (non-GAAP) of 5.371 billion yuan, a year-on-year increase of 32%, exceeding market expectations. It can be seen that Baidu, as one of China's Internet giants, still has strong profitability in the market. Moreover, after a series of measures to reduce costs and increase efficiency, Baidu has continuously improved its operational efficiency, investing in technology and professionals, and promoting high-quality development. As a result, studying its financial competitiveness has high reference significance in the entire Internet industry.

3.2 Analysis of Internet Industry Characteristics

Baidu belongs to the typical Internet industry. Since the beginning of the 21st century, the Internet industry has developed rapidly and the number of global users has increased year by year. It has also become an important part of the world's industry, driving continuous growth in various fields. The Internet industry is different from traditional industries and has the following outstanding characteristics:

Technology Research and Development is the Core Competitiveness. Taking Baidu as an example, Baidu's R&D expenses will be 2.33 trillion yuan in 2022. Since most Internet companies provide services through online platforms to obtain revenue, the service experience of users is crucial, and updating and upgrading products and services is one of the ways to improve user satisfaction. Achieving this goal depends on R&D and innovation, so the Internet industry often invests a lot of money in this field to enhance its core competitiveness.

Asset-Light is the Main Business Model. Internet enterprises mainly rely on the provision of Internet-related services to obtain income, so compared with a large number of fixed assets such as factories, machinery, and equipment, Internet enterprises pay more attention to patents, technological innovation, user resources, and other intangible assets. Taking Baidu as an example, its fixed assets accounted for about 6% of its total assets in 2022. It can be seen that to achieve rapid development, Internet companies often choose to focus more on technology-intensive products and services and outsource other low-value-added businesses, thereby reducing corresponding costs.

High Return and High Risk are Characteristics of Profitability. Compared with traditional industries, there are many differences in the profit model of Internet companies. In the early stage of development of Internet enterprises, they often invest a lot of costs in research and development, publicity, attracting customers, etc., due to the small number of users and less income, they are prone to continuous losses. With the high speed of enterprises and the increase in the number of users, cost input slows down, revenue gradually rises, losses improve, and corporate profits continue to increase. However, although well-run enterprises can obtain a lot of benefits, the Internet revenue conversion process is not stable enough, it is easy to break the capital chain, and coupled with high investment, therefore there is a high risk of bankruptcy, which brings bigger challenges to companies entering the Internet industry.

4 Baidu Financial Competitiveness Analysis

4.1 Analysis of Financial Competitiveness Under DuPont Analysis

Return on equity (ROE) is a key ratio in DuPont analysis and an important indicator of corporate profitability. Line charts are often used to show the trend and degree of difference in values over time. Generally, in 2018–2022, Baidu's ROE showed a downward trend, and changes in total assets and net profit were the direct cause of this phenomenon. Baidu's ROE in the past five years is detailed below in Table 1:

Table 1. Baidu 2018–2022 ROE analysis. Unit: million RMB.

Year	2018	2019	2020	2021	2022
Net income	27,573	2,057	22,020	18,830	20,680
Total asset	297,566	301,316	332,708	380,034	390,973
Total liability	121,814	128,501	140,865	156,082	153,168
Net asset	175,752	172,815	191,843	223,952	237805

In 2018, the ROE was 15.69%, the highest in the past five years; in 2019, ROE was 1.2%, the lowest in nearly 5 years. Compared with 2021, although Baidu's total assets increased by 2.9% in 2022, its net profit margin also increased by 9.8%, which increased more than its total assets, making Baidu's ROE in 2022 increase compared with 2021. However, compared with 2018, Baidu's total assets in 2022 increased by 31.3%, but its net profit fell by 25%, resulting in Baidu's ROE in 2022 being lower than in 2018.

Taking advantage of the opportunity of China's economic recovery, Baidu gradually resumed various business activities in 2022. Although Baidu's core and online marketing revenue has declined to varying degrees due to the recurrence of the epidemic in some regions, iQIYI's non-online marketing revenue has increased, which has led to a relative decrease in Baidu's annual net profit compared with 5 years ago, which not only means that Baidu has not yet recovered from the impact of the epidemic, but also indicates that

Baidu's strategic problems have led to a decline in profitability. As for costs, in addition to increasing long-term investment in AI, Baidu has also strengthened cost control and operational efficiency. In 2022, Baidu's cost of revenue fell by 46% year-on-year, and R&D expenses decreased by 23% year-on-year.

Google is an American multinational technology company, the world's largest search engine, and also provides various Internet products and services such as cloud computing. From the perspective of enterprise type, Google and Baidu have similarities, so this article also uses Google's 2022 data as a reference to conduct a horizontal comparative analysis of Baidu. The ROE situation of Google from 2018 to 2022 is as shown in Fig. 1:

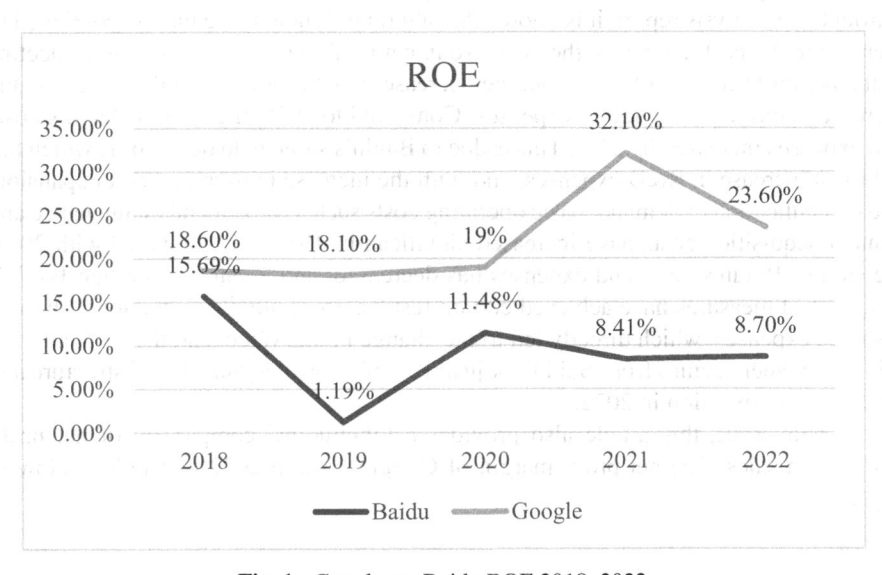

Fig. 1. Google vs. Baidu ROE 2018–2022.

As of December 2022, Google's ROE is 23.6%, which is significantly higher than Baidu. By comparison, Google's higher ROE is mainly due to higher net profit. Although the business composition is very similar, Google's net profit in 2022 is about 20 times that of Baidu. As an early international Internet company, the business structure is relatively mature, and the new business expanded in recent years has also created better performance, coupled with a larger user base than Baidu, it can be seen that Google's profitability is stronger than Baidu's.

4.2 Analysis of Net Profit Margin on Sales

The net profit margin on sales is one of the measures of profitability that can help investors assess whether a business has made enough profits from sales and control costs and expenses. By analyzing Baidu's net sales profit in the past five years, Table 2 is as follows:

It can be seen that except for the net profit margin of sales in 2019 due to the low net profit of 1.92%, the values in the remaining years generally show a decreasing trend. The

Table 2. Baidu 2018–2022 Net profit margin comparison. Unit: million RMB.

Year	2018	2019	2020	2021	2022
Total revenue	102,277	107,413	107,074	124,493	123,675
Net income	27,573	2,057	22,020	18,830	20,680
Baidu	26.96%	1.92%	20.57%	15.13%	16.72%

net profit margin on sales in 2022 decreased by about 10% compared to 26.96% in 2018. Through the analysis report, it is known that although Baidu's revenue has continued to increase in the past five years, the decrease in net profit has led to a continuous decline in the net profit margin of sales, and the decrease in net profit is directly caused by the increase in costs and operating expenses. Compared to 2018, the sum of Baidu's costs and expenses increased by 24%. This is due to Baidu's strategy to develop AI which has led to an increase in R&D expenses, and with the increase in users, market expansion, and diversification of demand, basic operating costs such as broadband maintenance and content acquisition costs have increased significantly. However, compared with 2021, the sum of Baidu's costs and expenses has decreased, and it can be seen that Baidu's cost control measures have achieved certain results, especially the reduction of human resource expenses, which directly led to the change in this value, and the realization of this achievement comes from Baidu's adjustment of its own organizational structure and personnel composition in 2022.

As with ROE, this article also provides a longitudinal comparison of net profit margins on sales. The net profit margin of Google sales in 2022 is detailed below in Fig. 2:

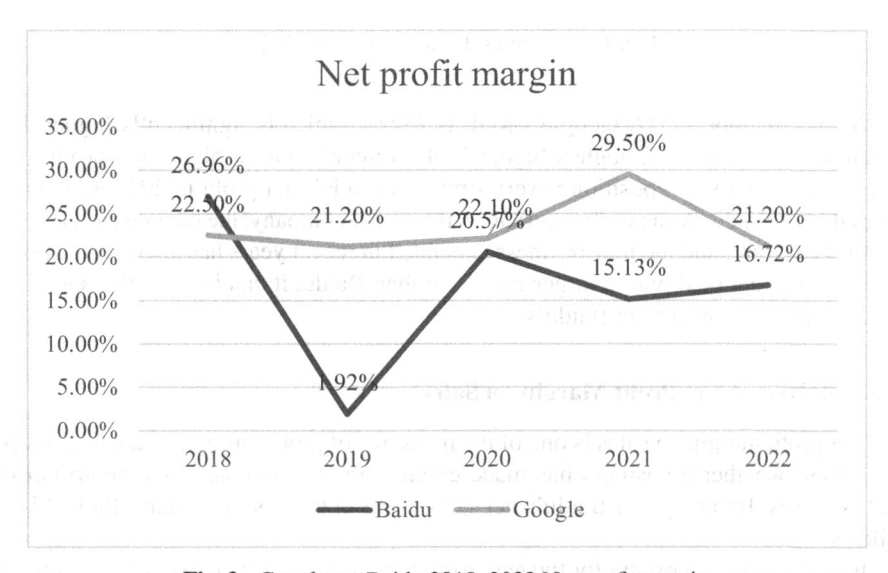

Fig. 2. Google vs. Baidu 2018–2022 Net profit margin.

Compared with the data of the past five years, Google's net sales profit margin is higher than Baidu, indicating that the overall profitability is stronger than Baidu's. In December 2022, Google's net profit margin on sales was 21.20%, slightly higher than Baidu's. Google's total revenue and net profit are more than ten times that of Baidu, but due to the cost of network maintenance and traffic to support its business, as well as the cost of maintaining its company scale, it finally shows a situation that is not much different from Baidu. Although Baidu's profitability is relatively weak through ROE analysis, comparing the net profit of sales shows that Baidu is not doing anything, but is adjusting its strategy to find a breakthrough in transformation and actively moving closer to the international level.

4.3 Total Asset Turnover Analysis

The total asset turnover ratio can reflect the number of times the total assets are turned over in a year, and the more times, the shorter the number of days to turn, the stronger the ability to generate income with assets. Similar to the above two index functions, the total asset turnover ratio can also be used to analyze the operation of enterprises. The specific data of Baidu's total asset turnover in the past five years are as follows in Table 3:

Table 3. Baidu's 2018–2022 Asset turnover analysis. Unit: million RMB.

Year	2018	2019	2020	2021	2022
Total revenue	102,277	107,413	107,074	124,493	123,675
Total asset	297,566	301,316	332,708	380,034	390,973
Baidu	0.37	0.36	0.34	0.35	0.32

Although Baidu's total asset turnover rate from 2018 to 2022 showed a downward trend overall, the highest was 0.37 in 2018 and the lowest was 0.32, but it was more stable, basically fluctuating between 0.30–0.37, and the value was not much difference between each adjacent two years. In general, total asset turnover around 0.8–1 is relatively healthy. From this point of view, Baidu's asset turnover speed is relatively slow, and the asset utilization rate is relatively low. Taking the 2022 data as an example, current assets accounted for 54% of Baidu's total assets, a decrease from 2021, and the decline in short-term investment was the main reason. Non-current assets rose 6.8%, with significant increases in long-term deposits and maturing investments. This is because Baidu has increased long-term investment due to strategic adjustments to cope with market competition, such as cloud services, which require enterprises to build a large number of servers. However, at present, Baidu's projects are slightly inferior compared with similar projects of other Internet giants, so Baidu's ability to generate revenue is still relatively weak.

To better understand Baidu's financial competitiveness, this article compares Baidu with Google, and the equity multiplier for the two from 2018 to 2022 is as follows in Fig. 3:

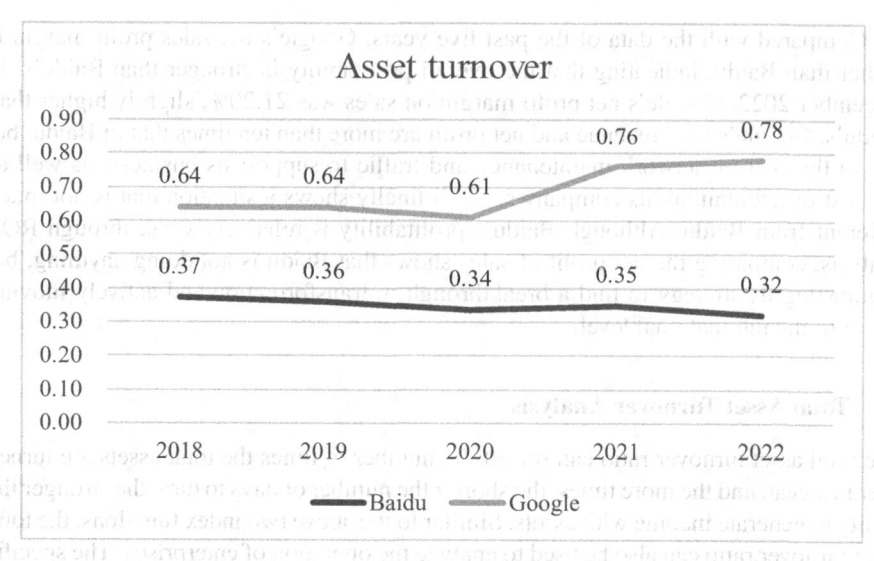

Fig. 3. Google vs. Baidu's 2018–2022 Asset turnover.

Compared with Google, Google's total asset turnover rate in the past five years has exceeded Baidu's, of which the total asset turnover rate in 2022 is 0.78 times, more than twice that of Baidu, indicating that Google's asset turnover is faster and its ability to generate revenue is stronger. Google has undergone a restructuring to streamline its original responsible business and reallocate its assets. The network infrastructure it has invested in has been put into use and achieved good benefits, and it has also achieved leading results in intangible assets such as patents. In addition, Google's total assets are about 6 times that of Baidu, and it is a larger operation.

4.4 Equity Multiplier Analysis

The equity multiplier is also an indicator of DuPont's analysis, which reflects corpo-rate leverage. Generally speaking, the larger the equity multiplier, the smaller the proportion of capital invested by shareholders in total assets, and the higher the degree of corporate debt. The specific data of Baidu's equity multiplier from 2018 to 2022 is as follows in Table 4:

Table 4. Baidu 2018–2022 Equity multiplier analysis. Unit: million RMB.

Year	2018	2019	2020	2021	2022
Total asset	297,566	301,316	332,708	380,034	390,973
Total liability	121,814	128,501	140,865	156,082	153,168
Liability to asset ratio	40.94%	42.65%	42.34%	41.07%	39.18%
Baidu	1.69	1.74	1.73	1.70	1.64

In the past five years, Baidu's equity multiplier has been relatively high, all above 1.6, but overall, it is relatively healthy. Among them, the highest equity multiplier in 2019 is 1.74, while the lowest equity multiplier in 2022 is 1.64. It can be seen that Baidu's borrowing to expand its operations has gradually increased, but in 2022, compared with last year, the total debt decreased by about 2%, indicating that Baidu began to pay attention to its leverage to strengthen financial management, and generated a relatively good cash flow after a year of operation, which can support Baidu to pay part of accounts receivable, bank borrowings and some long-term liabilities. Such results also show that Baidu's long-term solvency has been enhanced, operational risks have been reduced, and the rights and interests of shareholders and creditors have been more protected.

Google's equity multiplier in 2022 is 1.43, which is lower than Baidu's equity multiplier in the same year, and Google's total debt is about 5 times that of Baidu. According to the above, Google's asset-liability ratio is about 29.9%, while Baidu's asset-liability ratio is about 39.18%. Google's growth in recent years has increased investor confidence, relying heavily on equity financing. In addition, Google's free cash flow decreased in 2022, and a large amount of cash flow was spent to repay financing expenses such as deferred liabilities, which slowed down Google's total debt growth and better leverage than Baidu.

5 Analysis of the Problem of Weakening the Financial Competitiveness of the Enterprise

By comparing Baidu's net sales margin, total gearing ratio, and equity multiplier side-by-side, as well as comparing Google's indicators, it can be found that Baidu, as one of China's leading Internet companies, has relatively strong financial competitiveness. However, compared with the performance of recent years and international companies in the same industry, Baidu still has some problems in profitability, and asset management and risk control, the specific analysis is as follows:

Profitability Needs to be Improved. Although Baidu is involved in various fields, its main source of revenue is online marketing services. In 2022, this business revenue accounted for more than 60% of Baidu's total main business revenue, and other businesses accounted for only 40%. This phenomenon reflects Baidu's weakness in multi-line competition, and although Baidu's search position gives it a leading edge in the Chinese advertising market, other businesses are not strong in revenue generation, and once online marketing revenue is affected by the epidemic and other accidental events and significantly tightened, it is easy to lead to a decline in overall revenue. Baidu's profitability is also volatile, and its auction advertising model and new fee-based services have caused some users to turn to alternatives. In addition, compared with international search engines such as Google, Baidu mainly develops domestic users, which makes its user volume relatively small, which is why there is a large gap with Google's financial indicators.

In addition to search engines, Baidu has also expanded its video platform and artificial intelligence business. Baidu's iQIYI has an operating profit margin of 5% in 2022, up 20% from last year, and its revenue mainly relies on subscription members. Although iQIYI's profitability has increased, similar video websites such as Youku and Tencent have brought greater competitive pressure to iQIYI, and iQIYI's better reporting results are mainly reflected in the reduction of costs, so iQIYI's future revenue is still facing challenges. Unlike iQIYI, artificial intelligence started late is an emerging industry, and is in a period of strategic transformation, so the profitability of this type of business has not yet been fully utilized.

Low Asset Utilization. Baidu's total gearing ratio is relatively low, which is due to the increase in total assets and the decrease in total revenue. Baidu has invested heavily in bioscience, chip research and development, autonomous driving, and other fields, and established relevant subsidiaries. These areas require enterprises to invest a lot for a long time, the commercialization process is slow, the capital is not easy to return, the return period is long, and a large number of companies are established to consolidate assets, resulting in the current investment assets to create income is weak. In addition, Baidu's total cash accounts for about 44% of total assets, which means that Baidu may have a lot of idle cash, low utilization of working capital, and deficiencies in financial management.

Compared with Google, its Google cloud and hardware development business development is earlier. Their technology is more mature, coupled with the operation experience of massive servers and cheap data centers, making their asset revenue effect stronger than Baidu. It can be seen that Baidu needs to further tap its potential in developing high-tech emerging businesses.

Investment and Financing Risks are High. In terms of financing, equity multipliers can reflect the relationship between shareholders' equity and total assets. In 2022, Baidu's equity multiplier was the lowest in nearly five years, and the optimization of its gearing ratio was mainly due to the reduction of non-current liabilities, while current liabilities increased by 6.9%. This shows that Baidu has reduced its long-term liabilities and transferred more short-term liabilities, which means that Baidu is facing greater repayment pressure in the short term, and needs to be vigilant about whether it has enough cash to pay its debts to reduce financial risks.

In terms of investment, Baidu's current strategy is to broaden its track and cater to the new trend of AI. However, Baidu is facing competitive pressure from many aspects: Tesla in self-driving cars, Huawei Cloud and Xiaomi Cloud in cloud services, and other businesses such as online disks, games, navigation, and other markets are also fiercely competitive. In recent years, Baidu has continued to expand its scale and invested in and acquired many companies, but many companies have a small market share and are not very competitive, which has not achieved the expected results but has increased operating costs. Therefore, to seize market share as soon as possible in areas other than search engines, Baidu has invested a lot of money in research and development. However, it is unbeknown whether these inputs will bring benefits, and it is prone to continuous losses that consume funds to maintain basic operations. Once there is a problem in the company's operation and the capital chain is tight, it is difficult to quickly replenish the funds, which has a greater investment risk.

6 Conclusion

Through analysis, Baidu has the problems of weak profitability, low asset utilization rate, and high investment and financing risks. In response to these problems, this article believes that Baidu can improve in the following aspects:

Improve Revenue Structure. For its main business, although Baidu's online advertising still has a certain degree of competitiveness, the bidding model adopted has caused major social events and caused its consumer trust to decline. Therefore, considering long-term development, Baidu needs to change the original advertising model, assume corporate social responsibility, improve customer experience, and improve customer loyalty to enhance the revenue stability of this business. Baidu's main users are currently in China, and the threat to other domestic competitors in terms of search engines is relatively small, but Baidu cannot ignore these external threats and needs to actively transform to seize the potential market and develop mobile and information flow business.

For other businesses, video platforms such as Baidu's iQIYI are more effective in cost control, so they can focus on increasing revenue. In the face of fierce competition, these platforms should adhere to the content first, and increase user stickiness by launching high-quality output, to compete for market share and increase the number of users and the number of subscribers. At the same time, the department in charge of this platform can learn from the operation and management experience of other websites, attract active users, and improve sustainable profitability.

Select the Right Strategic Area. Baidu intends to develop the artificial intelligence market in line with the new development trend, but it needs more consideration in the selection of specific fields. Even if Baidu has more resources and a large number of talent advantages, the AI and smart car fields have a long payback period and are not easy to make profits in a short period, so Baidu can conduct market research to determine how to commercialize products in these fields as soon as possible and meet customer needs to stimulate potential profitability. In addition, to reduce the cost of silence, Baidu needs to clarify its advantages, conduct a multi-faceted evaluation of invested and future investment projects, select key areas for research and development, and promote problem products into star and cash cow products. At the same time, Baidu can reduce unnecessary capital expenditures by tightening mergers and acquisitions or appropriately abandoning underperformed companies.

Improve Risk Management Capabilities. The goal of risk management is to obtain maximum security assurance at the minimum cost, and the Internet industry has the characteristics of high risk, so risk management ability is very important for enterprises. Baidu can optimize its capital structure, adopt appropriate financing methods to reduce financial risks and prevent financial risks such as debt through multiple financing channels. In addition, Baidu can strengthen corporate governance, set performance targets and reward mechanisms, strengthen internal controls, and do a good job of dynamic monitoring to prevent strategic and operational risks.

References

1. Guo, X.M.: Research on the theory and comprehensive evaluation of the core financial competence of listed companies. Shenyang: Northeastern Univ. (7), 1–43 (2005)
2. Hao, C.L., Yao, Z.F.: Analysis of financial competitiveness and its constituent factors. Financ. Account. Monthly (9), 61–62 (2006)
3. Yu, W.L., He, Y.: Evaluation of financial competitiveness of internet enterprises. New Money Manage. **Z1**, 21–25 (2018)
4. Dimitriu, M.: Financial aspects of competitiveness in the sustainable development of the company. EIRP Proc. **4**(1), 498–502 (2009)
5. Herciu, M., Ogrean, C.: Does capital structure influence company profitability. Stud. Bus. Econ. **12**(3), 50–62 (2017)
6. Zhu, X.: Research and analysis on financial competitiveness of listed companies. Financ. Account. Bull. (7), 17–19 (2007)
7. Chen, Z.Y.: Financial competitiveness analysis of information technology industry—taking Zhongke Soft Technology Co.Ltd. as an example. Invest. Entrep. **33**(20), 141–143 (2022)
8. Herciu, M., Ogrean, C., Belascu, L.: A Du Pont analysis of the 20 most profitable companies in the world. In: The Proceedings of 2010 International Conference on Business and Economics Research. International Economics Development and Research Center, pp. 46–49. IACSIT Press (2010)
9. Chatzimanolis, G., Georgios, K.: Du Pont analysis of a bank merger and acquisition between Laiki bank from Cyprus and Marfin investment group from Greece. Is there an increase of profitability of the new bank?. MIBES (10), 157–176 (2011)
10. Han, Y.: Profitability analysis of China's listed commercial banks based on DuPont analysis method. Shanxi Univ. Financ. Econ. (10), 3–44 (2013)
11. Hu, Z.X.: Research on profitability of Q Group Co., Ltd. based on DuPont analysis method. Nanjing University of Aeronautics and Astronautics (8), 1–52 (2020)
12. You, Y.: Enterprise profitability analysis and research based on DuPont analysis method. Time-Honored Brand Mark. (5), 164–166 (2023)

The Impact of COVID-19 on the Aviation Industry: Event Study on U.S. Passenger Airline Stocks

Yuxin Chen[1(✉)] and Ziqing Gong[2]

[1] University College London (UCL), London WC1E 6BT, UK
ZCAHY67@ucl.ac.uk
[2] Macau University of Science and Technology, Macau 999078, China

Abstract. This study aims on analyzing the impact of the COVID-19 pandemic on the aviation industry by using stock data from the listed US Airline companies. The hypothesis is that the pandemic has a significant negative effect on these airline companies and is likely to have a different scale of impact on companies specializing in international flights to those specializing in domestic flights. Data is retrieved for both individual stocks and S&P 500 index (benchmark) for both pre-and post-pandemic outbreaks, based on which an event study using the Linear Regression Model was conducted. Using calculated daily returns as a performance indicator, robust results reveal a good level of match between the selected stocks and the market index, and the confidence interval test reflects that the pandemic has an additional negative effect on the aviation industry relative to the benchmark return, a stronger impact on companies specializing in international flights than those specializing in domestic flights, and effects are not identical across companies. The US aviation industry has a high market share worldwide, thus attracting our study interest. Results from our research provide a solid foundation for government to implement a recovery plan and would serve as a guide for potential investors.

Keywords: COVID-19 · Aviation Industry · Passenger Airlines · Civil Aviation · Equity Investment

1 Introduction

It took Columbus more than two months sailing to discover America and now it only takes 12 h flight from Beijing to JFK, New York City: All thanks to the development of the civil aviation industry. Yet the Civil Aviation Industry is a complex, gigantic sector instead of only the airline companies themselves. Besides the airline companies, the Civil Aviation Industry also includes aircraft manufacturers, telecom companies, internet service providers, service sectors, etc. The Civil Aviation Industry plays a crucial part in any economy, especially in the United States as it not only virtually links all countries together, but also boosts international trade and encourages international cooperation. According to the Federal Aviation Administration, the civil aviation-related industry has contributed to more than 5% of the Gross Domestic Product in the United States, has generated $1.8 trillion in revenue, and has supported nearly 11 million jobs.

However, a dramatic change happened over the past three years due to an unexpected pandemic outbreak that happened at the end of 2019. COVID-19 was first found in China in December 2019, yet the vast majority believe it was just another form of flu. The Chinese government took the initiative in disease control, the first-ever lockdown of many cities. Despite the initial success that the Chinese government has made, the disease soon spread out world-widely, on March 11, 2020, an official declaration of the pandemic has been made.

Suddenly, the pause button was pressed the world was not ready for such a big shock, especially for the airline companies.

In the pre-covid era, the public sees persistent prosperity and consistent expansion in the aviation industry. Billions of domestic and foreign direct investments are flowing into this industry every year, supporting the rapid growth in long-distance education, business, and travel. As a result of that, airline companies are being relatively profitable as indicated by TEKER et al. [1], though not comparable to many growth companies, a steady level of profit margin and healthy capital structure would also attract many value investors.

As per stock price data, the U.S. economy has gone through a few stages at the index level: as the secondary market is more sensitive to factor changes, at the beginning of the pandemic, we see a huge jump in the index level, followed by a recovering stage till its peak and then another abrupt jump starting from the end of 2021. The first two stages can be easily explained by the traditional technical analysis, while the recent drop would need more attention. A generic explanation for the last stage would be the inverse relationship between stock market performance and inflation rate which is somewhat like that of 1981 except for a lower possibility of soft-landing.

In this study, we use S&P 500 stock index as the benchmark for its positive correlation and high level of representation of the economy. As for individual stocks, Delta Airlines (DAL), United Airlines (UAL), Southwest Airlines (LUV), American Airlines (AAL), Alaska Airlines (ALK), Hawaii Airlines (HA), JetBlue (JBLU), SkyWest Airlines (SKYW), and Spirit Airlines (SAVE) are selected. Most of these securities are included in the S&P 500 index, which guarantees a high level of correlation and further provides a higher chance for robust casual relationships. Two companies on our list need extra attention: American Airlines (AAL) which is the largest airline company in the world, offering routes connecting all important terminals internationally. During the pandemic, AAL has been responsible for transporting passengers internationally when many other US companies discontinued their business. Another company is Southwest Airlines (LUV) which is the largest low-cost airline company in the world. Due to the increase in fuel costs combining the increase in inflation, airline companies are all facing a higher operating expense. Because of the competitive nature of this industry and the change in demand elasticity (in the pre-covid era, demand for air tickets is relatively elastic as it is closely related to recreational travel whereas, during the pandemic, recreational travel decreased dramatically leaving business travelers and other travelers for necessary reasons the main consumer, thus a more inelastic demand), it is interesting for us to analyze the performance of this famous low-cost airline company's performance during the pandemic.

However, it is worth noting that we are not going to analyze the effect of COVID-19 on individual stock price/return, as the result is most likely pre-determined. In contrast, we are going to analyze the additional effect of COVID-19 on airline companies by running a regression concerning index level and stock price level to isolate the systematic influence. In addition, among the selected airline companies, we are going to further divide them into two groups: companies specializing in domestic routes and international routes as we suspect COVID-19 would have a different impact on these two groups. For the group specializing in international flights, we have DAL, AAL, UAL, ALK, and SAVE while for the other group specializing in domestic flights, we have LUV, HA, JBLU, and SKYW.

It is only a matter of time before the pandemic comes to an end, and we must admit that it is very hard to answer the question 'When exactly?'. However, research is not all about prediction, it is more valuable to learn from the past and use our findings to guide future action. We hope our research can provide some suggestions for policymakers when making recovery plans, and we also hope investors would find our results helpful when making future investment decisions.

This paper is organized as follows: Previous related literature will be discussed in the next section, then we will cover the data and model we used. The later section presents the empirical results, conclusion, and future research interests will be discussed in the last part.

2 Literature Review

No one would doubt that the US stock market is the most active market on this planet for its long history, the number of the company listed, and high liquidity. When investing in stocks and shares, institutional investors are likely to classify them into value stock and growth stock. The former one is likely to be a large-cap stock with a high dividend payout rate, a steady operating performance, and a low P/E rate; while the latter one is likely to be a small-to-medium cap stock with high R&D expenditure, low dividend payout rate, and fluctuating profit margin. As for civil aviation companies, which group should they go into? Various research has been done, Fend and Wang [2] indicated in their research that aviation companies should be classified into value stocks. This finding supports our choice of using the S&P 500 index as our benchmark and guarantees a high positive correlation between the index and the selected underlying. In traditional financial analysis, financial ratios like profit margin, EV/EBITDA, turnover ratio, ROE, and ROA are frequently used. Each financial ratio is intended to provide a snapshot of a company's performance quantitatively, however, analyzing them separately can be troublesome. For instance, a company can be rated 'strong buy' for its outstanding profit margin. However, this same company may have trouble in collecting debt which indicates by a low A/R turnover rate.

To address this problem, Teker et al. [1] created a harmonic index in their analysis of the top 20 airline companies. The harmonic index model incorporates statistics from 4 aspects, namely profitability, operating, liquidity, and efficiency, within each category, a weighted average method is used. According to this research, Delta, American Airlines, Southwest, and JetBlue these four US companies on the list, indicating the profitability of the civil aviation industry. This finding is consistent with the results in the report from Bouwer, Krishnan, Saxon, and Tufft [3] that Delta, Southwest, United Airlines, American Airlines, and Alaska Airlines are among the top 10 value-creating airline companies.

The US Federation of Aviation Administration indicates the importance of the civil aviation industry to the US economy, this industry not only contributes to GDP and domestic employment but also attracts more than 8 billion dollars in annual R&D expenses over the past few years. Abbas et al. [4] reveal in their research that in the pre-covid era, the aviation industry fertilizes the travel industry by continuously improving service quality and lowering costs. Consequently, the shock from COVID-19 almost destroyed the travel industry and severely hurt the aviation industry as well. The United Nations [5] did a scenario analysis to analyze the impact of COVID-19 on aviation and international travel. In their experiment setting, scenario 1 represents the most pessimistic case, scenario 2 represents the less pessimistic case, and case 3 represents the neutral case, surprisingly in case 1, we see a 2.4 trillion dollar decrease in the world GDP, and in case 2, we see a 1.7 trillion dollar decrease in the world GDP. Bouwer et al. [3] also indicate in their report that among all aviation-related sectors, airlines are the biggest value destroyer during the pandemic, the airline companies suffered 167.9 billion dollars in economic loss in 2020.

COVID-19's impact on the aviation industry is obvious, but the world is not losing faith in the economy's recovery, humans have experienced different pandemics in the past and we all succeeded in the end. Thus, researchers and organizations have done much research on how to help the aviation industry to recover and what the future of the aviation industry should be. Bouwer, Saxon, and Wittkamp [6] predict that leisure trips will rapidly recover and reach around 80% of the pre-pandemic volume in 2024, on the other hand, business trips will take the longest to recover if it fully recovers at all. There are many different channels to answer this discrepancy, and the main one would be the changes in people's lifestyles caused by COVID-19. In the pre-pandemic era, only a minority of people work from home or do meetings online. However, after almost 3-years pandemic, online meetings and working from home have already become an unstoppable trend. Thus, many business trips will be unnecessary. Serrano and Kazda [7] are predicting what future airports should be like in their research, AI technology, and Less human intervention seem to be on top of their list. During this pandemic, we have already seen the power of Artificial Intelligence: Video cameras are analyzing passengers' identities even with the mask on, robots are helping people deliver supplies, digital travel files are gradually replacing the traditional paper-form file, etc. This assumption of a digital future is consistent with the suggestion from EU [8] in their project of relaunching transport and travel after COVID-19.

3 Methodology

3.1 Overall Explanation

The methodology applied to this research paper is Event Study coined by Ball and Brown [9], whose principle is based on the research purpose to choose a particular event and analyze the sample stock return rate before and after the research event. It explains the impact of the specific event on changes in sample stock prices and returns. Firstly, it uses the market model to estimate the normal return of sample stocks. Then the Abnormal Returns (AR) and Cumulative Abnormal Returns (CAR), which were summed up by AR both got from the event window, can measure the degree that stock prices abnormally react to the event, and the information disclosure and shows whether an event has any extra effect on sample stocks, compared to the fluctuation of the broader stock market.

3.2 Event Study Steps

1. Choose the Estimation window and the Event Window.
2. Calculate the daily returns separately on sample stocks and returns on the stock market index using the closing price for both the Estimation window and the Event Window.

$$R_t = \frac{P_t - P_{t-1}}{P_{t-1}} \quad (1)$$

where:
R_t is the Daily Returns on day t.
P_t is the Closing Price on day t.
P_{t-1} is the Closing Price on day t − 1.

3. Estimate the market model using the daily returns data of sample stocks (R_t) and the market index (R_{mt}) in the Estimation Window, by applying Ordinary Least Squares (OLS).

$$\hat{R}_t = \alpha + \beta \hat{R}_{mt} \quad (2)$$

$$\varepsilon_t = R_t - \hat{R}_t \quad (3)$$

whereby:
$\hat{R}_t$ is the estimated daily returns of the sample stocks.
R_t is the actual daily returns of the sample stocks
$\hat{R}_{mt}$ is the estimated daily returns of the market index.
R_{mt} is the actual daily returns of the market index.
In this way, we can obtain the variables: $\alpha, \beta, \varepsilon$.
Calculate the variance: σ^2

$$\sigma^2 = \frac{\sum(\varepsilon_t - 0)^2}{T} \quad (4)$$

where:
T is the number of days in the Estimation Window.
4. Compute the Abnormal Returns (AR) for everyday t in the Event Window.

$$AR_t = R_t - (\alpha + \beta R_{mt}) \quad (5)$$

Compute the Cumulative Abnormal Returns (CAR) for each t in the Event Window.

$$CAR_t = \sum_{s=1}^{t} AR_s \quad (6)$$

5. Confidence Intervals for the Cumulative Abnormal Returns compare CAR_t with $\pm 1.96\sigma\sqrt{t}$:

$$-1.96 \leq \frac{CAR_t - \mu}{\sqrt{t \times \hat{\sigma}^2}} \leq 1.96 \quad (7)$$

where:
$\mu = 0$: the average of $\hat{\varepsilon}_t$ based on the H_0.
t: the ordinal number from 1 to 21 in this study.
Standardize formula (7):

$$-1.96\sigma\sqrt{t} \leq CAR_t \leq 1.96\sigma\sqrt{t} \quad (8)$$

6. Plot CAR_t as time series plot along with the two confidence interval lines at $\pm 1.96\sigma\sqrt{t}$. Upper and lower confidence limits are separately presented by the formula below:

$$y = \pm 1.96\sigma\sqrt{t} \quad (9)$$

4 Data Analysis

4.1 Time Period Selection

This paper chose the whole year of 2019 (**January 1st, 2019, to December 31st, 2019**) when there was no COVID-19 outbreak as the Estimation Window. After a period as quarantine interval to make sure the data objectivity, the Event Window selected at the period spans from **March 5th, 2020, to April 2nd, 2020**. The specific event date is **March 19th, 2020**. The reason why the study chose this day is that the first COVID-19 Lockdown in the US was issued was California announced Statewide Stay-at Home Order on this day [10]. As early as January 20th, 2020, the US Centers for Disease Control and Prevention (CDC) announced 3 US airports, Los Angeles International Airport, California; San Francisco International Airport, California; and John F. Kennedy International Airport, New York City, New York would begin screening for coronavirus [11]. However, there are extremely many airports in the US and these 3 airports only account for a little part of it, which means they did not influence most people and draw enough attention among the public. Not until March 19th, 2020 the public realized the seriousness of COVID-19. In addition, since that day almost all the states in the US gradually issued Stay-at-Home directives such as Nevada, New Jersey, Illinois, and so forth. So, this specific day is an obvious turning point and quite a lot of people could not travel as conveniently as before. With this Event Window, the difference before and after the epidemic can be clearly shown.

4.2 Market Models of 9 American Aviation Stocks

After calculating the daily returns on all sample stocks which are 9 major U.S. aviation stocks including AAL, DAL, UAL, ALK, SAVE, LUV, HA, JBLU, and SKYW, the market models separately according to the 9 stocks are figured out by OLS. The different market models of sample stocks are shown in Fig. 1, 2, 3, 4, 5, 6, 7, 8 and 9. It presents changes in each sample stock along with the fluctuation of the S&P 500. Also, the formula obtained from the graph will be used to estimate the value of daily returns from March 5th to April 2nd, 2020, in the Event Window.

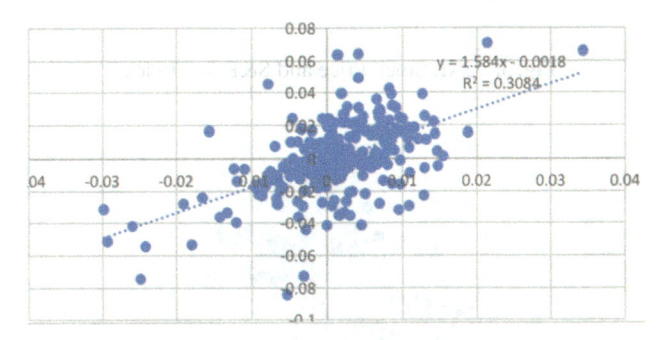

Fig. 1. AAL Stock Price and S&P 500 Index.

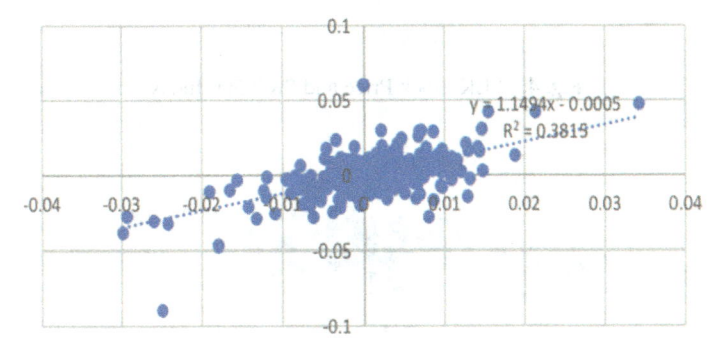

Fig. 2. DAL Stock Price and S&P 500 Index.

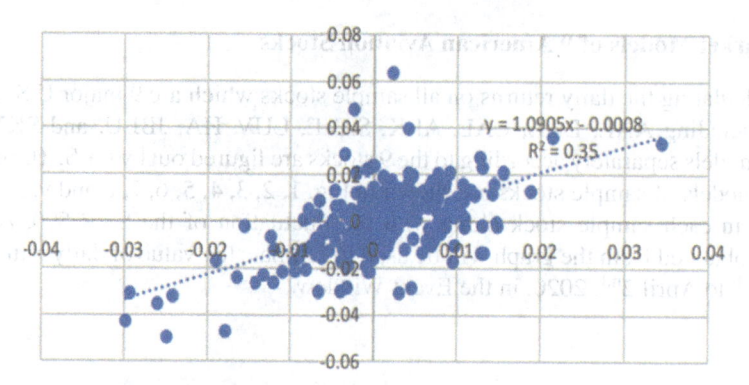

Fig. 3. UAL Stock Price and S&P 500 Index.

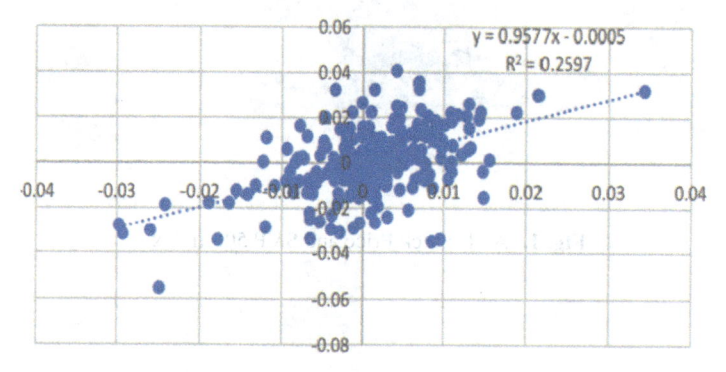

Fig. 4. ALK Stock Price and S&P 500 Index.

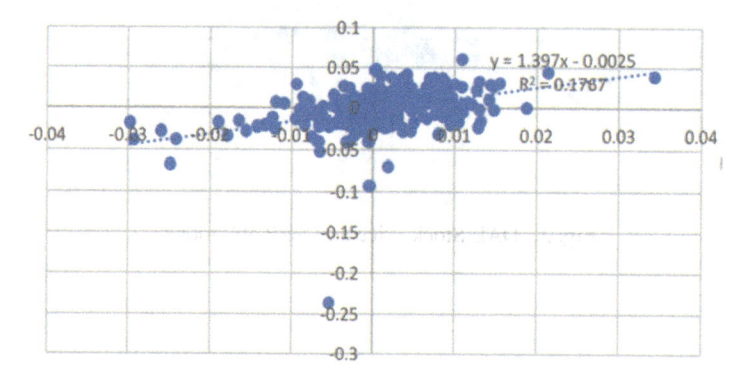

Fig. 5. SAVE Stock Price and S&P 500 Index.

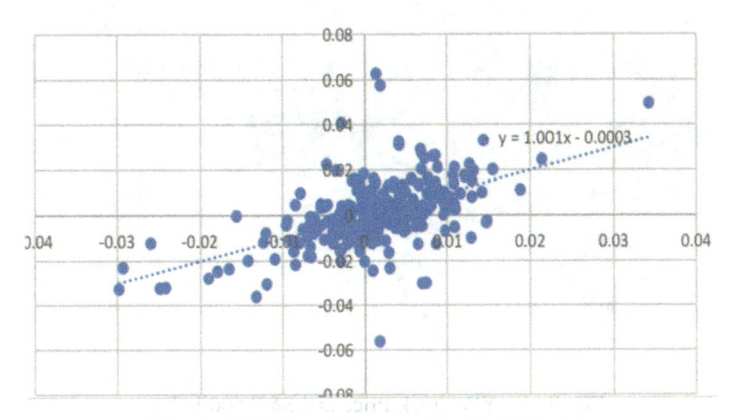

Fig. 6. LUV Stock Price and S&P 500 Index.

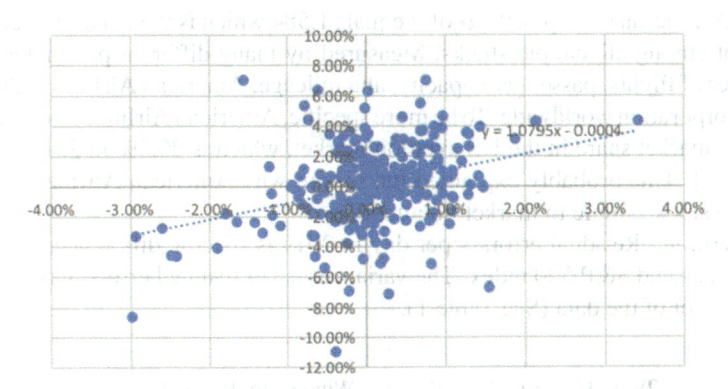

Fig. 7. HA Stock Price and S&P 500 Index.

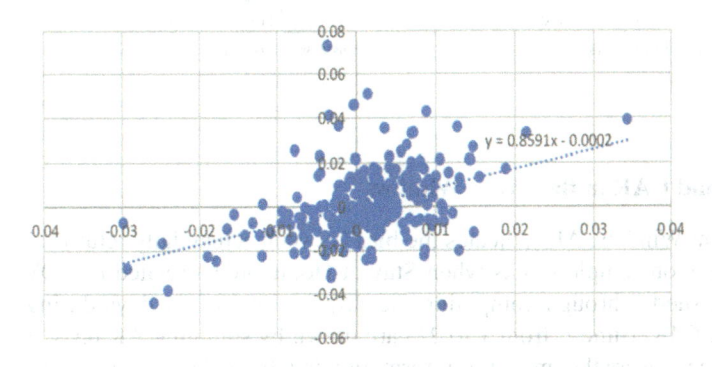

Fig. 8. JBLU Stock Price and S&P 500 Index.

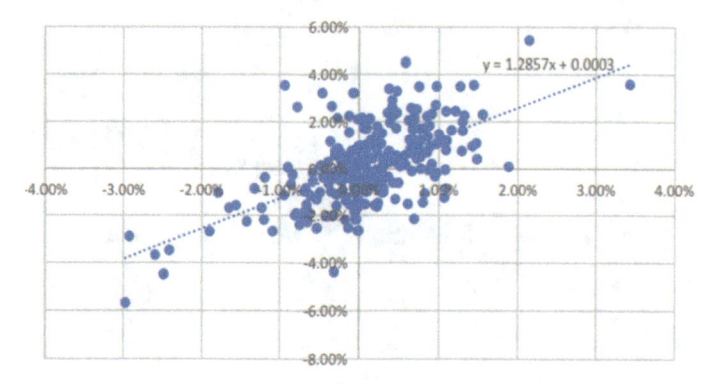

Fig. 9. SKYW Stock Price and S&P 500 Index.

Take AAL as an example, the α of it equals 1.584 which is the maximum correlation coefficient among all sample stocks. Measured by many different parameters such as the number of flights, passenger capacity, and mileage, American Airlines is the biggest aviation corporation worldwide. To be more specific, American Airlines has been holding the largest market share in the US aviation market, which is 20.3% in 2019 and 19.5% in 2021 [12]. This probably explained the reason why American Airlines is the most vulnerable stock sample to market fluctuations.

Furthermore, Residual errors ε per day in 2019 is specific differences between the sample stocks and S&P 500 index. The variances σ^2 of residual errors make known the deviation level of the data (See Table 1).

Table 1. $\varepsilon.\sigma$ in the Estimation Window for 9 sample stocks.

Stock	International					Domestic			
	AAL	DAL	UAL	ALK	SAVE	LUV	HA	JBLU	SKYW
σ^2	0.000345405	0.000131516	0.000135625	0.000160534	0.000558458	0.000148629	0.000602241	0.000202223	0.000172641

4.3 AR and CAR in the Event Window

In the Event Window, AR indicates the bias between actual daily returns and estimated daily returns on sample stocks when Stay-at-Home orders related to COVID-19 were formally issued. Through computing the AR_t for total of 21 days during the event's time span, CAR_t (time t: from 1 to 21) are drawn by summing AR up. CAR is a good indicator to measure the impact of information involving the Stay-at-Home directive on stock prices and daily returns.

4.4 Confidence Interval and CAR

Because it is assumed that ε shows a Normal Distribution, CAR should accordingly fit the Asymptotic Normality. In this case, CAR almost will follow a normal distribution as the sample number becomes infinitely high. When the Confidence Interval at which equals 95% Confidence Interval, it means there is a 95% probability that the true value of CAR will all be within the intervals between upper and lower confidence limits. If the null hypothesis (H_0) of the study is COVID-19 has no extra influence on individual stocks, CAR of them should be within this range which is presented by formula (7) mentioned before.

The relationship of CAR_t for sample stocks from March 5th, 2020, to April 2nd, 2020, in the Event Window and the confidence intervals are shown in Fig. 10, 11, 12, 13, 14, 15, 16, 17 and 18.

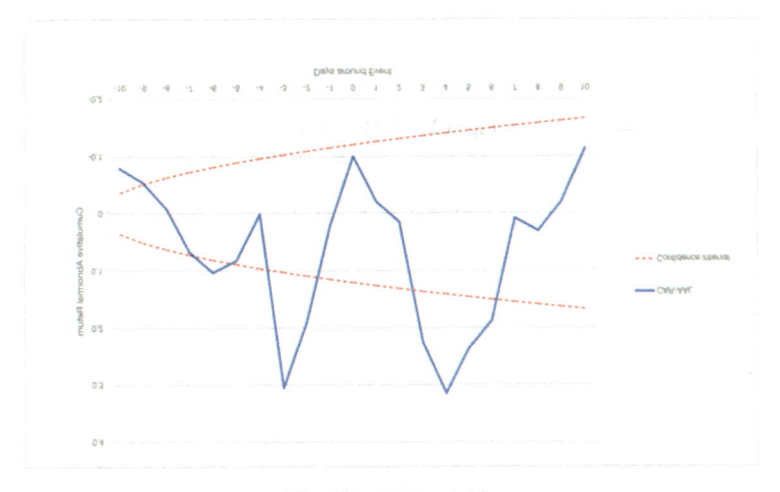

Fig. 10. CAR – AAL.

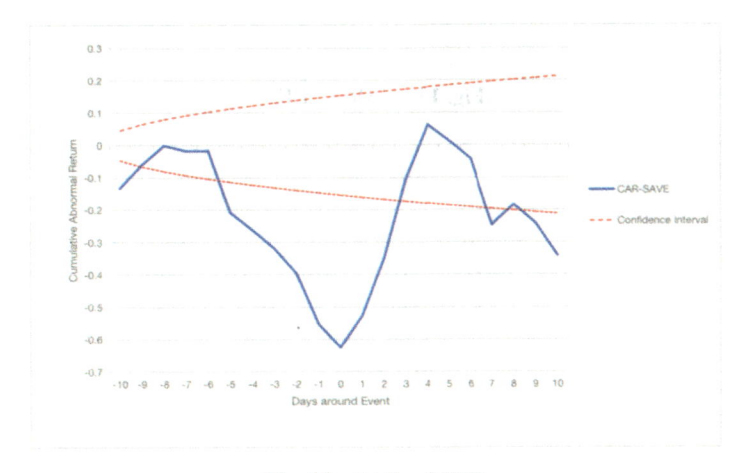

Fig. 11. CAR – SAVE.

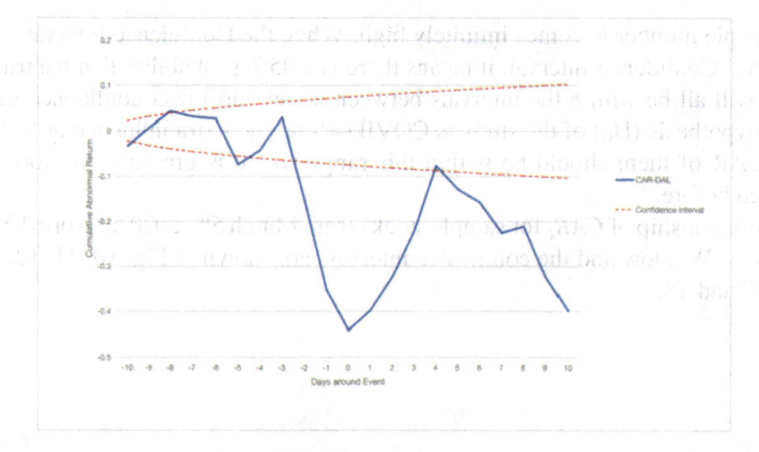

Fig. 12. CAR – DAL.

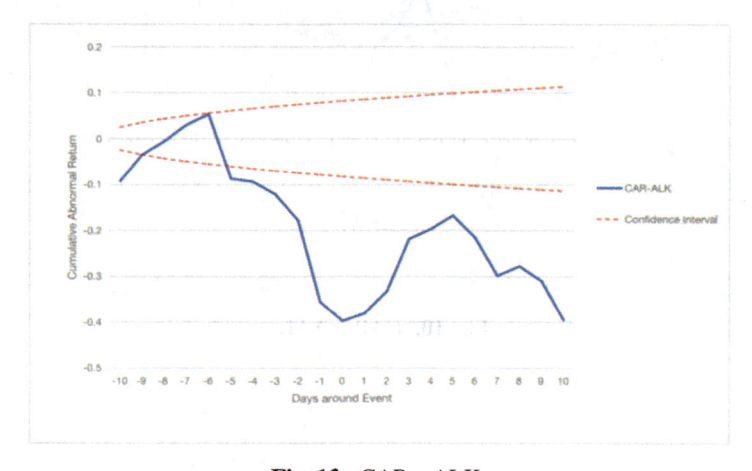

Fig. 13. CAR – ALK.

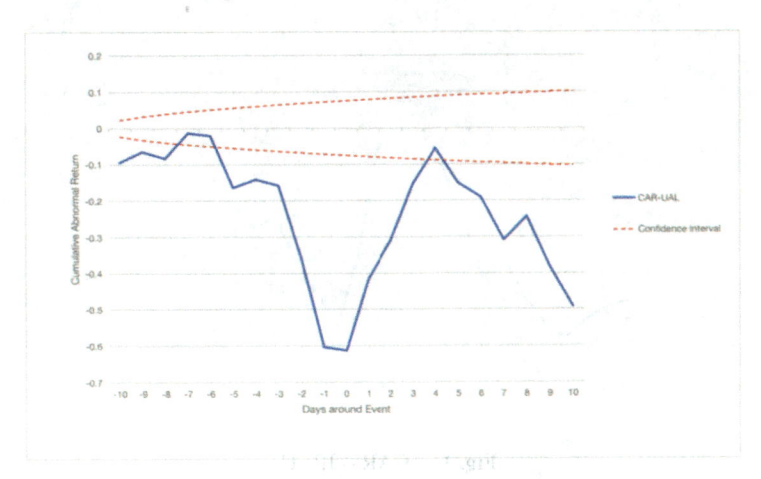

Fig. 14. CAR – UAL.

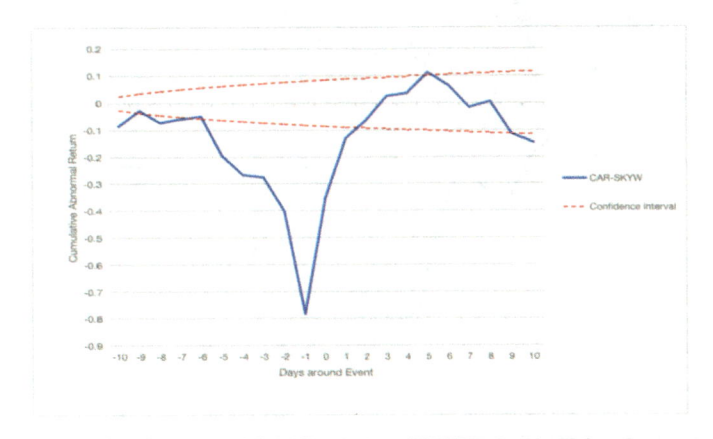

Fig. 15. CAR – SKYW.

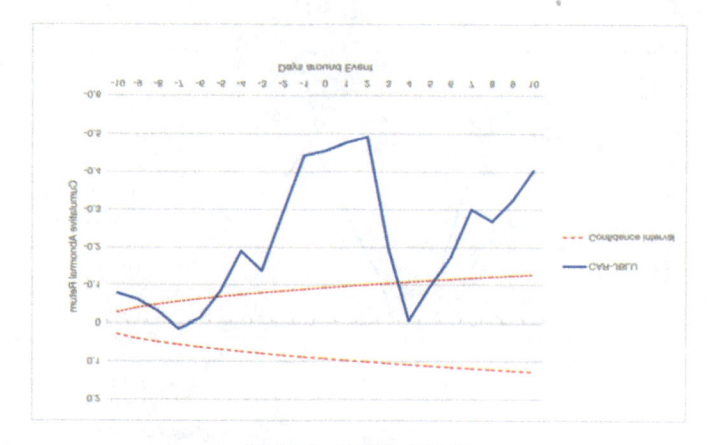

Fig. 16. CAR – JBLU.

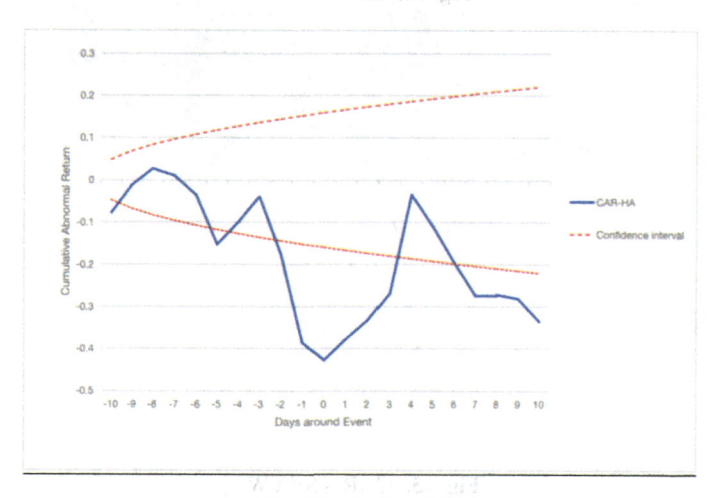

Fig. 17. CAR – HA.

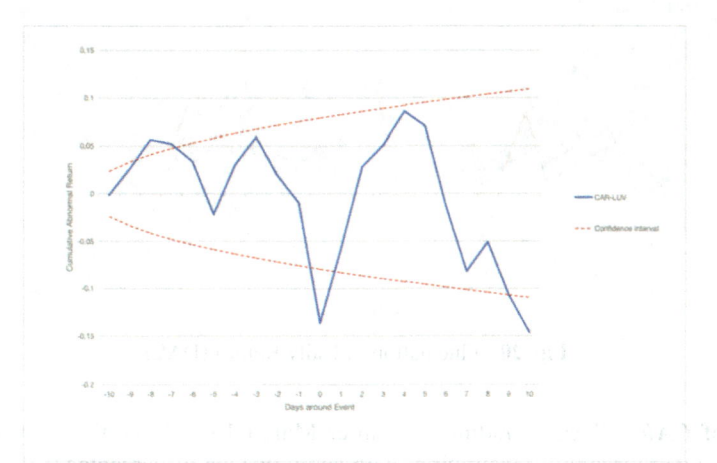

Fig. 18. CAT – LUV.

4.5 Slump and Upturn of CAR_t

Slump of CAR_t. After COVID-19 outbroken, the aviation industry around the world were affected negatively. Air passenger traffic went through a dramatic decrease. The report provided by International Air Transport Association Economics (IATA Economics) on February 5th, 2020, mentioned that "Air passenger traffic measured by revenue passenger-kilometers plunged by 66% in 2020 which was the biggest shock that the aviation industry has experienced" [13]. For instance, in Fig. 19 and 20 the daily return of AAL and DAL separately dropped 25.22% and 25.99% on March 19th, 2020, when the first Stay-at-Home directive in US issued.

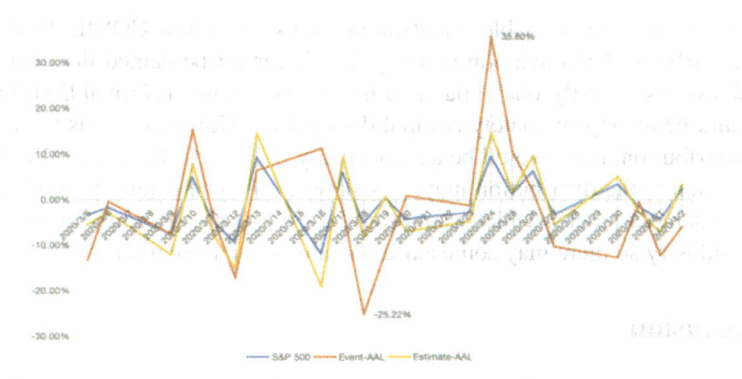

Fig. 19. Fluctuation of Daily Return (AAL)

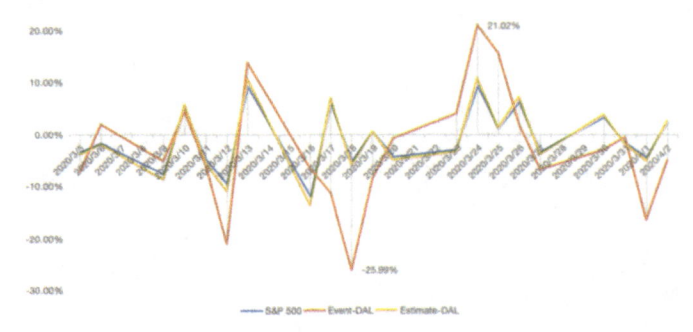

Fig. 20. Fluctuation of Daily Return (DAL)

Upturn of CAR_t. Several trading days after March 19th, 2020, the daily returns of all samples were strongly rebounding, with some dozens of percentages. Some of the policies released by the government may account for this. After a series of sharp falls, the Federal Reserve of US launched an unprecedented **Unlimited Quantitative Easing (Unlimited QE) policy** [14]. The rescue plan included US $25 billion in cash assistance to passenger airlines, another US $25 billion in loans and loan guarantees. On March 24th, 2020, under the anticipation that the US $2 trillion fiscal stimulus bill will be passed soon, the optimism of the US stock market soared, and the Dow Jones Index (DJI) hit the largest one-day percentage increase in nearly 90 years. The airline shares soared almost all over America, with AAL up 35.08% and DAL up 21.02% on the 24th. The reason why US government paid so much effort in aid of American Aviation industry is still its crucial status, for it concerns countless job positions, taxation and so on [15].

4.6 Limitations and Improvements

This paper presented reasonable statistical analyses about how COVID-19 effected on passenger airlines of US aviation industry. But it cannot be denied that there are still several drawbacks. Firstly, one of our assumptions is ε shows a Normal Distribution and CAR would be an approximately Normal distribution. However, if ε is not a perfectly normal distribution, there would be an inaccuracy in Fig. 10, 11, 12, 13, 14, 15, 16, 17 and 18, which is the distribution maybe is skewed to some extent. Second, this study invested 9 sample stocks, which cannot cover the whole passenger airlines also the aviation industry so there may some extra phenomena that we did not discover yet.

5 Conclusion

Based on analysis of the relationship between CAR_t and confidence interval, we have drawn four conclusions as follow:

5.1 Conclusion 1: Covid-19 Has Extra Negative Effect on Aviation Industry

For the conclusion 1, it is obvious that all the CAR_t exceed the confidence interval during the period. Therefore, we reject H$_0$, which means COVID-19 has extra influence on individual stocks. Also, the value of CAR_t that exceed confidence interval mostly are negative. For instance, the value of CAR_{11}-UAL is about -0.6133 and its absolute value is quite high. Observing those plots roughly, CAR_t's value, these minus numbers gradually decrease, that is, their absolute values gradually increase with time going from about 4 days before March 19th, 2020, to that very day. This is because actual daily returns of the sample stocks during the epidemic was lower than what we predicted due to the impact of the it. Those error items which are AR_t gradually added up to negative numbers that are CAR_t with relatively large absolute value. So, we can know all these aviation stock samples suffered the negative impact of the COVID-19.

5.2 Conclusion 2: Extra Negative Effect of COVID-19 on International Flights is Bigger that Domestic Flights

First, we averaged CAR_t across all sample stocks in the event window. The average of CAR_t-international (CAR_t of AAL, DAL, UAL, AKL, SAVE) is around -0.1493 and the average of CAR_t-domestic (CAR_t of LUV, HA, SKYW, JBLU) is around -0.1344, so the average of CAR_t-international is less than the average of CAR_t-domestic, in other words, the absolute value of the mean of CAR_t-international is higher than CAR_t-domestic one. It shows stocks of companies mainly engaged in international flights suffered more from the epidemic than those mainly engaged in domestic flights in general. This finding becomes more obvious after subtracting the minimum and maximum average value of CAR in international and domestic flights respectively. After deletion, the average of CAR_t-international (CAR_t of DAL, AKL, SAVE) is around -0.1913 and the average of CAR_t-domestic (CAR_t of HA, SKYW) is around -0.1584. The difference between them becomes much larger.

5.3 Conclusion 3: For the Stocks of Companies Mainly Engaged in International Flights, AAL is Less Negatively Affected by COVID-19 than the Other Four Stocks (DAL, UAL, AKL, SAVE)

For DAL, UAL, AKL, SAVE, the trend of their CAR_t and confidence interval graph is very similar in most of the time (from March 5th, 2020, to April 2nd, 2020) their CAR_t exceeded confidence intervals. However, looking at the graph corresponding to AAL it can be found that its CAR_t is within the confidence interval most of the time even on March 19th, 2020. Furthermore, the average of CAR_t-AAL is about 0.066552, which is also the only positive number among all sample stocks, and it is much higher than the other four stocks (DAL: -0.1624, UAL: -0.2393, AKL: -0.1941, SAVE: -0.2174). But it doesn't mean AAL did quite well during the period that COVID-19 outbroke, this appearance just presents that AAL relatively did not do as bad as the other four. Therefore, we drew the conclusion that AAL went through less extra influence by COVID-19 than the other four stocks.

5.4 Conclusion 4: For the Stocks of Companies Mainly Engaged in Domestic Flights, LUV is Less Negatively Affected by COVID-19 than the Other Three Stocks (HA, SKYW, JBLU)

The way of comparison in this conclusion is the same as what we did in the conclusion 3. The average of CAR_t-LUV is about -0.0055 which is the highest number compared to the other three (HA: -0.1831, SKYW: -0.1337, JBLU: -0.2152). Likes AAL, the CAR_t-LUV is within the confidence interval most of the time except two days, March 10th (CAR_4, when 7 days before the event) and March 19th (CAR_0, when the event happened), and the value of CAR_4 and CAR_0 that beyond the confidence interval is only around 0.0521 and -0.1364. The highest absolute value of CAR_t (beyond confidence intervals) of the other three (CAR_0-HA: -0.4271, CAR_{-1}-SKYW: -0.7830 and CAR_2-JBLU: -0.4920) are much higher than LUV's. So just like AAL in the group of international airlines, LUV suffered less extra influence by COVID-19 than the other three stocks.

Acknowledgements. Yuxin Chen and Ziqing Gong contributed equally to this work and should be considered co-first authors.

References

1. Teker, S., Teker, D., Güner, A.: Financial performance of top 20 airlines. Procedia Soc. Behav. Sci. **235**, 603–610 (2016). https://doi.org/10.1016/j.sbspro.2016.11.035
2. Feng, C.-M., Wang, R.-T.: Performance evaluation for airlines including the consideration of financial ratios. J. Air Transp. Manag. **6**(3), 133–142 (2000). https://doi.org/10.1016/s0969-6997(00)00003-x
3. Bouwer, J., Krishnan, V., Saxon, S., Tufft, C.: Taking stock of the pandemic's impact on global aviation. McKinsey & Company (2022). https://www.mckinsey.com/industries/travel-logistics-and-infrastructure/our-insights/taking-stock-of-the-pandemics-impact-on-global-aviation. Accessed 8 Oct 2022
4. Abbas, J., Mubeen, R., Iorember, P.T., Raza, S., Mamirkulova, G.: Exploring the impact of covid-19 on tourism: transformational potential and implications for a sustainable recovery of the travel and Leisure Industry. Curr. Res. Behav. Sci. **2**, 100033 (2021). https://doi.org/10.1016/j.crbeha.2021.100033
5. World Tourism Organization. International Tourism and Covid-19 | Tourism Dashboard (n.d.). https://www.unwto.org/tourism-data/international-tourism-and-covid-19. Accessed 11 Oct 2022
6. Bouwer, J., Saxon, S., Wittkamp, N.: Back to the future? Airline sector poised for change post-COVID-19. McKinsey & Company (2021). https://www.mckinsey.com/industries/travel-logistics-and-infrastructure/our-insights/back-to-the-future-airline-sector-poised-for-change-post-covid-19. Accessed 29 Sept 2022
7. Serrano, F., Kazda, A.: The future of airports post COVID-19. J. Air Transp. Manag. **89**, 101900 (2020). https://doi.org/10.1016/j.jairtraman.2020.101900
8. Directorate-General for Internal Policies of the Union (European Parliament), Panteia, Polis, Tre, U. degli S. R., Rodrigues, Teoh, Ramos, Winter, Knezevic, Marcucci, Lozzi, Gatta, Antonucci, Cutrufo, Marongiu, & Cré. Relaunching Transport and tourism in the EU after covid-19. Part I, overview. Photo of Publications Office of the European Union (2021). https://op.europa.eu/en/publication-detail/-/publication/d6c7e5cc-48e8-11ec-91ac-01aa75ed71a1. Accessed 29 Sept 2022

9. Ball, R., Brown, P.: An empirical evaluation of accounting income numbers. J. Account. Res. **6**(Autumn) (1968)
10. Governor Gavin Newsom Issues Stay at Home Order (2020). https://www.gov.ca.gov
11. Dollard, P., Griffin, I., Berro, A., et al.: Risk assessment and management of COVID-19 among travelers arriving at designated U.S. airports, January 17–September 13, 2020. MMWR Morb Mortal Wkly Rep **69**, 1681–1685 (2020). https://doi.org/10.15585/mmwr.mm6945a4externalicon
12. Salas, E.B.: Domestic market share - airlines in U.S. 2011–2021. Statista (2022). https://www.statista.com
13. New Covid Variants Pose a Risk to Air Travel Recovery. IATA Economics (2021). https://www.iata.org/economics
14. Robb, G.: Fed announces unlimited QE and sets up several new lending programs. MarketWatch (2020). https://www-marketwatch
15. Ni, H.: Empirical analysis of American aviation industry on national economic growth. China Civ. Aviat. (01), 47–49 (2004)

Predicting Customer Churn in a Telecommunications Company Using Machine Learning

Yinming Wu(✉)

School of Crowe Chinese Auditing, Nanjing Audit University, Nanjing, China
204070826@stu.nau.edu.cn

Abstract. In today's world, if a company is not equipped with clear analysis and foreseeing, endless customer churn will occur. This industry is highly competitive and the amount of customers is fundamental to a telecom company, which can help them to gain enough profits they want initially. Some data visualization will be realized to build up some relations between factors and churn by using heat maps and matrices. At last, some algorithms will be introduced and calculated in some train data to measure which model is the best one to predict churns, such as logic regression, random forest, and decision tree. They will be compared on different occasions and each of them will be given a quantitative score. From this research, the random forest has the best performance in accuracy score and PCA curve (2110 customers). This information can be used to develop targeted retention strategies to reduce churn rates and improve customer satisfaction.

Keywords: Machine Learning · Customer Churn · Random Forest · Logistic Regression · Decision Tree

1 Introduction

1.1 Background

Customers in the telecom sector have a variety of service providers to choose from and can actively switch between them. Instead of attempting to attract new customers, it is more successful to cultivate long-lasting relationships with existing ones. Once customer satisfaction increases by 5%, sales increase by 95% [1]. Customer churn is the loss of a client in favor of a rival, signifying the breakdown of the partnership [2]. The challenge for telecommunications companies is to identify customers who are at risk of churning and take proactive steps to retain them [3]. If they don't have enough customer flow, they are bound to struggle to live in this industry.

1.2 Related Research

Some previous studies made some progress in this field. For example, a study led by scholars at the University of West London explored churn under uncertain situations [4].

They have empirically assessed how the unknown samples affect the prediction model's effectiveness in the setting of TCI. Other scientists even considered two-hybrid data by neural networks to access their performance [5]. In another research, Olu Ojo conducted the relationship between service quality and customer satisfaction in Nigeria. Also, it is advised that businesses accept client feedback and develop additional programs to gauge customer happiness and service quality [6]. In 2018, Sigit Haryadi measured whether the telecommunication industry would benefit from an economic policy in Indonesia by conducting different forms of the test [7].

1.3 Objective

This paper aims to use machine learning techniques to predict customer attrition inside a telecoms company. Customers' call histories, billing histories, and demographic information may all be carefully examined to spot indicators and trends that point to a customer's propensity to leave. From the IBM sample dataset, 7073 consumers will be first chosen for analysis. This will answer some questions like: What is the ratio of customers who leave and those who remain active users of the services? Exist any gender-based patterns in terms of customer churn? Then, data will be gathered to inform businesses of their strengths and weaknesses. Churn prediction models used in predictive analytics can predict customer turnover by assessing a client's propensity for churn risk.

2 Methodology

2.1 Source of Data

In this paper, the data on the customer churn in a company is mainly from Kaggle [8], the dataset includes information in four parts. The dataset includes information on customer demographics, account information, service usage, and churn status as you can see in Fig. 1. Data about the customer is shown in each row, Each column includes the characteristics of the customer as indicated in the column metadata. It has 21 features and roughly 7043 customers. The percentage of males and females is fifty-fifty. In this dataset, each row stands for different meanings like gender, partner, tenure, and so on. (Table 1). The paper includes information on a number of different topics, including customer attrition, service usage, such as online backup and tech support, account information, including years, contract, and payment methods, as well as demographic information including age and gender. Moreover, demographic data relates to a group or market segment's characteristics, including predicted behavior. This data has historically included elements like social class, age, and gender; it now also includes fresh data on counties and gender.

2.2 Data Processing

Of knowledge loss and unpredictable data patterns, missing data affect statistical analysis [9].

When speaking of the missing value, we can visualize them as a matrix so that the pattern of missingness in the dataset is easy to be found. From the matrix, it is apparent

Table. 1. Information about dataset (Photo credit: https://www.kaggle.com/code/bhartiprasad17/customer-churn-prediction/notebook)

customerID	gender	SeniorCitizen	Partner	Dependents	tenure	PhoneService	MultipleLines	InternetService
7590-VHVEG	Female	0	Yes	No	1	No	No phone service	DSL
5575-GNVDE	Male	0	No	No	34	Yes	No	DSL
3668-QPYBK	Male	0	No	No	2	Yes	No	DSL
7795-CFOCW	Male	0	No	No	45	No	No phone service	DSL

that it has no particular pattern that stands out. As a matter of fact, there is no missing data. However, its precision should be checked through further research. In Table 2, the author found there were actually some missing values that are not easy to be noticed. In the column of a senior citizen, 0 means the missing value.

Table. 2. Result of missing value (Photo credit: https://www.kaggle.com/code/bhartiprasad17/customer-churn-prediction/notebook)

	gender	SeniorCitizen	Partner	Dependents	tenure	PhoneService	MultipleLines	InternetService
0	Female	0	Yes	No	1	No		No phone service
1	Male	0	No	No	34	Yes	No	
2	Male	0	No	No	2	Yes	No	
3	Male	0	No	No	45	No		No phone service
4	Female	0	No	No	2	Yes		No

After that, the author defined total charges as numeric variables and found that it has 11 missing values. After checking, there are no missing values left in the dataset. The next step is to delete the 11 missing values in order not to affect the process of the research. Now there are 7032 customers in the set and missing values in the column will be filled with the mean of total charges values.

In terms of data preprocessing, data will be split into train sets and test sets. To keep the balance of the research, three models will be accessed by the same approach.

2.3 Models

There are several machine learning techniques that can be used to predict customer churn in a telecommunications company. Here are some simple and feasible solutions:

The Definition of a Decision Tree
Each internal node in the decision tree is a splitting problem: a test for an instance attribute is defined, the samples arriving at the node are split based on a specific attribute, and each consecutive branch of the node corresponds to One potential value for this property.

The classification result is the mode of the output variable among the samples contained in the leaf nodes of the classification decision tree.

The Definition of Random Forest
A random forest is a collection of many strong trees. It will build many trees each has some randomness associated with it. It combines all the results by averaging or voting. Figure 1 shows a clear structure of a random forest.

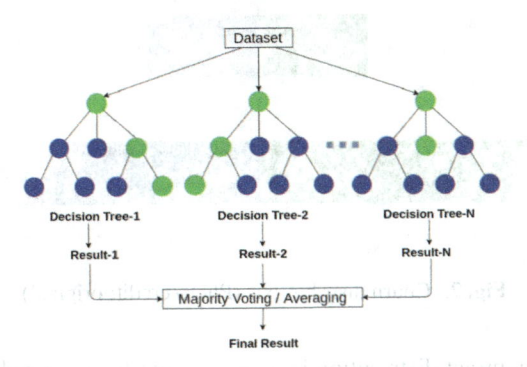

Fig. 1. Random forest (Photo credit: https://www.kaggle.com/code/bhartiprasad17/customer-churn-prediction/notebook)

Logistic Regression
A logistic regression transforms a linear regression surface logistically. It reduces the high region to a maximum of 1 and reduces the lower region to a minimum of 0. Linear regression is defined as:

$$y = b_0 + b_1 x_1 + b_2 x_2 + \cdots + b_n x_n = \sum b_i x_i \tag{1}$$

The output of the model y is the chance that the output y takes one of two values in binary classification situations when the output y takes one of two values. A logistic regression is more suited because the result y only ranges from zero to one.

A logistic regression (s-shaped curve) is:

$$y = \frac{1}{1 + e^{-\sum b_i x_i}} \tag{2}$$

3 Results and Discussion

3.1 Data Visualization

The first one in Fig. 2 is churn distributions. Domain type will work for pyramid layout. Through this method, two conclusions are reached: 26.6% of customers will switch to another corporation and customers are 49.5% female and 50.5% male. And 939 women churned while the number of men is 930. A concentric circle will be applied to tackle the problem of analysis. As a result, when it comes to switching or changing a telco company, both genders tend to show similar behaviors because there are subtle differences in proportion and amount.

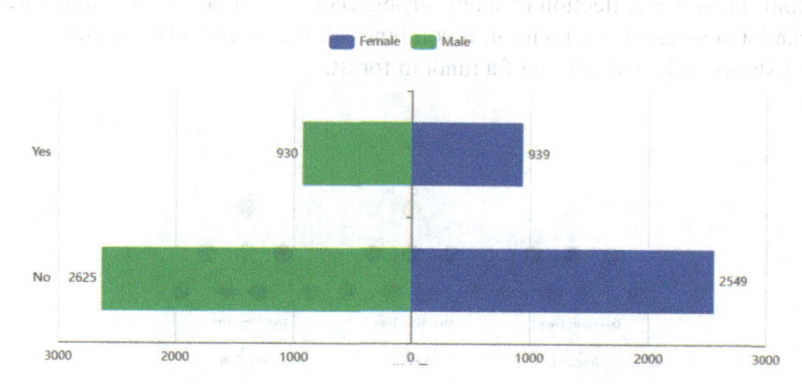

Fig. 2. Churn distributions (Photo credit: original)

The customer contract distribution is another point to be considered. From Fig. 3, about three-quarters of customers would like to select flexible plans with month-to-month contracts. In contrast to them, only 13% will choose one year, and 3% with two years.

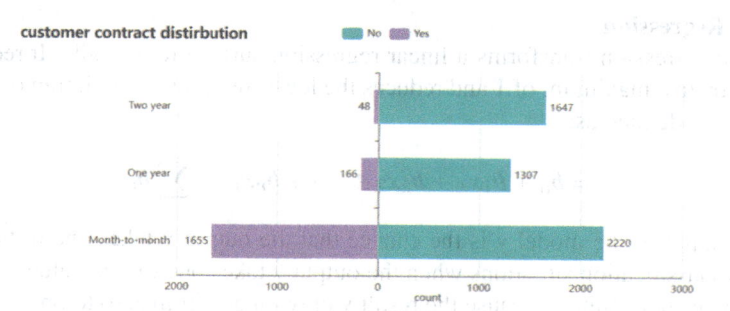

Fig. 3. Customer contract distribution (Photo credit: original)

Owing to the popular social trend in Fig. 4, more and more adults have a strong passion for new payment methods such as electronic checks. Sometimes they may have more novel ideas to get a higher quality of service from different companies. They always need to change their firm and contract for various reasons: promotion, moving to another community, or reducing some fixed costs from their expenditure. Turning to another group, they have gotten accustomed to traditional ways of payment like bank transfers or credit cards. Therefore, the majority of them are reluctant to change their contract. It is also obvious in the next chart: majors who moved out were choosing electronic checks while people who opted for a credit card were less likely to change their minds.

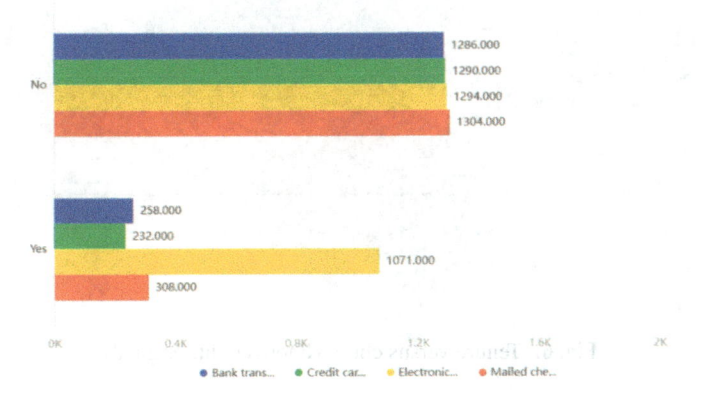

Fig. 4. Payment method and churn (Photo credit: original)

Despite the fact that the telco industry is developing at an astonishing speed, it is still lacking in online security. It is easy to explain the phenomenon in Fig. 5 of why most customers churn: without the strong protection of online security.

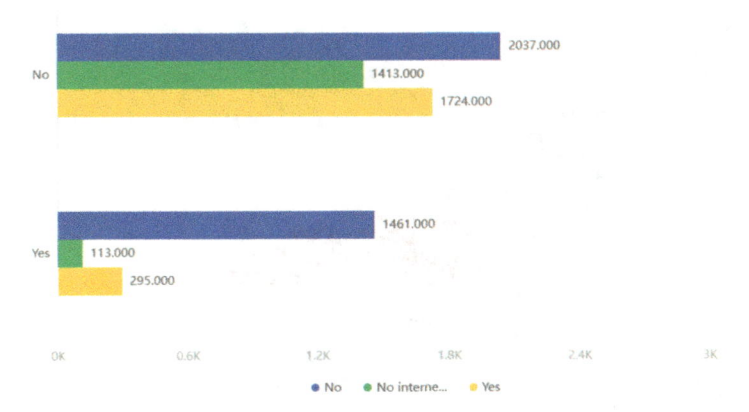

Fig. 5. Concerns about online security (Photo credit: original)

Also, from Fig. 6 (tenure vs churn), the median in group 'no' is 38 months, while 10 months in group 'yes'. In terms of current lives, new customers are willing to churn for lower prices and more discounts. So more and more companies are starting to have a reduction in prices and costs to attract more consumers.

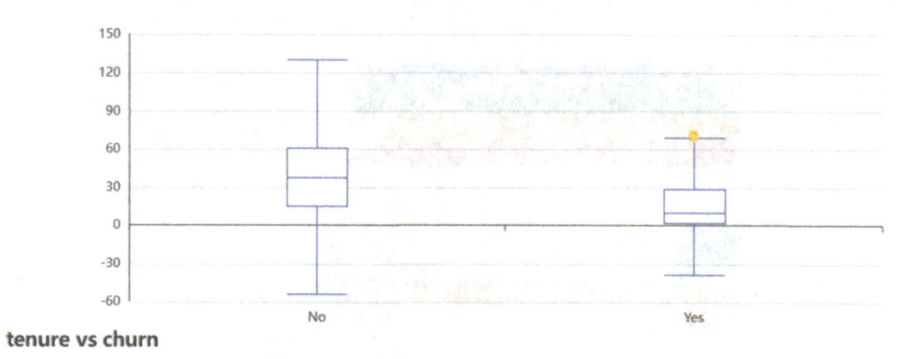

Fig. 6. Tenure versus churn (Photo credit: original)

3.2 Correlation Analysis

At last, the author drew a heat map just as in Fig. 7 to express the correlation between two different variables. From this table, the index of relations can be identified through color. In summary, streaming tv and movies have a strong relationship: the coefficient is 0.81, and next came online security and tech support (0.79).

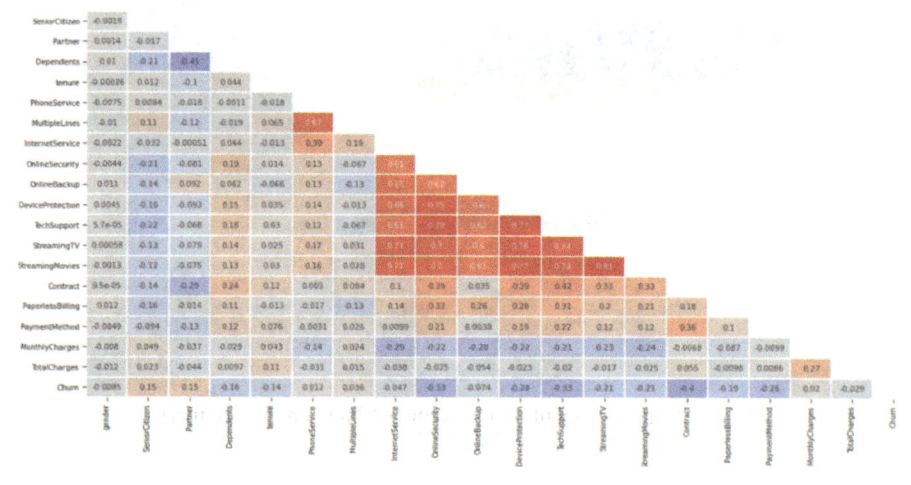

Fig. 7. Correlation matrix (photo credit: https://www.kaggle.com/code/bhartiprasad17/customer-churn-prediction/notebook)

3.3 Statistical Analysis

Following a review of distributions, a few predictive models will be presented and compared. The three most crucial algorithms are random forest, decision tree, and logic regression. Churn is one of the major problems affecting the telecom industry. The average monthly churn rate for the top 4 cellular carriers in the US is between 1.9% and 2%, according to studies.

Logistic Regression
Using LR, which produced an accuracy score of 0.809, the analysis aims to investigate the relationship between variables and churn. Two charts were also made to examine the relationship between various variables and churn, both positively and negatively. A negative correlation shows that the chance of churn reduces with that particular characteristic. Having a two-month contract lowers the possibility of churn. According to logistic regressions, tenure, and a two-month contract have the most adverse effects on churn. DSL internet service also lessens the likelihood of churn.

Also contributing to higher churn rates are total costs, monthly commitments, fiber optic internet services, and seniority. Although fiber optic services are faster, customers are more likely to churn as a result, which is an interesting fact. Some data is shown in Table 3, Fig. 8, and Fig. 9.

Table 3. The accuracy of LR (photo credit: original)

	Precision	Recall	F1-score	Support
0	0.86	0.89	0.87	1549
1	0.66	0.58	0.62	561
Accuracy	/	/	0.81	2110
Marco avg	0.76	0.74	0.75	2110
Weighted	0.8	0.81	0.81	2110

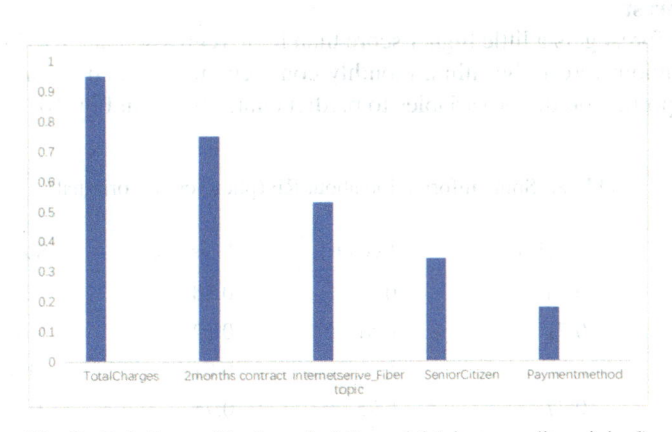

Fig. 8. Relations with churn in LR model (photo credit: original)

Decision Tree
The decision tree presents a very bad score at 0.7265 (in Table 4), although it is easy to interpret.

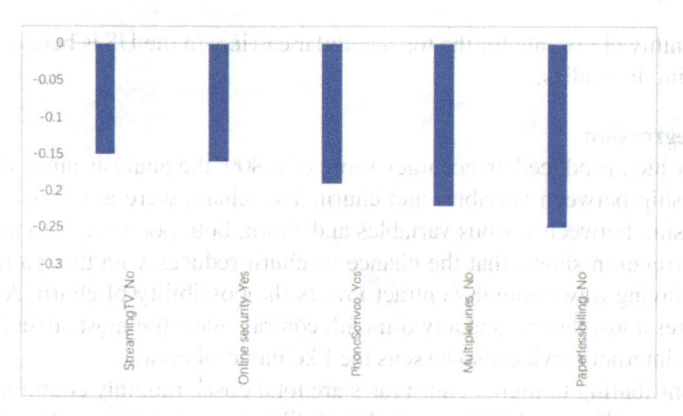

Fig. 9. Relations with churn in LR model (photo credit: original)

Table 4. The accuracy of DT (photo credit: original)

	Precision	Recall	F1-score	Support
0	0.82	0.8	0.81	1549
1	0.49	0.52	0.5	561
Accuracy	/	/	0.73	2110
Marco avg	0.65	0.66	0.66	2110
Weighted	0.73	0.73	0.73	2110

Random Forest

The random forest gets a little higher score than logic regression at 0.8137 (in Table 5). From the random forest algorithm, monthly contracts, tenure, and online security are the most important predictor variables to predict churn. See it in Fig. 10.

Table 5. Some information about RF (photo credit: original)

	Precision	Recall	F1-score	Support
0	0.84	0.92	0.88	1549
1	0.71	0.51	0.62	561
Accuracy	/	/	0.81	2110
Marco avg	0.77	0.75	0.75	2110
Weighted	0.8	0.81	0.8	2110

When it comes to the Roc curve, it has worse performance than logistic regression and random forest, also random forest scores more points in accuracy. The final result is in Fig. 11 and 12.

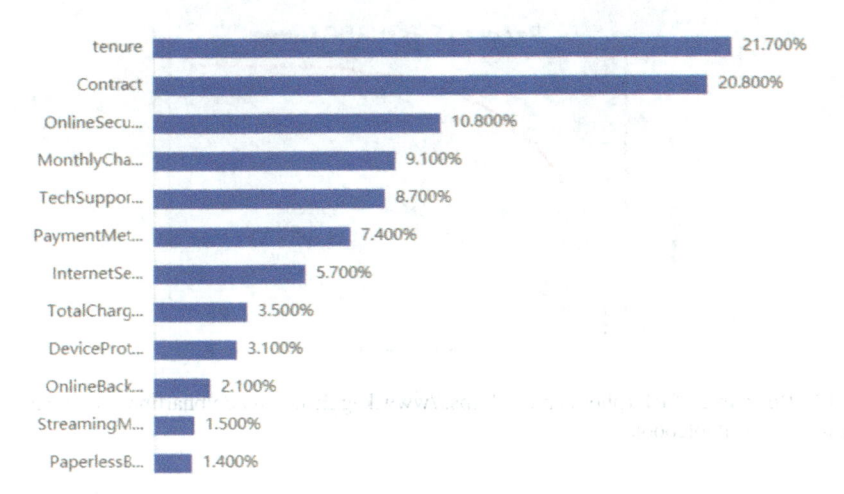

Feature	Importance
tenure	21.700%
Contract	20.800%
OnlineSecu...	10.800%
MonthlyCha...	9.100%
TechSuppor...	8.700%
PaymentMet...	7.400%
InternetSe...	5.700%
TotalCharg...	3.500%
DeviceProt...	3.100%
OnlineBack...	2.100%
StreamingM...	1.500%
PaperlessB...	1.400%

Fig. 10. Some information about RF (photo credit: original)

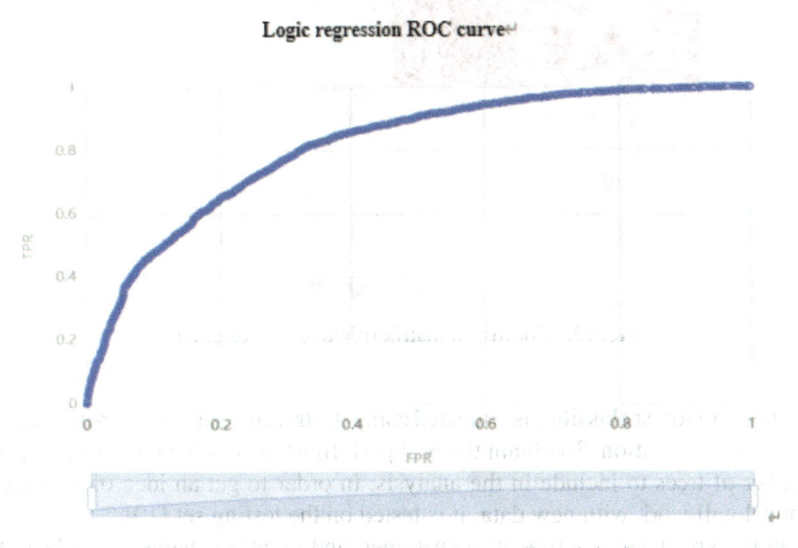

Fig. 11. Roc curve of LR (photo credit: original)

Based on the confusion matrix, there are 105 churn values and 1428 predicted non-churn values in Fig. 13, totaling 1533 genuine non-churn values. Although 261 non-churn values and 319 churn values are misclassified by the algorithm as churn and non-churn, respectively. Among these incorrectly identified values, there are actually 580 churn values.

It is obvious that the random forest has the best performance because it scores the most point in accuracy, so random forest is the most suitable one for prediction. Though it has a subtle edge when compared to logistic regression.

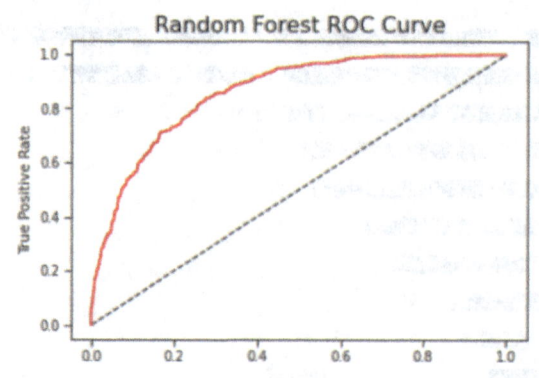

Fig. 12. Roc curve of RF (photo credit: https://www.kaggle.com/code/bhartiprasad17/customer-churn-prediction/notebook)

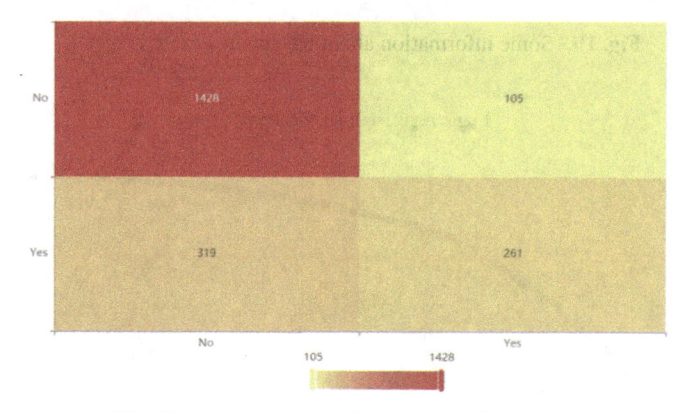

Fig. 13. Confusion matrix (photo credit original)

The random forest classifier is educated using the training set, and then it is fine-tuned by using cross-validation. To obtain the best performance possible on the validation set, the number of trees to include in the analysis. In order to get an idea of how well the final model will work with new data, it is tested on the testing set [10].

Contract type, length of time as a customer, and monthly charges have been found to be the most important factors in predicting customer churn. Customers who have low tenure, contracts that are for a short period of time, and high monthly fees are more likely to churn. This information can be put to use in the development of customer retention strategies that are specifically geared toward these customers, such as the provision of discounts or other inducements to remain loyal.

3.4 Limitation

There is no doubt that it has some limitations. The sample includes only 7000 citizens whose genders are taken into account rather than their lifestyle and regions. Different customers in different countries may not have a similar tendency to products. Also, it is not persuasive enough because 7000 customers cannot stand for a universal situation in the world. Moreover, as everybody knows decision tree is not a good model because it scores a lower point, it is feasible to add some explanations about its performance to strengthen integrity, which can give readers a better dimension to understand different algorithms.

Despite the fact that random forest is the best one to predict churn, it can only be accessed by scores and graphs. To be more specific, the author did not give his own opinions or did a transparent comparison between these three models.

It is necessary to be mentioned that this data was not trained in balanced target classes (50:50). If a step of 'undersampling' can be developed for the majority class (not churn), the result will be more accurate.

4 Conclusion

This paper used data from Kaggle to predict customer churn in a telecom company by using machine learning. The dataset originates from the IBM sample dataset from November 2019. A series of methods and models are utilized to predict the churn and this experiment evaluated three algorithms in machine learning. Among all of them, random forest is the most precise one (for about 90%), using 2110 customers' data to test, which can help managers to make wise decisions when they are confronted with a churn crisis.

During that process, variables like a contract, online backup, and tech support are concerned with churn, while gender seems to have nothing to do with customer churn. Some of the customers with month-to-month contracts are more likely to change when compared to that with one or two years contracts.

In the foreseeable future, more and more companies will take on more responsibilities and take more actions to avoid potential customer churn. This essay aims to research customer churn and find whether churn has some relation to factors like gender, age, and payment, which can help readers and companies to know what is positive/negative, thus accelerating the speed of adopting plans. Last but not least, ensuring the quality of customer service is a top priority for tackling issues like churn and some similar troubles.

References

1. Mustafa, N., Sook Ling, L., Abdul Razak, S.F.: Customer churn prediction for telecommunication industry: a Malaysian case study. F1000Research **10**, 1274 (2021)
2. Zhang, T., Moro, S., Ramos, R.F.: A data-driven approach to improve customer churn prediction based on telecom customer segmentation. Future Internet **14**(3), 94 (2022)
3. Ascarza, Retention futility: Targeting high-risk customers might be ineffective. J. Mark. Res. **55**(1), 80–98 (2018)
4. Amin, A., Al-Obeidat, F., Shah, B., et al.: Customer churn prediction in the telecommunication industry using data certainty. J. Bus. Res. **94**, 290–301 (2019)
5. Tsai, C.F., Lu, Y.H.: Customer churn prediction by hybrid neural networks. Expert Syst. Appl. **36**(10), 12547–12553 (2009)

6. Ojo, O.: The relationship between service quality and customer satisfaction in the telecommunication industry: Evidence from Nigeria. BRAND Broad Res. Account. Negot. Distrib. 1(1), 88–100 (2010)
7. Haryadi, S.: Applied statistics for assessment of the regulation and policy: case study in telecommunication industry. DOI10 13140 (2018)
8. Prasad, B.: Customer churn prediction, 29 June 2021. https://www.kaggle.com/code/bhartiprasad17/customer-churn-prediction/notebook. Accessed 14 Mar 2023
9. Ahmad, A.K., Jafar, A., Aljoumaa, K.: Customer churn prediction in telecom using machine learning in big data platform. J. Big Data 6(1), 1–24 (2019)
10. McDonald, R.P.: Test Theory: A Unified Treatment. Psychology Press (2013)

Research on Real Estate Price Index Forecasting Based on ARIMA Model: Taking Los Angeles as an Example

Xiao Han(✉)

University of Sydney, Camperdown, NSW 2006, Australia
xhan0721@uni.sydney.edu.au

Abstract. This study uses the ARIMA model to forecast and analyze potential future changes in the Los Angeles housing price index. Los Angeles, as a large city in the United States, has a significant impact on the U.S. economy due to its real estate market fluctuations. For the purpose of providing investors and decision-makers with meaningful data, this study forecasts future changes in the Los Angeles house price index using the ARIMA model. This approach can provide investors and policy makers with reliable forecasting results to better understand the future trends of the Los Angeles real estate market. The findings suggest that the Los Angeles house price index is likely to remain stable in the future, but may fluctuate due to various factors such as economic changes, government policies, and natural disasters. Investors are advised to focus on long-term investments and diversify their portfolios to reduce risk. Investors are advised to diversify their portfolios and take a long-term investment view to reduce the potential impact of short-term market volatility.

Keywords: House Price Index · ARIMA · Time Series

1 Introduction

1.1 Background

Individuals and the economy are significantly impacted by housing prices. The state of the global economy has significantly changed as a result of recent developments in the real estate industry. It is consequently more important than ever to predict the real estate market. There has recently been a lot of interest in the Los Angeles real estate market in the United States. Los Angeles' real estate market ups and downs have a significant impact on both the local and national economies. Because of its geographic location and economic circumstances, the market has experienced significant volatility over the years. Yet, there has been considerable uncertainty in the Los Angeles real estate market in recent years, which has worried investors and decision-makers. It has become more crucial than ever to be able to anticipate future changes in the Los Angeles home price index.

1.2 Objective

This study will use an ARIMA model to investigate the time series of the Los Angeles house price index in order to accurately anticipate future changes. In order to forecast future trends, this model can examine patterns like trends and seasonality and capture changes in the real estate market. By examining historical data from the Los Angeles real estate market and making predictions for the future home price indices, this article will examine the accuracy of the ARIMA model. In order to help investors and decision-makers better comprehend the future patterns of the Los Angeles real estate market, this study aims to deliver trustworthy forecasting results.

1.3 Literature Review

For the research on the real estate industry, scholars have used a variety of suitable analysis and prediction models from various aspects and perspectives in terms of house price forecasting analysis, in 1957, Holt first proposed the Exponential Smoothing Model to analyze and predict time series [1]. On this basis, Brown (2004) proposed the high-order exponential smoothing model [2]. Time series analysis, which is used in statistics, economics, and signal processing, is the most common application of vector autoregressive models to describe time-varying processes [3]. Malpezzi (1999) applied a straightforward error regression model to 133 American cities' general economic indicators throughout the period from 1979 to 1996 [4]. Luttik (2000) used a vector autoregressive VAR model to predict house prices based on 3000 transactions in the Netherlands and found that the model had a good predictive effect [5]. After that, by randomly picking 200 homes in Christchurch, Limsombunchai et al. (2004) examined the impact of the artificial neural network model and characteristic pricing model on house price prediction [6]. In terms of prediction impact, the results showed that the artificial neural network model outperformed the characteristic pricing model, and that the model held great promise for predicting home prices in New Zealand. Cook (2003, 2005) introduced an asymmetric response to the rise and fall of house prices through research on the convergence and coordination of house prices [7, 8]. Holemes (2008) analyzed the differences in house prices across a range of regions using unit root tests [9]. Rangan Gupta (2009) forecasted house price growth rates in four U.S. regions using a time-series model based on dynamic factor analysis and Bayesian shrinkage estimation [10]. According to Selim's (2008) comparison of the feature regression and artificial neural network prediction performances for house prices in Turkey, artificial neural network models are a better option for house price prediction [11].

The following research were carried out by international academics in response to the diversification of house price forecasting models in order to compare the predicting efficacy of various models: Regime-Switching model fits better on the training set, according to Crawford and Fratantoni's (2003) comparison of the forecasting ability of three distinct univariate time series models, the error of fitting on the test set is greater, and overfitting occurs [12]. In contrast, the generalization error of the ARIMA model is smaller, but the model is better only in the case of short-term forecasting. In order to estimate home values across 50 states, Lasse and Stig (2015) used dynamic model averaging and dynamic model selection and the prediction accuracy was significantly increased [13].

1.4 Framework

First, descriptive analysis will be used in this study to comprehend the fundamental characteristics of the data, such as their range, standard deviation, and degree of skewness. In time series analysis, the ARIMA model is frequently utilised. The smoothness and white noise of the data will be evaluated before modelling. The ACF and PACF functions plot autocorrelation and partial autocorrelation plots to reveal the smoothness of the time series. If the original series is not stationary, this research will use differencing and other techniques to make it stationary.

After the smoothness test and white noise test, the Los Angeles house price index will be simulated, and its future trend will be projected using the ARIMA model. By applying a differencing operation to the non-stationary time series, the ARIMA model converts it into a smooth series and uses the time sequence of the projected target historical data to estimate future values. It will consider how the time series' long-term trends, seasonal swings, and other stochastic elements affect the series' volatility.

2 Method

2.1 Data Collection

The House Price Index (HPI), an indicator that gauges changes in the cost of residential real estate, is used to assess the value of homes in Los Angeles. The data of HPI of Los Angeles from January 2000 to December 2022 are extracted from Fred Economic Fata with total of 276 months, utilized for analysis.

2.2 Data Descriptive Analysis

To begin with, it is essential to comprehend the fundamental characteristics of the data set under consideration. The data comprises house price indices for 276 months spanning from January 2000 to December 2022. The data ranges from 101.03 to 305.04, as shown in Table 1, with 211.88 as the average, 215.08 as the median, and 45.63 as the standard deviation. During the early 2000s, the housing price index in the Los Angeles area has been steadily rising, albeit experiencing a brief downturn during the financial crisis in 2008 and the COVID-19 pandemic in 2020.

Furthermore, an examination of the distribution of the dataset reveals a right-skewed pattern in the house price indices. The majority of the data is concentrated between the 150 and 250 range, as depicted in Fig. 1. A box plot was used to show the house price index's dispersion and outliers in order to acquire further understanding of the data. The results indicate significant variation in the distribution of the house price index, with several outliers present. Although the Los Angeles region's house price index growth rate has fluctuated since the early 2000s, there seems to be a long-term declining tendency. It's worth noting that the monthly growth rate data for the house price index show. In conclusion, despite a decelerating trend, the house price index in the Los Angeles area has been increasing with considerable volatility over the last 20 years, warranting further investigation.

In conclusion, the Los Angeles region's house price index has been on an upward trend for the past two decades, albeit at a slower pace.

Table 1. Descriptive analysis of the house price index in Los Angeles.

Mean	223.9972
Maximum	418.9189
Minimum	101.0312
Standard deviation	4.3944
Skewness	0.5162
kurtosis	−0.0141
Number of observations	276

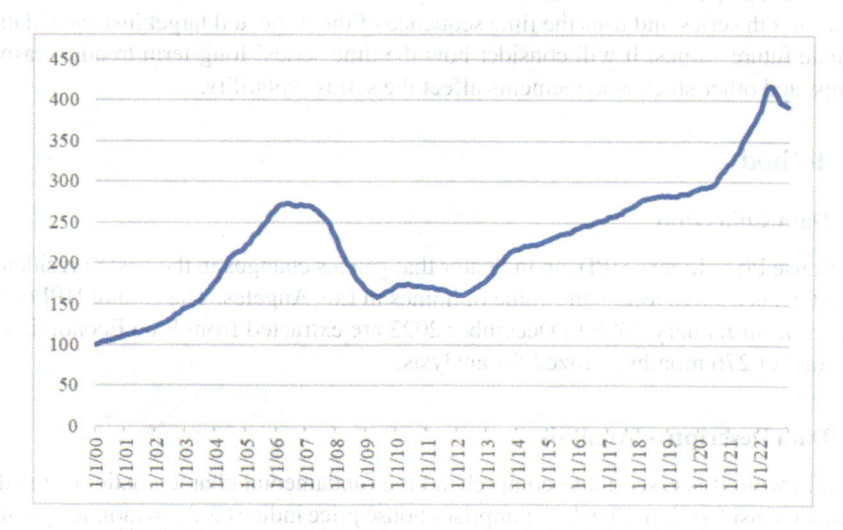

Fig. 1. Time series plot of the house price index in Los Angeles.

2.3 Stationary Testing

Before modeling, it needs to perform the stationary test and white noise test on the data, as shown in Fig. 2 and Table 2. ACF and PACF functions could be used to view plots of autocorrelation and partial autocorrelation functions of time series to understand the stationary of the series.

There is some autocorrelation and partial autocorrelation in the series, according to the ACF and PACF plots. However, based on the test results, the p-value is 0.3609, which is greater than the commonly used 0.05 threshold. Therefore, the original hypothesis cannot be rejected that the series has a unit root. Therefore, differencing is required, which is a common way to remove trends and seasonal variations from time series, making time series easier to model and forecast.

An ADF test (Augmented Dickey-Fuller test) can be used to determine the stability of the differenced time series, as shown in Fig. 3 and Table 3. The differenced time series' p-value, which is 0.3383 in Table 3, has a high significance level and cannot be used to invalidate the original claim that the differenced time series is not stationary.

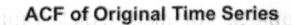

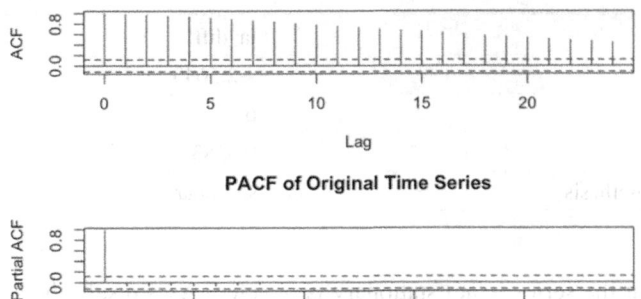

Fig. 2. ACF and PACF of original time series.

Table 2. The augmented dickey-fuller test.

Data	df$price
Dickey-Fuller	−2.5107
Lag order	6
p-value	0.3609
Alternative hypothesis	stationary

Higher-order differencing or other techniques could be used to make the time series stationary.

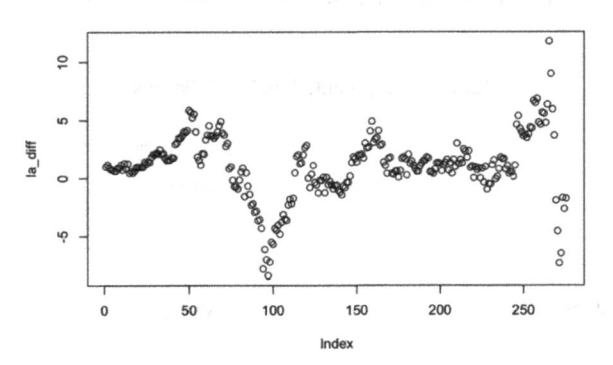

Fig. 3. First difference of LA house price index.

The series after the second-order difference has converged to stationery. The series has reached stationary after the second-order difference. Also, we can verify its stationary by ADF test from Fig. 4 and Table 4. Because the p-value is less than 0.01, the original

Table 3. Augmented dickey fuller test.

data	la_diff
Dickey–Fuller	−2.5643
Lag order	6
p-value	0.3383
Alternative hypothesis	stationary

hypothesis that the series is not stationary is rejected. As a result, the series after the second-order difference has reached the stationary level.

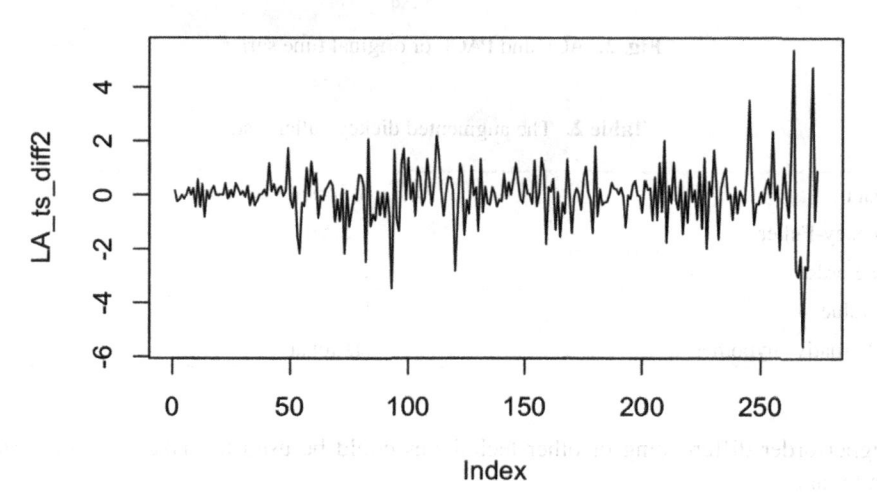

Fig. 4. Second difference of LA house price index.

Table 4. Augmented dickey fuller test.

data	LA_ts_diff2
Dickey–Fuller	−7.9284
Lag order	6
p-value	0.01
Alternative hypothesis	stationary

White noise detection is conducted with Ljung-Box test as in Fig. 5.

From Table 5 and Fig. 6, he p-value is very small (less than 0.02979), indicating that the residual series is autocorrelated under the Ljung-Box test and is not a white noise series.

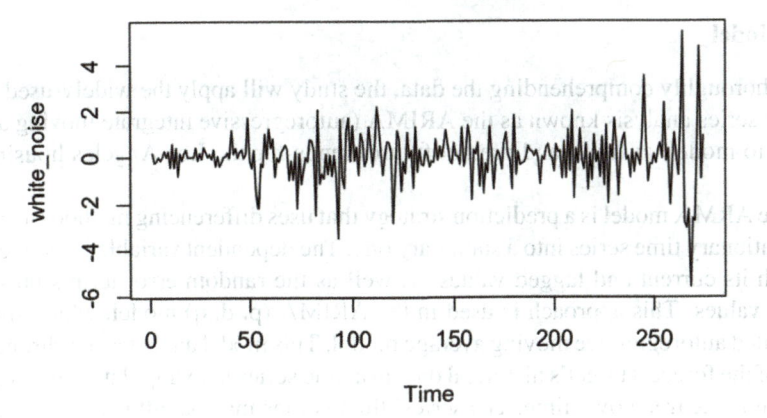

Fig. 5. White noise detection.

Table 5. Augmented dickey fuller test.

data	Residuals
Q*	19.944
df	10
p-value	0.02979
Model df	0
Total lags used	10

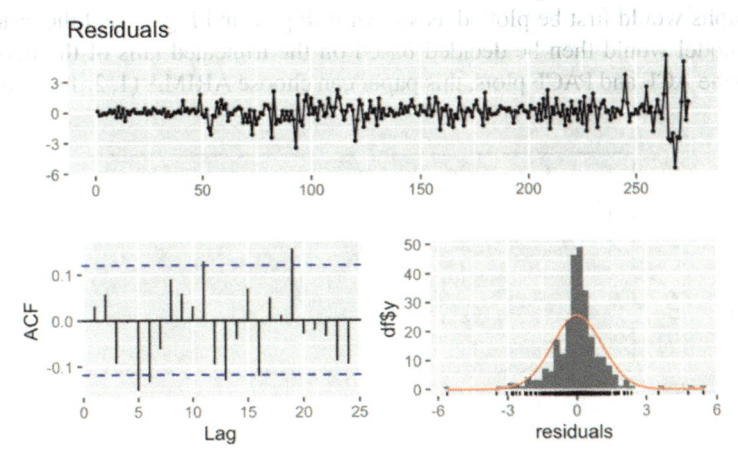

Fig. 6. Check residuals.

2.4 Model

After thoroughly comprehending the data, the study will apply the widely-used method of time series analysis known as the ARIMA (autoregressive integrate moving average) model to model, analyse, and predict future trends for the Los Angeles housing price index.

The ARMA model is a prediction strategy that uses differencing methods to change a non-stationary time series into a stationary one. The dependent variable is then regressed on both its current and lagged values, as well as the random error term's present and lagged values. This approach is used in the ARIMA (p, d, q) model, which stands for summated autoregressive moving average model. This model analyzes the chronological order of the forecast target's historical data in a time series to extrapolate future values by examining the trend over time. The series' fluctuations may be influenced by long-term trend changes, seasonal variations, and other stochastic factors.

The study will perform a stationary test on the obtained time series data. If the data fails to pass the stationary test, it indicates the presence of seasonality or trend in the data, requiring a difference operation to transform it into a stationary state. Additionally, the data will be evaluated for white noise to ensure that the series is correlated before and after time.

3 Results

3.1 Research Results

This research builds ARMA models to forecast the future volatility of Los Angeles house price data after differencing. For the city's weekly house price index series, ACF and PACF graphs would first be plotted as shown in Fig. 7 and Fig. 8, and the order of the ARMA model would then be decided based on the truncated tails of the two graphs. Based on the ACF and PACF plots, this paper can choose ARIMA (1, 2, 1) as our model.

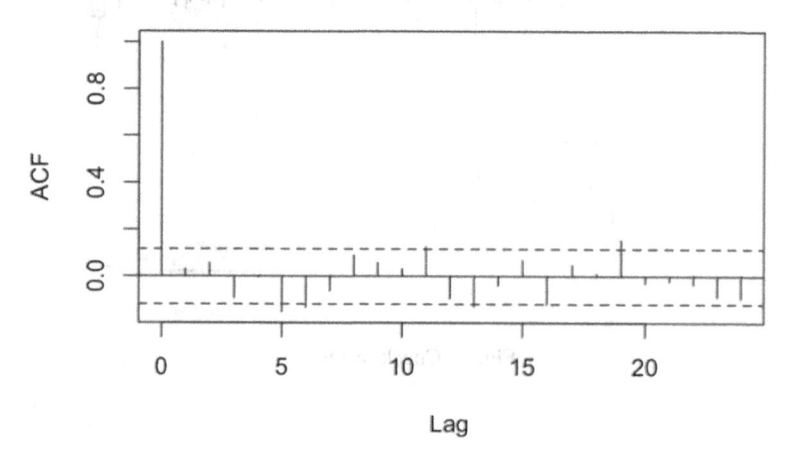

Fig. 7. Differenced time series - ACF plot.

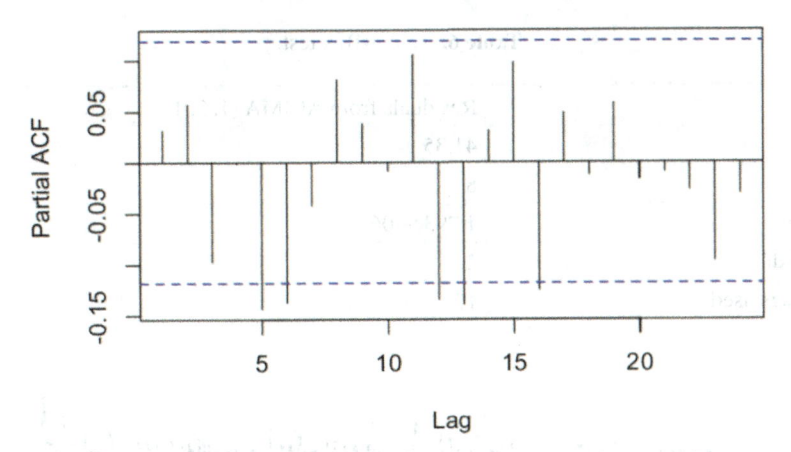

Fig. 8. Differenced time series - PACF plot.

As shown in Fig. 9, the forecast results show a downward trend in the house price index in the coming months.

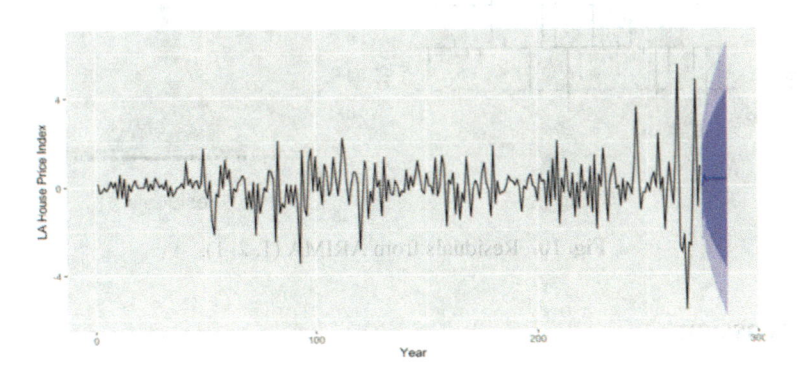

Fig. 9. Forecast of Los Angeles house price index.

3.2 Model Testing

As in Table 6 and Fig. 10, white noise test on the model residuals would also be conducted after the modeling is completed to ensure that the model has fully extracted the correlation in the weekly house price index series. Then, the model residuals could be checked whether meet the white noise assumption.

Table 6. Ljung-Box test.

data	Residuals from ARIMA (1, 2, 1)
Q*	41.35
Df	8
p-value	1.793e−06
Model df	2
Total lags used	10

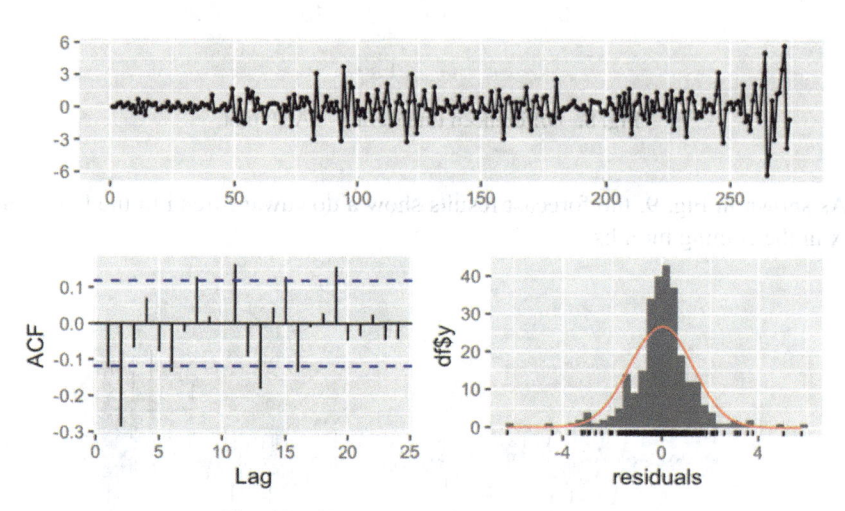

Fig. 10. Residuals from ARIMA (1, 2, 1).

4 Discussion

Based on the ARIMA model, the future trend of the Los Angeles housing price index is predicted to be stable, with occasional fluctuations. The model demonstrates that the discrepancy between the observed data and the anticipated data is within the permissible range, demonstrating a good fit. The model is reliable if the model parameters are statistically significant and the p-values are less than 0.05.

The Los Angeles house price index is anticipated to remain constant in the short term, according to the projection results. However, it is important to note that there may be occasional fluctuations due to various factors such as economic changes, government policies, and natural disasters. Therefore, it is necessary to monitor the index closely and adjust investment strategies in a timely manner.

Considering the investment strategies, it is suggested to focus on long-term investment in the Los Angeles housing market. Although there may be short-term changes in the market, the long-term trend is solid, and real estate values are often anticipated to rise over time. It is also recommended to diversify investment portfolios, including investing in different types of properties, such as residential and commercial real estate, and in different geographic locations within the Los Angeles area.

However, there are also some limitations to the ARIMA model. Firstly, the model assumes that the future trend of the Los Angeles housing price index will be similar to the historical trend, which may not always be the case. The housing market may be significantly impacted by external factors such as important economic events, geopolitical shifts, and natural disasters. Second, the model ignores the possible effects of unforeseen circumstances or modifications to governmental regulations, which could impose a considerable impact on the housing industry. Finally, this model assumes that the relationships between the variables in the model are linear, which may not be the case in reality.

In conclusion, the ARIMA model is a useful tool for predicting the future trend of the Los Angeles housing price index. However, it is important to use the results of the model as a reference and to closely monitor external factors that may affect the housing market. Diversifying investment portfolios and taking a long-term investment perspective is recommended to mitigate the potential impact of short-term fluctuations in the market.

5 Conclusion

For the purpose of providing investors and decision-makers with meaningful data, this study forecasts future changes of house price index in the area of Los Angeles using the ARIMA model. This ARIMA model uses patterns, trends, and seasonality in the real estate market to analyse historical data and predict future trends. Using historical data, the model's validity is confirmed, as is its capacity to deliver accurate forecasting outcomes for the Los Angeles housing market.

The main findings of the study indicate that the Los Angeles house price index is likely to remain stable in the near future, with occasional fluctuations due to various factors such as economic changes, government policies, and natural disasters. It is recommended that investors focus on long-term investments and diversify their portfolios to mitigate risks.

Despite the encouraging findings, the study had certain drawbacks. Future trends will be identical to current trends and correlations between variables are linear, which may not always be the case. The macro-environment and housing market's possible effect from unforeseen circumstances or modifications to governmental regulations are also not taken into consideration by the model. In addition, due to the restriction of access to data resources, the sample size could be enlarged and weekly data or even daily data could be considered to increase the accuracy in future studies.

By including outside variables and examining nonlinear interactions between variables, the future study may be able to overcome these restrictions. To further increase prediction accuracy, additional forecasting models could be evaluated and contrasted with the ARIMA model. To provide a more thorough picture of home price changes and their effects on the economy, the study's findings could also be applied to other major cities or areas.

References

1. Holt, C.C.: Forecasting seasonals and trends by exponentially weighted moving average. Int. J. Forecast. **20**(1), 5–10 (2004)
2. Taylo, J.W.: Volatility forecasting with smooth transition exponential smoothing. Int. J. Forecast. **20**(2), 273–286 (2004)
3. Time, B.: Generalized autoregressive conditional heteroskedasticity. Econometics 32–35 (1986)
4. Malpezzi, S.: A simple error correction model of house prices. J. Hous. Econ. **8**(1), 27–62 (1999)
5. Luttik, J.: The value of trees, water and open space as reflected by house prices in the Netherlands. Landsc. Urban Plan. **48**(3), 161–167 (2000)
6. Limsombunchai, V., Gan, C., Lee, M.: House price prediction: hedonic price model vs. artificial neural network. Am. J. Appl. Sci. **1**(3), 193 (2004)
7. Cook, S.: The convergence of regional house prices in the UK. Urban Stud. **40**(11) (2003)
8. Cook, S.: Detecting long-run relationships in regional house prices in the UK. Appl. Econ. **19**(1) (2005)
9. Holmes, M.J.: Is there long-run convergence among regional house prices in the UK?. Urban Stud. **45**(8) (2008)
10. Rangan, G., Marius, J., Alain, K.: The effect of monetary policy on real house price growth in South Africa: a factor-augmented vector autoregression (FAVAR) approach. Econ. Model. (2009)
11. Selim, H.: Determinants of house prices in Turkey: hedonic regression versus artificial neural network. Dogus Univ. J. (1), 65–76 (2008)
12. Crawford, G.W., Fratanton, M.C.: Assessing the forecasting performance of regime-switching, ARIMA and GARCH models of house prices. Real Estate Econ. **31**(2), 223–243 (2010)
13. Lasse, B., Stig, V.M.: Forecasting house prices in the 50 states using dynamic model averaging and dynamic model selection. Int. J. Forecast. **31**(1), 63–78 (2015)

Research on the Reasons for Abnormal Changes in the Operation Status of Domino's Pizza

Yining Feng[1], Yunong Li[2], Jingyu Qin[3], and Yuankai Tao[4](✉)

[1] School of Financial Management, Shanghai University of International Business and Economics, Shanghai 201620, China
[2] School of Business Administration, Beijing Normal University Hong-Kong Baptist University United International College, Zhuhai 519001, Guangdong, China
[3] School of Economics and Management, Changsha University of Science and Technology, Changsha 410076, Hunan, China
[4] School of Accounting, Zhongnan University of Economics and Law, Wuhan 430037, Hubei, China
202021080133@stu.zuel.edu.cn

Abstract. The spread of COVID-19 in 2020 had a huge negative impact on the catering industry, with the stocks of almost all catering companies falling. However, Domino's Pizza shares rose sharply in the early days of the pandemic. Based on the financial statements of Domino's Pizza in the past three years, the purpose of this study was to make a financial analysis of the changes in the data and to explore the impact of corporate decisions of catering enterprises on the stock index under the epidemic environment. The research concluded that the contactless delivery service of Domino's pizza during the epidemic period had a positive impact on its stock price. A complete distribution network was an important guarantee for the good operation of Domino's pizza; and the geographical advantages brought by the increase in offline stores also have a positive impact on their business performance. Therefore, the impact of COVID-19 was a significant reason why Domino's Pizza sales rose. The construction of Domino's Pizza's online ordering system and the development of offline stores will be discussed later.

Keywords: COVID-19 · Catering enterprises · Distribution network · Domino

1 Introduction

1.1 Research Background

In the first half of 2020, COVID-19 spread around the world. Governments around the world had taken strict steps to slow the spread of the virus, such as traffic controls and the requirement for people to wear face masks. While these measures were effective in stopping the spread of the epidemic, they had a huge negative impact on economies around the world. Among the industries hurt by the pandemic, the catering industry

---

Y. Feng, Y. Li, J. Qin and Y. Tao—These authors contributed equally.

© The Author(s), under exclusive license to Springer Nature Singapore Pte Ltd. 2024
X. Li et al. (Eds.): ICEMGD 2023, AEPS, pp. 796–803, 2024.
https://doi.org/10.1007/978-981-97-0523-8_74

suffered particularly. For safety reasons, people preferred eating at home rather than going out. This trend resulted in a decrease in profit in the catering industry. Water expense, electricity expense, and store rent fees increased significantly in restaurants. The food and beverage industry faced difficulties.

The United States had the world's largest catering market. The pandemic had a significant impact on the restaurant industry in the United States as well. Employment in full-service and limited-service restaurants fell 65% and 23%, respectively, in two months [1]. Due to COVID-19, more than 110,000 restaurants in the United States closed for long or permanent periods [2]. Fast food is a vital segment of the restaurant industry in the United States. Under the epidemic situation, almost all stocks in the fast-food industry were down entirely. However, as one of the top ten fast food brands, Domino's Pizza's stock price rose sharply. Domino's Pizza is a leading pizza delivery company in the world, operating through a network of over 17,600 locations in more than 90 countries [3]. The stock price increased, which meant investors were optimistic about the company's current business performance and future development prospects. The abnormal change in the business situation of the company caught people's attention.

There have been many previous studies of the fast-food industry. In order to explore the relationship between transformation leadership and human resources, Ntlhanngoe and Chipunza studied small fast-food restaurants in one region of South Africa in 2021 [4]. Syah et al. studied fast-food restaurants in Indonesia to determine the relationship between product quality, service quality, physical environment quality, perceived price, satisfaction, loyalty, happiness, and trust in the customers [5]. Veeresh Kumar et al. used Domino's Pizza in India as a research object to study the impact of product development and marketing on the Domino's Pizza market size [6].

1.2 Research Gap

During the epidemic, the stock price of Domino's Pizza rose sharply, which shows the strength of its business approach. Although there is a lot of research on the fast-food industry, there is little research on the stock price fluctuations of American local fast-food companies, which account for a certain proportion of the US catering industry. Most of the catering industry was hit hard by the epidemic, but Domino's Pizza has been able to keep running well, and its share prices have gone up. There is currently no relevant research on this abnormal phenomenon, which is a research gap that needs to be filled. Thus, this paper sets up the research question as: Why can Domino's Pizza remain unscathed during the pandemic and maintain good profitability?

It is forward-looking to analyze the principal contributors to Domino's Pizza's thriving during the pandemic, as this is an instructive case for most of the operators in this sector and worthy of being learned from. It is necessary to analyze its financial statements during the epidemic to explore the reasons for maintaining good profitability. In addition, as Domino's is a leading enterprise in the fast-food industry, exploring the reasons why it maintains profitability can provide a reference for other fast-food companies.

1.3 Fill the Gap

Due to this lack of research, it is important to figure out why the Domino's Pizza stock price index changed. The data from Domino's Pizza's financial statements for the past three years was analyzed. Through the analysis of Domino's Pizza, how to make major decisions during the COVID-19, and pizza's special position in the catering industry, explore the reasons why the market was optimistic about Domino's Pizza at the beginning of the COVID-19.

2 Case Description

Domino's Pizza, Inc., which goes by the brand name Domino's, is an American pizza restaurant chain that was started in 1961 and has its headquarters at the Domino's Farms Office Park in Ann Arbor. It has locations in the United States (including the District of Columbia, Guam, Puerto Rico, and the U.S. Virgin Islands) and in 83 other countries, including overseas territories such as the Cayman Islands and states with limited recognition such as Kosovo and Northern Cyprus. It has stores in 5,701 cities worldwide (2,900 internationally and 2,800 in the U.S.). As of the first quarter of 2018, Domino's had approximately 15,000 stores, with 5,649 in the U.S., 1,232 in India, and 1,094 in the U.K. [7].

During the coronavirus pandemic, the catering industry was hit hard. Statistics from Yelp's website show that more than 15,000 restaurants closed as a result. Texas Roadhouse, Inc., which was one of the most representative full-service operators and serves mostly steak, did not do well during the epidemic. This was reflected in its earnings Before Interest, Taxes, Depreciation and Amortization (EBITDA) and share price, which fell from 326.7 to 144.0 and from 63.18 to 33.86 between February 21 and April 3 [8, 9]. The comparable sales of Darden Restaurants, Inc. Had also slid from 44.7% year-on-year through April 19th [10]. Even though the sector as a whole did well, the performance of the share prices of limited service and fast-casual operators showed a different picture. Domino's Pizza, one of the quick-service restaurants (QSR) operators, did very well. Its sales revenue went up by 5.42% and its EBITDA went up by 14.93% [11]. And as for the profitability of Domino's, though the growth rate of EBITDA slightly narrowed from 10.01% and 10.12% to 7.98%, it still outstripped most of its rivals [12]. Having seen Domino's good performance, investors offered a higher price of $287.56, which rose to $406.68 only half a year later [13]. Another QSR restaurant, Papa John's, had experienced a similar growth trend, with a slight decline from 66.64 on February 20 to 47.42 on March 18, but steadily rising to 66.82 within a month, followed by stable and sustained growth in the next six months [14].

3 Analysis on Problems

3.1 Domino's Pizza's Tech Innovation on Supply Chain Centers and Food Delivery Devices had Attracted More Customers

Consumers mostly preferred to order food from a well-established channel with which they are familiar, either through carryout or delivery. However, market opportunities arose in the early stage of the pandemic, which allowed restaurants to expand their effect area in which the purchases for off-premises consumption would increase, since the fierceness of the competition in this industry kept subsiding with the disclosures of stores being trapped in a poor situation [15]. While most restaurants were not prepared for the emergency, Domino's Pizza jumped at the chance. Its tech-based innovation helped make improvements to how they get their products to customers, which benefited the company a lot and strengthened its market position. In the year before the emergency, Domino's Pizza tested a new service that originally aimed at time-pressed customers: On arriving, customers can get their pizza without having direct contact with the staff; an employee would deposit the pizza they had ordered via the brand's app on their phone in the trunk of their cars, and this was quite useful to protect customers from being infected during the pandemic [16]. This service had been put into use since the breakout of COVID-19, together with a series of innovations dedicated to their "digital-first" strategy, which included the autonomous delivery car in partnership with Ford in 2019 and their "launch delivery e-bike" developed with "Rad Power Bikes" in 2020. Though the bike had not yet been widely put into use, it led to a direct savings on fuel costs since the direct comparison of running costs is set at 9 dollars per 100 km. Those off-premise infrastructures enabled Domino's to offer adaptive services effectively and efficiently.

As a result, people who weren't allowed to talk to each other would like to use the delivery giant's services during the public health emergency. This is shown by a change in the number of times people search for the brand's name online, as shown in Google Trends [17]. The lockdown of the United States most major cities was carried out around March 20th and lasted for one month. And it is during this month that, after the lockdown, from March 14th to April 11th, the number of people searching for 'Domino's Pizza' in the US exactly doubled [18]. Given its self-owned delivery chain, Domino's generates nearly two-thirds of its revenues through its online platform, and the growing sales revenue has helped the company realize rapid cash accumulation [19].

3.2 Domino's Investment in Development of Delivery Network Enable it to Set Price and Margin More Flexibly

Most of Domino's competitors have to pay the huge fees that delivery aggregators charge, which end up being passed on to the customers. It is investigated that the delivery and pickup fee on each delivery that Doordash, which was considered to be the largest food delivery platform, charged were 15% and 6% for a basic subscription in 2020, while this set a limitation for most of the franchisees to adapt their margins and were forced to narrow the margins [20]. By contrast, Domino's Pizza had established its own online ordering system, affiliated with a series of technological innovations. As Domino's said, it had launched its own mobile application, which covered almost 95% of smartphones and tablets on the market, and it also introduced a voice-ordering application named "Dom", which was used to monitor every stage of a customer's order in real-time. Apart from these improvements, the company also enhanced a lot of its ordering profile platform, allowing consumers to have a better user experience.

During the pandemic, Domino's set up ways to order on popular social media sites like Facebook, Twitter, etc., as well as on its own website, so that it could handle the situation better. It was stated that during the second quarter of 2019, 65% of U.S. sales came through digital channels, and during the same quarter in 2020, this figure had risen to 75% and even as high as 80% in some weeks [21]. Domino's Pizza was able to get more pricing flexibility and control over their products' margins because more and more customers used the company's own delivery network. Domino's Pizza's EBITDA per franchisee went from $700,00 in 2015 to $1,180,000 in 2019, as profit margins continue to rise steadily [21].

However, it is apparent that while the coronavirus-related economic downturn limited the pricing headroom, Domino's product margins shrank as a result of the company's decision to refocus on those price-conscious customers. Amid global store closures, the decrease in those high-margin international franchisees' revenue brought bad effects to the overall margins despite the low contribution they had to the top line. While the year-on-year growth rate of sales had risen by 7.1% during the second quarter, international retail sales, conversely, had declined 3.2% on that rate during the three weeks up to April 12 [22]. Considering the negative effect that international franchisees had on the overall margins, the store openings planned for 2020 were delayed, and this helped the company maintain firm control over the margins of their products.

3.3 Domino's Stores' Diversified Geographical Presence Allow it to Recover Fast at the Beginning of the Outbreak

Despite the decision to delay the stores' opening plan in early 2020, transitorily, Domino's Pizza raised its new strategy after its preliminary restoration. The strategy was called "fortressing,", and it basically meant the building of more stores, even in areas that already had existing locations [23]. This enabled the company to shrink delivery radii and make it easier to deliver its products to its customers quickly and at a lower cost, meeting the ever-growing demand for speed and convenience in food delivery. Unlike its rivals, who were trying to promote their delivery range, Domino's kept building out new stores, with a net growth of 44 and 51 restaurants in the U.S. during the third and fourth quarters of 2020, respectively [24]. The diversity of its domestic stores' locations was useful to ascertain objects scientifically and cut logistic costs, and it was also helpful to the realization of its "30 min or it's free" policy.

4 Suggestions

4.1 Balance Online Services and Offline Stores

In this case, Domino's Pizza should find a good balance between its online services and its stores in order to grow in a coordinated way. Because of the pandemic, people tended to eat at or near their homes. Full-service restaurants spend most of their money on store construction and employee expenses. They don't have sufficient money or human resources to develop online platforms for delivery. In this context, some QSR, such as Domino's Pizza, have increased their performance through their digital order system. The increase in QSR was short-lived. In fact, in 2020, Domino's Pizza has been adding more than 100 stores a year in the United States, but profit growth has been disappointing. Domino Pizza reported $4117.4 million in revenue, a 13.8% increase from 2019 [25]. That year, the company's operating profit margin was 17.6%, and its net profit margin was 11.9% [25].

However, in 2021, Domino's Pizza's revenue was $4357.4 million, an increase of only 5.8% from 2020 [3]. The operating profit margin of the company was 17.9%, and the net profit margin was 11.7% [3]. Domino's Pizza's operating profit margin and net profit margin haven't changed much over the past few years. The fact that Domino's Pizza's sales growth has slowed down suggests that the company has reached a plateau. The company's revenue growth is expected to approach zero over the next few years. As the company's stores increase every year, Domino's Pizza needs to adjust online ordering and offline business to keep up with its rapid development. For online ordering services, companies should maintain regular lists of dishes. A variety of dishes can meet the needs of more consumers and attract people with different tastes. In this way, maintain the status of Domino's pizza in the fast-food industry. For offline stores, internal human resource management is necessary. Through the reasonable management of employees, it can effectively reduce the expenses of the store. Stores should also conduct market research on consumers to understand the unique needs of customers of different ages. As a matter of fact, older people have been concerned that pizza may be too greasy for their health. Domino's Pizza could use that to create a lighter fruit pizza. By this way, Domino's Pizza can introduce fresh products to adapt to the fierce competition in the fast-food industry. Through the control and management of online services and offline stores, Domino's Pizza is expected to maintain an annual profit growth rate of about 10% in the future, so as to achieve the purpose of coordinated development.

4.2 Suggestion on the Delivery Routes

The pickup distance, pickup time, and pickup method in logistics delivery services have significant correlations with perceived logistics delivery service quality, and logistics delivery service quality perception can promote consumers' online shopping willingness [26]. The logistics experience has a big effect on customer loyalty, which means that a good logistics experience is good for customer loyalty. The efficiency of the logistics experience has a big effect on customer loyalty, which means that a fast and efficient logistics experience can win customers over for new retail businesses [27].

Therefore, Domino's Pizza should plan the delivery routes ahead of time and train the delivery personnel [28]. Every delivery clerk needs to become familiar with the transportation conditions of the community they deliver to. Also, the company needs to develop alternative routes to allow the delivery clerks to choose Plan B. It is important for delivery clerks to pay attention to safety and follow the rules of the road when making deliveries. The company should figure out how many pizzas each community needs each month and send out the right number of delivery people based on that. This measure aims at maximizing the use of manpower to reduce costs and improve efficiency.

4.3 Suggestion on Stores Expansion

At the beginning of the outbreak, sales at Domino's in the second quarter of 2020 increased by 7.1%. Despite some of the impact of the epidemic, sales have now soared to 75–80% of total revenue. By the end of 2020, the company had posted its strongest quarterly performance in decades; it largely attributed the success of the fourth quarter to growing delivery demand and loyal members [29]. At the ICR conference, Levy stated that using his own internal delivery driver has given Delta Music greater flexibility in terms of fees and customer experience, which has allowed Domino's Pizza to stand out from many competitors in large chains [23].

Many of its competitors are focused on expanding their distribution areas, but Domino's Pizza sticks to its solid growth strategy [29]. Focus on opening more stores so that it can meet the needs of customers who want delivery or takeout and keep the promise to deliver in 30 min. In contrast, this approach enhances relationships with local customers, making them more trusting and inclined to choose a Domino's pizza.

The company's plan to open more stores gives it a geographical advantage, which helps it build good relationships with customers and keep their trust. This strategy has brought considerable benefits to Domino's, especially during the pandemic, where the positive effect is even more evident. Because of this, it is suggested that Domino's Pizza keep using these strategies to make more money.

5 Conclusion

In the first half of 2020, under COVID-19, almost all stocks in the fast-food industry fell. However, as one of the top ten fast-food brands, the share price of Domino's Pizza has soared. This means that investors are optimistic about the company's current operating performance and future development prospects. The abnormal changes in the company's operating conditions have attracted people's attention.

In response to the performance of Domino's, this research studied the factors that kept it in good operating condition during the pandemic. This research has analyzed three aspects of this phenomenon. The first is that it has its own delivery website. Secondly, the benefit of the delivery service that has been tested in advance by Domino's Pizza Finally, there is the geographical advantage of the expansion of stores for Domino's Pizza.

This research came to the conclusion that during the time of the epidemic, stock prices went up because the company improved its own delivery networks, started using contactless delivery services, and opened more stores in different parts of the country.

This article looked at the research on how the epidemic affected the fast-food industry in the United States. It also looked into why Domino's Pizza kept running well during the epidemic and filled a gap in the research on how the epidemic affected the fast-food industry. Since Domino's Pizza is one of the biggest fast-food chains in the US, the research results can be used as a guide.

Some limitations are present in the analysis. Only through the website to search for literature is the available information limited, and some of the problems are based on subjective speculation based on limited reports with only qualitative analysis rather than quantitative analysis. In future research, it is necessary to improve the way of accessing information and try to obtain as much data as possible. Additionally, utilize appropriate approaches to analyze problems qualitatively and quantitatively in order to make the conclusion more reliable.

References

1. Ansell, R., John, P.: COVID-19 ends longest employment recovery and expansion in ces history, causing unprecedented job losses in 2020. Monthly Labor Rev. 1–49 (2021)
2. Restaurant Hospitality. http://restaurant-hospitality.com. Accessed 17 Mar 2023
3. MarketLine Company Profile: Domino's Pizza, Inc. (2022). https://search.ebscohost.com. Accessed 17 Mar 2023
4. Ntlhanngoe, L., Chipunza, C.: Owner-managers' transformational leader-ship behaviours and human resource strategies: a case of small fast-food restaurants in South Africa. South Afr. J. Hum. Resour. Manage. **19**(1) (2021)
5. Syah, T., Alimwidodo, P., Lianti, L., Hatta, H.: Perceived price as antecedent of satisfaction and loyalty: learn from fast food international restaurants. Cent. Eur. Bus. Rev. **11**(4), 63–84 (2022)
6. Veeresh Kumar, W., Vetrivel, P., Sumukha Krishna, S., Suresh, E., Murthy, M.: An icon of pizzas: domino's in India - a case study. Aweshkar Res. J. **28**(2), 86–99 (2021)
7. Domino's, Wekipedia. https://en.wikipedia.org/wiki/Domino%27s. Accessed 17 Mar 2023
8. Texas Roadhouse, Inc., Koyfin. https://app.koyfin.com/chart. Accessed 18 Mar 2023
9. Texas Roadhouse, Inc/Profitability, Alpha seeking. https://seekingalpha.com/symbol. Accessed 18 Mar 2023
10. Darden Restaurants, Inc., Alpha seeking. https://seekingalpha.com/symbol/DRI/income-statement. Accessed 18 Mar 2023
11. Domino's Pizza, Inc./profitability, Alpha seeking. https://seekingalpha.com/symbol/DPZ/profitability. Accessed 18 Mar 2023
12. Domino's Pizza, Inc./growth, Alphaseeking. https://seekingalpha.com/symbol/DPZ/growth. Accessed 18 Mar 2023
13. Domino's Pizza, Inc./Overview, Koyfin. https://app.koyfin.com/chart. Accessed 20 Mar 2023
14. Papa John's Inc./Overview, Koyfin. https://app.koyfin.com/chart-template. Accessed 21 Mar 2023
15. Special Report, QSR. https://www.qsrmagazine.com/reports. Accessed 21 Mar 2023
16. The Wall Street Journal. https://www.wsj.com/articles. Accessed 21 Mar 2023
17. Domino's, Google Trends. https://trends.google.com/trends/explore. Accessed 21 Mar 2023
18. Pizza, Google Trends. https://trends.google.com/trends. Accessed 22 Mar 2023
19. Domino's Pizza/Analysis. Alphaseeking, https://seekingalpha.com/article. Accessed 22 Mar 2023
20. BestReferralDriver.com. https://bestreferraldriver.com/doordash. Accessed 5 Apr 2023
21. Fast Food News, Quick-Service and Fast Casual Restaurant News and Information. https://www.qsrmagazine.com/fast-food. Accessed 24 Mar 2023
22. Domino's Pizza/Analysis, Alphaseeking. https://seekingalpha.com/article. Accessed 25 Mar 2023
23. Pizza News, Pizza Marketing Quarterly. https://www.pmq.com/dominos. Accessed 1 Apr 2023
24. Events/Events Reviews, Chief Executive. https://chiefexecutive.net. Accessed 1 Apr 2023
25. MarketLine Company Profile: Domino's Pizza, Inc. (2021). https://search.ebscohost.com. Accessed 30 Mar 2023
26. Xu, C.H.: Research on the impact of logistics and distribution services on consumer product purchase decisions, p. 61 (2017)
27. Lin, X.Q.: The relationship between logistics experience and consumer loyalty in the context of "new retail". **2022**(07), 94–98 (2022)
28. NETEASE, NETEASE account. https://www.163.com. Accessed 5 Apr 2023
29. Nation's Restaurant News. https://www.nrn.com/quick-service. Accessed 3 Apr 2023

Detect the Change Points in the Growth Rate of US Real Export Data Based on Mean and Variance

Yiwei Zhang(✉)

University of Sydney, Camperdown, NSW 2006, Australia
jmatsumura81667@student.napavalley.edu

Abstract. When analyzing time series data, it is common to 'ssume the data was generated form a consistent distribution or process. However, many global epidemic and financial problems caused great shake on the global economy. The shake may change the environment of US exports and thus determining the change points of statistic properties in the time series data of US exports is important. This article transforms the original US export data into the growth rate of US exports and provides researches on detecting the multiple change points in the growth rate of US real export data from 1947 to 2022. This article detects change points from the aspects of mean, variance and mean-variance under the normal distribution assumption. The algorithms utilized to identify change points in this article are the segment neighborhood and the PELT. This article verifies that the segment neighborhood can give the exact results based on fewer assumptions than the PELT. The mean-variance method gives the best results, finding 9 change points. The 9 change points corresponds to 7 segments of the entire data and the segments are coincided with the recession periods from the National Bureau of Economic Research.

Keywords: Mean and Variance · Unite States · Export

1 Introduction

Time series data is analyzed in many subjects. When dealing with time series data, researchers commonly suppose the sample has a consistent data generating process. It is important to detect whether there are change points in the sample. This article provides the research on detecting the multiple change points in the growth rate of United States (US) real export data.

The US as the world's largest economy play a critical role in the global trade. The exports of US are a remarkable index when analyzing the economy state. There are many researches investigate and forecast the exports of US [1, 2]. In past years, the global economy has experienced a huge vibration caused by a series of "black swans", including the subprime mortgage crisis and the Covid-19. These events have strong impact on the environment of the exports of US, more and more attention is attracted to inspect that whether the trend of the US exports is different from that in past.

Many models have been proposed to detecting the structural change in time series data. Some models focused on the change of a specific statistic property, such as Variance. Some models exploit instrumental variables to analyze the structural breaks. Other models perform regression analysis. Some researches can be seen in, Chen and Gupta, Perron, and Aue and Horvath [3–5].

This article detects change points from the aspects of mean, variance and mean-variance under the normal distribution assumption. The algorithms used in this article are the segment neighborhoods and the Pruned Exact Linear Time (PELT) [6, 7]. After finding the change points, this article compares the results with the business cycle turning points determined by the National Bureau of Economic Research (NBER) to see if they are reasonable [8].

2 Method

This article analyzes the US export time series data to identify change points based on the mean and variance. First, this article describes the collected data and process the data for further analyzing. The data is the US export data in billions of chained 2012 dollars from 1947 Q1 to 2022 Q4 [9]. This article also collects the turning points determined by NBER, which are contrasted with the change points detected by the statistic method. NBER defines the turning points by determining the recession periods of US economy. Second, this article introduces and employs the multiple change point detect approach suggested by Killick and Eckley [10]. This approach detects the change point from three aspects, such as mean, variance and combined mean-variance.

2.1 Exploratory Data Analysis

This article analyzes the US real quarterly exports of goods and services from 1047 Q1 to 2022 Q4. The exports data is in billions of chained 2012 dollars and seasonally adjusted. The real export data indicates that the data has been adjusted to remove the impact of inflation. The chained 2012 dollars reveals that the dollar values in all years are equal to the dollar value in 2012. Another impact should be considered is the seasonality. The seasonality causes the variation of data due to the effect of weather or holiday. The seasonality adds extra volatiles on the data and make other movements unclear, such as trends. The Fig. 1 shows the real exports in billions of chained 2012 dollars after seasonal adjustment.

The series presents an exponentially increasing trend while at the beginning it shows a short time decreasing. In recent 30 years, the series also reveals a cyclical pattern for around 10 years. This article is going to detect the change point in mean but it is meaningless for an increasing trend. This article transforms the original data to the quarterly growth rate of the US exports. The formula is below while y_t is the export at time t:

$$Growth\ Rate = \left(\frac{y_t}{y_{t-1}} - 1\right) * 100 \qquad (1)$$

The Fig. 2 displays the growth rate. It can be found that the mean of the growth rate is 1.1758 and the variance is 17.8904. The positive mean indicates an increasing trend in

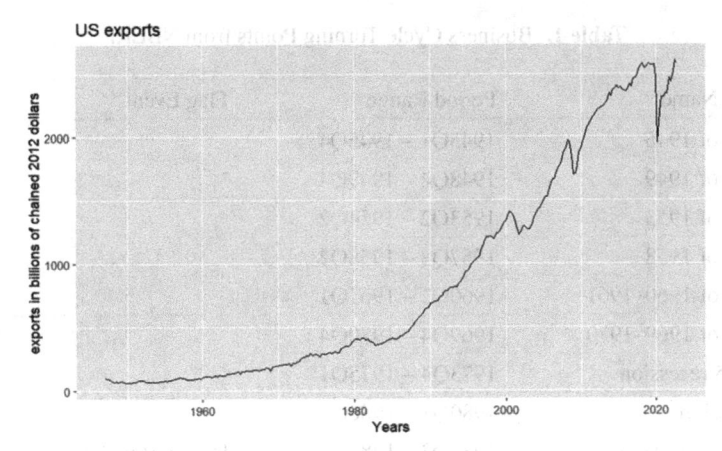

Fig. 1. US Exports.

the long run which is consistent with the result in the Fig. 1. It is should be noticed that the downside of growth rate does not mean the decreasing of the US exports. Another information implied by the Fig. 2 is that the variances are very different in different periods. For example, the period before 1980 has a relatively high variance and from 1980 to 2020 the variance is low. After 2020, the variance seams to go up but it is not clear because there is no enough data.

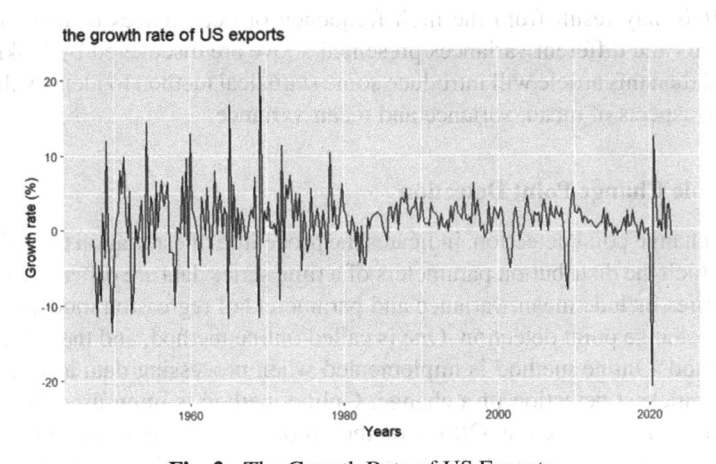

Fig. 2. The Growth Rate of US Exports.

By checking the Fig. 1 and 2, the change points are supposed to exist. These change points are caused by many reasons. Considering the high relationship between US export data and the US economic state, this article intends to compare the date of change points with the occurrence time of recessions in US. The Table 1 displays the turning points and recession periods announced NBER [8].

Table 1. Business Cycle Turning Points from NBER.

Recession Name	Period Range	Flag Event
Recession of 1945	1945Q1 – 1945Q4	
Recession of 1949	1948Q4 – 1949Q4	
Recession of 1953	1953Q2 – 1954Q2	
Recession of 1958	1957Q3 – 1958Q2	
Recession of 1960–1961	1960Q2 – 1961Q1	
Recession of 1969–1970	1969Q4 – 1970Q4	
1973–1975 recession	1973Q4 – 1975Q1	
1980 recession	1980Q1 – 1980Q3	
1981–1982 recession	1981Q3 – 1982Q4	Iranian Revolution
Early 1990s recession	1990Q3 – 1991Q1	Gulf War recession
Early 2000s recession	2001Q1 – 2001Q4	"Dot-com bubble"
Great Recession	2007Q4 – 2009Q2	subprime mortgage crisis
COVID-19 recession	2019Q4 – 2020Q2	COVID-19 pandemic

According to the Table 1 and Fig. 2, the great drops of the growth rate are coincided with the recessions in 2001, 2008 and 2020. The high variance of the growth rate from 1950 to 1970 may result from the high frequency of occurrences of recessions. The change points and different variances presented above are discovered by looking at the figures, and then this article will introduce some statistical method to identify the change points from aspects of mean, variance and mean-variance.

2.2 Multiple Change Point Detection

The name, change point detection, indicates the procedure of estimation the point before and after which the distribution parameters of a time series data are different. The statistical properties include mean, variance and parameters of regression models. There are two type of change point detection. One is called online method, and the other is called offline method. Online method is implemented when processing data as it arrives and the goal is quickest detection of a change. Online method is often used in processing control and intrusion detection. Offline method processes all the data in one go and the goal is accurate detection of a change. This article focuses on the offline method.

This paragraph gives the formal definition of the change point. The observations of a time series data are denoted as $y_{i:n} = (y_1, \ldots, y_n)$. Supposing at a time τ, $\tau \in \{1, \ldots, n-1\}$, the distribution parameters of $\{y_1, \ldots, y_\tau\}$ and $\{y_{\tau+1}, \ldots, y_n\}$ are different before and after the time τ, so the time τ is the location of a change point. Then, this idea can be extended to multiple changes. Supposing m change points exist, their locations are $\tau_{1:m} = (\tau_1, \ldots, \tau_m)$. Each change point location is an integer between 1 and $n-1$ inclusive. This article defines $\tau_0 = 0$ and $\tau_{m+1} = n$, and the time monotonically increases from τ_1 to τ_m. As a consequence, there will $m+1$ segments in total which are separated by m change points, and the i th segment contains observations $y_{(\tau_{i-1}+1):\tau_i}$. This article wants to identify the number of segments required to split the sample data.

The literature utilizes many methods to discover multiple change points. Among these methods, minimization approach which minimizes the blew equation is commonly accepted:

$$\sum_{i=1}^{m+1} [\mathcal{C}(y_{(\tau_{i-1}+1):\tau_i})] + \beta f(m) \tag{2}$$

In Eq. (2), the upper letter $\mathcal{C}$ denotes the cost function and this article employs negative log-likelihood as the cost function. $\beta f(m)$ is a penalty to guard against over fitting.

To solve the minimization problem, 2^{n-1} solutions should be considered. If m is known, the number of solutions reduces to $\binom{n-1}{m}$. This article chooses the maximum number of change points $Q = 13$, since there are 13 recession periods in the data set according to NBER. Another two thing should be determined before solving the minimization problem are penalty functions and algorithms for minimizing Eq. (2). In terms of penalty functions, the most common criteria are Bayesian Information Criterion (BIC) and Akaike's Information Criterion (AIC). For a larger dataset, AIC is more likely to select a more complex model in comparison with BIC. This article will choose BIC as the penalty function to control the complexity of models. In terms of Algorithms, the following paragraphs will briefly introduce three algorithms and then determine which algorithm will be used in this article.

Binary segmentation first tries to identify a single change point in the entire data. If a change point can be found, the data set is separated to two subsets at the changepoint location. Then, Binary segmentation repeats this procedure on the two new data sets until no change points are found. This algorithm is an approximate minimization of Eq. (2) as finding new change points are conditional on that identified previously. The details are described by Edwards and Cavalli-Sforza [11]. This algorithm has the highest speed with the lowest computational complexity, $\mathcal{O}(n\log n)$, among three algorithms. However, the highest speed sometimes generates wrong change points. For example, if the first point is estimated wrongly, the else points are all wrong.

The segment neighborhood algorithm minimizes the Eq. (2) exactly using a dynamic programing technique [6]. This algorithm finds change points based on an iteration method. This method reduces the computational complexity from $\mathcal{O}(2^n)$ to $\mathcal{O}(Qn^2)$. This algorithm is exact but computationally slowest.

The PELT algorithm also provides an exact segmentation. In contrast to the segment neighborhood, the PELT is more computationally efficient by exploiting dynamic programing and pruning which leads to an $\mathcal{O}(n)$ complexity subject to certain assumptions [7]. The main assumption is that the number of change points is proportional to the size of data sets, while in practices it is not common.

This article will apply the segment neighborhood and the PELT algorithms to detect change points. The following sections present some assumptions when detecting change points for different statistic properties.

Change Points in Mean. When detecting change points in Mean, this article assumes that the variance of whole data set is constant. In addition, this article also assumes that the observations are normally distributed with different means in different segments.

Change Points in Variance. When detecting change points in Variance, this article assumes that the mean of whole data set is constant. Another assumption is that the observations are normally distributed with different variance in different segments.

Change Points in Mean and Variance. Detecting change points in mean and variance needs the fewest assumptions. The assumption is that the observations are normally distributed with respective means and variances in each segment.

3 Results

This article reveals the results in three sub sections which follows the sequence of different statistic properties mentioned in the previous section. The result of each section contains the change points and comparison with the business cycle turning points from NBER.

3.1 Change Points in Mean

Figure 3 and Fig. 4 are change points in mean detected by the segment neighborhood and the PELT respectively. It shows the PELT method is over-fitting. One possible reason is that the assumption for PELT is not satisfied. Thus, this article compares the result of the segment neighborhood with the business cycle turning points of NBER.

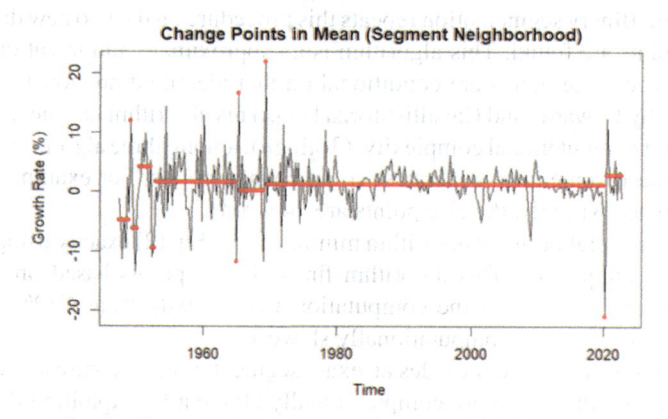

Fig. 3. Change Points in Mean (Segement Neighborhood).

Table 2 summarizes the comparison. This article considers that the change points coincides with a recession period if the change points is next to or in that recession period range. It can be found that only two recessions are detected and the performance of this model is bad. The high variances from 1950 to 1970 impedes the ability of the model to detect the change points while the change points in this period are the points with extreme values.

Change Points in Mean (PELT)

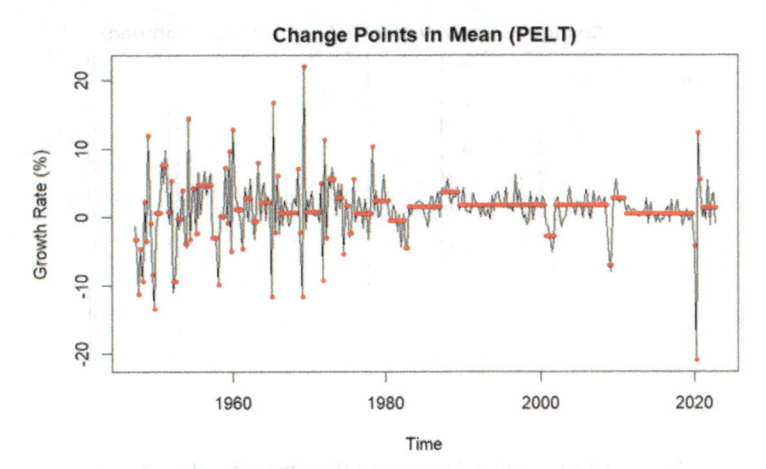

Fig. 4. Change Points in Mean (PELT).

Table 2. Summary of Change Points in Mean.

Change Points in Mean	Coincide or not	Recession Name	Period Range
1948Q4	Yes	Recession of 1949	1948Q4 – 1949Q4
1949Q1	Yes		
1950Q1	Yes		
1952Q1	No		
1952Q3	No		
1964Q4	No		
1965Q1	No		
1965Q2	No		
1968Q4	No		
1969Q1	No		
1969Q2	No		
2020Q1	Yes	COVID-19 recession	2019Q4 – 2020Q2
2020Q2	Yes		

3.2 Change Points in Variance

Figure 5 and Fig. 6 displays the detected change points in variance by the segment neighborhood and the PELT method respectively. The results from two methods are same. And the results are consistent with the intuitive discovery by looking at the figure.

Table 3 summary the comparison between change points in variance and the recession periods from NBER. 5 of 6 changes points are coincide with the recession periods, and the one outside the period is as well close to the period. Thus, change points in variance give the better result than change points in mean. One possible reason is that assumptions

Change Points in Variance (Segment Neighborhood)

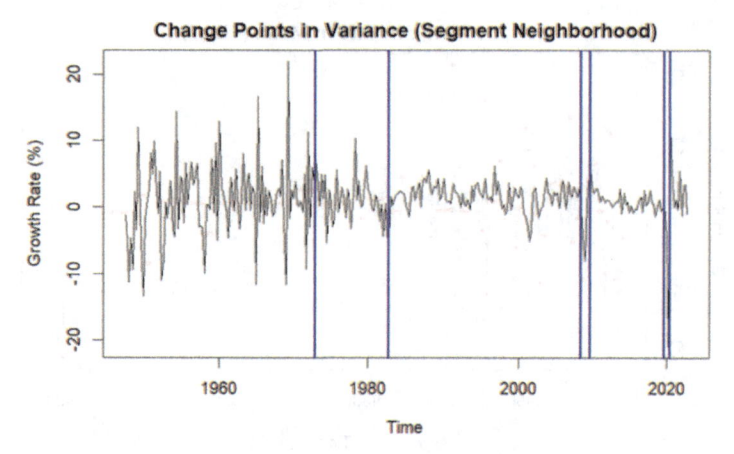

Fig. 5. Change Points in Variance (Segment Neighborhood).

Change Points in Variance (PELT)

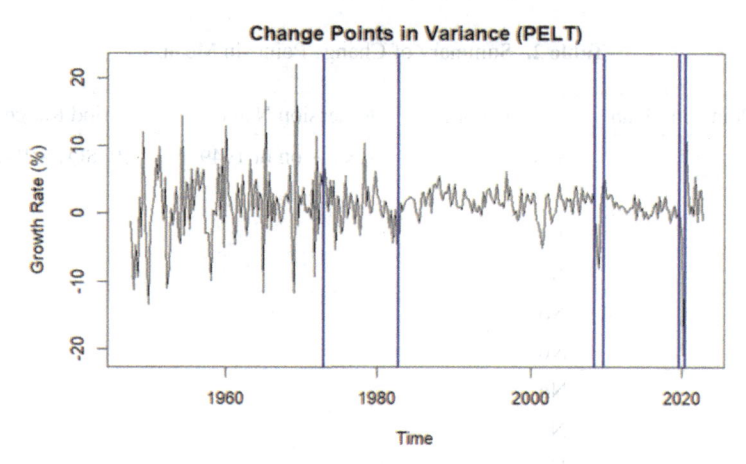

Fig. 6. Change Points in Variance (PELT).

for change points in Variance are more reliable compared to that for change points in mean.

3.3 Change Points in Mean-Variance

Figure 7 and Fig. 8 shows the change points in mean and variance for the segment neighborhood and the PELT methods respectively. The results for two methods are the same.

Compared to the recession periods from NBER, 6 of 9 change points are coincide with the recession period, presented in Table 4. Although 1973Q1 is not in the recession period, it is very close to the 1973–1975 recession. Thus, setting 1973Q1 as a change point is acceptable. Referring to 2000Q3 and 2008Q4 change points, it can be found that these two change points result from the high volatile caused by the Early 2000s

Table 3. Summary of Change Points in Variance.

Change Points in Variance	Coincide or not	Recession Name	Period Range
1973Q1	No but close	1973–1975 recession	1973Q4 – 1975Q1
1982Q4	Yes	1981–1982 recession	1981Q3 – 1982Q4
2008Q3	Yes	Great Recession	2007Q4 – 2009Q2
2009Q4	Yes		
2019Q4	Yes	COVID-19 recession	2019Q4 – 2020Q2
2020Q3	Yes		

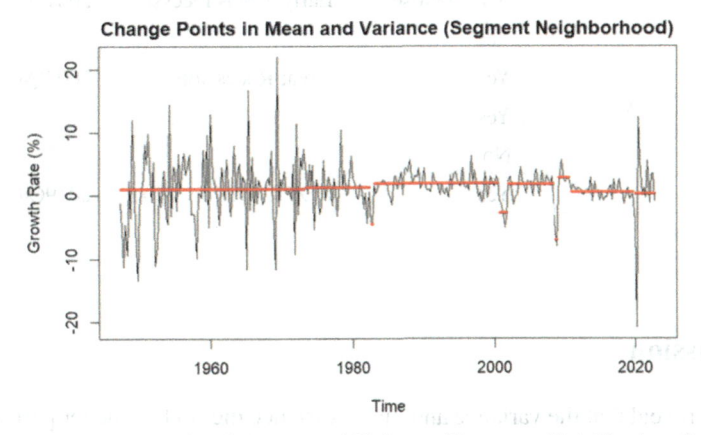

Fig. 7. Change Points in Mean and Variance (Segment Neighborhood).

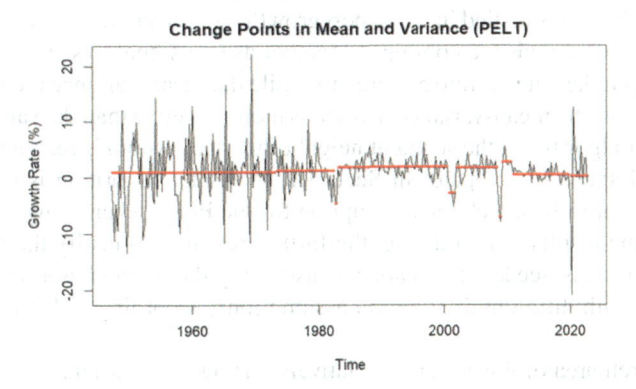

Fig. 8. Change Points in Mean and Variance (PELT).

recession and the Great recession (2008 Financial Crisis). The period between change point 2019Q1 and change point 2010Q4 records subsequent effect of the Financial Crises and the growth rate comes to a normal state after change point 2010Q4. In other words, the data set is split into 7 segments. Thus, change points in mean and variance provides a reliable reflection about some remarkable recessions.

Table 4. Summary of Change Points in Mean and Variance.

Change Points in Mean and Variance	Coincide or not	Recession Name	Period Range
1973Q1	No but close	1973–1975 recession	1973Q4 – 1975Q1
1982Q2	Yes	1981–1982 recession	1981Q3 – 1982Q4
1982Q4	Yes		
2000Q3	No but close	Early 2000s recession	2001Q1 – 2001Q4
2001Q4	Yes		
2008Q3	Yes	Great Recession	2007Q4 – 2009Q2
2009Q1	Yes		
2010Q4	No		
2019Q4	Yes	COVID-19 recession	2019Q4 – 2020Q2

4 Discussion

The results reveal that the variance and mean-variance method are better performed than the mean method in detecting the change points in US export growth rate. The possible reason is that the mean method relies on the assumption that the data set has a constant variance, which is not satisfied in US export growth rate. In addition, if the change points in same recession periods are combined together as one signal to segment the data set, the variance split the date set into 5 segments while the mean-variance method generates 7 segments. Thus, the mean-variance method is more sensitive than the variance method.

In terms of algorithms, the segment neighborhood algorithm is recommended, if the computational speed is accepted. In Sect. 3.1, the PELT algorithm is over-fitting, so people should carefully check the assumption for the PELT when using this algorithm.

To make the results more reliable, the further research to justify the normal distribution assumption is needed. Scholars can also apply the method used in this article to other data set with different distribution assumptions, according to Killick and Eckley [10].

The research area of this article is relatively narrow. This article detects the change points only considering the mean and variance, while there are many other statistic properties. For example, researchers can investigate the change on trend. They can first fit the data with a forecasting model and then check changes on parameters of the model [12]. In addition, the growth rate data set used in this article is univariant data, but the growth rate can be affected by many other factors, such as the employment rate and the interest rate. Further researches may consider the regression analysis.

5 Conclusion

This article utilizes change points analysis proposed by Killick and Eckley detects the change points in the growth rate of US export data. The mean-variance method gives the best results. The data set is split into 7 segments. The 7 segments are coincided with the recession periods from NBER. The mean method overestimates the number of change points while the variance method underestimates the number of change points. In terms of the algorithms, although the segment neighborhood is computationally slow, it provides more exact results. The reason is that the segment neighborhood needs fewer assumptions than the PELT.

The result that there are 7 segments in the data set can be used to build more complex models. Researchers can fit different model for the 7 segments. Other people can investigate the causes which producing this result. This article has some limits. The normal distribution assumption should be carefully checked in further researches. The relationship between the growth rate of US export with other factors, such as the employment rate and the interest rate, is the area this article doesn't cover.

References

1. Salvatore, D.: Growth and trade in the United States and the world economy: overview. J. Policy Model. **42**(4), 750–759 (2020)
2. Benguria, F., Taylor, A.M.: After the panic: are financial crises demand or supply shocks? Evidence from international trade. Am. Econ. Rev. Insights **2**(4), 509–526 (2020)
3. Chen, J., Gupta, A.K.: Testing and locating variance changepoints with application to stock prices. J. Am. Stat. Assoc. **92**(438), 739–747 (1997)
4. Perron, P.: Macroeconometrics and Time Series Analysis. Palgrave Macmillan, London (2010)
5. Aue, A., Horváth, L.: Structural breaks in time series. J. Time Ser. Anal. **34**(1), 1–16 (2013)
6. Auger, I.E., Lawrence, C.E.: Algorithms for the optimal identification of segment neighborhoods. Bull. Math. Biol. **51**(1), 39–54 (1989)
7. Killick, R., Fearnhead, P., Eckley, I.A.: Optimal detection of changepoints with a linear computational cost. J. Am. Stat. Assoc. **107**(500), 1590–1598 (2012)
8. NBER. https://www.nber.org/research/business-cycle-dating/business-cycle-dating-procedure-frequently-asked-questions. Accessed 5 Apr 2023
9. St. Louis Fed (stlouisfed.org). https://fred.stlouisfed.org/series/EXPGSC1. Accessed 5 Apr 2023
10. Killick, R., Eckley, I.: Changepoint: an R package for changepoint analysis. J. Stat. Softw. **58**(3), 1–19 (2014)
11. Bai, J., Perron, P.: Estimating and testing linear models with multiple structural changes. Econometrica **66**(1), 47–78 (1998)
12. Li, A., Qin, Z.: On-line segmentation of time-series data. J. Softw. **15**(11), 1671–1679 (2004)

Forecasting the Stock Market Index with Dynamic ARIMA Model and LSTM Model

Siyuan Zhu(✉)

Southwestern University of Finance and Economics, Cheng Du, China
41634047@smail.swufe.edu.cn

Abstract. With the development of the machine learning method, there are a lot more time series model being invented and applied to mimic the real-world data. The interpretation and prediction of time series in financial markets is a hot topic in current research. This thesis conducts dynamic ARIMA model and the Long-short term model to forecast the stock market index in America and check the causal inference between the residual of the forecasting and the federal fund rate, which could explain the abnormal increase in the period 2021–2022. Thus, this paper provides a hybrid explanation of the structure of the time series forecasting, which will be helpful with the predicting. And this thesis also shows that the epoch for long-short term need to be considered when concluding in a common result of forecast. The deep learning method should be more accurate with a vast data set and become more helpful. This study provides a new idea for the prediction of the US stock market index through the comparison of prediction results between models, expanding the current research field.

Keywords: Dynamics ARIMA model · LSTM model · Stock market index

1 Introduction

The stock index and individual stock price are always main concern of the investment, a huge set of financial derivatives are generated based on them, such as the option and ETF fund. Till now, there are already over 40 trillion dollars securities are traded on the stock market (Fig. 1). Therefore, the forecast of the index or the price many help with the portfolio investment and the derivatives performance, then get a better return of investment. However, the stock market is sensitive to the change of the economics and vulnerable to the economic shocks, resulting in the urgent need to figure out potential factors that can affect the stock price index.

The ARIMA model, which combines auto-regressive and moving average models, is the traditional way of forecasting in economics. It is based on time series analysis. The primary focus in the area of econometrics is on constructing and analyzing the elements of economic time series, such as trends and cycles. The two basic domains of the time series analysis model—time and frequency—were then described by Nerlove in 1964 [1]. The Forecasting Economic Time Series, a later publication, provides advancements in forecasting theory and practice as well as time series analysis [2]. Roh proposed hybrid

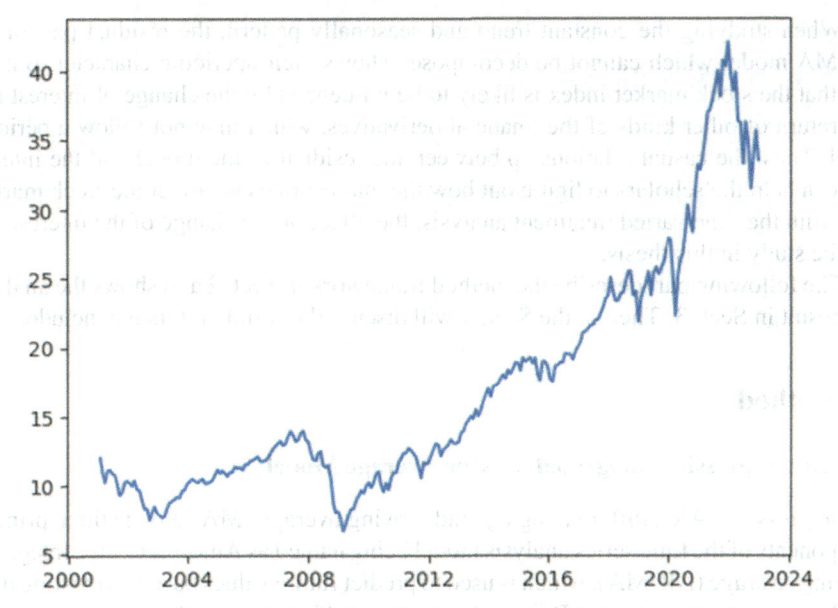

Fig. 1. The total value of the portfolio on S&P index (in trillion dollars).

models in 2007 that combine time series and neural network models for forecasting stock price index volatility from two angles: deviation and direction [3]. Moreover, other significant literature that has influenced the field's research, such as studies of outliers, level shifts, and variance changes in time series analysis, has also contributed [4]. The ARIMA model is widely used in other economic areas, such as inflation and GDP forecasting [5, 6].

In compared with the traditional data the machine learning approach based on the BP network, recurrent neural network and its adapted form, the long-short term model are becoming a better and more accurate method in the time series forecasting especially in the vast data set. Such hybrid model which connect the traditional ARIMA model to machine learning validation method are recently being discussed in both statistics and econometrics field. Du discussed the application of the ARIMA and BP network, while Rathnayaka et al. presented analysis of hybrid model of ARIMA and artificial neural network [7, 8]. The support vector machine and LSTM are also mentioned in the hybrid model [9, 10]. Furthermore, pure LSTM has been already used in the time-series prediction, as well as its applications in economics and finance data such as predicting the volatility of the S&P 500 [10–12].

This thesis applied the dynamic ARIMA model to forecast the stock index and price of individual stocks and figure out that there is a casual inference of the residual part of the forecast with the federal fund rate, which can partly explain the abnormal growth in 2022. Then this thesis conducts long-short term model to check whether the application of deep learning can improve the forecasting, and finally find that with the increasing of the data set, the accuracy of the forecasting is improved, which reveals that the Long-short term model can perform better in big data set.

When studying the constant trend and seasonally pattern, the residual part of the ARIMA model which cannot be decomposed shows their aperiodic character. But the fact that the stock market index is likely to be influenced by the change of interest rate and return of other kinds of the financial derivatives, which may not follow a periodic trend. Thus, the casual relationship between the residual of the model and the interest rate can help the scholars to figure out how the interest rate can affect the stock market. And with the time varied treatment analysis, the effect of the change of the interest rate will be study in this thesis.

The following part describe the method framework in Sect. 2 and shows the analysis and result in Sect. 3. Then in the Sect. 4 will discuss the result and then conclude.

2 Method

2.1 Autoregressive Integrated Moving Average Model

Autoregression (AR), differencing (I), and moving average (MA) are the three primary components of the time series analysis model being named as Auto-regressive Integrated Moving Average (ARIMA), which is used to predict future values based on existing data.

The auto-regression, or AR. a model running self-regression that makes advantage of the relationships between a single observation and many lagged observations (p) of the observed variable. *I* stands for integrated. Determining the disparities between observations made at various times in order to render the time series steady (d).

Moving Average, or MA. a method for using a series lagged observation to get a smooth indicator that considers the dependence between the observations and the residual error terms (q). Thus, the function form of a simple ARIMA (p, 0, q) model could be written as follows:

$$y_t = c + \sum_{i=1}^{p} \phi_i y_{t-i} + \epsilon_t + \sum_{i=1}^{q} \theta_i \epsilon_{t-i} \tag{1}$$

In this thesis, y_t is variable which indicate stock index, the ϵ_t is assumed to be a white noise follows standard Gaussian distribution.

2.2 Long-Short Term Model

The long-short-term memory (LSTM) neural network is a neural network model modified and optimized on the recurrent neural network (RNN) cyclic neural network. By introducing a four-layer neural network interaction layer on the basis of the RNN repeated neural network module, it greatly optimizes the long-term dependence on information. The learning process provides a better solution for machine learning of long-term random process sequence data.

The three gate layers are the core of the LSTM neural network, including the forget gate layer that decides to discard information from the cell state, the input gate layer that determines the information added to the cell state, and the output gate layer that confirms the content of the filtered output information. The core concepts and functions of the three gate layers are as follows:

Forget Gate Layer. For each input value in the previous state matrix, a corresponding vector is generated, and the vector with a constant interval [0,1] indicates the degree of information forgetting in the cell state. The function of the forget gate is:

$$f_t = \sigma\left(W_f \cdot [h_{t-1}, x_t] + b_f\right) \tag{2}$$

Input Gate Layer. In terms of input logic, first use the input gate layer to filter the information that needs to be updated, and then use an internal tanh layer to obtain new candidate cell information. Next, this gate will filter and forget a part of the old information (σ) which is already in the cell through the forget gate layer, and then select and add a part of the candidate cell information through the input gate layer (the remaining part after forgetting is summed with the weight of the newly added information), so as to update the obtained New cell information.

$$i_t = \sigma\left(W_i \cdot [h_{t-1}, x_t] + b_i\right) \tag{3}$$

$$\tilde{C}_t = tanh\left(W_c \cdot [h_{t-1}, x_t] + b_C\right) \tag{4}$$

$$C_t = f_t \cdot C_{t-1} + i_t \cdot \tilde{C}_t \tag{5}$$

Output Gate Layer. Following the updating of the cell state, the input data is routed via the sigmoid function of the output gate layer to derive the judgment conditions, and the cell state is then activated through the tanh layer to derive a vector of values ranging from −1 to 1. The output result of the LSTM network of this layer is obtained by multiplying the vector by the judgment condition that was obtained by the output gate.

$$o_t = \sigma\left(W_o \cdot [h_{t-1}, x_t] + b_o\right) \tag{7}$$

$$h_t = o_t \cdot tanh(C_t) \tag{8}$$

At the same time, the overall process is obviously: forget → update the state according to the new input and the latest out-put of the last cell → output the predicted value based on the existing state.

And the residuals of the forecast will also be examined as the dynamic ARIMA model to figure the relationship between the stock prices and the exogenous variables.

2.3 The Dynamic Time Series Model

But in the real effect, the variable and the residuals are often influenced by the exogenous factors, which may work as identification of different forecast result based on different assumption provided. And the government policies are main factors that can cause the shift of the stock index.

Since the count of the GDP is by the formula below:

$$Y = C(r) + I(r) + G + NX \tag{8}$$

$$S - I = CA \qquad (9)$$

Based on the formula above, any factor that can affect the civil investment I will have an influence on the stock market and the bond market. Once the fiscal and monetary policies work, the M2, government consumption G, and interest rate which works as an exogenous variable will change, which will cause investment changing. And big pandemics which could affect private consumption and net export also have an impact on the investment.

So, in real practice, the assumption could be made that if the interest rate increase, the investment I will also increase in response. So, in regarding with the constant trend and seasonal pattern, the residual which cause shift of the final data, could related to the interest rate and other policies. Thus, in the empirical analysis, the relationship between residual and the factors could be single regression, which works as the formula below:

$$\epsilon_t = \alpha + \beta x_i + \mu_i \qquad (10)$$

Thus, this thesis is going to conduct the dynamic ARIMA model to forecast and study the cases that can help with the more precise result.

2.4 Time Varied Treatment Effect Analysis

In the 2.3 section this thesis discussed the casual relationship between the federal fund interest rate. But whether the effect of the interest rate change will decrease or not in the time dimension is still an exciting topic of the casual inference study. The main focus is that whether the effect of the treatment will be weakened or strengthened during the application period of the conference paper. The meetings of the Federal Open Market Committee usually take place 8 times per year, which will decide the federal fund rate and this thesis will mainly focus on the residual of the ARIMA model around these time points and try to figure out the time varied treatment by ranking the time dimension of the treatment period, and finally get the formula that:

$$stock_t = \phi_{-3}T_{t-3} + \phi_{-2}T_{t-2} + \phi_{-1}T_{t-1} + \phi_0 T_t + \phi_1 T_{t+1} + \phi_2 T_{t+2} + \epsilon_t \qquad (11)$$

In which T_{t-i}, $i = 1, 2, 3$ refers to the binary variable which represent the i-th epoch before treatment execution, which T_{t+i}, $i = 1, 2, 3$ refers to the binary variable which represent the i-th epoch after treatment execution. T_t is the binary variable working as the treatment indicator. And the coefficients ϕ will be the effect measurement.

3 Result

3.1 The Stock Data

In the empirical analysis, this thesis used the S&P 500 index to figure to study the accuracy ARIMA and LSTM to test whether those time series method can be applied to the stock index forecast. The monthly data is collected from the Wharton Research Data Services database and contains over 22 years data.

Figure 2 below shows the general view of the stock index data in logarithm. From the graph, there are a constant trend of the stock index and the seasonal pattern is not significant. There are two huge drops in the stock index which happened in 2003 and 2008, referring to the financial crisis. Since the crisis is a part of the economic cycle, it still can be predicting in the time series model.

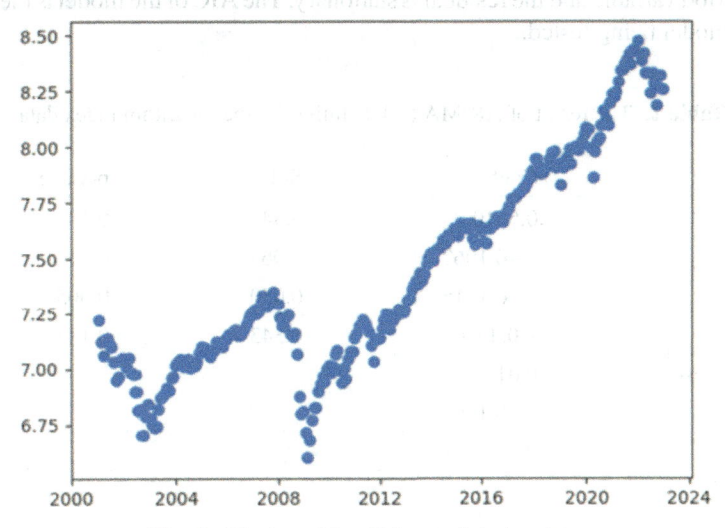

Fig. 2. The logarithm if the stock index data.

The monthly data ranges from January, 2001 to December, 2022, which is not stationary in original sequence and its 1st order difference is stationary (Table 1). In the Table 1 ADF test is unit root test and the KPSS test is sequence stationary test. Interestingly, the ADF test and the KPSS test get different lags as results.

Table 1. The stationary test.

	stats	lag	p-value
ADF test	−1.847	6	0.6404
ADF test (1st diff)	−4.795	6	< 0.01
KPSS test (level)	3.577	5	< 0.01
KPSS test (trend)	0.900	5	< 0.01
KPSS test (1st diff)	0.337	5	> 0.1

3.2 The ARIMA Model Without the Dynamic Part

The empirical analysis examined the ARIMA(p,d,q) model with different parameter and finally choose the ARIMA(3,1,1) as the best model in fitting the logarithm of the index data.

Table 2 shows the result of the ARIMA (3,1,1), which shows a significant coefficient of lag 3 period variable and the residual is stationary. The AIC of the model is the smallest of all the model being tested.

Table 2. The result of ARIMA (3,1,1) fitting for the logarithm index data.

	Coef.	Std.	p-value
AR (1)	0.5610	0.345	0.104
AR (2)	−0.1062	0.067	0.112
AR (3)	0.1415	0.050	0.005
MA (1)	−0.4980	0.343	0.147
Ljung-Box test	0.01		
MSE	0.199		
AIC	880.1		

The Fig. 3 shows the forecast of the data by model generated by the training data and tells us that the forecast without the seasonal factor is still not enough for the forecasting since it could not explain the sharply increase of the stock index in 2022. And the seasonal ARIMA got relatively the same result.

3.3 The ARIMA Model with the Dynamic Part

The Table 3 shows the result of the dynamic ARIMA model. And the dynamic model improves the accuracy of the model fitting proofed by the smaller MSE, while the model reveals a clear and significant relationship between the residual of ARIMA model and the Federal Fund interest rate, agreeing with the opinion that the stock market is related with the monetary market. So, the coefficient of the federal fund interest rate reveals that once the interest rate increases by 1%, the stock index will increase to 1.0342 times on its original value, which means that there will be an upward shift of 30–60 index point in response to a one-percent interest rate increase. Thus, the result of the dynamic ARIMA model does provide with a strong evidence that the federal fund interest rate has a great influence on the stock market index, showing that the monetary policies has an efficient impact on the stock market.

Thesis also chose some stock to test the ARIMA model and the result is shown in Table 4 The Federal Fund rate only has a significant result with the residual of the ARIMA model of Boeing and Ford, which result in a causal inference between these individual stocks and the Federal Fund rate, which shows the instability of residual in forecasting the stock.

Table 3. The result of dynamic ARIMA (3,1,1) fitting for the logarithm index data.

	Coef.	Std.	p
Federal Fund interest rate	0.0342	0.01	0.001
AR (1)	0.5666	0.401	0.158
AR (2)	−0.1089	0.063	0.086
AR (3)	0.1415	0.050	0.005
MA (1)	−0.4980	0.343	0.147
Ljung-Box test	0.02		
MSE	0.188		
AIC	882		

Table 4. The result of dynamic ARIMA model for the stock price data.

Company	AR (1)	MA (1)	SMA (1)	Federal Fund rate
Boeing	−0.8823	0.9686	0.1578	19.4984
	(0.0422)	(0.0209)	(0.0645)	(5.2883)
IBM	-	−0.1169	-	2.1610
	-	(0.0651)	-	(2.3947)
Ford	0.9695	-	-	0.7535
	0.0164	-	-	(0.3994)
General Electrics	0.9437	-		2.8592
	0.0215	-		(1.7871)
Microsoft	−0.4843	−0.6034	-	−0.2198
	0.0776	0.0714	-	(2.9228)
Oracle	−0.4867	-	-	1.6866
	(0.0544)	-	-	(1.5073)
Intel	-	−0.0283	−0.0411	−0.7104
	-	(0.0639)	(0.0684)	(0.8633)

3.4 The Study of Time Varied Treatment Effect Analysis

Since the dynamic model part above get the result that the change of the interest rate has significant effect on the stock market index, but the coefficient is constant. This thesis conduct time varying treatment analysis to figure out whether the effect of the interest rate change, which is discussed in Sect. 2.4

Table 5 shows the result of the regression of the model due the lack of the data we cannot find useful result of the time varied effect between the interest rate and the stock price index.

Table 5. Time varied treatment analysis.

	Coef.	Std. Err	t	P > |t|	[0.025,	0.975]
Const	8.2531	0.057	145.656	0	8.138	8.368
T-3	−0.0747	0.085	−0.879	0.385	−0.247	0.098
T-2	−0.0845	0.093	−0.913	0.367	−0.272	0.103
T-1	−0.0145	0.106	−0.137	0.892	−0.23	0.201
T0	−0.0941	0.106	−0.888	0.381	−0.309	0.121
T + 1	−0.0748	0.106	−0.705	0.485	−0.29	0.14
T + 2	−0.0812	0.093	−0.877	0.386	−0.269	0.107

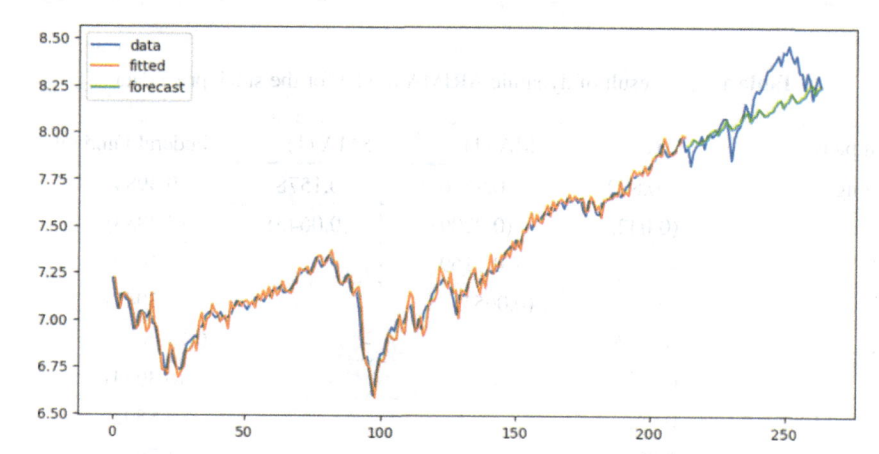

Fig. 3. The plot of the train set and test of the ARIMA model.

3.5 The Machine Learning and LSTM Model

As for the LSTM model, this thesis reveals that for a small data set, the deep learning, performance better than the traditional econometrics model and the Fig. 4 shows the result in the LSTM fitting. But the loss-epoch figure also that the performance cannot be improved and the validation loss grows larger when the epoch reaches a large number.

So, in order to get more accurate forecast, this thesis introduced daily data to the LSTM model. In the daily trend fitting and forecasting, this paper can find that the LSTM performance better in the fitting and forecasting, the MSE of the ARIMA model is 0.1883, while the MSE of the monthly LSTM model is 0.025 (in Fig. 5), and the loss-epoch figure show that the validation loss reach minimum at epoch 75, a bigger epoch will cause the overfitting of the train data, which will cause the validation loss grows larger in the validation part. But the Fig. 4 and 6 still shows that in comparing with the forecast data, the real data still shown an abnormal increase which may due to the increase of the federal fund interest rate decided by the recent conferences of the Federal Open Market Committee (Fig. 7).

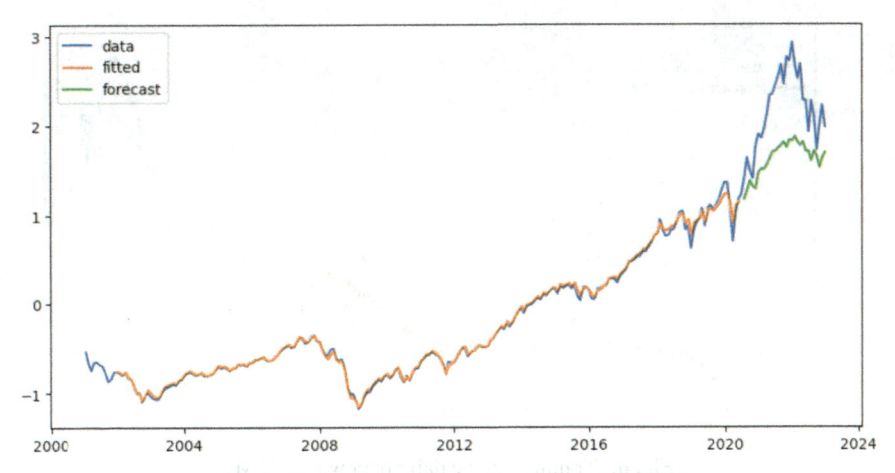

Fig. 4. Training on the monthly data with LSTM.

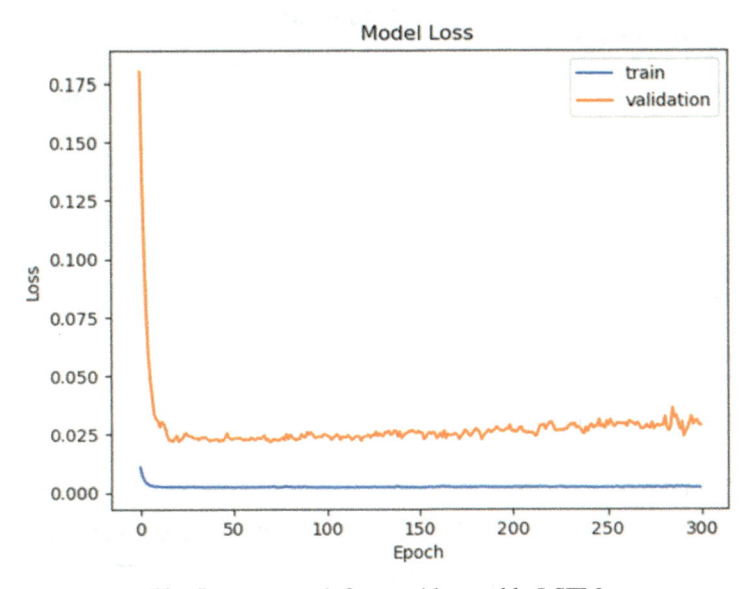

Fig. 5. Loss-epoch figure with monthly LSTM.

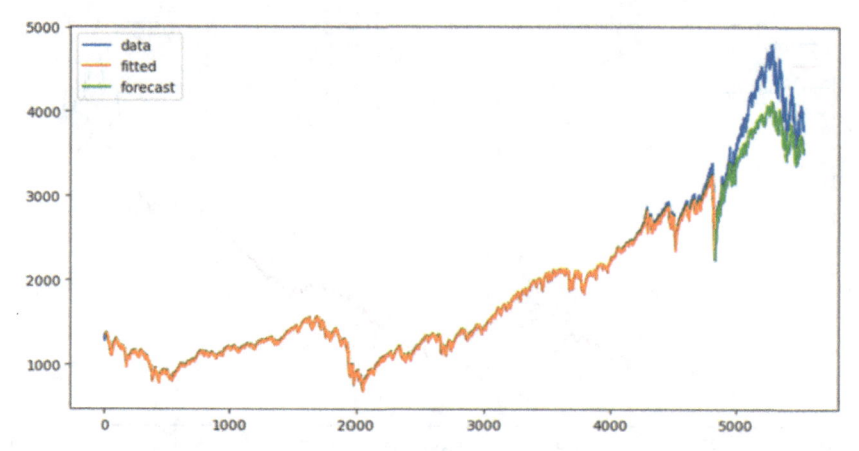

Fig. 6. Training on the daily data with LSTM.

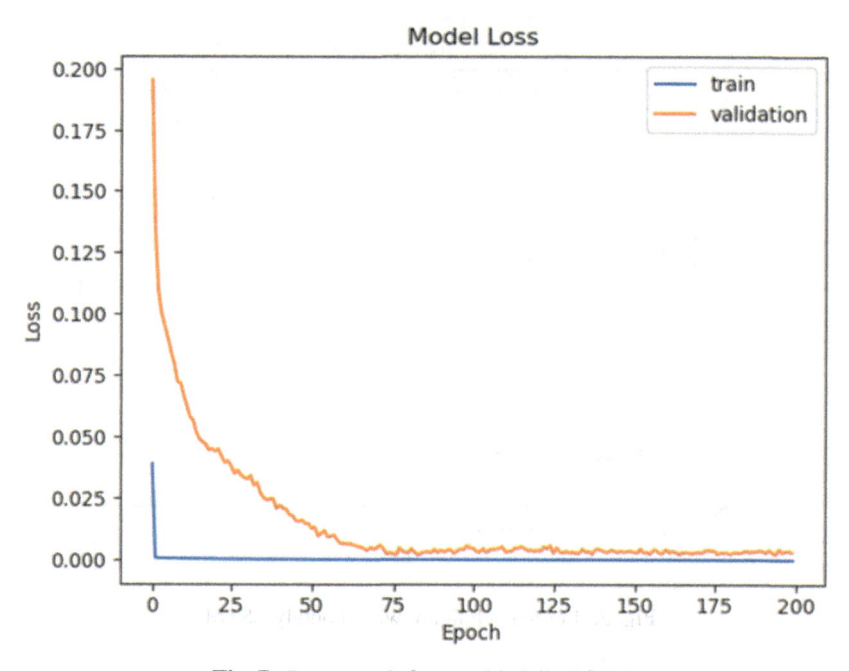

Fig. 7. Loss-epoch figure with daily LSTM.

4 Conclusion

This thesis mainly discussed the forecasting of the new machine learning method and the traditional econometrics method, which get the same result of other scholars that although being not interpretable, the machine learning can forecast the stock index and it does perform better than the traditional method. With the data set grows larger, the LSTM can performance even much better than the traditional method. In the traditional model, the forecast of the test data set is not as good as it was expected. The daily LSTM model did provide an accurate forecast of the index trend but the predicted value does not reach that high as the real data does. This may be caused by the abnormal fiscal and monetary policy by the FOMC.

The casual inference of the Federal Fund interest rate is also being found significant in the dynamic model which examined the relationship between monetary policy and stock market index. This thesis provides strong evidence to the fact that the stock index can be predicted and the government policy can also affect the stock index. The high interest rate attracts more savings, which result in more investment, and then the portfolio manager will use the investment in the bond market and stock market. So, the stock market index will increase in response to the strong confidence by the investor. But the time varied treatment analysis does not show any feature of the effect of the treatment being dependent on the time. So, this thesis cannot conclude that the effect of monetary policy is weakened or strengthened during the time, maybe both mechanisms exist in the treatment application due to spread of the information and the momentum effect, but further study can research these issues and try to figure out the two mechanisms.

As it is shown in the thesis, the overfitting and underfitting problem is mainly needed to be discussed. So, the time series validation is applied in the model to get the best epoch, from the loss and epoch curve, we can find that the speed of reach the best epoch is highly correlated with the size and density of the data set when monthly model reaches its best performance, the daily model shows a relatively slow speed in getting the best fit, although the absolute loss of the train data already became small. From the graph with real data and fitted data, the residual part is obviously smaller than the residual from the ARIMA part, so this thesis could not study the casual inference between the residual of the model and the federal fund rate, since the factor may be counted in to the black-box model.

However, there are still shortage in this thesis since the data of this thesis contains the data from the pandemic period during these periods the frequent changes of M2 and the interest rate along with the willing of investment from people who lose their job and wants to earn money from the stock, the stock market fall into the spurious blooms, which resulted in the sharply increase of the stock index, so this phenomenon cannot be explain by the model. Also, the Covid-19 cases can also be treated as a 'treatment' which will affect the estimation of the casual relationship between the interest rate and the stock index. Finally, the S&P 500 index can only be reference of the whole stock market since it only contains 500 relative healthy company which will seldomly encounter the bankrupt. So, this model, in the meanwhile can only forecast only a few stocks and the index, which could not give a big over view on the whole stock market.

Further study should focus on the cross-validation of the time series model and multi-factor panel model which could figure out the relationship between the residuals of the fitting of the ARIMA model and a variety of factors which are potential issues affecting the market index. And the accuracy and overfitting problem of the LSTM model in forecasting the economics can also be discussed in the further studies.

References

1. Nerlove M.: Spectral analysis of seasonal adjustment procedures. Econometrica: J. Econometr. Soc. 241–286 (1964)
2. Clements, M., Hendry, D.: Forecasting Economic Time Series. Cambridge University Press, Cambrige (1998)
3. Roh, T.H.: Forecasting the volatility of stock price index. Expert Syst. Appl. **33**(4), 916–922 (2007)
4. Tsay, R.S.: Outliers, level shifts, and variance changes in time series. J. Forecast. **7**(1), 1–20 (1988)
5. Abonazel, M.R., Abd-Elftah, A.I.: Forecasting Egyptian GDP using ARIMA models. Rep. Econ. Finan. **5**(1), 35–47 (2019)
6. Nyoni, T.: Modeling and forecasting inflation in Kenya: recent insights from ARIMA and GARCH analysis. Dimorian Re. **5**(6), 16–40 (2018)
7. Du, Y.: Application and analysis of forecasting stock price index based on combination of ARIMA model and BP neural network. In: 2018 Chinese control and decision conference (CCDC), pp. 2854–2857. IEEE (2018)
8. Rathnayaka, R.K., Seneviratna, D.M., Jianguo, W., Arumawadu, H.I.: A hybrid statistical approach for stock market forecasting based on artificial neural network and ARIMA time series models. In: 2015 International Conference on Behavioral, Economic and Socio-cultural Computing (BESC), pp. 54–60. IEEE (2015)
9. Ping-Feng, P., Chih-Shen, L.: A hybrid ARIMA and support vector machine model in stock price forecasting. Int. J. Manag. Sci. **33**, 497–505 (2005)
10. Brownlee J., 2016. Time Series Prediction with LSTM Recurrent Neural Networks in Python with Keras. https://machinelearningmastery.com/time-series-prediction-lstm-recurrent-neural-networks-python-keras/. Accessed 9 Apr 2023
11. Fischera T., Kraussb C. deep learning with long short-term memory networks for financial market predictions. FAU Discuss. Papers Econ. 11(2017)
12. Roondiwala, M., Patel, H., Varma, S.: Predicting stock prices using LSTM. Int. J. Sci. Res. (IJSR) **6**(4), 1754–1756 (2017)

Public Goods Game Based on the Combination Model of Reputation and Punishment

Qing Liu[✉]

Leicester International Institute, Panjin Campus of Dalian University of Technology, Panjin 116086, China
`ql132@student.le.ac.uk`

Abstract. There are many ways to improve players' dominant strategies in the public goods game, most of which introduce reward and punishment mechanism or use reputation to improve the result of the game. Motivated by these researches, this paper introduces a model combining punishment and reputation. In the process of repeating the public goods game, the model will give a higher reputation value to the partner and a lower reputation value to the defector and this value is going to add up. At the end of each game, the defectors will be punished by someone with a low overall ranking reputation. Through some simulations and calculations, it can be verified that the model is effective, which is useful in promoting cooperation and reducing defections. Additionally, the model can be applied in real life, which is related to social norms. It is found that real results show the same trend as the model results.

Keywords: Public Goods Game · Reputation · Punishment

1 Introduction

1.1 Background

Public goods gaming has always been a hotly discussed game problem. Many papers have proposed various models, such as using manipulators to reward or punish players, introducing reputation to evaluate each player so that enhancing the tendency to cooperate, putting forward heterogeneous or punishment strategies to reduce defectors. These models or strategies show certain advantages on the basis of the original traditional public goods game, enhancing cooperation or reducing defection. However, the introduction of third parties is usually costly and it is difficult to guarantee the impartiality of manipulators in real life. For the introduction of reputation, while low reputation puts psychological pressure on defectors to cooperate with other players, it does not affect the real payoff in essence. In a reward and punishment system, punishment and reward always come at a cost. There are also questions about who will pay these costs.

1.2 Related Research

On the basis of the original punishment and reward mechanism, Sun et al. researched that the situation of combination of rewards and punishments could promote cooperation. Manipulators is proposed, which are similar to a third party. And they no longer participate in cooperation or betrayal, but only provide rewards for collaborators, while punish those who defect [1]. The researched conducted by Feng et al. proposed the penalty pool and set it to be finite. This means that a player who wants to continue playing as a punisher will passively exit after the punisher fills up the punishment pool and receive a small fixed income accordingly. Feng proved it promotes cooperation and discourages defections [2]. Wang et al. also pointed out that the cost of punishment and reward is high, then he combined with the tax in reality, which is the pure reward and pure punishment based on tax. Because of the existence of a dedicated body to manage taxes, players do not have to pay penalties and rewards, but simply pay taxes, thus promoting cooperation [3]. Yang and Fu also proposed a punishment mechanism, in which everyone would punish the person who contributed the least to the game, and the cost would be shared by everyone. Through evolutionary simulation, the relationship between the number of punished and the number of cooperators in the group is illustrated. The more the number, the less cooperation, and the less the number, the more cooperation [4]. Jiao proposed that punishment and reward are not executed 100%, but with certain probability, which can reduce part of the cost of punishment and reward. Finally, through a series of numerical simulations, it is concluded that when the probability is 0.6, cooperation can be best promoted [5].

In a traditional game, players simply care about whether they have a high payoff. Wang et al. adopted the second angle, starting from the perspective of others' evaluation and introduces the evaluation coefficient. Players are thinking not only about the payoff, but also about how they will be evaluated if they cooperate or defect. Wang proved this is effective [6]. Similar to Wang et al. [6], Quan et al. has introduced the concept of reputation into the game and there is a reputation threshold, which can be understood as a standard for dividing players from bad players. Good players have a high reputation and bad players have a low reputation. After the simulation prediction of the game in the case of reputation, the conclusion is drawn: reputation can be used as a way to promote cooperation. The larger the threshold, the closer the cooperation relationship, the more the number of collaborators [7]. The research conducted by Shen et al. not only introduced the concept of reputation, but also analyzed the influence of individuals with high reputation on the group. Reputation along with payoff will be a consideration for players. When the proportion of reputation is higher, the probability of cooperation will be improved, and the high reputation will play a certain role model [8]. Lim and Zhang proposed that before the game starts, players first choose authority in the group. Similar to real life, a figure with certain influence is elected through election. In fact, it has something in common with the high reputation mentioned by high-reputation. And showed that the larger the group, the more the presence of authority promotes cooperation [9].

On the basis of the basic game, Lv and Wang added the exclusion strategy. The player who chooses this strategy can force the free rider to quit the game and no longer participate in the contribution or revenue. In this way, collaborators and exclusions can coexist. Of course, exclusion like punishment comes at a price [10].

1.3 Objective

Getting a third-party manipulator into the game is not easy. Who acts as the manipulators and who reciprocates the manipulators needs to be considered. The problem posed by pure reward and punishment mechanisms is similar to the second-order prisoner's dilemma. Who bears the cost of punishment or reward? And the problem with pure reputation mechanics, where high or low reputation can change players' strategies. But perhaps only for those who care about reputation. Because the payoff will not be reduced by the defection. In order to improve the shortcomings of a single model, the goal is to establish a compound or hybrid model. No longer consider adding manipulators. Allowing high and low reputations to play a role, which can make an influence on payoff for each player. And solve the conundrum of who will administer the punishment. The following article presents the model of combining reputation and punishment.

2 Method

The traditional public goods describes that there are N players, each player can choose to contribute a portion of the money. Then, all the money in public goods is multiplied by a factor r and the multiplied amount is divided equally among each player. In this situation, it is easy to see that all player's dominant strategy is defection. Hence, publishment mechanism is introduced to avoid this phenomenon. In this paper, the model is constructed by combining reputation with punishment. Suppose that people with low reputations must impose punishment. For every game played, the partner's reputation will plus 1, the traitor's reputation will remain unchanged. Ranking all players according to their reputation. At the end of each game, those in the bottom 30% of reputation rankings were selected for implementing punishment.

Suppose there are N players. If the player chooses to contribute, assuming the contribution value is a and the coefficient is r, where $1 < r < N$. The penalty is going to cost b and the penalty amount is going to be c.

We chose to use table evolution to analyze and discuss the situation of 2, 3, 4 players. And then by induction to get the general solution, and then the conclusion.

3 Results

When there are two players, the original situation without using model will be represented in Table 1.

Since $1 < r < 2$, $(r-1)a < \frac{ar}{2}$, $\left(\frac{r}{2} - 1\right)a < 0$

Then the Nash equilibrium is {0, 0}, which is two players both choose defection.

When there are two players and the model is applied, after one game, players who choose defection will be punished and the pushier is the one who has the low reputation. The amount of penalty is b and the price of punishment is c. Then, the table will be represented in Table 2.

Table 1. Two players without model.

		P2	
		cooperation	defection
P1	cooperation	$\{(r-1)a, (r-1)a\}$	$\{(r/2-1)a, ar/2\}$
	defection	$\{ar/2, (r/2-1)a\}$	$\{0, 0\}$

Table 2. Two players with model.

		P2	
		cooperation	defection
P1	cooperation	$\{(r-1)a, (r-1)a\}$	$\{(r/2-1)a, ar/2-(b+c)\}$
	defection	$\{ar/2-(b+c), (r/2-1)a\}$	$\{0-(b+c), 0-c\}$

Since when player 1 choose cooperation and player 2 choose defection, the later will be punished and also get the low reputation, his payoff will be $\frac{ar}{2} - (b+c)$. It is similar when player 1 choose defection and player 2 choose cooperation. When both players choose defection, since they both have the same low reputation, player 1 is randomly selected for implement punishment. Hence, their payoff will be $\{0 - (b+c), 0 - c\}$.

Setting $\left(\frac{r}{2} - 1\right)a + (b+c) > 0$, $\left(\frac{r}{2} - 1\right)a + c < 0$, then the Nash equilibrium is $\{(r-1)a, (r-1)a\}$, which is two players both choose cooperation.

When there are 3 players, the original situation without using model will be represented in Table 3.

Table 3. Three players without model.

		P3			
		cooperation		defection	
		P2		P2	
		cooperation	defection	cooperation	defection
P1	cooperation	$\{(r-1)a, (r-1)a, (r-1)a\}$	$\{(2r/3-1)a, 2ar/3, (2r/3-1)a\}$	$\{(2r/3-1)a, (2r/3-1)a, 2ar/3\}$	$\{(r/3-1)a, ar/3, ar/3\}$
	defection	$\{2ar/3, (2r/a-1)a, (2r/a-1)a\}$	$\{ar/3, ar/3, (r/3-1)a\}$	$\{ar/3, (r/3-1)a, ar/3\}$	$\{0, 0, 0\}$

Since $1 < r < 3$, $(r-1)a < \frac{2ar}{3}$, $\left(\frac{2r}{3} - 1\right)a < \frac{ar}{3}$, $\frac{ar}{3} < 0$, $\left(\frac{r}{3} - 1\right)a < 0$

Then the Nash equilibrium is $\{0, 0, 0\}$, which is all players choose defection.

When there are 3 players and the model is applied, similar as the 2 players' situation, the table will be represented in Table 4.

Setting $\left(\frac{r}{3} - 1\right)a + (b+c) > 0$, $\left(\frac{r}{3} - 1\right)a + c < 0$, then the Nash equilibrium is $\{(r-1)a, (r-1)a, (r-1)a\}$, which is all players choose cooperation.

Table 4. Three players with model.

		P3 cooperation		P3 defection	
		P2 cooperation	P2 defection	P2 cooperation	P2 defection
P1	cooperation	{(r−1)a, (r−1)a, (r−1)a}	{(2r/3−1)a, 2r/3−(b+c), (2r/3−1)a}	{(2r/3−1)a, (2r/3−1)a, 2r/3−(b+c)}	{(r/3−1)a, ar/3−(b+c), ar/3−c}
	defection	{2r/3−(b+c), (2r/3−1)a, (2r/3−1)a}	{ar/3−(b+c), ar/3−c, (r/3−1)a}	{ar/3−(b+c), (r/3−1)a, ar/3−c}	{0−(b+c), 0−c, 0−c}

When there are 4 players, the original situation without using model will be represented in Table 5.

Table 5. Four players without model.

				P4 cooperation		P4 defection	
				P2		P2	
				cooperation	defection	cooperation	defection
3	cooperation	P1	cooperation	{(r−1)a, (r−1)a, (r−1)a, (r−1)a}	{(3r/4−1)a, 3ar/4, (3r/4−1)a, (3r/4−1)a}	{(3r/4−1)a, (3r/4−1)a, (3r/4−1)a, 3ar/4}	{(r/2−1)a, ar/2, (r/2−1)a, ar/2}
			defection	{3ar/4, (3r/4−1)a, (3r/4−1)a, (3r/4−1)a}	{ar/2, ar/2, (r/2−1)a, (r/2−1)a}	{ar/2, (r/2−1)a, (r/2−1)a,ar/2}	{(r/4−1)a, (r/4−1)a, ar/4, (r/4−1)a}
	defection	P1	cooperation	{(3r/4−1)a, (3r/4−1)a, 3ar/4, (3r/4−1)a}	{(r/2−1)a, ar/2, ar/2, (r/2−1)a}	{(r/2−1)a, (r/2−1)a, ar/2, ar/2}	{ar/4, (r/4−1)a, (r/4−1)a, (r/4−1)a}
			defection	{ar/2, (r/2−1)a, ar/2, (r/2−1)a}	{(r/4−1)a, (r/4−1)a, (r/4−1)a, ar/4}	{(r/4−1)a, ar/4, (r/4−1)a, (r/4−1)a}	{0, 0, 0, 0}

Since $1 < r < 4$, $(r-1)a < \frac{3ar}{4}$, $\left(\frac{3r}{4}-1\right)a < \frac{ar}{2}$, $\left(\frac{r}{2}-1\right)a > \left(\frac{r}{4}-1\right)a$, $\frac{ar}{4} > 0$
Then the Nash equilibrium is {0, 0, 0, 0}, which is all players choose defection.

When there are 4 players and the model is applied, similar as the 2 players' situation, the table will be represented in Table 6.

Table 6. Four players with model.

				P4			
				cooperation		defection	
				P2		P2	
				cooperation	defection	cooperation	defection
P3	cooperation	P1	cooperation	{(r-1)a, (r-1)a, (r-1)a, (r-1)a}	{(3r/4−1)a, 3ar/4-(b + c), (3r/4−1)a, (3r/4−1)a}	{(3r/4−1)a, (3r/4−1)a, (3r/4−1)a, 3ar/4-(b + c)}	{(r/2−1)a, ar/2-(b + c), (r/2−1)a, ar/2-c}
			defection	{3ar/4-(b + c), (3r/4−1)a, (3r/4−1)a, (3r/4−1)a}	{ar/2-(b + c), ar/2-c, (r/2−1)a, (r/2−1)a}	{ar/2-(b + c), (r/2−1)a, (r/2−1)a, ar/2-c}	{(r/4−1)a, (r/4−1)a, ar/4-(b + c), (r/4−1)a}
	defection	P1	cooperation	{(3r/4−1)a, (3r/4−1)a, 3ar/4-(b + c), (3r/4−1)a}	{(r/2−1)a, ar/2-(b + c), ar/2-c, (r/2−1)a}	{(r/2−1)a, (r/2−1)a, ar/2-(b + c), ar/2-c}	{ar/4-(b + c), (r/4−1)a, (r/4−1)a, (r/4−1)a}
			defection	{ar/2-(b + c), (r/2−1)a, ar/2-c, (r/2−1)a}	{(r/4−1)a, (r/4−1)a, (r/4−1)a, ar/4-(b + c)}	{(r/4−1)a, ar/4-(b + c), (r/4−1)a, (r/4−1)a}	{0, 0, 0, 0}

Setting $\left(\frac{r}{4} - 1\right)a + (b + c) > 0, \left(\frac{r}{4} - 1\right)a + c < 0$, then the Nash equilibrium is $\{(r-1)a, (r-1)a, (r-1)a, (r-1)a\}$, which is all players choose cooperation.

After the application of the model, in all cases, the Nash equilibrium changes from all defection to all cooperation.

4 Discussion

The above results show that in the combination of punishment and reputation, the dominant strategy of players has changed from defection to cooperation, indicating that this mechanism is very effective.

In real life, the mechanism of combining punishment and reputation can be understood as respect theory or the competition for respect. For those who do not abide by social norms, the corresponding reputation is lower in the game of public goods. People who conform to social norms, on the other hand, think they have earned respect, which corresponds to a higher reputation. Naturally, those who fail to win the respect will be published to some extent. For example, accepting the pressure of public opinion, and even worse, may suffer legal sanctions, which is equivalent to a person with a low reputation accepting punishment and paying it. However, the person who wins the respect doesn't have to take on the publicity, and so doesn't have to pay the price of punishment and accept it.

In fact, the public generally follows social rules and moral standards to earn respect. This is consistent with the evolution of our model. The tendency to have a high reputation, and the reduction of the penalty for having a low reputation, means that the dominant strategy of players has changed to cooperation.

5 Conclusion

Most of the previous researches on public goods game are about reputation or rewards and punishments, and the model structure is relatively simple. This paper proposes a model combining reputation and punishment mechanism. The defector is supposed to be punished by someone with a low reputation. After table evolution, the dominant strategy of all players changes from defection to cooperation. While no more assumptions have been made in terms of player numbers, we can see a clear trend towards collaboration. This verifies that the combined reputation and punishment model can promote cooperation. In addition, the model also has some practical significance. Whether people abide by social norms or not will be related to their personal reputation. And those who violate norms will naturally get lower evaluation and reputation, which will accumulate or decrease with the behavior of people. At the same time, those who break the rules will be punished.

References

1. Sun, X.P., Li, M.Y., Kang, H.W., Shen, Y., Chen, Q.Y.: Combined effect of pure punishment and reward in the public goods game. Appl. Math. Comput. **445** (2023)
2. Feng, S.N., Liu, X.S., Dong, Y.D.: Limited punishment pool may promote cooperation in the public goods game. Chaos Solitons Fractals **165**(Part 2) (2022)
3. Wang, S., Liu, L., Chen, X.: Tax-based pure punishment and reward in the public goods game. Phys. Lett. A **386** (2021)
4. Yang, H.X., Fu, M.J.: A punishment mechanism in the spatial public goods game with continuous strategies. EPL (Europhys. Lett.) **132**(1), 10007 (2020)
5. Jiao, Y., Chen, T., Chen, Q.: Probabilistic punishment and reward under rule of trust-based decision-making in continuous public goods game. J. Theor. Biol. **486** (2020)
6. Wang, J.W., Wang, R., Yu, F.Y.: Fitness of others' evaluation effect promotes cooperation in spatial public goods game. Chin. Phys. B **30**(12), 128701 (2021)
7. Quan, J., Cui, S.H., Chen, W.M., Wang, X.J.: Reputation-based probabilistic punishment on the evolution of cooperation in the spatial public goods game. Appl. Math. Comput. **441**, 127703 (2023)

8. Shen, Y., Yin, W., Kang, H., Zhang, H., Wang, M.: High-reputation individuals exert greater influence on cooperation in spatial public goods game. Phys. Lett. A **428**, 127935 (2022)
9. Wooyoung, L., Zhang, J.: Endogenous authority and enforcement in public goods games. B.E. J. Theor. Econ. **20** (2020)
10. Lv, S., Wang, X.: The impact of heterogeneous investments on the evolution of cooperation in public goods game with exclusion. Appl. Math. Comput. **372** (2020)

The Stylized Facts of Income Inequality in Mainland China, Korea and Taiwan: Development and Comparison

Yanshu Wang[✉]

European Institute, London School of Economics and Political Science, London WC2A 2AE, UK

chentai@mail.sdufe.edu.cn

Abstract. This article explores Taiwan and Korea's development path with income inequality and compares mainland China's growth path with that of the two economies to explain why mainland China failed to prevent the intensifying income inequality. The land reform in Taiwan promoted income equality in the agricultural sector, while the decentralised industrialization model established the labour-intensive sector in both urban and rural areas to absorb the labour surplus. Korea also had land reforms to help its rural area grow and it developed human capital via universal elementary and secondary education which avoided high unemployment. Urban-rural disparity accounts for much of mainland China's inequality. Land and agricultural reform alleviated the problem to some extent, but the Hukou Registration System allowed urban inhabitants' exclusive welfare rights to persist. Marketisation and privatisation created a huge workforce excess. In rural areas, excessive workers could not easily find non-farm jobs outside the village and town businesses, while in urban areas, labour surplus from shrinking state sectors could not fulfil the demand of the newly forming private sector owing to poor skill and productivity. Geographic and institutional factors differed mainland China from Taiwan and Korea. Unlike tiny territories, mainland China has different areas with varying natural circumstances, making industrialization and modernization harder in certain places than others. Institutionally and politically, mainland China emphasised economic development and rapidly developed its capital-intensive and service industries. Labour-intensive industries, which suit low-skill employees, did not grow proportionally. Meanwhile, mainland China's Hukou Registration System hindered labour mobility, limiting certain employees' income-boosting job possibilities.

Keywords: Income Inequality · Urban-Rural Disparity · Kuznets Curve · Labour Surplus

1 Introduction

In 2021, due to the achievement that the nation had abolished absolute poverty, as determined by the daily consumption criterion of $2.3 per person daily, the Chinese government established the goal of reaching common prosperity by 2035. Inequalities in income, resources, and services continue to pose severe risks to social welfare and the attainment of shared prosperity, notwithstanding the progress made in eradicating poverty over the previous few decades. In recent decades, the fruits of economic prosperity have yet to be distributed fairly among the population. Mainland China has one of the most uneven income distributions in the world, with the richest decile receiving 43.4% of total income and the lowest 50% receiving 13.7% [1]. Measured with the World Bank's $5.5 daily consumption criteria for upper-middle-income countries, mainland China still has 180 million impoverished people [2].

The increasing inequality accompanying rapid economic growth is often recognised as a natural process in the early phase of industrialisation. After remaining at a controllable level of approximately or below 0.3, a similar level to Korea and Taiwan in the ending period of the planned economy before 1980, the income inequality measured by the Gini coefficient in mainland China rose to around 0.45 in the early 2000s. Kuznets implies that opportunities for people possessing capital abound as marketplaces grow, while salaries are held down by an inflow of low-cost labour from the early stage of agricultural sector development, deepening the disparities in income [3]. Piketty asserts that income would become increasingly concentrated in the hand of capitalists (the rich) as long as the return on capital is higher than the overall economic growth [4].

However, located geographically close to mainland China, a cluster of modern advanced capitalist economies, including Japan, South Korea, and Taiwan, has been identified not to follow the predicted pattern of scholars that generates much inequality in the path of advancement. Among the group, Taiwan and Korea, the two societies with relatively comparative conditions with mainland China, having short histories of modernisation after the Second World War and large agricultural sectors in the initial stages of development, as illustrated in Fig. 1, do not see their Gini coefficients in the 2000s significantly higher than in the 1960s. The growth model without inequality deepened in these economies has been recognised as a unique achievement in the literature [5, 6].

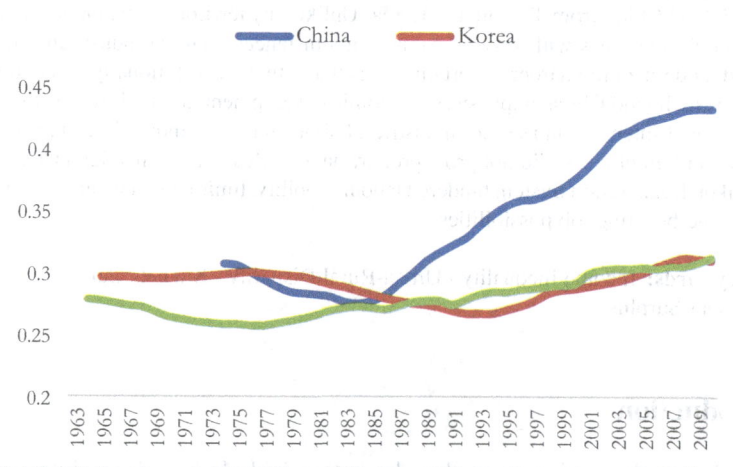

Fig. 1. Gini Coefficient in mainland China, Taiwan, and Korea. Data source: Solt, F. (2018). "The Standardized World Income Inequality Database v1-v7" [7]. Photo credit: Original

A detailed study on the growth model with equity and comparing the paths of development of mainland China after the reform in 1978 and these economies may provide insights into the factors leading to the inequality and potential solutions for the issues of inequality in mainland China and, potentially, into how the developing counties can avoid the worsening of inequality during the fast growth of the economy. The following sections of this paper are organised as follows: Sect. 2 analyses the history of industrialisation in Korea and Taiwan and the reasons why the growth avoided inequity, while Sect. 3 introduces the reasons why the development in mainland China ended up with rising inequality. Section 4 compares different societies and attempts to find the determinants of the income inequality in the Eastern Asian growth model. Section 5 concludes the study.

2 Comparative Asian Societies

2.1 Taiwan

Equalized and Productive Agricultural Sector. One source of expanding income disparities in the early phase of industrialization, according to Kuznets, is that the rural and agricultural sectors lose factors for growth, with labour and capital concentrated in the urban and industrial sectors [3]. However, during this period, Taiwan endeavored to enhance equality and income level in the rural area with major land reforms. After the reversion of Japanese ruling, Taiwan witnesses a series of land reforms by its government throughout the 1950s and 1960s. The reforms were executed in three distinct phases. With the passage of the 37.5% Arable Rent Reduction Act in 1949, farm rents were restricted at 37.5% of yields and in 1951, the government began to sell public land to tenant farmers whereas, beginning in 1953, vast landholdings were divided and redistributed to tenant farmers as part of the "Land to the Plough" programme. As a result, in 1961, 84% of Taiwanese farmers owned land, compared to 23% in 1949 [8]. Meanwhile, for labour absorption, Taiwan increased the planting of double-cropping, labour-intensive, and higher-value commodities such as mushrooms and asparagus, particularly among impoverished families [9]. In addition, with a series of projects that facilitated irrigation and livestock vaccination projects, agricultural productivity increased by approximately 50%, and the net income of farmers more than tripled throughout the 1950s [8, 10]. The equalisation of land resources and investments that enhanced productivity improved income equality within the agricultural sector and avoided the effect of being 'left behind' for the rural area compared to the urban area.

Decentralized Industrialization. Another factor for the deviation of the Taiwanese pattern from the prediction with Kuznets's theory is decentralised industrialisation. The dispersed industrial development and the land reform that raised agricultural productivity avoided the Kuznets effect of the deteriorating functional distribution of income by enhancing the labour share in the total income against the capital share [6]. Such a process is a result of the unique historical legacies of Taiwan. As part of the drive to extract surpluses the local agriculture, mainly in the form of crops for the home country, Japanese colonists focused substantially on rural road construction, basic industrial facilities that served agricultural production in the rural area, rural electrification as well as the dense railway system covering the whole island [10]. With financial aid from the U.S. that amounted to US$1.5 billion within the 15 years since 1950, the Nationalist government expanded the infrastructure and supported both the state-owned and private industrial enterprises under the policy of import substitution before 1958 and export expansion thereafter [9, 11]. As a result, the rural industry flourished. Instead of crowding into the urban area as Kuznets [3] assumes, rural families could easily find employment opportunities in the labour-intensive rural industrial sectors or engage in urban non-agricultural jobs without leaving the countryside. By 1972, the proportion of the non-agricultural income of rural families climbed from 33% in 1964 to 53% [9]. In the rural area, only 16% of male and 24% of female workers migrated to the urban for employment in 1972. Daily commuting accounted for 24% of male and 35% of female labour reallocation, while the figures for seasonal participation were 60% of males and 40% of females [12]. Meanwhile, the non-agricultural activities contributed to the more even rural income distribution. The rural poor (land area below 0.5 chia) earned 70% of their total household income from non-agricultural activities, while the figure for the rural rich (land area larger than two chia) was 25% [9].

2.2 South Korea

Land Reform Labour-intensive Industry. The post-war growth in Korea started with the equalisation of wealth. The partition of the Korean Peninsula immediately after the Second World War in 1945 and the Korean War destroyed the South's meagre industrial wealth, and a radical land reform dramatically altered the distribution of agricultural wealth. Before the land reform, 94% of farmers were either full or partial tenants. Redistribution of Japanese-owned land in 1947 and subsequent land reform in 1949 virtually ended tenancy, capped paddy holding at three hectares and established a system of relatively tiny owner-operated farms. Approximately 62% of Korea's 2.5 million agricultural families at the time benefited from the land reform, among which around 970,000 tenant farmers and landless agricultural labourers became proprietors, while 570,000 minor farmers were able to expand their holdings [13]. Consequently, over 80% of farm families owned land smaller than 1.5 Hectares between the 1960s and 70s, leading to egalitarian rural income distribution measured by Gini as low as 0.244 in 1970 [13, 14].

Like Taiwan, South Korea in the 1950s adopted labour-intensive industrialisation with import substitution policies and export expansion, which increased employment opportunities and kept income inequality low in the subsequent decades. High labour intensity in the initial development phase in Korea avoided the exclusion of unskilled labour when the market growth was favourable for capitalists as predicted by Kuznets's model. However, the rural-urban gap was not avoided in Korea as was in Taiwan. The factor that may explain the slightly higher Gini index in Korea than in Taiwan is that centralised industrialisation limited rural families' access to complementary sources of income. In Taiwan, the proportion of total farm household income generated from non-farm activities increased dramatically from 25% in 1962 to 43% in 1975. In Korea, which, like Taiwan, has witnessed accelerated development since the early 1960s, the proportion of total farm household income generated from non-farm activities has remained approximately constant at 23% since 1962 [14]. An average Korean rural household earned 54% as much as an urban household, while the figure in Taiwan was 71.7% in 1970 [14, 15].

Universal Education During the Capital-Intensive Growth. What prevented income inequality in Korea from further expansion is universal education. In the late 1970s, according to Kuznets, South Korea and Taiwan were both perceived to have reached the theoretical turning point along the Kuznets curve, at which the situation of labour surplus lost ground to labour deficit [6]. In practice, the two economies replaced the labour-intensive model with a capital-intensive one. Although the demand for skilled labour by capital-intensive sectors increased, while the demand for unskilled labour decreased among small businesses, Korea still eliminated unemployment in the 1980s [16].

Table 1. The gross enrollment rate of different levels of education in Korea and Taiwan.

Country/Region	Primary		Secondary		Higher Education	
	1965	1982	1965	1982	1965	1982
Korea	101	100	35	89	6	24
Taiwan	98	100	32	85	6	19
Upper-middle-income countries	96	102	26	51	5	14

Data source: Word Bank (1985). *World Development Report 1985* [17]

Universal education helps the two East Asian societies, probably to a greater extent in Korea, to meet the changing labour market demand for skilled labour. As shown in Table 1, Korea and Taiwan showed an advantage in school enrollment at different levels of education over the world's upper-middle-income countries' average in 1965. In 1982, Korea enlarged its lead over Taiwan and the upper-middle-income group in secondary and higher education enrollment. Immediately after the Korean War, South Korea initiated the first 6-year plan for compulsory primary education in 1954, leading to the attainment of universalisation (net enrollment rate of 95%) of primary education in 1960, and universalised junior secondary education by 1980, 17 years earlier than Taiwan did as shown in Table 2, despite a 1965 enrollment rate at 41.4%. Senior secondary education universalisation, which did not take place in Taiwan, was achieved by Korea in 1998. The effort by the Korean government is reflected in the proportion of government expenditure on education, which reached 19.5% in Korea, compared to 5.6% in Taiwan, in 1982 [17].

Table 2. The years in which universalisations of different levels of education were achieved.

	Primary	Junior Secondary	Senior Secondary
Korea	1960	1980	1998
Taiwan	1960	1997	–

Data source: Ministry of Education (1996, 2011). *Education Statistics in the Republic of China* [18, 19], Kim et al. (2015). *Education for All 2015 National Review Report: Republic of Korea* [20]

3 Path of Mainland China

3.1 Incremental Change in Rural Sector

Before the land reform, the Chinese agricultural sector under the planned economic regime was subordinated to the overall economic aims of the central government, with little autonomy and rights of decision for farmers. Farmers were managed under the Hukou Registration System and People's Commune System during the planned economy era. The establishment of the two systems in the 1950s was part of the state's heavy industry-focused economic "catch-up" strategy. The government imposed extremely stringent constraints on rural-urban migration, and people's household status was predetermined, typically following their mother's household, with only a handful of fortunate individuals being able to alter their household status [21]. Through the policy of centralised purchasing and marketing under the planned economy and the unequal exchange between the agricultural and industrial sectors, the state was able to obtain the surplus of production from the agriculture, which provided the initial accumulation necessary for industrialisation [22, 23]. The Hukou Registration System and the People's Commune System tied peasants to the land. Moreover, farmers do not have access to wages, food and oil stamps, housing allocation, medical care, and various other benefits that urban residents receive from the planned economic system, which constitute the exclusive rights of urban residents [24].

Mainland China's land and agricultural reform was incremental rather than radical and complete, as in the two neighbouring counterparts. The Household Contract Responsibility System introduced in 1978, the first year of mainland China's economic reform, changed the ownership of two productive assets: the power of the peasants to dispose of their own labour forces and the right to use land. The contractual system returned the peasants' autonomy in agricultural production activities [25]. Nevertheless, the urban-rural divide associated with the hukou system and the mechanism for capturing production surpluses from farm did not end until 1994, and the agricultural tax was not abolished until 2006 [25]. Only then did the mechanism of appropriation and transfer of agricultural surpluses from rural to urban areas disappear. Nonetheless, the welfare exclusivity of the urban hukou still remained in place for many years. For example, the collective purchase and sale system partially persists. The class mobility barrier still remained as a result of the hukou system in that the majority of migrant workers who migrate to the cities still could not enjoy the same social benefits and state subsidies as urban residents and that the discrimination against registered rural residents is prevalent in the urban labour market [26, 27].

The role of agricultural reform is vitally important in the evolution of the urban-rural gap and hence the overall inequality. As shown in Fig. 2, the initiation of three major reforms corresponds to the three periods when the urban-rural income gap shortly narrowed, namely the introduction of the Household Contract Responsibility System and cancellation of the People's Commune System in the late 1970s and the early 1980s, the raise of government-procurement price of crops to the market level regarding the fixed quotas that farmers obliged to sell in the mid-1990s, and the removal of agricultural tax in the late 2000s. The urban-rural income gap exerts considerable influence to the overall level of inequality. As shown in Fig. 2, the three periods coincide with the three periods when the overall Gini of the country declined. However, the incremental and intermittent policy changes have not addressed the chronic and intensifying issue of urban-rural inequality. A sharper overall decline in the proportion of rural income in total national income than in the share of rural population is observed in the recent decades. In 1984, rural China received 66% of national income with 78% of total population, while in 2016, it received 20% of income with 40% of population [27].

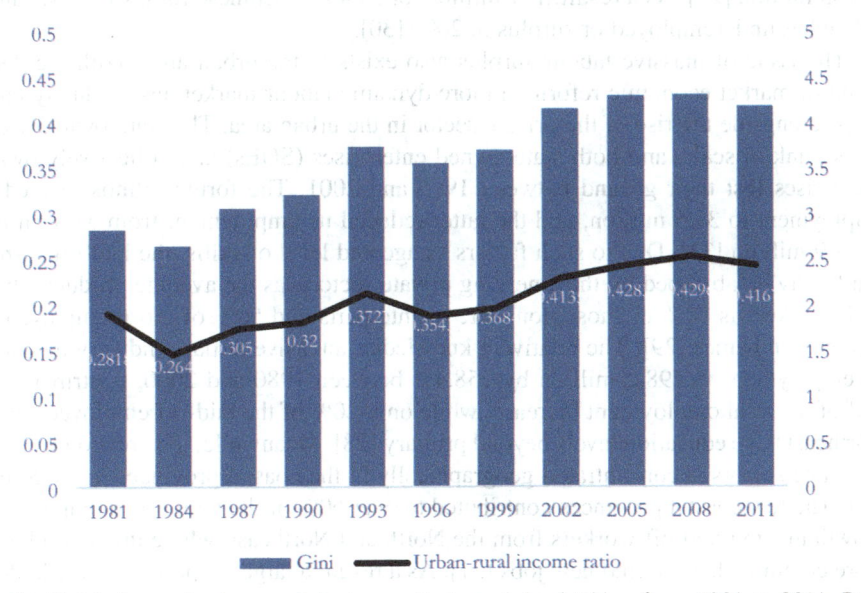

Fig. 2. Gini index and urban-rural income ratio in mainland China from 1981 to 2011. Data source: Ravallion, M. and Chen, S. (2022). *Is that really a Kuznets curve? Turning points for income inequality in China* [27]. Photo credit: Original

3.2 Marketisation and Privatisation and Generation of Labour Surplus

Apart from the urban-rural income gap, the inequality within the rural area is another significant component of the overall inequality in mainland China owing to the undigested labour surplus. The rural Gini coefficient has been constantly higher than in the urban, rendering mainland China a special case in contrast to Taiwan and Korea and the assumption of Kuznets [3, 12, 14, 27]. When the land distribution was in progress and immediately after its completion, mainland China was experiencing the period when the baby boomers of the 1960s entering into the working age, significantly increasing agricultural employment and adding pressure to the tightly allocated land to absorb labour. Between 1980 and 1990, agricultural employment increased by 17.38%, reaching a historical peak of 341.8 million [29]. After the reform, the primary goal of economic activities of farm households, as units in the market, is to maximize household economic interests rather than to fulfil the production targets specified under the planned economy. When the land allocated to households cannot absorb excess labour, the marginal output of additional household members on the farm would be minor. The newly emerged village and town enterprises under the market mechanism first took the role in absorbing excess labour, with employment in these firms increased from 30 million in 1980 to 128.6 million in 1995; midway through the 1990s, however, village and town enterprises began to experience financial difficulties due to weak management and increasing competition from the private counterparts, limiting their ability to digest the labour surplus. Employment in these enterprises thus has declined marginally from since the 1996 peak of 135 million [29]. As a result, 171 million, or 34.4% of Chinese rural workers, can be defined as underemployed or surplus in 2000 [30].

The issue of massive labour surplus also exists in the urban area. With the deepening of market economic reform, a more dynamic labour market has gradually taken shape alongside the rise of the private sector in the urban area. The state-owned sector has shrunk in scale, and both state-owned enterprises (SOEs) and collectively owned enterprises lost their ground between 1995 and 2001. The former almost halved its employment to 39.5 million, and the latter reduced its employment from 31.5 million to 12.9 million [31]. Due to such factors as age and level of skills, the laid-off surplus can hardly be absorbed by the emerging private sectors, as the average productivity of SOE workers is 71% of those non-state counterparts and 50% of those employed by foreign companies [29]. The relatively knowledge-intensive tertiary industry increased its employment to 198.2 million by 258.4% between 1980 and 2000, contributing to half of the total employment increase, while only 20% of the laid-off employees in the Northeast have education levels beyond primary [28]. Meanwhile, job creation from the non-state sectors is concentrated geographically in the coastal provinces in the Southeast. The few coastal provinces contributed to over 60% of the total urban employment growth making laid-off workers from the North and Northeast, where urban job loss is more common, hard to find new jobs [31]. As a result, a large proportion of the laid-off workers ended up joining the informal sectors with little and unstable working hours, not covered by social welfare policies.

4 Comparison and Discussion

4.1 Geographical Issue

The compact territories were the first factor that benefited Korea and Taiwan but not mainland China. Unlike in regions of small islands or peninsulas with the relatively homogeneous geographical condition across the territory, geographical location plays a vital role for different Chinese regions. Areas with lower incomes tend to be landlocked and border other low-income countries. Many are located in rough terrains, such as mountains or deserts, unsuitable for industrialisation and urbanisation. It is also expensive to build infrastructure and link these areas to others. However, coastal towns are more exposed to industry and commerce since they are adjacent to wealthier neighboring nations and are thus well-suited for urbanisation and infrastructural development, especially seaports. As a result of opening policy to foreign commerce and the fast development in national revenues, the coastal provinces, such as Guangdong and Jiangsu, have become industrial centres.

Likewise crucial has been the work of municipal administrations in making the most of advantageous locations. Since the strategy set at the initial phase of the reform was to allow some people and places to get rich first to aid the national economic development [32], local authorities in coastal areas have more incentives to attract foreign direct investment and to aid the establishment and growth of local enterprises to participate in the global competition, as the Chinese central government has adopted the directing policy in allowing some coastal provinces to develop first.

Consequently, further divergent trajectories typically set in motion once regional inequalities emerge. As coastal areas flourished and the establishment of various economic zones accelerated their development, an increasing number of labourers and entrepreneurs would migrate to these regions in pursuit of opportunities for prosperity. On the other hand, inferior business climate and dwindling fiscal revenues from tax in the interior regions have left local authorities with fewer financial resources and possibly less motivation to remedy the issues such as inefficient enterprises and widening pension system deficits. Today, the per capita income in Gansu province is almost one-fourth of that in Beijing or Shanghai [33].

4.2 Institutional and Policy Issues

Another difference between mainland China and the two neighbouring economies lies in the institutional settings before and during the reform. Unlike in Taiwan and Korea, where the economic reform involves establishing a modern capitalist institutional system from scratch after the end of colonialism or the destruction of the war, the reform in mainland China involved correcting one path of modernisation and the transition to another. Before the reform, mainland China eradicated urban unemployment with the administrative measure of centralised allocation and fixed permanent tenure and tied rural labour workers to the field with the Hukou Registration and People's Commune System [34]. The enterprises were forced to hire more workers than the economically efficient level. Once the competitive market mechanism is introduced, enterprises tend to adjust their use of labour by redundancy.

During the course of the reform, both Korea and Taiwan adopted a gradual path of industrialisation that involved a incremental transition of focus from labour-intensive first to capital-intensive and finally to knowledge- or skill-intensive production. For example, in Taiwan, the proportion of the secondary sector expanded from 18% in 1952 to over 40% in 1978, with the majority of the contribution made by labour-intensive light industries, while the following 12 years witnessed a further reallocation of the industrial sector labour to the capital-intensive heavy industry and the expansion of service sector to over 50%. Afterwards, high-tech industries became the pillar, supported by the service sector after the 1990s [35]. The central government directed the gradual change of economic structure with the accumulation of human capital to meet the demand for labour reallocation. In mainland China, however, the first ten years since the reform even witnessed a decline in the proportion of the secondary industry in the total national output and no significant increase after that, while the proportion of labour-intensive sectors stabilised at slightly over 60%, owing to the continued catch-up policy prioritising some capital-intensive sectors and the service sector [36, 37]. Although as Taiwan and Korea did, or to some extent more successfully, mainland China accomplished the goal of universalisation of compulsory primary and junior secondary education in the 2000s in less than 20 years, the pace of improvement of education still cannot catch up with that of the upgrading of domestic industries to achieve better employment [38].

Mainland China also faced the conflict between the gradual social policy adjustment and radical social changes that was not encountered in the two neighbours. Although Korea did not possess the unusually decentralised industrial infrastructure left by colonialists to facilitate the industrialisation of rural area as Taiwan did, and the rural income level was once left behind, Korean excessive rural labour could easily flow into the urban area and be absorbed by the urban sectors without creating massive hidden rural unemployment. As shown in Fig. 3, Korea had reduced its proportion of the rural population from 72% to approximately 20% in three decades, while mainland China halved the figure in 40 years from 82%. Evidence shows that despite the improvement in urban economic conditions and decreasing population in poverty, the number of people in poverty in the urban area increased proportionate to the rate of urbanisation between 1957 and 1980, indicating the flow of rural poor to the urban area [39]. The mobility of labour in Korea provides people experiencing poverty with more choices in the labour market and diluted the influence of low rural income on overall inequality. However, the Hukou Registration System in mainland China has kept impeding the rural-to-urban flow of people seeking employment despite the reform. To remain in cities and obtain preferential services such as social security, education, and healthcare, a registered hukou in the city was required. Urban enterprises were not allowed to recruit labour from another province if local labour was available. It was not until 2000 that the central government started allowing registered rural residents with stable jobs in one of the twenty thousand small cities and towns to obtain the hukou in the workplace without giving up the land use right in the hometown [29].

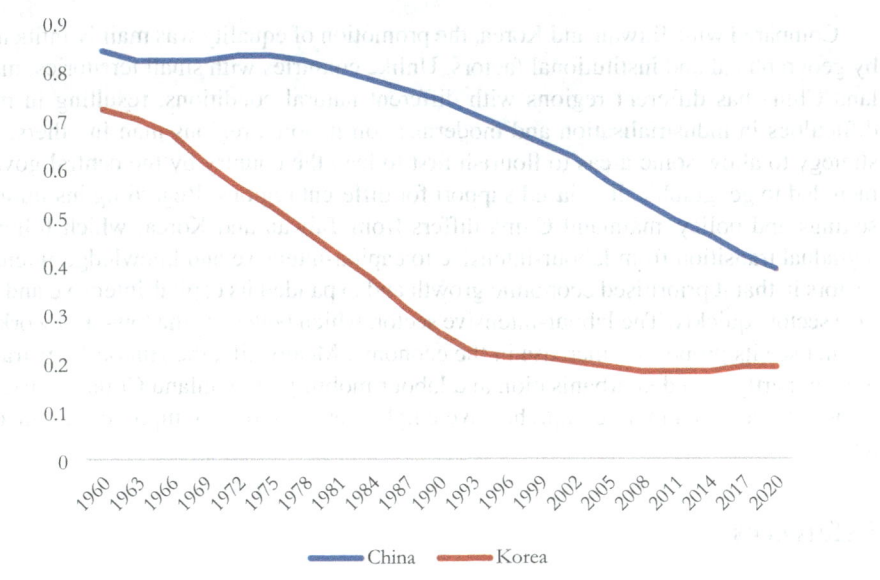

Fig. 3. The proportion of rural population in mainland China and Korea. Data source: World Bank. (2021). *Rural population (% of total population)* [40]. Photo credit: Original

5 Conclusion

This paper examines the contributing factors to the model of growth with equity in two East Asian economies, namely Taiwan and Korea. It attempts to compare mainland China's development path with those of the two economies to explain why mainland China failed to avoid the expanding income disparities as the two neighbours did. In Taiwan, the land reform promoted income equality in the agricultural sector. The decentralised industrialisation based on the legacy of the colonial period enabled the labour-intensive sector to be established both in the urban and the rural area to absorb the labour surplus. Korea did not have the unusually dispersed industry sites to promote the rural economy. As Taiwan did, it also paved the road for equal growth throughout the rural area through land reform. Universalised primary and secondary education enabled Korea to accumulate human capital for development with a low unemployment rate. The issue of the urban-rural gap was not resolved in Korea as in Taiwan, which may explain the slightly higher Gini coefficient in Korea than in Taiwan before 1990. In mainland China, urban-rural inequality explains a considerable part of the overall inequality. Land and agricultural reform also took place, and the gradual process temporarily alleviated the issue before the income gap widened again. However, the exclusive welfare rights for urban residents as a result of the Hukou Registration System remained. The marketisation and privatisation process generated a massive labour surplus. In the rural area, excessive labour could not easily find non-farm employment further than village and town enterprises, whose scale was limited due to poor management and the competition from the private sector, while in the urban area, labour surplus from the downsizing state sectors could not meet the demand of newly emerging private sector due to the low skill level and productivity.

Compared with Taiwan and Korea, the promotion of equality was mainly influenced by geographical and institutional factors. Unlike countries with small territories, mainland China has different regions with different natural conditions, resulting in more difficulties in industrialisation and modernisation in some regions than in others. The strategy to allow some areas to flourish first to lead the country by the central government led to geographically biased support for different regions. Regarding institutional settings and policy, mainland China differs from Taiwan and Korea, which followed a gradual transition from labour-intensive to capital-intensive and knowledge-intensive sectors in that it prioritised economic growth and expanded its capital-intensive and service sectors quickly. The labour-intensive sector, which better fits the low-skill workers, did not see its proportion increase in the economy. Meanwhile, the Hukou Registration System partly impeded urbanisation and labour mobility in mainland China, restricting some workers from more comprehensive employment options to improve their income level.

References

1. World Inequality Database. World (2022). https://wid.world/world/#anninc_pall_z/CN/last/eu/k/p/yearly/a/false/85.39449999999988/20000/curve/false/country
2. Lugo, M.A., Raiser, M., Yemtsov, R.: What's next for poverty reduction policies in China? (2021). https://www.brookings.edu/blog/future-development/2021/09/24/whats-next-for-poverty-reduction-policies-in-china/
3. Kuznets, S.: Economic growth and income inequality. Am. Econ. Rev. **45**(1), 1–28 (1955)
4. Piketty, T.: Capital in the Twenty-First Century. The Belknap Press of Harvard University Press, Cambridge (2014). Translated by A. Goldhammer
5. Wang, F.: The end of 'growth with equity'? Economic growth and income inequality in East Asia. In: Analysis from the East-West Center. East-West Center, Honolulu (2011)
6. Kuznets, P.W.: An east Asian model of economic development: Japan, Taiwan, and South Korea. Econ. Dev. Cult. Change **36**(3), S11–S43 (1988)
7. Solt, F.: The standardized world income inequality database v1-v7 (2018). https://doi.org/10.7910/DVN/WKOKHF. Harvard Dataverse, V20
8. Koo, A.Y.C.: Economic consequences of land reform in Taiwan. Asian Surv. **6**(3), 150–157 (1966)
9. Ranis, G.: Equity with growth in Taiwan: how 'special' is the 'special case'? World Dev. **6**(3), 397–409 (1978)
10. Bowden, T.R.: Land reform and rural development on Taiwan. Univ. Coll. Rev. **1**(1), 34–40 (1961). http://www.jstor.org/stable/41965668. Accessed 12 Apr 2023
11. Chu, W.: Catch-up and learning in Taiwan. How Nations Learn 107–124 (2019). https://doi.org/10.1093/oso/9780198841760.003.0006
12. Fei, J., Ranis, G., Shirley: Growth with Equity. Oxford University Press, USA (1979)
13. Rao, D.C.: Economic growth and equity in the Republic of Korea. World Dev. **6**(3), 383–396 (1978)
14. Renaud, B.: Economic growth and income inequality in Korea. In: Conference of the Population and Development Studies Center on Population and Development. International Bank for Reconstruction and Development (World Bank), Seoul (1975)
15. Bourguignon, F., Fournier, M., Gurgand, M.: Fast development with a stable income distribution: Taiwan, 1979–94. Rev. Income Wealth **47**(2), 139–163 (2001)

16. Oshima, H.T.: Kuznets' curve and Asian income distribution trends. Hitotsubashi J. Econ. **33**(1), 95–111 (1992). https://www.jstor.org/stable/43295931. Accessed 12 Apr 2023
17. Bank, W.: World Development Report 1985. Oxford University Press, USA (1985)
18. Ministry of Education: Education Statistics in the Republic of China 1995. R.O.C. Government Publications, Taipei (1996)
19. Ministry of Education: Education Statistics in the Republic of China 2010. R.O.C. Government Publications, Taipei (2011)
20. Kim, J., et al.: Education for All 2015 National Review Report: Republic of Korea. Incheon, Republic of Korea (2015)
21. Wu, X., Treiman, D.J.: Inequality and equality under Chinese socialism: the Hukou system and intergenerational occupational mobility. Am. J. Sociol. **113**(2), 415–445 (2007)
22. Chan, A., Madsen, R., Unger, J.: Chen Village Under Mao and Deng: Expanded and updated Edition. University of California Press, Berkeley (1992)
23. Nee, V., Oi, J.C.: State and peasant in contemporary china: the political economy of village government. Contemp. Sociol. **20**(2), 205 (1991)
24. Wang, F.-L.: Organizing Through Division and Exclusion. Stanford University Press (2005)
25. Lin, T., Wu, X.: Institutional changes, class structural transformation, and income inequality in China: 1978–2005. Chin. J. Sociol. (CJS) **30**(6), 1–40 (2010)
26. Research Group of the State Council. Research Report on Chinese Migrant Workers. Yanshi Publishing House, Beijing (2006)
27. Ravallion, M., Chen, S.: Is that really a Kuznets curve? Turning points for income inequality in China. J. Econ. Inequality (2022)
28. Liu, W., Wang, C., Zhao, X. and Zhang, H.: The income distribution disparity in china: a study on the status, causes, and solutions. J. People's Univ. China (5) (2018)
29. Brooks, R., Tao, R.: China's labor market performance and challenges. IMF Working Papers, vol. 03, no. 210, p. 1 (2003)
30. Imai, H.: China's growing unemployment problem. RIM **2**(2), 22–39 (2002)
31. National Bureau of Statistics. China labour statistical yearbook 1989–2015. China Statistic Press, Beijing (2016)
32. Dunford, M.: The Chinese path to common prosperity. Int. Crit. Thought 1–20 (2022)
33. Poonpatpibul, C.: From Shanghai to Gansu: growing regional disparities in China – causes and remedies. AMRO ASIA (2019). https://www.amro-asia.org/from-shanghai-to-gansu-growing-regional-disparities-in-china-causes-and-remedies/
34. He, X.: The choice of history: from the central allocation system to the market two-way choice - 50 years review of the talent resources allocation. Chin. Talents (8), 7–9 (1999)
35. Cai, C.: Reflections on industrial structure upgrading and policy effects in Taiwan. Mod. Econ. Res. (8), pp.89–92 (2008)
36. Deng, Z., Yu, C.: Structural changes in the industrial economy in the 70 years of the new China. China Econ. **14**(4), 14–39 (2019)
37. Rozelle, S., Boswell, M.: Complicating China's rise: rural underemployment. Wash. Q. **44**(2), 61–74 (2021)
38. Park, S.: Analysis of Saemaul Undong: a Korean rural development programme in the 1970s. Asia-Pac. Dev. J. **16**(2), 113–140 (2012)
39. Word Bank. Rural population (% of total population) - Korea, Rep., China | Data (2021). https://data.worldbank.org/indicator/SP.RUR.TOTL.ZS?locations=KR-CN. Accessed 12 Apr 2023
40. Cai, F.: Insist on expanding employment in the structural adjustment. Qiushi **5**, 27–29 (2009)

Factors Influence Loan Default–A Credit Risk Analysis

Xianya Qi[✉]

School of Business, Economics and Law, University of Queensland, Brisbane 4072, Australia
`xianya.qi@uqconnect.edu.au`

Abstract. Loan default has been a severe and critical issue for both lenders and borrowers. Default on loan payments not only reduces the profitability for lenders but also affects the credit rating of borrowers. This work aims to analyze the factors that influence loan default status, which closely determines credit default risks. To answer this question, this paper first regresses the data to explore the variables which have a significant effect on loan status. Secondly, it conducted a comparison analysis between loan defaulters and non-defaulters, to find the main characteristics of the two groups. Then, a factor analysis is exercised to reduce the dimensions of the continuous variables and to seek the correlation between them. At last, this work regresses the data using variables after dimension reduction. The results show that credit default can be affected by several factors, which can be used to determine credit decisions for lenders.

Keywords: Credit Risk Analysis · Binary Regression · Comparison Analysis · Factor Analysis

1 Introduction

Financial institutions provide several kinds of loans to customers, such as business loans, housing loans, and consumer loans, which generate significant credit risks to financial institutions if loans are not paid back in full amount. Therefore, evaluating loan applications play an essential role for financial institutions when it comes to loan applications. This research aims to evaluate the factors that influence credit risk, mainly focusing on personal characteristics. However, information such as economic condition is not involved in this data research. In this work, a binary regression is first conducted to examine factors that significantly affect loan default. Then, comparison analysis is exercised to observe the different characteristics between loan defaulters and non-defaulters. Finally, after a factor analysis that reduces the dimension of regression, the data is regressed to improve predictability. The results show that loan defaults are significantly impacted by age, income, home ownership, loan grade, loan intent, and other factors. The default group especially differs from the non-default groups in terms of the loan amount, personal income, loan intent, and home ownership status. Furthermore, prediction is improved, and some noises are reduced with dimension reduction. Therefore, lenders can estimate the credit risk of borrowers according to these important factors under the improved model.

© The Author(s), under exclusive license to Springer Nature Singapore Pte Ltd. 2024
X. Li et al. (Eds.): ICEMGD 2023, AEPS, pp. 849–862, 2024.
https://doi.org/10.1007/978-981-97-0523-8_79

2 Regression

This section aims to discuss the result of the binary logistic regression on loan status. Firstly, to contrast the predicted dependent variable with the true loan status, a confusion matrix is firstly conducted under a cut value of 0.5. According to Fig. 1, the accuracy is at 86.8%. While recall ratio is at 55.6% and precision is at 76.3%. Therefore, the F1 Score would be 64.3% (Table 1).

Table 1. Classification Table[a]

	Observed		Predicted		Percentage Correct
			loan_status		
			0	1	
Step 1	loan_status	0	21312	1055	95.3
		1	2716	3402	55.6
	Overall Percentage				86.8

Source: SPSS Statistics
a. The cut value is .500

Table 2. Classification Table[a]

	Observed		Predicted		Percentage Correct
			loan_status		
			0	1	
Step 1	loan_status	0	19754	2613	88.3
		1	1714	4404	72.0
	Overall Percentage				84.8

Source: SPSS Statistics
a. The cut value is .300

To lower the occurrence of Type II error, the threshold of cut value is reduced to 0.3. According to Table 2, under this threshold, accuracy is lower at 84.8%. However, the recall ratio increases by 16.4%. The number of people who are not default but labeled as default decreases by more than 1000. Though, this is at the cost of a slightly lower precision, at 62.8%. As a result, the F1 Score is improved to 67.1%, which implies that 0.3 is a better threshold to regress the data.

Table 3. Variables in the Equation

		B	S.E.	Wald	df	Sig.
Step 1[a]	person_age	−.013	.006	4.076	1	.043
	person_income	.000	.000	8.328	1	.004
	person_home_ownership			851.821	2	.000
	person_home_ownership(1)	.829	.043	372.991	1	.000
	person_home_ownership(2)	−1.790	.113	251.243	1	.000
	person_emp_length	−.014	.005	8.065	1	.005
	loan_intent			527.054	5	.000
	loan_intent(1)	−.646	.063	106.532	1	.000
	loan_intent(2)	−.875	.061	204.483	1	.000
	loan_intent(3)	−.155	.058	7.203	1	.007
	loan_intent(4)	−1.129	.067	287.356	1	.000
	loan_intent(5)	.053	.068	.610	1	.435
	loan_grade			1187.527	5	.000
	loan_grade(1)	−2.786	.274	103.662	1	.000
	loan_grade(2)	−2.677	.230	135.591	1	.000
	loan_grade(3)	−2.546	.207	151.407	1	.000
	loan_grade(4)	−.455	.194	5.495	1	.019
	loan_grade(5)	−.286	.200	2.047	1	.153
	loan_amnt	.000	.000	557.518	1	.000
	loan_int_rate	.088	.018	23.619	1	.000
	loan_percent_income	13.133	.251	2727.254	1	.000
	cb_person_default_on_file(1)	−.022	.053	.169	1	.681
	cb_person_cred_hist_length	.011	.009	1.250	1	.264
	Constant	−1.308	.408	10.266	1	.001

Source: SPSS Statistics

Table 3 above interprets that in terms of loan intent, home improvement does not have a significant effect on loan status. Similarly, a loan grade of E, historical default, and credit history length also have no significant impact on default.

By contrast, renting real estate, loan amount, loan interest rate, and loan percentage on income all have a positive significant effect on loan default. Among those variables, loan percentage on income has the largest coefficient magnitude. Firstly, raising loan interest rate limit borrowers' repaying capacity, which in turn growing the probability of default [1]. Intuitively, a high loan percentage on income implies a high debt-to-income ratio [2], which demonstrates that the borrowers are unlikely to manage the debt repayment, thus increasing the chance of default. Furthermore, renting than buying a

Table 4. Loan_status * person_home_ownership Crosstabulation.

Count		person_home_ownership			Total
		Rent	Own	Mortgage	
loan_status	not default	11254	2391	11754	25399
	default	5192	193	1690	7075
Total		16446	2584	13444	32474

Source: SPSS Statistics

place to live may denote the renter's financial condition and repayment capacity: people who have real estate as collateral are more prone to pay back than people who do not have any physical assets. In addition, a high rent-to-income ratio shows the disability to pay for other living expenses thus a high probability of default [3].

Moreover, loan intent and loan grade have a negative significant effect on loan default. Specifically, venture loan has the lowest default risk compared with loans for other purposes. Most venture loans are backed with collateral such as intellectual property. Also, venture loans satisfy the short-term needs of cash for borrowers that support them to operate for a longer period, until the borrowers earn more funds to repay the debt. Therefore, venture loans have a lower default risk [4]. When it comes to loan grades, it is evident that higher-grading loans such as A loans, B loans, and C loans are much safer than lower-grading loans in terms of default risk. Higher-grade loans have a lower rate of risk and a lower loan-to-value ratio, which makes the payment of the borrower more reliable [5].

3 Comparison Analysis

This section aims to conduct a comparison analysis between loan status and different discrete variables and continuous variables, to figure out more details of the default population characteristics.

Table 5. Chi-Square Tests

	Value	df	Asymptotic Significance (2-sided)
Pearson Chi-Square	1904.727[a]	2	.000
Likelihood Ratio	1994.250	2	.000
Linear-by-Linear Association	1607.346	1	.000
N of Valid Cases	32474		

Source: SPSS Statistics

Table 6. Loan_status * loan_intent Crosstabulation.

Count		loan_intent						Total
		Personal	Education	Medical	Venture	Home Improvement	Debt Consolidation	
loan_status	not default	4423	5342	4450	4872	2664	3722	25473
	default	1098	1111	1621	847	941	1490	7108
Total		5521	6453	6071	5719	3605	5212	32581

Source: SPSS Statistics

Firstly, a cross tabulation (Table 4) is created of the dependent variable and personal home ownership. It is shown that people who default are only one-fifth of the total number of people being tested. However, among the defaulted people, about 73.4% of them are the renter of real estate, while 23.9% of them pay the mortgage. Only 193 defaulters own the home. The chi-square test (Table 5) also verifies that there is a distinct difference in home ownership between the two groups. Rental and mortgage default can be correlated with inflation, higher living expenses, stagnant economic condition, and lagging welfare systems. In the United States, 20% or more renters default under the constraint of growing inflation and daily expenses, and the national eviction ban [6]. Another research on Hongkong mortgage default probability investigates that mortgage default is positively correlated with current loan to value ratio (CLTV), mortgage rate, and unemployment rate. In addition, it is negatively correlated with stock prices. Specifically, a higher CLTV implies a higher mortgage amount and even negative equity of the borrower, thus restraining the borrower's ability to pay. Furthermore, at the same level as CLTV, a large drop in stock prices strongly increases the probability of mortgage default [7].

Table 7. Chi-Square Tests

	Value	df	Asymptotic Significance (2-sided)
Pearson Chi-Square	520.512[a]	5	.000
Likelihood Ratio	526.237	5	.000
Linear-by-Linear Association	139.269	1	.000
N of Valid Cases	32581		

Source: SPSS Statistics

When comparing the loan intent between the default group and the non-default group, the chi-square test (Table 7) also displays that diverse loan purposes affect default status significantly. As Table 6 shows, most defaulted people borrow the loan for the purpose of personal use, education, medication, and debt consolidation, among which education and debt consolidation are the most important factors, accounting for more than 20% of the total number of defaulters.

Educational default can be related to the program they borrow money for. Studies found that an increasing number of large-loan-balance people borrow educational loans for attending for-profit schools in which students have unsatisfactory loan repayment and labor market condition compared with other institutions. In addition, they are more likely to be parents and independent undergraduates, who have a risker financial outlook [8].

When it comes to debt consolidation, when combining multiple debts into a larger one, it is possible that total interest payment is increased if combining a new loan with a longer repayment term and a higher interest rate. Moreover, people who borrow more loan to consolidate loans implies that they have a higher amount of loans. Therefore, debt consolidation increases loan to income ratio thus restricting the debt borrower's ability to repay.

Table 8. Tests of Normality

	loan_status	Kolmogorov-Smirnov[a]		
		Statistic	df	Sig.
person_age	0	.158	22367	.000
	1	.165	6118	.000
person_income	0	.216	22367	.000
	1	.147	6118	.000
person_home_ownership	0	.311	22367	.000
	1	.460	6118	.000
person_emp_length	0	.116	22367	.000
	1	.160	6118	.000
loan_intent	0	.165	22367	.000
	1	.164	6118	.000
loan_grade	0	.221	22367	.000
	1	.197	6118	.000
loan_amnt	0	.133	22367	.000
	1	.124	6118	.000
loan_int_rate	0	.107	22367	.000
	1	.076	6118	.000
loan_percent_income	0	.092	22367	.000
	1	.073	6118	.000
cb_person_default_on_file	0	.516	22367	.000
	1	.440	6118	.000
cb_person_cred_hist_length	0	.216	22367	.000
	1	.231	6118	.000

Source: SPSS Statistics
a. Lilliefors Significance Correction

A test of normality (Table 8) is conducted to compare the continuous variables with loan status, and the results show that the loan status is not normally distributed under the seven variables. The Mann-Whitney U test (Table 9) also verifies that the distribution of the seven continuous variables is different under different categories of loan status.

Table 9. Hypothesis Test Summary

	Null Hypothesis	Test	Sig.[a,b]	Decision
1	The distribution of person_age is the same across categories of loan_status	Independent-Samples Mann-Whitney U Test	.000	Reject the null hypothesis
2	The distribution of person_income is the same across categories of loan_status	Independent-Samples Mann-Whitney U Test	.000	Reject the null hypothesis
3	The distribution of person_emp_length is the same across categories of loan_status	Independent-Samples Mann-Whitney U Test	.000	Reject the null hypothesis
4	The distribution of loan_amnt is the same across categories of loan_status	Independent-Samples Mann-Whitney U Test	.000	Reject the null hypothesis
5	The distribution of loan_int_rate is the same across categories of loan_status	Independent-Samples Mann-Whitney U Test	.000	Reject the null hypothesis
6	The distribution of loan_percent_income is the same across categories of loan_status	Independent-Samples Mann-Whitney U Test	.000	Reject the null hypothesis
7	The distribution of cb_person_cred_hist_length is the same across categories of loan_status	Independent-Samples Mann-Whitney U Test	.000	Reject the null hypothesis

Source: SPSS Statistics
The significance level is .050.
Asymptotic significance is displayed.

Evidently, as Table 10 shows, non-default people have 21,678.71 more income than defaulted people on average. The minimum personal income of the defaulted group is only 4,000. In addition, both the personal income data of the default group and the non-default group are highly right-skewed, with skewness at 5.471 and 33.531 respectively. Furthermore, defaulters have an average of 1,613 higher loan amounts than non-defaulters. Though the maximum loan amount in the two groups is the same, the defaulted group has a minimum of 900 loans. Therefore, it is concluded that the default group has a lower income and more loan amount to be repaid. In addition, this also implies that people who default have a higher loan percentage on income at 10% higher than non-defaulters on average.

Table 10. Descriptives of personal_income, loan_percent_income and loan amount.

	loan_status		Statistic		loan_status		Statistic		loan_status		Statistic
person_income	0	Mean	70804.36	loan_percent_income	0	Mean	.1488	loan_amnt	0	Mean	9237.46
		Minimum	7000			Minimum	.00			Minimum	500
		Maximum	6000000			Maximum	.83			Maximum	35000
		Skewness	33.531			Skewness	1.025			Skewness	1.270
	1	Mean	49125.65		1	Mean	.2469		1	Mean	10850.50
		Minimum	4000			Minimum	.01			Minimum	900
		Maximum	703800			Maximum	.78			Maximum	35000
		Skewness	5.471			Skewness	.355			Skewness	.899

Source: SPSS Statistics

4 Factor Analysis

This section aims to conduct a factor analysis to reduce regression dimension, improve prediction and study the intercorrelations between the observed variables which determine default status.

Firstly, to examine the correlations among a set of variables, two measured are conducted. The Kaiser-Meyer-Olkin is a measure of the adequacy of the sample size. In terms of the Bartlett's Test of Sphericity, the null hypothesis that variables are not correlated. Therefore, the data can be assessed if rejecting the null hypothesis (i.e., the significant value is less than 0.5) [9].

Table 11. KMO and Bartlett's Test

Kaiser-Meyer-Olkin Measure of Sampling Adequacy		.435
Bartlett's Test of Sphericity	Approx. Chi-Square	64564.398
	df	21
	Sig.	.000

Source: SPSS Statistics

According to Table 11, Bartletts' Test of Sphericity has a significant value smaller than 0.5. Therefore, the variables are not orthogonal, and the factor analysis can be conducted (Table 13).

Firstly, the factor analysis is conducted with the eigenvalues over 1. Table 12 demonstrates the communalities before and after extraction. According to Table 12, the communalities of loan interest rate and personal employment length are relatively small at 15.5% and 33%. The other variables have communalities at more than 75%. Specifically, personal age and personal credit history have the highest variance that can be explained by the retained factors, at 92.5% and 92.8% respectively.

Before extraction, there are seven linear components in the dataset. Before extraction and rotation, the variance explained by the first component is 28.56%. After extraction and rotation, the seven components are reduced to three main factors with eigenvalues

Table 12. Communalities

	Initial	Extraction
person_age	1.000	.925
person_income	1.000	.753
person_emp_length	1.000	.330
loan_amnt	1.000	.870
loan_int_rate	1.000	.155
loan_percent_income	1.000	.830
cb_person_cred_hist_length	1.000	.928

Source: SPSS Statistics
Extraction Method: Principal Component Analysis.

Table 13. Total Variance Explained.

Comp-onent	Initial Eigenvalues			Extraction Sums of Squared Loadings			Rotation Sums of Squared Loadings		
	Total	% of Variance	Cumulative %	Total	% of Variance	Cumulative %	Total	% of Variance	Cumulative %
1	1.999	28.555	28.555	1.999	28.555	28.555	1.850	26.432	26.432
2	1.633	23.330	51.885	1.633	23.330	51.885	1.627	23.246	49.677
3	1.160	16.567	68.453	1.160	16.567	68.453	1.314	18.775	68.453
4	.978	13.973	82.425						
5	.850	12.149	94.574						
6	.242	3.463	98.037						
7	.137	1.963	100.000						

Source: SPSS Statistics
Extraction Method: Principal Component Analysis.

larger than 1. The first component and the second component can both explain more than 20% of the variance. In addition, the cumulative percentage of variance explained by the three factors is 68.453%. Since at least 50% of the total variance explained by the retained factor is necessary [10], the three factors show a relatively strong performance in terms of explaining about 70% of the total variance out of the seven linear components.

A scree test is conducted to determine a more appropriate eigenvalue and to increase the total variance explained. The first step of the screen test is to plot the eigenvalues against the number of components. Then, observe the graph and find where the point on the curve moves dramatically. This point determines the maximum number of components to retain [11]. From the Fig. 1, it is seen that the curve experiences a significant reduction after the second and the fifth component. Then the eigenvalue decreases to less than one after the fourth component. In addition, the eigenvalue of the fourth and the fifth

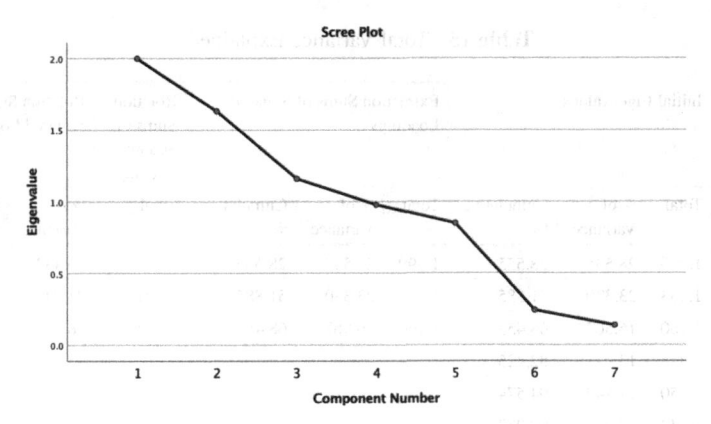

Fig. 1. Scree Plot.

component is very close to 1, which explains approximately 14% and 12% of the variance respectively. Since the variance explained by the sixth and the seventh component is only 3.46% and 1.96%, they are excluded from the components retained. Therefore, an eigenvalue great than 0.85 is reset and the first five components are retained.

Table 14. Communalities (eigenvalue over 0.85).

	Initial	Extraction
person_age	1.000	.930
person_income	1.000	.956
person_emp_length	1.000	.999
loan_amnt	1.000	.900
loan_int_rate	1.000	1.000
loan_percent_income	1.000	.904
cb_person_cred_hist_length	1.000	.932

Source: SPSS Statistics
Extraction Method: Principal Component Analysis.

Table 14 above shows the communalities of the variables after extraction and before rotation with the eigenvalue larger than 0.85. It is shown all of the variables have a communality larger than 0.90, which indicates the retained factors can explain at least 90% of the variance of the remaining variables.

Table 15 shows the total variance explained with the eigenvalue greater than 0.85. There are five factors left after extraction and rotation, which account for 94.57% of the total variance, shared by the seven variables. The variance explained by the retained factors improves by 26% if the eigenvalue is greater than 0.85.

Table 15. Total Variance Explained.

Component	Initial Eigenvalues			Extraction Sums of Squared Loadings			Rotation Sums of Squared Loadings	Rotation Sums of Squared Loadings	
	Total	% of Variance	Cumulative %	Total	% of Variance	Cumulative %	Total	% of Variance	Cumulative %
1	1.999	28.555	28.555	1.999	28.555	28.555	1.85	26.432	26.432
2	1.633	23.330	51.885	1.633	23.330	51.885	1.627	23.246	49.677
3	1.160	16.567	68.453	1.160	16.567	68.453	1.314	18.775	68.453
4	0.978	13.973	82.425						
5	0.850	12.149	94.574						
6	0.242	3.463	98.037						
7	0.137	1.963	100						

Source: SPSS Statistics
Extraction Method: Principal Component Analysis.

Table 16. Rotated Component Matrix[a]

	Component				
	1	2	3	4	5
cb_person_cred_hist_length	.963				
person_age	.958				
loan_percent_income		.893			
loan_amnt		.879			
person_income			.972		
person_emp_length				.992	
loan_int_rate					.996

Source: SPSS Statistics
Extraction Method: Principal Component Analysis.
Rotation Method: Varimax with Kaiser Normalization. [a]
a. Rotation converged in 5 iterations.

To interpret the result of the analysis more comprehensively, a rotated component matrix is conducted. Rotation makes it possible that each variable is explained by different factors, while each factor explains the variables in an overlapping way. Here a factor loading value larger than an absolute value of 0.4 is selected for easier interpretation.

As Table 16 shows, personal credit history and personal age have the highest loadings with the first factor, at 0.963 and 0.958 respectively. Therefore, the first factor is highly correlated with time. In addition, loan percent on income and loan amount load highly on the second factor. Consequently, the second factor can be labeled as loan size. Furthermore, the rest of the three variables are explained by the other three factors respectively, with the loadings all close to 1. Therefore, the seven variables can be reduced to five main factors to regress the data (Tables 18 and 19).

5 Regression After Dimension Reduction

Table 17. Classification Table[a]

	Observed		Predicted		
			loan_status		Percentage Correct
			0	1	
Step 1	loan_status	0	21388	979	95.6
		1	2841	3277	53.6
	Overall Percentage				86.6

Source: SPSS Statistics
a. The cut value is .500

Table 18. Classification Table[a]

	Observed		Predicted		
			loan_status		Percentage Correct
			0	1	
Step 1	loan_status	0	19683	2684	88.0
		1	1734	4384	71.7
	Overall Percentage				84.5

Source: SPSS Statistics
a. The cut value is .300

This section aims to show the results of the binary logistic regression using the five variables (and discrete variables) provided by the factor analysis. The classification matrix (Table 17) displays that under a cut value of 0.5, the accuracy is similar to the previous model. However, the precision value is improved to approximately 78%.

When the cut value is 0.3, the recall ratio increases from 53.56% to 71.66%. The number of people who are not defaulted but labeled as default decreases by more than 1000. Compared to the results under a cut value of 0.5 (which has a F1 score of 63.18%), the F1 score grows to 66.49%.

The table above illustrates the results of the variables under a cut value of 0.3 after dimension reduction. It is shown that the positive and negative correlations between the discrete independent variables and loan status are not changed. In addition, the time factor, income factor, and personal employment length factor have a negative relationship

Table 19. Variables in the Equation.

		B	S.E.	df	Sig.
Step 1[a]	person_home_ownership			2	.000
	person_home_ownership(1)	.835	.043	1	.000
	person_home_ownership(2)	−1.611	.109	1	.000
	loan_intent			5	.000
	loan_intent(1)	−.628	.061	1	.000
	loan_intent(2)	−.857	.060	1	.000
	loan_intent(3)	−.185	.057	1	.001
	loan_intent(4)	−1.088	.065	1	.000
	loan_intent(5)	.066	.067	1	.324
	loan_grade			5	.000
	loan_grade(1)	−2.860	.278	1	.000
	loan_grade(2)	−2.733	.236	1	.000
	loan_grade(3)	−2.561	.214	1	.000
	loan_grade(4)	−.506	.202	1	.012
	loan_grade(5)	−.313	.209	1	.134
	cb_person_default_on_file(1)	−.015	.053	1	.771
	REGR factor score 1 for analysis 1	−.142	.019	1	.000
	REGR factor score 2 for analysis 1	.758	.019	1	.000
	REGR factor score 3 for analysis 1	−1.294	.034	1	.000
	REGR factor score 4 for analysis 1	−.186	.020	1	.000

a. Variable(s) entered on step 1: person_home_ownership, loan_intent, loan_grade, cb_person_default_on_file, REGR factor score 1 for analysis 1, REGR factor score 2 for analysis 1, REGR factor score 3 for analysis 1, REGR factor score 4 for analysis 1, REGR factor score 5 for analysis 1

Source: SPSS Statistics

with loan status. While loan size factor and loan interest rate factor is positively correlated with loan default, which is generally consistent with the results of section one. More importantly, after the dimension result, all five factors are statistically significant, which greatly develops the reliability and accuracy of the prediction.

6 Conclusion

Compared to business loans, consumer loans have a higher default rate in general. Therefore, credit risk evaluation plays a significant role for financial institutions. The binary logistic regression result in section four shows that credit default can be affected by home ownership, loan intent, loan grade, personal income, loan size, and other factors. The factors impacting credit default in this work have strong similarities with the factors of the qualitative model of default risk evaluation, in which the evaluation of the creditworthiness of the borrowers focuses on four main fields: reputation, leverage, volatility of earnings, and collateral. In more detail, the character (purpose), capacity, cash, collateral, conditions (e.g., the occupation of the borrowers), and control of the creditor are analyzed [12]. However, there are several limitations to the logistic regression model. Firstly, the parameter estimates are unstable when there is a considerable separation between the different classes of the dependent variable. Secondly, generative models are more accurate when the independent variables are normally distributed in each class within a small sample size [13]. Moreover, when evaluating credit risk, other factors other than borrower-specific factors should also be considered. For example, different industries perform differently in the distinct business cycle. In recession periods, the non-durable goods industry is more profitable than the durable goods sector [12]. Therefore, employees in the durable goods sector have a higher probability of default. In conclusion, to predict credit risk, financial institutions can put more focus on the significant factors, while taking the other factors such as the business cycle into account.

References

1. Divino, J.A., Lima, E.S., Orrillo, J.: Interest rates and default in unsecured loan markets. Quant. Finan. **13**(12), 1925–1934 (2013). https://doi.org/10.1080/14697688.2012.738932
2. Murphy, C.B.: Debt-to-income (DTI) ratio: What's good and how to calculate it. Investopedia (2023). Accessed 17 Feb 2023. https://www.investopedia.com/terms/d/dti.asp
3. Rohde, J.: How to Determine The Rent to Income Ratio Required for Tenants. Stessa (2021). https://www.stessa.com/blog/rent-to-income-ratio/
4. Totty, M.: Lending to Startups: Not as Risky as You'd Think. UCLA Anderson Review (2018). https://anderson-review.ucla.edu/venture-debt/
5. Armstrong, B.: About Loan Grading (2019). https://blog.groundfloor.com/groundfloorblog/about-loan-grading
6. Dore, K.C.: These are the 10 states where renters are most behind on payments — and high-cost California didn't make the list. CNBC (2022). https://www.cnbc.com/2022/10/07/renters-are-most-behind-on-payments-in-these-states.html
7. Wong, J., Fung, L., Fong, T., Sze, A.: Residential mortgage default risk and the loan-tovalue ratio (2005). https://www.hkma.gov.hk/media/eng/publication-and-research/quarterly-bulletin/qb200412/fa3.pdf
8. Yannelis, A.L.A.C.: Most students with large loan balances aren't defaulting. They just aren't reducing their debt. Brookings (2022). https://www.brookings.edu/research/most-students-with-large-loan-balances-arent-defaulting-they-just-arent-reducing-their-debt/
9. Shrestha, N.: Factor Analysis as a Tool for Survey Analysis (2021). http://pubs.sciepub.com/ajams/9/1/2/
10. Birmingham City University. Advice on Exploratory Factor Analysis (2014)
11. Ledesma, R.D., Valero-Mora, P., Macbeth, G.: The Scree test and the number of factors: a dynamic graphics approach. Spanish J. Psychol. **18**, E11–E11 (2015). https://doi.org/10.1017/sjp.2015.13
12. Saunders, A., Cornett, M.M.: Chapter 10 Credit risk I: individual loan risk. in Financial Institutions Management: A risk management approach. New York, NY: McGraw-Hill Education (2014)
13. James, G., et al.: Classification in An Introduction to Statistical Learning: With Applications in R. Springer, Boston (2022)

An Empirical Analysis of the Causal Relationship Between Equity Incentives and Idiosyncratic Volatility in Chinese A-Share Listed Companies

Zhaoxuan Gan[✉]

School of Management, Zhejiang University, Hangzhou 310058, China
3200105821@zju.edu.cn

Abstract. In recent years, the relationship between equity incentives (EI) and idiosyncratic volatility (IV) has become an increasingly important topic in corporate finance research. By creating a measure of EI using the entropy approach and researching the link between EI and IV in Chinese A-share listed corporations from 2016 to 2019, this study adds to the body of literature. The regression analysis results show that EI are positively correlated with IV, suggesting that EI may increase company-specific risk. This finding adds to the "IV puzzle" by providing evidence of a potential driver of non-systematic risk. The use of the entropy method to construct a measure of EI is another innovation of this study. This method provides a comprehensive measure of EI that considers both the size and structure of EI, which is more accurate than traditional measures. The empirical analysis also controls for other potential factors that may influence IV, such as firm size, leverage, and profitability. Overall, this study provides empirical evidence of the relationship between EI and IV, which has important implications for corporate governance and risk management. The results suggest that managers should carefully consider the potential risks associated with EI when designing compensation schemes, and investors should pay attention to the potential impact of EI on company-specific risk.

Keywords: Idiosyncratic Volatility · Equity Incentives · Asset Pricing

1 Introduction

In financial asset pricing, the traditional theory holds that a stock's expected return is only influenced by systematic risk, and non-systematic risk can be diluted through diversified investment portfolios. However, as research has deepened, scholars have gradually discovered that the real stock market cannot achieve complete idealization. On the one hand, investors cannot be completely rational, and on the other hand, there is some deviation in the transmission of market information, which means that non-systematic risk cannot be well diversified. Therefore, scholars have started to use IV to study company-specific risk, hoping to control and measure non-systematic risk.

Based on the incomplete information capital market equilibrium model established by Merton, researchers have conducted numerous research on the connection between IV and expected returns [1]. Ang et al. found that high IV stocks in the US stock market had lower future returns on average, indicating a negative correlation between the two [2]. Fu proposed a positive correlation between IV and stock expected returns [3]. These opposing viewpoints have long been debated in the academic community and are known as the "mystery of idiosyncratic volatility." In addition, scholars have also conducted numerous studies on the estimation models, methods, and influencing factors of IV. Investor preferences, company information disclosure levels, extreme downside risks, and management rights can all affect changes in IV [4]. With the deepening of research, the measurement of IV is becoming more and more accurate. However, there is still a lot of research space to explore the factors that affect IV.

Meanwhile, as a widely adopted compensation incentive by companies since the 21st century, EI motivate managers or employees to create financial benefits for the company, improve its performance, and increase shareholder value by allocating company stocks or equity to them. The role of EI in corporate management is also a hotly debated topic in academia. There are currently two main arguments. On one hand, Jensen & Meckling believe that implementing EI has the power to tie managers' and shareholders' interests by making them share the distribution of surplus wealth and bear the costs of agency, which can encourage managers to improve company performance [3]. Long-term EI can also effectively alleviate the problem of managers' short-term vision [5]. EI can also play an important role in attracting and retaining talent for the company. Lazear pointed out that EI can help companies attract better management teams, which can help companies make better strategic decisions, improve performance, and develop potential [6]. Research by Zong et al. shows that EI play a crucial role in reducing the frequency of managerial turnover, stabilizing management teams, and helping companies develop stably, thereby strengthening investor confidence [7]. In addition, EI have a positive impact on improving company cash flow, promoting innovation output, and can serve as a positive signal to the market, conveying that the corporation has good operating conditions and development prospects [8–10].

On the other hand, scholars such as Randall argue that the defects of equity incentive systems and market imperfections can easily lead to managers' opportunistic behavior, which reduces enterprise value [11]. Li also pointed out that managers may cause negative effects on company performance by abusing excessive control rights due to their high stock ownership, which may harm the interests of other investors [12].

However, although the respective studies on IV and EI have a long history, no research has directly established the relationship between the two, and analyzed its impact on IV from the perspective of EI. But in fact, the impact of EI on IV is worth discussing through its impact on investor expectations, market information transmission, company performance and many other aspects. The establishment of the connection between the two is theoretically transmissible and practically reliable. Therefore, this paper intends to describe the company's EI and other factors, examine their impact on IV, and reveal the inextricable connection behind the two to explore the theoretical mechanism and transmission path of EI on IV. Based on this, this paper proposes Hypothesis 1, which is that the degree of EI is positively correlated with IV.

2 Methodology

2.1 Data Sources and Sample Selection

Chinese A-share listed corporations from 2015 to 2019 are used as the research sample in this paper. To avoid extreme values affecting the accuracy of statistical results, this paper excludes ST (including ST*) listed companies, companies that lacked index data during the study period, financial listed companies. And companies with abnormal financial indicators during the sample period. After the screening, 14604 pieces of valid data were finally obtained, and the data came from the CSMAR database. Stata 16.0 software was used for data analysis and processing, and the data were standardized and winsorized.

2.2 Modelling

This research develops the following regression model to confirm the effect of EI on IV:

$$IVOL3_{i,t} = \beta_0 + \beta_1 EI_{i,t} + \sum \beta_j Control_{i,t} + \mu_i + \mu_t + \varepsilon_{i,t} \quad (1)$$

Among them, the dependent variable $IVOL3_{i,t}$ represents the IV of enterprise i in year t measured by the Fama-French three-factor model (FF3) method. $EI_{i,t}$ is the company's equity incentive degree, and $Control_{i,t}$ is a company-level characteristic variable that may affect the dependent variable, including company size, company age, asset-liability ratio, price-to-book ratio, return on assets, the balance of equity, marketing expenses. If the coefficient β_1 is significantly positive, it means that the company's equity incentive is positively related to IV, and hypothesis 1 is proved.

2.3 Variable Definitions

Explained Variable. This paper draws on the practice of Ang et al. to measure the IV by the standard deviation of the regression residual sequence of the FF3 [13]. On this basis, referring to the practice of Li et al., through the Fama-French five-factor model (FF5), the IV is measured more accurately, and the robustness test is carried out [13, 14]. Equations (2) and (3) represent the daily data to estimate the FF3 and FF5.

$$R_{i,m,t} = \alpha_{i,m} + \beta_{i,m} MKT_{m,t} + \gamma_{i,m} SMB_{m,t} + \delta_{i,m} HML_{m,t} + \varepsilon_{i,m,t} \quad (2)$$

$$R_{i,m,t} = \alpha_{i,m} + \beta_{i,m} MKT_{m,t} + \gamma_{i,m} SMB_{m,t} + \delta_{i,m} HML_{m,t} + \theta_{i,m} RMW_{m,t} + \rho_{i,m} CMA_{m,t} + \varepsilon_{i,m,t} \quad (3)$$

where $R_{i,m,t}$ is expressed as the excess rate of return of stock i on day m, month t, which is the daily actual rate of return minus the daily risk-free rate of return. $MKT_{m,t}$, $SMB_{m,t}$, $HML_{m,t}$, $RMW_{m,t}$, $CMA_{m,t}$ respectively is the market risk premium factor, the market value factor, the book-to-market value ratio factor, the profitability factor, and the Investment model factor on day t of month m. $\beta_{i,m}$, $\gamma_{i,m}$, $\delta_{i,m}$, $\theta_{i,m}$, $\rho_{i,m}$ are the risk factors corresponding to each factor. $\varepsilon_{i,m,t}$ is the disturbance item of stock i on day t of month m. Further, it uses Eqs. (4) and (5) to mensisize the regression residual standard deviation of Eqs. (2) to (3) to obtain the measurement index of IV:

$$IVOL3_{i,m} = \sqrt{N_{i,m} Std^2(\varepsilon_{i,m,t})} \quad (4)$$

$$IVOL5_{i,m} = \sqrt{N_{i,m}Std^2(\varepsilon_{i,m,t})} \tag{5}$$

where $Std^2(\varepsilon_{i,m,t})$ represents the variance of the regression residual of stock i on day t of month m, and $N_{i,m}$ is the number of trading days of stock i in month m. Further, this paper calculates the annual value of IV by summing the calculated monthly variance data on a monthly basis.

Explanatory Variables. This paper uses the entropy approach to measure the degree of corporate EI by using the entropy approach to calculate the comprehensive index of the weight of the four dimensions of equity incentive breadth, depth, and core technical personnel and executives' EI [15]. The weights are calculated by the entropy method (see Table 1). Among the four dimensions of EI, executive EI are the highest (weight is 0.4506), followed by the breadth of EI (weight is 0.2537), and the third is the core technical personnel EI (0.1573), and finally the equity incentive depth (0.1384).

Table 1. Weights of evaluation indicators obtained by entropy method.

Variable Index	REI	DEI	CTEI	EEI
Weights	0.253697224	0.138428131	0.157284253	0.450590391

Control Variables. This paper refers to the practice of Chai et al., and other scholars, and selects enterprise size, enterprise age, profitability, financial leverage, price-to-book ratio, the top ten shareholders' percentage of shares outstanding, and marketing expenses as control variables [16]. The selection and measurement of each variable are shown in Table 2.

Table 2. Variables definition.

Variable Type	Variable Name	Symbol	Variable Definitions
Dependent Variable	Idiosyncratic Volatility	IVOL3	Idiosyncratic Volatility based on Fama-French three-factor model
Independent Variable (EI)	Breadth of Equity Incentives	REI	The number of motivated employees (Pnumber)/total number of employees
	Depth of Equity Incentive	DEI	granted equity incentive rights (Grtstkta) / total share capital

(*continued*)

Table 2. (*continued*)

Variable Type	Variable Name	Symbol	Variable Definitions
	Depth of Equity Incentive	DEI	granted equity incentive rights (Grtstkta) / total share capital
	Executive Equity Incentives	EEI	The number of equity incentives granted to executives (Exustkta) / total share capital
Control Variables	Enterprise Size	SIZE	the natural logarithm of total assets
	Enterprise Age	AGE	Ln(the establishment year + 1)
	Profitability	ROA	return on corporate assets
	Financial Leverage	LEV	assets and liabilities
	Price-to-book Ratio	PB	price per share/net assets per share
	Equity Checks and Balances	EB	The shareholding ratio of the top ten shareholders
	Marketing Costs	MS	sales expenses/business operating income

3 Empirical Results

3.1 Summary Statistics

According to Table 3, the variables' descriptive statistics include Mean, Median, Std. Dev, Min. Value, and Max. Value, etc. IV situation: the Avg. Value is 4.19, the Std. Dev is 1.404, the Min. Value is 1.33, and the Max. Value is 7.851, which is at a relatively high level overall. EI: The Avg. Value of EI is 0.084, the Std. Dev is 0.254, the Min. Value is 0, and the Max. Value is 1.564, indicating that the current A-share companies have a relatively large degree of differentiation in implementing EI.

Table 3. Descriptive statistics.

variable	mean	sd	p50	min	max	cv	N
EI	0.0840	0.254	0	0	1.564	3.046	14658
SIZE	22.23	1.307	22.06	19.89	26.24	0.0590	14658

(*continued*)

Table 3. (*continued*)

variable	mean	sd	p50	min	max	cv	N
AGE	7.605	0.00400	7.606	7.597	7.611	0.00100	14658
LEV	0.414	0.204	0.401	0.0590	0.908	0.493	14658
PB	3.947	3.623	2.873	0.550	24.18	0.918	14658
ROA	0.0370	0.0680	0.0380	−0.329	0.192	1.843	14658
EB	59.65	14.83	60.89	24.97	90.47	0.249	14652
MS	0.0770	0.0910	0.0460	0	0.482	1.175	14658
IVOL3	4.190	1.404	4.074	1.330	7.851	0.335	14604

By examining the correlation coefficients between the variables in Table 4, it is found that IV is positively correlated with the degree of EI, and the correlation coefficient is 0.028, which preliminarily verifies the positive correlation between the two. At the same time, except for the asset-liability ratio and enterprise size, the correlation coefficients between different variables are all less than 0.5, which is reasonable to believe that the correlation between variables is weak, so it can be considered that almost no multicollinearity exists between the variables.

Table 4. Pairwise correlations.

Var	IVOL3	EI	SIZE	AGE	LEV	PB	ROA	EB	MS
IVOL3	1.000								
EI	0.028	1.000							
SIZE	−0.268	−0.031	1.000						
AGE	0.156	0.107	−0.402	1.000					
LEV	−0.051	0.012	0.525	−0.354	1.000				
PB	0.311	−0.039	−0.450	0.110	−0.063	1.000			
ROA	−0.032	0.004	−0.019	0.179	−0.360	0.044	1.000		
EB	0.031	−0.048	0.101	0.342	−0.100	0.008	0.249	1.000	
MS	0.006	0.029	−0.177	0.115	−0.239	0.088	0.062	0.030	1

3.2 Regression Results

The OLS regression's findings, which measures EI and IV, are shown in Table 5. Column 1 reports the results without the control variable and column 2 reports the result with the control variable included. According to the regression results, the EI coefficient is significant at the 1% level with a value of 0.159. That is to say, IV and EI are significantly positively correlated. That is, The larger the level of EI, the higher the stock's IV, thus verifying Hypothesis 1.

Table 5. Regression results.

	IVOL3	IVOL3
EI	0.215***	0.159***
	(5.22)	(4.06)
SIZE		−0.229***
		(−19.62)
AGE		29.22***
		(8.95)
LEV		0.625***
		(9.06)
PB		0.0536***
		(15.33)
ROA		−0.322*
		(−1.96)
EB		0.00624***
		(8.07)
MS		−0.711***
		(−6.19)
Cons	4.888***	−212.9***
	(75.57)	(−8.55)
Year fixed effects	Yes	Yes
Industry fixed effects	Yes	Yes
N	14604	14604
R-squared	0.205	0.293

3.3 Robustness Check

Based on the fact that the correlation coefficient between the asset-liability ratio and the size of the enterprise is greater than 0.5 in the previous correlation analysis, a multicollinearity test is carried out on the independent variables. Table 6 displays the test results. Each variable's VIF value is less than 5, hence multicollinearity is not present.

The way to replace the measure of the explained variable. Learn from the practice of Li Zhibing et al., and use the FF5 [14] to measure the IV more accurately, so as to conduct a robustness test, the regression results are shown in Table 7. Columns (3, 4) are

Table 6. VIF inspection.

Variable	VIF	1/VIF
SIZE	2.340	0.428
LEV	1.870	0.534
AGE	1.490	0.669
PB	1.440	0.692
EB	1.290	0.772
ROA	1.280	0.779
IVOL3	1.150	0.869
MS	1.070	0.934
Mean VIF		1.490

the regression results of using the FF5 to measure IV. The EI coefficient of EI is 0.147, which is significant at the 1% level. It is proved that EI and IV are still significantly positively correlated, consistent with the above conclusions, and the results are robust.

Table 7. Robustness test.

	IVOL3	IVOL3	IVOL5	IVOL5
EI	0.215***	0.159***	0.199***	0.147***
	(5.22)	(4.06)	(5.24)	(4.06)
SIZE		−0.229***		−0.220***
		(−19.62)		(−20.37)
AGE		29.22***		26.14***
		(8.95)		(8.68)
LEV		0.625***		0.602***
		(9.06)		(9.46)
PB		0.0536***		0.0476***
		(15.33)		(14.78)
ROA		−0.322*		−0.305**
		(−1.96)		(−2.01)

(*continued*)

Table 7. (continued)

	IVOL3	IVOL3	IVOL5	IVOL5
EB		0.00624***		0.00572***
		(8.07)		(8.02)
MS		−0.711***		−0.630***
		(−6.19)		(−5.95)
Cons	4.888***	−212.9***	4.453***	−190.0***
	(75.57)	(−8.55)	(74.60)	(−8.27)
Year fixed effects	Yes	Yes	Yes	Yes
Industry fixed effects	Yes	Yes	Yes	Yes
N	14604	14604	14604	14604
R-squared	0.205	0.293	0.195	0.285

4 Conclusion

Based on previous studies, this paper has carried out an effective literature review and induction, sorting out and summarizing relevant theories and research results on EI and IV at home and abroad. Based on these results, based on the data of China's A-share market, after a reasonable theoretical derivation and mechanism analysis, an empirical analysis is made on the relationship between EI and IV. This paper selects the data of China's A-share listed corporations from 2015 to 2019 as a sample, with a period of 5 years, and uses EI as explanatory variables to explain the changes in IV. After investigation, the hypothetical conjecture is verified, thus confirming that there is a positive correlation between EI and IV. This is explained from the following path. Affected by the EI plan, executive performance, corporate financial indicators, and investor information will all change accordingly. At the same time, due to information asymmetry, market noise increases and IV increases. This study builds a bridge between EI and IV, further improves the influencing factors of IV, provides new considerations for exploring the mystery of IV, and helps to further explore the measurement of IV.

At the same time, there are still some deficiencies and shortcomings in this paper. For example, in the measurement of IV, this paper uses the FF3 and the FF5 to describe IV. Reliability. However, with the deepening of research, the limitations of these early theories are gradually revealed. Further research in the future can consider using more cutting-edge theoretical models to test the conclusions, and appropriately increase the control variables in the model to achieve more rigorous and perfect purpose. At the same time, this article discusses the transmission mechanism of the impact of EI on IV. In the future, it can be further refined and explored on this basis, with in-depth analysis and inspection of the transmission path, and further improvement and enrichment of conclusions.

References

1. Merton, R.C.: A simple model of capital market equilibrium with incomplete information. J. Finan. **42**(3), 483–510 (1987)
2. Ang, A., Hodrick, R.J., Xing, Y., Zhang, X.: The cross-section of volatility and expected returns. J. Finan. **61**(1), 259–299 (2006)
3. Fu, F.: Idiosyncratic risk and the cross-section of expected stock returns. J. Financ. Econ. **91**(1), 24–37 (2009)
4. Lou, X.Y.: The impact of managerial power on the idiosyncratic volatility of stocks. Zhejiang University (2022)
5. Murphy, K., Zimmerman, J.L.: Financial performance surrounding CEO turnover. J. Account. Econ. **16**(1–3), 273–315 (1993)
6. Lazear, E. P.: Output-Based Pay: Incentives or Sorting? Social Science Research Network (1999)
7. Zong, W.L., Wang, Y.T., Wei, Z.: Can equity incentives retain executives? Empirical evidence from the Chinese securities market. Account. Res. **9**, 58–63, 97 (2013)
8. Fazzari, S.M., Petersen, B.C., Hubbard, R.G.: financing constraints and corporate investment. Brookings Papers Econ. Activity **1**, 141 (1988)
9. Wang, S.X., Fang, H.Y., Rong, Z.: Does stock option incentives promote corporate innovation? Evidence from patent output of listed companies in China. Finan. Res. **3**, 176–191 (2017)
10. Hu, G.Q., Gai, D.: Executive stock option incentives and bank lending decisions: empirical evidence from China's private listed companies. Account. Res. **4**, 58–65, 96 (2014)
11. Morck, R., Shleifer, A., Vishny, R.W. management ownership and market valuation: an empirical analysis. Soc. Sci. Res. Netw. (1998)
12. Li, X.J.: An empirical study on the impact of equity incentive intensity on the performance of listed companies. J. Soc. Sci. Hunan Normal Univ. **5**, 126–132 (2017)
13. Fama, E.F., MacBeth, J.D.: Risk, return, and equilibrium: empirical tests. J. Polit. Econ. **81**(3), 607–636 (1973)
14. Li, Z.B., Yang, G.Y., Feng, Y.C., Jing, L.: Empirical testing of the Fama-French five-factor model in the Chinese stock market. Finan. Res. **06**, 191–206 (2017)
15. Wu, Y.T.: The impact of equity incentives on financial performance from the perspective of innovation investment intermediation: a comparative study of technology-based and non-technology-based enterprises. Accoun. Finan. Commun. **14**, 39–43 (2021)
16. Chai, X., Hu, L.S.: Equity incentives, international R&D cooperation, and innovation performance: empirical evidence from a-share listed companies. J. Hubei Univ. Econ. (Human. Soc. Sci.) **20**(02), 71–75 (2023)

An Empirical Analysis of the Relationship Between Chinese GDP and Deposit Savings

Yichuan Bai(✉)

School of Business, Central University of Finance and Economics, Beijing 100081, China
2020311296@email.cufe.edu.cn

Abstract. The phenomenon of a high savings rate in China has been receiving much attention from the academic and policy communities. The research on the causes of high savings rates has become increasingly diversified, including studies on the impact of GDP on savings. In this paper, we use the econometric analysis method and Eviews software to analyze the data of total savings and Gross Domestic Product (GDP) in China from 1952 to 2021. It establishes a simple linear regression model, which indicates the existence of heteroscedasticity and autocorrelation. To eliminate heteroscedasticity, it takes the logarithm of both sides of the equation and uses the Generalized Method of Moments (GMM) to eliminate autocorrelation, which results in an ideal GMM regression model. Our research shows that the value of GDP in China does not affect the total savings, but the growth rate of GDP is significantly positively correlated with the growth rate of total savings. Based on these findings, we propose some relevant policy recommendations.

Keywords: GDP · Savings · Correlation · Regression Model

1 Introduction

The relationship between savings and GDP has been studied in the economic growth literature, but a consensus has not been reached. Empirical analyses have also produced varying results. Mehrara, Musai, and Nasibparast have examined the causal relationship between Iran's domestic savings and GDP using annual data from 1970 to 2008 and found that higher economic growth leads to increased savings [1]. Other research analyzing data from 123 countries has found that economic growth precedes an increase in the savings rate [2]. In Bangladesh, a Granger causality test showed bidirectional causality between savings and economic growth [3]. However, Agrawal and Sahoo have suggested that there is a positive correlation between savings and GDP growth in third-world countries, where higher GDP growth rates lead to increased savings [4].

The phenomenon of the coexistence of high savings and high economic growth in the process of Chinese economic development has attracted wide attention from academia and policy circles. However, existing economic growth theories have not reached a unified understanding of the relationship between savings and GDP. As a result, many studies have used different methods and data to arrive at different empirical analysis results. Wei have used data from 1992 to 2016 and established an empirical regression model based on linear least squares method, pointing out that the balance of savings of urban and rural residents is the main driver of GDP growth in China [5]. However, Xi, Chen, and Lei have found that the variation in actual GDP growth rate is the main reason for changes in savings rate, and this relationship exists universally across 28 provinces in China without significant differences between individuals. After excluding two resource-based provinces, the savings rate is not a determining factor for actual GDP growth rate [6]. In addition, Liu and Guo have used Granger causality tests to find that the savings rate in China has little effect on economic development at the moment, but there is a significant impact of actual GDP level on savings increment, and the rate of savings and that of GDP growth are not causally related. [7]. Bonham and Wieme have also found through empirical analysis that income growth has always been the leading factor behind the sharp rise in China's savings rate [8]. Furthermore, Fang and Fu have argued that the percentage of Chinese citizens who save and the pace of GDP growth are not positively correlated, and the same direction of variation should be in terms of the amount of savings held by residents. Moreover, to ensure that savings growth and economic expansion are positively correlated, some special conditions must be met, such as continuous increase in residents' income and the ability to smoothly transform savings into investment [9]. Therefore, despite the various research results on the relationship between savings and GDP, further exploration is still needed.

Policymakers and academics are both interested in how high savings and rapid economic growth coexist in China's economic growth process. However, there is no consensus among existing economic growth theories on the relationship between savings and GDP. As a result, numerous studies have adopted different methods and data, leading to varying empirical analysis results. Wei has used data from 1992 to 2016 and established an empirical regression model based on the linear least squares method, demonstrating that the balance of savings of urban and rural residents is the primary driver of China's GDP growth [5]. Conversely, Xi, Chen and Lei have found that the variance in the real GDP growth rate is the main cause of changes in the savings rate, which is a universal relationship across all 28 provinces in China without significant differences among individuals. After excluding two resource-based provinces, the savings rate was not found to be a determinant of actual GDP growth rate [6]. In addition, Liu and Guo have employed Granger causality tests, finding that China's economic growth isn't significantly affected by the savings rate at present. Nevertheless, there is a significant impact of the actual GDP level on savings increment, and no causal relationship exists between the savings rate and GDP growth rate [7]. Bonham and Wiemer have used empirical analysis to reveal that income growth has always been the leading factor behind the sharp rise in China's savings rate [8]. Further, Fang and Fu argue that Chinese residents' savings rate and GDP growth rate do not correlate well, and the amount of savings held by residents should vary in the same direction. Moreover, to ensure a positive correlation between savings and economic growth, some special conditions must be met, such as continuous increases in residents' income and the ability to transform savings into investment smoothly [9]. As such, despite various research results on the relationship between savings and GDP, further exploration is necessary.

This study strives to investigate the connection between Chinese savings and GDP growth. Initially, a simple linear regression model was established by analyzing the absolute indicators of total savings and GDP to explore the relationship between the two. However, through empirical analysis, it was found that the model had many shortcomings and could not accurately describe the relationship between savings and GDP growth. Therefore, this paper made a series of modifications to the model, improving it from multiple angles, and ultimately found that GDP growth could better explain the changes in savings growth. Based on this, this paper proposes relevant suggestions to help promote the coordinated development of China's macroeconomy.

2 Methodology

2.1 Data Selection

To ensure the accuracy and reliability of the data, all savings data used in this study were obtained from the National Statistical Yearbook, while all GDP data were obtained from the National Bureau of Statistics. Given that China is currently undergoing significant changes, and the impact of the 2022 Russia-Ukraine conflict and changes in China's epidemic prevention and control policies on the Chinese economy is not yet fully understood, this study did not include 2022 data in the sample. This study selected the total savings and GDP data from 1952 to 2021 in China as the research sample.

2.2 Modelling

This study conducted data analysis and modeling using Eviews econometric software. The variable "savings in China" studied in this paper is referred to as "Y" and is measured in units of RMB 100 million. Based on the scatter plot and economic knowledge analysis, there exists a positive correlation between total savings deposits and GDP. To further investigate the relationship between the two, this study established a linear regression model and conducted model testing. However, the results showed that the model had problems of heteroscedasticity and autocorrelation. Therefore, this study used the method of taking the logarithm of both sides to eliminate heteroscedasticity and used the generalized difference-in-difference method to eliminate autocorrelation, resulting in a second-order generalized difference-in-difference linear regression model.

2.3 Testing

In this study, the goodness of fit and significance of the simple linear regression model was tested first. Through graphical analysis, it was determined that the model exhibited heteroscedasticity, which was further verified using the White test. In addition, the LM test based on the AIC criterion was employed to investigate the presence of second-order autocorrelation in the model. Therefore, a series of modifications were made to the model, and the presence of heteroscedasticity and autocorrelation was reexamined.

Furthermore, the study took the implementation of China's reform and opening-up policy in December 1978 as an important node and divided the data into two groups: the period from 1952 to 1978 and the period from 1979 to 2021. From a temporal perspective, stability tests were conducted on the model. While performing regression according to the modified model, the goodness of fit, significance, and presence of heteroscedasticity and autocorrelation were also tested by group to investigate whether the major change of reform and opening-up had an impact on the stability of the model.

3 Empirical Results

3.1 One-Dimensional Linear Regression Model

In addition to GDP, Y may be affected by other variables and random factors. The influence of other variables and random factors is attributed to the random variable μ, and a univariate linear regression model is established.

$$Y = a + b \cdot gdp + \mu \tag{1}$$

The obtained results are displayed in Table 1, as follows.

Table 1. One-dimensional linear regression results.

Variable	Coefficient	Std. Error	t-Statistic	Prob.
Y	−9591.291	3021.208	−3.174655	0.0023
GDP	0.825265	0.009020	91.49146	0.0000

The estimated coefficient of GDP is 0.82, indicating that for every one hundred million yuan increase in GDP, the savings in China will increase by 82 million yuan. The constant term is negative, indicating the existence of autonomous savings behavior that is not influenced by GDP. The positive relationship between Y and GDP is consistent with economic theory.

3.2 Model Correction

This study established a univariate linear regression model by taking the logarithm of both Y and GDP to eliminate heteroscedasticity.

$$lnY = a + blnGDP + \mu \tag{2}$$

Following is a representation of the findings in Table 2.

The econometric interpretation of this model is that, holding other variables constant, an increase of 1% in China's real GDP is associated with an average increase of 1.54% in its corresponding savings. As the economy develops, the savings also increases accordingly. The model has been corrected for heteroscedasticity, which enables a more accurate representation of the relationship between the two variables.

Table 2. OLS estimation after taking the same logarithm on both sides.

Variable	Coefficient	Std. Error	t-Statistic	Prob.
lnY	−7.125863	0.211223	−33.73614	0.0000
lnGDP	1.544663	0.020846	74.09719	0.0000

3.3 Second-Order Generalized Difference Regression Model

This paper uses the Eviews software to establish a GMM linear regression model to eliminate the impact of autocorrelation on the model. Firstly, the autocorrelation coefficient is estimated, and the Generalized Difference Method (GDM) is used to eliminate the autocorrelation, resulting in autocorrelation-free data. The residual sequence is then fitted to obtain the second-order autocorrelation coefficient, with the following results (in Table 3).

Table 3. Second-order autoregressive results.

Variable	Coefficient	Std. Error	t-Statistic	Prob.
C	−0.210358	0.041722	−5.041903	0.0000
GDLNGDP	1.283217	0.073053	17.56554	0.0000

The generalized difference transformation was applied to lnY and lnGDP, and the following equations were obtained, as follows.

$$gdlnY_t = lnY_t - 1.37 lnY_{t-1} + 0.42 lnY_{t-2} \qquad (3)$$

$$gdlnGDP_t = lnGDP_t - 1.37 lnGDP_{t-1} + 0.42 lnGDP_{t-2} \qquad (4)$$

Based on Eqs. (3) and (4), a generalized difference linear regression model can be constructed and the outcomes are displayed in Table 4.

Table 4. Generalized differential linear model regression results.

Variable	Coefficient	Std. Error	t-Statistic	Prob
C	−0.210358	0.041722	−5.041903	0.0000
GDLNGDP	1.283217	0.073053	17.56554	0.0000

Transforming the variables, we obtain the generalized least squares estimates of the original model as follows.

$$lnY = -4.2 + 1.28 lnGDP \qquad (5)$$

The regression model, processed by the Generalized Difference Method, shows that when China's GDP increases by 1%, the average increase in China's savings is 1.28%. This model has corrected autocorrelation and heteroscedasticity, providing a more accurate description of the relationship between China's savings deposits and GDP.

4 Testing Results

4.1 Goodness-Of-Fit and Significance Tests

In this study, we evaluated the goodness of fit of our model using R-squared and tested its significance using t-tests and F-tests.

Table 5. Summary of regression models.

	Model(1)	Model(2)	Model(5)
R-squared	0.991942	0.987766	0.823788
Adjusted R-squared	0.991823	0.987586	0.821118
S.E. of regression	21920.61	0.417263	0.085860
Prob(F-statistic)	0.000000	0.000000	0.000000

As Table 5 shown, the R2 value is 0.9919, and the adjusted R2 is 0.9918, indicating a very small difference between them. This suggests that the regression equation can explain 99% of the variation in the savings amount due to changes in GDP. Performing an F-test on model (1), The critical value for F distribution is F0.05 (1,70) = 3.978. Since the calculated F-statistic is 8370.69, which is greater than 3.978, we can conclude that the overall regression equation is significant, indicating a significant correlation between GDP and savings.

The model (1) is also subjected to a t-test. The critical value for t distribution with 68 degrees of freedom (70–2) is t0.025(68) = 1.995. From Fig. 1, we obtain the t-statistics for the regression coefficients as ta = −3.17 < −1.995, tb = 91.49 > 1.995. Therefore, we can conclude that the regression coefficients are significantly different from zero, indicating a significant effect of GDP on the savings amount and the inclusion of a constant term in the regression model. Similarly, it concludes that the sample regression lines of models (2) and (5) have a very high degree of fit to the sample data, and the regression coefficients are significantly non-zero with a constant term included in the regression models.

4.2 Heteroskedasticity Test

After conducting regression analysis using Eviews, we obtained a residual plot. As shown in the plot, the simulated results are quite close to the actual data, and most of the residual values are distributed within one standard deviation from zero, indicating a good fit for the model. However, the residual plot appears to show some kind of curvilinear shape, which suggests the need for further heteroscedasticity testing to determine the reliability of the model.

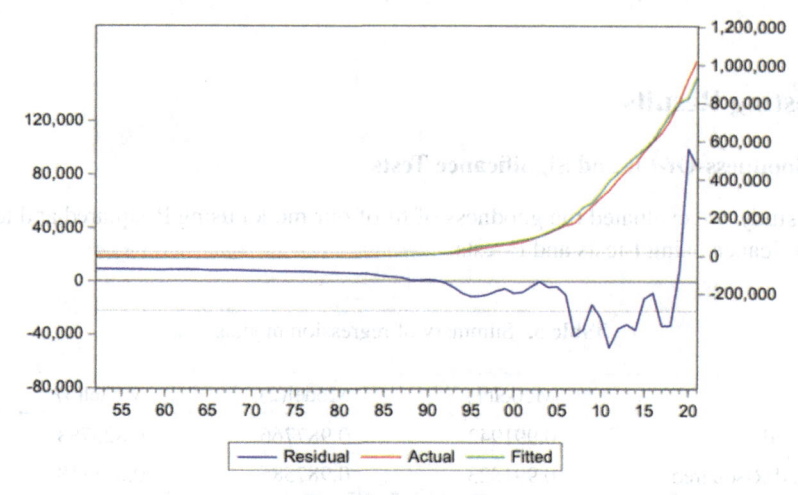

Fig. 1. Residual plot.

After calculating the residuals ei (i = 1, 2, 3,...54) using Eviews, scatter plots were generated with Y as the vertical axis and GDP as the horizontal axis, and with ei as the vertical axis and GDP as the horizontal axis, as shown in Fig. 2 and Fig. 3, respectively.

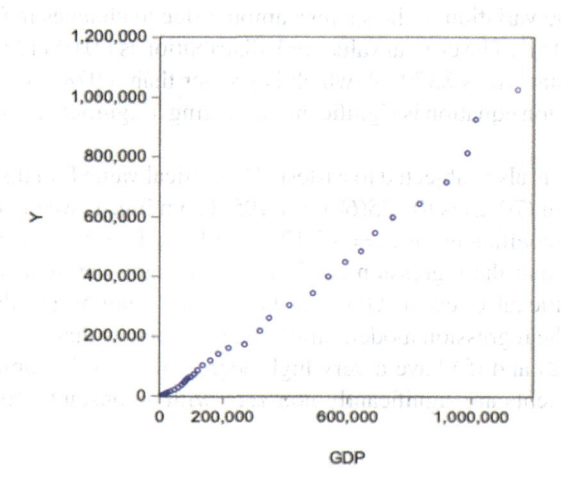

Fig. 2. Scatter plot with GDP as the horizontal axis and Y as the vertical axis.

Figure 2 illustrates how the dispersion of Y steadily rises as GDP grows. Figure 3 indicates that the dispersion of the residual term also increases with the increase of GDP.

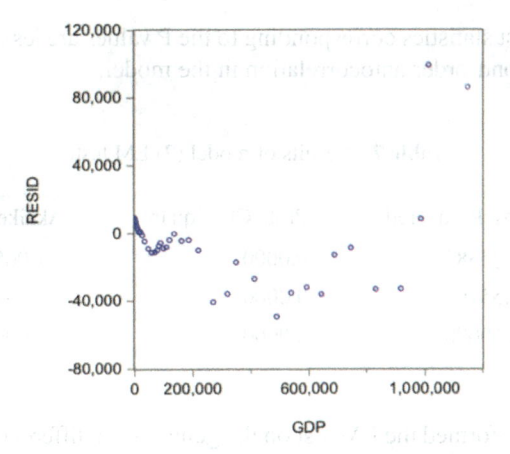

Fig. 3. Scatter plot with ei as the vertical axis and GDP as the horizontal axis.

Combining the two figures, it can be inferred that there exists heteroskedasticity in the error term.

The White test is a classic method for heteroskedasticity testing, which constructs a chi-square statistic based on an auxiliary regression equation to conduct a hypothesis test.

Table 6. White test results on model (2).

	Model(1)	Model(2)	Model(5)
Obs*R-squared	38.09483	2.659721	2.204146
Prob. Chi-Square(2)	0.0000	0.2645	0.3322

As Table 6 shown, the P-value corresponding to TR^2 was found to be 0, rejecting the null hypothesis and indicating the presence of heteroskedasticity in Model (1). A White test was also performed on the logarithmically transformed Model (2), which was modified by taking the logarithm of both sides of the equation. According to the results, the heteroskedasticity problem has been successfully eliminated by the logarithmic transformation. Similarly, Model (5) does not exhibit heteroskedasticity.

4.3 Autocorrelation Test

LM test is one of the testing methods based on generalized linear models. The principle of this test method is to construct a test statistic based on the sum of squared residuals, and then judge whether there is autocorrelation based on the AIC criterion. In order to test whether there is autocorrelation in model (2) with logarithmic correction, this study conducted LM test and determined the order of autocorrelation based on the AIC criterion. When the order of autocorrelation is 2, the AIC value is smallest (see Table 7).

Furthermore, the test statistics corresponding to the P values are less than 0.05, showing the presence of second-order autocorrelation in the model.

Table 7. Results of model (2) LM test.

	Obs*R-squared	Prob. Chi-Square	Akaike info criterion
Order of 1	62.25383	0.0000	−1.065400
Order of 2	62.55160	0.0000	−1.997880
Order of 3	62.60078	0.0000	−2.009500

Similarly, we performed the LM test on the generalized difference regression model (5) and obtained P-values for the chi-square statistic corresponding to TR^2 that were all greater than 0.05, indicating that this model does not exhibit autocorrelation (see Table 8).

Table 8. Results of model (5) LM test.

	Obs*R-squared	Prob. Chi-Square	Akaike info criterion
Order of 1	0.414538	0.5197	−2.019924
Order of 2	0.910664	0.6342	−1.997880
Order of 3	3.607730	0.3071	−2.009500

4.4 Stability Test

When conducting research on data spanning a long period of time, it is often necessary to conduct tests from a temporal perspective in order to better understand the stability and effectiveness of the model. In this study, the implementation of the reform and opening-up policy by China in December 1978 was taken as an important dividing point, and the data studied was divided into two groups according to time, one group from 1952 to 1978 and the other from 1979 to 2021. The stability of the model was tested from a temporal perspective. This grouping method can divide the time span of the research object into different time periods, thus better exploring the changes in different periods. The generalized difference regression model eliminates autocorrelation and heteroscedasticity and is the most effective model to truly reflect the situation of Y and GDP in the models involved in this study. Therefore, the generalized difference regression model for the two groups of data was directly tested.

The first group is the model established by data from 1952 to 1978. The results of second-order autoregression results and the generalized difference regression model are shown in Table 9 and Table 10, respectively.

Table 9. Second-order autoregression results for the first data set.

Variable	Coefficient	Std. Error	t-Statistic	Prob.
RES(−1)	1.117824	0.198521	5.630764	0.0000
RES(−2)	−0.321986	0.190529	−1.689958	0.1045

Table 10. Results of generalized difference regression for the first data set.

Variable	Coefficient	Std. Error	t-Statistic	Prob.
C	0.960821	0.074502	12.89656	0.0000
GDLNGDP	0.625560	0.081733	7.653668	0.0000

Similarly, for the model established by data from 1979 to 2021, the results of second-order autoregression results and the generalized difference regression model are shown in Table 11 and Table 12, respectively.

Table 11. Second-order autoregression results for the second data set.

Variable	Coefficient	Std. Error	t-Statistic	Prob.
RES(−1)	1.303864	0.143712	9.072731	0.0000
RES(−2)	−0.394654	0.129803	−3.040416	0.0042

Table 12. Results of generalized difference regression for the second data set.

Variable	Coefficient	Std. Error	t-Statistic	Prob.
C	−0.166240	0.074985	−2.216983	0.0325
GDLNGDP	1.110194	0.064532	17.20380	0.0000

Similarly, a series of tests are conducted to determine their stability. The results indicate that the sample regression lines of both models fit the data well; the overall regression equation is significant; the regression coefficient is significantly non-zero, and the regression model includes a constant term.

The White test (1952–1978) was conducted, the results indicate that the model does not suffer from heteroscedasticity. Similarly, the second-order LM test was performed, and result indicates that the model does not suffer from autocorrelation. Likewise, it was found that the data from 1979 to 2021 also does not suffer from heteroscedasticity or autocorrelation.

5 Discussion

The final and preferred model obtained in this study is as follows.

$$lnY = -4.2 + 1.28lnGDP \qquad (6)$$

When other variables are held constant, a 1% increase in China's GDP corresponds to an average increase of 1.28% in total savings. This suggests that the increase of real GDP influences total savings in a favorable manner, and the growth rate of savings exceeds that of GDP, which reflects the high marginal propensity to save among Chinese residents. From a macroeconomic perspective, this phenomenon may be due to the increase in people's income brought about by the growth of real GDP, and the increase in income may promote savings behavior. Some scholars point out that due to a combination of a declining share of the dependent population and rapid GDP development, China's national savings rate increased in the 2000s [10]. In addition, GDP growth also brings about an increase in investment opportunities, and people may choose to use their savings for investment in order to obtain higher returns. Therefore, the government should continue to support economic growth to create more employment and income growth opportunities and to promote people's savings behavior.

However, savings may be detrimental to the development of the economy. Excessive savings may lead to a shortage of investment opportunities, thereby suppressing economic growth. Therefore, the government should also take measures to encourage people to use their savings for investment and consumption, in order to promote economic growth. At the policy level, the government can take a series of measures to promote consumption and investment, such as reducing taxes, expanding the consumption sector, and improving the level of education, medical care, and social security. In addition, the government can use fiscal and monetary policies to stimulate economic growth, increase investment opportunities, and further promote the virtuous cycle between savings and economic growth.

6 Conclusion

This paper establishes an econometric model of the relationship between GDP and total savings using Eviews software. The results indicate that GDP cannot explain the changes in total savings well, but GDP growth can effectively explain the growth of total savings. Additionally, the model reflects that Chinese residents have a relatively high marginal propensity to save. However, this relationship is not absolute. This study is only based on data from China. In some cases, if a government's savings policy is too strict or excessively enforced, it may inhibit personal savings, resulting in a growth rate of total savings lower than that of GDP growth. Moreover, in some regions, such as developing countries, people may not want to save due to a lack of confidence, and even economic growth may not necessarily promote the growth of total savings. Therefore, when studying the relationship between savings and GDP, it is necessary to consider the impact of factors such as policy and culture on savings behavior.

This paper mainly focuses on the impact of GDP on total savings and finds that factors other than GDP growth also affect savings growth. The rise in China's national savings rate in the 2000s can be attributed to the combination of a decreasing proportion of the dependent population and a high GDP growth rate Empirical studies indicate that the national savings rate and the uncertainty of economic policy have a strong positive correlation, and there are apparent heterogeneity characteristics among countries with different income levels. Further research can explore other factors that may affect savings growth, such as policy environment, income level, social and cultural factors, etc. At the same time, it is feasible to carry out thorough analysis of the mechanism by which economic policy uncertainty affects the national savings rate and explore how policy uncertainty affects personal and corporate savings behavior.

References

1. Mehrara, M., Musai, M., Nasibparast, S.: The causality between savings and GDP in Iran. Int. J. Adv. Res. Eng. Appl. Sci. (2012)
2. Attanasio, O., Picci, L., Scorcu, A.E.: Saving, growth, and investment: a macroeconomic analysis using a panel of countries. Rev. Econ. Stat. **82**(2), 182–211 (2000)
3. Agrawal, P., Sahoo, P.: Savings and growth in Bangladesh. J. Developing Areas **42**(2), 89–110 (2009)
4. Saltz, I.S.: An examination of the causal relationship between savings and growth in the third world. J. Econ. Finan. **23**(1), 90–98 (1999)
5. Wei, G.L.: Analysis of the contribution rate of urban and rural residents' savings to GDP growth. Statistics and Decision **16**, 103–105 (2017)
6. Xi, J., Chen, K., Lei, Q.L.: Research on the relationship between high economic growth and high savings in China: granger causality test based on provincial panel data. Econ. Geogr. **05**, 143–148 (2016)
7. Liu, J.Q., Guo, Z.F.: Research on the relationship between the savings rate of Chinese residents and economic growth. China Soft Sci. **02** (2002)
8. Bonham, C., Wiemer, C.: Chinese saving dynamics: the impact of GDP growth and the dependent share. Oxford Econ. Pap. New Ser. **65**(1), 173–196 (2013)
9. Fang, S.J., Fu, W.L.: Analysis of the correlation between Chinese residents' savings and GDP growth. Forecasting **05**, 29–32 (2001)
10. Modigliani, F., Cao, S.: The Chinese saving puzzle and the life-cycle hypothesis. J. Econ. Lit. **42**(1), 145–170 (2004)

FinTech Promotes the Development of Green Finance

Heqing Huang[1(✉)] and Qijie Yang[2]

[1] School of Physics, Dalian University of Technology, Dalian 116024, Liaoning, China
1455808907@mail.dlut.edu.cn
[2] School of Civil Engineering, Changsha University of Science and Technology, Changsha 410114, Hunan, China

Abstract. Achieving the goals of "carbon peaking" and "carbon neutrality" and achieving high-quality economic development are important policies around the world. As an efficient means to collect, monitor and analyze environmental related financial data through technology, and use finance to innovate development models to achieve sustainable development goals, FinTech has also been used to achieve the "dual carbon goals". Regarding the impact of FinTech on a carbon-neutral economy, this paper analyzes the role of FinTech in promoting green finance in three ways. First, Fintech uses big data to promote the circulation of green financial products. Second, Fintech effectively helps banks to realize green credit and reduce credit risks. Third, Fintech is committed to building an information platform to disclose the environmental protection situation of enterprises. As well as makes references to the specific cases provided by the bill provided by the Swiss laboratory to provide FinTech-related methods for the amplitude or enterprise development of green finance in the future.

Keywords: FinTech · Green Finance · Financial System Innovation · Sustainable Development

1 Introduction

In recent years, as the environmental problems brought by global warming have become increasingly prominent to reduce carbon emissions, carbon neutrality has become the goal of the global countries carbon neutrality has gradually become the goal of economic transformation and economic development of all countries in the future, as countries have launched carbon neutrality and debt financing tools in the market. It promotes more transfer of capital allocation and flows into the field of carbon emission reduction. These carbon neutral bonds also broaden the channels for enterprises to obtain green funds, and enterprises are also supported in terms of capital. While enterprises develop the green economy, investment consumers also pay close attention to the flow of green funds from enterprises and the market.

H. Huang and Q. Yang—These authors contributed equally.

© The Author(s), under exclusive license to Springer Nature Singapore Pte Ltd. 2024
X. Li et al. (Eds.): ICEMGD 2023, AEPS, pp. 885–892, 2024.
https://doi.org/10.1007/978-981-97-0523-8_82

At the same time, the ESG standards have emerged. Focusing on ESG standards has also become the investment standard for investors to meet the concept. Since achieving the sustainable development goals requires significant investment, any the financial system serves as one of the main levers for mitigating climate change, which has been of fundamental and global importance since then. But digitalization has always been the core driving force of financial development, because digitalization defines products and processes. Digitization is covering all areas of financial processes, from payments to investment to financing, in a renewed description of trends closely related to innovation. So that's why it's here known as the financial technology (FinTech) revolution [1, 2].

Even at an early start, Financial technology focused on innovation in startup companies such as Ripple, Wealthfront, or LendingClub, existing banks and so-called big tech companies (GAFA consists of the following four companies, Google, Amazon, Facebook, Apple) have recently started working with these startups, or they are offering their own Financial technology services [3]. At the intersection of climate change and FinTech comes the so-called "green FinTech". The combination of green economy and FinTech produces the whole industrial chain that runs through the whole social and financial system, including banks, insurance companies, startups, large technology companies and so on. FinTech is also increasingly supporting other industries, such as the energy sector that provides digital infrastructure through peer-to-peer. At present, through our research on scholars and the collation of relevant papers, we find that the industry's current impact on how FinTech affects the green financial performance of enterprises has provided a great boost to the sustainable development of the financial industry by improving financial efficiency. FinTech improves the overall efficiency of enterprises to reduce carbon emissions and peak carbon peaks for enterprises and at the whole level of society. We in this paper from various scholars through all levels of models and examples from the positive and side to directly and indirectly shows that financial technology is from the bank's green financial performance and reduce enterprise carbon emissions, etc., review the financial technology through all aspects of society today carbon and economic impact, finally achieve the goal of sustainable development. In the future, it may continue to study the influence of FinTech on the green economy and financial performance of the whole society.

Finally, to achieve the problem of sustainable development. In previous literature, the research of Dorfleitner have verified that FinTech and sustainable economy have common ground in many aspects [4], so FinTech can enhance the potential of green finance [5]. The research proves that FinTech and blockchain technology can expand the investor base, improve the efficiency of capital operation and reduce the cost, thus promoting the development of green finance. Based on the characteristics of FinTech, this paper analyzes the role of FinTech in promoting green economy, as well as the specific cases provided by the bill provided by the Swiss laboratory to provide FinTech-related methods for the amplitude or enterprise development of green finance in the future.

2 The Impact of FinTech on the Green Economy

At present, the impact of FinTech on green economy in 2020 by Swiss scholars on Switzerland focused on the impact of economic technology on carbon neutral and future sustainable development. It points out that FinTech has had a significant impact on the banking sector, suggesting that Standard Chartered Bank in the UK is committed to making banking practices sustainable, which are helpful for having better social and environmental impacts in financial work. The bank has set sustainable development goals, such as reducing carbon emissions, investing development of renewable energy sources. It also offers sustainable financial solutions such as green bonds and green financial products to realize a transition to a low-carbon economy for their customers. In addition, the bank conducts a risk assessment of its lending activities to make sure they are sustainable and works with their customers to incorporate sustainability considerations into its business strategy [3]. ING Bank (The Netherlands), which takes lead in all financial institutions, puts sustainability in the first place. It has three pillars as its sustainable approach to banking: decreasing environmental footprint of itself, subsidizing sustainable economic activities and fostering a culture of sustainable development. Aiming at decreasing its influences on environment, ING Bank has set grand goals to reduce emissions of greenhouse gas, improve energy use ratio and move to more sustainable workplaces. To fund sustainable economic activities, it provides several financial methods, including green bonds and loans, and provides suggestions and financial help to customers seeking to transition to a low-carbon economy.

In addition, this article also explores how green FinTech can unleash its own potential in the future to reduce the impact of climate change to promote sustainable development. First, transportation and construction are the main levers of change. Transport is Switzerland's largest source of emissions, accounting for about a third of all emissions. And then construction (Urban heating), industry, agriculture and waste disposal. While no significant progress has been made in transportation, construction and industrial emissions have dropped significantly from 1990 levels. Thus, transportation and construction remain huge levers for change. Second, Switzerland's environmental footprint is significantly overshadowed by greenhouse gas emissions from imported goods and services. Secondly, the greenhouse gas emissions of imported goods and services cast a significant shadow over Switzerland's environmental footprint. Two-thirds of Switzerland's total carbon footprint is due to imported emissions. Another, even greater lever of change is imported emissions. Finally, according to the 2017 climate test, 79 pension funds and insurance companies that have not yet invested in green energy and account for 65% of the total capital market participated in the first test in 2017. Coal, oil and gas account for about 60% of their exposure, but renewables account for only 10% of their total. As a result, the investment plans of the listed stock and corporate bond portfolios of pension funds and insurance companies are still on the path of rapid development. So changing these portfolios is a huge leverage for change. Swiss scholars in 2020 research shows that the phenomenon of the green economy has received extensive attention, but the capital is still insufficient and the proportion of investment in the financial industry is still low, Swiss research on carbon emissions and carbon neutral economy and the green financial technology release future potential to meet the challenge of future climate change has greater reference significance. We have also compared the development of green economy in African countries with Switzerland [6]. We can clearly find that there are obvious imbalance and different proportions in the development of green economy in developing and developed countries.

3 How FinTech Promotes a Carbon-Neutral Finance

3.1 Promoting the Circulation of Green and Low-Carbon Wealth Management Products

Through big data and artificial intelligence technology to enterprises or individual customers to instill green ideas, so as to promote [7]. Alibaba, an e-commerce platform, has opened a "carbon account" in Alipay, The carbon emissions generated by users' trading behavior can be observed through the carrier of "ant Forest"; MyBank issued the first order of 2 billion Yuan to support the development of small and micro green assets to financial institutions at a lower interest rate than the marketization level [8]; Catering company KFC also made donations through its own online platform to reduce the benefits of excessive packaging; In the 2022 two-stage SEM-artificial neural network approach of Bangladesh Scholars, studying FinTech adoption has a positive and positive impact on the sustainable performance of banking companies [9]. The study shows that FinTech's integration of new technologies and funding for environmental projects into banking improves bank sustainability performance, while the government and banks encourage the prudent use of technologies such as blockchain to motivate and expand digital lending to continuously empower environmental and green projects. Through ANN model, the linear-nonlinear correlation of FinTech, green innovation, green finance and sustainability performance was successfully verified the positive impact of FinTech adoption on the sustainability performance of the banking industry [10].

3.2 Risk Prevention and Control of Green Credit by FinTech

Affected by the lack of information feedback ability, the blind pursuit of high profit margin, improper decision-making and other factors lead to the occurrence of credit risk, which seriously affects the credit business of banks [11]. At present, credit crises are frequently encountered in high-pollution and high-efficiency enterprises, which not only seriously affects the credit structure of the whole market, but also seriously hinders the development of carbon neutral economy. FinTech can effectively reduce the risk of bank credit, and is conducive to the implementation of green credit. First, FinTech can improve the ability of banks to assess the credit risks of enterprises. By obtaining credit signals of customers, they can assess the possible risk index, and alleviate the problems of where information arising in credit transactions. Second, FinTech can also improve the efficiency of commercial banks' information collection, convenient for banks to obtain better customers with smaller costs, and improve the scale and quality of credit transactions. Third, as mentioned above, it can promote the circulation of green credit products in the market. Previous studies have shown that green credit can effectively reduce the capacity utilization rate of highly polluting enterprises, but can reduce the cost of enterprises with excellent environmental awareness, so as to improve the competitiveness of enterprises [12].

3.3 Establish a Unified Information Platform

Financial institutions can use big data, cloud computing and AI technologies to conduct ESG evaluation of enterprises and projects and integrate the whole business process, so as to realize the credit risk application and management of non-financial information. Financial institutions can use big data portrait to reveal the ESG risk of customers, improve the quality and efficiency of business approval due diligence; use the deep learning technology to explore the relationship between customer ESG evaluation and customer credit risk, and advance risk control. By establishing the ESG evaluation system for corporate credit customers, Huzhou Bank integrates the "business development" and "risk management" objectives deeply into the ESG evaluation standard in the evaluation system design; in the system development, the digital technology realizes the functions of 100% automatic calculation, ESG risk dynamic monitoring and automatic generation of standardized ESG information disclosure statistical data. In recent years, FinTech has made significant progress in supporting the construction of a green financial system, but compared with the potential market demand of carbon peak and carbon neutral target, it still needs to be further developed and improved.

4 Analyze the Enlightenment of FinTech to Green Finance from the Selected Examples

With today's rise of FinTech around the world, in the new study, whether the B2B/B2C business model adopted by Spanish FinTech, Insutech and PropTech companies are related to the sustainability plans of these companies [6]. FinTech is considered as a disruptive, competitive and sustainable industry [10]. The FinTech category is shown in Fig. 1 below.

Experts in FinTech generally agree with the same view and concerns about sustainability. The ultimate consumer (B2C) requires FinTech companies to provide service-related strategies to meet other related company requirements with financial services (B2B) related to each other. With the discovery of research, more and more financial companies change from B2B to B2C, and the increasing proportion is also higher. Among them, the leading role are the disrupters in the FinTech industry, who prefer the B2B model to provide a platform for financial institutions. Sustainability is a multi-angle and multi-dimensional concept in both socioeconomic and environmental dimensions. FinTech can assist companies in assessing and reducing their impact on the environment through advanced data analysis, blockchain, and artificial intelligence technologies [9]. Meeting ESG standards is now a goal for more and more investors and consumers to pay attention to, choosing and buying and related companies. Some studies point directly to '66% of global consumers' (and 77% of millennial)' are willing to choose environmentally friendly products even at higher prices. According to the current research, FinTech-related enterprises and providers have a good reputation for green finance, which can make consumers feel satisfied and trust in participating in online banking and other related activities. The method used in the correlation studies is the Logit regression. Scholars received 55 valid answers [6]. The basic summary summarizes the new capital that FinTech companies that meet ESG standards find more likely to attract new customers and green investors. FinTech can pursue a digital sustainable model with its powerful innovative functions. Take the green economy of African countries to explore the relevant performance of FinTech on green economy [14].

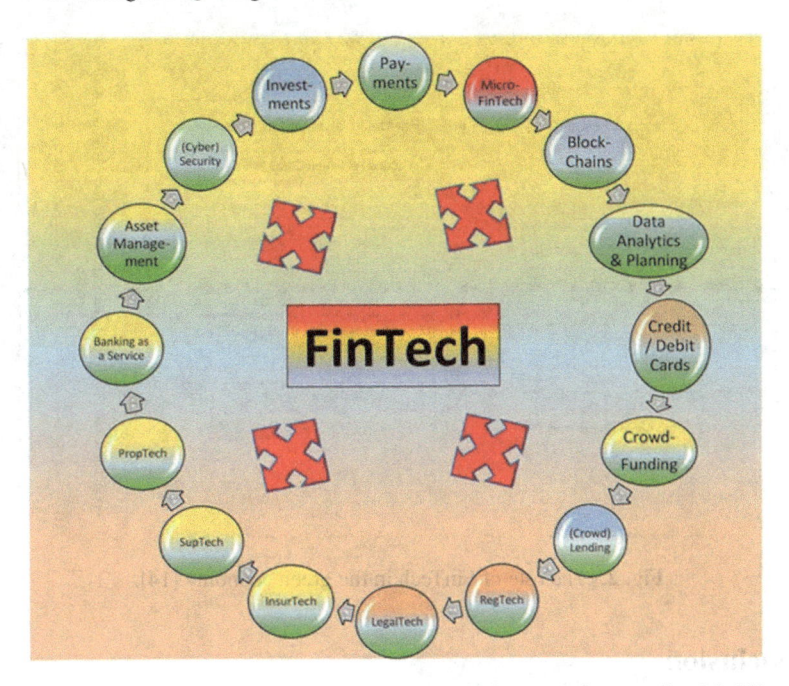

Fig. 1. The FinTech Classification was adapted from previous studies [6, 13].

According to related research, FinTech may act by integrating them into finance through the integration of communication between machines and the Internet of things to indicate reduced carbon emissions. In this study, the keyword co-occurrence analysis of the cited author and the country, and the clusters from large to small are red, green, blue, yellow and purple. This comprehensive framework shown in Fig. 2 is about driving sustainable development in Africa.

These discussions found that FinTech provides a stage for clean energy, and the scholar green finance policy has been found to reduce China's carbon dioxide emissions [1, 15]. The author points out that the higher the level of green finance innovation in a country, the lower its carbon emissions and the lower the climate risk. So FinTech can indeed be a way to reduce the risk of climate change and achieve green economic growth.

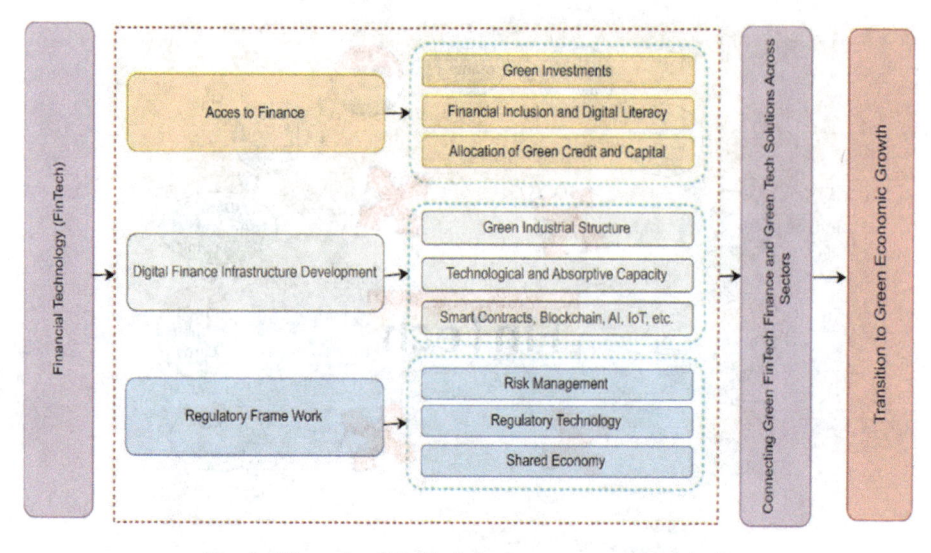

Fig. 2. The role of FinTech in the green economy [14].

5 Conclusion

In order to realize sustainable development, this paper demonstrates the role of FinTech in promoting carbon neutral economy by analyzing Swiss examples and the principles of FinTech. Through big data, artificial intelligence and cloud computing, the labeled green credit and other data can be accurately identified, so as to realize the timely generation, statistics and push of regulatory data. Big data is used for data mining, analysis and integration to accurately, timely and multi-dimensional panorama of green financial data, and achieve business insight and decision support. Therefore, FinTech will promote the development of green finance in many aspects. In the future, we will study how to build a big data platform to better use FinTech to promote the development of green finance.

References

1. Tufano, P.G.M., Harris, M., Stulz, R.M. (eds.): Financial innovation. In: Handbook of the Economics of Finance, Constantinides, pp. 307–335. Elsevier, Amsterdam, The Netherlands (2003)
2. Frame, W.S., White, L.J.: Technological change, financial innovation and diffusion in banking. NYU Working Paper No. 2451/33549 (2014)
3. Puschmann, T., Hoffmann, C., Khmarskyi, V.: How green FinTech can alleviate the impact of climate change—The case of Switzerland. Swiss Finance Institute Research Paper Series 21-20 (2020)
4. Dorfleitner, G., Braun, D.: FinTech, digitalization and blockchain: possible applications for green finance. In: Migliorelli, M., Dessertine, P. (eds.) The rise of green finance in Europe. Palgrave Studies in Impact Finance. Palgrave Macmillan, Cham (2019)

5. Vergara, C.C., Agudo, L.F.: FinTech and sustainability: do they affect each other? Sustainability **13**(13), 7012 (2021)
6. Department of Professional Orientation, Instituto de Estudios Bursátiles (IEB), C/Alfonso XI: Special issue Insurtech: PropTech and FinTech Environment, 14(19), 12088 (2022)
7. Ma, J.: Green finance roadmap under carbon neualization vision. China Financ. **20**, 12–14 (2021)
8. Song, J., Feng, X., Lu, Y.: FinTech enables green finance to support carbon peak and carbon neutrality. Banker **11**, 117–120 (2021)
9. Cheng, L.: Computational modelling methods for financial and FinTech innovations. Financ. Innov. **10**(5), 148 (2022)
10. Moro-Visconti, R., Pascual, J.L.: Sustainability in FinTech: explained by business model scalability and market valuation. Sustainability **12**(24), 10316 (2020)
11. Pu, S.: Analysis of bank credit risk management problems under the new situation. Mod. Bus. **33**, 70–73 (2022)
12. Lu, W., Su, L.: How does the green credit policy affect the capacity utilization rate of enterprises?; Empirical evidence from Chinese micro-enterprises. Financ. Econ. 1–12 (2023)
13. Moro-Visconti, R.: MicroFinTech: Expand Financial Inclusion through Cost-Cutting Innovation. Palgrave Macmillan, Cham (2021)
14. School of Chemical Engineering, University of Birmingham, Edgbaston, Birmingham B15 2TT, UK, 15 (22), 8658 (2022)
15. Nenavath, S.: Impact of FinTech and green finance on environmental quality protection in India: by applying semi-parametric differences-in-differnece (SDID). Renew. Energy **193**, 913–919 (2022)

Comprehensive Analysis of China's Local Government Financing Vehicle Debt

Zihao Tang[✉]

School of Banking and Finance, University of International Business and Economics, Beijing 100029, China

202141091@uibe.edu.cn

Abstract. The total amount of unpaid debt in China's Local Government Financing Vehicles ("LGFVs") has reached a staggering 65 trillion yuan, highlighting the need for a thorough analysis of the country's local debt problem and financial development model. This paper focuses on the crisis of China's LGFV debt, systematically analyzes the causes of debt formation, risks faced by local investment companies, the social impact of debt defaults, and measures to respond to the debt crisis. Additionally, it explores the commonalities of debt problems with other typical cases worldwide. Results show that: (1) China's LGFV debt reflects an unhealthy development model, involving problems such as unreasonable financing, excessive credit, and poor government decision-making; (2) Resolving the debt problem requires addressing short-term debt relief and long-term financial system reform, local financing development model reform; (3) The debt problem is due to reasons such as an unreasonable economic structure, an unsound financial system, unscientific government decision-making, and an irrational fiscal system, causing a chain reaction globally; (4) China needs to deepen financial and fiscal reform, strengthen local government fiscal capacity, promote financial services for the real economy, and pay more attention to financial regulation.

Keywords: LGFVs · Debt Crisis · Financial System · Financial Regulation

1 Introduction

Since the 1990s, Local Government Financing Vehicles ("LGFVs") have emerged in large numbers in China. They are also known as Urban Investment Companies and are designed to raise funds for municipal infrastructure construction through bank loans, bond issuance, and non-standard financing. LGFVs are essentially closely related to local governments and assume their responsibilities while reducing the financial pressure on local governments and completing urban construction. Also, due to government support, the debt of LGFVs is generally considered to have a high credit rating and low default risk. In the past two decades, the emergence of LGFVs has effectively solved the problem of insufficient funds for urban construction, promoted the construction and optimization of large-scale infrastructure, and provided opportunities for the improvement and development of China's communication and rail transportation networks, directly promoting the long-term high-speed development of the Chinese economy [1].

However, since 2018, more and more LGFV debt is facing debt repayment risks. According to a report by CaiLian News, as of the end of February 2023, the balance of local government debt in China was 36.2269 trillion yuan [2]. According to the "usually the balance of urban investment debt is about twice the explicit debt of local governments", the interest-bearing debt balance of China's LGFVs may have reached 65 trillion yuan. The pressure of short-term debt repayment in local areas is high, and debt risk is significant, which seriously affects the stability of the economy and society.

The emergence of the crisis in LGFV debt is mainly due to excessive and unreasonable financing by LGFVs, as well as many projects failing to achieve expected returns, leading to their inability to repay debts. Once a large number of defaults occur in LGFV debt, it will inevitably cause serious consequences, including: government credit collapse, difficulties in local refinancing, lack of funds to develop the local economy, and triggering systemic financial risks. This problem has caused concerns among the Chinese government and investors. The Chinese government has taken measures to address these issues, including strengthening supervision of LGFVs, debt restructuring, and market-oriented debt-to-equity swaps to alleviate their debt pressures [3].

This paper will systematically elaborate on the issues related to LGFV debt by combining existing research results and similar economic development cases in other countries. It will analyze the development process and causes of urban investment debt, as well as the social impact and preventive measures of debt crisis. Finally, it will provide strategies and recommendations for the ultimate resolution of LGFV debt problem.

2 Formation of LGFV Debt

As China's urbanization process advances, local governments urgently need continuous investment in infrastructure funds. After the reform of the central-local fiscal revenue sharing system, local government finances have remained relatively tight, leading to the emergence of the land finance and LGFVs. The operating mechanism of LGFVs is as follows: the local government injects land into the LGFV in the form of registered capital or sells it to the LGFV at a low price. The LGFV then uses the land as collateral to finance its various infrastructure projects, or transfers the money to the local government in the form of land purchases. This mechanism essentially enables local governments to monetize their land through LGFVs, obtain funding from banks and the public, and complete urban construction tasks [4]. This not only maintains the relatively low fiscal deficits of local governments, but also meets the needs of local development.

There are four main reasons for the emergence of LGFV debt problems:

2.1 Implicit Government Debt Guarantees

From the operating mechanism of LGFVs, it can be seen that the legal status of urban investment and construction companies is not clear enough. As a means of off-balance-sheet financing for local governments, LGFV debt is usually regarded as implicit debt of local governments. Banks lend because of the implicit endorsement and even administrative intervention of local governments, but local governments do not have joint legal responsibilities, which brings risks of implicit government guarantees.

In reality, the amount of debt borrowed by LGFVs far exceeds their ability to generate cash flow and profits, and their own repayment capacity is insufficient [5]. The inflated credit ratings of the bonds and the blind borrowing by banks have led to the disorderly expansion of credit bonds, which is the main reason for the outbreak of LGFV debt crises.

2.2 Insufficient Profitability of Investment Projects

LGFVs mainly engage in urban infrastructure construction and public service investments. The public nature of their projects means that the income from many urban investment and construction projects cannot cover the repayment of principal and interest, as well as related financing costs, increasing the risk of debt default.

At the same time, many local investments are characterized by blindness and a desire for quick results. Due to the ease of LGFV borrowing and lack of supervision, some officials blindly pursue GDP growth and large-scale infrastructure construction, resulting in a lot of waste and unreasonable decision-making during the investment process. The investment direction lacks scientific and reasonable planning. Some projects are not in line with market demand, wasting a large amount of social resources.

2.3 Unreasonable Operating Model of LGFVs

Firstly, there is no clear separation between the government and the enterprise. Most urban investment companies are funded or controlled by local governments and closely linked with them. Local governments may support LGFV projects by intervening in market prices, tax policies, etc., affecting the market competition mechanism and increasing the risks of LGFV projects. Secondly, the source of funding is opaque, and supervision is lacking. LGFVs' financing channels are not transparent, and their funding sources are unclear with non-standard procedures. Additionally, the governance structure of LGFVs is complex, with a lack of effective regulatory and restraint mechanisms, which may lead to violations or corruption during their operations. Thirdly, the debt lacks evaluation, and the risk is too high. The massive financing of LGFVs has resulted in a large amount of LGFV debt. Their income mainly depends on government approval and support, and once government support decreases or stops, LGFVs may face the risk of default.

2.4 Economic Downturn Under the Epidemic

In recent years, due to the impact of the epidemic and other factors, the global economy has faced increasing downward pressure. Economic downturns lead to a decrease in urban construction investment demand, which inevitably affects the investment demand of LGFV projects. A large number of projects may be postponed or stagnated, affecting the company's profitability and development prospects. Moreover, economic downturns may also lead to a decrease in market demand, making it difficult for LGFV projects to sell and finance.

Moreover, the economic downturn increases the debt risk of LGFVs. LGFVs usually rely on debt financing to support project construction, and during an economic downturn, financing costs rise, increasing debt risk and possibly facing debt repayment pressure and the risk of a fund chain breakdown. Additionally, the economic downturn may cause a decline in land market prices, thereby affecting LGFVs' land acquisition and project construction.

3 Risk Hazards Faced by LGFVs

3.1 Debt Risk

Due to the special nature of LGFVs, they face different debt risks from other enterprises. Firstly, the debt scale of Chinese LGFVs is enormous, reaching trillions of yuan, mainly due to their main business of urban infrastructure construction and public utility operation, which requires substantial financial support. This also means that LGFVs have a greater debt repayment pressure, and once the economic situation is unfavorable or funding sources become problematic, they may face the risk of debt default [6]. Secondly, the debt structure is complex. LGFVs' debt structure is usually complex, including bank loans, bonds, financing leases, and various financing methods, including different types of government bonds and corporate bonds. This makes LGFVs face greater challenges in debt management and risk control.

3.2 Fluctuation Risk in Land Market

The debt of LGFVs is mainly financed through land reserve financing, and fluctuations in the land market have a direct impact on the operation and financial situation of LGFVs. If the land market experiences a significant downturn, the financial situation of LGFVs will be severely affected.

Firstly, investment returns will decrease. A decline in land prices will reduce the cost of land purchase for LGFVs, but it will also lower the investment return rate and profit level of the projects after land conversion, which may have a negative impact on the company's performance. Secondly, the quality of land reserve will decline. A decline in land prices means that the value of land reserves purchased by LGFVs will decrease, and the quality of land reserves will also decrease accordingly. This will have an unfavorable impact on the company's future project planning and layout, affecting the sustainable development of the company. Thirdly, financing difficulties will increase. A decline in land prices will result in a decrease in the value of land mortgaged, thus increasing the difficulty of LGFVs in financing. Under the circumstances of restricted financing channels, a decline in land prices may have adverse effects on the company's project construction and operation [7]. Fourthly, competition intensifies. A decline in land prices may attract more competitors to enter the market, and intensified competition may further shrink the difficulty of LGFVs in project development and profit space, also having an unfavorable impact on the company's market share and competitiveness.

3.3 Local Government Risk

LGFVs are platforms of local governments, and their development is often highly managed by local governments. They mainly face the following risks: Firstly, policy risk.

The development of LGFVs is often influenced by policies, especially in land transfer, financing, and financial support. Policy changes may have a significant impact on the business and finance of LGFVs. Therefore, LGFVs need to closely monitor policy changes and adjust their business strategies and risk control measures in a timely manner. Secondly, local financial risk. The funding source of LGFVs mainly comes from local governments. Once local government finance encounters problems, LGFVs may be unable to obtain sufficient financial support, leading to business stagnation and debt default. Thirdly, political risk. The development of LGFVs is often influenced by local political factors, such as changes in government leadership and local political instability. The investment and construction of LGFVs may rely heavily on the decision-making of local government leaders, and the change of leadership may cause changes in financial support and even project termination [8].

3.4 Market Risk

The main business of LGFVs is urban infrastructure construction and public utility operation, and these businesses have a greater market risk. Factors such as changes in market demand, intensified competition, and a decline in project investment return rates may have an impact on the debt risk of LGFVs.

Firstly, the fluctuation risk of the urban economic cycle. The main business of LGFVs is mainly around urban infrastructure construction and public utility operation. When the urban economy is in a downturn, the business of LGFVs will be affected, and they may not be able to complete the established investment tasks. Secondly, market competition risk. LGFVs' business is mostly focused on urban infrastructure construction and public utility management. As urban development continues, market competition will become increasingly fierce. Thirdly, interest rate fluctuation risk. LGFVs usually need to obtain financial support through bank loans and other means. If interest rates rise, LGFVs' borrowing costs will also increase, which will have adverse effects on their business and finances.

4 Social Impact of LGFV Debt Defaults

4.1 Impact on Investors

LGFV debt defaults will cause losses to investors. If LGFV debt defaults, investors may face losses in their invested principal and interest. More seriously, a large number of LGFV defaults may trigger market panic, negatively affecting investor confidence, especially in the bond market. This will further induce shock waves throughout the entire financial market.

4.2 Impact on LGFVs

First, it will be difficult for the company to refinance. LGFV debt defaults will reduce investors' confidence in LGFVs and LGFV debt, leading to a credit rating downgrade for subsequent bond issuances, increasing financing costs. Second, it will be difficult for the company to maintain operations. After LGFVs default, they may face the risk of being unable to timely repay the principal and interest of maturing bonds, which may cause their funding chain to break, and they will be unable to conduct business as usual. Third, internal management will be difficult. After LGFVs default, they may be subject to regulatory focus, increasing the difficulty and cost of company management. In addition, default events may cause internal management chaos and business adjustments, increasing operational risks for the company.

4.3 Impact on Local Development

The problems with LGFV operation mechanisms will further transmit to the overall development of the government and local economy. First, LGFV debt is essentially local government debt. If LGFV debt defaults on a large scale, local governments may have to help LGFVs repay their debts, which will bring a heavy debt burden to local governments. Second, LGFV debt is one of the main channels for urban financing. LGFV debt defaults will cause government credit collapse and local refinancing difficulties, making it difficult for the government to obtain financing through LGFVs, inevitably exacerbating the fiscal crisis of local governments, and even affecting local government investment and construction, making it difficult for them to fulfill their basic functions and provide public services, leading to stagnation and obstruction of urban projects.

4.4 Impact on Financial Markets

Default on LGFV debt could lead to increased credit risk in the bond market, causing market volatility and rising interest rates, making it difficult for other LGFV debt issuances. At the same time, it could also affect the capital adequacy and debt-servicing ability of banks and other financial institutions, leading to an increase in non-performing loans and market liquidity tightening, thereby affecting the stability of the entire financial market and economic development [9].

4.5 Social Impact

The crisis of LGFV debt could have a negative impact on social fairness and justice. Due to the lack of transparency in the issuance and use of LGFV debt, some local governments may use LGFVs for improper capital operations and rent-seeking, resulting in unfair distribution of wealth and resources. LGFV debt defaults will also bring real economic losses to a large number of investors, leading to social conflicts and dissatisfaction. More seriously, credit tightening and reduced investment will further lead to economic recession, affecting people's production and life, and triggering social instability and political risks.

5 Measures to Address the LGFV Debt Crisis

The response to LGFV debt should focus on both the urgent debt crisis resolution and the formation of a new, more scientific and reasonable local financing development mechanism for long-term development.

5.1 Resolving the Current Debt Risk

To solve the LGFV debt problem, we must first do "debt-to-equity, debt reduction" [10]. The subject responsibility of local governments in preventing and resolving implicit debt must be strengthened, the disposal of existing implicit debt should be intensified, the debt structure should be optimized, the interest burden should be reduced, and the supervision of implicit and statutory debts of local governments should be merged and regulated to resolutely curb incremental debt and resolve stock debt.

The central government should take measures to retain LGFVs that truly engage in public welfare, benefit people's livelihoods, and promote economic development, promote market-oriented debt restructuring, use debt extension, debt-to-equity swaps, and other methods to replace debt with lower-interest-rate debt and gradually return it to the government's balance sheet for regulation. For LGFV companies that are non-compliant, seeking profit, with excess capacity, or outdated, the implicit endorsement of local governments should be denied, the moral dilemma of "too big to fail" should be rejected, and their bad debts should be written off or they should be liquidated [11].

5.2 Establishing a More Scientific and Rational Local Financing Mechanism

Long-term structural reforms should be carried out while resolving the debt crisis. All disguised borrowing behaviors should be prohibited, and the "platformization" of local state-owned enterprises and institutions should be prevented. The local financing mechanism must be more transparent and scientific, with strengthened project transparency and information disclosure to reduce information asymmetry. A transparent financing mechanism can increase the confidence of market participants, thereby reducing market uncertainty and risk. The financing structure should be continuously optimized, and financing channels should be regulated and expanded. Through market-oriented supervision, the review and evaluation of LGFV debt projects should be strengthened to avoid implicit government guarantees [12], promote the optimal allocation of market resources, and prevent excessive financing and non-performing loans. Local financing platforms should achieve a greater degree of marketization, reducing government influence on LGFVs.

5.3 Deepening Fiscal and Taxation System Reforms

The transformation of the local financial system should be promoted. The fiscal transfer payment system should be improved, the provincial and sub-provincial fiscal systems should be sound, and the construction of the local tax system should be steadily advanced to solidify local basic financial resources and self-development capabilities. The central government should appropriately grant greater financial and taxation powers to local governments, strengthen local government's own financial capabilities, and reduce their dependence on LGFVs.

Moreover, the government should vigorously develop the real economy, optimize the fiscal structure, and increase the level of fiscal revenue. The virtual economy should serve the real economy to avoid large amounts of capital being idle in the financial system. The development of the real economy can promote economic structural adjustments, transforming from resource and capital-intensive to labor-intensive, technology-intensive, and knowledge-intensive, improving economic quality and efficiency, and increasing economic growth potential.

6 Comparative Analysis of Debt Problems in Various Countries

From 2007 to 2009, the US experienced a severe subprime mortgage crisis, which then triggered a global financial crisis. The fundamental cause was the housing market bubble and excessive lending. From 2001 to 2006, low-interest rates, loose lending standards, high housing prices, and mortgage securitization jointly promoted the prosperity of the US real estate market. As the US housing bubble burst, borrowers defaulted in large numbers [13]. Studies have found that before the subprime crisis erupted, the policies of the US government and the Federal Reserve were short-sighted, and the credit process lacked regulatory review. The financial market operated irregularly, and financial institutions leveraged high and ignored financial risks, resulting in excessive lending. These problems are similar to those encountered in the Chinese LGFV debt crisis.

After the 2008 financial crisis, Greece also faced serious debt problems and eventually applied for an emergency bailout program from the International Monetary Fund (IMF) and the European Union in 2010. The fundamental cause of the Greek debt crisis was the imbalance in its economic structure and the inaction of the government. For a long time, Greece's economic income mainly relied on tourism and shipping, while manufacturing and industry lagged behind. With the external impact of the financial crisis, Greece's tourism and shipping industries both fell into recession. The government failed to take timely measures to cope with this situation. On the contrary, the Greek government overspent for a long time, resulting in a continuous increase in the country's fiscal deficit and debt. Tax collection was unfavorable, leading to a large number of illegal tax evasion incidents, and even financial fraud. Domestic and external troubles pushed the Greek economy into the abyss.

Similarly, many countries, such as Japan, Argentina, Spain, and Venezuela, have also faced serious debt problems, causing long-term economic stagnation in these countries. There are many commonalities in the reasons, which are worth exploring. First, the national economic structure is unreasonable. Many countries rely too much on certain industries or fields, leading to unbalanced economic development and weak resistance to external risks. Second, the financial system is not sound. Many countries' financial industries have structural problems, and some financial institutions may be overly exposed to certain risks for short-term interests; regulatory agencies may not have sufficient capacity or willingness to regulate financial institutions. Third, poor policy decision-making and an unreasonable fiscal system. The economic policies of many countries are too short-sighted, only seeing the prosperity in front of them, disregarding the long-term consequences. An unsound fiscal system and improper government management of fiscal revenue and expenditure may also lead to national debt problems. Fourth, economic cycles and the global economic environment. In today's world, countries are increasingly interconnected, and one country's economic and financial problems may seriously affect other countries, and even trigger a global financial crisis.

7 Conclusion

This article focuses on the recent attention-grabbing LGFV debt problem in China, and discusses it from the perspectives of causes, impacts, and responses, and analyzes it in combination with typical debt problems worldwide. The research results show that:

First, China's LGFV debt crisis is a product of the times, a manifestation of the phenomenon of local governments living beyond their means, and a microcosm of China's economic development model since the reform and opening up. Since the reform and opening up, China's economy has grown at an astonishing speed, and promoting development through administrative means is an important feature of China's economic development. On the one hand, this is a manifestation of the superiority of socialism, which has achieved rapid development in the short term, and LGFVs have also enabled rapid construction of infrastructure throughout the country; but on the other hand, some officials only care about their political achievements and do not attach enough importance to sustainable development. The government and enterprises are not separated, resulting in unhealthy economic development.

Second, to address the issue of LGFV debt in China, on the one hand, current debt risks should be resolved by using measures such as debt extension and debt-to-equity swaps to firmly control the stock of debt and resolve the increment [14]. More importantly, in the longer term, it is necessary to establish and improve local financing mechanisms, explore fiscal and taxation system reforms, and develop new and healthier ways for local financing and development. Overall, it is necessary to strengthen the financial capacity of local governments themselves and reduce their dependence on LGFV platforms.

Third, debt issues are problems faced by many countries globally, with similar underlying causes, such as an unreasonable economic structure, an unsound financial system, unscientific government decision-making, and an irrational fiscal system, as well as being affected by economic cycles and the global economic environment. The impact of debt issues on a country is very complex and may lead to economic recession. Governments may need to adopt austerity policies and reduce public expenditure to address debt problems, which could exacerbate social discontent. Debt issues may also lead to a loss of national sovereignty, as it may require external institutions such as the International Monetary Fund to regulate and intervene.

Fourth, the financial system is of great significance for a country's economic development, and all countries worldwide need to continually improve and strengthen their financial systems. Vulnerabilities in the financial system have led to phenomena such as excessive credit, non-performing loans, and inadequate supervision, seriously threatening the security of national development and creating financial risks. Different countries need to combine their national conditions and development status, continually improve their financial systems, and handle the relationships between financial institutions, regulatory authorities, and market participants. For China, it is necessary to promote the financial sector to serve the real economy, effectively prevent and control financial risks, advance the construction of a modern financial regulatory framework, improve the financial market system, and promote the healthy and sound development of the Chinese economy, transitioning from high-speed development to high-quality development.

Currently, the Chinese government is taking various measures to address local debt issues, and in the future, research can be conducted from the perspectives of the consequences of debt defaults, the impact of LGFVs shutting down, and reforms in the local financing system.

References

1. Zhang, Y.: Study on the impact of city investment bonds on local economic growth. Contemp. Manag. **4**, 27–37 (2022)
2. Ministry of Finance of the People's Republic of China: Newly issued local government bonds in February nationwide total 441.9 billion Yuan. https://www.cls.cn/detail/1304883. Accessed 11 Apr 2023
3. Clarke, D.C.: The law of China's local government debt crisis: local government financing vehicles and their bonds. GWU Law School Public Law Research Paper (2016)
4. Xia, S.Y.: City investment bonds: origin, risks, and regulatory research. Financ. Theory Teach. **2022**(6), 44–50 (2022)
5. Wang, R.H., Hu, C.Y.: Analysis of the spillover effect of implicit local government debt risk in China based on the risk network perspective. Humanit. J. **2**, 129–140 (2023)
6. Xu, X.F.: Research on the spillover effect of local debt risk among provinces in China. Nankai University, Tianjin (2022)
7. Ji, Y.Y., Fu, W.L., Yang, Y.H.: Land financing, imbalance of urbanization, and local debt risk. Stat. Res. **36**(7), 91–103 (2019)
8. Zhou, L., Ren, J.: Causes and countermeasures analysis of local debt problems in China. J. Hunan Univ. Financ. Econ. **36**(5), 94–101 (2020)
9. Luo, H., Chen, L.: Bond yield and credit rating: evidence of Chinese local government financing vehicles. Rev. Quant. Financ. Account. **52**(3), 737–758 (2019)
10. Zhang, X.R.: Urban investment company optimizes debt with early redemption "Lightening the Burden" in progress. Shanghai Securities News, 2023-03-27 (004)
11. Zhang, X.R.: Local debt risk resolved with warmth: city investment bonds' downward strategy may be timely. Shanghai Securities News, 2023-02-20 (004)
12. Li, Y.H., Li, L.W.: Bank competition, implicit guarantees, and credit spreads of city investment bonds. Stat. Inf. Forum **38**(2), 74–85 (2023)
13. Ackermann, J.: The subprime crisis and its consequences. J. Financ. Stab.Financ. Stab. **4**(4), 329–337 (2008)
14. Shi, J.: Where will city investment bonds go: Strengthening regulations while controlling incremental growth. China Business News, 2023-01-16 (B07)

The Relationship Between ESG Ratings and Financial Performance of Coal Firms — the Case of China Shenhua and China Coal Energy

Aimiao Zhang(✉)

College of Business Administration, Chongqing Vocational and Technical University of Mechatronics, Chongqing 402760, China
zhangyong14.cq@chinatelecom.cn

Abstract. Since the concept of ESG was explicitly introduced, Chinese coal companies have paid more attention to the three aspects of environmental, social and corporate governance (ESG). This paper mainly adopts a case study approach to elaborate on the three aspects of ESG performance of China Shenhua and China Coal Energy respectively. The ESG rating scores of the two companies are compared and analysed through the WindESG rating system, and the three types of financial performance of the two companies, namely return on assets, net sales margin and asset turnover ratio, are compared and analysed using the DuPont analysis respectively. Two conclusions were drawn from the study: firstly, the analysis of the financial performance of the companies showed that the return on assets was mainly influenced by the net sales margin of the companies; secondly, from a short-term perspective, the financial performance of the companies was positively correlated with the ESG ratings.

Keywords: ESG rating · Corporate Financial Performance · Coal Companies

1 Introduction

ESG has been a topic of great interest to governments and companies since it was first introduced in the UN Global Compact in 2004. ESG is a comprehensive analysis of the sustainability of a company's operations and its impact on social values from three perspectives: environmental, social and governance. In addition, ESG integrates these three dimensions to help companies achieve long-term sustainability goals for the environment, society and corporate governance while maximising profits. In September 2020, China put forward a "double carbon" target plan, clearly stating the "carbon peak" by 2030 and the "carbon risk" by 2060. In September 2020, China put forward a "double carbon" target plan, clearly proposing a "carbon peak" by 2030 and a "carbon neutral" target by 2060. Coal companies, which are part of the polluting industry, need to pay more attention to this policy in order to fulfil their social responsibility to protect the environment and continue to vigorously promote ESG implementation, which will not only create more opportunities for enterprises in the new era, but also achieve high-quality development. The significance of this paper is fourfold: first, topicality. This paper follows the development of the times and explores the relationship between ESG ratings and the financial performance of coal companies in the context of China's "double carbon" development goal, and provides suggestions for modern coal companies to achieve the national "double carbon" strategic plan. Secondly, it is catalytic. Although there are many academic studies on the relationship between ESG and corporate performance in China and abroad, researchers have not been able to unify their views, and the development of ESG in China is still in its infancy, so more reasonable suggestions are needed to promote its development. The data indicates that only a few researchers at home and abroad have studied the relationship between ESG ratings and corporate performance in the pollution industry today, and the research in this paper has the significance of opening up new ideas and can bring more researchers to think in different directions; fourth, extensibility. This paper only compares the data of two companies, China Shenhua and China Coal Energy, but there are still many coal companies in the market. Based on the content of this paper, researchers can conduct research and analysis on more coal companies or polluting industries to strengthen the verification of the relationship between ESG ratings and corporate performance.

This paper focuses on data analysis and comparative analysis of China Shenhua and China Coal Energy ESG ratings, ESG performance and financial performance respectively using a case study approach, where financial performance indicators are analyzed using DuPont analysis.

2 Literature Review

Firstly, through the results of Xia Jiao's study, it is indicated that a large number of research results show that ESG has a positive impact on corporate performance, especially a significant impact on financial indicators represented by ROA and ROE [1]. Friede et al. found that 90% of the results of 2,200 papers on ESG and financial performance as a research subject proved that there is that there is a positive relationship between ESG and financial performance and concluded that the impact of ESG on financial performance will become more stable over time [2]. According to MH Shakil's research, companies with good ESG performance have lower overall risk [3]. Not only that, through S Chouaibi et al. study indicated that ESG strengths possessed by firms increase the value of the firm itself, while ESG weaknesses possessed by firms decrease the value of the firm [4]. Secondly, the public recognition of ESG has gradually increased in China, and people's evaluation of the development ability of enterprises has changed from a single financial statement analysis to the current way of combining financial reports with ESG reports, which makes the evaluation of enterprise value more objective [5]. How to study the relationship between ESG and financial performance is one of the research points in this paper. According to the global research literature, it is indicated that there is less research on the relevance of financial indicators based on industry characteristics and more research on traditional financial indicators [6]. According to the results of the empirical study by Liu Ping et al. indicated that the evaluation indexes of the financial performance of the chemical industry based on the concept of environmental protection are mainly divided into quick ratio, current ratio, total assets return, cost margin, sales margin, fixed assets turnover, operating income growth rate, waste gas emission per unit of profit, waste emission per unit of profit and COD emission per unit of profit [7]. Combined with the analysis results, this paper focuses on the financial performance using the DuPont analysis. The DuPont analysis is a decomposition of return on net assets into two parts: return on assets and equity multiplier, which in turn can be divided into sales margin and total asset turnover [8]. A study by Zhang Yuan et al. suggested that enterprises must invest a large amount of money to ensure good quality ESG reports, which will have a certain impact on their production and operation in the short term, but has a positive effect on their long-term sustainable development [9]. Overall, ESG has a positive effect on the financial performance of enterprises, and enterprises should strengthen their long-term attention to ESG and make proper use of the ESG system to bring more opportunities for enterprises and achieve sustainable development.

3 Comparison of ESG Performance and Ratings of Companies

3.1 Introduction to ESG Rating

With the release of the ESG Evaluation Criteria Report by the China Biodiversity Conservation and Green Development Foundation on 29 September 2021, many companies in China are beginning to pay attention to the ESG rating system. There are currently about 600 ESG rating agencies worldwide, but the ESG rating systems of China's rating agencies have not yet reached world standards and the internationally accepted ESG rating systems cannot be fully applied to China. According to the data of the "Report on ESG Development of Listed Companies in China 2022", it indicates that ESG information disclosure of A-share listed companies has been on the rise in recent years, with a total of 1,431 companies releasing ESG-related reports for 2021, accounting for 31.34% of the total (as shown in Fig. 1). As a result, the importance attached to ESG in China is increasing and the establishment of an ESG rating system with Chinese characteristics has become an important topic of development today.

Under the influence of this, Wind ESG Rating System, which is suitable for the development characteristics of Chinese enterprises and the current situation of the capital market, and is in line with international standards and assessment frameworks, has been launched to assess the substantive ESG risks of enterprises and their ability to operate sustainably in a scientific, rigorous and predictable manner. In particular, the rating system analyses over 400 ESG indicators covering environmental, social and governance dimensions, reflecting the long-term ESG fundamentals, and over 1,200 controversial event labels covering news, regulatory penalties and legal proceedings, reflecting the impact of short-term emergencies, and combines them with the performance of companies in the same industry. In this paper, China Shenhua and China Coal Energy are compared and analysed with data from the Wind ESG rating system.

3.2 China Shenhua

Introduction to China Shenhua. China Shenhua Energy Company Limited (hereinafter referred to as China Shenhua) was exclusively sponsored by Shenhua Group

Disclosure of ESG-related reports for A-share listed companies

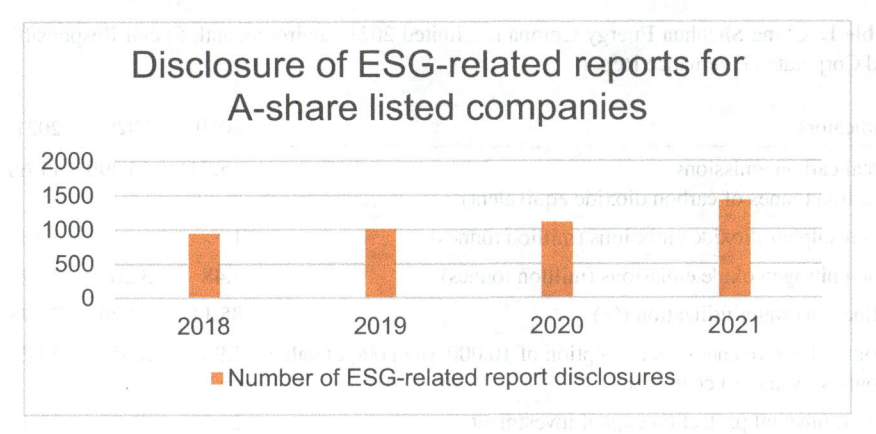

[Bar chart showing Number of ESG-related report disclosures: 2018 ~950, 2019 ~1000, 2020 ~1100, 2021 ~1450]

Fig. 1. Disclosure of ESG-related report for A-share listed companies.

Company Limited and was incorporated in Beijing, China on 8 November 2004. China Shenhua's A shares were listed on the Shanghai Stock Exchange in October 2007. China Shenhua is the world's leading integrated coal-based energy company, with its main businesses being the production and sale of coal and electricity, and the transportation of coal by rail, port and fleet, etc. In December 2021, China Shenhua became one of the first ESG demonstration companies in China and was awarded AA rating in the latest Wind ESG Rating results in April 2022, ranking No. 1 in the industry and tops the list among its domestic counterparts.

China Shenhua's Performance in Environment (E). From the data provided in the "China Shenhua Energy Company Limited 2021 Environmental, Social Responsibility and Corporate Governance Report" we can obtain Table 1. Firstly, from the pollutant emissions we can analyze that although the total carbon emissions of China Shenhua in the three years from 2019 to 2021 are increasing year by year, the total emissions of sulfur dioxide and nitrogen oxides of the company as a whole show a decreasing trend; secondly, the data of the company's mine Secondly, the company's mine water utilisation rate figures have been decreasing year on year, the utilisation rate of waste water has increased by 1.2 percentage points, and the comprehensive energy consumption consumption of 10,000 Yuan output value has also shown a decreasing trend; in terms of investment in environmental protection funds, the company's overall investment volume is high, and the investment volume in 2021 has risen by 11.72% compared to 2020, which can be inferred that the company has a strong awareness of environmental protection.

China Shenhua's Performance in Social (S) Aspects. In terms of social welfare, firstly, China Shenhua has been upholding the concept of giving thanks to the motherland, repaying society and giving back to the people, and fulfilling its social obligations through various forms of environmental protection, emergency relief and voluntary help. By the end of 2021, the company had donated a total of approximately RMB 389 million to the outside world, giving back its own resources to the development of society. Not only that, the Company also actively participates in social events such as the ESG China Forum 2021 Spring Summit and organises large-scale conferences on low-carbon clean

Table 1. China Shenhua Energy Company Limited 2021 Environmental, Social Responsibility and Corporate Governance Report.

Indicators	2019	2020	2021
Total carbon emissions (million tonnes of carbon dioxide equivalent)	15,741	13,490	17,665
Total sulphur dioxide emissions (million tonnes)	1.5	1.16	1.18
Total nitrogen oxide emissions (million tonnes)	3.48	3.26	3.42
Mine (pit) water utilization (%)	85.11	74.76	73.73
Comprehensive energy consumption of 10,000 Yuan output value (tonne of standard coal/yuan)	2.96	3.05	2.92
Environmental protection capital investment (billion yuan)	14.24	20.99	23.45

coal utilization technologies to share industry experience and professional insights. Secondly, in terms of safeguarding the interests of its employees, the Company continues to improve its remuneration mechanism and is committed to providing better pay and benefits for its employees. In 2021, China Shenhua effectively conducted up to 26,439 professional training sessions for 76,239 employees in conjunction with its employee training programme, with a staff training ratio of 97.90% and a total of 8,052,800 h, and established a comprehensive employee assessment mechanism to motivate employees and help them develop so that they can make more contributions to the company. Finally, China Shenhua actively promotes the construction of the company's culture and continuously carries out activities such as condolence to the families of employees in difficulties and care for the disabled to help employees solve practical problems. Not only that, China Shenhua focuses on protecting the rights and interests of female employees and providing equal employment development opportunities to create a harmonious working environment.

China Shenhua's Performance in Terms of Governance (G). In terms of corporate governance, China Shenhua has always focused on building a world class listed energy company with global competitiveness, improving its corporate governance mechanism, enhancing compliance management and promoting integrity building. In addition, China Shenhua has introduced an ESG governance structure that is closely integrated with the company's development. By connecting the Board of Directors, the Safety, Health and Environmental Protection Committee, the company's management (including: the Safety and Environmental Protection Group, the Social Contribution Group and the Corporate Governance Group) and the ESG Governance Working Office, and formulating more than 30 special institutional articles, the company's ESG governance work is carried out in an orderly manner. Secondly, the Company provided ESG training to more than 300 management staff in order to enhance their ability to perform their duties. The company also added 316 CDP indicators and 50 annual report indicators to the ESG information system to achieve financial coherence of multi-system indicators and implement the 14th Five-Year Plan.

3.3 China Coal Energy

Introduction of China Coal Energy. China Coal Energy Group Limited (hereinafter referred to as China Coal Energy) is a key state-owned backbone enterprise managed by the State-owned Assets Supervision and Administration Commission of the State Council, formerly known as China National Coal Import and Export Corporation, which was established in July 1982 and returned to A-share in February 2008. The Company is a large energy enterprise integrating four main businesses: coal production and trading, coal chemical industry, power generation and coal mining equipment manufacturing. It is committed to building a clean energy supplier with strong international competitiveness, becoming a leader in safe and green production, a demonstrator in clean and efficient utilization, and a practitioner in providing quality services, creating comprehensive economic, social and environmental values for corporate development. In the latest Wind ESG rating in April 2022, China Coal Energy was rated BBB, ranking 25th in its industry in China.

China Coal Energy's Performance in Environment (E). According to the data provided in the 2021 China Coal Energy Company Limited Environmental, Social and Governance Report, Table 2 shows that, firstly, China Coal Energy's emissions of pollutants such as sulphur dioxide and nitrogen oxides are on a downward trend from 2019 to 2021; secondly, the company's comprehensive mine water utilisation rate is on an upward trend and remains at a high level; not only that, the company's comprehensive energy consumption per 10,000 Yuan of output value Secondly, the comprehensive utilization rate of mine water has been on the rise and has remained high. It can be seen that China Coal Energy has a high level of environmental protection and a strong awareness of environmental protection.

Table 2. 2021 China Coal Energy Company Limited Environmental, Social and Governance Report

Indicators	2019	2020	2021
Sulphur dioxide emissions (tonnes)	2,976	2,724	2,299
Nitrogen oxide emissions (tonnes)	4,002	4,006	3,978
Integrated mine water utilization (%)	89.8	93.3	90.5
Comprehensive energy consumption of 10,000 Yuan output value (tonne of standard coal/yuan)	1.371	1.396	1.295

China Coal Energy's Performance in Social (S) Aspects. Firstly, China Coal Energy attaches great importance to the economic development of its operating locations and actively carries out public welfare activities to fulfill the company's social responsibility. The Company has assisted 21 villages, townships and towns, implemented 32 projects and invested approximately RMB25.99 million in support of its rural revitalisation policy. In addition, the company will also increase the implementation of local procurement projects. In 2021, the annual procurement contract value of China Coal

Shaanxi was RMB 4.186 billion, with local procurement accounting for 94.03% of the total. Secondly, the company adheres to the employment concept of "people-oriented and sharing achievements", and carries out professional training for employees around the deployment of the 14th Five-Year Plan, in which 70% of professional and technical staff are trained, with 20 h of training per capita, and 75% of skilled employees are trained, with 22.5 h of training per capita. The company has trained 70% of its professional and technical staff, with 20 h of training per capita. By the end of 2021, the company had trained 67 "master craftsmen in the coal industry", 4 "excellent technical experts in the coal industry", 1 person was selected as one of the "100 outstanding craftsmen" of the central enterprises, and 12 people were selected by the national human resources department. One person was selected as one of the "100 Outstanding Artisans" of the central enterprises, and 12 persons were awarded the honorary title of "National Technically Competent Person" by the Ministry of Human Resources and Social Security.

Performance of China Coal Energy in Terms of Governance (G). In terms of corporate governance, China Coal Energy standardizes the company's operational system, continuously integrates ESG concepts into the company's industrial chain, blends stakeholders and integrates sustainable development, and actively explores an ESG management system suitable for the company. At the same time, China Coal Energy also attaches great importance to the company's risk management capability, focusing on the main line of "target, risk and control", to sort out the weak points in the company's operation and management process, and monitor the control of major risks on a quarterly basis, so as to reasonably eliminate the hidden dangers caused by major risks. Secondly, China Coal Energy insists on transparent operation, and the company publishes timely information reports through its corporate website, WeChat public number and other information platforms every year.

3.4 Comparison of ESG Rating Scores

This article compares the ESG scores of China Shenhua and China Coal Energy using the latest data from the Wind ESG Rating System. From the ESG score chart of China Shenhua and China Coal Energy, it is clear that China Shenhua's scores in E, S and G are much higher than those of China Coal Energy, and the overall ESG score of China Shenhua is also higher than that of China Coal Energy. According to the previous section, China Shenhua is ranked first in its industry in the Wind ESG Rating System, while China Coal Energy is only ranked 27th. From the data in Fig. 2, it can be deduced that China Shenhua is stronger than China Coal Energy in terms of ESG implementation capabilities and is the leader in the same industry, while China Coal Energy needs to strengthen its ESG management system and has more room for improvement in all aspects of ESG. The company should pay more attention to ESG implementation efforts in order to improve its ESG rating score and achieve sustainable corporate development.

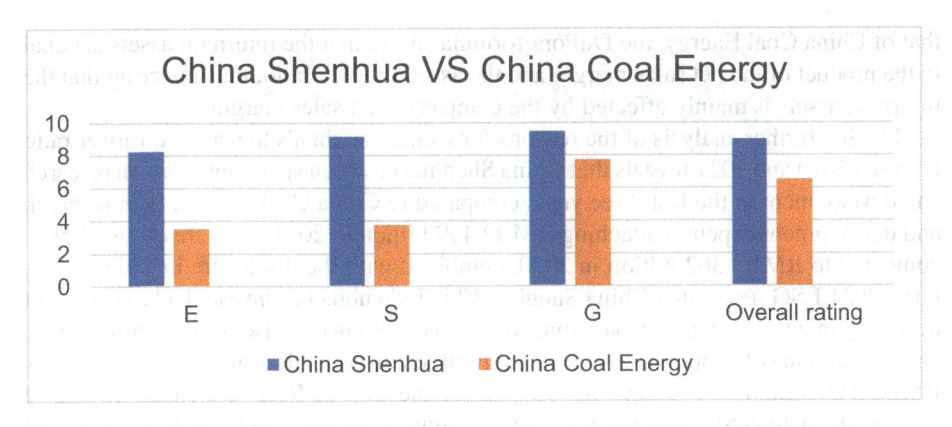

Fig. 2. China Shenhua VS China Coal Energy.

4 Comparative Analysis of the Financial Performance of the Two Companies

4.1 Explanation of Reasons for Comparison

Firstly, both companies are mainly engaged in coal production and operation, and they are both leading coal companies in China. In addition, China Shenhua and China Coal Energy were listed on the A-share market in similar years, with China Shenhua listed in October 2007 and China Coal Energy listed in February 2008. Secondly, both companies' financial data and ESG reports can be collected on their official websites, and both companies present different rating scores on the Wind ESG Rating System. In summary, China Shenhua and China Coal Energy have good comparability.

4.2 Analysis of Financial Data Using DuPont Analysis

This paper focuses on comparing the financial performance of China Shenhua and China Coal Energy based on the data provided in their annual reports for 2019 to 2021.

Firstly, it is clear from Fig. 3 that from 2019 to 2021, China Shenhua's return on assets is significantly higher than that of China Coal Energy, with both companies showing an upward trend in return on assets, and it can be inferred that China Shenhua is stronger than China Coal Energy in terms of capital utilisation and has achieved good results in terms of increasing revenue and saving capital usage.

Secondly, according to the DuPont analysis, return on assets can be decomposed into net sales margin and asset turnover rate multiplied by each other [10]. Analysis of the data in Fig. 4 clearly shows that China Shenhua's net sales margin is much higher than that of China Coal Energy, which can be analysed to show China Shenhua's high ability to obtain sales revenue during the period; Fig. 5 shows that China Shenhua's asset turnover ratio is lower compared to that of China Coal Energy, but shows an overall upward trend, which indicates that China Coal Energy has better sales capacity and asset utilisation efficiency, and both companies' sales capacity has The sales capacity of both companies improved during the study period. As China Shenhua's return on assets is higher than that of China Coal Energy, the DuPont formula shows that the return on assets is equal to the product of the net sales margin and the asset turnover ratio, thus inferring that the return on assets is mainly affected by the company's net sales margin.

Finally, further analysis of the reasons for China Shenhua's low asset turnover ratio between 2019 and 2021 reveals that China Shenhua has been spending more on research and development in the last three years compared to China Coal Energy, with research and development expenses reaching RMB2.499 billion in 2021, an increase of 45.50% compared to RMB1.362 billion in 2020, combined with the disclosure in China Shenhua's 2021 ESG report that China Shenhua China Shenhua has invested a large amount of money in environmental protection, which has continued to rise over the three years, and the amount of money invested in environmental protection in 2021 is as high as RMB2.345 billion, accounting for 93.83% of the overall R&D expenses. It can be inferred that China Shenhua has a strong ESG implementation and a high awareness of environmental protection, which can not only strengthen the fulfillment of China Shenhua's social responsibility, but also enhance the public's goodwill towards the enterprise, thus indirectly Based on the ROA data, we can see that China Shenhua's asset quality is high and stable. From the above information, it can be inferred that China Shenhua has strengthened its research and development intensity in order to build better quality assets, thus affecting the operating cycle and resultingin a relatively low asset turnover ratio.

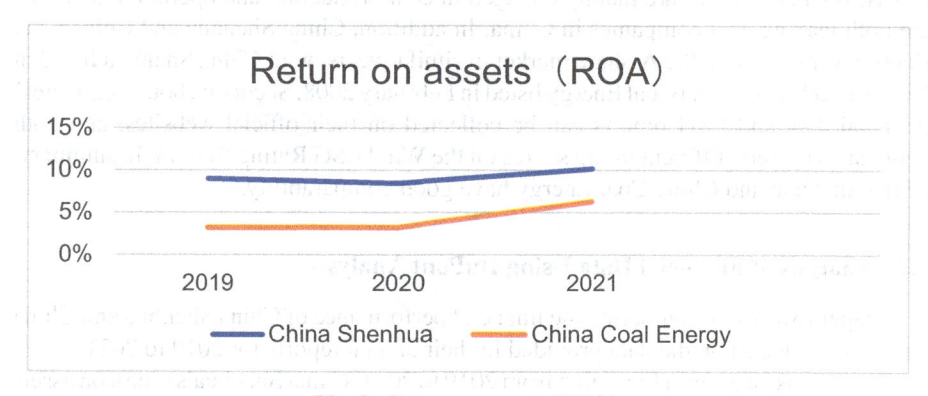

Fig. 3. Return on assets (ROA).

$$Return\ on\ Assets = Net\ profit\ /\ Total\ Average\ Assets \times 100\%$$

$$Total\ average\ assets = (Total\ assets\ at\ the\ beginning\ of\ the\ year + Total\ assets\ at\ the\ end\ of\ the\ year)/2$$

$$Net\ profit\ from\ sales = Net\ profit\ /\ Sales\ revenue \times 100\%$$

$$Asset\ turnover\ ratio = Sales\ revenue\ /\ Average\ total\ assets \times 100\%$$

Asset turnover ratio =
(total assets at the beginning of the year + total assets at the end of the year)/2

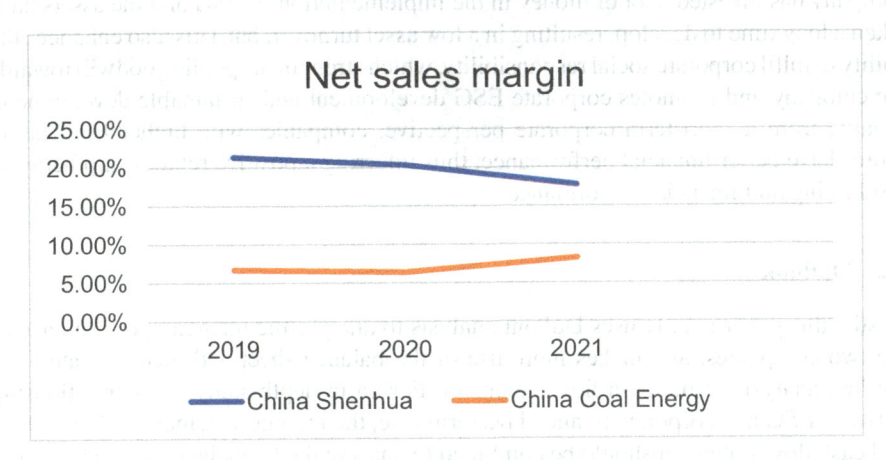

Fig. 4. Net sales margin.

Fig. 5. Asset turnover rate

5 Conclusion

5.1 Results

This paper firstly elaborates on the ESG performance of China Shenhua and China Coal Energy separately and compares their ESG rating scores to obtain the result that both China Shenhua's ESG rating scores are higher than China Coal Energy's. Secondly, this paper uses DuPont analysis to compare the data on the financial performance of China Shenhua and China Coal Energy. By decomposing the return on assets, we arrive at the result that net sales margin has a greater impact on return on assets than asset turnover, and deduce that the lower asset turnover of China Shenhua is due to the fact that the company has invested a lot of money in the implementation of ESG and the assets have taken a long time to develop, resulting in a low asset turnover, but This also enhances the ability to fulfil corporate social responsibility, which strengthens public goodwill towards the company and promotes corporate ESG development and sustainable development. Finally, from a short-term corporate perspective, companies with higher ESG rating scores have better financial performance, thus inferring a positive relationship between ESG rating and financial performance.

5.2 Outlook

Firstly, this paper mainly uses DuPont analysis to analyse the financial performance of the two companies, and makes more use of the balance sheet and income statement, but less analysis of the cash flow statement. For an in-depth study of the relationship between ESG and corporate financial performance, the income statement, balance sheet and cash flow statement should be combined to analyse the financial performance more comprehensively. Secondly, this paper only provides a comparative analysis of the financial performance of the two companies from 2019 to 2021, and subsequent studies could lengthen the time line of the study so as to provide a more convincing positive and research on coal companies in terms of sustainable development. Finally, based on the content of this paper, researchers can conduct more in-depth research and analysis on the relationship between financial performance and ESG ratings of more coal companies, suggest more development suggestions for coal companies in the domestic ESG environment, and strengthen the verification of the relationship between ESG ratings and financial performance of coal companies.

References

1. Xia, J.: Analysis of the impact of ESG on corporate performance–China Shenhua as an example. New Account. **162**(06), 31–34 (2022)
2. Wang, H.: A review of the literature on the impact of ESG ratings on corporate performance. Mod. Enterp. **432**(09), 86–87 (2021)
3. Shakil, M.H.: Environmental, social and governance performance and financial risk: moderating the role of ESG controversies and board gender diversity. Resour. Policy (2021)
4. Chouaibi, S., Chouaibi, J., Rossi, M.: ESG and corporate financial performance: the mediating role of green innovation: UK common law versus German civil law. Eur. Med. J. Bus. (2021). ahead-of-print (ahead-of-print)
5. Yi, Z.: The relationship between ESG performance and corporate financial performance: the case of Baosteel. Invest. Entrep. **33**(12), 55–57 (2022)
6. He, W., Zhao, X.: An empirical study on the impact of environmental performance on financial performance in a low-carbon economy: empirical evidence from the oil industry. Low Carbon Res. (4), 26 (2018)

7. Liu, P., Yu, J.X.: Construction of financial performance evaluation index system in chemical industry under the concept of environmental protection. Sci. Technol. Manag. **22**(01), 58–64 (2020)
8. Yan, Z.: The application of DuPont analysis system in corporate financial management–an example of M Group. Mark. World **17**, 167–169 (2022)
9. Zhang, Y., Liu, R.: A comparative study on the impact of social responsibility report and ESG report disclosure on financial performance of mining companies. Rental Sales Intell. **820**(10), 92–94 (2022)
10. Liang, W.: The establishment of an evaluation system based on ROE and ROA corporate profitability. Hebei Enterp. **270**(01), 24 (2012)

Research on the Impact of Regulatory Inquiries Related to Information Disclosure of Listed Companies – A Case Study of ANDON HEALTH

Miaoxuan Ma[✉]

Business School, Beijing Technology and Business University, Beijing 102488, China
2002020108@st.btbu.edu.cn

Abstract. With the rapid development of China's capital market, many problems arise. Among them, the violation of information disclosure is particularly significant, such as inadequate information disclosure, misleading statements, omission of important matters and other behaviors are common in major listed companies. In this paper, by studying the inquiry of ANDON HEALTH information disclosure by Shenzhen Stock Exchange, the effectiveness of regulatory inquiry is studied by using event study method. It is found that the cumulative excess rate of return of ANDON HEALTH is significantly affected by the inquiry behavior of Shenzhen Stock Exchange. This inquiry behavior caused widespread concern in the market, resulting in the stock price in the short term to produce an obvious callback phenomenon, has a certain incentive effect. However, when ANDON HEALTH admitted that there was a problem of incomplete disclosure of information disclosure, the stock market's response to the quality problem of ANDON HEALTH information disclosure was not significant.

Keywords: Andon Health Co., Ltd · Information Disclosure · Regulatory Inquiry · Market reaction

1 Introduction

1.1 Research Background

With the change of times and the progress of science and technology, China's capital market is moving towards high-quality development, but it is also closely related to information disclosure. Because the establishment time of Chinese capitalist market is not as long as developed countries, compared with its mature capital market, there is still a gap, there are still widespread information disclosure non-standard, illegal and other chaos. Such behavior seriously affects investors' interests and the fairness of market transactions. Thus, the importance of the regulatory body emerges, in order to shape the true, accurate, complete, timely and fair information disclosure environment. Since the exchange launched the "information disclosure through train" in 2013, the regulatory system of inquiry letter has been formally implemented. By using this regulatory method, strict requirements and high standards are set for the information disclosure behavior of enterprises, which alleviates the problem of information asymmetry to a certain extent and enables investors to obtain more reliable, true and comprehensive information.

1.2 Research Significance

In terms of theoretical significance, this paper enriches the existing literature, takes the incomplete information disclosure of ANDON HEALTH Medical and the concern letter received from Shenzhen Stock Exchange as the research object, and analyzes the effectiveness of inquiry supervision combined with market reaction. Using the method of case analysis, analyze the market reaction caused by the inquiry regulation from the perspective of individual companies and analyze the reasons.

In terms of practical significance, this paper can further improve the intensity of supervision and punishment of the exchange on corporate information disclosure and promote the awareness of listed companies to improve the quality of information disclosure and improve its integrity. It can serve as a warning to investors, and it is hoped that through this article, investors can improve their prevention and attention to the problems existing in the company's information disclosure.

2 Theoretical Foundation and Literature Review

2.1 Review of the Literature on Regulatory Inquiry and Information Disclosure

Regulatory Inquiry. The regulatory inquiry system provides direct and targeted behavior rules for enterprise operation, management and information disclosure. It has become an emerging interpretation method to re-understand the company and discover the problems existing in the disclosure of company information through regulatory inquiry. The influence of regulatory inquiry on enterprises involves many aspects, so the conclusions of the studies are different. Yu and Zheng studied the effectiveness of the inquiry supervision of the stock exchange and found that the inquiry supervision of the stock exchange can realize its supervision function by improving the quality of information disclosure of listed companies in the short and medium term, improving the quality of reorganization of listed companies, and making early warning of violations of listed companies [1]. Guo and Li believe that correspondence has a significant impact on information improvement, market response, and behavior of companies and stakeholders [2]. Liu found that the stock exchange inquiry letter system played a positive role in improving the information efficiency of the capital market, maintaining the steady development of the stock market, and protecting the legitimate rights and interests of investors [3]. Yang and Li proved through empirical research that inquiry supervision has a significant impact on the cumulative average excess return rate of the company under inquiry [4].

In the research on inquiry supervision, scholars pay more attention to the characteristics of enterprises that are easy to be queried. Some studies have found that when corporate governance is low, business performance is poor, audit quality is low and information disclosure quality is poor, enterprises are more likely to receive inquiry letters. Zhang et al. found through research that listed companies with sustained losses, continuous profit growth, risk warnings, irregularities and other characteristics are more likely to receive inquiry letters [5]. Zhao et al. found that the worse the quality of internal control of listed companies, the more likely the annual report is to be questioned by the exchange [6]. Kubick et al. found that firms found to have potential for tax evasion were more likely to receive regulatory inquiries [7].

Information Disclosure. The quality of disclosure is closely related to regulatory inquiries. A large number of studies at home and abroad show that regulatory inquiry is beneficial to optimize the information disclosure level of listed companies. Johnston proved that inquiry letters played a positive role in improving the quality of information disclosure [8]. Liu analyzed and found that the inquiry letter system of the stock exchange can play a supervisory role in the information disclosure system, thus improving the quality of information disclosure [3]. Zhai and Wang found that inquiry letter affects the quality of information disclosed by enterprises by reducing the level of information asymmetry [9].

2.2 Comment

This paper reviews the relevant literature from the aspects of the value and effect of regulatory inquiry, the characteristics of enterprises liable to be queried, and the influence of regulatory inquiry on information disclosure. It has proved that the regulatory inquiry is effective and has certain influence on the information disclosure of enterprises. It can improve the information disclosure content of listed companies and improve the accuracy of their disclosure, so as to provide more authentic information to the outside world. The existing literature mainly analyzes the role of regulatory inquiries from the analysis and disclosure content of listed companies' annual reports. This paper takes ANDON HEALTH Medical as an example to carry out research, and uses relevant theories to analyze the impact of regulatory inquiries caused by the quality of information disclosure on enterprises, and draws conclusions.

3 A Review of ANDON HEALTH Inquiries

3.1 Ask About Developments

The letter of inquiry is one of the most important non-administrative punishment measures in our country. Zhang conducted inquiry statistics on Shenzhen Stock Exchange and found that it only issued three inquiry letters in 2014, but the number of letters issued later increased by about 40% [10]. The frequency of sending letters is gradually increasing at the same time that the number of various types of letters is also growing.

The pharmaceutical industry combines traditional industry with modern industry, and is an important part of our national economy. Among them, the phenomenon of information disclosure violation is common, which not only damages the interests of the people but also hinders social development, and the frequency of receiving letters is high.

3.2 General Situation of ANDON HEALTH

ANDON HEALTH is a global provider of household medical and health electronic products, specializing in home-based testing, personalized, professional physiotherapy and home-based. We are committed to allowing everyone to have a simple and accurate understanding of their own body, and provide the most advanced and convenient blood pressure diagnostic tools for doctors and medical institutions around the world. ANDON HEALTH integrates research and development, production and sales at home and abroad. Since its establishment in Tianjin Nankai New Technology Industrial Park in 1995, ANDON HEALTH has successfully promoted physiological parameter testing instruments including electronic sphygmomanometer, electronic thermometer, far infrared thermometer, blood glucose meter, etc. And low-frequency therapy instrument, multi-channel low-frequency therapy instrument, far infrared heating instrument, handheld massage instrument and other health equipment, occupy an important share of global HHCE related medical instruments. At the end of 2007, the company underwent shareholding reform, and has been listed on the Shenzhen Stock Exchange SME edition on June 10, 2010.

3.3 The Inquiry Process of ANDON HEALTH

On January 7, 2022, ANDON HEALTH Medical issued the Announcement on the subsidiary's receipt of the experimental report on the performance of iHealth's Home Self-testing OTC kit for the Novel Coronavirus Antigen against Omicron mutated Virus. It said the report showed that "iHealth-Covid-19 Antigen Rapid Test detected Omicron active virus samples with a maximum CT value of 21.59 (n = 5) 100% of the time in the experiment". However, only part of successful test results were disclosed, but not all experimental results were disclosed, and the disclosure information was incomplete.

On the evening of January 12, Shenzhen Stock Exchange expressed in the letter of concern to ANDON HEALTH Medical, hoping that ANDON HEALTH Medical could explain several matters, the main contents of which are shown in Table 1 (data from Shenzhen Stock Exchange):

Table 1. The main contents of inquiry.

Order	Inquiry content
1	Explain the specific meaning of the CT value of the virus sample in this experiment and the distribution of the CT value of the Omicron virus population (if applicable)
2	Explain why your company's Announcement only discloses the test results of four samples with CT value less than or equal to 21.59, but does not disclose the test results of seven samples with CT value greater than 21.59. Is it possible to mislead investors by confusing the positive detection rate of all samples with the positive detection rate of some samples? Whether the above announcement has disclosed the test results of the experimental report completely, whether there is any selective disclosure of part of the information to hype the stock price, and explain the reasons
3	Explain whether "100% of the iHealth kit detected Omicron active virus samples with the maximum CT value of 21.59 (n = 5)" stated in your company's Announcement is consistent with the actual results of the experiment report. Whether there is any contradiction with the US FDA's claim that "early data show that antigen detection kit can detect Omicron mutated virus, but its sensitivity may be reduced", further explain whether the relevant statements in your company's Announcement are accurate or misleading, and explain the reasons

(*continued*)

Table 1. (*continued*)

Order	Inquiry content
4	Supplementary disclosure of the details of the experiment, including but not limited to the experimental group and control group 3 sample selection methods, experimental process, positive detection rate of all experimental samples, reliability of experimental results, and combined with the experimental sample size, experimental methods and other factors, to explain whether the experimental results can represent the overall situation. The corroborative relationship between the experimental results and the sensitivity and specificity of the iHealth kit to detect Omicron virus, on the basis of which the experimental results were adequately suggested for risk
5	Combined with the answers to the above four questions, explain whether the disclosure of your company's Announcement is true, accurate and complete, whether there are misleading statements or major omissions, whether it is clear, appropriate and easy to understand. Whether it complies with the provisions of Rules 2.1.1, 2.1.4, 2.1.5, 2.1.6 and 2.1.9 of the Stock Listing Rules (2022 Amendment), and explain the reasons
6	State the procedures that your company's iHealth kit needs to follow if it wants to obtain emergency approval from Tianjin Drug Administration, state whether your company's proposed program is inconsistent with the characteristics and prevention and control strategies of the epidemic in China, and fully indicate the uncertainties and related risks
7	Explain whether the contents of the Record Form mentioned above are prudent and objective, and whether there are exaggerated propaganda or misleading tips to cater to hot market concepts and hype up stock prices. Whether it complies with the relevant provisions of Article 7.1.1, 7.5.2 and 7.5.3 of the Guidance on Self-Regulation of Listed Companies No.1 – Standardized Operation of Listed Companies on the Main Board

4 Analysis of the Impact of Regulatory Inquiry on ANDON HEALTH Medical

Event studies were pioneered by Ball & Brown and Fama et al. [11, 12]. The principle is to select a specific event according to the research purpose, study the change of the sample stock return rate before and after the event, and then explain the influence of the specific event on the sample stock price change and return rate, which is mainly used to test the price change before and after the event or the reaction degree of the price to the disclosed information. This paper uses the market model to establish the market model equation $R_{it} = \alpha_i + \beta_i \times R_{mt}$ for the index rate of return (R_{it}) and the daily rate of return (R_{mt}) of JIU' an Medical stock price. In the extracted data, the actual rate of return and market rate of return data selected in this paper are from Juchao.com and EastMoney.com.

Event I was set as: Tianjin ANDON HEALTH Co., Ltd. Disclosed on January 7, 2023 "Announcement on the subsidiary's receipt of the experimental report on the performance of iHealth's Home Self-testing OTC Kit for Novel Coronavirus Antigen against Omicron mutated virus"; Event II is set as: Shenzhen Stock Exchange issued a letter of concern to ANDON HEALTH on January 12, 2023.

With the help of the event study method, this paper studies the stock price fluctuations and market returns caused by the announcement of ANDON HEALTH and the behavior of the exchange concern letter in a certain period of time, and analyzes its market effect. The event window period and estimation window are set as follows (see Table 2):

Table 2. The event window period and estimation window.

Events	Working day	Event window	Estimation window
Event I ANDON HEALTH issued a notice	2022-01-07	2022-01-06 to 2022-01-10	2021-04-29 to 2021-12-08
Event II Shenzhen Stock Exchange inquiry process	2022-01-12	2022-01-11 to 2022-01-24	2021-04-29 to 2021-12-08

Since the estimation Windows selected for event I and event II are the same, the scatter chart is the same. Excel is used to generate a scatter chart, and the values of parameters α and β are obtained. The scatter chart is shown in Fig. 1:

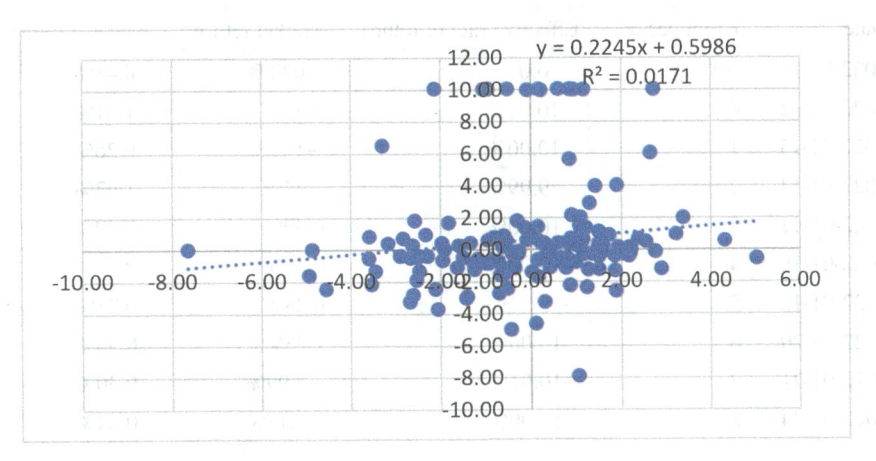

Fig. 1. Equation of event I and event II estimation window.

Table 3. Final parametric equation.

Events	Estimation window	Parameter equation	α	β
Event I ANDON HEALTH issued a notice	2021-04-29 to 2021-12-08	y = 0.2245x + 0.5986	0.5986	0.2245
Event II Shenzhen Stock Exchange inquiry process	2021-04-29 to 2021-12-08	y = 0.2245x + 0.5986	0.5986	0.2245

From the point of view of β value (see Table 3), ANDON HEALTH daily rate of return (R_{it}) and market rate of return (R_{mt}) showed a positive correlation.

The daily market rate of return (R_{mt}) of the event period can be substituted into the regression equation $R_{it} = 0.2245\ R'_{mt} - 0.5986$ to obtain the daily expected rate of return

R'_{it} of ANDON HEALTH. The expected return of event I is shown in Table 4, and the expected return of event II is shown in Table 5:

Table 4. Correlated returns of event I.

Date	Event period	Effective rate of return	Market return	expected return
2022-01-06	−1	2.04%	−0.90%	0.40%
2022-01-07	0	6.05%	−1.06%	0.36%
2022-01-10	1	1.82%	0.99%	0.82%

Table 5. Correlated returns of event II.

Date	Event period	Effective rate of return	Market return	expected return
2022-01-11	−1	10.00%	−0.86%	0.41%
2022-01-12	0	10.01%	2.71%	1.21%
2022-01-13	1	10.00%	−1.52%	0.26%
2022-01-14	2	9.99%	1.47%	1.47%
2022-01-17	3	10.00%	0.49%	0.49%
2022-01-18	4	−10.00%	0.06%	0.06%
2022-01-19	5	−5.27%	0.28%	0.28%
2022-01-20	6	10.00%	1.53%	0.94%
2022-01-21	7	−10.01%	−3.99%	−0.30%
2022-01-24	8	−10.00%	−1.17%	0.34%

The excess rate of return AR is directly formed by the behavior of information disclosure. It is the rate of return beyond the normal market return. The excess rate of return is the actual rate of return of JIU' an Medical in the event period minus the expected rate of return under the market model:

$$AR_{it} = R_{it} - R'_{it} \quad (1)$$

The cumulative abnormal return rate is the sum of the ultra long daily return rate of ANDON HEALTH stock in the event period. Compared with the excess rate of return, the cumulative abnormal rate of return can better reflect the influence of information disclosure behavior and regulatory inquiries on ANDON HEALTH:

$$CAR_{it} = \sum_{t2}^{t1} AR_{it} \quad (2)$$

(t_1, t_2) is the calculation interval of cumulative excess return, this paper selects event I $T_1 = (-1, 1)$ and event II $T_2 = (-1, 8)$.

The income rate of event I during the event window is shown in Table 6 and Fig. 2:
The yield of event II during the event window is shown in Table 7:

Table 6. Correlated returns of event I.

Date	Event period	Effective rate of return	Expected return	Yield advantage	Excess cumulative return
2022-01-06	−1	2.04%	0.40%	1.64%	1.64%
2022-01-07	0	6.05%	0.36%	5.69%	7.33%
2022-01-10	1	1.82%	0.82%	1.00%	8.33%

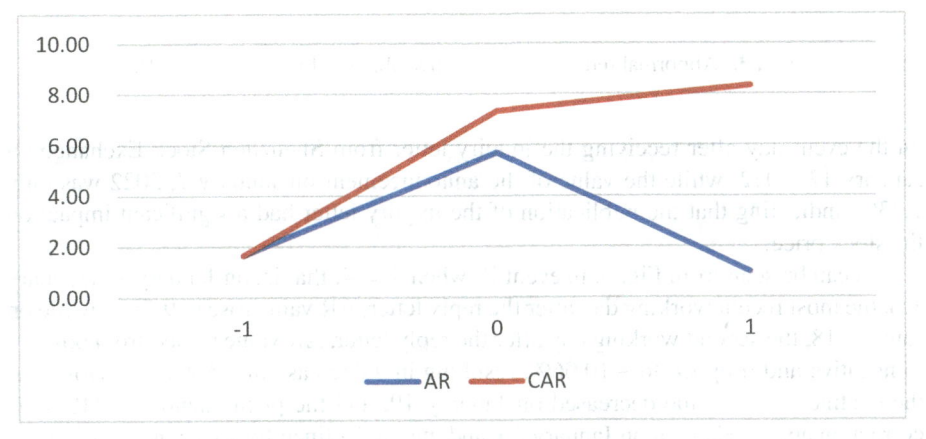

Fig. 2. Abnormal return and cumulative abnormal return of Event I.

Table 7. Correlated returns of event II.

Date	Event period	Effective rate of return	Expected return	Yield advantage	Excess cumulative return
2022-01-11	−1	10.00%	0.41%	9.59%	9.59%
2022-01-12	0	10.01%	1.21%	8.80%	18.39%
2022-01-13	1	10.00%	0.26%	9.74%	28.13%
2022-01-14	2	9.99%	1.47%	8.52%	36.65%
2022-01-17	3	10.00%	0.49%	9.51%	46.16%
2022-01-18	4	−10.00%	0.06%	−10.06%	36.10%
2022-01-19	5	−5.27%	0.28%	−5.55%	30.55%
2022-01-20	6	10.00%	0.94%	9.06%	39.61%
2022-01-21	7	−10.01%	−0.30%	−9.71%	29.91%
2022-01-24	8	−10.00%	0.34%	−10.34%	19.57%

Through a comprehensive analysis of the abnormal rate of return and the cumulative abnormal rate of return of event I and II, the value of ANDON HEALTH rose to 18.39%

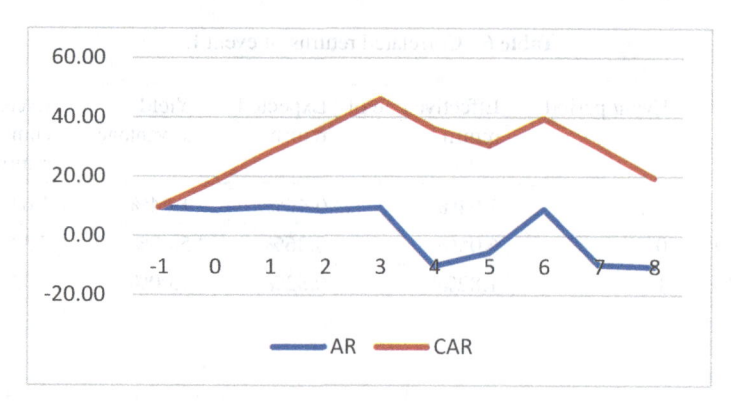

Fig. 3. Abnormal return and cumulative abnormal return of Event II.

on the event day after receiving the inquiry letter from Shenzhen Stock Exchange on January 12, 2022, while the value of the announcement on January 7, 2022 was only 7.33%, indicating that the publication of the inquiry letter had a significant impact on the stock price.

As can be seen from Fig. 3, in event II, when T = 4, that is, on January 17 (January 15), the most recent working day after the reply letter, AR value rose to 9.51%, while on January 18, the second working day after the reply letter, AR value turned from positive to negative and dropped to -10.06%, resulting in a decrease in CAR value. However, the decline of AR value decreased on January 19, and the phenomenon of AR value correction appeared again on January 20, and then it declined for two consecutive days. The excess rate of return showed obvious fluctuations after the reply, but overall, the accumulated excess rate of return was still positive and reached 19.57% on January 24.

The fact that ANDON HEALTH has received the inquiry letter from Shenzhen Stock Exchange has a far greater incentive effect on the stock price than its own information disclosure. Investors still hold a positive attitude towards this stock and continue to invest more. However, ANDON HEALTH disclosed more complete experimental results to investors after the letter, which alleviated the asymmetry of information and prevented the further fermentation of negative information. But on January 18th and the following days, investors sold stocks, causing prices to fall and generating negative excess returns. However, from the perspective of cumulative excess rate of return, the whole stock market has no significant response to the quality problems of ANDON HEALTH information disclosure.

5 Conclusion

The inquiry behavior of Shenzhen Stock Exchange has significantly affected the cumulative excess yield of ANDON HEALTH. This series of inquiries by causing widespread concern in the market, so that the stock price in the short term produced a huge correction phenomenon. This paper is consistent with the conclusion of Yang's empirical analysis on inquiry regulation. After the inquiry letter announcement is issued by the regulator, the cumulative average excess return rate of the companies queried is positive and shows an obvious positive effect.

Thus, for market participants and regulators, exchange inquiry letters improve the quality of information disclosure, enhance the orderly flow of information, and reduce information asymmetry. In the short term, regulatory inquiries can affect the psychology of investors, raising their interest in the companies being questioned and, in turn, investing more and chasing shares higher. However, in the long run, it is necessary for the enterprise to reply as soon as possible, improve the information disclosure, improve the quality of information disclosure and build investors' confidence in order to stabilize the stock price in the long run, so that it will not be affected by inquiries and produce negative trends. At the same time, the supervision office should also strengthen the supervision and improve the feedback mechanism, so as to improve the quality of information disclosure of enterprises.

References

1. Yu, X., Zheng, J.: Research on the effectiveness of stock exchange inquiry regulation – an empirical test based on inquiry letter. Res. Financ. Regul. Res. (2020)
2. Guo, Z., Li, Y.: Review and prospect of research on effectiveness of stock exchange regulatory inquiry. Financ. Regulatory Res. (2020)
3. Liu, C.: Stock exchange regulation and stock price crash risk: a heterogeneity analysis based on inquiry letters. South. Financ. (2019)
4. Yang, H., Li, J.: Market reaction of inquiry regulation – an empirical analysis based on the data of shenzhen stock exchange. J. Beijing Technol. Bus. Univ. (Soc. Sci. Edit.) (2018)
5. Zhang, K., Hu, W., Li, X.: Who is more likely to be regulated by a letter of regulation for year-end surprise profits? – Also on the effect of letter regulation. Secur. Mark. Guide (2019)
6. Zhao, L., Fu, X., Li, Y., et al.: Can exchange inquiry letter identify internal control risk? – Empirical evidence based on the inquiry letter of annual report. South. Financ. (2020)
7. Kubick, T.R., Lynch, D.P., Mayberry, M.A., Omer, T.C.: The effects of regulatory scrutiny on tax avoidance: an examination of SEC comment letters. Account. Rev. (2016)
8. Johnston, R., Petacchi, R.: Regulatory oversight of financial reporting: securities and exchange commission comment letters. Contemp. Account. Res. **34**(2), 1128–1155 (2017)
9. Zhai, S., Wang, M.: Does non-punitive supervision improve the quality of corporate performance prediction? Evidence from financial report inquiry letter. J. Shanxi Univ. Financ. Econ. **41**(04), 92–107 (2019)
10. Zhang, M.: Research on the effectiveness of inquiry regulation from the perspective of market response. Dongbei University of Finance and Economics (2022)
11. Ball, R., Brown, P.: An empirical evaluation of accounting income numbers. J. Account. Res. 159–178 (1968). Autumn
12. Fama, E.F., Fisher, L., Jensen, M.C., Roll, R.: The adjustment of stock prices to new information. Int. Econ. Rev. 10(1), 1–21 (1969)

Research on Financial Competitiveness of a Listed Company Based on DuPont Analysis Method

Yile Kong[1(✉)] and Xitong Zhu[2]

[1] DeGroote School of Business, McMaster University, Hamilton L8S 4L8, Canada
kongy15@mcmaster.ca

[2] College of Economics and Management, Nanjing University of Aeronautics and Astronautics, Nanjing 211100, China

Abstract. Based on the DuPont analysis method, this paper analyzes the financial data and competitiveness of the well-known Chinese beer brand, Tsingtao Brewery. Studying the "financial competitiveness" of Tsingtao Brewery and DuPont analysis method not only helps the company's financial management but also provides innovative directions for traditional catering and food companies under the COVID-19 pandemic. Meanwhile, the thesis also provides a representative case for researchers to explore the application of financial analysis methods in practice and expanding research perspectives.

Keywords: Financial Competitiveness · DuPont Analysis · Tsingtao Brewery

1 Introduction

This thesis analyzes the financial data of Tsingtao Brewery, a well-known Chinese beer brand, using the DuPont analysis method. By effectively decomposing the core indicator of return on equity, and analyzing the company's balance sheets, cash flow statements, and income statements from 2012 to 2017, both before and during the COVID-19 pandemic. The study found that Tsingtao Brewery's asset profitability ratio and equity multiplier are at a relatively high level in the industry, while its debt multiplier is relatively low. This indicates that the company has higher asset quality and less financial risk. In addition, the company's profitability, debt-servicing ability, and operational efficiency are also outstanding, which enhances its "financial competitiveness" and market competitiveness.

2 Literature Review

2.1 Definition of "Financial Competitiveness"

The concept of "core competence" of enterprises was first proposed by Prahalad and Hamel [1]. Porter M. E. a professor at Harvard Business School, pushed the research wave on "financial competitiveness" in the economic field with the publish of his book

---

Y. Kong and X. Zhu—These authors contribute equally.

"Competitive Advantage", which discussed how enterprises can create and maintain their competitive advantages [2].

The essence of "financial competitiveness" of enterprises lies in achieving financial innovation by changing their development direction and management concepts Wang, Guo [3]. This competitiveness mainly manifests in various aspects such as the enterprise's ability for technological innovation, profitability, operating and production costs, and reflects the actual management situation of the enterprise comprehensively. Therefore, taking "financial competitiveness" as an evaluation criterion can encourage enterprises to not only consider reducing costs and creating value but also attach importance to improving the efficiency of fund operation. This can prevent enterprises from adopting strategies such as retaining uneconomical assets due to a single-minded focus on core competitiveness Hao et al. [4].

2.2 Related Theories

In 1920, the DuPont Company in the United States created and used this system to analyze the financial situation of enterprises and evaluate their operational effectiveness. Return on equity, as the most core indicator of the DuPont analysis system, fully reflects the impact of an enterprise's profitability and equity multiplier.

Zvi and Alex, professors at Boston University in the United States, improved and extended the DuPont model by adding interest expense and tax two indicators, forming the five-factor DuPont model, and using tax burden rates, interest expenses, and other indicators to more comprehensively reflect the financial condition and capital structure of enterprises [5]. The DuPont analysis system, improved by Smith, proposed using indicators such as underwriting profit margin, revenue rate, revenue coefficient, and Kenni coefficient to measure the profitability of R&D business, investment business, future investment scale, and solvency of enterprises [6].

2.3 Literature Review

Research on Financial Competitiveness

International Research. "Financial competitiveness" has always been an important part of international economic competitiveness. Through a comprehensive study of relevant literature at home and abroad, this paper summarizes the following points: innovation in financial technology can promote financial inclusion and enable more people to access financial services. A cross-country study shows that innovation in financial technology has a positive effect on promoting financial inclusion by Sui, [7]. Therefore, the development of financial technology is of great significance to improving a country's "financial competitiveness".

The development of financial markets has a significant positive relationship with economic growth, which has been confirmed by multiple studies. For example, Beck and Levine's study shows that the development of stock markets and the banking industry has a significant positive relationship with economic growth [8]. Demirguç-Kunt and Levine also pointed out that the development of financial markets plays an important role in long-term economic growth [9].

The deepening and diversification of financial markets play an important role in promoting economic growth and development. Laeven and Valencia's research found that the deepening and diversification of financial markets can promote financial stability and economic growth [10]. The deepening of financial markets can improve capital allocation efficiency and resource allocation efficiency, thereby promoting economic growth.

Chinese Research. Corporate "financial competitiveness" arises from the theory of core competitiveness in the management economics, and is a financial innovation based on this theory. "Financial competitiveness" includes multiple aspects with profitability and growth as the core, determining the vlue of the enterprise. Zhu taking maximizing sustainable growth as financial goals can benefit enterprise by better balancing profitability, development and sustainability [11].

Meng believed that "financial competitiveness" is the sum of survival and development abilities relative to other competitors in the market, and can promote sustained development of enterprises [12]. It is not only external market performance and innovation ability of the enterprise, but also an internal control capability.

Huang discussed the necessity of improving corporate competitiveness in financial strategies [13]. Her thesis made suggestions for improving the level of self-financing, such as reasonably determining the scale of financing, controlling the cost of financing or expanding financing channels through analyzing the relationship between corporate competitiveness and financial strategies.

Mu and Wang proposed the importance of financial flexibility [14]. They believed that improving the utilization rate of corporate funds and controlling the cash-to-debt ratio can ensure the enterprises to obtain financial resources at the lowest cost and fastest speed when making strategic adjustments. Meanwhile it can also avoid overinvestment or insufficient investment and improve corporate performance.

Yu Miao believed that R&D investment is positively correlated with corporate performance [15]. Excellent early R&D will be conducive to the sustained development of the enterprise, and continuous adjustment and transformation in the later stage will bring sustained benefits in terms of cost and market share to the enterprise.

Application of DuPont Analysis. The DuPont analysis method is an important method for evaluating corporate "financial competitiveness" from a financial perspective with return on equity as the core, and can comprehensively evaluate the efficiency of enterprise-owned capital. In 1919, DuPont Company created the DuPont financial analysis method and found the method useful since it can analyze financial conditions more intuitively, adjust financial strategies timely and enhance market competitiveness. Even now the DuPont analysis method is still been used as a classic financial analysis method.

However, due to the limitations of traditional DuPont analysis, it is often combined with other financial innovation tools. For example, the informationization application of DuPont analysis can establish a risk warning mechanism and improve the enterprise's anti-risk ability [16].

Literature Review. According to the domestic and foreign research reviewed above, it can be observed that there is increasing attention being paid to factors such as the cost of capital, return on investment, capital utilization, and sustainable growth of enterprises.

The field of economics has begun to consider more and more development factors when assessing a company's "financial competitiveness". Therefore, companies should keep up with the times and develop corresponding innovative financial strategies to enhance their core "financial competitiveness".

Currently, China is in the phase of post-pandemic recovery, and the catering and food industry is gradually recovering. During the pandemic, the sales channels and methods of these companies were greatly affected, and numerous innovations emerged. The integration and development of these excellent innovative points are crucial to promoting the healthy development of the market and improving the recovery speed of the entire industry. This thesis takes Tsingtao Brewery, a state-owned time-honored enterprise, as a case study, and conducts an in-depth analysis of the company's financial situation, innovative points, and shortcomings before and after the pandemic, which can serve as a reference for other companies in the same industry.

3 Case Company Introduction

3.1 Company Overview

Qingdao Beer Co., Ltd. (Tsingtao Brewery) is a Chinese beer manufacturer and distributor. Its predecessor was the state-owned Tsingtao Brewery Factory, established in 1903, which is one of the oldest beer production plants in China. The company was registered in China on June 16, 1993, and was listed on the Hong Kong Stock Exchange on July 15 of the same year, becoming the first Chinese company to be listed overseas. In addition, Tsingtao Brewery issued A shares in China in July of the same year and was listed on the Shanghai Stock Exchange on August 27.

Tsingtao Brewery's main business is the manufacture and sale of beer. Currently, the company has 58 wholly-owned or controlled beer production enterprises, as well as two joint venture beer production enterprises, located in 20 provinces, municipalities, and autonomous regions across the country. Its scale and market share are in a leading position in the Chinese beer industry.

As one of the most well-known beer brands in China, Tsingtao Brewery has been marketed to more than 100 countries and regions around the world. Its main products include Tsingtao Brewery, Finest Beer, Draft Beer, and Tsingtao Brewery Classic. Tsingtao Brewery also actively participates in social public welfare undertakings, such as environmental protection initiatives, sports events, and cultural activities, making contributions to society.

3.2 Reasons for Case Selection

Based on the principle of typicality, Qingdao Beer Co., Ltd. was selected as the case company for this article (hereinafter referred to as Tsingtao Brewery). The reasons for this selection are as follows:

Tsingtao Brewery is China's first modern beer production enterprise. In 1947, Tsingtao Brewery became the protagonist of China's first film advertisement, famous throughout the country for its clean and hygienic transparent production process and authentic

German flavor, laying the foundation for the brand's growth and internationalization. In 2022, Tsingtao Brewery and its subsidiaries topped the World Brand Lab's 2022 "China's 500 Most Valuable Brands" list with a total brand value of 218.225 billion yuan. Also it maintained its position as the most valuable brand in the Chinese beer industry for the 19th consecutive year.

In addition to the brand effect, Tsingtao Brewery also has strong patent research and development capabilities. From Fig. 1, as of October 2021, Tsingtao Brewery's patent applications totaled 233, ranking fifth in the global beer industry in terms of the number of patents. Compared to other Chinese domestic brands, Tsingtao Brewery's number of effective patents is far ahead, with 114 of them being invention-type patents, including four PCT patent applications, as shown in Fig. 1 below.

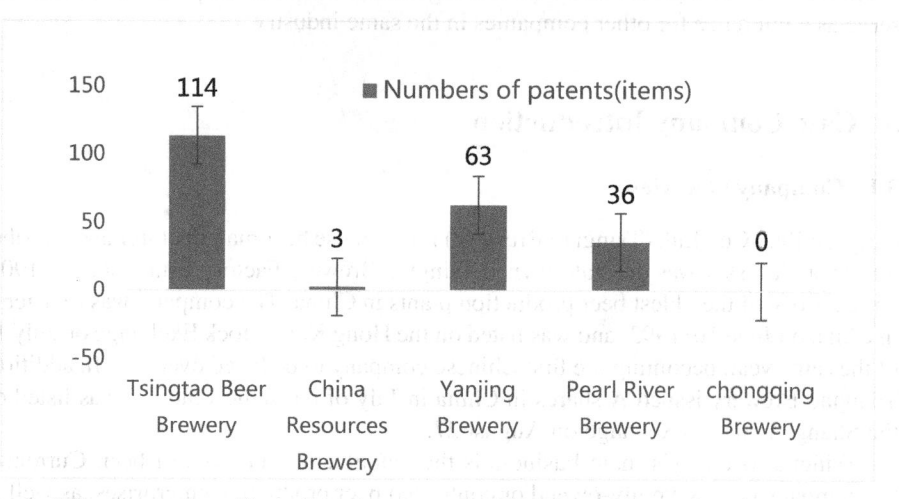

Fig. 1. Effective number of invention-type patents for China's top five beer brands as of February 2023.

3.3 Industry Analysis

Beer Industry Mergers and Acquisitions Are Accelerating, and Market Share Competition is Intense. In terms of expanding scale, the beer industry has adopted several different methods, including mergers and acquisitions, building new factories, and expanding existing ones. Among them, the most effective method is mergers and acquisitions because it has additional effects that new construction and expansion cannot achieve, namely the double effect of simultaneous reduction and increase. Therefore, from an economic perspective, this expansion method is also a common practice internationally.

The Market Share of the Chinese Beer Market Shows a Characteristic of Stability, and the Competitive Position in the Market is Relatively Stable. Currently, the Chinese beer market presents a competitive pattern of five major beer companies' monopoly, namely China Resources Brewery, Tsingtao Brewery, Budweiser Brewery, Beijing Yanjing Brewery and Chongqing Brewery. Among them, China Resources Brewery is the company with the largest market share, which reached 32.5% in 2020. The market share of Tsingtao Brewery, Budweiser Brewery, Beijing Yanjing Brewery, and Chongqing Brewery is 22.9%, 20%, respectively. Chongqing Brewery completed asset restructuring and obtained assets injection from Carlsberg China, which resulted in nearly triple growth in its sales volume and revenue. This has further promoted the concentration of the Chinese beer market.

At the same time, the production and sales volume of the Chinese beer market has reached its peak, and the number of beer companies has shown a trend of decreasing year by year. In 2020, the number of beer companies above a certain scale in China was 346, which was 124 less than the 470 in 2015. Due to the intensified competition in the beer market, many small companies are unable to survive and have to withdraw from the market. This intensified market competition has also prompted beer companies to increase their investment and innovation, improve the quality of their products and services, and better meet the needs of consumers.

High Transportation Cost of Beer Industry and the Phenomenon of Local Monopolies is Significant. Due to the fact that the packaging of beer mostly uses fragile glass or metal, and the beer itself has the characteristic of releasing gas easily under vibration, it is necessary to avoid collision during transportation and use shock-resistant and pressure-resistant packaging. However, such packaging materials, such as plastic and sponge, mostly have the characteristics of low density and large volume, which occupy a large transportation space.

In addition, as a liquid product, beer has the characteristics of large weight and short preservation time, and needs to be transported throughout the cold chain to ensure its taste. These factors have resulted in high transportation costs for long-distance beer logistics. In addition, local beer brands often face administrative and technological barriers when entering local markets due to the protection policies of local governments, resulting in most products of various beer brands being sold only in their production areas, which leads to a significant phenomenon of regional monopolies.

4 Financial Competitive Analysis

4.1 DuPont Analysis on Financial Competitive Analysis

The DuPont analysis method uses the return on equity (ROE) as an indicator of a company's profitability. It reflects the efficiency of the company's use of its own capital and is equivalent to the return on investment for ordinary shareholders. When a company's ROE exceeds 10%, it is generally considered a low-growth stock with potential.

Vertical Comparison: Net Asset Return on Investment (ROE) Comparison of Tsingtao Brewery. From Table 1, it can be seen that Tsingtao Brewery's average ROE has shown a rapid upward trend in the past five years. This indicates that the company's efficiency in using shareholder funds has been continuously improving, and the return on investment for shareholders has gradually increased. In 2020, Tsingtao Brewery's ROE reached 11.23%, exceeding the 10% standard. This also indicates that Tsingtao Brewery has great potential for future growth. In addition, after the epidemic, the company's gross profit margin gradually recovered, and it is expected to recover to 38%

in 2022. The effects of organizational structure and product structure optimization are expected to gradually become apparent. In the long term, revenue growth recovery may be transmitted to the profit side and improving company's profitability.

Horizontal Analysis: Net Asset Return on Investment (ROE) Comparison of Tsingtao Brewery and Two Other Companies in the Same Industry. From Table 1, it can be seen that although Tsingtao Brewery was overtaken by China Resources Brewery in 2021, its overall profitability is still in a leading position among local beer brands in the Chinese beer industry, and it is worth noting that Tsingtao Brewery's ROE growth rate has been fast in the past five years and was less affected by the epidemic. After the epidemic, with the gradual implementation of the company's high-end product transformation plan and the continuous expansion of overseas markets, Tsingtao Brewery's ROE is expected to further increase.

Table 1. Comparison of return on equity of Qingdao Brewery with two industry peers 2017–2021. Unit: %

Return on equity	2017	2018	2019	2020	2021
Tsingtao Brewery	7.55	8.10	9.97	11.13	14.47
China Resources Brewery	6.52	5.24	6.81	10.24	20.10
Yanjing Brewery	1.26	1.39	1.76	1.49	1.71

4.2 Sales Net Profit Margin Analysis

Longitudinal Comparison: Sales Net Profit Margin Comparison of Tsingtao Brewery. This article selects sales net profit margin as an indicator to measure the company's profitability level of sales revenue, reflecting a company's ability to convert sales into actual profits. According to industry data, the average sales net profit margin in the beer industry is between 9% and 15%. Although Tsingtao Brewery's sales net profit margin is still below the industry average, it has made significant progress in the past few years.

As shown in Table 2, the sales net profit margin of Tsingtao Brewery has shown an upward trend in the past five years, indicating that the company is more efficient in obtaining net profits when selling products or providing services than before. Since 2019, Tsingtao Brewery's sales net profit margin has increased year by year, reaching 6.62% in 2019, 7.93% in 2020, and 10.46% in 2021. This indicates that Tsingtao Brewery has improved its profitability in the past few years through optimizing production costs, strengthening product innovation, and other methods. As for the relatively low sales net profit margin in 2017 and 2018, which were 4.81% and 5.35%, respectively, this may be due to factors such as intensified market competition and incorrect cost choices.

From the Table 2, it can be seen that the profit conversion ability of Tsingtao Brewery is actually somewhat inferior to China Resources Beer, but far higher than other local beer brands. Although China Resources Beer has a higher net profit margin than Tsingtao Brewery, Tsingtao Brewery also has a good growth performance in this indicator, with

Table 2. Comparison of Tsingtao Brewery's net interest rate in sale with two industry Peers, 2017–2021. Unit: %

Net interest rate in sale	2017	2018	2019	2020	2021
Tsingtao Brewey	4.81	5.35	6.62	7.93	10.46
China Resources Brewery	3.95	3.07	3.95	6.66	13.74
Yanjing Brewery	1.44	1.59	2.00	1.80	1.91

a growth rate of 2.53 percentage points compared to 2020, indicating that the company has made significant progress in profitability. Tsingtao Brewery is one of the leaders in China's beer industry, and its performance in net profit margin also reflects the company's efforts and investment in product innovation and brand building. Although there is still some gap with competitors in certain aspects, Tsingtao Brewery is still steadily improving its profitability and market position, maintaining its leading advantage in the industry.

4.3 Analysis of Total Asset Turnover

This article selects total asset turnover as a measure of a company's operational capability. The return on total assets reflects the actual operating efficiency of a company's total assets by calculating the operating income generated by each unit of assets, and is essentially the number of times a company's assets can be invested in one year. As beer belongs to a capital-intensive industry, the asset turnover rate is generally less than 1.

As shown in Table 3, the overall trend of Tsingtao Brewery's total asset turnover rate is declining, which is largely due to the annual growth of accounts receivable. Although the company's cash flow income is considerable and higher than the industry average, the data shows that the company's utilization efficiency of assets such as fixed assets is not high, and the company still needs to strengthen asset management and formulate more efficient utilization plans.

Table 3. Comparison of Tsingtao Brewery's total asset turnover with two industry peers, 2017–2021. Unit: %

Total assets turnover	2017	2018	2019	2020	2021
Tsingtao Brewery	0.86	0.82	0.78	0.7	0.69
China Resources Brewery	0.73	0.78	0.81	0.76	0.71
Yanjing Brewery	0.62	0.63	0.64	0.6	0.63

4.4 Analysis of Equity Multiplier

This article selects equity multiplier as a measure of the proportion of a company's capital to its total assets. The higher the equity multiplier, the higher the degree to which the company relies on debt financing and the less capital the owner invests; conversely, the smaller the ratio, the more capital the owner invests and the lower the company's debt level, resulting in better protection for creditors' rights. As beer belongs to a capital-intensive industry, the equity multiplier is generally between 2 and 3.

As shown in Fig. 2, the overall trend of Tsingtao Brewery's equity multiplier is increasing, which is due to the increase in the financial leverage ratio of the company's external financing. Tsingtao Brewery's debt scale is continuously increasing, while also constantly undertaking capital expenditures and investment expansion. Although the annual increase in the equity multiplier indicates an increase in the proportion of borrowing by the company, it also means that the company has achieved good results in terms of investment return.

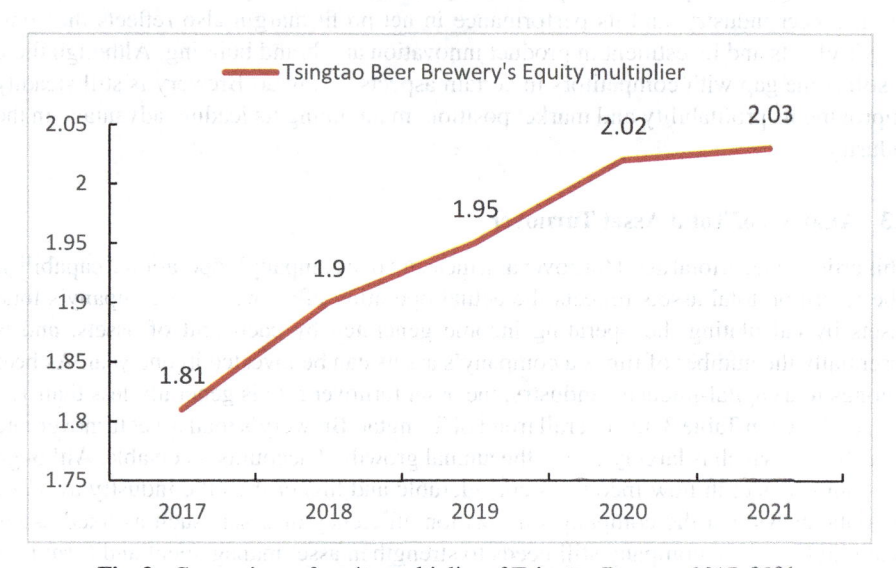

Fig. 2. Comparison of equity multiplier of Tsingtao Brewery 2017–2021.

5 Analysis of Issues Weakening the "Financial Competitiveness" of the Company

5.1 Decrease in Beer Demand Due to COVID-19 and Decrease in Gross Profit

The COVID-19 pandemic and related lockdowns have significantly reduced people's frequency of going out, affecting industries related to social dining, and beer products, which mainly rely on offline sales channels, have been hit the hardest. While economics also slowdown, which may affect consumers' spending on non-essential items. Additionally, due to vaccination programs and other factors such as virus infections, there has been a shift in consumer preferences towards craft beers, healthier beers and other alcoholic drinks. This may have affected the demand for ordinary beers and resulting in lower sales. Moreover, the increase in labor costs and the purchasing and transportation expenses of imported raw materials have resulted in a decrease in gross profit, further squeezing the profits of China's capital-intensive and low-margin beer industry.

5.2 Relatively Low Net Profit Margin and Need for Improvement in Profit Conversion Ability

Overall, Tsingtao Brewery's net profit margin has shown an upward trend over the past five years, indicating that the company's profitability in product sales and services has improved year by year. Particularly in 2021, Tsingtao Brewery's net profit margin reached 10.46%, demonstrating the significant progress the company has made in sales strategies and cost management over the past five years. However, it is worth noting that the net profit margin was relatively low in 2017 and 2018, affected by factors such as intensified market competition and erroneous cost choices. Therefore, the company needs to continue to address these issues and adopt appropriate strategies to improve its net profit margin and profitability. The factors contributing to the gap in profit conversion ability relative to China Resources Beer include differences in market share, cost control, and production efficiency.

5.3 Large Total Assets, High Proportion of Fixed Assets, and Poor Asset Liquidity

According to the 2021 annual report of Tsingtao Brewery, fixed assets such as factories and production equipment accounted for approximately 57.6% of non-current assets, while non-current assets accounted for 37.8% of the company's total assets, which is relatively high, resulting in poor asset liquidity. Additionally, accounts receivable has consistently accounted for a high proportion of current assets since 2018, which has weakened the company's operational ability to some extent, but it can be seen that this has decreased in 2021, indicating that the company is managing this consciously.

Due to the low-margin, high-volume nature of the Chinese beer industry, the company has adopted a cautious investment strategy, with only a small amount of funds used for investment and financial management, taking into account the cost of packaging materials, the price fluctuations of raw materials such as barley, and other risks in the production process.

It can be seen that the company's trading financial assets have been increasing year by year and made a leap in 2021, but the proportion of income from this part of assets is still relatively small compared to total assets. The overall growth rate of operating income is still lower than the growth rate of total assets, which cannot reverse the downward trend of the total asset turnover rate.

5.4 Strengthened "Financial Competitiveness" but Increased Financial Risk

It can be seen that Tsingtao Brewery's "financial competitiveness" is steadily increasing. The current ratio has been increasing from 1.81 in 2017 to 2.02 in 2021, reflecting that the company's liquidity in operating activities has become healthier. At the same time, the quick ratio of Tsingtao Brewery has also been on the rise, increasing from 1.14 in

2017 to 1.50 in 2021, indicating that the company's short-term solvency is strengthening year by year. This indicates that the company has made progress in expansion, but it has also increased the company's financial risk, debt management, and risk control. The increase in the company's financial risk may result in the company being unable to repay debts or pay interest on time, which may lead to creditors taking legal action against the company or even causing the company to go bankrupt. In addition, when the company's financial leverage increases, the company may face higher interest costs and financial expenses, which may affect the company's profitability and cash flow situation.

6 Conclusion

From the research above, we can conclude that like many other brewery companies in China during the COVID-19 epidemic, Tsingtao Brewery, like other beer companies, initially faced problems such as declining sales, reduced asset liquidity, and increased production and transportation costs. However, due to Tsingtao Brewery's focus on patent research and development, as well as a conscious expansion of online sales channels, the company's net asset return rate continues to rise. Based on the above characteristics of the company, we suggest the following recommendations:

6.1 Expand the Market for Non-Alcoholic and Low-Alcohol Beer

Given the current impact of the pandemic and the significant potential for growth in the female beer market, the demand for non-alcoholic beer is gradually increasing. Female consumers prefer innovative beer flavors that are sweet and have a light taste, especially fruit-flavored beer. Tsingtao Brewery can increase the creation of other innovative flavors on the basis of its best-selling fruit-flavored beers, such as peach and lemon, to respond to current market demand and tap into emerging markets.

6.2 Sell and Renovate Idle Fixed Assets

Considering the characteristic of the beer industry that cash accounts for a small proportion of total assets and the need to retain cash to respond to fluctuations in raw material prices and other risks, the increasing amount of trading financial assets of Tsingtao Brewery indicates that the company is consciously managing assets for appropriate investment. However, the decreasing fixed asset turnover ratio shows that the company's utilization efficiency of fixed assets is not high, which may result in idle or low production efficiency. The company can sell some idle assets to increase asset liquidity. Also renovate some factories and production equipment with historical value higher than their realization value and open them to the public as museums can be a good idea, which can increase its brand awareness and obtaining additional revenue. Additionally, the company should also pay attention to the quality of fixed assets and improve their production efficiency through maintenance or replacement to eliminate the existence of low-quality mass products.

6.3 Control Costs and Expenses

The sales expenses of Tsingtao Brewery constitute a significant proportion of its main business income. Cost and expense control are fundamental and essential for companies to maintain their core competitiveness. However, despite this, the sales expenses of Tsingtao Brewery have remained high year after year, mainly due to the high costs of transportation, advertising, and promotions. To address this issue, the company needs to enhance the utilization rate of expenses while concurrently improving market share. This can be achieved through a series of measures, such as improving the one-time supply rate to reduce transportation costs, using advertising to promote new products, implementing consumer promotions for mature products, and adopting a combination of advertising and promotion strategies for growth products. These measures will help to strengthen cost control and enhance the company's overall competitiveness.

References

1. Prahalad, H.: The core competence of the corporation. Harv. Bus. Rev. (5), 79–91 (1990)
2. Porter, M.E.: Competitive Advantage: Creating and Sustaining Superior Performance (1985)
3. Wang, Y.H., Guo, X.M.: Financial competitiveness and core financial competitiveness of enterprises. J. Shanxi Univ. Financ. Econ. **27**(4), 131–133 (2005)
4. Hao, C.L., Qi, R.G., Guo, J.S.: Research on financial competitiveness of enterprises. J. Field Actions **341**(6), 70–72 (2006)
5. Bodie, Z., Alex, K., Alan, J.M.: Essentials of Investments. McGraw-Hill Higher Education, New York, NY, USA (2004)
6. Smith, B.D.: Using a modified DuPont system of analysis for understanding property-liability insurance company financial performance lJl. Risk Manag. Insur. Rev. **3**, 141–151 (1999)
7. Sui, Y.: Fintech innovation and financial inclusion: evidence from cross-country data. J. Financ. Serv. Res. **57**(3), 209–234 (2020)
8. Beck, T., Levine, R.: Stock markets, banks, and growth: panel evidence. J. Bank. Financ. **28**(3), 423–442 (2004)
9. Demirgüç-Kunt, A., Levine, R.: Finance, financial sector policies, and long-run growth. World Bank Policy Research Working Paper (4469) (2008)
10. Laeven, L., Valencia, F.: Systemic banking crises revisited. IMF Work. Pap. **18**(206), 1–63 (2018)
11. Zhu, K.X.: Financial management goals and core financial capabilities of enterprises. Financ. Econ. Forum **5**, 50–56 (2001)
12. Meng, C.M.: On the core competitiveness of enterprise finance. Friends Account. **22**, 32–33 (2009)
13. Huang, Y.Y.: Discussion on the financial strategy to improve the competitiveness of enterprises. Mod. Econ. Inf. **21**, 106–107 (2020)
14. Mu, Q.B., Wang, M.X.: The impact of financial flexibility on firm performance. Account. Friend **3**, 55–62 (2023)
15. Yu, M.: The impact of R&D on firm performance: a case study of Hengrui medicine. Value Eng. **42**(5), 26–28 (2023)
16. Cao, K.C., Li, X.G., Mao, S.N.: Financial analysis promotes enterprise quality and efficiency: application of DuPont analysis in Kunlun Gas financial analysis. Financ. Account. **24**, 21–23 (2017)

Time Series Analysis in Pfizer Stock Prices in the Pre- and Post-COVID-19 Scenarios

Rixin Su[✉]

International Business School, Brandeis University, Waltham 02453, USA
rixinsu@brandeis.edu

Abstract. Pfizer is a multinational pharmaceutical company that specializes in the research, development, manufacturing, marketing, and sale of pharmaceuticals. When it comes to the pharmaceutical industry, Pfizer is a major player, and it has developed phase-3 study COVID-19 vaccine on November 9, 2020, which provided a positive impact on stock prices and distinguishes Pfizer stock price trends from other companies. This research focus on the Pfizer stock price which comes from Yahoo Finance website to compare difference model performance of Pfizer stock price forecasting and test if the stock market's trend before and after the COVID-19 outbreak is distinct. The result shows the LSTM had a best performance and in the next year, Pfizer stock price will stay at around 43 after a sharp decrease. And the vaccine has a statistically significant effect on the stock price. This essay provides a forecast regarding the pattern of recovery throughout the period after the COVID-19 pandemic.

Keywords: Stock Price · Time Series · COVID-19

1 Introduction

Pfizer is a multinational pharmaceutical company that specializes in the research, development, manufacturing, marketing, and sale of pharmaceuticals. Pfizer has created, manufactured, and introduced a wide variety of pharmaceuticals and vaccines that have been crucial in preventing, managing, and curing some of the world's most debilitating diseases through its three core businesses: Consumer Healthcare, Upjohn, and Pfizer Biopharmaceutical Group. Today, it is still providing new and innovative therapies for treating different symptoms. In Pfizer's three business, Consumer Healthcare is responsible for over-the-counter pain relievers and other OTC medications, while Upjohn is responsible for all generic medications sold in the United States and other countries. Pfizer Biopharmaceutical Group is in charge of all operations related to science-based therapeutics across six different business categories, including vaccines and oncology. The stock market has rewarded the pharmaceutical companies as the best with some of the highest returns industries. And in order to produce effective new medications and vaccinations, the pharmaceutical industry must consistently fund R&D. If the pharmaceutical company is successful in developing a patentable product, they will have the opportunity to recoup the costs of developing the drug at an accelerated rate. It is now an essential step to take in order to acquire a better understanding of the organization based on its performance and direction [1]. As a pharmaceutical company, Pfizer stock price is worth analyzing. Therefore, this paper chose Pfizer sock price from 2006 March 6th to 2023 March 6th as research data set and tried to research for the potential pattern of the stock price.

Several studies have shown that the stock market is considered hard to be analyzed since high noise, nonlinearity, complex influencing factors, and participation of many human factors [2]. Experts and industry insiders have been looking for a system that may give a scientific basis and lessen financial risks for a significant amount of time in the hopes of discovering a stock price forecasting technique that is more practical and effective. Yet, because of the features of the stock market, stock values are affected by a wide variety of factors. Predicting stock prices with any degree of precision is made substantially more difficult by the abrupt nature, nonlinearity, and randomness of price movements in the stock market [3–5]. This paper focus on comparing predicted results' accuracy using ARIMA, SARIMA and LSTM model and choose best fitted model to forecast Pfizer stock price.

Compared with these technology and trade companies, Pfizer is specific. Pfizer made the exciting statement that they were successful in their phase-3 research on November 9, 2020. According to the findings of the study, the vaccination potentially decreased the likelihood of infection by almost 90 percent [6]. The effect of the vaccine news on the stock markets of different businesses varies widely, and this also increases the gap between different industries [7]. In order to determine whether or not there was a discernible shift in the price of Pfizer stock before and after COVID-19, an interrupted time series analysis was selected as the method of investigation.

This paragraph introduce the structure of this paper. After the introduction, the paper will introduce the resource of dataset, model and test methods in Sect. 2. In Sect. 3, research results and discussion will be presented. And Sect. 4 concludes and presents policy recommendations.

2 Method

2.1 Data

Data Description. This study aims to investigate the predictability of Pfizer's closing prices both pre- and post- the COVID-19 pandemic, as well as to determine whether the current pandemic produces higher uncertainty within the price structure. To analyze whether there was a significant change in stock prices before and after the COVID-19 outbreak, March 16, 2006 to March 06, 2023 period is selected in this research. The dataset is downloaded from Yahoo Finance (https://finance.yahoo.com), which is the Nasdaq Real Time Price of Pfizer Inc.

Data Visualization. Data wrangling was done before separating the dataset into training and validation sets in order to develop deep learning models. The general trend in the stock price is depicted in Fig. 1. The adjusted close price is chosen to present the stock price. By making a volume- and price-weighted interest fix available, adjusted close price aids in avoiding errors in determining whether or not a stock's movement is abnormal

[8]. The effect of the financial crisis and its recovery may be seen in the sharp drop that occurred around 2008–2009, followed by the gradual increase in volatility over the subsequent six years. Starting in 2015, Stock prices had a stabile pattern, until 2020. After the COVID-19 outbreak in 2020, there was a clear upward trend in stock prices, which was because during the COVID-19, mRNA vaccine and potent drug Pfizer produced to against the coronavirus was widely recognized and used worldwide, which is one of the parts this research focus on. In the next sections, a comparison will be made between pre- and post- the breakout of COVID-19, and the past financial crisis will be used to make predictions on the future path of stock prices and the recovery of the economy.

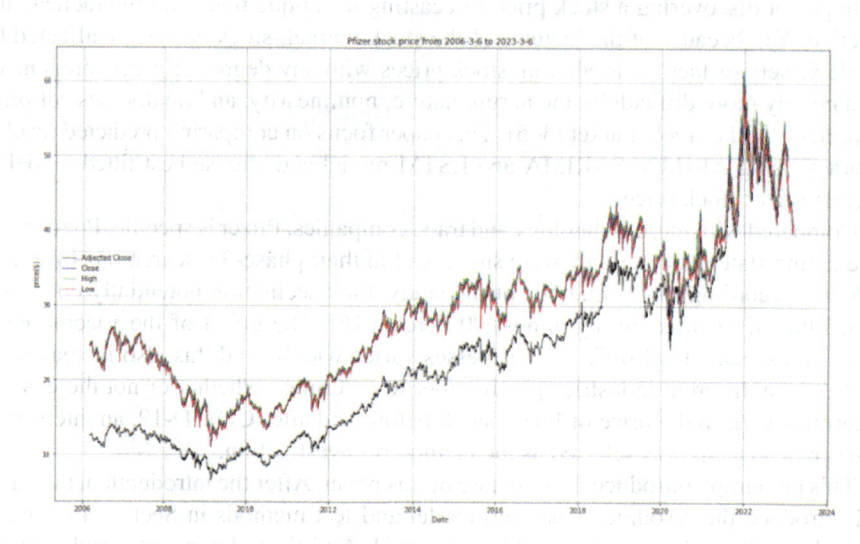

Fig. 1. Pfizer stock price from 2006-3-6 to 2023-3-6.

2.2 ARIMA

ARIMA model is autoregressive integrated moving average. It has a solid foundation in the statistical research community [9]. The ARIMA model is an extension of the MA and AR method of analyzing time series [10]. ARIMA model is an empirical approach that allows for the fitting of a model that best captures the data of interest [9]. This information can be discovered during the process. For the purpose of determining whether or not the application of an ARIMA model is adequate, a method that consists of three stages is necessary. These stages include model identification, parameter estimation, and diagnostic check. The difference in values between observations should be employed to make the time series that are being used in the ARIMA model stationary [11], which will allow the model to satisfy the stationary assumption.

The standard implementation of the ARIMA model for making forecasts can be described as follows:

$$S_t = C + \varphi_1 S_{t-1} + \varphi_2 S_{t-2} + \cdots + \varphi_q S_{t-q} + \gamma_t - \alpha_1 \gamma_{t-1} - \alpha_2 \gamma_{t-2} - \cdots - \gamma_{t-r} \tag{1}$$

S_t is the true worth, and $C\&\gamma_t$ indicating the random and constant part, φ and α is ARMA parameter, autoregressive moving average and γ_{t-r} is periodic white noise mistake.

Figure 2 demonstrates that the strategy was at first conceived as an ARIMA model (p, q, d). The ACF plot reveals that the stock price exhibits a significant degree of autocorrelation. ARIMA (p, 1, d) method parameters for the autoregressive delay p1 and the moving average delay q1 were selected for each possible combination as the appropriate model.

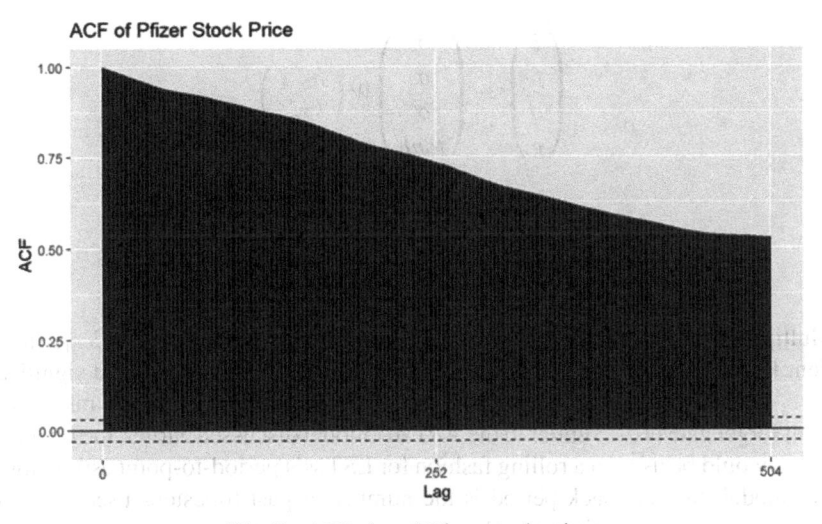

Fig. 2. ACF plot of Pfizer stock price.

2.3 SARIMA

The SARIMA model is the other kind of model that was evaluated here because it possesses a number of benefits that are not shared by other types of models. These benefits include the explicitness of the model structures, the high accuracy of the forecasting results, and the availability of software packages such as Matlab, R, and SAS. In this study, the SARIMA model was fitted in R, and R was also used to evaluate the model's performance. ARIMA models can be extended in order to include a seasonal factor using the SARIMA notation. The basic SARIMA model is $ARIMA(p, d, q)(P, D, Q)\{m\}$, which has an additional four parameters to capture the seasonal component, in which m is the seasonality period.

2.4 LSTM

In time series analysis area, Long Short Term Memory (LSTM) performs well. As an expansion of RNN (the recurrent neural network) approach.

When modeling data at a given time step, traditional neural networks are unable to make use of information learned at earlier time steps. This is a significant limitation of conventional neural networks. Recurrent neural networks attempt a solution to this issue by employing loops that carry data from one stage of the network to the next.

LSTMs are a subclass of RNNs that can be trained to understand both immediate and remote dependencies. LSTM networks are made up of memory blocks connected via layers. Gates within each block control the output and the state of that particular block.

LSTM can be express as following equation:

$$\begin{pmatrix} i \\ f \\ o \\ g \end{pmatrix} = \begin{pmatrix} \sigma \\ \sigma \\ \sigma \\ tanh \end{pmatrix} W \begin{pmatrix} h_{t-1} \\ x_t \end{pmatrix} \qquad (2)$$

$$C_t = f \odot C_{t-1} + i \odot g \qquad (3)$$

$$h_t = o \odot tanh(C_t) \qquad (4)$$

Multiplying elements together yields C_t when backpropagating from C_{t-1}. Since the gradient flow wouldn't be interrupted like it is in RNN, the speed would significantly improve. In addition, at each time step in an LSTM, the gradients may be multiplying a different forget gate [10]. Similar to the ARIMA model discussed earlier, the Pfizer stock price data would be used in a rolling fashion for LSTM's period-to-point estimation. For a given model, the lookback period is the number of past timesteps used for making predictions about the next timestep. An approximation might be computed using period-to-point estimation, and both the approximation and the real value may be plotted on a line chart for comparison. The LSTM models were analyzed with a Rolling-Window technique to spot the pattern.

The stock price was rescaled to a range of (0, 1) before being input into the model. The following equation describes how to carry out the rescaling operation:

$$x_{new} = \frac{x_{original} - x_{min}}{x_{range}} \qquad (5)$$

2.5 Interrupted Time Series Analysis

As there is just one batch in the dataset and no controls, the following form is suitable for the conventional ITSA regression model [12], ITSA regression model are shown formula (6) and Fig. 3.

$$Y_t = \beta_0 + \beta_1 T_t + \beta_2 X_t + \beta_3 X_t T_t + \epsilon_t \qquad (6)$$

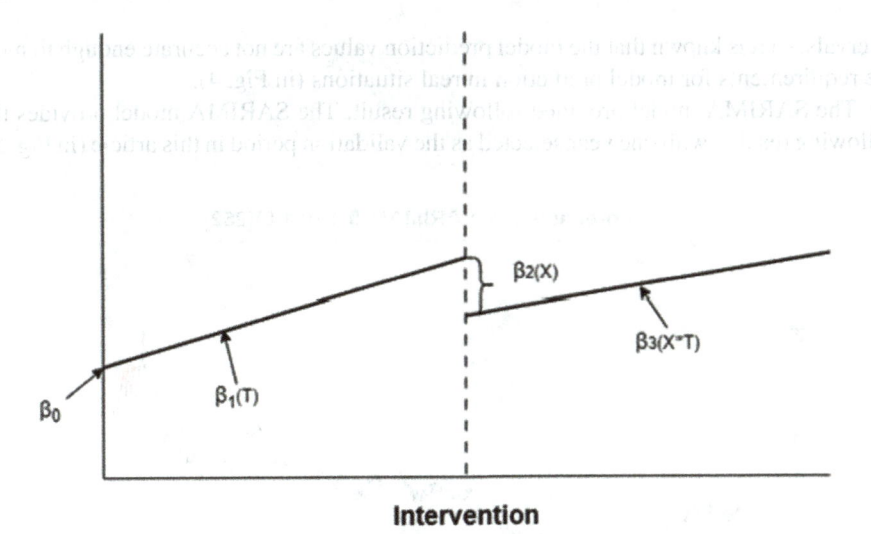

Fig. 3. ITSA regression model.

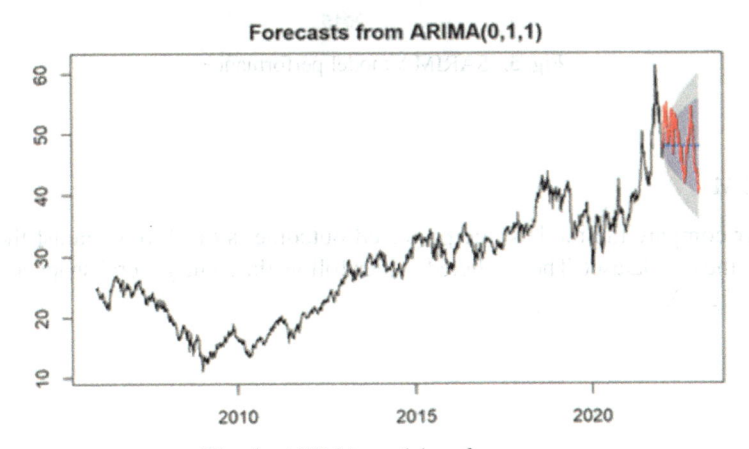

Fig. 4. ARIMA model performance.

3 Result

3.1 Time Series Analysis

The ARIMA model provides the following results, with one year selected as the validation period in this article (in Fig. 4).

The model fits in a statistical sense, but does not perform well in the actual forecasts. The forecast suggests that Pfizer stock price should show a flat trend, which is the blue line, but due to the 2008 economic crisis, COVID-19, global economic instability and other factors, the trend of the forecast and the observed values do not overlap well. Both the 99.5% and 99% confidence levels (Shaded section) have a wide range of prediction intervals, so it is known that the model prediction values are not accurate enough to meet the requirements for model prediction in real situations (in Fig. 4).

The SARIMA model provided following result, The SARIMA model provides the following results, with one year selected as the validation period in this article (in Fig. 5).

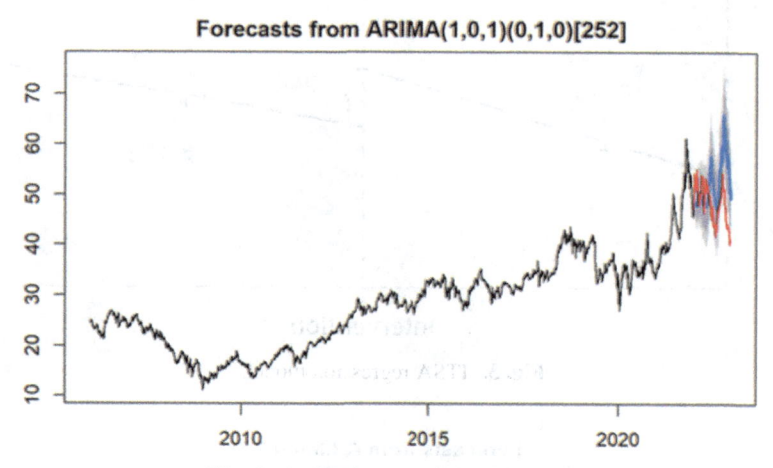

Fig. 5. SARIMA model performance.

3.2 LSTM

To further compare the models, the projected outcome is displayed against the actual data from the test dataset. The predicted values follow the same general shape as the real data (see Fig. 6).

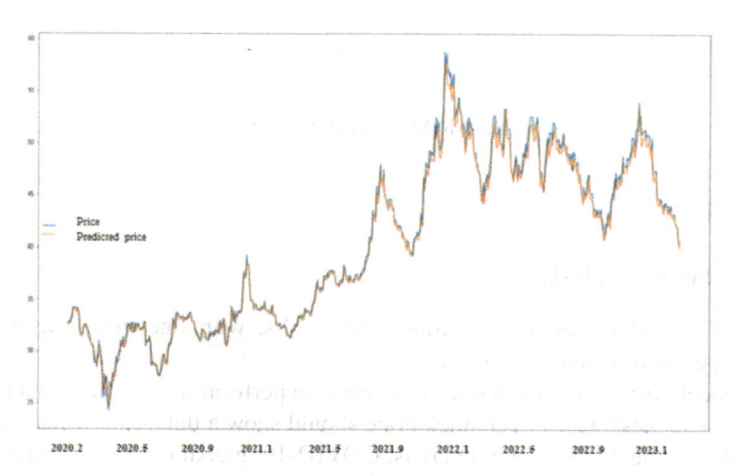

Fig. 6. LSTM model performance.

3.3 Comparison Between SARIM and LSTM

To choose the best model, MSE (Mean squared error) is chosen to o evaluate models. MSE displays the difference between the real value and prediction values for each observation. MSE can be a number not less than 0, with a lower value indicating a better performing model [13]. The equation is shown below:

$$MSE = \frac{1}{n}\sum_{i=1}^{n}(\hat{y}_i - y_i)^2 \qquad (7)$$

The MSE of there three models is presented in the Table 1:

Table 1. MSE of the three models.

Model	MSE
ARIMA	12.9607
SARIMA	48.2447
LSTM	0.7479

Compared these models, ARIMA model has the 12.96072 MSE while SARIMA model has 48.24472. Term Memory (LSTM) performed better than the other two models since it has smaller MSE than for the validation dataset. Thus, LSTM model is chosen to do the prediction, and the predicted value is as Fig. 7.

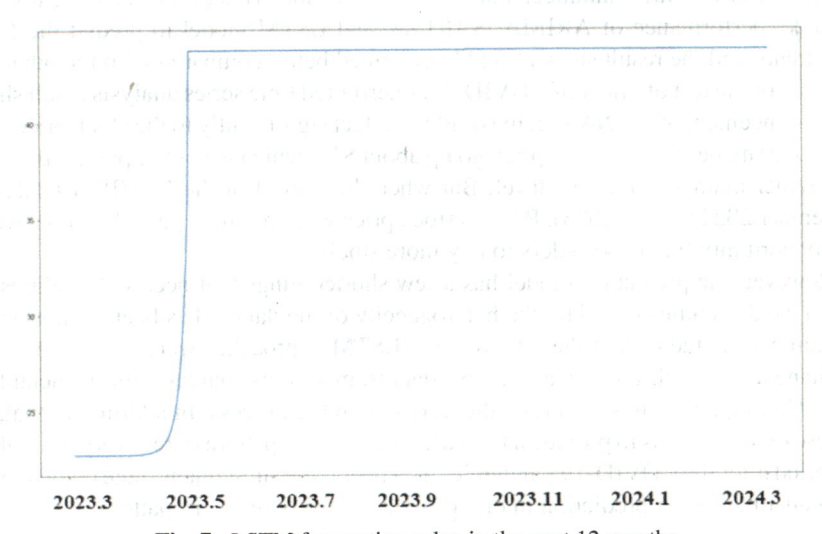

Fig. 7. LSTM forecasting value in the next 12 months.

From the end of 2022, the stock price has shown a sharply downward in Fig. 7, so as the model prediction shows, in March, 2023, the stock price will be very low, which is 22.7119. But in May 2023, the stock price will return to normal levels, which is about 43 and remain at that price.

3.4 Interrupted Time Series Analysis

The result of interrupted time series analysis is as Table 2. There is a positive coefficient of β_3 (24.21), which indicates the mRNA vaccine announcement has a positive effect on Pfizer stock price. And the P-value is approximately 0.00, which shows the coefficient is statistically significant, and the effect of mRNA vaccine is significant.

Table 2. OLS Regression results.

	Coef	Std err	t	P > |t|	[0.025 0.975]
const	19.4550	0.133	146.461	0.000	19.715
After-intervention	24.2100	0.360	67.216	0.000	24.916
R-squared: 0.514	F-st.atistic: 4518				

4 Conclusion

Because of the outbreak of COVID-19, the world economy has been hit hard and stock prices of majority companies have different degrees of decline. But Pfizer make a difference because of the announcement of mRNA vaccine. This paper did some research on model performance of ARIMA, SARIMA and LSTM model to predict the Pfizer stock trend, and the result shows LSTM performed better compared with the other two models. For the test of effect of COVID-19, interrupted time series analysis result shows the announcement of mRNA vaccine of Pfizer affect significantly to the stock price. And COVID-19 made Pfizer's stock price go up about $10, which is not temporary, the stock price rather maintained at this level. But when the impact of the COVID-19 subsides (November 2022 to May 2023), Pfizer's stock price will drop for a period of time, which is an opportunity for stockholders to buy more stock.

However, the prediction model has a few shortcomings that need to be addressed. Due to the difficulties posed by the heterogeneity of the data, it has been demonstrated in a number of studies that the ARIMA and LSTM approaches were not successful in simultaneously synchronizing alternative data from various sources with financial time series. Consequently, this would be the next step in the process. In addition to that, the purpose of this essay is to provide a forecast regarding the pattern of recovery throughout the period after the COVID-19 pandemic. As a result, the subsequent stage could consist of conducting further prediction in order to see the likely recovery pattern.

References

1. Alkhyeli, S., et al.: Financial analysis and performance evaluation of Pfizer. Available at SSRN 3896385 (2021)
2. Aggarwal, R.K., Wu, G.: Stock market manipulations. J. Bus. **79**(4), 1915–1953 (2006)

3. Kapar, B., Buigut, S., Rana, F.: Winners and losers from Pfizer and Biontech's vaccine announcement: evidence from S&P 500 (sub) sector indices. PLoS One **17**(10), e0275773 (2022)
4. Baker, S.R., Bloom, N., Davis, S.J., Kost, K.J., Sammon, M.C., Viratyosin, T.: The unprecedented stock market impact of COVID-19 (No. w26945). National Bureau of Economic Research (2020)
5. Zaremba, A., Kizys, R., Aharon, D.Y., Demir, E.: Infected markets: novel coronavirus, government interventions, and stock return volatility around the globe. Financ. Res. Lett. **35**, 101597 (2020)
6. Thompson, M.G., et al.: Interim estimates of vaccine effectiveness of BNT162b2 and mRNA-1273 COVID-19 vaccines in preventing SARS-CoV-2 infection among health care personnel, first responders, and other essential and frontline workers—eight US locations, December 2020–March 2021. Morb. Mortal. Weekly Rep. **70**(13), 495 (2021)
7. Bradley, C., Stumpner, P.: The impact of COVID-19 on capital markets, one year in. McKinsey & Company (2021)
8. Wei, J., Xu, Q., He, C.: Deep learning of predicting closing price through historical adjustment closing price. Procedia Comput. Sci. **202**, 379–384 (2022)
9. Ho, S.L., Xie, M.: The use of ARIMA models for reliability forecasting and analysis. Comput. Ind. Eng. **35**(1–2), 213–216 (1998)
10. Weilin, F., et al.: Time series analysis in american stock market recovering in post COVID-19 pandemic period. arXiv preprint arXiv:2212.05369 (2022)
11. Forecasting: Principles and Practice, 2nd edn. Chapter 8 ARIMA models (n.d.). Accessed 3 Dec 2022
12. Linden, A., Adams, J.L.: Applying a propensity score-based weighting model to interrupted time series data: improving causal inference in programme evaluation. J. Eval. Clin. Pract. **17**(6), 1231–1238 (2011)
13. Zhou, D., Zheng, L., Zhu, Y., Li, J., He, J.: Domain adaptive multi-modality neural attention network for financial forecasting. In: Proceedings of the Web Conference 2020, pp. 2230–2240 (2020)

Stacking-Based Model for House Price Prediction

Yiqian Zhou[✉]

Department of Mathematics and Information Science, Nanchang Normal University, Nanchang, Jiangxi, China
hangzoudeyu@huagejun.com

Abstract. As a pillar industry of the economy, real estate has a significant impact on social and economic development. Therefore, accurate prediction of house prices has always been a focus of attention. This study is based on the Kaggle House Prices dataset and constructs a relatively reliable house price prediction model through data cleaning, feature engineering, and machine learning algorithms. Firstly, the data was preprocessed to remove outliers and missing values. Then, feature engineering and principal component analysis were performed to extract more meaningful data features. Finally, the stacking model was used to train the data, and a high-accuracy house price prediction model was established. The research results of this study can help homebuyers make more informed decisions, assist investors in making more favorable investment decisions, aid governments in formulating more effective policies and plans, and help the real estate industry develop more targeted marketing strategies, among others.

Keywords: House Price Prediction · Machine Learning · Stacking Ensemble Model

1 Introduction

1.1 Background

Nowadays, due to the continuous growth of the population and the shortage of housing resources, the real estate market has become a hot topic of concern. People use machine learning technology and data analysis techniques to analyze the characteristics and sales prices of houses and can obtain accurate house price prediction results, which is of great significance to related industries such as homebuyers, banks, and real estate companies. For example, homebuyers can obtain accurate reference prices for houses through the house price prediction model, thereby avoiding the occurrence of excessively high or low house prices, reducing investment risks, and avoiding investment losses caused by market fluctuations; real estate companies can use this model to understand the sales situation of different regions and different types of houses, better understand market demand, make reasonable pricing strategies, increase sales, and reduce losses; banks can use house price prediction models to evaluate the risk of real estate projects, improve the accuracy and scientificity of loan strategies, attract more customers and business, and avoid the risk of non-performing loans. Therefore, the house price prediction model conforms to the trend of social development and is a beneficial model.

1.2 Related Research

Some scholars conducted experiments to compare the performance of individual models and ensemble models [1, 2]. The results indicated that the prediction method based on the stacking regression model had better performance than independent machine learning models. Madhuri, Anuradha, and Pujitha conducted a comparative study on regression techniques for predicting house prices using Multiple Linear Regression, Ridge Regression, Lasso Regression, Elastic Net Regression, Ada Boosting Regression, and Gradient Boosting models [3]. The research results showed that the Gradient Boosting algorithm has higher performance than all other algorithms in terms of predicting house prices.

Ali and Zaman carried out a study on the impact of housing prices on stock prices in European Union countries. They found that housing prices can significantly decrease the stock prices of a region. The study confirmed that in the short term, these two variables move together over a period of time, whereas in the long term, there is a bi-directional causality between the two variables [4]. This suggests that there is a certain relationship between the real estate market and the stock market, which has a certain reference value for investment decisions and risk control. Based on the mortgage contracts and housing price data in England during 2005–2015, Cloyne, Huber, Ilzetzki, and Kleven have come to the conclusion that housing prices have a significant impact on household borrowing. Specifically, they found that a 10% increase in house prices would lead to a 2–3% increase in borrowing [5]. This study sheds light on the connection between the real estate market and household borrowing behavior and provides valuable insights into the assessment of household borrowing risk.

Liu constructed multiple machine learning models by collecting house features and rental price information, and compared their performance in predicting rental prices [1]. The results show that the main factors affecting rental prices are the area of the house, location, and transportation convenience.

1.3 Objection

To sum up, people are increasingly inclined to use housing price prediction models to make investment and purchasing decisions. Housing price prediction models can help people understand current real estate market trends and future price changes, and serve as an important basis for policy-making and regulation, in order to achieve better results in investment and purchasing activities. However, traditional prediction models are subject to various factors, resulting in errors and limiting their accuracy and reliability. In this case, machine learning technology can be used to build more accurate prediction models. Therefore, this study aims to use the Stacking model in machine learning to predict housing prices, in order to ensure the reliability and stability of the prediction results.

In Sect. 2, the distribution of the target variable was transformed into a normal distribution using log transformation. Outliers and missing values were also handled. Feature encoding was performed, and the distribution of other variables was analyzed. Furthermore, feature selection was conducted to select the variables for model training. In Sect. 3, the limitations of this study were discussed, and experimental results were presented. The results indicated that the proposed model was effective for house price prediction. Section 4 summarized the main findings of this study.

2 Methodology

2.1 Source of Data

The test set and training set data were both sourced from Kaggle [6], providing detailed information on 2919 houses in Ames, Iowa from 2006 to 2010. The dataset includes 81 features related to house prices, such as nearby geographical factors, layout, and style of the house, and internal and external features of the house. The first variable is ID, and the last variable is the target variable (SalePrice). This study randomly divided 70% of the dataset into training sets and 30% into testing sets, with the aim of using the feature data in the dataset to predict the sales price of houses.

2.2 Data Processing

Distribution of Target Variables

By observing Fig. 1, it can be seen that the original housing price data shows a significant right deviation distribution. According to Python's calculation, the average value is 180921.20, and the standard deviation is 79415.29. Because in machine learning algorithms, many algorithms require data to conform to a normal distribution, logarithmic transformations are performed on the target variable to fit it with a normal distribution.

(a) Original 'SalePrice' distribution (b) Original Probability Plot

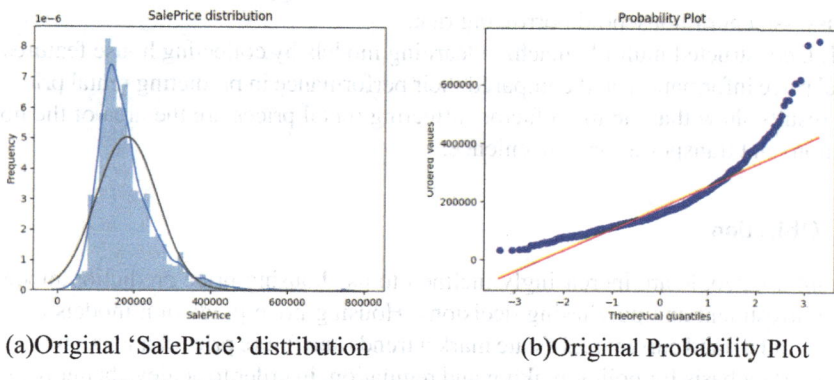

Fig. 1. Original data distribution chart (Photo credit: Original).

As shown in Fig. 2, the logarithmic transformation is used to process the right biased housing price data. After the logarithmic transformation, the distribution of the target variable has approached a normal distribution, with a mean value of 12.06 and a standard deviation of 0.29.

Cleaning Outliers

This study used Python to generate a heatmap and identified 18 variables highly correlated with the target variable from the heatmap. To better understand the correlation coefficients between these variables and the target variable, a correlation matrix was plotted. For ease of description, some variable names were abbreviated: 'OverallQual'

(a) SalePrice distribution after change

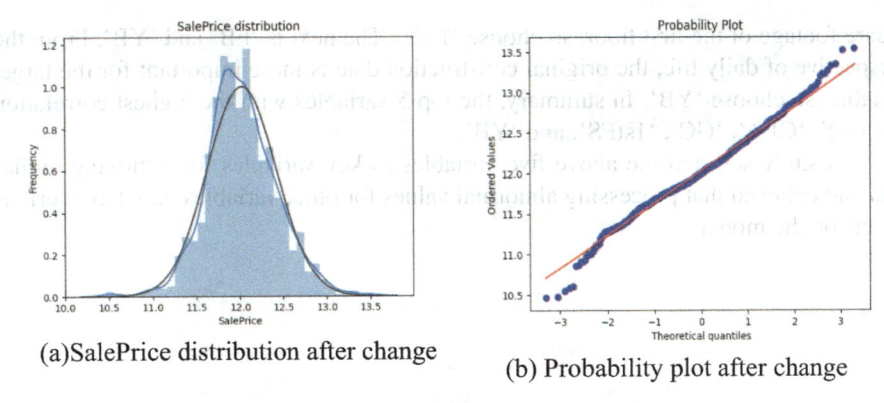

(b) Probability plot after change

Fig. 2. Transformed data distribution chart (Photo credit: Original).

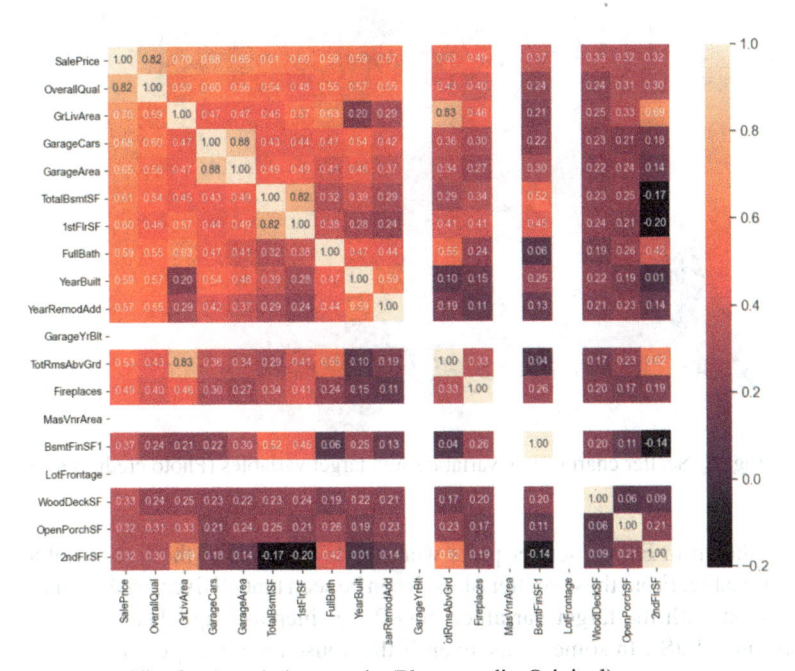

Fig. 3. Correlation matrix (Photo credit: Original).

as 'QQ', 'GrLivArea' as 'GLA', 'GarageCars' as 'GC', 'Garage Area' as 'GA', 'TotalBsmtSF' as 'BS', '1stFrSF' as '1stS', 'FullBath' as 'FB', and 'YearBuilt' as 'YB'. It can be seen from Fig. 3 that the top 5 variables with the highest correlation coefficients can be identified as 'OQ', 'GLA', 'GC', 'GA' and 'TBS'. As 'GC' and 'GA' have similar meanings, but 'GC' has a higher correlation coefficient, it is chosen over 'GA'. The sixth variable consists of '1stS' and 'TBS' and there is a relationship between these two variables. In general, the difference in square footage between the first floor and the basement is not very large, and there is not a big difference between the correlation coefficients of 'TBS' and '1stSF'. In daily life, people should pay more attention to the square footage of the first floor, so choose '1stS'. The next is 'FB' and 'YB'. From the perspective of daily life, the original construction date is more important for the target variable, so choose 'YB'. In summary, the top 5 variables with the highest correlation are 'OQ', 'GLA', 'GC', '1stFS', and 'YB'.

This study selected the above five variables as key variables for removing outlier data and believed that processing abnormal values for other variables may have serious effects on the model.

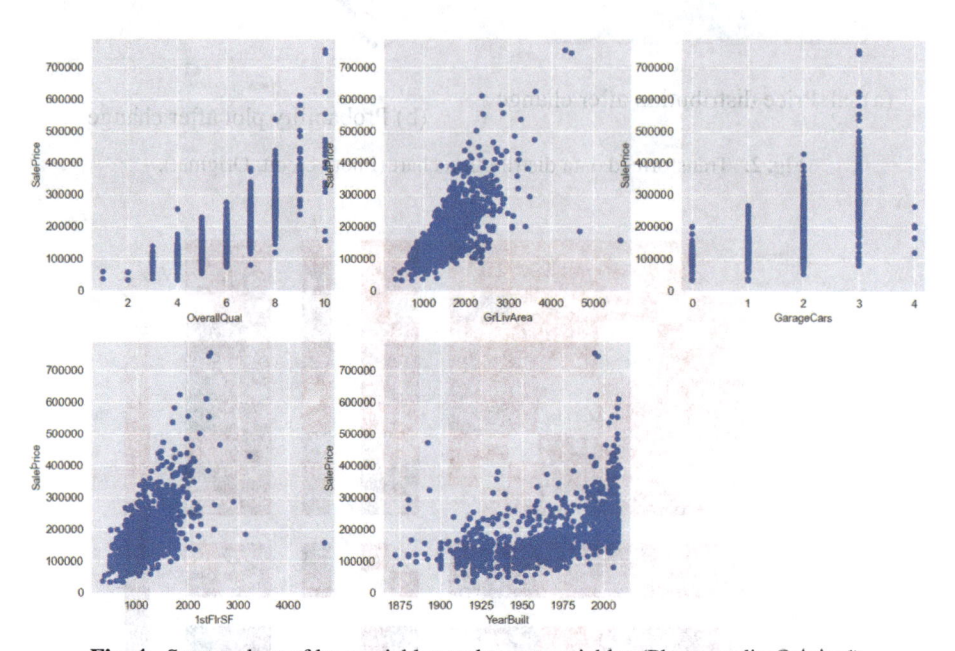

Fig. 4. Scatter chart of key variables and target variables (Photo credit: Original).

As shown in Fig. 4, scatter plots were made for each of the five variables with the target variable. From these scatter plots, it can be seen that all five variables have a positive correlation with the target variable. 'SalePrice' increases quickly with an increase in 'GLA' and '1stS'. In some areas, even if the house area is large, the price may still be low, possibly due to their location far from the city center. This paper considers these points deviating from the main distribution as outliers and removes them.

Cleaning Missing Data. Cleaning missing data helps to avoid building high-risk models, and the missing rates of variables can be clearly seen in Fig. 5.

The original data had many missing values, which seriously affected data prediction and analysis of the data. If the missing values of a variable exceeded 20%, it would significantly affect the readability and interpretability of the data. Therefore, this study removed 'PoolQC', 'MiscFeature' 'Alley', 'Fence', and 'FireplaceQu'. Some variables related to various parts of the household, and their missing values may be due to the absence of corresponding facilities in the house. For example, variables related to the garage, interior quality of the house, and basement. The missing values of these variables

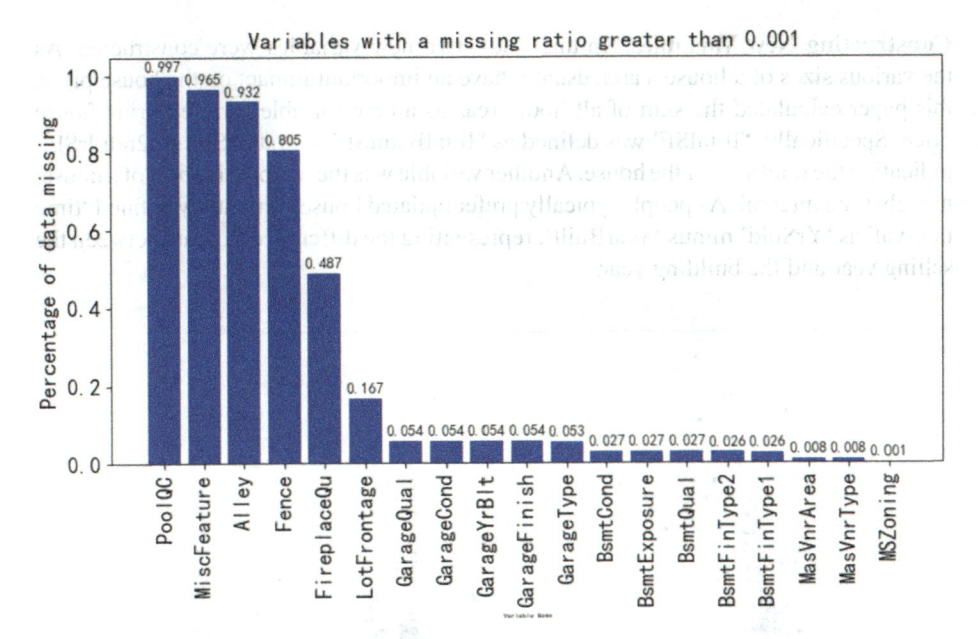

Fig. 5. Variable missing rate visualization (Photo credit: Original).

were filled with 'NA'. For variables such as 'MSZoning', 'BsmtHalfBath', and 'Utilities', missing values can be filled with the mode of each variable. For numeric variables such as 'GarageArea' and 'GarageCars', the mean filling method is used. The median value is used to fill in the missing values for 'LotFrontage'. Similarly, The number of missing values for 'MasVnrType' and 'MasVnrArea' are very similar, and their meanings are also very similar. If a house's 'MasVnrType' is missing, but its 'MasVnrArea' is not missing, the median value of 'MasVnrArea' with the same type of 'MasVnrType' is taken for the missing value of 'MasVnrArea'. For 'Functional', the 'Typ' is used to fill in missing values because it assumes typical.

Feature Coding. One-hot encoding is a process of transforming categorical data into numerical data so that it can be used for machine learning purposes. However, sometimes the categorical data has a large number of unique values, which can lead to a high dimensional feature space. Therefore, it is helpful to sort the categories by frequency and then merge the categories with very low frequency into a single category, in order to reduce the dimensionality of the feature space. This can make the data set more manageable and reduce the risk of overfitting.

Some of these features, are represented as numeric features but lack actual meaning, such as categories and time. Therefore, these features were converted to string format, namely categorical variables. Compared to one-hot encoding, LabelEncoder can convert temporal data into integer format, reducing the dimensionality of the data and better capturing the information in the data. Therefore, in this study, LabelEncoder was used to encode temporal data.

Constructing New Variables. In this study, two new variables were constructed. As the various sizes of a house's area usually have an important impact on the house price, this paper calculated the sum of all floor areas as a new variable for measuring house price. Specifically, 'TotalSF' was defined as 'TotalBsmtSF' + '1stFlrSF' + '2ndFlrSF', indicating the total area of the house. Another variable was the temporal aspect of a house, namely time interval. As people typically prefer updated houses, this study defined 'time interval' as 'YrSold' minus 'YearBuilt', representing the difference in years between the selling year and the building year.

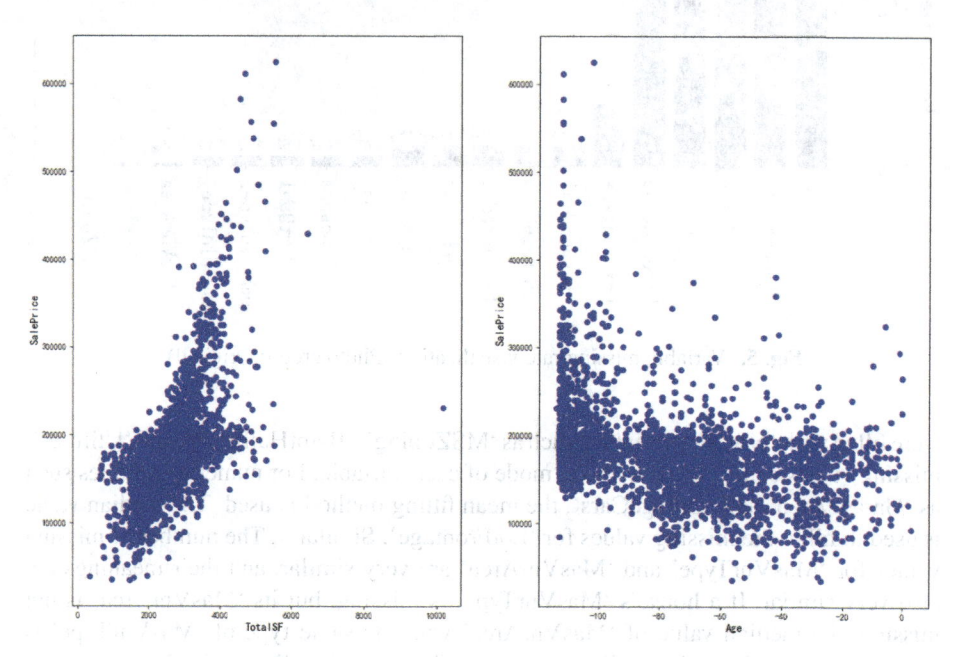

Fig. 6. New variables (Photo credit: Original)

According to Fig. 6, there is a positive correlation between the total area of a house and the price of the house, and the price of the house increases as the size of the house increases. The closer the selling time is to the construction time, the higher the house price.

Process Other Variables. Logarithmic transformations can be used to alter the distribution of raw numerical variables, improving heavily skewed data and introducing correlations that allow models to better utilize the data. This study examined the skewness of each variable using the Scipy library in Python. Among the numerical variables, about 60% of them have an absolute skewness value exceeding 0.75, indicating highly skewed distributions. To ensure better accuracy of the model, this study set the threshold for skewness to be 1. Variables with absolute skewness values above the threshold were subjected to logarithmic transformation to improve the quality of the data.

Feature Selection and Dimensionality Reduction Processing. To make the model more accurate, principal component analysis is used to reduce the dimensionality of variables. PCA is a common data reduction method with broad applications in machine learning. Its main purpose is to transform high-dimensional data into low-dimensional data while retaining as much information as possible and reducing computational complexity [7]. PCA projects the original data onto a new coordinate system through linear transformation, and the principal components ranked at the forefront can retain as much original data information as possible. Therefore, selecting the first n principal components as the new feature representation can achieve the goal of dimensionality reduction.

According to the research results, 53 principal components were selected and preserved as the final feature space size in this paper. These principal components were used for subsequent stacking model training and prediction.

2.3 Models

In machine learning classification and regression problems, the stacking model has been widely used to improve the performance of prediction models. The idea behind the stacking model is to use the prediction results of the previous layer model as the input data of the next layer model, gradually improving the overall prediction accuracy of the model.

In this study, five base classifiers, including Lasso, ElasticNet, LinearSVR, BayesianRidge, and KernelRidge, were utilized along with a final Gradient Boosting Regressor. The model divided the training data into five different subsets, where each subset served as a validation set once while the remaining subsets were used for training to obtain first-level outputs. The model then concatenated the five predicted results by column to form a feature matrix to be trained and predicted by a second-level model. Finally, the trained model was evaluated on the test set to obtain the root mean square error (RMSE). The structure is shown in the following Fig. 7.

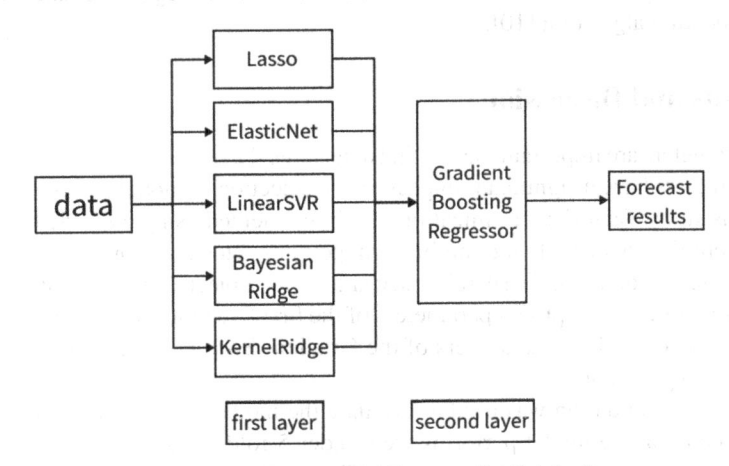

Fig. 7. Stacking model (Photo credit: Original).

Lasso. Lasso is a biased estimation method. Based on the premise that the sum of absolute values of variable coefficients is less than a constant, Lasso minimizes the residual sum of squares. This results in some regression coefficients that can be precisely shrunk to zero, which can eliminate multicollinearity to a certain extent and perform more accurate predictions of the target variable [8].

ElasticNet. ElasticNet is a combination of lasso and ridge, which randomly selects two algorithms in the algorithm and inherits some of the stability of ridge regression under cyclic states [1]. When there is severe multicollinearity, ElasticNet can achieve variable selection and obtain good coefficient compression results [8].

LinearSVR. Linear Support Vector Machine Regression is a method of performing regression analysis using support vector machine algorithms. The computational cost of linear SVM is relatively low and requires less memory, making it an ideal choice for dealing with large-scale datasets.

BayesianRidge. BayesianRidge is a linear regression model based on Bayesian statistical inference, which is a biased estimation regression method specifically designed for analyzing collinear data. It calculates posterior probabilities by introducing prior probabilities of the model parameters. In the process of applying the model, the Bayesian model optimizes the minimum error rate, that is, selects the class with the largest posterior probability as the predicted category of the object [1].

KernelRidge. Kernel Ridge Regression combines the linear least squares with L2 norm regularization with kernel tricks to find the objective function that minimizes the loss. Kernel Ridge Regression can handle nonlinear data by introducing a kernel function between data samples, mapping the original data into a more complex kernel space, and giving the model enough expressive power to fit the training data [9].

Gradient Boosting Regressor. The domain of Gradient Boosting Regressor is the set of all feasible base functions. It first sets a target loss function and gradually approaches the local minimum by iteratively selecting a base function on the negative gradient direction through boosting algorithm [10].

3 Results and Discussion

Model parameters are important factors that determine the prediction performance, while hyperparameters have a significant impact on the selection of model parameters. Therefore, in this study, Bayesian optimization was implemented using the TPE algorithm in the Hyperopt library of Python to optimize hyperparameters. The optimization process was completed by defining the search space and search object, as well as calling the min function. In Table 1, the optimal parameters of the first five models are obtained through a hyperparameter, and the parameters of the Gradient Boosting Regressor are obtained through pre-experiments.

5-fold cross-validation was used to evaluate the model in this study, From Table 2, it can be seen that the model performs well under 5-fold cross-validation, with a high predictive ability and small predictive errors. Therefore, it can be considered an effective prediction model suitable for the analysis and prediction of the correlation between the target variable and the independent variables.

Table 1. The optimal parameters of each algorithm.

Algorithm	Optimal parameter
Lasso	alpha = 0.14
ElasticNet	alpha = 0.3, l1_ratio = 0.74, tol = 1e−5
LinearSVR	C = 0.9, tol = 1e−5
BayesianRidge	n_iter = 400, tol = 1e−6, alpha_1 = 1e−5, alpha_2 = 1e−4, lambda_1 = 1e−7, lambda_2 = 1e−7
KernelRidge	alpha = 6.29, gamma = 7.17
Gradient Boosting Regressor	max_depth = 3, learning_rate = 0.01, n_estimators = 300

Table 2. RMSE of each algorithm on the train set and test set.

dataset	R^2	RMSE
train set	0.9357	0.1001
test set	0.8984	0.1255

3.1 Limitation

This study shows that using a stacking model can effectively improve prediction accuracy, but this method also has some limitations. Firstly, using multiple complex models may lead to overfitting, which can affect the generalization performance of the model. Secondly, in practical applications, the selection of models and hyperparameters needs to be tuned, which requires a lot of computational resources and expertise. Finally, even with multiple models, there may still be collinearity issues between variables that require special treatment.

Based on the Kaggle notebook, a stacking model was used to further optimize the model in this study. For the final prediction, Serigne combined the stacking averaged model, XGBoost, and LightGBM to obtain better prediction results [11]. This suggests that the stacking model can be combined with other models for improved prediction performance.

DŽEROSKI and ŽENKO proposed two novel stacking techniques, namely probability distribution extension stacking and multi-response linear regression stacking [12]. Experimental results demonstrate that the multi-response linear regression stacking method outperforms existing stacking methods and selects the best classifier from the ensemble via cross-validation.

In machine learning, feature engineering is an experience-rich step. However, due to time constraints, the optimal feature processing method was not identified in this study, which affects the model's performance to some extent. Secondly, it is necessary to further investigate the data from different regions and countries to explore their universality. Therefore, in the subsequent research, data from different cities and countries should be included as research objects.

4 Conclusion

This study constructed an effective house price prediction model using data cleaning, feature engineering, and machine learning algorithms. Predicting house prices aims to provide a reference price scheme to assist homebuyers, real estate developers, and banks in making better investment and transaction decisions. In this study, we addressed outlier and correlation issues using a heatmap, correlation coefficient matrix, and scatter plot, treated missing data with imputation and deletion methods, and extracted 53 features for modeling and predicting house prices using principal component analysis. For modeling and prediction, we used the stacking algorithm with Lasso, ElasticNet, LinearSVR, BayesianRidge, and KernelRidge as the first-layer algorithms and Gradient Boosting Regressor as the second-layer algorithm. We performed hyperparameter tuning for each algorithm in the first layer and evaluated the model with 5-fold cross-validation. The R^2 values of the training set and test set were 0.9357 and 0.8984, respectively, and the RMSE of the training set and test set were 0.1001 and 0.1255, indicating good model performance. Therefore, this model can be considered an effective prediction model.

References

1. Yutian, L.: Predicting the prices of luxury houses based on ensemble regression models. Lanzhou University (2020). https://doi.org/10.27204/d.cnki.glzhu.2020.001975
2. Xu, L., Li, Z.: A new appraisal model of second-hand housing prices in China's first-tier cities based on machine learning algorithms. Comput. Econ. **57**, 617–637 (2021). https://doi.org/10.1007/s10614-020-09973-5
3. Madhuri, C.R., Anuradha, G., Pujitha, M.V.: House price prediction using regression techniques: a comparative study. In: 2019 International Conference on Smart Structures and Systems (ICSSS), Chennai, India, pp. 1–5 (2019). https://doi.org/10.1109/ICSSS.2019.8882834
4. Ali, G., Zaman, K.: Do house prices influence stock prices? Empirical investigation from the panel of selected European Union countries. Econ. ResearchEkonomska Istraživanja **30**(1), 1840–1849 (2017). https://doi.org/10.1080/1331677X.2017.1392882
5. Cloyne, J., Huber, K., Ilzetzki, E., Kleven, H.: The effect of house prices on household borrowing: a new approach. Am. Econ. Rev. **109**(6), 2104–2136 (2019)
6. Shuyu, L.: Analysis of factors affecting urban rental prices based on machine learning methods. Nankai University (2021). https://doi.org/10.27254/d.cnki.gnkau.2021.000080.
7. Kaggle: House Prices: Advanced Regression Techniques (2017). https://www.kaggle.com/c/house-prices-advanced-regression-techniques/data
8. Zhan, C., Wu, Z., Liu, Y., Xie, Z., Chen, W.: Housing prices prediction with deep learning: an application for the real estate market in Taiwan. In: 2020 IEEE 18th International Conference on Industrial Informatics (INDIN), Warwick, United Kingdom, pp. 719–724 (2020). https://doi.org/10.1109/INDIN45582.2020.9442244
9. Junyang, W.: Study on influential factors of residential prices in China based on elastic net. Hunan Normal University (2018)
10. Siyang, S.: Study on inversion of water quality parameters of Miyun reservoir based on multi-source remote sensing and machine learning. Beijing Forestry University (2019). https://doi.org/10.26949/d.cnki.gblyu.2019.000505.
11. "Comparison of kernel ridge and Gaussian process regression — scikit-learn 1.2.2 documentation." scikit-learn.org. https://scikit-learn.org/stable/auto_examples/gaussian_process/plot_compare_gpr_krr.html. Accessed 08 Apr 2023

12. Lianlian, F., Wu, J.: Forecasting pig prices based on gradient boosting regression model. Comput. Simul. **37**(01), 347–350 (2020)
13. Serigne. "Stacked Regressions: Top 4% on Leaderboard." Kaggle (2018). https://www.kaggle.com/code/serigne/stacked-regressions-top-4-on-leaderboard#Modelling. Accessed 08 Apr 2023
14. Džeroski, S., Ženko, B.: Is combining classifiers with stacking better than selecting the best one? Mach. Learn. **54**, 255–273 (2004)

A Dynamic Game Study on the "Big Data Discriminatory Pricing" Behavior of E-commerce Platforms Under Government Regulation

Zhuang Yao[✉]

Department of International Education Cooperation, Tianjin University of Commerce,
Tianjin 300133, China
zyao005@fiu.edu

Abstract. The emergence of big data killing behavior is essentially a "differentiated pricing" behavior. The effective use of big data can promote the digital transformation of enterprises, bringing greater benefits to enterprises compared to the past price discrimination. However, "big data discriminatory pricing" also has widespread harmfulness, which has a huge negative impact on the welfare of consumers and the entire society. This article explores the reasons for the e-commerce platform's "discriminatory pricing" behavior from the perspective of consumers and e-commerce platforms under government control. This article draws on domestic and foreign literature to establish an evolutionary game model of e-commerce platform "discriminatory pricing" behavior and user consumer "loyalty behavior", and introduces government regulation and punishment mechanisms. Research has shown that when reputation losses and penalties are high, by "discriminatory pricing" they not only effectively curb the platform's behavior of paying too much attention to the more benefits and thus encroach on the rights and interests of consumers, but also help improve the scope of government regulation of the degree of "discriminatory pricing" of the platform. In addition, a government consumer coordination and supervision mechanism's introduction has a significant inhibitory effect on the "killing" behavior of e-commerce platforms.

Keywords: E-Commerce Platform "Discriminatory Pricing" Behavior · Consumer "Loyalty Behavior" · Government Regulation · Dynamic Game Evolution

1 Introduction

The news of the "discriminatory pricing" experience of e-commerce platform big data, which has been frequently exposed in many fields such as hotel booking, ticket sales, and online shopping, has begun to spread crazily in various major media, causing people's interest in similar experiences in e-commerce consumption fields such as booking rooms, buying tickets, and taking taxis on the Internet. Since big data discriminatory pricing was selected as one of the top ten popular words in 2018 which Total sound volume is 109535, the word has officially entered the public's attention. Big data killing refers to the use of big data by e-commerce platforms or enterprises to collect and consumer's historical information, and analyze their consumption preferences, purchasing habits, income degree, and other information. In the purpose of selling the same product or service to different consumers according to different prices to get higher returns, Using the path dependence and information asymmetry of loyal customers, price discrimination is implemented.

It is widely recognized that fair trading should abide by the rule of equal price for equal goods. However, with the long-term commercial development history of human society, a large number of "differentiated pricing" behaviors have evolved, which roughly include three types: the so-called generalized "price discrimination" in economics, dynamic pricing caused by deterministic premium or discount factors, and tidal pricing caused by tidal demand. There is a fundamental difference between big data savvy and traditional differentiated pricing behavior: In traditional differentiated pricing, there is generally no behavior of merchants concealing information, and information is usually transparent to consumers. Consumers, knowing that there are different prices, make behavioral decisions based on their own circumstances and voluntarily choose to pay high or low prices. However, in the "big data killing" scenario, platform companies hide price differences from consumers, who are kept in the dark about the existence of price differences, let alone whether they have paid a high price or a low price. In this case, the consumer's high price payment behavior is involuntary because he is not aware of the price difference. Although the era of big data has created more possibilities for businesses to implement differentiated pricing, "big data discriminatory pricing" behavior has widespread harms: On the one hand, consumers need to spend more time and energy to "counter killing" in order to avoid being "killed". On the other hand, big data fraud can also have a negative impact on the social image of platform companies, leaving the impression of abusing consumer personal data and abusing market dominance. At the same time, " big data discriminatory pricing" can also undermine the sense of social fairness and justice, endanger the order of commercial circulation, raise transaction costs in the circulation sector of the economy, and thereby reduce the overall welfare of society. The prevalence of phenomena such as "selling fake goods, false discounts, promotional traps, and scalping orders to stir up trust" has exposed the potential for platform moral hazard behavior in the e-commerce market, undoubtedly reducing the credibility of e-commerce platforms, leading to a credit crisis in the e-commerce market. These phenomena are inextricably linked to the phenomenon of "killing acquaintances" in platform big data. In the context of big data killing and government regulation, this article adopts an evolutionary game approach to analyze the stability of the two evolutionary game models between e-commerce platform "discriminatory pricing" behavior and consumer "loyalty behavior, and This paper explains that discusses the factors that affect the platform's" discriminatory pricing "behavior selection. Based on this, this article proposes suggestions to crack the platform's "killing" pricing.

2 Literature Review

Firstly, the reason why enterprises are increasingly capable of large-scale "killing" consumers is precisely due to the development of computer and communication technology, which makes data analysis and other aspects more mature; Secondly, the increasing motivation of enterprises to implement big data "killing off" behavior is due to the bottleneck encountered by e-commerce platform enterprises in the development of incremental markets. Third, consumers' attitudes towards "killing off" corporate big data. The black box characteristic of the algorithm makes the "killing" behavior of enterprises towards consumers covert. Even if it is found that issues such as high cost of rights protection and difficulty in providing evidence will deter consumers, which undoubtedly encourages e-commerce platform enterprises to violate the rules [1]. Fourth, there are still problems in government departments such as a lack of professional personnel, unclear law enforcement boundaries, high regulatory costs, small regulatory efforts, and the need for innovation in regulatory methods, which make it difficult to curb the "killing" motivation of enterprises [2].

In foreign countries, research is mainly conducted from the perspective of game theory between enterprises and consumers, as well as between competitive enterprises and supply chain enterprises. Zhou proposes that although enterprises will make corresponding price decisions based on the big data of consumers' past purchasing behavior, consumers will use anonymous methods to protect their rights and interests in the game with enterprises in order to avoid being identified as regular customers [3]. Although this method benefits consumers, the effect will reverse after reaching a certain level because consumers need to bear the cost of anonymity. Chen found that the discriminatory pricing caused by big data "big data discriminatory pricing" in the mainstream e-commerce field abroad has been developing slowly, mainly because there are relevant and strictly regulated legal measures and systems outside the market to curb such discriminatory pricing behavior, while this discriminatory pricing within the market not only leads to differences in product quality, but also causes enterprises to formulate different pricing strategies [4]. Bai believes that foreign countries attach great importance to and take legal measures to curb this discriminatory pricing behavior, so this discriminatory pricing has been slow to develop in mainstream e-commerce abroad [5].

2.1 The Perspective of Analyzing Government Regulatory Policies

Consumer Perspective. Peng analyzed the issue from the perspective of consumer rights protection, and the effective way to solve the problem is for the government to appropriately tilt the protection and regulate the liability of operators for damages [6]. In addition, Zhang's improvement in the market situation of big data "discriminatory pricing" should be based on the unified role of the market and the government [7]. Zhong believes that compared with the situation of unified pricing, the enterprise's practice of discriminatory the familiar will inhibit technological innovation, which is mainly due to price discrimination against consumers, which reduces operating efficiency, reduces consumer surplus and intensifies price competition between enterprises [8]. From the view of government regulation and governance, Wang analyzed the behavior of both trying to shield platform sellers in the "Alibaba VS Industry and Commerce Bureau" incident and establishing a regulatory agency to govern platform sellers in Alibaba [9]. He concluded that the entrusted agency relationship within the organization consists of platform e-commerce and platform sellers, enabling platform e-commerce to actively protect platform sellers from external accusations, "We also need to impose severe penalties on platform sellers for their violation strategies. The credit problems in the e-commerce market cannot be solved through internal supervision. Therefore, the construction of an effective platform e-commerce credit supervision mechanism depends on the internal supervision of platform sellers by platform e-commerce and the external supervision of the government on platform e-commerce. Therefore, it is necessary to strengthen the rationality of various entities on credit supervision issues to solve the platform e-commerce's credit" regulatory dilemma ", Lei and others explored the impact of consumer behavior on government regulation from the perspective of scholars, and constructed an evolutionary game model of citizen strategy and enterprise environmental protection strategy based on the perspective of public participation, pointing out that the formation of enterprise green production paths is positively correlated with citizen strategy [10].

Perspective of a Third Party. Wang and others introduced fund managers into evolutionary game analysis to analyze the cognitive bias of violation penalties, and found that fund managers' behavior is related to increasing the intensity of violation penalties and increasing the frequency of investigation and punishment [9]. Yang and others found that a tripartite static game model with incomplete information was built for enterprises, government regulators and dealers, and concluded that regulatory strength, regulatory costs and opportunity cost would have an impact on whether they would strictly regulate their own strategies, and further concluded that it is urgent for the government to establish a strict regulatory mechanism and punishment measures to ensure industry self-regulation [11]. Bei and other researchers have found that by creating an evolutionary game model between government regulators and enterprises and introducing public supervision, when consumers participate in supervision, effective strategies to curb corporate violations benefit from rational decision-making and strategic choices adopted by government departments [12]. Public supervision is an effective complement to government regulation, and can form a good interactive mechanism with government regulation and market regulation. Li and others analyzed the necessity of involving government, media, consumers, and other parties in the governance of this behavior, and found that by introducing an asymmetric evolutionary game model between government regulatory agencies and enterprises under new media coverage, enterprise violations can be suppressed by efficient new media regulation, It is believed that the degree of consumer trust in the platform can affect the evolutionary game relationship between consumer and platform killing behavior, which is related to the degree of consumer trust in the platform [13]. Ma and others have found that to avoid e-commerce dishonesty, they can improve credit deposits, strengthen credit supervision, and increase disguise costs [14]. Therefore, how to implement appropriate supervision is the key to solving the "regulatory dilemma" of platform e-commerce credit.

From the perspective of research methods, the issue of platform e-commerce credit regulation is a repeated game problem randomly matched by two large groups, which is suitable for evolutionary game analysis. Most scholars' research on platform e-commerce credit issues mainly focuses on the theoretical research level of improving laws and regulations and government regulation system. Few literature uses evolutionary game methods, starting from the perspective of bounded rationality of the three participants of platform e-commerce, consumers and government, Disclose the internal reasons for the widespread violations of platform e-commerce in shielding platform sellers. From a theoretical research perspective, the following points deserve attention. The innovation of this article lies in the following: Firstly, the regulatory bodies involved in the study should be more comprehensive. Most of the existing literature adopts the idea of bilateral game, which studies the collaborative efforts of consumers and governments to more effectively achieve the big data "discriminatory pricing" behavior's governance. Most of the existing literature adopts ideas of bilateral game. Secondly, in the past, most of the industry fields involved in research were mainly concentrated in areas such as food safety regulation, coal mine safety regulation, and rural labor transfer, while the e-commerce industry was less involved, which was not conducive to enhancing the persuasiveness of research conclusions. The research on regulatory issues in existing research should be broader. Thirdly, when constructing model parameters, this article not only sets up a punishment mechanism to directly reflect government regulation, but also sets up subsidies as an indirect means. When e-commerce engages in fraud, the subsidies generated are also different. It is also an innovation of this article to reflect government regulation through the differences in subsidies under different behaviors.

3 Evolutionary Game Between Platform E-commerce and Consumers Under Government Regulation

3.1 Problem Description and Model Assumptions

With consumers and e-commerce platforms as participants in the evolutionary game, considering that the relationship between the two e-commerce platforms in government governance is a principal-agent contract under the condition of asymmetric information, there may be serious "moral hazard" and "adverse selection" problems in the product pricing process. There are two types of pricing strategies for e-commerce platforms to choose from: non "discriminatory" pricing and "discriminatory" strategy. "non-discriminatory" pricing strategy refers to the e-commerce platform which can set a fair and reasonable price by market demand and without damaging on the legitimate rights and interests of consumers; The anti-familiar pricing strategy refers to that the e-commerce platform conducts differential pricing and price discrimination for different consumers through the opaque information in the online transaction process and the technical support of big data and complex algorithms. For a certain e-commerce platform, consumers will adopt different behavioral strategies to deal with "discriminatory" pricing: active control and passive control strategies. The active control strategy refers to consumers' awareness of the harm of "big data discriminatory pricing" pricing on their own, and effective control of the "discriminatory" behavior of big data on e-commerce platforms through complaints from e-commerce and government platforms, phone complaints, as well as public opinion pressure generated by major media exposure and active cooperation with government management systems; "Non active supervision strategy refers to consumers' lack of awareness of supervision or rights protection, and their negative attitude towards the platform's" discriminatory "pricing behavior." This article is to discuss the evolutionary game effect on platform e-commerce and consumers under the introduction of government regulation.

The following reasonable hypothesis can be made between consumers and e-commerce platforms.

(1) Participants in the game process involve platform e-commerce and consumers, and the game players are bounded rationality.
(2) Game players adopt two strategies. Platform e-commerce adopts two strategies: "discriminatory price" and "don't discriminatory price", and the strategy set is {discriminatory price, not discriminatory price}; Consumers adopt two strategies: "active control" and "non active control". The strategy set is {active control, non-active control}.
(3) Assuming that the probability of platform e-commerce choosing the "discriminatory" strategy is x ($0 \leq x \leq 1$), and the probability of choosing the "not discriminatory" strategy is 1−x; The probability of consumers choosing the "active control" behavior strategy is y ($0 \leq y \leq 1$), and the probability of choosing the "non active control" behavior strategy is 1−y.
(4) Construction of platform e-commerce and consumer income matrix.

Table 1. Game Model between E-commerce and Consumers.

consumer	E-commerce platform	
	Not discriminatory y	discriminatory 1−y
active control x	$R_1 + R_3 + S_1 - C_3 - C_2$ $R_2 - S_1$	$R_1 + R_3 + S_1 - C_3 - C_1$ $R_2 + \omega\alpha - P\alpha^2 - L - S_1$
non-active control 1−x	$R_1 + S_1 - C_1$ $R_2 - S_1$	$R_1 - C_2 + S_1$ $R_2 + \omega\alpha - S_1 - P\alpha^2$

In Table 1, the benefits obtained when e-commerce platforms adopt a "discriminatory" pricing strategy are $\omega\alpha$, parameter ω is marginal revenue of pricing the platform [15]. The basic benefits of normal operation of e-commerce platforms are R_1 and R_2, The basic utility of consumers in online consumption channels is R, The platform's subsidies for loyal and disloyal consumers are respectively S_1 and S_2 The punishment imposed by the government on the pricing behavior of "discriminatory" of the platform is $C(p, \alpha) = p\alpha^2$ Penalty cost and platform "familiarity" degree α in connection with the government's punishment level P, the normal cost that consumers pay when e-commerce platforms do not "kill" customers with big data is C_1[16]. But when encountering price discrimination, the cost is C_2. $C_2 > C_1$ When consumers and government actively monitor the platform's pricing behavior and expose and complain about the "kill familiar" phenomenon, the platform will face certain reputational losses L The main performance is the loss of social signal effect (the "Matthew effect" formed by attracting new customers to join) and social network effect (the "lock in effect" formed by cultivating old customers' stickiness) [17]. Consumers need to pay a certain amount of time and energy to cooperate with the government's "active supervision" platform's "killing mature" behaviorC_3 (Altruistic punishment cost), punishing behaviors that violate social norms at the expense of one's own interests [18]. The social benefits of consumers' active supervision of the platform include improved service levels, transparent and reasonable price settings, and protection of consumers' right to know and fair trade in goods or services is R_3 [19, 20].

3.2 Equilibrium Points and Analysis of Evolutionary Games

Obtained as follows:

$$U_{E1} = x(R_1 + S_1 + R_3 - C_2 - C_3) + (1 - Y)(R_1 + R_3 - C_2 + S_1)$$
$$U_{E2} = y(R_1 + S_1 - C_1) + (1 - y)(R_1 - C_2 + S_1)$$
$$U_E = xU_{E1} + (1 - x)U_{E2}$$

The replication dynamic equation for consumers to choose an active monitoring strategy is

$$U_1 = x(1-x)(R_3 - G) \tag{1}$$

Similarly, the replication dynamic equation for e-commerce platforms to choose a normal pricing strategy is

$$U_2 = y(1-y)\left(Lx - w\alpha + P\alpha^2\right) \tag{2}$$

The replication dynamic Eqs. (1) and (2) describe the evolution process of consumer monitoring strategies and platform pricing strategies, respectively. According to the replication dynamic equation, the Jacobian matrix of the evolutionary game can be obtained:

$$J_1 = \begin{pmatrix} (1-2x)(R_3 - C_1) & 0 \\ y(1-y)L & (1-2y)(Lx - \omega\alpha + P\alpha^2) \end{pmatrix}$$

Proposition 1: When the cost of altruistic punishment paid by consumers for "killing off" big data on e-commerce platforms is less than the social benefits generated by their active supervision $R_3 > C_3$ and $L - \omega\alpha + P\alpha^2 > 0$, (1, 1) is a saddle point.
Prove that when $R_3 > C_3$ and $L - \omega\alpha + P\alpha^2 > 0$, $x = 1, y = 1$, determinant $|J| = (L - \omega\alpha + P\alpha^2)(R_3 - C_3) > 0$ $\mu_1 = C_1 - R_3 < 0$, $\mu_2 = -L + \omega\alpha - P\alpha^2 > 0$ of a function, when $L > \omega^2/(4P)$, $\Delta < 0. G(\alpha) = 0$ is no solution. Therefore, for $\alpha > 0$, $\omega\alpha - L - P\alpha^2 < 0$, equation holds good under all circumstances. When $L = \omega^2/(4P)$, $\Delta = 0$, $G(\alpha) = 0$ is a unique zero solution $\alpha = \omega/(2P)$. Therefore, for $\alpha \neq \omega/(2P)$, $\omega\alpha - L - P\alpha^2 < 0$, equation holds good under all circumstances; When $L <$

$\omega^2/(4P)$, $\Delta > 0$, $G(\alpha) = 0$ are two zero solutions, $\alpha_1 = \left(-\omega + \sqrt{\omega^2 - 4pL}\right)/ - 2p$, $\alpha_2 = \left(-\omega - \sqrt{\omega^2 - 4PL}\right)/ - 2F$.

So for $\alpha > max\left\{\left(-\omega + \sqrt{\omega^2 - 4PL}\right)/ - 2P, 0\right\}$, $\omega\alpha - L - P\alpha^2 < 0$ equation holds good under all circumstances.

This conclusion indicates that the regulatory mechanism can effectively regulate the degree of "familiarity" of e-commerce platforms α related to the value of penalty parameters L and P, when reputation losses L and penalties P are high they not only effectively curb the platform's behavior of paying too much attention to the additional benefits brought by "discriminatory price" and thus damaging on the legitimate rights and interests of consumers, but also help improve the scope of government supervision α over the degree of " discriminatory price " of the platform.

4 Conclusions

4.1 Conclusion

The e-commerce platform's price discrimination against different consumers through big data algorithm analysis technology is a suicidal behavior, which will overdraw consumers' loyalty and trust in the platform, cause losses to consumers' welfare and even cause the government to increase investment in e-commerce supervision costs. This article mainly constructs an evolutionary game model between consumers and e-commerce platforms. By conducting an evolutionary game analysis of the potential "discriminatory price" behavior in the e-commerce market under the guidance of government regulation, it explores the impact of government punishment and the "discriminatory price" behavior of e-commerce platforms' big data on their own reputation on consumer behavior strategies and platform pricing behavior strategies. Further exploring the influencing factors and evolutionary paths of different behavioral strategies of each participant, it is found through research that:

The Impact of Government Punishment on "Discriminatory Price" Behavior. When other parameters remain unchanged, in response to the plight of the e-commerce market in which only platform self-discipline behavior and government regulation are considered, a new mechanism is proposed to consider the joint supervision of consumers and governments on the phenomenon of "discriminatory price" e-commerce platforms, and an evolutionary game model is established to regulate the "discriminatory price" behavior of e-commerce platform big data, When government punishment P plays a decisive role in promoting a win-win cooperation mechanism between e-commerce platforms and consumers, weaker punishment P will not help curb the "discriminatory price" phenomenon in the e-commerce market. Only by implementing greater punishment P can the government effectively curb the "killing" pricing behavior of e-commerce platforms.

The Influence of Government Consumer Coordination and Supervision Mechanism on "Discriminatory Price" Behavior. Similarly, when other parameters and conditions remain unchanged, after the selection of e-commerce platforms and consumers, the original evolutionary game model, based on the introduction of a government consumer coordinated regulatory mechanism, has a significant inhibitory effect on e-commerce platforms' "discriminatory" behavior. It is necessary to increase platform reputation losses L and government penalties P, especially when government penalties P are insufficient, the pressure of public opinion brought about by consumers' active supervision could effectively curb the platform's the "discriminatory price" pricing behavior, thereby avoiding the harm of platform differential pricing behavior.

4.2 Recommendations

Solving the pricing dilemma of big data in the e-commerce market requires a combination of technology, regulation, and mechanisms:

(1) In terms of technology, the era of big data urgently requires the government to innovate the control technology for the development of big data, build a landing regulatory framework to enhance the transparency of personalized pricing algorithms, guide platform companies to explain the main parameters and mechanism of pricing algorithms, and ensure the reasonable transparency of enterprise pricing algorithms through systematic regulatory methods such as algorithm audit and algorithm impact assessment in the future, It also protects consumers' right to opt out of personalized pricing options, reduces consumers' supervision costs, and determines whether the supervising enterprise is suspected of "killing off", thereby providing consumers with convenient and efficient rights protection channels.

(2) In terms of regulation, the object of regulation is not the enterprise's autonomous pricing behavior itself, but rather various algorithms for analyzing data and completing pricing. To build a flexible and professional digital law enforcement team, regulatory authorities urgently need to include big data "killing" behavior within a clear legal governance scope, clarify who is responsible for supervision, impose huge fines on illegal enterprises, increase their illegal costs, and stipulate that platform service agreements and payment rules, as well as network platforms, should be publicized. If there is a lack of in-depth understanding of the operation of the digital market, and a lack of deep understanding of the application of digital technology, "There may be a problem of" shooting an arrow at a target while triggering supervision. Therefore, it is necessary to develop and deploy an online detection system with real-time evaluation and dynamic detection functions".

(3) In terms of model, "personalized pricing" has been widely criticized, which is related to both consumers' distrust of pricing algorithms and the current imbalance between consumers and platform companies in the era of algorithms. Relying solely on government led administrative supervision is difficult to correct this structural imbalance in game forces, reshape the chain of trust among consumers, and form a new model of government consumer collaborative supervision. It is vital to give enough play to the administration supervision' power and public opinion supervision, and require multiple participation in common governance.

References

1. Zou, K., Liu, J.: The legal regulation dilemma and outlet of big data "killing maturity" - only from the perspective of the consumer rights protection law. Price Theory Pract. **410**(08), 47–50 (2018). https://doi.org/10.19851/j.cnki.cn11-1010/f.2018.08.012
2. Lei, L., Chen, R.: How can big data "kill" be broken? Evolutionary game based on government consumer collaborative regulation. J. Syst. Manage. **30**(04), 664–675 (2021)
3. Bai. S., Xu, W., Jiang, M.: Research on collaborative governance of big data "killing off" behavior on e-commerce platforms - based on evolutionary game analysis among e-commerce companies, consumers, and government. Price Theory Pract. **462**(12), 141–144+203 (2022). https://doi.org/10.19851/j.cnki.cn11-1010/f.2022.12.404
4. Xuhui, W., Xiaoxue, R.: A dynamic evolutionary game study of platform e-commerce credit regulation from the perspective of government governance. China Manage. Sci. **29**(12), 29–41 (2021). https://doi.org/10.16381/j.cnki.issn1003-207x.2019.1875
5. Ding, P., Han, X.: The evolutionary game between government regulation and the "killing off" behavior of e-commerce enterprises in the digital economy. Econ. Manag. **35**(01), 77–84 (2021)
6. Zhao, X.: Research on the evolutionary game between government, platform e-commerce, and consumers under the dynamic reward and punishment mechanism. Bus. Econ. Res. **855**(20), 96–98 (2022)
7. Liu, C.: Analysis of big data pricing issues. Libr. Inf. Knowl. **169**(01), 57–64 (2016). https://doi.org/10.13366/j.dik.2016.01.057
8. Feicheng, M., Xiaoguang, W.: Information economics (IX) lecture 9: pricing strategies and methods for information goods. Intell. Theory Pract. **03**, 285–287 (2003). https://doi.org/10.16353/j.cnki.1000-7490.2003.03.029
9. Yang, C., Luo, X.: Preliminary study on comprehensive governance of algorithmic discrimination. Sci. Soc. **8**(04), 1–12+64 (2018). https://doi.org/10.19524/j.cnki.10-1009/g3.2018.04.001
10. Liu, Y., Zhang, W., Hui, D.: Research on the impact of online word of mouth on consumer price sensitivity. Price Theory Pract. **336**(06), 77–78 (2012). https://doi.org/10.19851/j.cnki.cn11-1010/f.2012.06.038
11. Emerald: A focus on consumer behaviors and experiences in an online shopping environment.Emerald Group Publishing Limited, UK (2015)
12. Fehr, E., Schmidt, K.M.: A theory of fairness, competition, and cooperation. Q. J. Econ. **114**(3), 817–868 (1999)
13. Friedman, D.: A simple testable model of double auction markets. J. Econ. Behav. Organ. **15**(1), 47–70 (1991)
14. Lei, L., Gao, S.: Evolutionary game analysis of ride sourcing companies and passengers under new policies of ride sourcing. IEEE Access **6**, 71918–71931 (2018)
15. Mark, J.T.: Pareto price discrimination. Econ. Lett. **183**, 108559 (2019). https://doi.org/10.1016/j.econlet.2019.108559
16. Chen, Y.: Paying customers to switch. J. Econ. Manage. Strat. **6**(4), 877–897 (1997)
17. Shi, H., Liu, Y., Petruzzi, N.C.: Consumer heterogeneity, product quality, and distribution channels. Manage. Sci. **59**(5), 1162–1176 (2013)
18. Wang, X.Q., Yuen, K.F., Wong, Y.D., et al.: It is green, but is it fair? Investigating consumers' fairness perception of green service offerings. J. Clean. Prod. **181**, 235–248 (2018)
19. Peng, W., Xun, C., Xiaochen, Z.: Weak tax market tax regulation based on consumer supervision. Syst. Eng. Theory Pract.Pract. **35**(04), 847–856 (2015)
20. Wang, X., Zhang, Q.: Building a reputation for platform based e-commerce: a perspective of value co-creation between platform enterprises and platform sellers. China Ind. Econ. **356**(11), 174–192 (2017). https://doi.org/10.19581/j.cnki.ciejournal.2017.11.013

Analysis on Marketing Strategy of Chinese Online Music Platform–QQ Music

Jiayi Hong[✉]

College of Humanities, Beijing University of Chinese Medicine, Beijing 102401, China
20210621036@bucm.edu.cn

Abstract. Today, as various music apps gradually become the "infrastructure" on people's mobile phones, the future development of music apps has become an important issue. As a representative music platform in China, QQ Music has the common advantages of streaming media platforms and faces the general problems of online music platforms. This article is based on the literature, adopts document analysis to expose the deficiencies of QQ Music. The study shows that QQ Music has a social model that is too old-fashioned. And QQ Music has a problem with the over-collection of users' personal information. In addition, QQ Music's copyright protection measures are inadequate and its hardware industry chain is not well developed. The company's social networking model is too dated, and QQ Music needs to regulate the scope of information collection and protect user privacy. Apart from that, QQ Music should try to improve the other two problems by using digital protection system technology and extending the related hardware industry chain.

Keywords: Online Music Platforms · Social Networking · Digital Protection · Industry Extension

1 Introduction

In primitive societies, music was used as a way to pray to gods. Today, people listen to music to soothe their moods, express their individuality, and find like-minded partners. It can be said that music has become an indispensable part of human daily life. With the continuous development of science and technology, the form of music transmission is also constantly changing. Digital music breaks the constraints of time and space with the characteristics of "dematerialization" [1]. From 1972, when Andreas Pavel, a German-Brazilian, built the prototype of the Walkman, to the advent of the first music app, technology has made the music carriers smaller and smaller. Up to this day, everyone has a mobile phone. People can almost meet all their needs of life through the app on their mobile phone. Uber can solve transportation problems, Alibaba can offer daily necessities, and Just Eat can meet dietary needs. "Online" and "Internet" are unavoidable trends in all service industries. The research object of this paper - QQ Music is an app that can meet people's needs for listening to music. Portable and low-cost, digital music has fundamentally changed the shape and consumption of music paraphernalia [1]. As

---

© The Author(s), under exclusive license to Springer Nature Singapore Pte Ltd. 2024
X. Li et al. (Eds.): ICEMGD 2023, AEPS, pp. 969–976, 2024.
https://doi.org/10.1007/978-981-97-0523-8_90

one of the representative online music platforms in China, QQ Music has registered 800 million users since its establishment in 2005. As more and more people discover the benefits of digital music, emerging online music platforms such as NetEase Cloud Music, Qianqian Music, and Soda Music have tried to challenge the existing market structure. At the same time, the development of the online music industry has entered the era of stock dividends from the era of incremental dividends, which means QQ Music is facing huge challenges [2].

This article will briefly introduce QQ Music. At the same time, the advantages of QQ Music and the disadvantages of QQ Music will be mentioned. It also analyzes the inconvenient interactive methods, the phenomenon of collecting personal information beyond the scope, copyright disputes, and the insufficient development of the hardware industry of QQ music. The article would also points out the causes of problems and gives solutions through literature analysis. It will take QQ Music as an example to discuss the dilemma and direction of online music platforms' developments and provide reference for the development of streaming media platforms.

2 Brand Story

2.1 Development Process

Since 2005, Tencent Group has seized the opportunities brought by the times and established QQ Music shortly after the online music platform entered the Chinese market. In the era that the online music platform was immature, QQ Music became a leader in the industry under the huge copyright advantage brought by Tencent Group and accumulated a group of loyal users. To face the challenges brought about by development of market, QQ Music merged with Kuwo Music and Kugou Music in 2016 to form "Tencent Music Entertainment Group" (TME). The number of authorized music copyrights exceeds 1 million. Due to copyright disputes and the collection of personal information beyond the scope, QQ Music has been questioned. In November 2021, QQ Music was included in China's List of Application Software Notified by the Ministry of Industry and Information Technology of Existing Problems.

2.2 Target Market

QQ Music claims to be "China's latest and most complete, free, genuine, high-quality, lossless music platform" [3]. QQ Muaic adopts the operation mode of "free most users + charging fewer users" [3]. This means, most users can listen to basic songs for free, and paid users can listen to and download more songs with higher quality and enjoy more services [3]. QQ Music takes advantage of its huge music library, rich copyright resources, and large user base brought by Tencent Group. And it is committed to meeting customers' needs for specific tracks, higher music playback quality, and diversified music types. QQ Music's target customer groups are first-tier and second-tier male and female urban residents aged 20–29, who pursue a quality of life, focus on efficiency, love reading, and have certain investment and financial management skills.

3 Advantages Analysis

QQ Music obtains a large amount of copyrights through cooperation with a large number of companies. QQ Music established cooperative relations with more than 200 companies around the world. At the same time, it has exchanged copyrights with Netease Cloud Music, Kugou Music, and other platforms. As of 2019, QQ Music has 17 million songs with valid copyrights [4].

QQ Music raises awareness by working with multiple brands across borders. QQ Music cooperated with commercial banks to launch co-branded bank cards [5]. It also united China Unicom to launch an exclusive traffic package. QQ Music provides users with a high-quality listening experience. QQ Music collaborated with Dolby and added Dolby Atmos to the platform. Launched the Hi-Res lossless version of the sound effect.

QQ Music actively holds offline activities, combining online and offline. The QQ Music Premiere Concert QQ Music is one of QQ Music's ground-level branding activities. Founded in December 2008, QQ Music Premiere is a brand of premiere concerts in the mainland music industry, with the fundamental aim of promoting new and hot artists, regularly inviting famous artists with newly released albums to meet with QQ Music fans across the country. QQ Music participated in the production of music variety shows, cooperating with Akiyay and Youku Video respectively to launch popular variety shows such as "Summer of the Band", "Tomorrow's Son" and "This is Original". QQ Music innovatively provides exclusive electronic pets for clients. The client could adopt pet eggs for free, listen to songs to incubate eggs, and make pets grow at the same way [6].

4 Problems Analysis

4.1 Insufficient Social Attractiveness

QQ Music's social approach is rigid. Although there is a special social platform for people to communicate, it is useless. There are many ways to socialize in the contemporary era, and platforms that simply publish pictures and daily routines are not favored by young people. For example, on the QQ music social platform, the discussion group of world-renowned Chinese singer Jay Chou has only 605,000 followers. The antiquated social model has made QQ Music less socially attractive. This lack of social appeal further creates an inactive community culture. This inactive community culture does not bring much benefits to QQ Music. Therefore, QQ Music did not pay enough attention to the community culture, and accordingly did not invest enough in the social culture. Without the corresponding funding, it is difficult to innovate the social model. Thus, here comes to a vicious circle.

Though the social platform of QQ Music has lowered the threshold and invited many independent musicians to settle in, the independent has also created difficulties in building a social and civilized environment. First, due to the lack of QQ Music's support, independent musicians inevitably hope to earn extra money by any means necessary. Secondly, the zero distance between music creators and listeners also makes it easy to create some "overly intimate" relationships. Finally, human character is unpredictable and unassessable. Vanity and greed can easily drive people to post messages that show off their wealth and fraud on social media platforms. The most important thing is that QQ Music's lack of supervision of social platforms has contributed to a bad social culture.

Besides, although QQ Music has a live broadcast function, it does not focus on well-known musicians who attract the main customers. The platform itself is not attractive enough to attract well-known weblebrities to reside. QQ Music does not pay much attention to the construction of live streaming function. And it does not use its close relationship with many musicians to invite them into the live streaming platform. In addition to the reasons for QQ Music itself, external competitors are also the reason for QQ Music's lack of social appeal. Platforms such as TikTok and BiliBili are powerful and attractive for live streaming. These platforms have seized the live streaming market and compressed the living space of QQ Music live streaming.

4.2 Unprotected User Privacy

The problem of apps collecting personal information beyond the scope currently consists of seven main scenarios: First, the declaration of sensitive permissions exceeds the necessary scope. Second, the request for permission exceeds the necessary scope. Third, the sensitivity of the collected data exceeds the necessary scope. Fourth, the specific content of the collected data exceeds the necessary scope. Fifth, the collection method exceeds the necessary scope. Sixth, the collection frequency exceeds the necessary scope. Seven, the collection scenario exceeds the necessary scope [7]. Second, QQ Music should check the content of the authorization information forms to ensure that they are legal and legitimate, and QQ Music should collect limited information in limited ways and in limited scenarios.

Due to QQ Music's infringement of customers' privacy rights, it was listed on China's List of Application Software Notified by the Ministry of Industry and Information Technology in November 2021 [8]. QQ Music collects the information of users who listen to songs beyond the scope, and it still runs in the background of the device after the user closes its running page. It also illegally pirated songs published on other platforms without the authorization of independent musicians. The boundary between collecting customer preferences and violating customer privacy is a problem that every social platform and even artificial intelligence Chat GPT needs to face recently.

4.3 Disputed Copyrights

According to a report published by the European union intellectual property office in 2017, The economic cost of IRP infringement in the recorded music industry, the conclusion can be summed up that piracy brings the music industry [9]. As a commercial music platform, QQ Music inevitably pursues profits. And its free trial listening, free download, and even paid download to attract customers all provide conditions for music piracy [3]. Because downloaded music can be used not only for research but also for profit. The large number of copyrights owned by QQ Music objectively saves the cost of pirated music and facilitates the development of illegal activities. As an intermediary of music copyright, QQ Music lacks attention to digital music copyright issues. After users download music, the unlimited use right to music has caused hidden losses to music copyright suppliers to a certain extent. From the perspective of the sustainable development of the music market, this is not conducive to protecting the enthusiasm of creators and the stability of the music market.

4.4 Blank Hardware Industry Chain

Limited Advertising Profitability and Single Advertising Method. Although digital music profitability models are becoming increasingly abundant, there are not many ways to really bring in significant revenue. Relevant data reveals that advertising is still the main source of revenue for mobile music clients, with most mobile music clients generating around 50% of their revenue from commercials, and this proportion is even as high as 90% in some streaming music [4]. In contrast, Spotify and Deezer's advertising revenues are as low as 10% and 3.7% respectively, in stark contrast to China's online music platforms [4].

The Lack of Payment for Music. In addition to this, the low level of user payment is also a serious problem. The difference between QQ Music members and non-members is mainly in the quality of the music. However, for most casual users, the slight difference in sound effects does not affect music listening. As a result, most users do not have much desire to pursue high quality music when they can listen to it, and there is little incentive to convert from free users to paid members.

E-commerce Profitability Gap. In recent years, QQ Music has actively cooperated with car and electrical appliances brands such as NIO and Xiaomi to expand broadcasting channels. But its brand derivatives are consistently absent. On the other hand, Netease Cloud Music, a comparable music brand in China, has launched the "Netease Yanxuan" app. Not only sell some NetEase brand mobile phone accessories in this online mall: such as earphones, data cables, mobile phone holders, mobile phone cases, and other music-related items. It also focuses on empowering the "Netease Yanxuan" brand itself. QQ Music is completely blank in this regard.

5 Solutions

5.1 Innovating Social Model and Strengthening the Supervision of the Platform

QQ Music should strengthen the "Virtual Community" of the music community, and link users with the same interests in the form of a group "Music Public Model", which promotes client communication in the community, and meet the requirements of user expression and sharing [10]. With music content as the core, QQ Music could try to connect customers with content, enhance the emotional connection of users, and establish a community culture with interest as the core final goal.

Based on the advantages of massive exclusive copyrights, QQ Music could maintain close cooperation with cooperating musicians. QQ Music should endeavor to strive for the right to release music and appropriate concert welfare tickets to increase user activity. And this online music platform could try to invite more well-known musicians to interact live online to improve the overall style of the platform at the same time.

In order to rectify the chaos around the social platform showing off wealth and selling at excessively high prices illegally, QQ Music could increase the supervision and management personnel of the platform. In addition, QQ Music can offer genuine peripherals, concert tickets and more by collaborating with well-known musicians. This is a great way to combat the pirate peripheral market with genuine peripherals and to clean up the messy market.

5.2 Actively Rectifying to Protect User Privacy

First of all, QQ Music needs to listen to the rectification opinions of the Ministry of Industry and Information Technology of China in a timely manner, and corrects the act of collecting personal information beyond the scope. Secondly, the person in charge of QQ Music needs to carefully read the relevant Civil Law, Economic Law and other laws to clarify the definition of citizens' right to privacy to avoid doing anything illegal. At the same time, QQ Music needs to clarify relevant authorization issues when cooperating with other music intermediary companies or copyright holders, so as to avoid the problem of uploading music without authorization. QQ Music needs to explain authorization issues to customers accurately and in a timely manner and obtain corresponding information on the premise of customers' informed consent.

In order to give customers a customized experience within the limits of legality, QQ Music could learn from NetEase Cloud Music to use user song lists more systematically to organize songs and develop personalized recommendations for music from past recommendations and private music broadcasts. QQ Music can imitate NetEase Cloud Music to provide users with personalized personal homepages to help them express their emotions and feelings easier [11].

5.3 Strengthening Copyright Protection

QQ Music can properly use DRM and digital watermarking technology. DRM system uses a special DRM file encryption format and can configure the relevant permission template and encryption verification method, which can effectively realize the digital copyright protection of enterprise scientific research achievement documents [12]. QQ Music can restrict the use of downloaded music through a DRM system by limiting the digital key to six aspects: digital media encryption, blocking illegal content registration, user environment monitoring, user behavior monitoring, permission authentication mechanism, payment mechanism and storage management. Digital watermarking technology is a method of embedding watermark information into the encoding of the original media file using spread spectrum, discrete Fourier, discrete cosine, discrete wavelet or transform domain hybrid algorithms to achieve copyright protection [13]. QQ Music can also learn from Apple's music digital copyright encryption protection technology—Fair Play, to limit the number of times music copying or use, so as to alleviate the hidden loss of the copyright owner.

5.4 Expanding the Hardware Industry Chain

On the one hand QQ Music could expand the forms of ad insertion. For example, it could allow non-paying customers to listen to a certain number of songs before being forced to insert an ad, while paying customers would not be bothered by the ads. Or let non-paying customers listen to a song only after a certain length of ad, etc.

On the other hand, the survey shows that the mobile music penetration rate among university students is over 90%, and the percentage of them willing to pay for music products is 40.8%, with an average monthly spending of $20. A generational survey showed that 5.8% of the "post-70s" were willing to pay for music products, 9.2% of the "post-80s" were willing to pay, and 13.2% of the "post-90s 13.2% of the "post-90s" group are willing to pay for music products [4].

QQ Music could be segmented according to listening age as well as preference to expand the range of paid songs. Expanding the proportion of paid songs that are popular with younger people, as well as older, more popular songs could help to target specific fee behaviours to those who are more willing to pay. To increase the incentive for people to switch from free to paid users QQ Music could also endeavour to expand the proportion of paid songs.

In addition, QQ Music could cooperate and co-brand with other brands to attract customers in the form of multiple IPs. QQ Music can also try to cooperate with industrial brands, such as companies that make earphones and water cups, to make up for technical deficiencies. Launching peripherals with logos is also a good method to expand new revenue growth points. Expanding the intelligent hardware industry chain is the final goal of QQ Music needs to achieve.

6 Conclusion

With online music apps gradually becoming the "infrastructure" of people's cell phones, QQ Music as a typical streaming platform is of great importance to study. After the above analysis, this article can conclude that QQ Music, which was once brilliant but is now declining, can improve its own problems in four aspects: building a music community culture, improving user privacy protection measures, using an anti-piracy system to reduce piracy, and expanding the industry chain. The privacy protection and copyright disputes it faces are also common problems faced by digital platforms after the development of science and technology.

Correctly solving these problems can provide a reference for the development of digital music platforms in the future. The source of the development of the music platform is good music, and the in-depth development of high-quality IP is the driving force for development. As a listed company, in order to become more profitable, QQ Music needs to update its advertising methods and attract other brands to advertise on the QQ Music online platform. In order to face competition from other music platforms, QQ Music needs to increase its users' desire to spend by widening the difference in service between free users and members. In order to increase awareness and expand the industry chain, QQ Music should actively collaborate with light industrial companies to launch a range of QQ Music peripherals.

This article briefly describes the background, current situation, problems and solutions of QQ Music, a representative streaming platform in China. As a classic online music platform, QQ Music has problems that are common of all online music platforms. The digitalization of music is an unstoppable trend of the times. How to create a better digital music platform should be summarized in practice. This article can provide some reference for the future development of digital music, represented by QQ Music.

References

1. Fan, X.P.: From music platform to content ecology: The business model innovation of Tencent music. Beijing Cult. Creativity **04**, 22–28 (2021)
2. Zhang, C.L.: Analysis on the development model of online music platform——Taking NetEase cloud music and QQ music as examples. Sci. Technol. Commun. **23**, 155–157 (2020)
3. Jia, L.L., Li, Q.: Analysis on the real difficulties and development strategies of digital music copyright protection in my country——Taking QQ music as an example. Publishing Res. **01**, 80–82 (2019)
4. Yang, F.: Exploration of opportunities, dilemmas and optimization strategies for the development of China's digital music industry in the new media era. J. Guiyang Coll. (Soc. Sci. Edn.) **03**, 111–114 (2019)
5. Jian, Y.F., Shi, J.L.: Analysis of music platform business models in the context of the Internet - Taking QQ music as an example. Mark. World, 19–20 (2021)
6. Li, Y.: Fun with QQ music pet M-PETS. Comput. Netw. Netw. **22**, 33 (2021)
7. App collecting personal information in excess of the scope of "seven types" of hidden problems need to be closely watched. Xinhua Daily Telegraph, 2, (2021)
8. Ministry of Industry and Information Technology of the People's Republic of China. https://wap.miit.gov.cn/xwdt/gxdt/sjdt/art/2021/art_1b4410dcdc9743edae30b6429bd76d22.html. Accessed 16 Apr 2023
9. European Union Intellectual Property Office, The economic cost of IPR infringement in the recorded music industry. https://euipoeuropa.eu/himportal/en/web/observatory/ IPR infringement music. Accessed 16 Apr 2023
10. Liu, T., Zhao, O.Y.: A study on the "music social" model of mobile music platforms: the example of netease cloud music and QQ Music". Today Media **27**(4), 58–61 (2019)
11. Huo, L.L.: Exploring the development of Netease cloud music APP market. Publishing Wide Angle **12**, 82–84 (2020)
12. Deng, Y., Huang, W.J., Xu, N.: Digital copyright management and protection of enterprise scientific and technological achievements based on DRM technology. In: Proceedings of the 2021 Academic Annual Conference of China Civil Engineering Society, p. 91 (2021)
13. Luo, Y.F.: Research on key technology of adaptive audio and video watermarking based on media feature analysis. Sichuan University (2021)

The Causality Between Executive Compensation, Equity Concentration, and Corporate Performance: A Multiple Regression Analysis

Xiao Rao[✉]

Faculty of Business and Management, Beijing Normal University-Hong Kong Baptist University United International College, Zhuhai 519087, China
q030001080@mail.uic.edu.cn

Abstract. Academics, practitioners, and politicians have all become increasingly interested in and engaged in discussion about the correlation between executive compensation, equity concentration, and corporate performance in recent years. This growing attention can be attributed to the critical role that effective executive compensation and equity structures play in shaping a company's success, as well as their potential impact on the overall economy. This research paper is to examine the interplay between executive compensation, equity concentration, and corporate performance through multiple regression analysis on 4652 non-financial A-share listed companies in China between 2018 and 2022. By exploring the underlying mechanisms and interactions among these three factors, this paper aims to shed light on their influence on corporate success and provide practical recommendations for companies to optimize their management strategies. Through this analysis, it hopes to contribute to the current body of literature on this subject and support the development of more effective and sustainable corporate governance practices.

Keywords: Executive Compensation · Equity Concentration · Corporate Performance

1 Introduction

Corporate performance has taken on a central role in shareholders' attention and their pursuit of interests in the context of the principal-agent relationship. To achieve this goal, shareholders employ top executives and use remuneration contracts as incentives to improve corporate performance. Therefore, executive compensation, as a key regulatory factor in the principal-agent problem, has attracted widespread attention from scholars regarding its relationship with corporate performance. According to the supervision theory, a higher concentration of equity ownership usually implies stronger shareholder supervision and constraint on executives, thereby encouraging executives to work towards achieving corporate performance goals. In contrast, companies with lower equity concentration tend to have numerous small and medium-sized shareholders who are less enthusiastic about supervising executives, making it difficult to effectively control executives' self-serving behaviors. Based on this, the impact of equity concentration on corporate performance has also become a focal point for scholars both domestically and internationally.

This paper aims to investigate the causality between executive compensation and corporate performance, providing a scientific basis for formulating executive compensation policies and leveraging the incentive effects of executive compensation. Meanwhile, by exploring the relationship between equity concentration and corporate performance, this essay offers reference suggestions for companies to appropriately introduce major shareholders and leverage the incentive effects of equity concentration.

2 Literature Review and Research Hypotheses

Extensive research has been done on the effect of CEO salary at listed businesses on corporate performance by foreign academic groups. Early research findings suggested that executive salary and corporate performance were not significantly correlated [1, 2]. More and more researchers have discovered a favorable causality between CEO salary and business success, nevertheless, as a result of changes in the business governance environment. Conyon and Schuabach used British and German corporate annual reports as samples and concluded that executive annual salaries in both countries were significantly positively correlated with performance of corporates, but degree of impact varied [3]. According to research by Gabaix and Landier, there is a stronger correlation between CEO pay and company performance in large companies [4]. The study on the causality between CEO salary and business performance has advanced in domestic academic circles, but the conclusions have not yet been agreed upon. Early research findings indicated that there was no meaningful relationship between executive pay and corporate success [5, 6]. Recent studies have started to empirically explore the causality between executive compensation and business performance, though, as a result of listed companies' increasing emphasis on executive salary incentives. In their empirical analysis of listed companies in the SSE and SZSE from 2009 to 2014, Chen Guanghui and Zhao Dongfeng discovered a substantial positive link between CEO pay and corporate performance [7]. A similar empirical study by Li Minghua and Zhang Qiang from 2010 to 2016 on listed companies on the SSE and SZSE came to the same result with a positive association between CEO pay and corporate success [8]. According to the principal-agent theory and optimal contract theory, shareholders can minimize moral hazard and agency costs by negotiating optimal compensation packages with executives, which will incentivize them to boost business performance and maximize shareholder wealth. Corporate compensation agreements relate executive pay to business success, and when executive pay rises, business success can be enhanced by changing executive conduct. Thus, the following hypothesis is put forth in this paper:

Hypothesis 1: The executive compensation in a company is positively correlated with corporate performance.

Shleifer and Vishny suggested that when a company increases its equity concentration to a relatively concentrated state, increasing the proportion of shares held by major shareholders can improve overall work performance [9]. After conducting an empirical study with data from 500 manufacturing companies, Myeong-Hyeon discovered an inverted U-shaped curve association between corporate performance and the percentage of internal shareholders' shares in each of the three equity concentration intervals [10]. After that, some scholars collected data from 11 listed national joint-stock commercial banks from 2006 to 2009, and the empirical results indicated that equity concentration was negatively correlated with corporate performance. According to this paper, variations in the choice of indicators and changes in the macroenvironment are to blame for the results above's contradictions. More academics have come to agree in recent years that there is a favorable correlation between equity concentration and business performance. According to the supervision theory, increased equity concentration can enhance the oversight and restrictions imposed by major shareholders on executives, thereby averting financial risks arising from executive actions detrimental to shareholder wealth. This encourages executives to work towards improving corporate performance and minimizing agency costs. Conversely, when equity concentration is low, scattered ownership may lead to reduced management supervision enthusiasm by small and medium-sized shareholders, which in turn results in "free-riding" and adversely affects the enhancement of corporate performance. Thus, the following hypothesis is put forth:

Hypothesis 2: The equity concentration of a company is positively correlated with corporate performance.

3 Methodology

3.1 Data Selection

This essay uses empirical research based on the data of all A-share listed companies in China from 2018 to 2022. The data is sourced from the CSMAR database, and Excel 2010 is used for data collection and preprocessing. During the empirical analysis phase, Stata 17.0 is utilized for data experimentation. For the sample data, the following measures are followed to ensure the validity and precision of the data: (1) exclusion of financial stocks such as brokerages, banks, and insurance companies; (2) exclusion of ST and ST* type loss-making companies; (3) exclusion of samples with missing data. The data is ultimately subjected to a 1% winsorization in order to guarantee the consistency and accuracy of the data and to reduce the influence of outliers. After the screening process, a total of 7,578 sample data points are collected.

3.2 Variable Definition

Dependent Variable (Corporate Performance). Previous foreign studies often used Tobin's Q, which reflects market performance, as an indicator of corporate performance, while domestic research often used indicators such as ROA and ROE to measure corporate performance. Because the Chinese securities market is still in its early stages of development, this study uses ROE to indicate the level of corporate performance.

Independent Variable (Executive Compensation and Equity Concentration). Executive compensation is the independent variable in Hypothesis 1. This study assesses the overall compensation level of the company's executive team by employing the total salary of the top three executives of listed businesses, and uses the natural logarithm of the total salary of the top three executives of listed businesses to lessen the negative effects of heteroskedasticity and skewness on the coefficient estimate in the regression model. Equity concentration serves as the independent variable in Hypothesis 2. This study analyzes the percentage of shares held by the largest shareholder as a proxy for equity concentration, in line with most previous research.

Control Variable. The size, financial leverage, operating capability, and growth capability of a company can also impact corporate performance. Therefore, this paper selects the above items as control variables. Following most mainstream studies, this paper uses total assets as an indicator to measure company size, the debt-to-asset ratio for financial leverage, total asset turnover for operating capability, and total asset growth rate for growth capability. Table 1 displays the definitions of the variables.

Table 1. Variable definition.

Type of Variable	Symbol	Construction
Explained variable	ROE	Dividing net income by shareholders' equity
	ROA	Dividing net income by total assets
Explanatory Variable	SALARY	The natural logarithm of the sum of the top three executive salary
	CR1	Shareholding ratio of the largest shareholder
Control Variable	LEV	Dividing total liabilities by total assets
	SIZE	The natural logarithm of total assets
	TAT	Dividing net sales by total assets
	TAG	(Ending Total Assets - Beginning total assets)/Beginning total assets

3.3 Modelling

To test the hypotheses regarding the impact of executive compensation and equity concentration on corporate performance, this study establishes two regression models. Model 1 considers the effect of executive compensation on firm performance, while Model 2 considers the effect of equity concentration on firm performance.

$$ROE = \alpha + \beta_1 SALARY + \beta_2 LEV + \beta_3 SIZE + \beta_4 TAT + \beta_5 TAG + \varepsilon \quad (1)$$

$$ROE = \alpha + \beta_1 CR1 + \beta_2 LEV + \beta_3 SIZE + \beta_4 TAT + \beta_5 TAG + \varepsilon \quad (2)$$

In the above models, α is a constant, β_1, β_2, β_3, β_4, and β_5 are the regression coefficients of the equation, and ε is the residual of the model.

4 Empirical Results

4.1 Descriptive Statistics

As shown in Table 2, the study contains 7,578 valid data points for each indicator. The mean of ROE is 0.04, indicating that the overall operating capability of listed companies is satisfactory. However, the ROE of well-performing companies reaches 0.342, while poorly performing companies suffer losses with a minimum of -1.491. The standard deviation of ROE is 0.233, indicating significant differences in financial performance among listed companies.

The top three executives of publicly traded businesses receive an average total compensation of 14.67 after taking the logarithm, with a range of 12.91 to 16.71 and a standard error of 0.714. The actual difference would be much larger since the data is processed logarithmically in this paper. According to the analysis of the percentage of shares held by the largest shareholder of each listed company, it shows that both a high level of overall equity concentration among Chinese listed companies and a wide range of individual differences.

According to the analysis of the natural logarithm of total assets, it shows that significant asset disparities among listed businesses. The average debt-to-asset ratio for publicly traded corporations is 0.414, with the range being 0.069 to 0.894 and a standard deviation of 0.189. This implies that listed corporations generally have high levels of financial leverage and fluctuating degrees of financial risk. The mean total asset turnover for listed businesses is 0.613, with a range of 0.083 to 2.361 and a standard error of 0.380, showing generally good asset management with high asset utilization but significant individual variation. The total asset growth rates which has an average of 0.182 also and standard error of 0.315 also differ significantly among listed companies, with the worst-performing company having a negative total asset growth rate of -0.392 and the best-performing company having a positive total asset growth rate of 1.746.

Table 2. Descriptive statistics.

Variable	N	Mean	p50	SD	Min	Max
ROE	7578	0.0400	0.0790	0.233	−1.491	0.342
ROA	7578	0.0350	0.0440	0.0910	−0.441	0.220
SALARY	7578	14.67	14.65	0.714	12.91	16.71
CR1	7578	0.306	0.291	0.133	0.0810	0.671
SIZE	7578	22.34	22.25	1.101	20.18	25.68
LEV	7578	0.414	0.411	0.189	0.0690	0.894
TAT	7578	0.613	0.534	0.380	0.0830	2.361
TAG	7578	0.182	0.111	0.315	−0.392	1.746

In order to initially assess the viability of the hypotheses, this study first performs an analysis of correlation of the sample data. As shown in Table 3, the correlation coefficient between executive compensation and company performance, which determined by ROE and the logarithm of the total compensation of the top three executives, respectively, is 0.152 with a P value less than 0.01. The correlation coefficient is significant at the 1% level, indicating that executive performance and firm performance are probably positively correlated, which provides preliminary support for Hypothesis 1. Also displayed in Table 3 is the correlation coefficient between equity concentration and company performance, which is 0.158 with a P value less than 0.01. This correlation uses the shareholding ratio of the largest shareholder as the measure of equity concentration. This suggests that the correlation coefficient is significant at the 1% level and that equity concentration and firm performance are probably positively correlated, offering preliminary support for Hypothesis 2.

Table 3. Correlation matrix.

Var.	ROE	ROA	SALARY	CR1	SIZE	LEV	TAT	TAG
ROE	1.00							
ROA	0.89***	1.00						
SALARY	0.15***	0.16***	1.00					
CR1	0.16***	0.19***	0.01	1.00				
SIZE	0.08***	0.03**	0.44***	0.02*	1.00			
LEV	−0.28***	−0.33***	0.11***	−0.00	0.49***	1.00		
TAT	0.12***	0.13***	0.12***	0.10***	0.04***	0.12***	1.00	
TAG	0.34***	0.38***	0.05***	0.08***	−0.02*	−0.07***	0.01	1.00

Note: *** $p<0.01$, ** $p<0.05$, * $p<0.1$.

4.2 Multicollinearity Test

According to Table 3's correlation test, all of the explanatory variables' correlation coefficient values are less than 0.5, with the majority being less than 0.3. Therefore, the explanatory factors in this study do not appear to be multicollinear. The outcomes of a more thorough investigation of the variables' collinearity are displayed in Table 4. The VIF of each variable in the two models is less than 10, indicating that the two models constructed in this essay do not exhibit multicollinearity.

4.3 Multiple Regression Analysis

Table 5 displays the regression results. According to results (1), there is a 1% level significant positive correlation between executive compensation and company performance. Corporate owners link executive compensation levels with corporate performance, encouraging managers to work harder. This result further verifies the validity of Hypothesis 1. According to results (2), equity concentration and corporate performance also have a positive correlation at 1% significance level. Higher equity concentration

Table 4. Multicollinearity results.

Variable	VIF	1/VIF
SIZE	1.640	0.610
LEV	1.360	0.734
SALARY	1.280	0.778
TAT	1.040	0.958
CR1	1.020	0.983
TAG	1.020	0.985

makes major shareholders more willing to supervise managers, effectively reducing managers' opportunistic and self-interested behavior, and ultimately improving corporate performance. This result further verifies the validity of Hypothesis 2.

Table 5. Multiple regression results.

Variables	(1) ROE	(2) ROE
Constant	−1.276***	−1.182***
	(0.058)	(0.051)
SALARY	0.0181***	
	(0.004)	
CR1		0.198***
		(0.017)
LEV	−0.485***	−0.492***
	(0.014)	(0.014)
SIZE	0.0516***	0.0568***
	(0.003)	(0.002)
TAT	0.0903***	0.0872***
	(0.006)	(0.006)
TAG	0.234***	0.229***
	(0.007)	(0.007)
Observations	7578	7578
F-statistic	536.8***	565.1***
R-squared	0.262	0.272

Note: Standard errors in parentheses; *** $p<0.01$, ** $p<0.05$, * $p<0.1$.

4.4 Robustness Test

In this article, the explained variables in the test model are swapped out to reduce the impact of variable selection bias on the regression analysis and to confirm the validity of the empirical results: using ROA as the measure of corporate performance. The robust test results in Table 6 show that the regression results using ROA as the explained variable are consistent with the results of using ROE. The original hypotheses still hold, further verifying the reliability of the study's results.

Table 6. Robustness results.

Variables	(1) ROA	(2) ROA
Constant	−0.457***	−0.395***
	(0.022)	(0.019)
SALARY	0.0111***	
	(0.001)	
CR1		0.0974***
		(0.007)
LEV	−0.210***	−0.214***
	(0.005)	(0.005)
SIZE	0.0168***	0.0200***
	(0.001)	(0.001)
TAT	0.0396***	0.0385***
	(0.002)	(0.002)
TAG	0.100***	0.0985***
	(0.003)	(0.003)
Observations	7578	7578
F-statistic	706.1***	752.2***
R-squared	0.318	0.332

Note: Standard errors in parentheses; *** $p<0.01$, ** $p<0.05$, * $p<0.1$.

5 Conclusion

This essay looks into the information for Chinese A-share listed firms from 2018 to 2022. The first part of this study looks at the connection between executive pay and business success in publicly traded corporations. According to the research, there is a considerable incentive impact between the two, which suggests that the executive remuneration scheme used by listed businesses in China can help to improve corporate performance. Second, this study examines the relationship between listed companies' equity concentration and firm performance and finds that equity concentration has a favorable effect. It is primarily because major shareholders can use their higher shareholding ratios to exert stronger supervision and control over executive behavior, thereby improving corporate management efficiency and ultimately enhancing corporate performance.

This study presents the following suggestions for the management and operation of listed firms in China based on the aforementioned research findings: First, companies can use executive salary incentives to motivate leaders to contribute more to the development of the business. Second, corporations can gradually raise equity concentration so that large shareholders can monitor executive behavior and help the company operate better. Additionally, they should control the shareholding ratio of major shareholders to avoid the occurrence of major shareholders "hollowing out" the company or impeding the proper management decisions of executives.

References

1. Fama, E.F., Jensen, M.C.: Separation of ownership and control. J. Law Econ. **26**(2), 301–325 (1983)
2. Jensen, M.C., Murphy, K.J.: Performance pay and top-management incentives. J. Polit. Econ. **98**(2), 225–264 (1990)
3. Conyon, M.J., Schwalbach, J.: Executive compensation: evidence from the UK and Germany. Long Range Plan. **33**(4), 504–526 (2000)
4. Gabaix, X., Landier, A.: Why has CEO pay increased so much? Quart. J. Econ. **123**(1), 49–100 (2008)
5. Zhang, W.: An empirical analysis of the relationship between executive compensation and corporate performance. Econ. Res. **4**, 62–69 (2001)
6. Wang, H.: An empirical study of the relationship between executive compensation and corporate performance in China's listed companies. Account. Res. **11**, 40–45 (2002)
7. Chen, G., Zhao, D.: An empirical study of the relationship between executive compensation incentives and corporate performance: evidence from A-share listed companies in Shanghai and Shenzhen. J. Finance and Econ. **9**, 57–64 (2015)
8. Li, M., Zhang, Q.: An empirical study of the relationship between executive compensation and corporate performance: evidence from A-share listed companies in Shanghai and Shenzhen. Friends Account. **3**, 55–58 (2017)
9. Shleifer, A., Vishny, R.W.: A survey of corporate governance. J. Finance **52**(2), 737–783 (1997)
10. Cho, Myeong-Hyeon.: Ownership structure, investment, and the corporate value: an empirical analysis. J. Financ. Econ. **47**(1), 103–121 (1998)

Exploring the Interplay Between Inflation, Energy Prices, and COVID-19 Amidst the Ukraine Conflict

Zeyao Li[✉]

Richard A. Chaifetz School of Business, Saint Louis University, Saint Louis City, MO 63103-2097, USA

1811000614@mail.sit.edu.cn

Abstract. The main purpose of this paper is to study the economic problems and difficulties of the three major economies (China, the European Union, and the United States) in the context of the Russia-Ukraine conflict in the post-epidemic era. The purpose is to analyze economic indicators such as GDP, CPI, unemployment rate, inflation rate, and exchange rate of these three economies in different periods, with auxiliary analysis based on the gold price, commodity index, and oil and gas price of the global market. It tries to study the specific economic difficulties faced by the three major economies and their countermeasures, and according to the response of the above data after the implementation of the policies, to judge the effect of the implementation of various policies in each economy and try to analyze the possible potential risks and try to propose whether there is a better solution. According to the analysis of this paper, the conflict between Russia and Ukraine has a certain impact on the three major economies, especially the European Union. All three economies were hit in the short term by sharp rises in raw materials and energy prices. However, the three major economies shave adopted timely policies to stabilize the economic downturn indirectly caused by the conflict between Russia and Ukraine. The United States and China have also ensured price stability to a certain extent. However, the EU needs to further deal with inflation due to the energy structure and other reasons.

Keywords: Economic Indicators · Global Capital Market · COVID-19 Pandemic

1 Introduction

The Russia-Ukraine conflict broke out on February 24, 2022. The conflict has had a huge impact not only on the economic conditions of Russia and Ukraine but also on the economies of China, the United States, the European Union, and the world. The first is energy prices. Russia is the world's third-largest oil producer and the largest oil exporter. Russia exports 5 million barrels of crude oil a day, accounting for 12% of the world's crude trade. Russia produces 28,500 barrels of gasoline and accounts for 15% of the world's trade in refined products. Russia exports 60% of its oil to Europe and 10% to China. According to the official website shows that the conflict broke out on February

24, and the WT crude oil price index soared from $91.59/BBL on February 25, before retreating from a high of $123.7/BBL on March 8. It dropped to $95.04 per barrel on March 16 and recovered to $111.76 on March 22 [1].

These figures alone show that Russia, as one of the world's largest energy exporters, has the capacity to make huge swings in world energy prices. Not only that, but Russia is also a major producer and exporter of key strategic minerals such as titanium, palladium, neon, nickel, platinum, and aluminum. Russia is the world's leading producer of nickel, copper, and iron, and it controls 10% of global copper reserves. Since February 27th the prices of coal and nickel have soared, and palladium, steel, aluminum, and iron have also, to varying degrees, risen markedly [2]. Meanwhile, Russia and Ukraine together account for more than a third of global grain exports. Planting season has arrived in Ukraine and the conflict between Russia and Ukraine means food shortages will have lasting effects. Therefore, in general, in the current background of economic globalization, the rising prices of raw materials and energy will increase the cost of global enterprises on a large scale, which will have a huge impact on the world economy [3].

This paper first hopes to analyze the recent fluctuations of oil prices, natural gas prices, CRB Index, Commodity Research Bureau Index, and gold prices worldwide. The reasons for choosing these factors as our analysis objects are as follows: First, as mentioned above, Russia is an important exporter in the world no matter in precious metal raw materials or energy represented by oil and natural gas. This Russia-Ukraine conflict is highly likely to have a huge impact on the prices of the three factors mentioned above. Second, whether it is energy represented by oil and gas, or commodity prices represented by Reuters CRB, if these three indicators have a huge fluctuation, it will have a huge impact on the economies of our three target economies (the United States, the European Union, China) and the economies and countries around the world. Thirdly, the reason why the price of gold should be taken into account is that a large increase in the three indexes selected this time is likely to lead to Pentium inflation, that is, the annual inflation rate is more than 10% and less than 100%. Because gold can resist hyperinflation, from the simple market supply and demand relationship, if individual or national investors find that surging inflation is possible or has already happened, they may buy a large amount of gold to resist the surging inflation. Assuming that the supply of gold is unlikely to increase dramatically in a short time, the price of gold will rise to a certain extent.

2 Energy Prices

First, this paper firstly observes the fluctuation of energy prices represented by crude oil prices and natural gas prices. It can be seen that both crude oil prices (see Fig. 1) and natural gas prices (see Fig. 2) rose sharply in the early stage of the conflict between Russia and Ukraine. In particular, the price of natural gas soared all the way. But there have also been very significant increases, but then prices have all fallen back to near pre-conflict levels, so you can assume that the policies adopted by the world's major economies have had some effect in bringing energy prices back down.

As for the Reuters CRB index, it is extremely timely because it covers commodities of the nature of raw materials and because its prices are derived from the futures market. Therefore, the index has a special role in reflecting the general dynamics of world

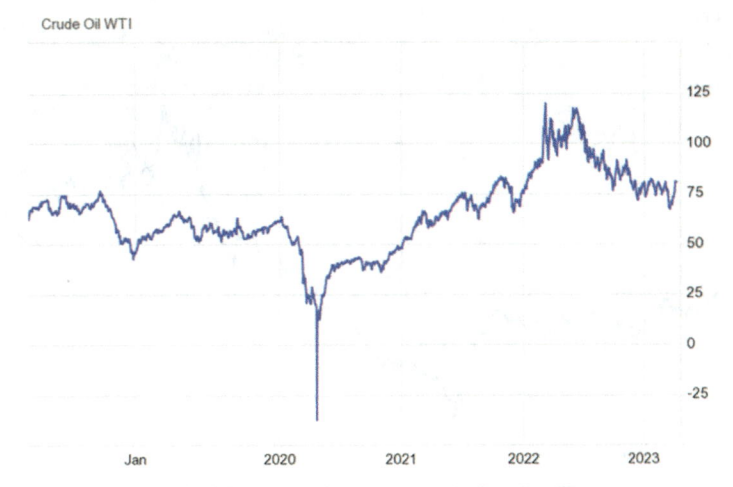

Fig. 1. Crude oil prices from 2020 to 2023 [4].

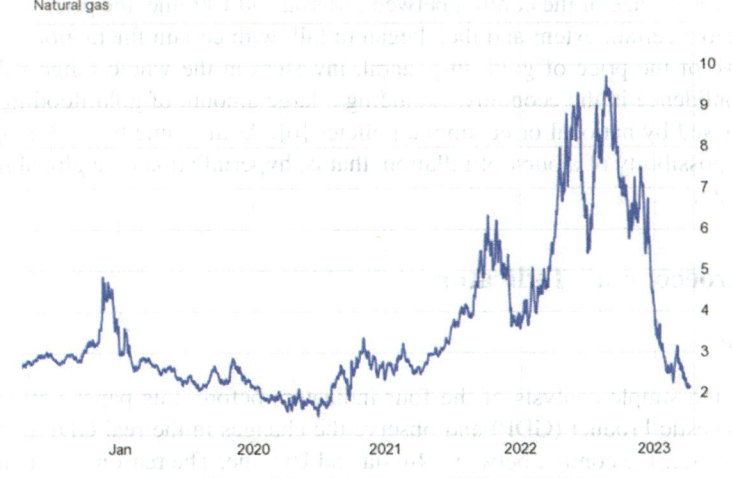

Fig. 2. Natural Gas Prices from 2020 to 2023 [4].

commodity prices. It can not only better reflect the changes of the producer price index (PPI) and consumer price index (CPI) but is even more advanced and sensitive than the indicator function of CPI and PPI, so it can be regarded as an indicator of inflation. Studies show that the CRB index is a better indicator to reflect inflation, it fluctuates in the same direction as the inflation index, and at the same time, it fluctuates in the same direction as the bond yield. To some extent, it reflects the trend of economic development. As can be seen from Fig. 3, the CRB index is almost consistent with the price fluctuations of crude oil and natural gas, which also skyrocketed at the beginning of the conflict between Russia and Ukraine and then slowly dropped [5].

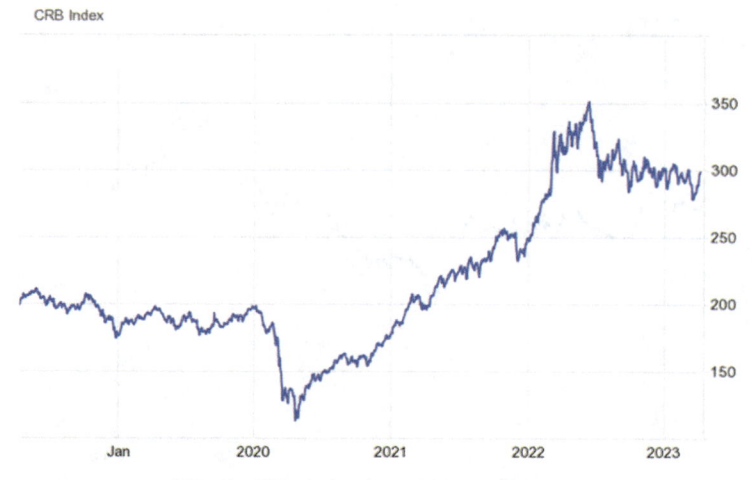

Fig. 3. CRB index from 2020 to 2023 [4].

In the early stage of the conflict between Russia and Ukraine, the price of gold also increased to a certain extent and then began to fall, with certain fluctuations. From the perspective of the price of gold, in general, investors in the whole range still have a certain confidence in the economy, excluding a large amount of gold flooding into the market caused by national or economic policies [6]. At the same time, it is optimistic about the possibility of a burst of inflation, that is, hyperinflation on a global scale will last too long.

3 Macroeconomic Indicators

3.1 GDP

Based on the simple analysis of the four indicators before, this paper will start with Gross Domestic Product (GDP) and observe the changes in the real GDP of the three economies after the conflict between Russia and Ukraine. The reason why real GDP is chosen is that This paper hopes to analyze the inflation factor separately, and the real GDP of inflation can better reflect the real economic state of an economy. First, in Fig. 4, this is the real GDP of the United States from October 1, 2017, to October 1, 2022. The sharp drop in REAL GDP at the beginning of 2020 was largely due to the outbreak of COVID-19. After a series of policies implemented by the US government, real GDP began to turn around. As can be seen from Fig. 4, the growth rate of real GDP began to slow down from the fourth quarter of 2021, although the overall trend was still rising. But the scale is slowing.

China's real GDP has shown a great fluctuation in the past five years (2017.10.01–2022.10.01). In my opinion, the fluctuation of the international economy, the impact of the epidemic, and the government's intervention are the main reasons for such drastic fluctuations. As can be seen from Fig. 5, China's real GDP experienced a sharp decline at the beginning of 2022, mainly due to the impact of the epidemic, the bursting of the real

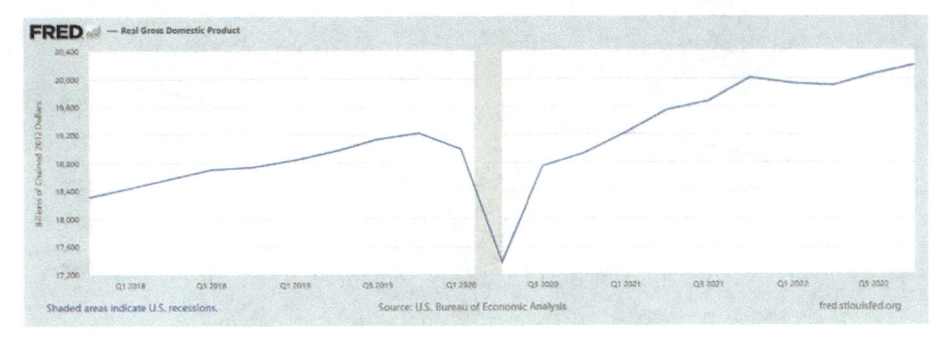

Fig. 4. Real GDP of US from 2018 to 2022 [7].

estate bubble, and the Russia-Ukraine conflict. Three kinds of negative factors occurred at the same time, which greatly destroyed the confidence of investors from all walks of life and caused many entrepreneurs and investors to take a negative and pessimistic view of the future [3].

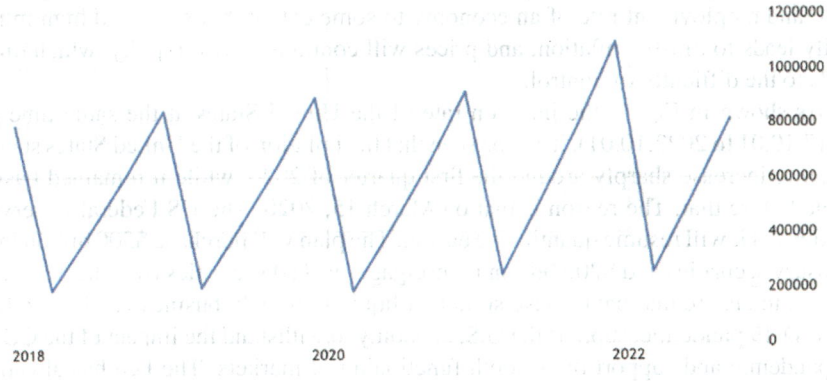

Fig. 5. Real GDP of China from 2018 to 2022 [4].

In this paper, the real GDP of Europe is selected in the same period, as shown in Fig. 6. In my opinion, Europe's real GDP can maintain such a real GDP growth despite such a huge change in energy sources, which shows that the measures taken by EU countries are very timely and effective under the condition that the data are correct. However, it is necessary to make a judgment and analysis by observing the inflation situation at the same time.

3.2 Inflation

In terms of the selection of the inflation rate, this paper chooses inflation instead of core inflation. As mentioned above, core inflation is the inflation rate excluding the price fluctuations of energy and food. However, in the conflict between Russia and Ukraine, the biggest cause of impact on the global economy includes the sharp price fluctuations of

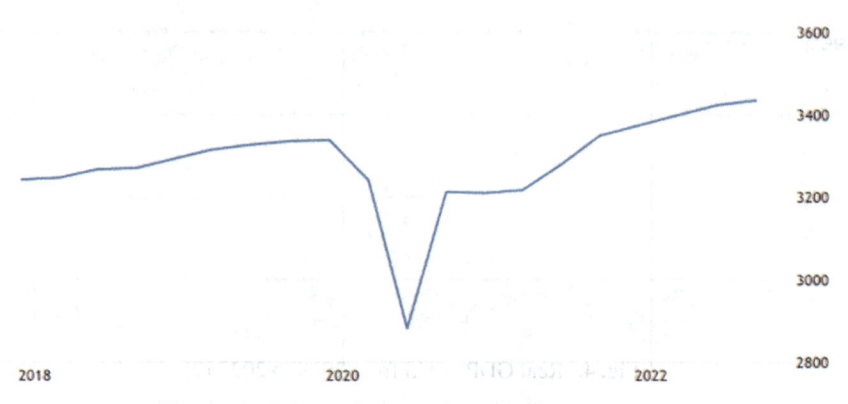

Fig. 6. Real GDP of Europe from 2018 to 2022 [4].

food and energy. Therefore, Personally, it is a more sensible choice to choose the inflation rate as the reference and research object. In addition, this paper needs to emphasize that the inflation rate is a concept of time periods rather than time points, so sustained high inflation is very fatal to a country. As is known to all, moderate inflation is helpful to the GDP and employment rate of an economy to some extent, but sustained high inflation easily leads to drastic inflation, and prices will continue to rise rapidly, which directly leads to the difficulty of control.

As shown in Fig. 7, the inflation rate of the United States at the same time point (2017.10.01 to 2022.10.01), it can be seen that the inflation of the United States suddenly began to increase sharply around the first quarter of 2020, while it remained basically stable before that. The reason is that on March 15, 2020, The US Federal Reserve has announced it will resume quantitative easing. The plan will purchase $500 billion in U.S. Treasury securities and $200 billion in mortgage-backed securities over the next several months to ensure that banks have sufficient liquidity to help businesses affected by the COVID-19 pandemic, support the U.S. economy to withstand the impact of the COVID-19 pandemic and support the smooth functioning of markets. The Fed has already cut rates twice, taking its target range for the federal funds rate to between 0% and 0.25% [8]. This massive stimulus led to a sharp increase in inflation. Similarly, we can say that in the first quarter of 2022, there was a substantial increase in U.S. inflation and then a decline. From here alone, the inflation rate in the United States is still affected by the Russia-Ukraine conflict, but not to an unacceptable and manageable extent, which can be controlled through appropriate and correct fiscal or monetary policy.

Based on the special status of the US dollar, this paper makes a separate analysis here, because the US dollar is the world currency and many countries' currencies are indexed against the US dollar. For example, Hong Kong introduced a currency board system on October 17, 1983. Under this system, when issuing and redeeming certificates of indebtedness to support bank notes, the issuing banks must deal in US dollars at a fixed rate of HK $7.80 to US $1. This means that Hong Kong's central bank does not have the right to issue Hong Kong dollars separately, but rather to link them directly to the dollar in its foreign exchange reserves. So, if there is inflation in the United States, on the one hand, it can be interpreted as rising prices in the United States, but on the other hand,

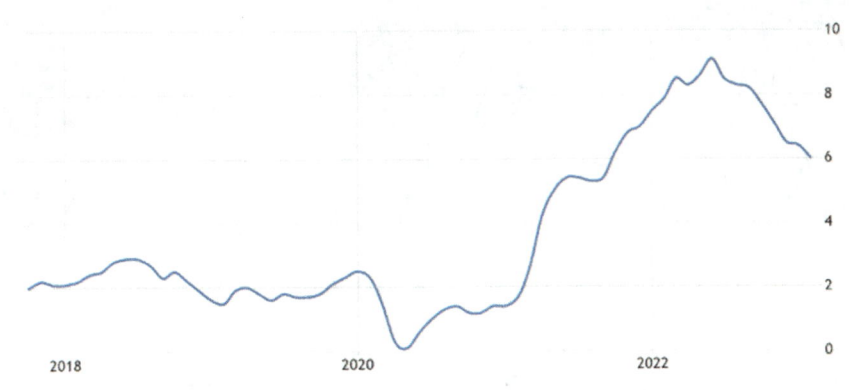

Fig. 7. Inflation rate of the US from 2018 to 2022 [4].

it can be interpreted as the depreciation of the dollar. But many countries around the world have currencies that are directly linked to the dollar or hold many dollar reserves. According to this paper, from a certain point of view, if the dollar depreciates, massive inflation occurs in the United States, which also means that the currencies of a large part of the countries in the world have depreciated. In a sense, it can be understood that many countries share a part of the inflation for the United States. On this basis, America still has such a high inflation rate compared with the past, indicating that the after-effects of quantitative easing are indeed serious. The author believes that there are two aspects to explain the change in inflation in the United States. First, a large amount of money flows into the market, leading to an increase in the supply of money, which leads to the devaluation of the currency. Second, many hard dollars have damaged the interests of individual investors holding dollars as well as the country or economy, so individual or national investors have lower confidence in the dollar, leading to the depreciation of the dollar.

The inflation rate in China is shown in Fig. 8. It can be seen that at the beginning of 2022, the inflation rate has risen significantly. It can be concluded that this is due to the rising prices of raw materials, energy, and food caused by the conflict between Russia and Ukraine, which leads to the sustained high inflation rate. Previous drops in inflation can be attributed to the effects of the economic downturn caused by the pandemic. After analysis and verification, this paper believes that the possible reasons are as follows: although China, as the world's second-largest economy, is far less dependent on Russia's energy, food, and raw materials than the EU, the Russia-Ukraine conflict still has a certain impact on the world's energy and raw materials price market. As a famous "world processing plant". China is still heavily dependent on imported energy and raw materials, although it has been trying to increase investment in new technologies and shift some energy-intensive industries abroad. So, some impact is inevitable, but because of China's abundant sources of energy and raw material imports and its small dependence on Russian energy, the impact on inflation is arguably limited and manageable for now.

The following paper will focus on inflation in Europe because it has been mentioned above that the main source of energy supply (including oil and natural gas) in Europe is Russia [9]. From the perspective of economics, the increase in energy price will directly

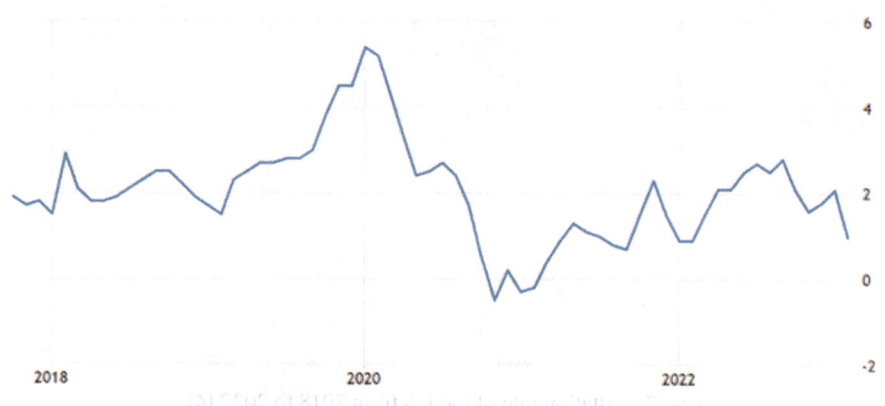

Fig. 8. Inflation rate of China from 2018 to 2022 [4].

lead to a sharp increase in the cost of enterprises in an economy or a country, resulting in the left shift of the supply curve. In this case, there is a certain probability that prices will rise and the economy will fall, which is commonly known as stagflation. There are two basic explanations for stagflation in contemporary economic theories: one is based on the consequences of surging aggregate demand, and the other is based on the constraints of aggregate supply caused by the scarcity of certain resources [10]. Generally, economists believe that macroeconomic regulation has a more direct and easier effect on the AD curve. According to the discretionary theory proposed by the Keynesian school, discretionary means that the fiscal authorities adjust fiscal expenditure according to the state of economic operators to achieve the goal of economic and price stability. However, in the view of the traditional Keynesian school, the adjustment of prices is very limited in the period of less than full employment, which means that, in a period of insufficient employment, the fiscal authorities have a single goal of controlling fiscal revenue and expenditure, that is, stabilizing output. Simply put, when the economy overheats, it uses tight fiscal and monetary policies to restrain the economy, shifting the AD curve to the left and causing prices to fall. When the economy is depressed, expansionary monetary policy and expansionary fiscal policy should be adopted to restore it to the optimal equilibrium state and make the unemployment rate reach the natural rate of unemployment [9]. However, the emergence of stagflation can be said to have once made the Keynesian school down from the altar. Therefore, economists believe that if the AS curve shifts to the left, it will easily lead to high inflation accompanied by an economic recession, and at this time, fiscal and monetary policies are difficult to have good effects or bad consequences. For example, in the case of skyrocketing prices of raw materials and energy, the cost of enterprises has skyrocketed. If the government adopts tight monetary and fiscal policies at this time due to extremely high inflation, the AD curve is forced to shift to the left. However, if the AD-As curve reaches a new equilibrium again, the already fragile economy will be further weakened. If we leave it alone according to the theory of the classical school, theoretically the AS curve will automatically return to the original position over time, and the market will reach the original equilibrium state again. However, this time is too long, and it is only a theoretical possibility. Personally, it is not a wise decision [11]. The last resort is for the government to use expansionary fiscal policy and expansionary monetary policy to force the AD curve to the right, allowing the economy to recover, but the consequences are obvious, further increasing inflation in the country or economy [12]. Therefore, although it is found in the previous part of this paper that the GDP growth of the EU can be said to be quite good, the effect of its policies obviously needs to be judged considering its inflation situation. As shown in Fig. 9, the inflation of the EU can be said to have risen all the way since 2021 due to the impact of the epidemic and the Russia-Ukraine conflict, which is almost impossible to control. Given its GDP, there is a high probability that the EU has adopted a massively expansionary economic policy.

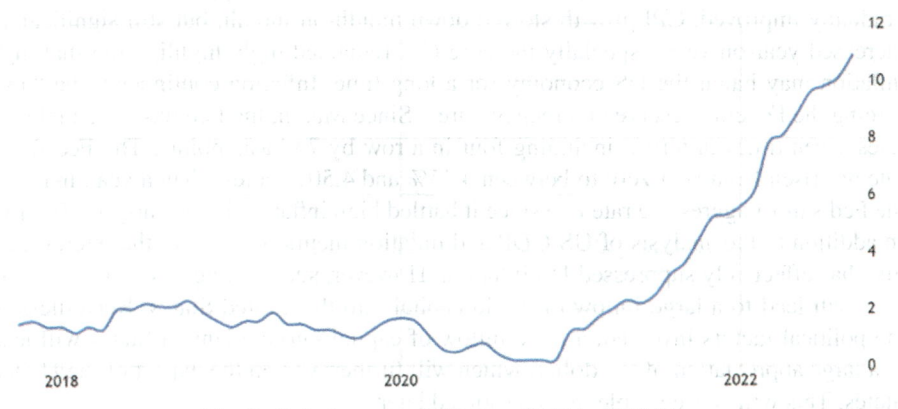

Fig. 9. Inflation rate of EU from 2018 to 2022 [4].

This article now wishes to explore the various policies adopted by various economies after the outbreak of the Russia-Ukraine conflict in 2022, as well as their objectives and effects. First, look at the policies adopted by China. Relevant government departments said that special debt is an important policy of China's fiscal policy this year. In fact, the Chinese government introduced a similar policy in 2008. In September 2008, after the full outbreak of the international financial crisis, China's economic growth slowed down rapidly, with negative export growth and many migrant workers returning to their hometowns, putting the economy at risk of a hard landing. In response to this crisis, the Chinese government introduced ten measures in November 2008 to further expand domestic demand and promote steady and fast economic growth. According to preliminary calculations, the implementation of these ten measures will require an investment of about RMB 4 trillion by the end of 2010. By expanding government spending, to ensure economic growth. The result has been soaring prices. But the Chinese government has learned its lesson from the last one, and this time the stimulus has been significantly toned down [13]. On April 15, 2022, the People's Bank of China announced a cut in the reserve requirement ratio for financial institutions, which will release about 530 billion yuan of long-term funds [14]. The point of this move is to increase investment by lowering interest rates and releasing liquidity into the market through expansionary monetary policy. It is obvious that this measure has reduced the cost of some enterprises. For some enterprises, the high cost caused by the conflict between Russia and Ukraine has been mitigated by the reduction of taxes and fees. This measure is undoubtedly very helpful.

Combined with the previous analysis of China's GDP and inflation in this paper, under the assumption that there are no major errors in relevant data, the policies of the Chinese government are undoubtedly very effective. Despite the economic impact caused by the conflict between Russia and Ukraine, some advantages of its own economic structure and energy structure, as well as appropriate policies, It's got a good handle on what's going on in the economy and what's going on in inflation.

In the US, "inflation" is the most important keyword for the US economy in 2022. Consumer prices in the US soared in the first half of this year, pushing up prices across the board for staples from petrol to meat, eggs, and milk. In the second half of the year, as the Federal Reserve continued to raise interest rates and supply chain bottlenecks gradually improved, CPI growth slowed down month-on-month, but still significantly increased year-on-year, especially the core CPI remained high, highlighting that high inflation may haunt the US economy for a long time. Inflation continues to be "hot" forcing the Federal Reserve emergency "fire". Since March, the Fed has raised interest rates seven times in a row, including four in a row by 75 basis points. The Fed funds rate has risen from near zero to between 4.25% and 4.50% in less than a year, marking the Fed's most aggressive rate rise since it battled high inflation in the early 1980s [15]. In addition to the analysis of US GDP and inflation mentioned above, the interest rate hike has effectively suppressed US inflation. However, such an aggressive interest rate hike will lead to a large inflow of world capital into the United States. Regardless of the political factors involved, a large inflow of capital into the United States will lead to a large appreciation of the dollar, which will further worsen the export of the United States. This will cause problems to be solved later.

In European Union, the EU has proposed an economic stimulus package worth about 2 trillion euros. It includes the EU's Long-Term Budget for 2021–2027, worth about €1.2tn, and the Next Generation EU, worth about €800bn in the short term. This is very close to the situation analyzed above in this paper. Massive government expenditure is used to stimulate the economy and ensure its development of the economy, but the consequences are also very obvious. The extremely high inflation leads to many problems.

Here, the author wishes to mention the reason why China and the European Union, the two major economies, simultaneously put economic stimulus policies on fiscal policies and adopted monetary policies like interest rate cuts. In the author's personal opinion, since the world's largest economy, the United States is carrying out such a radical interest rate hike, if the other two economies choose to further cut interest rates to stimulate the economy at this time, that can have very serious consequences. First, the local currency will be severely depreciated. Although a moderate depreciation is beneficial to foreign trade, a substantial depreciation is not good news for China and the European Union, the two largest economies. Second, there will be a massive flight of domestic capital to the United States, which will deal a further blow to a domestic economy already suffering from soaring raw material and energy prices.

4 Conclusion

In general, the research results of this paper are as follows: firstly, the conflict between Russia and Ukraine has indeed caused a great impact on the three major economies (the United States, China, and the European Union) in a short period of time. The main reason is that the Russia-Ukraine conflict caused a short-term spike in energy prices such as oil and natural gas. Secondly, the prices of international heavy metals and raw materials also rose sharply, which directly led to an impact on the global economy. The three major economies controlled the economic impact caused by the Russia-Ukraine conflict through different policies for a certain period of time. At the same time, China and the United States through a series of policies ensure economic recovery while keeping prices relatively stable.

In general, this paper has basically achieved the research objective. However, there are still some shortcomings. First, the conflict between Russia and Ukraine is in the post-COVID-19 era. But there is no doubt that the impact of the pandemic continues. Therefore, it is difficult to say which part is caused by the epidemic and which part is caused by the Russia-Ukraine conflict, or the combination of the epidemic and the Russia-Ukraine conflict. Second, this paper focuses on the macroeconomic perspective and analysis of objective facts and data, but for some reason, political factors cannot be considered. Third, because the overall perspective of this paper is novel and the topic is sensitive, it is difficult to find much literature for reference. Therefore, there is a possibility that the research results and some actual conditions may be biased. In the future, it is hoped that it will be more appropriate to select more targeted data in the appropriate time period for stage analysis, and at the same time prove that more detailed and diversified data will be more appropriate.

References

1. Yu, Y.: The impact of the Russia-Ukraine conflict on the world economy. J. Financ. Econ. **4** (2022)
2. Ballentine, K., Nitzschke, H.: The political economy of civil war and conflict transformation. Berghof Res. Cent. Constr. Conflict Manage. **39**(3), 430–455 (2005)
3. Lewis, W.A.: Theory of Economic Growth. Routledge eBooks (2013)
4. Trading Economics. https://tradingeconomics.com/. Accessed 1 Apr 2023
5. Chevallier, J.: Carbon futures and macroeconomic risk factors: a view from the EU ETS. Energy Econ. **31**(4), 614–625 (2009)
6. Ghosh, D., Levin, E.J., Macmillan, P., Wright, R.E.: Gold as an inflation hedge? Stud. Econ. Financ. **22**(1), 1–25 (2004)
7. Federal Reserve Economic Data. https://fred.stlouisfed.org/. Accessed 1 Apr 2023
8. Inflation, interest rate hikes, recession: Analysis of high-frequency words in the US economy in 2022. Xinhua News Agency. http://www.xinhuanet.com/english/2022-12/23/c_1310683 243.htm. Accessed 1 Apr 2023
9. Knopf, B., Nahmmacher, P., Schmid, E.: The European renewable energy target for 2030–an impact assessment of the electricity sector. Energy Policy **85**, 50–60 (2015)
10. Banerjee, A., Marcellino, M., Masten, I.: Leading indicators for euro-area inflation and GDP growth. Oxford Bull. Econ. Stat. **67**, 785–813 (2005)

11. Chatziantoniou, I., Duffy, D., Filis, G.: Stock market response to monetary and fiscal policy shocks: multi-country evidence. Econ. Model. **30**, 754–769 (2013)
12. Afonso, A., Sousa, R.M.: The macroeconomic effects of fiscal policy. Appl. Econ. **44**(34), 4439–4454 (2012)
13. Mountford, A., Uhlig, H.: What are the effects of fiscal policy shocks? J. Appl. Economet. **24**(6), 960–992 (2009)
14. Notice of the National Health Commission on the Publication of the Fifth Batch of National Traditional Chinese Medicine Key Promotion Counties. National Health Commission. http://en.nhc.gov.cn/2022-05/31/c_87054.htm. Accessed 1 Apr 2023
15. Bernanke, B.S., Reinhart, V.R.: Conducting monetary policy at very low short-term interest rates. Am. Econ. Rev. **94**(2), 85–90 (2004)

An Empirical Analysis of Asset Pricing Models

Ziqi Chen[1], Zhenwu Sun[2(✉)], and Xiaoyu Wang[3]

[1] College of Business, University College Dublin, Dublin D04 V1W8, Ireland
[2] School of Economics and Management, East China Jiaotong University, Nanchang 330013, China
2020041002000224@ecjtu.edu.cn
[3] Faculty of Economics and Finance, University of Melbourne, Melbourne 3010, USA

Abstract. This paper presents a comparative analysis of three asset pricing models, namely, the Capital Asset Pricing Model (CAPM), the Fama-French Three Factor Model (FF3), and the Fama-French Five Factor Model (FF5), using six market portfolios generated from NYSE, AMEX, and NASDAQ stocks. The research aims to investigate which model has the best performance in terms of goodness of fit using ANOVA testing. Contrary to the traditional assumption that FF5 outperforms the other two, the study reveals that FF3 has the best performance in terms of the smallest RRS in ANOVA testing. The paper also discusses the effect of adding more regressors to CAPM and transitioning to FF5. The results confirm that FF models have general improvements from CAPM in accuracy and completeness, but there is a trivial increase in performance by adding the additional investment factor and profitability factor to FF3. The success of various asset pricing models is better understood due to this research, which can help with investing choices and portfolio management tactics. The findings have implications for practitioners and policymakers in the financial industry.

Keywords: Empirical Asset Pricing Models · the US Stock Market · Explanatory Power

1 Introduction

The empirical asset pricing models are statistical techniques used by financial econometrists to observe and explain the performance of the underlying financial assets. Due to a continuous change in asset prices reflected by the expectation of various investors, asset pricing models are necessary and critical to be introduced to understand how asset prices behave in the market and to assess the performance of different investment strategies. This report will especially focus on exploring and assessing the performance of one six factors model and the established asset pricing models including three asset pricing models CAPM, FF3, and FF5 on six different portfolios generated from NYSE, AMEX, and NASDAQ stocks [1–4].

Z. Chen, Z. Sun and X. Wang—These authors contributed equally.

© The Author(s), under exclusive license to Springer Nature Singapore Pte Ltd. 2024
X. Li et al. (Eds.): ICEMGD 2023, AEPS, pp. 998–1007, 2024.
https://doi.org/10.1007/978-981-97-0523-8_93

The CAPM, created by Sharpe and Lintner, is the earliest asset pricing model. It makes the assumption that the market is efficient and utilizes beta to measure the systematic risk of the underlying asset. Beta is obtained by regressing a managed portfolio against a benchmark portfolio. Then, using a function of beta along with market risk and premium, the projected return on the asset is determined. As the model was highly used as a substrate by a wide range of scholars, a number of extension forms were introduced soon later. In order to further explain the unusual variations in data and adjust for the imperfect asymmetric market which cannot be interpreted by the beta value, the D-CAPM was first introduced by Hogan and Warren [5]. Paster and Stambaugh proposed the A-CAPM which considers market liquidity risk [6]. Besides, Hansen and Richard developed the C-CAPM to adjust for the unexpected changes in market conditions and inhomogeneous expectations of investors [7]. Moreover, the I-CAPM was proposed by Merton, which includes a function of estimating the long-term effect of variations in macroeconomics [8]. Furthermore, Co-CAPM was introduced by Lucas and Breeden, which focuses on predicting the expected return of risky assets affected by its own sensitivity to consumers' wealth and consumption [9, 10].

Criticism of the standard CAPM of its accuracy and efficacy in testing with only one coefficient has been aroused since the 1980s [11]. According to Reilly and Brown, empirical evidence has indicated that the CAPM model performs poorly due to the model's linear relationship and questionable beta stability [12]. Fama and French tested the beta performance of CAPM on empirical grounds using Fama-Macbeth cross-sectional regression method. They found beta cannot be able to explain the abnormalities caused by the value effect and size effect on the US stock market [3]. Firm size and book-to-market ratio, which are important determinants of risk and return in the stock market, have a substantial correlation with a company's systematic profitability and growth, according to Fama and French. By introducing the size factor and value factor to the conventional CAPM, Fama and French created a three-factor model.

The three-factor model was still biased by omitted variables, though. In further research, Fama and French uncovered proof that profitability and investment are essential in understanding a company's book-to-market ratio [4]. Therefore, they updated the model and introduced a five-factor model which contains elements of the market, size effect, value effect, profitability and investment [4]. After the model was released, it was tested on various empirical grounds and showed great performance superior to both CAPM and FF3. In more recent empirical studies, Cochrane claimed that the procedure of asset pricing is not necessarily to be a linear multifactor model, and he introduced the SDF method which performs closely precise estimation on risk premia and pricing error testing [13]. However, little evidence has shown that recent studies examined the omitted variable biased of FF5.

The remainder of the essay is structured as follows. The methodology is introduced in Sect. 2. Empirical findings are described in Sect. 3. The conclusion is presented in Sect. 4.

2 Methodology

2.1 Data Selection

The study's sample includes returns for all NYSE, AMEX, and NASDAQ equities from 1963 to 2019, gathered monthly using returns from the first trading day of each month. The portfolios are created at the end of each June by intersecting three portfolios based on the book equity to market equity ratio (BE/ME), three portfolios based on market equity, and two portfolios based on size (market equity, ME). The median NYSE market equity at the end of June in year t serves as the size breakpoint for that year. BE/ME for June of year t is calculated by dividing ME for December of year t − 1 by the book equity for the fiscal year that ended in June of year t − 1. The 30th and 70th NYSE percentiles are the BE/ME breakpoints. The final data collected included a sample of 675 observations per return portfolio, for a total of 4050 observations.

2.2 Modelling

Sharp et al. first suggested CAPM and noted there really some relationship between predicted stock market returns and asset risk as the following formula derived [1].

$$E[R_i] - R_F = \beta_i E[R_M - R_F] \tag{1}$$

Later, when Fama and French analyzed the factors that lead to different returns of different stocks in US, They develop a new model as follows because they think that stock pricing and returns will be impacted by both the market's systematic risk and the market value of capital [3].

$$R_{it} - R_{ft} = \alpha_i + (R_{mt} - R_{ft}) + \beta_S SMB + \beta_H HML + e_{it} \tag{2}$$

Later, many studies have found that the three factors cannot effectively explain the returns of many stock markets in many cases. So Fama and French proposed in 1995 to add investment and profit factors to FF3 to form FF5, as follows [4].

$$R_{it} - R_{ft} = \alpha_i + (R_{mt} - R_{ft}) + \beta_S SMB + \beta_H HML + \beta_R RMW + \beta_C CMA + e_{it} \tag{3}$$

3 Empirical Results

3.1 Descriptive Statistics

Table 1 shows the mean, variance, 25th, 50th and 75th quartiles, minimum, maximum, and t-statistics of the data, and it can be clearly found that the monthly return of 0.53% is higher than the risk-free return, this corresponds to 6.36% per year. The size impact refers to the notion that smaller businesses typically produce higher returns than larger ones. The average return on size for SMBs is 0.90%, slightly under the market factor. Correspondingly, the average return on U.S. stocks typically declines as market capitalization declines. Smaller companies tend to perform better than larger companies in terms of returns. The corresponding t-statistic of 1.9 standard deviations is the lowest among these factors.

Table 1. Summary statistics of 5 factors.

Variables	mean	sd	p25	p50	p75	min	max	t-statistics
MKT	0.53	4.39	−0.02	0.01	0.03	−23.24	16.10	3.14
SMB	0.23	3.01	−0.02	0.00	0.02	−14.91	18.32	1.96
HML	0.31	2.81	−0.01	0.00	0.02	−11.18	12.87	2.86
RMW	0.26	2.16	−0.01	0.00	0.01	−18.33	13.33	3.15
CMA	0.28	1.99	−0.01	0.00	0.02	−6.86	9.56	3.60

Table 2. Correlation matrix of 5 factors.

	MKT-RF	SMB	HML	RMW	CMA
MKT	1.00				
SMB	0.28	1.00			
HML	−0.25	−0.06	1.00		
RMW	−0.23	−0.35	0.06	1.00	
CMA	−0.39	−0.10	0.69	−0.03	1.00

HML has a mean monthly change of 0.31% and a standard deviation of 2.81% compared to SMB. The low t-statistic suggests that there is no discernible difference in the spread between value and growth equities. As a result, the value effect is minimal on the American market, and the returns from a value portfolio are unquestionably negligible for investors. The average premiums for both the conservative-aggressive portfolio and the robust-weak profitability portfolio are statistically non-zero, similar to the value factor. The correlation coefficient matrix (Table 2) showed that the five factors showed different degrees of positive and negative correlation with each other, among which the positive correlation between factor HML and CMA had the strongest correlation coefficient (0.69), ranking top, and the negative correlation between factor CMA and factor MKT was the highest, with a correlation coefficient of −0.39.

3.2 Comparison of Model Performance Based on the Significance Level

This section explores which of the six portfolios can fit the data better under the three asset pricing models from Table 3, Table 4 and Table 5. If Portfolio 1 is used as an example, it can be seen that Model 1 and the CAPM model effectively reflect the impact of market risk. These five variables are used to account for variations in returns brought on by anomalies that are not taken into account by the CAPM model, such as asset size and book-to-market ratio. It can find the adj. R^2 by looking at the correlation coefficient (R^2) after adding SMB and HML is significantly higher, improved from 0.761 to 0.981, so it can be said that the addition of these two factors better explains the variability of stock returns.

Model (3) tests the generalizability of the FF5 to the U.S. stock market. RMW and CMA factors to FF3, FF5 aims to obtain the average return relationships related to size, book value, profitability, and other factors and investment. With the addition of RMW and CMA, the correlation coefficient (adj. R^2) of FF3 improved slightly, from 0.981 to 0.984.

Table 3. Comparison of model performance based on the Portfolio 1 and Portfolio 2.

Var	Portfolio 1			Portfolio 2		
	CAPM	FF3	FF5	CAPM	FF3	FF5
MKT	1.336***	1.077***	1.056***	1.072***	0.957***	0.971***
	(46.31)	(126.13)	(124.94)	(47.35)	(139.45)	(137.55)
SMB		1.029***	0.991***		0.820***	0.841***
		(85.16)	(84.04)		(84.52)	(85.36)
HML		−0.394***	−0.350***		0.252***	0.217***
		(−30.67)	(−21.59)		(24.39)	(16.06)
RMW			−0.170***			0.0931***
			(−10.29)			(6.74)
CMA			−0.0957***			0.0749***
			(−3.96)			(3.71)
Cons.	0.186	0.212***	0.289***	0.666***	0.463***	0.417***
	(1.46)	(5.95)	(8.50)	(6.65)	(16.2)	(14.67)
Obs.	675	675	675	675	675	675
R^2	0.7611	0.9819	0.9844	0.7692	0.9816	0.9829

Table 4. Comparison of model performance based on the Portfolio 3 and Portfolio 4.

Var	Portfolio 3			Portfolio 4		
	CAPM	FF3	FF5	CAPM	FF3	FF5
MKT	1.057***	0.985***	0.997***	1.000***	0.984***	0.993***
	(39.78)	(160.75)	(155.83)	(101.34)	(141.28)	(148.19)
SMB		0.864***	0.877***		−0.144***	−0.110***
		(99.71)	(98.26)		(−14.62)	(−11.72)
HML		0.574***	0.541***		−0.270***	−0.260***

(continued)

Table 4. (continued)

Var	Portfolio 3			Portfolio 4		
	CAPM	FF3	FF5	CAPM	FF3	FF5
		(62.31)	(44.12)		(−25.80)	(−20.28)
RMW			0.0574***			0.156***
			(4.59)			(11.92)
CMA			0.0732****			−0.0242
			(4.00)			(−1.26)
Cons.	0.791***	0.455***	0.421***	0.379***	0.504***	0.455***
	(6.73)	(17.82)	(16.37)	(8.69)	(17.36)	(16.86)
Obs.	675	675	675	675	675	675
R^2	0.7016	0.9863	0.9869	0.9385	0.9735	0.9785

Table 5. Comparison of model performance based on the Portfolio 3 and Portfolio 4.

Var	Portfolio 5			Portfolio 6		
	CAPM	FF3	FF5	CAPM	FF3	FF5
MKT	0.894***	0.977***	1.006***	0.958***	1.076***	1.052***
	(63.67)	(85.35)	(85.62)	(46.64)	(104.89)	(99.22)
SMB		−0.136***	−0.108***		0.0204	0.00452
		(−8.40)	(−6.57)		(1.40)	(0.31)
HML		0.356***	0.265***		0.761***	0.849***
		(20.65)	(11.77)		(49.29)	(41.78)
RMW			0.127***			−0.0714***
			(5.54)			(−3.44)
CMA			0.198***			−0.194***
			(5.88)			(−6.38)
Cons.	0.443***	0.320***	0.238***	0.564***	0.261***	0.322***
	(7.14)	(6.71)	(5.04)	(6.21)	(6.09)	(7.55)
Obs.	675	675	675	675	675	675
R^2	0.8576	0.9181	0.9242	0.7637	0.9489	0.9522

3.3 ANOVA Multi-Sample Testing

In this paper, when comparing the goodness-of-fit of multiple models, the multiplot function of the coefplot package in R language is used to carve multiple models together, and the results are shown in the figure below. After that, it uses ANOVA to perform multiple sample tests. Although it is not advocated to use ANOVA to do multiple sample tests, it is feasible to test the strengths and weaknesses of different models, and to do ANOVA analysis on multiple models, and the returned results are a table including the sum of squared residuals (RSS), and the smaller its value is, the better. The results are shown in Table 6.

Table 6. Variance Analysis of Portfolios.

	Res. Df	RSS	Df	Sum of Sq	F	Pr(>F)
Portfolio 1						
CAPM	673	7256.7				
FF3	671	487.8	2	6768.9	5492.405	<2.2e−16***
FF5	669	412.2	2	75.6	61.335	5.513e−11***
Portfolio 2						
CAPM	673	4428.2				
FF3	671	303.9	2	4124.2	4975.772	<2.2e−16***
FF5	669	277.3	2	26.7	32.197	4.465e−14***
Portfolio 3						
CAPM	673	6112.3				
FF3	671	237.8	2	5874.6	8757.372	<2.2e−16***
FF5	669	224.4	2	13.4	19.935	3.894e−09***
Portfolio 4						
CAPM	673	822.39				
FF3	671	322.55	2	499.84	666.598	<2.2e−16***
FF5	669	250.82	2	71.73	95.656	<2.2e−16***
Portfolio 5						
CAPM	673	1667.29				
FF3	671	958.82	2	708.48	268.575	<2.2e−16***
FF5	669	882.38	2	76.44	28.977	8.533e−13***
Portfolio 6						
CAPM	673	3582.4				
FF3	671	734.8	2	2847.6	1391.103	<2.2e−16***
FF5	669	684.7	2	50.1	24.475	5.513e−11***

As Fig. 1 shown, the smallest value of value is FF3 in four of the six coefficient figures, while the results of the ANOVA multi-sample test indicate that the FF5 has the smallest RSS, which means that it is the best among these models, so in the selection of models, we believe that the third model is able to fit the six data sets better.

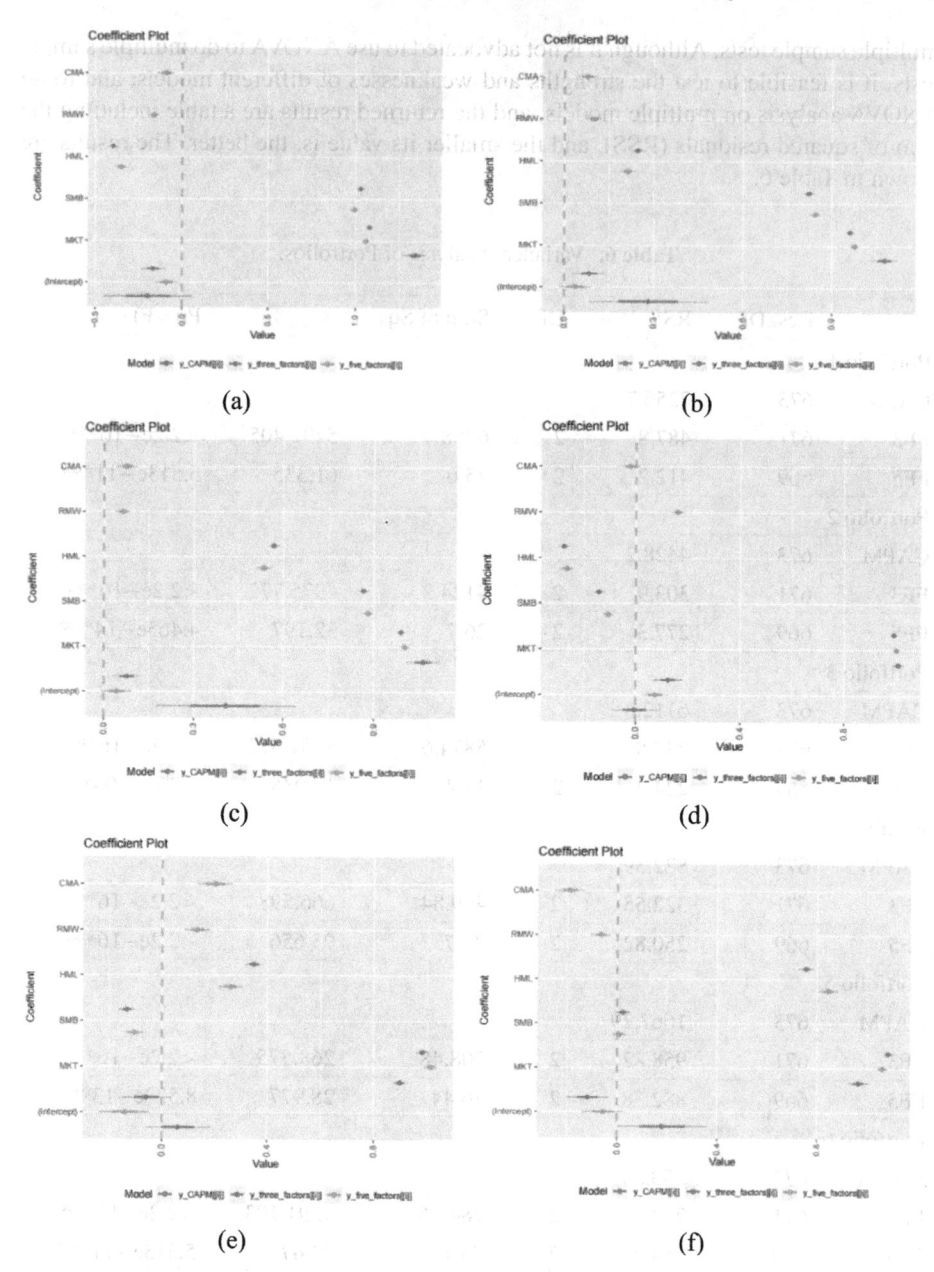

Fig. 1. Coefficient Plot of 6 portfolios.

3.4 Robustness Test

After concluding that the third model is the best model, we perform a robustness test on the model. In this paper, we select the U.S. stock market return data for 2020–2022 to test whether FF5 uses generalizability for the U.S. stock market stock return under the impact of the epidemic. Table 7 shows that the coefficients of the robustness test are significant to some extent, but the estimates of the factor CMA are largely insignificant, but it can be seen that the model can fit and predict to some extent the stock return returns of the US stock market.

Table 7. Regressive results of 6 portfolios from 2020 to 2022.

	(1)	(2)	(3)	(4)	(5)	(6)
MKT	1.070***	1.004***	1.011***	0.999***	0.980***	1.084***
	(12.36)	(18.63)	(13.59)	(28.43)	(30.97)	(19.72)
SMB	1.415***	1.071***	1.228***	0.305***	0.341***	0.394**
	(7.36)	(8.23)	(5.23)	(4.01)	(4.17)	(3.46)
HML	−0.417**	−0.0230	0.250	−0.137*	0.347***	0.897***
	(−3.33)	(−0.28)	(1.73)	(−2.43)	(6.36)	(11.39)
RMW	−0.620***	−0.249*	−0.319*	−0.0447	0.0868	−0.181*
	(−3.88)	(−2.23)	(−2.38)	(−0.39)	(0.92)	(−2.20)
CMA	−0.00721	0.0398	0.256	−0.158*	0.0081	−0.314*
	(−0.04)	(0.28)	(0.93)	(−2.21)	(0.10)	(−2.55)
Cons.	0.137	0.0898	1.020*	−0.00148	−0.0588	0.459
	(0.35)	(0.27)	(2.34)	(−0.01)	(−0.30)	(1.89)
Obs.	36	36	36	36	36	36

4 Conclusion

In summary, the FF3 contains elements of MKT, SMB and HML and FF5 includes additional RMW and CMA factors generally perform better than CAPM in analysing market portfolios. In addition, the results generated from ANOVA test show that the RMW and CMA factors have little improvement in the accuracy of the parameters but deteriorates the SSR which influences the model's goodness of fit on the contrary. In other words, the FF3 is identified as the best model in matching with the six portfolios. However, the limitation of this study is that all data analysed is formed as portfolios rather than individual stocks, which can lead to biases in conclusion as the lack of evidence on comparing the performance in terms of these three models on separate stock returns. That is to say, the study only focuses on six market portfolios extracted from the US stock markets, which is hard to provide precise empirical and general assumption in terms of the three models. Nevertheless, this study contributes to the formation of comparable vertical and horizontal analysis of different asset pricing models, which is beneficial to the further study on furnishing the research on CAPM variations or Time Series Analysing Models by using simulated analysing process.

References

1. Sharpe, W.F.: Capital asset prices: a theory of market equilibrium under conditions of risk. J. Financ. **19**(3), 425–442 (1964)
2. Lintner, J.: Security prices, risk, and maximal gains from diversification*. J. Financ. **20**(4), 587–615 (1965)
3. Fama, E.F., French, K.R.: Common risk factors in the returns on stocks and bonds. J. Financ. Econ. **33**(1), 3–56 (1993)
4. Fama, E.F., French, K.R.: A five-factor asset pricing model. J. Financ. Econ. **116**(1), 1–22 (2015)
5. Hogan, W.W., Warren, J.M.: Toward the development of an equilibrium capital-market model based on semivariance. J. Financ. Quant. Anal. **9**(1), 1–11 (1974)
6. Pástor, Ľ., Stambaugh, R.F.: Liquidity risk and expected stock returns. J. Polit. Econ. **111**(3), 642–685 (2003)
7. Hansen, L.P., Richard, S.F.: The role of conditioning information in deducing testable restrictions implied by dynamic asset pricing models. Econometrica **55**(3), 587–613 (1987)
8. Merton, R.C.: An intertemporal capital asset pricing model. Econometrica **41**(5), 867–887 (1973)
9. Lucas, R.E.: Asset prices in an exchange economy. Econometrica **46**(6), 1429–1445 (1978)
10. Breeden, D.T.: An intertemporal asset pricing model with stochastic consumption and investment opportunities. J. Financ. Econ. **7**(3), 265–296 (1979)
11. Raei, R.: A study on developing of asset pricing models. Int. Bus. Res. **4**(4), 139–152 (2011)
12. Reilly, F.K., Brown, K.C.: Investment Analysis and Portfolio Management, 6th edn. The Dryden Press, Harcourt College Publishers, New York (2000)
13. Cochrane, J.H.: Asset Pricing. Princeton University Press, Princeton (2005)

The Empirical Analysis of Asset Pricing Models in the Asia-Pacific Stock Market Under COVID-19

Hui Wang(✉)

School of Business and Economics, Universiti Putra Malaysia, 43400 Selangor Darul Ehsan, Malaysia
1811000807@mail.sit.edu.cn

Abstract. Through comparative analysis, this paper verifies that Fama and French Five-Factor Model (FF5) is more explanatory than other asset pricing models in analyzing the stock pricing in the Asia-Pacific region from the end of 2016 to the end of 2019. But at the end of 2019, covid-19 was ushered in, which broke the economic situation at that time. Therefore, this paper analyzes the data from December 2019 to December 2022 and verifies that the explanatory power of FF5 is still high compared with other models under the influence of the epidemic. However, because each country implemented different policies in controlling the epidemic during the epidemic period, which indirectly affected the development of enterprises of different scales, FF5 was used to study the stock pricing of companies of different scales and book-to-market value, and it was found that FF5 had changed the explanatory power of stock pricing for enterprises of different scales.

Keywords: Asset Pricing Models · Asia-Pacific Market · COVID-19 Pandemic

1 Introduction

The new coronavirus first appeared in Asia around the end of 2019, which was highly mobile and infectious and quickly spread to all countries and region. Due to the sudden outbreak of the epidemic and the uncontrollable nature of the virus, various countries have taken corresponding import, export, and cross-border transportation control measures. The emergence of the epidemic not only affects the development of enterprises but also affects the development of individuals. The risk factors leading to the global economy have significantly increased. Developed countries and regional economic markets in the Asia Pacific region (excluding Japan) cannot be spared. The stock markets of Australia, New Zealand, Singapore, and Hong Kong have all been affected and implemented different policies. Although the number of infected individuals and deaths in Australia is not significant, the stock market is one of the countries most affected [1]. Small-scale enterprises with high investment are more susceptible to impact [2]. As the Australian economy cope with the coronavirus, the Reserve Bank Board convened yesterday and settled on a comprehensive plan to assist employment, earnings, and enterprises. [3].

After the outbreak of the epidemic, market volatility increased, and the Singapore stock market has been in a sluggish state due to the impact of COVID-19 [4].

The capital asset pricing model, developed in 1964, focuses on how the equilibrium price is determined as well as the relationship between the predicted return rates of safe and risky assets [5]. Banz discovered, however, that a stock's return is also correlated with its market value [6]. Later, they discovered that the B/M ratio and P/E ratio of capital would greatly affect and explain stock pricing. This also indicates that these two ratios can be used as factors for analyzing stock pricing [6]. In a 1993's article by Fama and French, they used annual market risk data, enterprise market value data, and book value data to comprehensively calculate three coefficients that can measure market risk, enterprise size, and enterprise book value to represent these three influencing factors as independent variables and put them into the equation [7]. However, we discovered that in some equities, is significantly not zero based on the empirical research that academics conducted on the three elements. This suggests that the three variables are invalid. In addition to the threats listed above, Fama & French's article discovered that there exist risks at the profit margin and risks at the investment margin that can result in excess returns for specific stocks [8]. As a result, on the basis of FF3, they added profit factor (RMW) and investment factor (CMA).

FF5 is a financial model used to quantify investors' investment risk. It decomposes investors' investment risk into five basic factors: market factors, industry factors, company-specific factors, financial reporting factors, and financial policy factors. These five factors decompose investors' investment risks into factors that can be understood and controlled, enabling investors to assess investment risks [9]. However, FF5 also has certain flaws. The compensation explanatory power of the model is not strong enough. FF5 only considers five factors and fails to consider other factors, such as the impact of natural or man-made disasters on overall economic development trends and national policies [10]. At the same time, the implementation of FF5 requires a large amount of data and calculations, and the data used for empirical model effectiveness are all from the US stock market. Due to the different economic policies and stock market backgrounds of each country or region, the explanatory power of the FF5 varies in different countries and regions' stock markets.

This article uses the asset pricing models to conduct an empirical analysis of the stock markets of developed countries in the Asia Pacific region without Japan during the epidemic period, to test whether the FF5's explanatory power on the stock market remains stable despite the huge risks brought by the emergence of COVID-19. The rest sections are: Sect. 2 is about data sources, data analysis results, and adopted models; Sect. 3 is about the empirical analysis; Sect. 4 is a conclusion.

2 Methodology

2.1 Data and Variables

The data adopts six portfolio returns of 2 * 3 combinations proposed by Fama and French according to different scales and book-to-market ratios. The data used is the daily data from December 2016 to December 2022, with a data of 1604 days. All the data are collected from Kenneth R. French Data Library. This article cites a traditional 2 * 3 investment portfolio. The division is based on the B/M value statistics based on size, and then 25% and 75% of the data are used as breakpoints to divide all data into three groups, namely low, medium, and high. Enterprises with a B/M value below 25% have significant development potential and are classified as growth-oriented enterprises (G). Enterprises that are more than 25% and less than 75% mature and enter a stable stage of development is called mature enterprises (N), and the last 25% of enterprises are quite successful in the development, with high returns and stability are called value oriented enterprises (V). Secondly, it is divided into large enterprises (B) and small enterprises (S) based on the size of the company. Table 1 specifically explains how these six combinations are divided [7]. The independent variables are also mentioned in the model. In Table 2, the five coefficients that can represent a market risk, size, book value, investment ability, and profitability are calculated based on company market value, book value, and other data, namely MKT-RF, SMB, HML, RMW, and CMA.

Table 1. Classification of the portfolios.

	low BM	Medium BM	High BM
Small	S&G	S&N	S&V
Big	B&G	B&N	B&V

Table 2. Independent variables.

Independent Variable	Definition
MKT-RF	Market risk minus the risk-free rate
SMB	The size factor: SMB is abbreviated from the "small-minus-big"
HML	The value factor: HML is abbreviated from the "high-minus-low"
RMW	The profitability factor: RMW is abbreviated from the "robust-minus weak"
CMA	The investment factor: CMA is abbreviated from the "conservative-minus-aggressive"

2.2 Modelling

Sharp et al. first suggested CAPM and noted there really some relationship between predicted stock market returns and asset risk. The return on a single security can be obtained from risk-free interest rates, but this portion of the return is relatively low and very stable. If you want a high income, you still need to obtain it from the risk premium of risky stocks, which is easy to gain and easy to lose. Through using a beta value as a coefficient of risk premium to measure the volatility or risk of securities or investment portfolios relative to the market.

$$E[R_i] - R_F = \beta_i E[R_M - R_F] \quad (1)$$

Later, when Fama and French analyzed the factors that lead to different returns of different stocks in US, they believe that not only the systematic risk of the stock market will affect stock pricing and returns, but also the market value of capital will affect stock pricing and returns. In subsequent research, Fama and French found that book value and stock market value can largely explain stock pricing and returns. So they constructed a new model as follows.

$$R_{it} - R_{ft} = \alpha_i + (R_{mt} - R_{ft}) + \beta_S SMB + \beta_H HML + e_{it} \quad (2)$$

Later, many studies have found that the three factors cannot effectively explain the returns of many stock markets in many cases. So Fama and French proposed in 1995 to add investment and profit factors to FF3 to form FF5, as follows.

$$R_{it} - R_{ft} = \alpha_i + (R_{mt} - R_{ft}) + \beta_S SMB + \beta_H HML + \beta_R RMW + \beta_C CMA + e_{it} \quad (3)$$

3 Empirical Results

3.1 Summary Statistics

Table 3 displays statistical information on risk factors such as lowest, quartile, mean, median, quartile, and maximum. The correlation between factors can be seen in Table 4. Table 3 shows that the average of Mkt-RF is 0.01812, and the impingement of it on the stock market is positive, as to the absolute value of t is not significant, indicating that it is not highly sensitive to the influence of market forces on the stock market.

Table 3. Summary statistics of variables.

Variables	min	1stQu	median	mean	3rdQu	Max	Sd	T-value
MKT-RF	−3.06	−0.32	0.05	0.01812	0.41	2.51	0.64	−0.302
SMB	−1.58	−0.2425	−0.035	−0.03893	−0.2	0.98	0.36	−5.380
HML	−1.48	−0.23	0	0.02935	0.23	1.88	0.38	−5.005
RMW	−1.65	−0.19	0.04	0.03292	0.25	1.75	0.33	−5.728
CMA	−1.23	−0.17	−0.01	−0.0048	0.17	1.02	0.28	−6.873

The average value of SMB is −0.03893, at the same time the value of standard deviation is 0.36, which shows that the stock market is more inclined to companies with large market value at this time, and the stock returns increase with the increase of market value. T value is −5.380, which shows that the stock market in Asia-Pacific region is very

Table 4. Correlation matrix of variables.

	MKT-RF	SMB	HML	RMW	CMA
MKT-RF	1.0000000				
SMB	−0.6679128	1.00000000			
HML	−0.2175209	−0.06647500	1.0000000		
RMW	0.2326124	−0.04624432	−0.7167577	1.00000000	
CMA	−0.2092591	0.10128136	0.3273109	−0.14084744	1.0000000

sensitive to the influence of scale factor. With regard to the influence of HML and RMW, we can see that the average mean is positive, and the standard deviation is very close to that of other factors, and both are very small. At the same time, because the absolute value of t is large enough, it shows that the fluctuation of the stock market is relatively small, and the return rate of the stock market is more inclined to companies with high B/M ratio and more profitability. At this time, the average mean of investment factor CMA is −0.0048, as to absolute value of t value is the largest among several factors, which shows that the stock market is obviously influenced by the investment ability of enterprises, and the return rate of enterprises with less total assets growth year-on-year is higher. The correlation analysis of variables in Table 4 shows that HML, RMW and CMA have high correlation and collinearity. That is to say, RMW and CMA coincide with HML to some extent. The correlation of other variables is relatively low.

3.2 Regression Results

From Table 5 and Table 6, we can know that the coefficients of HML, RMW and CMA are mostly negative, and CMA is not significant at the level of 0.05, which may be due to the small scale of the company, less profit but too high investment, so the explanatory power of the FF5 to this kind of capital will decline. Furthermore, as shown in Table 6, the impact of HML on the return rate is insignificant, indicating that the portfolio's performance is more oriented toward the growth stock portfolio. Of course, the B/M ratio may fluctuate in the future due to lagging in the publication of the company's market value data and the volatility of the stock.

However, from Table 7, it can be seen that before the epidemic, the coefficient of CMA was −0.08178, which was significant at the level of 0.05%, and it was negative with the coefficient of RMW −0.01243. This means the growth of RMW will leads to the negative growth of stock price. But following the outbreak, the coefficients of CMA and RMW became positively linked with the rate of return, with RMW considerably influencing the expected return at the level of 0.05% and CMA being insignificant. This may be due to the impact of the epidemic. For small-scale value-based capital, people began to focus on more profitable capital, rather than taking more risks and investing more.

From Table 8 and Table 9, the SMB are not significant, because Table 8 and Table 9 are large-scale companies, on this premise, investors are more inclined to pay attention to other factors.

Table 5. Comparison of model performance to the S&G portfolio before & after COVID-19.

Var.	Before COVID-19			After COVID-19		
	CAPM	FF3	FF5	CAPM	FF3	FF5
MKT-Rf	0.738***	1.077***	1.080***	0.993***	1.079***	1.102***
	(0.021)	(0.013)	(0.012)	(0.021)	(0.009)	(0.099)
SMB		1.024***	1.002***		1.120***	1.083***
		(0.023)	(0.021)		(0.017)	(0.017)
HML		−0.361***	−0.553***		−0.378***	−0.402***
		(0.017)	(0.022)		(0.013)	(0.017)
RMW			−0.318***			−0.152***
			(0.024)			(0.017)
CMA			−0.027			−0.053*
			(0.021)			(0.028)
Cons.	−0.039**	−0.005***	0.004	−0.013	−0.001	0.003
	(0.013)	(0.006)	(0.005)	(0.024)	(0.008)	(0.007)
Obs.	804	804	804	804	804	804
R^2	0.603	0.918	0.933	0.736	0.969	0.972

Table 6. Comparison of model performance to the S&N portfolio before & after COVID-19.

Var.	Before COVID-19			After COVID-19		
	CAPM	FF3	FF5	CAPM	FF3	FF5
MKT-Rf	0.705***	1.069***	1.065***	0.899***	1.105***	1.100***
	(0.016)	(0.011)	(0.011)	(0.015)	(0.008)	(0.086)
SMB		0.965***	0.971***		0.980***	0.976***
		(0.019)	(0.019)		(0.015)	(0.021)
HML		−0.051	−0.043*		−0.369***	−0.001
		(0.014)	(0.020)		(0.011)	(0.015)
RMW			−0.059**			0.022
			(0.022)			(0.015)
CMA			−0.027			−0.063**
			(0.019)			(0.020)
Cons.	−0.038**	−0.007***	0.009	−0.006	−0.002	0.003

(*continued*)

Table 6. (*continued*)

Var.	Before COVID-19			After COVID-19		
	CAPM	FF3	FF5	CAPM	FF3	FF5
	(0.010)	(0.005)	(0.005)	(0.018)	(0.006)	(0.006)
Obs.	804	804	804	804	804	804
R^2	0.697	0.929	0.930	0.799	0.970	0.970

Table 7. Comparison of model performance to the S&V portfolio before & after COVID-19.

Var.	Before COVID-19			After COVID-19		
	CAPM	FF3	FF5	CAPM	FF3	FF5
MKT-Rf	0.585***	0.911***	0.907***	0.563***	0.801***	0.804***
	(0.012)	(0.009)	(0.009)	(0.011)	(0.008)	(0.008)
SMB		0.775***	0.777***		0.681***	0.667***
		(0.016)	(0.016)		(0.015)	(0.015)
HML		0.254***	0.265***		0.240***	0.186***
		(0.011)	(0.016)		(0.011)	(0.015)
RMW			−0.012			0.103***
			(0.017)			(0.015)
CMA			−0.081***			0.045*
			(0.015)			(0.020)
Cons.	−0.018**	0.005	0.005	0.008	0.004	0.007
	(0.008)	(0.004)	(0.004)	(0.013)	(0.007)	(0.006)
Obs.	804	804	804	804	804	804
R^2	0.718	0.927	0.930	0.739	0.927	0.931

Table 8. Comparison of model performance to the B&N portfolio before & after COVID-19.

Var.	Before COVID-19			After COVID-19		
	CAPM	FF3	FF5	CAPM	FF3	FF5
MKT-Rf	0.101***	0.984***	0.991***	1.075***	1.127***	1.134***
	(0.009)	(0.013)	(0.012)	(0.008)	(0.011)	(0.010)
SMB		−0.073**	−0.068**		−0.043*	0.004
		(0.022)	(0.021)		(0.019)	(0.019)

(*continued*)

Table 8. (*continued*)

Var.	Before COVID-19			After COVID-19		
	CAPM	FF3	FF5	CAPM	FF3	FF5
HML		−0.050**	0.012		0.173***	0.205***
		(0.016)	(0.021)		(0.015)	(0.019)
RMW			0.171***			0.197***
			(0.023)			(0.019)
CMA			0.193***			0.067**
			(0.020)			(0.025)
Cons.	0.000	−0.001	−0.006	0.004	0.000	−0.005
	(0.005)	(0.005)	(0.054)	(0.010)	(0.009)	(0.008)
Obs.	804	804	804	804	804	804
R^2	0.937	0.932	0.490	0.948	0.956	0.962

Table 9. Comparison of model performance to the B&V portfolio before & after COVID-19.

Var.	Before COVID-19			After COVID-19		
	CAPM	FF3	FF5	CAPM	FF3	FF5
MKT-Rf	1.005***	1.098***	1.093***	0.822***	1.073***	1.062***
	(0.019)	(0.017)	(0.015)	(0.014)	(0.010)	(0.009)
SMB		−0.012	−0.028		0.096***	0.043*
		(0.029)	(0.026)		(0.018)	(0.017)
HML		0.745***	0.586***		0.638***	0.629***
		(0.020)	(0.027)		(0.014)	(0.018)
RMW			−0.325***			−0.188***
			(0.029)			(0.017)
CMA			−0.199***			−0.114***
			(0.025)			(0.023)
Cons.	−0.001	−0.005	0.004	0.012	−0.001	0.004
	(0.012)	(0.007)	(0.006)	(0.016)	(0.008)	(0.008)
Obs.	804	804	804	804	804	804
R^2	0.768	0.918	0.932	0.802	0.944	0.953

From the Tables 5, 6, 7, 8 and Table 9, the R Square of FF5 are always higher than the R Square of the other model, no matter before or after COVID-19. This shows that the explanatory power of FF5 is generally higher than that of asset pricing model and FF3 for small-scale capital and large-scale mature and large-scale value capital before the epidemic. Similarly, after the epidemic, the overall explanatory power of FF5 to stock pricing and yield is still strong, which proves that FF5 is stable enough. Market factors have always had a significant positive influence on the return of portfolios.

Table 10. Comparison of model performance to the B&G portfolio before & after COVID-19.

Var.	Before COVID-19			After COVID-19		
	CAPM	FF3	FF5	CAPM	FF3	FF5
MKT-Rf	1.115***	0.932***	0.923***	1.111***	0.767***	0.765***
	(0.017)	(0.016)	(0.015)	(0.016)	(0.012)	(0.012)
SMB		−0.262***	−0.254***		−0.343***	−0.373***
		(0.028)	(0.027)		(0.022)	(0.023)
HML		−0.639***	−0.595***		−0.743***	−0.780***
		(0.020)	(0.028)		(0.017)	(0.022)
RMW			−0.020			−0.140***
			(0.030)			(0.023)
CMA			−0.253***			−0.016
			(0.027)			(0.030)
Cons.	0.010	0.005	0.005	−0.011	0.004	0.008
	(0.010)	(0.007)	(0.007)	(0.019)	(0.010)	(0.010)
Obs.	804	804	804	804	804	804
R^2	0.839	0.927	0.935	0.842	0.953	0.933

From Table 10, we can see that the explanatory power of FF5 is slightly lower than that of the FF3, which probably can be due to the fact that large-scale growth companies need to continuously invest a lot of cash flow in order to maintain sustained growth, so they need a lot of investment to make profits and keep the company's funds running normally. During the epidemic period, investors are more inclined to stable enterprises, which leads to the decline of the explanatory power of FF5. Because of the multicollinearity among HML, RMW, and CMA, FF5 has weaker explanatory power than FF3.

4 Conclusion

Based on the analysis of stock portfolio returns using asset pricing models from December 2019 to December 2022, the COVID-19 epidemic has clearly had a big influence on the stock market in the Asia-Pacific area. FF5 proves to be more suitable for stock market analysis in this region, but the explanatory power is weak for small-scale companies, particularly those in the development and maturity stages. This is likely due to the susceptibility of such firms to the uncertainties brought about by the epidemic. Interestingly, the explanatory power of FF5 to the stock return rate of large-scale growth companies is also impinged by the uncertainty brought about by the epidemic. The year 2021, in particular, marked the widest spread of the epidemic and the highest number of patients. During this year, FF5 had the lowest explanatory power to the stock market return rate in the Asia-Pacific region. This suggests that the uncertainty brought by the epidemic does affect the model's robustness.

Overall, the analysis shows that the COVID-19 epidemic has had a profound impingement on the Asia-Pacific region's stock market, with companies of different scales and market value ratios affected differently. FF5 is better suited to analyze the stock market in this region, but its explanatory power is subject to uncertainties brought about by the epidemic. Investors and analysts must, therefore, carefully consider the impinge of the epidemic when analyzing stock market trends and making investment decisions.

References

1. Chiah, M., Chai, D., Zhong, A., Li, S.: A better model? An empirical investigation of the Fama-French five-factor model in Australia. Int. Rev. Financ. **16**(4), 595–638 (2016)
2. Rahman, L., Amin, A.S., Mamun, M.A.: The COVID-19 outbreak and stock market reactions: evidence from Australia. Financ. Res. Lett. **38**, 101832 (2021)
3. Philip, S.A.: Speech Responding to the Economic and Financial Impact of COVID-19. Reserve Bank of Australia. https://www.rba.gov.au/speeches/2020/sp-gov-2020-03-19.html. Accessed 1 Apr 2023
4. Yong, J.Y.J., Ziaei, S.M., Szulczyk, K.R.: The impact of Covid-19 pandemic on stock market return volatility: evidence from Malaysia and Singapore. Asian Econ. Financ. Rev. **11**(3), 191–204 (2021)
5. Sharpe, W.F.: Capital asset prices: a theory of market equilibrium under conditions of risk*. J. Financ. **19**(3), 425–442 (1964)
6. Banz, R.W.: The relationship between return and market value of common stocks. J. Financ. Econ. **9**(1), 3–18 (1981)
7. Fama, E.F., French, K.R.: Common risk factors in the returns on stocks and bonds. J. Financ. Econ. **33**(1), 3–56 (1993)
8. Fama, E.F., French, K.R.: A five-factor asset pricing model. J. Financ. Econ. **116**(1), 1–22 (2015)
9. Horváth, D., Wang, Y.: The examination of Fama-French model during the Covid-19. Financ. Res. Lett. **41**, 101848 (2021)
10. Zhang, H., Song, H., Wen, L., Liu, C.: Forecasting tourism recovery amid COVID-19. Ann. Tour. Res. **87**, 103149 (2021)

The Impact of Technological Change on Labour Market Outcomes and Income Inequality in China: An Empirical Analysis

Xueyao Tong[✉]

School of Business and Management, Hong Kong University of Science and Technology, Hong Kong 999077, China
Xtongae@connect.ust.hk

Abstract. As technological advances continue to advance, there is increasing concern about their impact on the labour market. This study aims to investigate the impact of technological change on income inequality and labour market outcomes in China. This paper used data from several reliable databases, such as the China Statistical Yearbook, and employs multiple regression analysis in terms of employment numbers and wage levels. The level of education received by workers in different industries was included as a control variable, as an increase in education within a given industry would theoretically also lead to an increase in employment rates and wages. The findings of this paper show that technological change had an impact on income inequality and employment opportunities and that the impact was not the same for the three industries. In general, the primary sector was negatively affected, the secondary sector was positively affected, and the tertiary sector was significantly positively affected.

Keywords: Technology · Labour Market · Employment · Inequality

1 Introduction

The technological changes caused by artificial intelligence and automation have been in the spotlight for a long time. Changes in technology are usually accompanied by increased productivity and economic growth. Recently, ChatGPT has become a tech sensation, with many people reporting that their productivity (especially coding jobs for programmers) has been improved with the aid of ChatGPT. But at the same time, many people are concerned about whether technological improvement will pose a threat to human beings. As technological changes, it is gradually possible for many jobs to be completely replaced by machines, which potentially leads to unemployment [1]. Elon Musk, Steve Wozniak, and Pinterest co-founder Evan Sharp are among those calling for a moratorium on advanced AI research and development. In this light, as the pace of technological change accelerates, it is important to understand how it will affect the labour market and how policymakers can design policies to support workers and mitigate possible negative impacts.

The relationship between technological change and the labour market has been studied in a number of works of literature both in China and overseas. A 2017 Chicago Booth poll showed that between 35 and 40% of economists in the US believe that technological change has negative effects, specifically leading to higher long-term unemployment rates [2]. Recent technological developments may also have an impact on the labour market in terms of the way firms organise production, labour market policies, and the form of labour market 'institutions', and through this channel may have a significant impact on the structure of wages, particularly on the wages and employment of workers in reproductive jobs in conventional task-intensive industries [3–5]. Specifically, it can have a seriously detrimental effect on the wages and employment of workers engaged in replication work in conventional task-intensive industries. The Chinese economy also shows this trend. Some empirical studies have found that automation reduces labour demand [6] and lowers overall labour compensation [6, 7]. In addition, Li Sainan shows that the extent to which income and employment are affected varies across industries [8]. On the other hand, it has also been shown that the impact of technology is positive, as the introduction of new technologies can help industries reduce costs, modernise and become more competitive in domestic and overseas markets [9]. Changes in technology do not necessarily mean that people's employment will be harmed but may instead lead to more new opportunities and create a new mechanism for employment.

There are relatively few studies on related topics based on the Chinese economy and market conditions, and the data used is relatively outdated. This paper, therefore, used several recent datasets from authoritative Chinese statistical agencies, splitting the data into three different industries, including the scale of R&D activity, income by industry, educational level of employed persons by industry, and disposable income per capita by industry. In order to estimate the relationship between technological change and labour market outcomes, multiple regression analysis models were used with the inclusion of educational level as a control variable. Thereby, building on previous research, the paper analysed the development of income and employment in different industries in the Chinese labour market under the influence of rapid technological advances and also further investigated whether technological change is exacerbating social inequality.

2 Data Description and Methodology

2.1 Model Design

In this paper, China Statistical Yearbook data for a total of ten years from 2012 to 2021 were selected for an empirical study to investigate the impact of R&D in technology on labour force employment, earnings and income inequality based on the results by building a multiple regression model for three different industries. The model equations are as follows, where i represents the first industry, the second industry, and the tertiary industry.

$$Employment_i = \beta_0 + \beta_1 R\&D + \beta_2 education_i \tag{1}$$

$$Wage_i = \beta_0 + \beta_1 R\&D + \beta_2 education_i \tag{2}$$

2.2 Data Source

The data for this study is drawn from the China Statistical Yearbook and the China Population and Employment Statistical Yearbook, which statistics reflect the economic and social development of China. They systematically collect the economic and social statistics of the previous year at the national level and at the level of all provinces, autonomous regions and municipalities directly under the Central Government, as well as major national statistics in several important historical years and recent years. Combined with literature in the relevant fields and tailored to the purpose of this research paper, data from three industries for the decade 2012–2021 were selected to make them an ideal source for investigating the research questions of this study.

2.3 Variable Setting

The multiple regression model in this study includes several variables that are assumed to be correlated with the outcome variable of interest.

Dependent Variables (Employment and Wage). According to relevant theory and literature, technological change is reflected in the labour market mainly in terms of income and employment, two indicators that are used by a wide range of scholars. Therefore, one of the dependent variables in this study is the number of employed persons counted at the end of each year in the three industries, in millions of people; the other dependent variable is the total wages of employed persons by the three industries, in billions of CNY. The three industries are the division of industrial structure according to the sequence of the historical development of social production activities. This paper selected forestry, husbandry, and fishery as the representative of the primary industry, manufacturing as the representative of the secondary industry, and information transmission, software, and information technology services as the representative of the tertiary industry. The following variables and control variables follow the same selection principle.

Independent Variables (R&D Expenditure). This paper takes the ratio of R&D expenditure to GDP as a variable to indicate the development and change of science and technology in China. Indicators of the scale and intensity of R&D activities are commonly used internationally to reflect a country's scientific and technological strength and core competitiveness. According to the Statistical Yearbook, R&D refers to creative, systematic work undertaken to increase the stock of knowledge and to design new applications of existing knowledge, including basic research, applied research, and experimental development.

Control Variables. The control variable selected in this paper is the education level of the employees in the three industries, which is expressed by the percentage of the employees with a junior college degree or above in the total industries, as Table 1 shown. From a theoretical and empirical perspective, those with higher levels of education are more likely to have access to more employment opportunities, as well as earn higher wages, compared to those with lower levels. Therefore, to isolate the effect of technological change on employment rates and wages, education level was chosen as a control variable to allow for a more accurate relationship between the independent and dependent variables.

Table 1. Variable descriptive statistics.

	Min.	Max.	Mean	S.D.
R&D (%)	1.91	2.44	2.144	0.17
First industry employment (in million)	17072	25535	20732	2675.06
Secondary industry employment (in million)	21234	23226	22196	774.75
Tertiary industry employment (in million)	27493	35806	32911.9	2898.72
First industry income (billions CNY)	410.6	949.9	715.55	183.18
Secondary industry income (billions CNY)	17668.1	35232.8	28358.53	4674.19
Tertiary industry income (billions CNY)	1769.4	10289	5386.46	2662.24
First industry education level (%)	0.16	1.02	0.749	0.24
Secondary industry education level (%)	11.3	17.3	15.236	1.82
Tertiary industry education level (%)	19.9	70.58	52.254	20.51

A collation of the data shows that the increase in the proportion of R&D to GDP reflects the progress of technology in China. According to the division of the three major industries, overall, there was a wide disparity in income and employment, and educational attainment between the different industries. In particular, the tertiary industry has significantly more educated and employed employees than the other two industries. In addition to this, there was also a large difference in the total wages of employees in the three industries. The indicators selected and the model built for this study can thus be justified, and the results will be clearer through the use of regression models.

3 Empirical Results

According to the regression results in Table 2 and Table 3, in terms of employment and wages, as mentioned in other literature, the three industries were affected to different degrees. In terms of employment, with the progress and change of technology, the number of employment in the primary industry decreased greatly, employment in the secondary industry also declined, and only the number of employees in the tertiary industry rose. In detail, for each unit increase in R&D expenditure would reduce employment in the primary industry by about 11,483 million, the number of employments in the secondary industry by 32.98 million, and that in the tertiary industry by 52.13 million. The results for primary industries were highly significant ($p < 0.01$), while the results for secondary and tertiary industries were not significant. Among them, the level of education had a statistically significant effect ($p < 0.01$) on employment in the tertiary industry, which was much higher than the other two industries, indicating that the improvement of education level increased the number of employees in the tertiary industry to a large extent.

In terms of wages, as with the number of people employed, the income of employees in the primary industry was negatively correlated with technological change. An increase in R&D expenditure by one unit would reduce the wages of employees in the primary sector by approximately 123.43 million yuan. However, both the secondary and tertiary sectors had a positive relationship between employee wages and technological change. In particular, the unit increase in R&D expenditure would increase wages in the secondary sector by about 162.691 million yuan, and increase wages in the tertiary sector by approximately 136.1486 million yuan. The results are more significant for the primary and tertiary industries and insignificant for the secondary industry.

This shows the different levels of dependence on technology in the three industries. The main reason for the decrease in employment in the primary industry is automation and increased productivity. Technological advances have made agricultural production more efficient so that producing the same amount of product can be achieved with a much smaller amount of labour. In addition, mechanised agricultural equipment has replaced many repetitive human jobs, and those who cannot learn or adapt to new technical skills and methods in time will face unemployment [10]. As a result, the reduced demand for labour has led to lower wages for them. Besides, the industry is more dependent on natural resources than on high technology compared to the other two industries, so technological change could not lead to higher wages for employees in the primary sector. In the case of the secondary industry, which is mainly manufacturing, in addition to the substitution of manpower by machines, the reduction in employment may also be due to the fact that the demand for talent levels in the secondary industry has become higher as technology has developed, eliminating a large proportion of the general workforce with only average skills. However, secondary industry workers' wages have increased a lot, probably due to increased productivity, which has led to increased economic welfare in the industry and consequently to higher payments for their labour. The increase in employment in the tertiary sector, which is dominated by services and highly skilled knowledge-intensive industries such as information technology, is mainly due to a surge in demand for information technology workers as a result of the development and use of online platforms and various mobile applications, as well as services (e.g., online customer service). However, even with the increase in employment, there was still more demand than supply in the labour market, resulting in higher wages for employees, thus revealing why the increase in income for employees in the tertiary sector was significant.

These results also show a gradual increase in income inequality among the Chinese. With technological change, the employment and wage gap between different industries has widened further. Industry-specific factors may be an important determinant of inequality. Technological change may lead to a reduction in demand for jobs in the primary industry, leading to an increase in unemployment. These jobs are usually low-skilled, and workers are correspondingly lower paid. Income in the secondary industry rose, but they may also be at risk of being replaced by robots and automated systems. On the other hand, high-skilled jobs in the tertiary industry may only be held by a small group of people who are paid higher wages, thus increasing income inequality in China.

Table 2. The impact of R&D and education on employment.

Variables	First industry	Second industry	Tertiary industry
R&D	−11483**	−3297.72	5212.62
	(2760.00)	(1622.35)	(2888.53)
Education	−2845	−19.59	97.97**
	(2005.00)	(154.29)	(24.40)
Constant	47482***	29564.72***	16616.54*
	(4829.00)	(2320.97)	(5212.63)
Observations	10	10	10
R-squared	0.9159	0.5971	0.9302

Note: ***p < 0.001, **p < 0.01, *p < 0.05, p < 0.1

Table 3. The impact of R&D and education on income.

Variables	First industry	Second industry	Tertiary industry
R&D	−1234.3*	16269.1	13614.86***
	(357.10)	(7400.00)	(1817.00)
Education	375.9	843.9	15.12
	(259.40)	(703.80)	(15.35)
Constant	3080.3**	−19380.6	−24593.64***
	(624.70)	(10586.70)	(3278.95)
Observations	10	10	10
R-squared	0.6997	0.7697	0.9672

Note: ***p < 0.001, **p < 0.01, *p < 0.05, p < 0.1

4 Conclusion

In summary, this paper examined the impact of technological change on the number of people employed and wages in the labour market, and tested whether it increases income inequality. Firstly, the regression model showed how technological change brought about changes in the number of people employed in each industry. The number of people employed in the primary and secondary sectors decreased, while only the number of people employed in the tertiary sector increased. In terms of wages, wages decreased in the primary sector and increased in the secondary and tertiary sectors, with the rise in wages in the tertiary sector being more significant. The combination of the two aspects exacerbated the problem of inequality. The main reasons for this inequality are the different levels of dependence on technology in different industries and the increased demand for advanced skills. In addition to this, education played a key role in the increase in employment and wages in the tertiary sector, which provides useful information for policy makers and practitioners. It may be possible for countries to increase spending on education (especially for low-skilled workers) and raise the level of national education to keep the knowledge of the majority of the population as up to date as possible with technological advances and changes, not only to reduce inequality to a certain extent but also to boost the overall economy. In future research, more control variables or other variables can be added to the model in this paper to make the results more accurate.

References

1. Feldmann, H.: Technological unemployment in industrial countries. J. Evol. Econ. **23**(5), 1099–1126 (2013). https://doi.org/10.1007/s00191-013-0308-6
2. Autor, D.H.: The Labor Market Impacts of Technological Change: From Unbridled Enthusiasm to Qualified Optimism to Vast Uncertainty. NBER (2022)
3. Acemoglu, D.: Technical change, inequality, and the labor market. J. Econ. Lit. (2002)
4. Bartel, A.P., Sicherman, N.: Technological change and wages: an interindustry analysis. J. Polit. Econ. **107**(2), 285–325 (1999)
5. Liu, J.: Technological change and the demand for new types of labor: how education can effectively respond. Educ. Econ. Rev. (02), 36–51 (2018)
6. Wang, Y., Dong, W.: How the rise of robots has affected china's labor market: evidence from China's listed manufacturing firms. Econ. Res. J. (10), 159–175 (2020)
7. Zhu, Q., Liu, H.: Research on the income distribution effects of technological change in artificial intelligence: frontier advances and review. Chin. J. Popul. Sci. (2), 111–125 (2020)
8. Li, S.: Research on the impact of artificial intelligence development on employment and income. Changzhou University (2021)
9. David, B.: Computer technology and probable job destructions in Japan: an evaluation. J. Jpn. Int. Econ. **43**, 77–87 (2017)
10. Jin, H., Sheng, R.: Literature review on the impact of artificial intelligence technology on labor employment. Value Eng. (02), 165–168 (2023)

The "Strong" Development of RMB

Shengran Huang[✉]

Economics and Management School, Beijing Forestry University, Beijing 100000, China
2200935063@stu.pku.edu.cn

Abstract. In this article, the author will focus on how the RMB has developed rapidly and exerted its real value in different transactions, such as China's balance of payments, China's GDP, and the real exchange rate changes of the RMB against the US dollar. In addition, by introducing investment methods, the author will provide some practical suggestions for US dollar investors to hedge long-term risks in the RMB. From an empirical perspective, an analysis of why the internationalization of the RMB has developed at a rapid level will clarify some suggestions for the relevant foreign exchange market. The research results show that although the RMB depreciated in the second quarter of 2022, due to the economic development under the socialist system with Chinese characteristics, the RMB remains strong in the foreign exchange market.

Keywords: CNY · the Balance of Payments · Finance · Investment · GDP

1 Introduction

Due to various policies led by the Chinese government, such as the "the Belt and Road" and the "Silk Road", the RMB plays an important role in world transactions. There is no doubt that the RMB is constantly internationalizing. However, this can be a double-edged sword. During the conflict between Ukraine and Russia, the prices of raw materials and oil experienced difficult increases, and the internationalization of currencies has closely linked the economies of various countries. Currency not only symbolizes the medium of purchasing goods, but also represents the purchasing power of a country.

In this article, the author will focus on assessing how the RMB has developed rapidly and how it can play its practical value in different transactions. The author will analyze China's international balance of payments, China's GDP, and the real exchange rate of the RMB against the US dollar. In addition, by introducing foreign exchange investment methods, the author will provide some practical suggestions for dollar based investors to hedge long-term RMB risks.

Most previous studies have focused on the one-sided analysis of the RMB, so the conclusions of these studies cannot reflect the complete development of the RMB. In order to explore the high-quality development of the RMB, the author provides a true valuation of the RMB by analyzing various data and papers. In addition, some suggestions will be made for the relevant foreign exchange market.

© The Author(s), under exclusive license to Springer Nature Singapore Pte Ltd. 2024
X. Li et al. (Eds.): ICEMGD 2023, AEPS, pp. 1025–1034, 2024.
https://doi.org/10.1007/978-981-97-0523-8_96

2 The Balance of Payment in China

Since 2020, under the COVID-19 invasion, many of the countries declared emergency. It had a huge influence on the traditional daily trading, therefore, it is quite obvious to see that the uncertainty of the global economic and trade situation has increased significantly. The world is undergoing great changes not seen in a century, countries are supposed to help each other. The common development of all countries is an important foundation for the sustainable development of the world [1].

In these special situations, despite the obstacles in cross-border business and trade activities and the severe turbulence in the financial market, China has continued to unswervingly expand reform and opening up. The cross-border business is an essential medium for the development of foreign economies. The changes in the use of foreign exchange have an important and far-reaching impact on the new pattern of the global monetary system which has majorly relates with data economy and the new era of China's economy.

International balance of payments is a comprehensive reflection of a country's foreign economic activities, and is one of the most important economic indicators for government decision-making in an open economy [1]. In this process, all transactions between residents and non residents are systematically recorded in currency through the balance of payments.

2.1 The Payments of Main Account in Current Account

(See Fig. 1).

As reflected by the red line above, China's current account continues to run a surplus. The green bar represents service trade, the blue bar represents commodity trade, and the purple bar represents original income.

It can be seen from the figure that commodity trade is the biggest determinant of China's current account deficit. The construction of China's "the Belt and Road" and "Silk Road", such as the export of tangible goods such as Chinese wheat and a series of fine textiles, as well as processing trade with Chinese characteristics, is an important driving force for the strong development and internationalization of the RMB.

Service trade includes transportation, tourism, communications, construction, insurance services, as well as commercial services such as consulting and advertising. The deficit narrowed. The revenue from the service trade increased by 48% from 2020 to 2021, reaching 338.4 billion US dollars, and China's service trade revenue also showed a positive trend. The high growth of transportation earnings was a major factor in the transportation deficit's $20.6 billion US decrease (46%). The travel project deficit was $94.4 billion US, a 22% decrease, showing the ongoing effects of the global pandemic on Chinese citizens' cross-border travel. This indicates that the foreign economy, especially those countries with tourism as their main economic source, or those with relatively abundant overseas education industry, has been incredibly hard hit by the epidemic, resulting in the devaluation of foreign currencies. Therefore, even during the relatively difficult epidemic period, compared to previous years' data and foreign economies, the RMB has maintained a certain growth rate, reducing the service trade deficit.

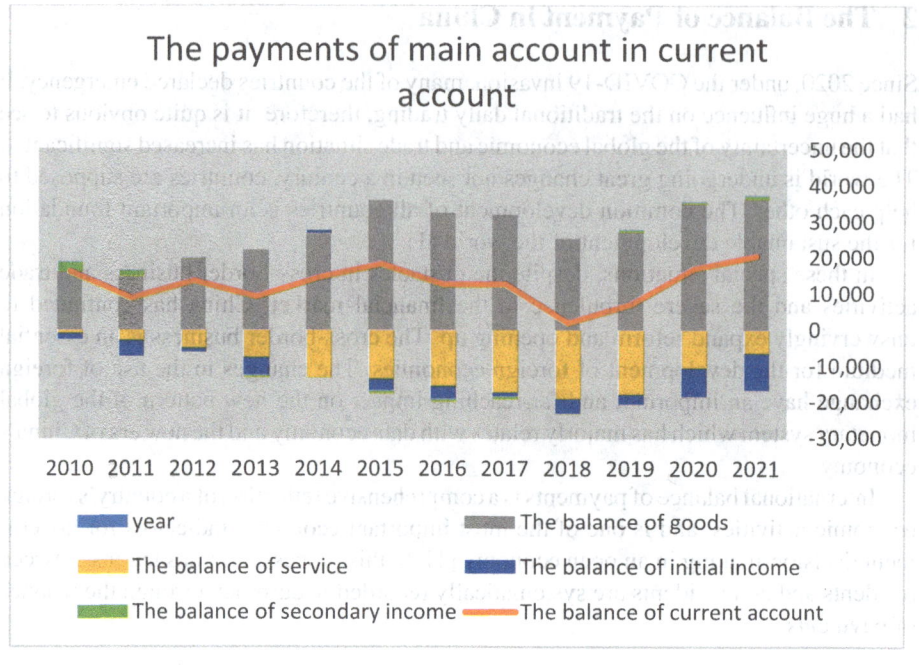

Fig. 1. The payments of main account in current account (100 million yuan) [2].

Initial earnings also showed a deficit. In 2021, the revenue under initial revenue was 274.5 billion US dollars, an increase of 12% compared to 2020. Expenditures amounted to $436.5 billion, an increase of 20% [2]. The deficit is $162 billion.

The amount of direct investment in excess rose. The direct investment surplus in 2001 was US $205.9 billion, compared to US $99.4 billion in 2020, according to statistics on the global balance of payments. China's foreign direct investment is down 17% from 2020 to $128 billion. In light of the epidemic, domestic business mergers and acquisitions and cross-border investment are typically reasonable and well-organized. China's economic growth has continued to be the fastest in the world, and the country's domestic market has become increasingly appealing to foreign capital [2], creating a critical environment for the rapid internationalisation of the RMB. Foreign direct investment in China has increased by 32% to US $334 billion.

As can be seen from the above, the current account has maintained a reasonable and balanced surplus model [1], enabling the RMB to develop rapidly under the promotion of internal and external circulation. The stable operation of China's current account mainly benefits from two factors.

The first is that the domestic processing trade market and supply chain continue to play a role, and foreign trade has achieved significant results in improving quality and efficiency. Currently, China's expanding variety of trading partners, ongoing optimisation of the composition of export commodities, and boosting the vitality of foreign trade operators are all significant guarantees for fostering the RMB's rapid development and further internationalisation [2].

The second is that the global epidemic continues to suppress the import of service trade. In 2021, the overseas epidemic broke out again, and the flow of cross-border personnel was hindered, which determined that consumer spending such as travel in the service trade status continued to decline, and the service trade deficit was at a low level.

3 The Relevant Data of GDP in China

GDP is the final result of the production activities of all permanent residents of a country in a certain period of time. GDP is not only an important value that can reflect CNY, but also an important indicator to measure the economic situation and development level of a country or region.

3.1 Analysis of the GDP in Recent Years

(See Fig. 2).

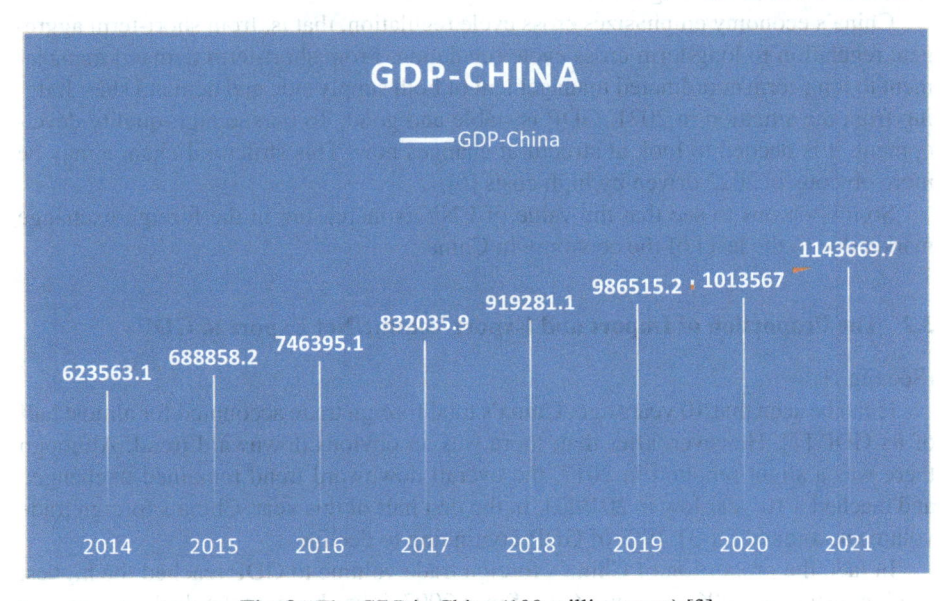

Fig. 2. The GDP in China (100 million yuan) [3].

The graph demonstrates how quickly China's economy has grown in recent years. The GDP increased by 101.36 trillion yuan from 2020 to 2021, or 8.1%, for a year-over-year gain of 2021 over 2020, to reach 114.37 trillion yuan [3].

After the impact of the COVID-19, China's annual GDP growth rate has increased from 2.3% in 2020 to 8.1% in 2021. Generally speaking, it is a relatively stable recovery process.

68.89 trillion yuan is China's economic total in 2014. Since then, China's economy has climbed six 10 trillion yuan steps, reaching 114.4 trillion yuan by 2021, ranking second in the world [4].

2022 is a big year for infrastructure investment [4]. In terms of policy, some investment projects in the 14th five year plan may be advanced to 2022. Various localities are launching large-scale infrastructure construction investment projects. The first batch of investment projects involves 3 trillion yuan, and more cities may launch them later.

The size of the US economy is also quickly nearing that of China. The size difference between China and the United States quickly shrunk from US $9.1 trillion to US $6.2 trillion between 2000 and 2020. Around 2030, China's economy will surpass that of the United States and surpass all other economies worldwide if its economic growth rate exceeds that of the United States in the coming years [5].

China's central economic work conference suggested that further supply-side structural reform is necessary, focusing on opening up all links of production, distribution, circulation, and consumption and removing supply limitations.

"Stability" is the overall situation of China's economy [4]. The central government has always insisted that the overall situation should be stable in the short term, that structural adjustment should be made in the medium term, and that high-quality development should be made in the long term.

China's economy emphasizes cross cycle regulation, that is, from short-term aggregate regulation to long-term cross cycle regulation. From short-term demand management to long-term coordinated management of both supply side and demand side. Judging from the situation in 2021, GDP is stable and good. To pursue high-quality development, it is needed to look at structural changes now. This structural change may be more obvious in 2022 driven by high costs [6].

So it is obious to see that the value of CNY is increasing in the foreign exchange market due to the level of the economy in China.

3.2 The Proportion of Import and Export Volume/Net Export to GDP

(See Fig. 3).

It can be seen that 10 years ago, China's total foreign trade accounted for almost half of its GDP [7]. However, after that, there was an obvious downward trend. Although there was a slight rebound in 2017, the overall downward trend remained unchanged and reached a 10-year low in 2019[2]. In the first half of this year, China's foreign trade volume accounted for 31.19% of GDP, continuing to decline.

In fact, the proportion of China's foreign trade volume to GDP reached the highest level in history in 2006, reaching 64%. Since 2007, it has been on the decline, and now the proportion is less than half of the highest level.

The proportion of China's net exports to GDP has not shown an obvious downward trend, and it has been rising for several years. However, in recent years, there has been a downward trend, and by 2019, it has been lower than the level in 2010. In addition, the highest proportion of China's net exports to GDP was also set in 2006, when the proportion reached 6.4%, more than twice that of now [7].

In the past 10 years, the proportion of China's net exports to GDP has not decreased significantly as the proportion of total foreign trade to GDP, which shows that the growth rate of China's exports in the past 10 years is faster than that of imports [7]. The reason behind this is mainly because the competitiveness of China's commodities in the world

THE PROPORTION OF IMPORT AND EXPORT VOLUMN/NET EXPORT TO GDP

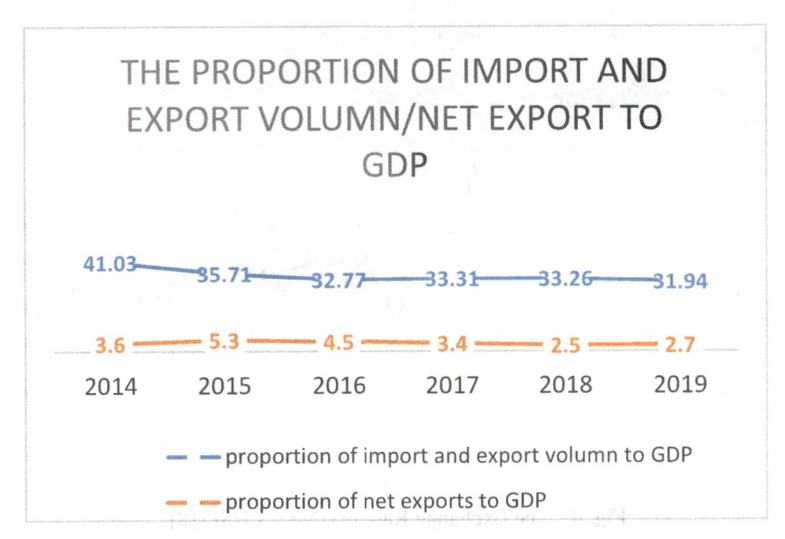

	2014	2015	2016	2017	2018	2019
proportion of import and export volumn to GDP	41.03	35.71	32.77	33.31	33.26	31.94
proportion of net exports to GDP	3.6	5.3	4.5	3.4	2.5	2.7

Fig. 3. The proportion of import and export volume/net export to GDP (100 million yuan) [7].

has become stronger. This is a manifestation of China's economic strength, and does not mean that China's economy has become more dependent on exports.

On the whole, in the past decade or so, the contribution of foreign trade to China's economic growth is declining, which is also in line with the direction of China's economic development. For a large economic country, it is impossible to achieve sustained economic growth by relying on foreign trade. There is no such large market outside China to support the export of goods. If China wants to achieve sustainable economic growth, it must rely on domestic demand.

The world's most populated nation and one with the highest per capita wealth has a lot of potential for boosting domestic demand, nevertheless. Despite having a per capita GDP that is currently just around one-sixth that of the United States, China has virtually caught up with the US in terms of social retail sales thanks to its larger population. It is evident how much room China's consumer growth has to grow. Therefore, completely stimulating China's internal demand may be the most important move to take if China's economy as a whole is to surpass that of the United States in the future.

4 The Exchange Rate in CNY vs USD

(See Fig. 4).

In the past two months, the relatively large changes in the exchange rate of CNY against the US dollar have aroused widespread concern. From the middle of April 2022, there will be a round of rapid depreciation of the CNY exchange rate. On May 16, the onshore CNY exchange rate closed at 6.7967 yuan, a new low since the current round of depreciation. Compared with the closing price on April 19, the accumulated depreciation of CNY exchange rate in this round exceeded 4000 basis points, with a range of more than 6% [9].

Fig. 4. The Exchange Rate in CNY vs USD [8].

Supported by various favorable factors, since May 17, 2022, the CNY exchange rate has stopped falling and rebounded. Among them, on May 17 and 20, the spot exchange rate of the onshore CNY against the US dollar has appreciated 495 and 938 basis points respectively [9]. On May 23, the central parity rate of CNY against the US dollar was raised by 731 points to 6.6756 compared with the previous trading day, the largest one-day increase since July 22, 2005. On May 24, the onshore CNY exchange rate closed at 6.6723 yuan.

According to the Purchasing Power Parity theory, the relative change of the inflation rate will affect the nominal exchange rate. When a country's currency depreciates internally, if the inflation rate of another country's currency remains unchanged, it often means that the currency depreciates externally, so the currency with higher inflation will also face greater possibility of exchange rate depreciation. In the first quarter of 2022, US inflation continued to reach a record high, of 8.5% in March, while China's inflation rate was only 1.5% in the same period. The US China inflation gap was the main factor supporting the resilience of the CNY exchange rate in the first quarter [9]. However, the U.S. CPI has probably peaked in March, and will continue to decline under the influence of the high base and weak core commodity prices. China's CPI is expected to continue to act under the situation of residents' hoarding and blocked supply under the epidemic, and the U.S. - China inflation gap will narrow, thus depressing the nominal exchange rate of RMB.

However, the depreciation of CNY is not a bad deal. The rapid depreciation of the RMB against the US dollar has caused the exchange rate index of the CNY against the CFETS currency basket to drop to about 102, which undoubtedly helps to eliminate the overvaluation of the exchange rate [9].

4.1 Investment in Foreign Exchange Market

(See Fig. 5).

Fig. 5. The Moving-Average Crossover Rules [10].

The introduction of the Moving-Average Crossover Rules is recommended in this section while making investments in the foreign exchange market [10]. Moving-averages of the currency rate are used. The sample average of the previous n trading days, which includes the present rate, is what makes up an n-day moving average. Using averages over both a short time (y days) and a long period (z days), a (y, z) moving-average crossover rule is used [10]. According to the method, one should buy foreign currency when the short-term moving average crosses the long-term moving average seen in the above (below) chart. One and five days (1, 5), one and twenty days (1, 20), and five and twenty days (5, 20) are common rules [10].

The short-run moving average line, which in this instance is the exchange rate itself because a 1-day rule is used, is picked up by the upward trend more quickly in the left-hand portion of the graph and is cut through the long-run moving average line from below, signalling a buy. This graph demonstrates how this happens (Figs. 6, 7 and 8).

Fig. 6. The Real Exchange Rate in USD vs CNY [8].

This figure shows the real exchange rate in USD vs CNY. The author chose the (5, 20). The pink line means the MA5 and the red one represents the MA20. Then just like the sign in the figure, it is supposed to buy CNY at 2022/04/07 and sell at 2022/05/25, which indicates that the investor could receive +5.0457% profits.

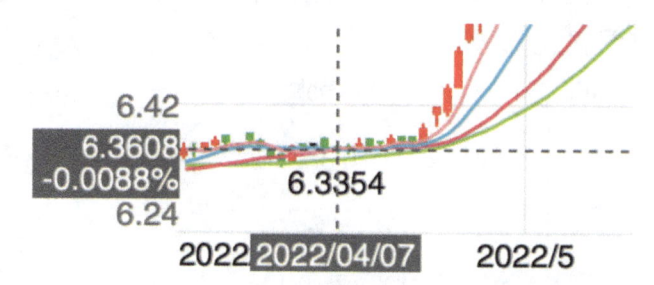

Fig. 7. The Condition in Buy Point [8].

Fig. 8. The Condition in Sell Point [8].

5   Conclusion

As the CNY is keeping its way to nationalizing, it becomes the strong power in the global trade market. Morever, it is needed to consider various panels relating to the currency as well as the power of China due to the formal data published by China's government.

International balance of payments is a comprehensive reflection of a country's foreign economic activities. In China, the service trade deficit narrowed while the initial income showed a deficit. Furthermore, the secondary income continued to run a small surplus and the direct investment surplus increased. And the current account maintained a reasonable and balanced surplus pattern which shows that the CNY is experiencing a stable appreciate in the mainland.

As introducing the proportion of import and export volume/net export to GDP, this part of data shows China's total foreign trade. For a large economic country, it is impossible to achieve sustained economic growth by relying on foreign trade. Though the contribution of foreign trade to China's economic growth is declining, there is no such large market outside China to support the export of goods. Therefore, it can reflect how esssential CNY is in the foreign trade.

The final study of the exchange rate can directly view the valuation of CNY when competing with USD at accurate moment. Then the following stocking method in foreign exchange market is quite practical when investing or change currency if it is needed.

There is one way of further improvement in this paper. First, when introducing the balance of payments, people pay little attention to the capital account, which reflects the purchases and sales of foreign assets by domestic residents and domestic assets by foreigners. Having considered the proportion of import and export volume/net export to GDP could simultaneously represent the foreign trade. If this part of content could be added in further study, it can give a more expansive view on the foreign market.

Also, the author only uses data from other studies. If any first-hand data is added, by testing the moving-average crossline rule, it could have helped readers process more clearly and the research more reliable.

Although CNY is experiencing depreciation in the second quarter of 2022, CNY is still powerful in the foreign exchange market due to the strong power of China's economy. With the introduction of the concept of "community with a shared future for mankind" by China, all of us can look forward to the development of CNY in the future.

References

1. Nan, L.: Steadily promoting RMB internationalization under the background of sustainable balance of payments. Banker (12), 73–75 (2020)
2. International balance of payments analysis group of the State Administration of foreign exchange (2022). The balance of payments in China. http://www.gov.cn/shuju/2022-03/25/5681503/files/23d8bc8aaf2347ddb0639de76ea3a11f.pdf
3. The class of mothers. Analysis of China's gross domestic product (GDP), GDP structure and per capita GDP in 2021 (2022). https://www.163.com/dy/article/GVRKAAR10526PA5O.html
4. Zhang, H.: China's GDP growth rate is expected to be around 8% this year, and it is expected to become a moderately developed country around 2035. Daily economic news (006) (2021)
5. Gao, Y.: Where does China's GDP continue to grow in 2022? CPPCC news (014) (2022)
6. Zhou, X.: In 2021, China's GDP exceeded 110 trillion yuan, and the stable growth policy promoted the smooth start of the first quarter of this year. 21st century economic report (002) (2022)
7. Feng, J.: What is the proportion of the China's foreign trade in GDP (2022). https://www.fengjinwei.com/blog-1101847.html
8. https://finance.sina.com.cn/money/forex/hq/CNYUSD.shtml
9. Pay attention to the trend of RMB exchange rate. Chin. Chief Accountant (05), 186–187 (2022)
10. Bekaert, G., Hodrick, R.: International Financial Management, p. 418. Cambridge University Press, Cambridge (2018)

Research on Business Value Assessment Model for New Generation Star

Ziyi Xing(✉)

School of Mathematical Sciences, Tianjin Normal University, Tianjin 300387, China
2030050142@stu.tjnu.edu.cn

Abstract. The popularity and hotness of new-generation TV series stars are important influencing factors for project investment and financing and commercial endorsement. In this paper, we address the market demand and field gap issues and literature research of artist evaluation and establish a commercial value evaluation model of new generation TV series stars. By investigating the necessity of various aspects required for artist evaluation, four dimensions of popularity, professionalism, endorsement, and image are constructed. Since Baidu, Tencent, and Sina have already achieved certain results in index heat using big data technology, this paper takes into full consideration the audience's habit of expressing opinions using new media platforms such as search engines, microblogs, and WeChat, and adopts the entropy value method to process the data, thus constructing a new generation This paper adopts the entropy method to process the data, and then constructs a new generation of TV stars' commercial value index evaluation system, which provides a reference tool for management decision and risk control. To test the model, Chinese new-generation TV actors were selected as an example for the experiment, and the four dimensions were analyzed separately by substituting them into the model calculation. From the experimental results, it can be seen that the assessment results of the artist assessment model are consistent with the mainstream assessment results in the market, which verifies the validity of the artist assessment model in assessing artists in all aspects.

Keywords: New Generation Star · Business Value · Index Evaluation System · Entropy method

1 Introduction

1.1 Introduction

With the rapid development of the data society, various industries are also innovating and integrating, and the development trends of station network linkage and multi-screen interaction have made data quantification, mining, and analysis an important support and driving force for the upgrading and transformation of various links in the industrial value chain. The popularity of the stars largely represents the commercial value of the whole project, and it has become a common practice for project investors and advertisers to use stars with high fan popularity and appeal as much as possible. The huge fan base

© The Author(s), under exclusive license to Springer Nature Singapore Pte Ltd. 2024
X. Li et al. (Eds.): ICEMGD 2023, AEPS, pp. 1035–1042, 2024.
https://doi.org/10.1007/978-981-97-0523-8_97

and brand effect accumulated by the stars are closely related to the scale of investment and financing that the project can attract. In the professional field, producers need to find artists with outstanding abilities to participate in their works, and in the commercial field, there is a constant demand for artists' market appeal. Therefore, a comprehensive and systematic analysis and evaluation of artists is necessary.

1.2 Related Research

Wang has sorted out the assessment methods of sports stars' commercial value at home and abroad and established a framework for the ex-ante assessment, ex-post assessment, and ex-post assessment of sports stars' commercial value based on consumer psychological changes. However, no quantitative assessment of sports stars' commercial value has been conducted [1]. Zhang added a second identity, that is, the identity of the star agent (including economic companies, brokers, agents, cooperation companies, etc.) combined with the identity of third parties (including but not limited to credible institutions, fan groups, market demand, etc.) to establish a star value evaluation system, extending the cost method, market comparison method, and income method in brand value evaluation, but no quantitative evaluation model is given [2]. Su applied the AHP method to systematically evaluate the value of artists, using the weighted average method, the concatenated multiplication method, and the mixed method to assign indicators and establish an index model to evaluate the value of artists. Ten Chinese actors were also selected for a comprehensive evaluation, and the assessment results were in line with the general public perception [3].

Zhao selected the real-time Baidu index, Weibo index, and WeChat index, and processed the data using the assumption of a normal distribution to calculate the Chinese top ten scored male and female TV series lead actor popularity composite scores. A quantitative approach was used to study the popularity index assessment system of TV drama lead actors [4]. Li and Chen believe that celebrities have personal brand values. They analyzed the characteristics of celebrity personal brand value assessment, and adjust the evaluation factors based on the Interbrand model as a way to assess celebrity personal brand value [5]. Han and Ki developed a measure of celebrity reputation, which was analyzed through questionnaires, and exploratory and confirmatory factors. Key dimensions were derived to evaluate different components of celebrity reputation, including personality, relationships, appearance, expert abilities, private life management, and reputation [6].

Based on the research data, Hu applied the AHP and KSF evaluation methods to screen the indicators of sports star brands, determine the corresponding weights, construct the evaluation index system, and conduct targeted and operable analysis of star brands [7]. Zhou and Bai used an 18-month ethnographic study of several fan communities and found that in the social media environment, the endorsement of emerging stars is no longer a linear transmission process of celebrity endorsement of brands, but a dynamic cycle of value creation among the three actors: fan community-brand-celebrity. A new mechanism of celebrity endorsement is revealed [8]. Yang and Xia conducted an empirical study on the relationship between the celebrity effect and consumer brand loyalty in branded Weibo based on the consumer integration perspective. The relationship between celebrity effect and brand loyalty on Weibo has a significant positive effect on consumer integration and brand loyalty, and consumer integration has a significant positive effect on brand loyalty [9]. Wang and Zhang took the problem of enterprise technology innovation capability evaluation ranking as an empirical example and did a comparative study on the credibility of the Delphi method, hierarchical analysis method, full value method, and fuzzy cluster analysis method to determine the evaluation index weights [10].

1.3 Objective

It is easy to see that the above star value assessment framework has the characteristics of system theory, treating star value as a complete closed-loop system and assessing one or more parts of the process separately, facilitating the systematic integration of fragmented measurement and evaluation. However, the shortcomings are also obvious, as it fails to further start from the relevant theories of cybernetics, and mostly focuses on performance, competitiveness, and other fields, and the assessment of people is only for specific groups such as sports stars, lacking systematic assessment and analysis of artists as a whole. To fill the gap in this field, this paper will build an assessment index system centering on new-generation TV actors, and conduct a comprehensive systematic assessment of them to effectively control the marketing risk, this paper will construct an evaluation index system focusing on new-generation TV actors and conduct a comprehensive systematic evaluation of them. To verify the effectiveness of the evaluation model, we will select examples and conduct experiments.

2 Celebrity Value Evaluation System

2.1 Determination of Evaluation Indicators

The FRDD Criteria Are Familiarity, Relevance, Esteem, Differentiation, and Deportment. It is believed that celebrities must be trustworthy, highly visible, responsible, less controversial, and compatible with their target audience. The classical meaning transfer model (MTM) suggests that when a company chooses a suitable celebrity to endorse a product, the celebrity's attributes will be transferred to the product and the consumer's attitude towards the endorsed product will then change, leading to purchase intentions and behavior, thus the value of the celebrity is transferred from the product to the consumer, who is the passive endpoint. With celebrity endorsements becoming increasingly common, fan communities are becoming an increasingly important factor in the performance of endorsements. Fan communities are becoming productive organizations, investing their own consumption and communication labor as productive resources to improve the performance of celebrity endorsements. Because of the prevalence of the fan economy, this paper establishes the popularity index, the professional index, the endorsement index, and the image index as the criteria for evaluation. It is also broken down into 8 specific indicators as shown in Table 1.

Table 1. The specific indicators in four indexes.

Index	Indicators
Popularity	Awareness
	Fanbase
Professional	Quality of work
	Awards
Endorsement	Number of endorsements
	Quality of endorsements
Image	Public welfare
	Lifestyle

The higher the popularity index, the more "traffic" the star can drive, the more influence it has on social media and fan communities, and the greater the familiarity of society and fans, the greater the commercial value of the star. The Professional Index consists of two indicators: the quality of their work and the awards they have received. They can be subdivided into TV stars, movie stars, singers, idols internet celebrities, etc. The higher the quality of their work and the more awards they have received in their field of expertise, the higher their Professional Index. The endorsement index includes both the number of endorsements and the quality of endorsements. In the era of the fan economy, advertisers pay more attention to the additive effect of fan productivity on celebrity popularity and commercial endorsements when choosing a spokesperson. The image index includes public welfare activities and lifestyle. Stars have great influence in society, and their image is closely related to their usual words, actions, and public welfare activities, when the positive image of a star is deeply rooted in people's hearts, the higher the social recognition of that star.

2.2 Determination of the Evaluation Method

After the evaluation indicators are selected, how to assign values to the indicators is the basis of quantitative assessment. There are various methods for assigning values to the indicators, the most commonly used are two major types: subjective assignment method and objective assignment method. The subjective assignment method takes a qualitative approach, and the weights are obtained by subjective judgment, which is relatively simple to operate but is highly subjective, has no unified objective standards, and is influenced by human factors, such as hierarchical analysis, fuzzy evaluation method, Delphi technique, weighted index method, and efficacy coefficient method. The objective weighting method is based on the weighted index method and the efficacy coefficient method. The objective weighting method is based on the correlation coefficient or coefficient of variation between the indicators to determine the weights, the evaluation results are relatively accurate, and multiple indicators need to be integrated through certain mathematical formulas or models to obtain an overall evaluation model, the evaluation method of indicator weights in this paper is the entropy weighting method. Splayed equations are centered and set on a separate line.

2.3 The Process of the Entropy Method

Data Normalisation. To eliminate the effects of differences in scale and order of magnitude, and to ensure the reliability of the results and the comparability of the data, the extreme value method was used to standardize the positive and negative indicators in the evaluation index system respectively. The formulae are as follows:

$$x_{ij}^{(1)} = \frac{x_{ij} - x_{min}}{x_{max} - x_{min}} \tag{1}$$

$$x_{ij}^{(1)} = \frac{x_{max} - x_{ij}}{x_{max} - x_{min}} \tag{2}$$

$x_{ij}^{(1)}$ is the standardized index value, x_{ij} is the raw data of the jth indicator of the ith star, x_{max} and x_{min} are separately the maximum and minimum values of the jth index.

To eliminate the effect of negative and zero values, the normalized data are appropriately panned. The equation after the translation is as follows:

$$y_{ij} = x_{ij}^{(1)} + K \tag{3}$$

y_{ij} is the value of the index after leveling, K is the indicator panning range.

Determine the Index Weight. The entropy method uses the degree of variation of each indicator to obtain the indicator weights, which can avoid the subjectivity of weight determination and the overlap of information among multiple indicator variables, increase the discriminative meaning and variability of indicators, and provide an objective basis for the evaluation process. The specific steps for calculating the weight of each indicator of star value using the entropy method are as follows:

Calculate the weight of the indicator y_{ij}

$$P_{ij} = \frac{y_{ij}}{\sum_{i=1}^{n} y_{ij}} \tag{4}$$

Calculate the entropy value of the jth indicator

$$e_j = -k \sum_{i=1}^{n} p \ln p_{ij} \quad k = \frac{1}{\ln n} \tag{5}$$

Calculate the coefficient of variation of the jth indicator

$$g_i = 1 - e_j \tag{6}$$

Calculate the weight of the jth indicator w_j

$$w_j = \frac{g_i}{\sum_{j=1}^{m} g_i} \tag{7}$$

Comprehensive Evaluation Index Calculation. Calculate the composite score of each star's value:

$$s_i = \sum_{j=1}^{m} g_i x_{ij} \tag{8}$$

According to Eqs. (1) to (8), the value composite index of the star i is obtained.

3 Experimental Study

3.1 Data Sources

The sample for this article was selected from 10 new-generation post-90s stars who have been active in the Chinese TV drama industry in recent years. The data for the indicators mainly came from more than 10 professional data output platforms such as Baidu, Sina, WeChat, Douban, AiMan Data, Detawen, Seeking Art, and Bone Data, which have high user activity and a large amount of data available for quantitative calculation. The main contents covered are public attention, media attention, star fan power, brand endorsement, search volume, media news coverage, public welfare activities, and public welfare organizations, etc., covering data sources for each element of star value assessment and specific analysis of the data for each indicator in Table 2.

Table 2. Data sources of each indicator.

Indicators	Data sources
Awareness	Search volume
Fanbase	Weibo followers
Quality of work	Representative work rating
Awards	Prestigious awards in the industry
Number of endorsements	Product endorsement status
Quality of endorsements	
Public welfare	Public service activities and donations
Lifestyle	Any life scandals

3.2 Result Analysis

According to the experimental study conducted by the above evaluation method, the value ranking results of these ten Chinese post-90s new-generation actors and actresses are in Table 3.

The top-ranked stars share characteristics such as having starred in phenomenal TV series, being highly recognized by the public and experts, having quickly accumulated a large fan base and a fan community that is actively engaged in the production of star value, having a longer acting age, having a better number and quality of endorsements, being passionate about charity work and performing well in all aspects, and can be described as quality artists who develop in all aspects;

The stars in the middle of the ranking are less experienced due to their short-acting age, but high popularity, fast growth in value performance, high reliance on brands, and easy renewal between groups. Their superb popularity makes them perform better in the endorsement index, but they rank slightly lower in the professional index due to their

Table 3. Chinese new-generation actors and actresses.

RANK	NAME	SCORE	YeonRANK
1	XZ	0.680846864	5
2	WYB	0.599054439	4
3	DLRB	0.539553598	7
4	YZ	0.439688535	2
5	WHD	0.38520963	8
6	YSX	0.333938451	6
7	WJK	0.310133395	9
8	YY	0.308336624	10
9	ZLS	0.26969221	1
10	GJ	0.215507166	3

lack of professional accumulation, young age and social experience, and insufficient quantity and quality of their works.

Among them, although YY has appeared in phenomenal TV series, it has been around for a long time, and although it has a high fan base, the fan community is less active, Making the star's effectiveness as a spokesperson volatile throughout for his career, leading to a decline in commercial value.

Comparing the commercial value of these top 10 post-90s drama actors released by Yeon Data in 2023, we can see that ZLS and GJ have moved up in rank from 9 and 10 to 1 and 3. Since both stars have had phenomenal hit dramas in the recent past, they have accumulated huge fans in a short period of time and the resulting commercial endorsement quantity and quality have increased significantly. Although they have not won mainstream awards and stable word of mouth, the increase in popularity index and endorsement index has increased the overall commercial value score, and we can launch that the popularity index and endorsement index in Yien data have contributed to the commercial value of new generation stars The popularity index and endorsement index contribute more to the commercial value of new generation stars.

4 Conclusion

From the practical point of view, advertisers have gradually changed from the traditional "looking for the most suitable spokesperson" to "looking for the most popular spokesperson", and the products endorsed by popular celebrities are more likely to attract public attention in terms of publicity and buzz, which has a great impact on the initial sales and brand image of the products. This has a great impact on the initial sales and brand image. In this paper, we address the market demand and the gap in the field of artist evaluation by investigating the necessity of various aspects required for artist evaluation, constructing four dimensions of popularity, professionalism, endorsement, and image, and using the entropy value method to assign weights based on the study of various index assignment methods, to build a complete model of Chinese artist evaluation index. To test the model, Chinese new generation TV drama actors were selected as an example for experiments, substituted into the model calculation, and analyzed the four dimensions separately. From the experimental results, it can be seen that the assessment results of the artist assessment model are consistent with the mainstream market assessment results, which verifies the validity of this artist assessment model for the all-around assessment of artists. In addition, this method can be applied to analyze the market influence of movie stars, singers, idols, and internet celebrities to help advertisers obtain sufficient data information to select the most suitable spokesperson, providing richer talent information and hot resources for product awareness enhancement, brand image improvement and consumer purchase intention strengthening.

References

1. Wang, G.: A study on the construction of the evaluation framework of the commercial value of the sport stars. J. Beijing Sport Univ. **32**(12), 38–41 (2009)
2. Zhang, Q.: An analysis of star value assessment. J. Ethnic Music **2**, 76–78 (2013)
3. Su, P., Tin, F., Xie, L., Liao, J.: A study of the Chinese artist evaluation index model. China New Telecommun. **18**(24), 142–145 (2016)
4. Zhao, D.: Research on the evaluation system of TV drama main actor popularity index. Southeast Commun. **3**, 100–102 (2018)
5. Li, X., Chen, X.: Exploring the personal brand value of celebrities based on the Interbrand model. Market Modernization Mag. **6**, 20–22 (2022)
6. Han, E., Ki, E.-J.: Developing a measure of celebrity reputation. Public Relat. Rev. **36**(2), 199–201 (2010)
7. Hu, X.: Construction and evaluation analysis of sport star brand value index system based on KSF method. Bull. Sports Sci. Technol. **27**(12), 12–15 (2019)
8. Zhou, Y., Bai, M.: The value co-creation mechanism of celebrity endorsement: netnography of multiple fan communities. Foreign Econ. Manag. **43**(1), 3–22 (2021)
9. Meng, Y., Xiahou, S.: Empirical study on the relationship between celebrity effect and consumers' brand loyalty—from the perspective of customer engagement. J. Chongqing Univ. Arts Sci. (Soc. Sci. Ed.) **39**(2), 43–52 (2020)
10. Wang, J., Zhang, J.: Comparing several methods of assuring weight vector in synthetical evaluation. J. Hebei Univ. Technol. (02), 52–57 (2001)

Fiduciary Duty Regime of Private Fund Managers: Insights from the US Regulatory Experience

Jia Cheng(✉)

Law School, Hunan University, Lu Shan Nan Road, Changsha 410000, China
jessiecheng0713@foxmail.com

Abstract. With the continuous development of China's financial market, private equity (PE) funds are playing an increasingly important role in the financial and investment sectors. The fiduciary duties of PE fund managers, who play a central role in the PE market, are of vital importance to the orderly development of the market and the protection of investors' interests. This article will adopt a comparative research method to explore the connotation and characteristics of the fiduciary duties of PE fund managers, analysis the problems of the fiduciary duties of PE fund managers under China's current legal framework and put forward corresponding suggestions for improvement, with a view to promoting the sustainable and compliant development of the PE industry.

Keywords: Private Equity Funds · Asset Management · Fund Managers · Fiduciary Duties

1 Introduction

In recent years, with the development of China's economy and the continuous opening of the financial market, the private equity (PE) fund investment market has developed rapidly. PE funds have flexible investment strategies and high return potential, but while they attract capital market participants, they also lay down many potential risks. Firstly, as PE funds often invest in unlisted companies, the lack of transparency in the disclosure of information about these companies makes them vulnerable to misconduct such as insider trading. In addition, many PE fund managers are also exposed to undesirable moral risks, such as misappropriation of funds and false advertising [1].

Against this background, how to regulate the PE fund market and prevent and mitigate risks in order to protect the interests of investors has become an issue of common concern for regulators and market participants. The difficulties and focus of these risks are focused on the regulation of fund managers, which are the key entities responsible for the investment management of PE funds [2].

PE fund managers are responsible for managing and operating PE funds to achieve asset appreciation and generate returns for investors. At the same time, private fund managers should also assume the relevant fiduciary duties to protect the interests of investors. However, under China's current legal framework, there are still problems and shortcomings in the fiduciary duty regime for PE fund managers, which require further strengthening of regulation and improvement of the fiduciary duty-related regime [3].

2 Overview of the Fiduciary Duties of Private Fund Managers

2.1 Content and Characteristics of Fiduciary Duties

As the core manager of a PE fund, the PE fund manager must comply with the corresponding fiduciary obligations in all aspects of fundraising, investment, management and exit, i.e. to serve investors faithfully and prudently and protect their interests, including but not limited to: faithfully fulfilling contractual agreements, making investments and obtaining maximum returns in accordance with the requirements of funders; complying with relevant laws and regulations and compliance requirements to ensure investment activities to comply with the relevant laws and regulations and compliance requirements to ensure that investment activities are legal and compliant; to treat contributors in good faith and protect their legitimate rights and interests; to strengthen internal controls to prevent internal risks and misconduct; to enhance information disclosure and provide contributors with necessary investment information to help them fully understand the fund's investments and make informed decisions, etc. [4].

The fiduciary duties of a PE fund manager include the duty of loyalty and the duty of care [5]. The duty of loyalty requires that PE fund managers should manage PE funds in good faith and should not engage in self-dealing, connected transactions or misappropriation of fund property that conflicts with the interests of investors. The purpose of the duty of loyalty is to prevent conflicts of interest, requiring the manager to safeguard the interests of the fund and its investors and not to use the fund's property for the benefit of himself or others other than the investors, the core of which is to prevent conflicts of interest and prohibit abuse of rights [6]. The duty of care requires a PE fund manager to exercise reasonable care in the conduct of its management, to devote sufficient effort and to make appropriate actions or decisions after being fully informed of all material information reasonably available at the time of the conduct. This includes the duty to invest prudently, the duty to manage personally, the duty to operate in compliance, the duty to keep proper records and reports, and the duty to liquidate. The Manager, as a body composed of professionals entrusted with the management of money on behalf of others, should have the knowledge, competence and experience normally expected of professionals in respect of the matters entrusted to them.

The fiduciary duty is based on a fiduciary relationship between the parties, where one party is the principal and the other is the fiduciary. The fiduciary relationship between the two parties within a PE fund, the investor and the PE fund manager, is typical. Based on the trust in the manager's business ability and professional conduct, the investor gives all the property and power to the manager and no longer enjoys control over the property; the manager provides professional asset management services and enjoys full control over the property; however, the manager may abuse its power and neglect to provide services for its own benefit and to the detriment of the investor [7]. It is difficult for investors to hedge such risks and protect their interests entirely by agreement and in the market, and private law rules of a mandatory nature are needed to govern the behaviour of fund managers.

Firstly, although the duty of loyalty presents itself as a negative duty of omission, while the duty of care focuses on a positive duty, neither of them, as a whole, constitutes a fiduciary duty, and therefore there is considerable scope for interpretation in determining the boundaries of the fiduciary duty.

Secondly, although fiduciary duties are essentially statutory obligations, when they come into play, they are often based on contractual obligations such as investment fund contracts. In practice, the basis for fiduciary duties is found in various laws, regulations and industry self-regulatory documents, but even though they are so widely available, they must ultimately be presented by way of agreement, and it is practically impossible to exhaust all agreements on fiduciary duties in advance.

Thirdly, in Article 94 of The Minutes of the National Court Work Conference for Civil and Commercial Trials (Law [2019] No. 254) (The Minutes) issued by the Supreme People's Court of China, it is stipulated that "if a principal of an asset management product requests the trustee to bear damages on the grounds that the trustee has failed to fulfill its obligations such as diligence and fair treatment of customers, which damage its legitimate rights and interests If the trustee fails to prove that it has fulfilled its obligations, the trustee shall prove that it has fulfilled its obligations. If the fiduciary cannot prove it and the principal requests it to bear the corresponding liability, the people's court shall support it in accordance with the law" [8]. In other words, for the judgment of the performance of fiduciary duty, the law affirms the reversal of the burden of proof, that is, if the PE fund manager has no evidence to prove that it has fully performed its fiduciary duty, it should bear the corresponding legal responsibility for its breach of trust. Therefore, the reversal of the burden of proof is also one of the typical features of the fiduciary duty regulatory path.

2.2 The Necessity of Fiduciary Duties to Regulate Private Fund Managers

By analysing the relevant adjudication cases of domestic PE disputes in recent years, we can clearly understand that PE fund managers have certain moral risks in the process of investment, which need to be strengthened and regulated. However, there are still obvious inadequacies in adjusting the legal relationship of PE funds using only the existing adjustment mechanism.

Firstly, the use of contract law to regulate fiduciary relationships in investment management is inadequate. Funds of all organisational forms are subject to the moral hazard of manager abuse and laziness and negligence. Investors entrust fund managers with the management of their investments, and good or bad management depends on the professionalism and due diligence of the manager, which is difficult to observe directly. For this reason, due to the limited rationality of human beings, the asymmetry of information and capacity of both parties and the complex and volatile nature of the private investment business environment, it is difficult for contract law, which is only used to regulate equal legal subjects, to play a full role in regulating and binding the legal relationship of private funds [9].

Secondly, In the legal relationship of PE funds, the fund manager has almost all the power to manage and operate the fund. How to prevent abuse of the manager's power and protect the interests of investors is the core of legal regulation. Fiduciary duties provide the most appropriate framework. However, the parties to PE funds are sophisticated and professional market participants who are concerned with privacy and market autonomy, and the intervention of public law should be restrained and passive. In the private law arena, where the regulatory effect of contract law is already insufficient and the regulation and adjustment of public law must remain modest, fiduciary duties can play an important role in filling the legal regulatory gap.

3 The Fiduciary Duties of Private Equity Fund Managers in China's Current Legislation

3.1 Laws and Regulations in the Field of Private Equity

China's legal regulatory system for PE funds is dominated by laws and regulations and supplemented by the self-regulatory system of industry associations [10]. 2003 Securities Investment Fund Law provides for the obligations of fund managers for securities investment funds as a matter of principle, and the 2012 amendments added provisions for PE funds, but as the regulatory authority of PE funds had not been determined at the time of the legislation, PE funds still do not fall within the Fund Law. It was not until August 2014 that the SFC issued the Interim Measures for the Supervision and Administration of Private Investment Funds, in which Article 4 provides in principle the obligations of fund managers "shall exercise due diligence and fulfill the obligations of honesty, credit, prudence and diligence. Practitioners of PE funds shall comply with laws and administrative regulations and abide by professional ethics and codes of conduct". In December 2014, the Securities Investment Fund Association issued the Self-Regulatory Code of Conduct for Fund Practitioners, which regulates the conduct of practitioners through industry self-regulatory codes and generally establishes a system for regulating the conduct of PE fund managers in China.

Generally, the laws and regulations on which the regulation of PE funds in China is based include the Securities Law, the Securities Investment Fund Law, the Company Law, the Partnership Law and the Interim Measures for the Supervision of Private Investment Funds. Among them, the Securities Law and the Securities Investment Fund Law clarify the legal status of PE funds and are the basic law for the healthy development of PE funds; the Company Law and the Partnership Law provide organizational protection for PE fund management institutions; the Interim Measures for the Supervision of PE Funds provide comprehensive regulation in terms of PE fund registration and filing, fund raising, investment operation, qualified investors, industry self-regulation, supervision and management, legal liability, etc. [11].

As for the self-regulation of PE funds, a general framework of "7 + 2" has been established for self-regulation by industry associations, including seven measures on fund raising, registration and filing, information disclosure, investment advisory business, outsourcing service management, custody business and qualification management, as well as internal control guidelines and fund contract guidelines [12].

In terms of the regulation and enforcement of PE funds, China is currently based on moderate regulation. In recent years, securities regulators have strengthened the supervision and enforcement of PE funds and increased administrative supervision and self-regulatory discipline to effectively prevent and mitigate the risks of PE funds.

3.2 Current Status and Deficiencies of the Application of the Fiduciary Duty Regime

Guiding Opinions on Regulating Asset Management Business of Financial Institutions (the "New Regulation on Asset Management") jointly issued by the People's Bank of China, the CBRC and the State Administration of Foreign Exchange on 27 April 2018 confirms for the first time in a regulatory document the fiduciary obligations that financial institutions must fulfill in their asset management business [13]. However, the regulation of fiduciary duties in asset management business in China is still not satisfactory. In terms of effect, China has not clarified whether the fiduciary duty regulation is arbitrary or mandatory, and judicial practice is inconsistent in determining this; in terms of content, the existing laws only provide general provisions on the fiduciary duty, which are too general and the relevant regulations are of low rank, making it difficult to play a role in the overall situation of the industry; in terms of system, the provisions on the fiduciary duty of capital management institutions are scattered in the Commercial Bank Law, the Trust Law and other laws. Due to the long-standing mode of separate regulation of China's financial industry, the regulation of fiduciary duties inevitably suffers from legislative omissions, duplication of provisions and inconsistent implementation of laws.

The introduction of Article 88 of The Minutes is seen as an important turning point in the characterisation of the legal relationship of asset management business. Prior to this, the legal relationship of asset management business was more often characterised as a fiduciary legal relationship, where the manager only assumed fiduciary obligations according to the contract. Article 88 of The Minutes clarifies that the essence of asset management business is "being entrusted by others and managing their wealth on their behalf", and its product structure is basically consistent with that of a trust. The nature of the underlying legal relationship. In the context of this change in legal characterisation, investors have found another route to exit the project, namely: claiming that the administrator has failed to fulfil its fiduciary obligations, pursuing the administrator's liability and recovering their investment.

The change in the characterisation of the legal relationship by the Supreme People's Court has its deep reflection on the regulation of the financial order [14]. Under the fiduciary relationship, the administrator is not only subject to contractual agreements, but also to statutory obligations such as due diligence, and in this context the market reaction has gradually become apparent. This is evidenced by the large number of claims by investors for improper performance of the administrator's duties.

Despite the above application of the duty of good faith in legislation and judicial practice, the connotation of the duty of good faith is not specifically reflected at the level of laws and normative legal documents, and different normative legal documents use such overly broad expressions as the administrator should assume the duty of "honesty, credit and diligence" [15]. The circumstances and boundaries of the application of the duty of good faith still need to be refined through judicial precedents.

4 Fiduciary Obligations of Private Fund Managers in the US Legal Perspective

4.1 The Legal Regulation and Practice of Fiduciary Duties

As one of the most mature PE markets in the world, the regulatory experience of the US is worth learning from. A systematic analysis of the fiduciary duties of fund managers in the US PE regulatory regime can help us better understand its regulatory mechanism and practical experience and provide us with references for formulating corresponding reform proposals.

The US enacted the Securities Act and the Securities Exchange Act in 1933 and 1934 to build a regulatory system with information disclosure as its core. However, with the continued development of the financial market, the regulatory instruments based on information disclosure obligations were no longer sufficient to effectively regulate the conduct of investment companies. As a result, the US law, in order to protect the interests of investors and to address the inherent conflict of interest in the investment management industry, built a regulatory system based on the disclosure system with the fiduciary duty as the core, and the Investment Companies Act and the Investment Advisers Act were enacted at the federal level in 1940. The Investment Companies Act is regarded as the cornerstone of the investment fund industry and the asset management industry [16].

Today, the regulation of investment practices in the US has developed a regulatory system that includes federal and state financial and securities regulatory laws, SEC rules, and state commercial organizations laws. Among them, the legal regulations related to investment funds are mainly concentrated in the Securities Act, the Securities Exchange Act, the Investment Company Act, the Investment Advisers Act and the Dodd-Frank Wall Street Reform and Consumer Act of 2010. The determination of rights and obligations between managers and investors is scattered throughout the Investment Advisers Act of 1940, which treats the anti-fraud provisions as a general constraint, and in legal provisions such as the Employee Retirement Income Security Act of 1974 (ERISA), the Uniform Prudent Investor Act of 1995 (UPIA), and the Uniform Trust Code of 2003.

In addition, as a case law country, the application of the fiduciary duty rule in the US is more often reflected in judicial precedent [17]. For example, in a series of financial consumer lawsuits arising from the subprime mortgage crisis, many decisions were based on the doctrine of fraud, using the duty of good faith as the basis for judicial discretion.

By doing so, US law specifies the fiduciary obligations of fund managers to protect the interests of investors, avoid conflicts of interest and disclose necessary information, and regulates them through the SEC and other regulatory bodies to ensure the lawful operation of fund managers and the transparency of their investment activities [18].

It is easy to see from the development of the regulation of investment institutions and PE funds in the US that although the lax attitude of the law towards the regulation of PE funds for a period of time has to a certain extent met the needs of the rapid development of the PE investment market [19], with the expansion and complexity of the investment business, if there are no corresponding measures to regulate them, the legitimate interests of investors are bound to receive damage, and even the integrity of the investment market and society as a whole will be shaken.

4.2 Insights from the US Fiduciary Duty Regime on the Regulation of Private Equity Funds in China

The US capital markets are a bottom-up market system that has been characterized by market autonomy since its inception. Compared with the US, the legal framework foundation and supporting system required for the healthy and orderly development of China's PE industry is generally lagging behind the current development of the industry. If we simply borrow from the US regulatory experience without considering our own legal system, economic development, cultural environment and other backgrounds, it is easy to form regulatory failures and bring about regulatory arbitrage by a large number of market institutions. Therefore, learning from advanced foreign experience must be based on the actual situation of China's capital market.

Firstly, the overall design of the US legal system has resulted in a very strict logic between the different laws, with consistent standards, effectively preventing regulatory arbitrage. For example, the US qualified investor system is a system that covers all types of securities, whereas the current laws in the Chinese capital market are not closely related, and currently there is only a certain system established for qualified investors in PE funds, but the system of qualified investor systems in other securities areas does not yet have legal applicability [20].

Secondly, to ensure strict enforcement. According to the US Dodd-Frank Act, the US Securities and Exchange Commission applies to private fund managers of a certain size or above the regulatory measures for public fund managers, and once an investment adviser is found to sell private products to unqualified investors, heavy penalties are imposed. At present, China's PE fund managers raise funds from unqualified investors mainly based on departmental regulations "Interim Measures for the Supervision and Administration of Private Investment Funds" for punishment, rarely based on the "Securities Investment Fund Law" Article 128, Article 136 to make punishment for illegal fund raising, resulting in weak punishment [21].

Thirdly, strict regulation ensures the authenticity of the data on record. True, accurate and complete financial data is the cornerstone for determining systemic financial risk. The US Form ADV and Form PF achieve the goal of comprehensive monitoring of product information, leverage levels, risk exposures, liquidity levels, governance, investment concentrations, violation records, etc. Also, through the 2012 on-site inspection special activities to ensure understanding of investment adviser operations and ensure data reporting in line with regulatory requirements, the US has achieved significant external influence on PE funds through Form PF and Form ADV Data monitoring of private funds with significant external influence is achieved in the US through Form PF and Form ADV. The authenticity of PE data has a significant impact on the determination of financial risk, but the large number and uneven quality of PE fund managers in China makes verification of data difficult [22].

5 Suggestions for Improving the Fiduciary Duty System of Private Equity Fund Managers in China

Both the inspiration from overseas experience and the current situation of China's PE market clearly shows that there are deficiencies in the market autonomy of the PE industry, and that the role of the fiduciary duty must be given full play in order to promote the healthy development of the industry. In view of the problems in the development of China's PE industry, a regulatory system with the fiduciary duty at its core should be improved as soon as possible, a long-term mechanism for standardized operation should be established, the governance level of PE funds should be improved, investor protection should be strengthened, and systemic risks should be prevented and controlled.

5.1 Clear and Appropriate Agreement Terms as an Entry Point to the Administrator's Fiduciary Duties

Article 20 of the Provisional Measures on Supervision and Administration of Privately offered Investment Funds refers to the fund contract, articles of association or partnership agreement drawn up and entered into by a PE fund as the fund contract [23]. The prevailing view is that, regardless of whether a PE fund takes the form of a contract, partnership or company, the essence of the agreement between the PE fund manager and the investor is a fiduciary legal relationship, and an appropriate contract design can reduce agency costs.

For example, mandatory distribution rules for profits received from investments could be included in the investment agreement. These provisions could discourage the possibility of managers reinvesting profits rather than distributing them to investors. Opportunistic managers prefer reinvestment to profit distribution because they can continue to earn management fees on the next investment. Mandatory distribution provisions can ensure that investors receive an immediate distribution of profits from a profitable exit liquidation, reducing the risk of abuse by the administrator.

In summary, in the relevant agreement of the PE fund, the connotation and extension of the rights and obligations of the manager, the calculation of liability and damages for breach of contract and the settlement of disputes should be clarified in the agreement as far as possible, taking into account the purpose and direction of the investor's investment, the situation of the underlying investment, the manager's own management capabilities and its profession.

5.2 Improve the Regulatory System and Clarify Regulatory Boundaries on the Basis of Uniform Legislation

According to incomplete contract theory, limited human rationality, information asymmetry and third party unverifiability make it impossible for PE fund managers, as fiduciaries, to fully plan in advance the specific content of their fiduciary obligations [24]. The current legal system for PE funds is mainly governed by the type of institution as the standard for binding, and the sources of regulation are rather fragmented.Therefore, the current regulatory system relating to the fiduciary duties of PE fund managers can be improved in the following ways.

Firstly, to ensure the uniformity of legislation. At the legislative level, PE funds of different organizational forms are regulated in a unified manner, and the content of the duty of care and diligence of various types of PE fund managers is unified. Based on this, and provided that the parties do not violate the statutory standards, the parties' autonomy is fully respected, and they are allowed to agree on the criteria for aggravating or mitigating the duty of care, and arrangements are made for the content of the duty of prudence and diligence.

Secondly, strengthen the collaborative governance role of fund associations. Develop guiding model clauses to clarify the compliance boundaries and scope of private fund managers and agree on specific ways and paths to protect the interests of investors who lack critical information in model clauses, so as to establish a uniform industry standard and establish a reasonable external boundary for the standard of duty of care.

5.3 Promoting the Transformation of Private Equity Funds from Passive to Active Management by Clarifying the Standards of Judicial Decisions

The history of the development of fiduciary duty regimes shows that courts have played an important role in interpreting the scope of a fiduciary's duty to perform. The substance of fiduciary duties in legislation can have very different outcomes depending on jurisdiction, but what remains constant is that the existence of fiduciary duties will generally protect investors from grossly negligent, reckless and intentionally harmful conduct. Therefore, the judiciary in China should play an active role in guiding judicial decisions related to PE disputes and promote PE fund managers to take the fiduciary duty as the standard of conduct and proactive compliance [25]. Specifically, this can be done in the following ways.

Firstly, the duty of fidelity should be implemented in the whole process of PE fund management, and conflicts of interest such as self-dealing and non-competition should be prohibited. Secondly, the misconduct of PE fund managers should be restrained and controlled especially in the fund raising process. Thirdly, in the investment and management process, the managers should be required to fulfill the obligation of continuous information disclosure in the process of property management, disposal and change. Fourthly, the liquidation phase can be drawed on the means of enforcement and exit under property law, so as to protect the rights of investors. Last but not least, the burden of proof should be shifted to the fund manager if there is a contractual obligation of fiduciary duty that is missing in the aforementioned aspects of the fund's investment management and that the investor is unable to prove.

6 Conclusion

The fiduciary duty of a private fund manager is a positive due diligence obligation that places the interests of private fund investors above its own and is the soul and foundation of the private fund industry. PE fund managers should abide by their fiduciary duty and make maximising the interests of PE fund investors the highest standard of conduct for their fund activities. At the same time, the fiduciary duty of PE fund managers is also the key to cracking legal risks throughout PE funds, and the process of fostering fiduciary duty should evolve in tandem with the development of the PE market. At present, there is already a scattering of fiduciary duties in China's legal and regulatory system, and fiduciary duties are reflected in the legal regulation of every aspect of PE fund raising, investment management and withdrawal. However, the regulations involved are rather vague and the current fiduciary duty system still needs to be improved. Therefore, it is necessary to build a unified code of fiduciary duty at the level of PE fund managers, so as to achieve fair and reasonable pricing for PE transactions through "sellers' due diligence and buyers' responsibility", and to make the fiduciary duty deeply rooted in the compliance construction of PE funds.

References

1. Asset Management Association of China. Compliance Management Manual for the PE Fund Industry. China Finance and Economy Press, Beijing (2021)
2. Qin, Z.: Fund Governance: Global Perspectives and Chinese Practices. Beijing University Press, Beijing (2022)
3. Wu, X.: The Theory and Practice of Investment Fund Law: Also, on the Revision and Improvement of Investment Fund Law. Shanghai Sanlian Press, Shanghai (2014)
4. Drury, L.L.: Private equity and the heightened fiduciary duty of disclosure. NYU J. **6**, 39–58 (2009)
5. Frankel, T.: Fiduciary Law. Oxford University Press, New York (2011)
6. Xu, K.: The unified theory of private fund managers' obligations. Northern Law J. **02**, 46–48 (2016)
7. Zhao, Y.: Study on the admission mechanism of PE fund managers. Legal Sci. **04**, 166–167 (2013)
8. Supreme People's Court of China. The Minutes of the National Court Work Conference for Civil and Commercial Trials (2019). https://www.court.gov.cn/zixun-xiangqing-199691.html. Accessed 20 Apr 2023
9. Hu, J., Wang, Q.: On the duty of fidelity of fund managers as fiduciaries: the regulation of "rat positioning" as an example. Financ. Innov. Law Rev. **02**, 22–24 (2017)
10. Huang, W.: PE Funds in China: Issues and Developments. China Development Press, Beijing (2015)
11. Li, S.: Chinese Style PE Funds: Raising and Setting Up. Legal Press, Beijing (2009)
12. Hong, L.: The logic of self-regulation of PE funds. Tsinghua Financ. Rev. **05**, 28–30 (2018)
13. The People's Bank of China. Guiding Opinions on Regulating Asset Management Business of Financial Institutions (2018). http://www.pbc.gov.cn/goutongjiaoliu/113456/113469/3529600/index.html. Accessed 30 Mar 2023
14. Shanghai Financial Court. Report on Legal Risks of Private Investment Funs Disputes (2022). https://mp.weixin.qq.com/s/GqcsrzP7wfeMGxJTpl1EvA. Accessed 10 Apr 2023
15. Xu, X., Liang, P.: A study of the principle of good faith in commercial law. Law Rev. **03**, 31–33 (2002)
16. Liu, Y.: The "name" and "reality" of asset management. Financ. Law Forum **02**, 21–22 (2018)
17. Wang, Q.: The use of fiduciary duties in UK and US financial regulation. The Financial Jurist, 2nd Series, pp. 581–582 (2010)
18. SEC. Private Funds Statistics: Second Calendar Quarter 2022 (2023). https://www.sec.gov/divisions/investment/private-funds-statistics. Accessed 20 Apr 2023
19. DeMott, D.A.: Fiduciary contours: perspectives on mutual funds and private funds. Res. Handb. Mutual Funds 26–38 (2016)

20. Liang, Q.: The evolution of the U.S. private placement registration exemption system and its implications: the construction of a qualified investor system in China. Legal Bus. Res. **05**, 144–152 (2013)
21. CSRC. Government Information Disclosure: Administrative Penalty Decisions, January 2001–April 2023. http://www.csrc.gov.cn/csrc/c101971/zfxxgk_zdgk.shtml?channelid=17d5ff2fe43e488dba825807ae40d63f. Accessed 3 Apr 2023
22. Yang, Y.: Another group of PE fund managers "cleared" by regulation (2023). https://mp.weixin.qq.com/s?src=11&timestamp=1682075459&ver=4482&signature=WNpXecdAnu3Pmo0DtwcFlYyQHo1FgVichmdpUcwILoGgi-8lMQnAWST2sVXfiGUMcwWgBIiXs0gziR*F-B7UZq*Lp8dRNnhRuH5e0mEtkZBq1BmvpJ0TSf7ttwe9VJAi&new=1. Accessed 15 Apr 2023
23. CSRC. Provisional Measures on Supervision and Administration of Privately-offered Investment Funds (2014). http://www.csrc.gov.cn/csrc/c106256/c1653981/content.shtml. Accessed 8 Apr 2023
24. Sitkoff, R.H.: The economic structure of fiduciary law. Boston Univ. Law Rev. **91**, 1039–1049 (2011)
25. Huang, T.: The legal path from "institutional regulation" to "functional regulation" of China's financial markets. Jurisprudence **7**, 105–119 (2011)

The Impact of Capital Globalization on Green Innovation: A Cross-Country Empirical Analysis

Yuyang Yuan(✉)

University of Toronto, Toronto, ON, Canada
yuyangevayuan@gmail.com

Abstract. Capital globalization has significantly changed the landscape of the global economy over the last few decades. As countries open their borders to foreign investment, multinational corporations are increasingly seeking out new opportunities to invest and expand their operations. This empirical study aims to investigate the impact of capital globalization on green innovation in eight countries: Australia, Canada, France, Germany, Japan, Korea, United Kingdom, and United States of America. In this research, the relationship between green innovation and capital globalization were analyzed through multiple regressions. To check the robustness of the findings, RANSAC and Quantile Regression are used. Endogeneity processing is also conducted by using the Propensity score matching and Gaussian Mixture Model. The results indicated that Foreign direct investment and outward FDI has a constructive impact on green innovation in all eight countries. Furthermore, R&D investment is found to mediate the relationship between FDI/OFDI and green patent, indicating the significance of capital globalization in promoting sustainable innovation. Based on the findings, the study suggests that governments can promote green innovation by providing incentives for firms to increase their FDI/OFDI, such as reducing corporate taxation and increasing subsidies. Additionally, governments can invest in education and human resource development and raise awareness of the importance of sustainable development and green innovation. This study concludes that promoting capital globalization is crucial in achieving the sustainable development and calls for more research in this area.

Keywords: Green Innovation · Capital Globalization · Sustainable Development

1 Introduction

The well-known 16 sustainable development goals listed by the United Nation and the prioritized objective of achieving carbon neutrality set by many countries indicating that sustainability and eco-friendly have become the key drivers of the global economic development. Green innovation, which enables firms to reduce environmental costs while enhancing energy efficiency, is seen as an effective approach to balancing economic growth and sustainable development. Given the increasing environmental pressures, promoting green innovation has become an important research topic.

Previous literature has examined the factors that influence green innovation on both microscopic and macroscopic levels and has provided policy recommendations, including environmental regulation, industrial structure reformation, and governmental support. However, it is found that relevant study on the relationship between globalization and green innovation is limited. With this growing trend of international trade and globalization become a defining characteristic of the modern world, it is crucial to investigate the impact of capital globalization on green innovation. Specifically, it is important to examine whether the capital globalization can promote green innovation.

This research will mainly focus on eight countries: Australia, Canada, France, Germany, Japan, Korea, UK, USA. It is hypothesized that when firms' capital globalizes, the influence of different cultures and the introduction of more advanced foreign technology are likely to increase the number of green innovations. This research aims to explore the reasons behind and analyze the impacts of capital globalization on green innovation under different conditions. This paper makes three significant contributions compared to the existing literature. Firstly, it provides a unique macroscopic perspective on the factors that drive green innovation, which contributes to the existing body of literature in this field. Secondly, this research identifies and analyzes in detail how capital globalization impacts green innovation, thereby offering a new theoretical model for policymakers. Thirdly, the empirical analysis presented in this study can serve as a reference for enterprises while making decisions regarding foreign direct investment or other forms of capital transactions in the international market.

2 Literature Review

After a thorough review of the existing literature, it is found that scholars have focused on three main aspects that affect green innovation: internal factors, external factors, and the market. Internal factors refer to the firm-level characteristics, such as the level of research and development investment, the size of the firm, and the degree of environmental management. Furthermore, it is found that R&D investment is positively related to green innovation in several studies [1, 2]. Similarly, larger firm is more likely to engage in green innovation since their greater resources and capabilities [3]. Environmental management practices, such as ISO 14001 certification, have also been found to have a constructive effect on green innovation [4]. External factors, on the other hand, refer to the external circumstances in which firms operate. These factors include government policies and regulations, market demand, and access to finance. For instance, government policies and regulations, such as carbon pricing and emission standards, have been found to be positively associated with green innovation [5]. Consumer demand for eco-friendly goods and services are also an important driver of green innovation [6]. And in terms of finance, green investment funds and green bonds have been identified as potential sources of finance for green innovation [7]. The conclusion of these studies is that it is essential for the government to pay attention to environmental protection and implement policies that promote green innovation based on factors that have a positive impact on it.

In addition to internal and external factors, globalization has also been identified as a key driver of innovation. Globalization can increase access to technology, knowledge, and resources, and promote competition and collaboration among firms. However, the impact of capital globalization on eco-friendly innovation is not well-defined. Some studies have found a positive relationship between capital globalization and green innovation [8], while others have found a negative relationship [9]. The contradictory findings suggest that the relationship between globalization and green innovation is complex and context specific.

In the context of the aforementioned eight countries, the influence of capital globalization on green innovation has not been extensively studied. Given the importance of these countries in the global economy, and the increasing attention to environmental sustainability, understanding the relationship between capital globalization and green innovation in these eight countries is important. Hence, this study endeavors to fill the gap by conducting an empirical investigation on a cross-country scale.

3 Hypothesis

It is believed that firms that participate in capital globalization, particularly when there is an increase in foreign investment and shareholders, are likely to be exposed to new ideas and cultural influences from foreign countries, as well as have access to more advanced technologies. This, in turn, can lead to an increase in the number of green innovations that a company produces. Therefore, it is hypothesized that there is a positive relationship between capital globalization and green innovation. Furthermore, this study will also investigate the relationship between capital globalization and green innovation under various conditions. And our second hypothesis suggests that R&D investment may act as a mediating variable between capital globalization and green innovation.

4 Research Design

4.1 Variable

To investigate the relationship between capital globalization and green innovation, this study employed several variables and measurement methods. As shown, the dependent variable, green innovation (GI), will be measured by the number of green patents applied in the given year. Meanwhile, the independent variable, capital globalization, will be represented by the monetary flow between the domestic firms and other countries, with the inward foreign direct (FDI) and outward foreign direct investment (OFDI) measured in USD. The mediating variable will be the R&D investment measured in USD. And to ensure a comprehensive analysis, five control variables that may impact GI will also be considered: gross domestic product, population, business confidence, tax revenue on corporate profit, and year. The following table provides an overview of the variables and measuring methods used in this research (Table 1).

4.2 Data and Descriptive Statistics

This research collected relevant data from the World Bank, United Nation database and Organization for Economic Co-operation and Development (OECD) database covering eight countries from 1969–2020. All used databases are authorized sources of data.

Table 1. Variables.

Variable type	Variable name	Symbol	Measure
Dependent variable	Green Innovation	GI	Number of green patents applied in a year
Explanatory variable	Foreign Direct Investment	FDI	Amount of inward FDI in a year in USD
	Outward Foreign Direct Investment	OFDI	Amount of outward FDI in a year in USD
Mediating variable	R&D investment	R&D	R&D investment in a year in USD
Control Variable	Gross domestic product	GDP	The total market value of all final goods and service produced in an economy in a year
	Population	P	Population of the country in the year
	Business confidence	IF	Investment forecast in USD
	Tax Revenue on Corporate Profit	TCP	Tax Revenue on Corporate Profit in USD
	Year	Y	Year

Table 2 shown below displays the descriptive statistics of the raw data. Prior to econometric analysis, the data were filtered by removing all data prior to 2005 due to excessive missing data. The R&D data for Australia was then filled in using a recursive function, as there appeared to be a recursive relationship between the data. Then, to account for differences in measuring standards for the variables, a z-score standardization was conducted. The following Table 3 summarizes the information for the data after normalization.

Table 2. Descriptive Statistics of raw data.

Variable	Obs.	Mean	SD	Max	Min
GI	120	17843.9	20484.6	69701.2	1433.83
FDI	120	6.7E + 10	9.1E + 10	4.8E + 11	-3E + 10
OFDI	120	8.5E + 10	1E + 11	4.2E + 11	-2E + 11
R&D	120	1.2E + 11	1.4E + 11	6.8E + 11	1.6E + 10
GDP	120	4.4E + 12	4.9E + 12	2.1E + 13	7E + 11
IF	120	0.019	0.043	0.115	−0.126
Population	120	9.5E + 07	8.8E + 07	3.3E + 08	2E + 07
TCP	120	1.2E + 11	1.2E + 11	4.7E + 11	1.8E + 10

Table 3. Descriptive Statistics after z-score standardization.

Variable	Obs.	Mean	SD	Max	Min
GI	120	0	1.004	2.542	−0.804
FDI	120	0	1.004	4.631	−1.051
OFDI	120	0	1.004	3.275	−2.349
R&D	120	0	1.004	3.915	−0.708
GDP	120	0	1.004	3.473	−0.748
IF	120	0	1.004	2.224	−3.347
Population	120	0	1.004	2.657	−0.851
TCP	120	0	1.004	4.7E + 11	1.8E + 10

4.3 Model Design

To test the first hypothesis regarding how capital globalization affects green innovation, an econometric model is developed as presented below:

$$GI_{it} = \beta + \beta_1 FDI_{it} + \beta_2 OFDI_{it} + \beta_3 C_{it} + Y_t + \varepsilon_{it} \tag{1}$$

where GI_{it} is the dependent variable representing the number of green patents applied in a year; FDI_{it} and $OFDI_{it}$ are the key independent variables representing the inward federal direct investment and outward federal direct investment in a year; C_{it} is the set of the control variables, including: GDP, P, IF, TCP; Y_t measures the fixed effect of year, ε_{it} is the residual [10].

5 Empirical Results

5.1 Multivariate Regression

Table 4 shows the result of regressions, in which column (1) is the result of the basic regression. It can be seen that both FDI and OFDI are significant to GI and has a positive relationship with GI, which indicates capital globalization can promote green innovation, and thus proved hypothesis one. However, the VIF of variable P is greater than ten which suggest a high collinearity. In order to address this issue, Ridge regression was conducted to the data, and the results are summarized in column (2). After adjustment, results are still significantly positive, indicating the explanatory variable has regression relationship with the dependent variable, which again, is in accordance with the hypothesis one.

5.2 Robustness Check

In order to check and improve the robustness of regression, two robustness test are carried out in the following section.

Table 4. Basic regression result.

Variable	GI (1)		GI (2)	
	Coefficient	P	Coefficient	P
FDI	0.054	0.015**		0.001***
OFDI	0.124	0.000***		0.000***
IF	3.536	0.002***		0.000***
GDP	0.254	0.000***		0.000***
P	−0.013	0.006***		0.000***
TCP	1.403	0.005***		0.073*
Constant	0.054	1.000		1.000
R-squared	0.124	0.834		0.866

Note: ***, **, * represent the significance under 1%, 5%, 10% significance level respectively

Random Sample Consensus (RANSAC). The first method selected for robustness check is the random sample consensus. Table 5 below presents the results, indicating that the p-values of all variables suggest they are statistically significant in relation to GI. Furthermore, the coefficients of FDI and OFDI remain positive, providing evidence of the favorable influence of capital globalization on green innovation, which is consistent with hypothesis one.

Table 5. RANSAC result.

Variable	GI (1)	
	P	B
FDI	0.012**	0.1
OFDI	0.028**	0.101
IF	0.000***	−3.876
GDP	0.001***	−0.008
P	0.017**	1.329
TCP	0.000***	−0.332

Quantile Regression. To ensure the robustness of the findings, a quantile regression analysis is also performed to examine how the relationship between the variables of interest and green innovation varies across different quantiles of the dependent variable. The results of this analysis are presented in Table 6 below. As evident from the p-values, once again, foreign direct investment (FDI) and outward foreign direct investment (OFDI) demonstrate a positive and significant association with GI, providing further evidence to support hypothesis one that globalization fosters green innovation.

Table 6. Quantile Regression result.

Variable	Quantile 0.2	Quantile 0.5	Quantile 0.75
FDI	0.160 (0.000***)	0.188 (0.000***)	0.199 (0.004***)
OFDI	0.919 (0.001***)	1.286 (0.000***)	1.112 (0.000***)
IF	0.061 (0.018**)	−0.054 (0.052*)	−0.075 (0.106)
GDP	2.995 (0.000***)	−3.859 (0.000***)	−3.443 (0.000***)
P	0.919 (0.001***)	1.286 (0.000***)	1.112 (0.000***)
TCP	0.641 (0.000***)	0.836 (0.000***)	0.605 (0.000***)
const	−0.276 (0.000***)	−0.097 (0.000***)	0.185 (0.000***)

5.3 Endogeneity Processing

Propensity Score Matching (PSM). To address the potential issue of endogeneity, propensity score matching (PSM) method is employed. Firstly, a binomial research variable is created using the mean value of foreign direct investment (FDI) as the threshold. If an observed FDI value is greater than the mean, it is coded as 1, otherwise it is coded as 0. Then, by taking the five control variables as the matching variable, GI as the outcome variable. Next, to match the control group and treatment group, the nearest neighbor PSM method is utilized. Finally, a balance test is performed to obtain the results, and it is observed that the p-values of all matching variables exceed 0.05. So, the null hypothesis cannot be rejected and thus there is no systematic difference between the treatment group and the control group. And thus, the result satisfies the homogeneity test. Table 7 (1) is a summary of the PSM result. It can be seen that the coefficient of FDI is positive which is consistent with the result of the basic regression.

Gaussian Mixture Model (GMM) - Instrumental Variable. Another way to deal with endogeneity is to conduct Gaussian Mixture Model (GMM). In specific, FDI and OFDI are set as the endogenous variable, GDP, IF, P and TCP are set as the instrumental variable, and location is set as the exogenous variable. Results are summarized in Table 7 (2), in which the P-value of Wald is 0.000***, suggesting it is significant at 1% level which this GMM model is effective. By inspecting the results, it can be seen that FDI and OFDI are both significant and positive at 5% level; therefore, it can be concluded that the endogeneity problem is improved after conducting GMM.

Table 7. Endogeneity processing.

Variable	PSM (1)	GMM (2)
FDI	0.0532***	0.029**
	(0.116)	(0.179)
OFDI	0.0713***	0.050**
	(0.164)	(0.108)
Control	YES	YES
Year	YES	YES
Constant		0.000***
R-squared		0.909
Wald		1680.885
		(0.000***)

5.4 Mediation Variable Testing

Furthermore, this research also tested the mediation effect for the factor R&D investment. In hypothesis two, it is hypothesized that R&D investment will act as a mediator variable between the FDI&OFDI and GI. Conducting the regression with the addition of variable R&D, the result of positive coefficient of FDI and R&D, showing in Table 8 (1) & (2), is indicating that R&D investment is acting as a mediator variable between FDI and green patent application. And therefore, hypothesis two is verified to be true.

Table 8. Mediator variable testing result.

Variable	(1) R&D	(2) GI
FDI	0.278***	0.678***
	(0.0028)	(0.0190)
R&D		0.0187***
		(0.0017)
Control	YES	YES
Year	YES	YES
Constant	3.0590***	−3.8560***
	(1.3173)	(0.2545)

6 Conclusion

This research studied the relationship between capital globalization and green innovation. The empirical analysis of eight countries has demonstrated that FDI and OFDI can measurably promote green innovation. Furthermore, the study found that increasing investment in research and development (R&D) can also lead to a greater emphasis on green innovation. As a result, governments may consider promoting capital globalization as a means of increasing green innovation and green patent activity.

There are several strategies that the government could implement to incentivize firms to increase FDI and engage in eco-friendly innovation. One approach could be to reduce the corporate tax rate, which would make it more attractive for foreign companies to invest in the country. Additionally, increasing subsidies for R&D and other forms of support for eco-friendly innovation could also incentivize firms to increase their green patent applications and other eco-friendly activities [11].

Another potential approach could be to invest in education and human resource development, particularly by promoting study abroad programs. As people become more aware of the importance of environmental protection, green innovation, and gain inspiration from different countries, there would be an increased likelihood of people engaging in environmental innovation.

However, the most critical step in promoting sustainable development and green innovation is to educate firms and raise public awareness of its importance. By emphasizing the value of eco-friendly practices and the benefits they can bring to both the environment and the economy, firms may be more likely to prioritize sustainable development in their operations. Ultimately, a combination of these strategies could be implemented to promote capital globalization and green innovation.

References

1. Wang, L., Pan, X., Zhu, D., Chen, G.: Research on the relationship between R&D investment and green innovation of manufacturing enterprises. In Proceedings of the 2018 International Conference on Industrial Engineering and Operations Management, pp. 834–844 (2018)
2. Xue, J., Yang, F., Chen, J., Wang, X.: R&D investment and green innovation: evidence from china's manufacturing industry. Sustainability **10**(10), 3439 (2018). https://doi.org/10.3390/su10103439
3. Lu, Y., Tao, R., Su, Y., Tan, K.: What drives green innovation? Evidence from China. J. Clean. Prod. **234**, 552–560 (2019). https://doi.org/10.1016/j.jclepro.2019.06.112
4. Yang, J., Sun, L., Liu, W.: The impact of environmental management practices on green innovation: empirical evidence from Chinese manufacturing firms. J. Clean. Prod. **226**, 439–448 (2019). https://doi.org/10.1016/j.jclepro.2019.04.190
5. Ghisetti, C., Quatraro, F., Rainoldi, A.: Green technologies and environmental productivity: a cross-sectoral analysis of direct and indirect effects in Italian regions. J. Clean. Prod. **172**, 4255–4268 (2018). https://doi.org/10.1016/j.jclepro.2017.10.163
6. Li, X., Liang, X., Xue, Y., Li, J.: The impact of consumer demand for eco-friendly products on green innovation: evidence from Chinese manufacturing firms. J. Clean. Prod. **223**, 1107–1116 (2019). https://doi.org/10.1016/j.jclepro.2019.03.085
7. Feng, T., Chen, Y., Wang, Y., Sun, C.: The role of financial support in green innovation: empirical evidence from China. J. Clean. Prod. **225**, 798–807 (2019). https://doi.org/10.1016/j.jclepro.2019.03.249
8. Tang, B., Chang, Y., Luo, J.: Capital globalization, green technology innovation and environmental governance: a panel data analysis of 56 countries. J. Clean. Prod. **174**, 1224–1234 (2018). https://doi.org/10.1016/j.jclepro.2017.11.054
9. Huang, Y., Wu, Y., Jin, B.: Capital globalization and green innovation: evidence from Chinese firms. J. Clean. Prod. **237**, 117649 (2019). https://doi.org/10.1016/j.jclepro.2019.117649

10. Feng, G.-F., Niu, P., Wang, J.-Z., Liu, J.: Capital market liberalization and green innovation for sustainability: evidence from China. Environ. Adv. **10**, 100102 (2022). https://doi.org/10.1016/j.eap.2022.06.009
11. Wen, H.W., Lee, C.C., Zhou, F.X.: How does fiscal policy uncertainty affect corporate innovation investment? Evidence from China's new energy industry. Energy Econ. **105**, 105767 (2022)

Financing Constraints, Local Government Debt, and Corporate Stock Returns: An Empirical Analysis

Yike Lu[✉]

School of Accounting, Central University of Finance and Economics, Beijing 102206, China

2020310480@email.cufe.edu.cn

Abstract. Against the background of expanding local government debt in China, it is inevitable that firms will be affected by local government debt in some aspects. Based on the relevant data of Shanghai and Shenzhen A-share companies from 2000 to 2020, this paper conducts an empirical analysis by constructing an OLS model. From the results, it can be seen that local government debt can, on the one hand, lead to higher corporate share price returns by alleviating financing constraints, which brings a positive boost to corporate share prices; at the same time, local government debt can increase corporate financing constraints, which indirectly leads to lower corporate share price returns and has a negative inhibitory effect on corporate share prices. The relationship between local government debt, financing constraints and stock price returns is still unclear in the current academic world. It is hoped that this paper can fill the gap in academic research through theoretical mechanism construction and empirical model analysis, so that local government debt can better play its effectiveness.

Keywords: Local Government Debt · Financing Constraints · Stock Prices

1 Introduction

After the reform and opening up, although the process of industrialization and urbanization in China has increased significantly, the pressure of local fiscal deficit in China has also been increasing, and issuing debt has become an important means and tool for the government to solve the financing problem. Examples of the government increasing fiscal spending and deficits to avoid the country falling into the vicious cycle of the economic downturn are also common. Take the 2008 financial crisis as an example, China formulated a $4 trillion investment plan to relieve the economic pressure; the United States launched a $1.9 trillion rescue plan when the new epidemic hindered economic development. The government's revenue is limited, and in the face of national infrastructure construction needs, local government debt can relieve financial pressure and provide additional funds for the treasury, thus improving the infrastructure and corporate financing environment and promoting high-quality economic development, which reflects the positive impact of government debt on corporate share prices.

However, at the same time, major enterprises also face financing problems for their development, and considering the credibility of the government and enterprises, funds will be more easily tilted to the government. In this case, the government, to a certain extent, crowds out the financing channels of enterprises. The financing constraint will directly affect the enterprises, forcing them to make adjustments in various aspects, such as financing structure, dividend policy, etc., which in turn will cause fluctuations in their share prices. Local government debt has been growing in recent years as the government continues to issue debt to improve infrastructure and increase the level of market access. As far as the "Local Government Bond Issuance and Debt Balance in February 2022" released by the budget department is concerned, the balance of local government debt nationwide has reached 3,163.64 billion yuan by the end of February 2022. Such rapid development of local government debt has also rapidly accumulated many problems in the process, such as too much government-issued debt, a large number of invisible and contingent debts, and the accumulation of government debt risks, which is not conducive to the development of local enterprises, which indicates that the impact of local government debt on corporate share prices is also negative.

To address the positive and negative aspects of local government debt issuance, the state has gradually paid attention to government debt and strengthened the standardized management of local government debt in order to resolve the risk of local government debt and reduce its negative aspects, while promoting the benign development of local government debt and sustaining its positive aspects.

To sum up, the study of local government debt is of great significance for the smooth implementation of policies and the reform of the fiscal system. On this basis, this paper will focus on the impact of local government debt issuance on enterprises, and explore in depth the mechanism of government debt acting on enterprise stock returns through financing constraints from both positive and negative aspects. At the micro level, the effectiveness of local government debt issuance is better examined and the intrinsic link between government debt and enterprise value is sorted out.

2 Literature Review

There are currently fruitful academic findings on the impact of local autonomy debt on the crowding out of firms' financial channels. Through an empirical study of both internal financing efficiency and the external financing environment, Ren demonstrated that the increased risk of local government debt ultimately reduces the financing capacity of firms [1]. Fan's study shows that the most fundamental reason for the repulsive effect of local government debt on business investment and financing activities is the financing constraint it imposes. The transmission mechanism behind the financing constraint of new enterprises can be explained by the reduction in the scale of business investment and the reduction in financing capacity. Shu & Gao pointed out that financing-constrained firms can choose to adjust their dividend policy to maintain the normal flow of funds in the firm, and dividends have a significant ameliorating effect on the financing constraint of the firm [2]. Wen also elucidates a detailed insight into this effect: the fact that a firm makes dividends reduces the number of funds under management's control, thus reducing the likelihood of generating agency problems [3]. In addition to this, according to signaling theory, a firm's stable distribution of cash dividends can convey to potential investors in the market that the firm is doing well, thus motivating investors to invest and ultimately promoting higher share prices. However, according to the tax differential theory, reducing the dividend payout is instead beneficial to raise the stock price. Therefore, the impact of local government debt on corporate share price returns through the crowding out effect is still subject to a variety of possibilities and cannot be consistently concluded based on the existing literature and theoretical review alone.

At the same time, some literature suggests that the increase in the level of local government debt also has a positive effect and is beneficial to the development of firms. Hu & Fan first proposed the "infrastructure crowding-in effect", which applies the infrastructure effect to the micro-firm component and uses it to define the utility of government debt in increasing firms' financing opportunities by improving the financing environment [4]. Chen et al. argue that local government debt issuance can improve infrastructure construction and increase the level of market openness, which provides an excellent financing environment for firms and helps them to increase the share of internal financing and the level of equity financing [5]. A study by Wang & Wang showed that economic growth is inextricably linked to the construction of infrastructure for economic growth [6]. The Bureau of Statistics of Rizhao City, Shandong Province, conducted a data analysis using the 2001–2016 to derive a positive relationship between infrastructure investment and economic growth. Through an empirical study, Li conclude that there is a long-run equilibrium relationship between economic growth and stock prices in China. It follows that the infrastructure crowding-out effect of local government debt may promote higher stock price returns [7].

In summary, there may be a crowding-in or crowding-out effect of local government debt that increases or decreases the financing constraint of firms, which ultimately has a positive or negative impact on the stock price returns of firms. Therefore, this paper starts from local government debt and explores its mechanism of affecting firm's stock price return through financing constraints.

3 Methodology

3.1 Sample Selection

This paper draws on the existing literature and selects the data of A-share listed companies in Shanghai and Shenzhen from 2000 to 2020 to form a sample for analysis, excluding the sample observations according to the following principles: (1) listed companies with operating income and expense changes lower than 1% and higher than 99%; (2) ST and *ST listed companies; (3) financial listed companies. At the same time, tailoring (winsorize) processes all continuous variables to eliminate the influence of outliers on regression results, thus improving data accuracy. The company data in the study are obtained from the wind database and relevant enterprise financial statements, and local data are obtained from the statistical yearbooks of each province and city to ensure the authenticity and reliability of the data sources.

3.2 Variable Definition

Explanatory Variable. Local government debt includes direct, contingent, explicit, implicit and other types. From the statistical perspective, it is difficult to accurately measure the debt scale of many financing platform enterprises, institutions and other sectors related to local governments, while contingent debt involves the problem of default probability which is difficult to quantify precisely. From the policy perspective, changes in national regulations and rules lead to the changing scope of local government debts, and governmental debt audit reports are released in provincial administrative regions, with a few prefecture-level cities released separately, making it difficult to support research at the prefecture-level city level. In summary, it is not possible to measure local government debt directly, and therefore draw on Hong et al.'s paper to use (local fiscal expenditure + fixed asset investment)/local fiscal revenue, an indirect measure of local government debt pressure, as a proxy variable for local government debt [8].

Explained Variable. Corporate share price return is the average weekly return (ret) is used to measure corporate share price returns.

Intermediary Variable. Degree of financing constraint is the degree of financing constraint is measured by the ww index.

Control Variables. In addition to the independent variables, there are some business operating characteristics variables that influence the dependent variables. Therefore, this paper introduces control variables such as year-end total assets (Size), year-end gearing ratio (Lev), operating cash flow percentage (Cf), whether audited by a Big 4 accounting firm (Big4), and management expense percentage (Mfee). Table 1 demonstrates the definition and calculation of each variable.

Table 1. Definition of variables.

Symbol	Variable	Variable Definition
ww	Degree of financing constraints	ww financing constraint index
ret	Average Weekly Return	ret = (dividend + sell price − sell price)/sell price*100%
debt	Local government debt	Debt = (local fiscal expenditure + fixed asset investment)/local fiscal revenue
Size	Total asset at the end of the year	Natural logarithm of total assets for the year
Lev	Gearing ratio at year end	Lev = total liabilities/total asset
Cf	Operating cash flow as a percentage	Cf = net cash flow from operating activities/total assets
Big4	Whether audited by the Big Four	1 if the company is audited by a Big Four accounting firm, 0 otherwise
Mfee	Administrative expenses as a percentage	Mfee = overhead/operating income

3.3 Hypothesis Development

The reasons for the infrastructure crowding-out effect of local governments on firms can be understood from two perspectives. From a macro perspective, local government debt raises funds through financial means to improve infrastructure construction and provide a good financing environment for enterprises, thus forming an infrastructure crowding-out effect; from a micro perspective, the threat posed by local government debt in financing will force enterprises to adjust their own financing structure, thus forming an infrastructure crowding-out effect. The infrastructure crowding-in effect will boost economic growth at the macro level and increase stock returns at the micro level.

The impact of local government debt on stock returns is studied separately for state-owned and non-state-owned enterprises. On the one hand, the special characteristics of SOEs are that they have less financing constraints under the guarantee of state credit than non-SOEs, and on the other hand, the infrastructure crowding-in effect is also beneficial to the future development of SOEs, and external investors' confidence in corporate development increases, raising stock price returns [9].

The impact of local government debt on corporate financing constraints is twofold: the reduction of financing channels and the intermediation problem. On the one hand, local government debt has an expulsion effect because it absorbs credit resources and reduces corporate financing channels in the financing process. After appropriating credit resources from firms, firms have less access to finance as part of the financing process, and financing costs and firm financing constraints are reinforced. On the other hand, local government debt makes local firms more distinct from industry characteristics and the institutional environment, decreases firm information, which in turn creates agency problems and increases the burden of corporate finance.

The impact of firms' financing constraints on stock price performance is examined from two different perspectives: cash flow expectations and incomplete contract theory. When analyzed from the perspective of cash holdings, the enhanced financing constraints faced by firms increase the cost of raising funds from capital markets to grow their business and increase the propensity to hold cash internally, making it more difficult for firms to maintain certain cash dividends [10]. The message of poor business conditions is conveyed to potential investors through signaling theory, making the firm's share price return lower. In addition, incomplete contract theory suggests that there are various constraints that make the act of concluding a complete contract impossible. Therefore, the management of the firm will make the decision to invest in the project with internal funds to reduce the financing cost, which will also make the share price return decrease through the signaling theory.

Therefore, hypotheses are formulated:

H1: Local government debt increases and share price return increases
H2: The effect of local government debt acts more significantly on state-owned enterprises than non-state-owned enterprises
H3: Local government debt increases and corporate financing constraints also increase
H4: An increase in corporate financing constraints decreases stock price returns

3.4 Modelling

This paper hopes to reveal the correlation between local government debt, corporate financing constraints and corporate stock price returns in China through OLS model construction and enterprise heterogeneity analysis, based on theoretical mechanism analysis, the following model is constructed:

$$Y_{it} = \beta_0 + \beta_1 X_{it} + \beta C + \varepsilon_{it} \tag{1}$$

where Y_{it} is the dependent variable, and financing constraints and weekly average returns are used in the paper respectively; X_{it} is the independent variable, and local government debt and financing constraints are used respectively; C is the control variable, as shown in Table 1 above.

4 Empirical Results

4.1 Descriptive Statistics

The results of descriptive statistics of the main variables in this paper are shown in Table 2. From the sample as a whole, the mean value of weekly average return (ret) is 0.004, which indicates the low level of share price returns of listed companies in China. Comparing the obtained data with the previous literature, it is found that the statistical values of these variables are within a reasonable range, and the values are all consistent with the previous literature.

Table 2. Descriptive statistics.

Variable	Mean	S.D.	Min.	Max.
ww	−0.861	0.538	−1.246	2.404
ret	0.004	0.012	−0.029	0.065
debt	−0.043	0.085	−2.230	0.067
Size	21.990	1.281	19.240	26.400
Lev	0.433	0.207	0.027	0.991
Cf	0.047	0.073	−0.224	0.283
Big4	0.059	0.235	0.000	1.000
Mfee	0.094	0.086	0.005	1.093

4.2 Regression Results

Table 3 reflects that local government debt has a positive effect on financing constraints and stock price returns, with a 1 unit increase in debt pressure, the degree of financing constraints and average weekly returns increase by 0.108 and 0.002 units, respectively, while a 1 unit increase in financing constraints decreases average weekly returns by 0.00003 units. That is, under our government and market system, the expansion of local government debt will tighten the financing environment and increase corporate financing constraints, at which time H3 is accepted; but at the same time, due to the expectation that government funds are used to boost economic growth, corporate share prices receive higher yields, at which time H1 is accepted, while the increase in financing constraints affects the level of corporate financing, thus affecting corporate development potential and expectations and adversely affecting share prices. It proves that H4 is correct.

Table 3. Baseline regression results.

	ww	ww	ret	ret	ret	ret
debt	0.120***	0.108**	0.002**	0.002**		
	(2.72)	(2.47)	(1.98)	(2.36)		
ww					−0.00004***	−0.00003**
					(−2.95)	(−2.38)
Size		−0.042***		−0.001***		−0.00114***
		(−11.68)		(−15.86)		(−16.56)
Lev		0.177***		0.003***		0.00149***
		(8.27)		(8.69)		(3.49)
Cf		−0.744***		0.016***		0.01695***
		(−13.96)		(15.74)		(15.98)
Big4		0.025		0.000		0.00047
		(1.55)		(0.41)		(1.50)
Mfee		0.206***		0.004***		0.00194*
		(4.08)		(4.91)		(1.92)
Cons.	−0.841***	0.020	0.004***	0.026***	0.00445***	0.02804***
	(−199.05)	(0.26)	(53.83)	(17.46)	(59.17)	(18.99)

4.3 Heterogeneity Analysis

The regressions are divided according to the nature of enterprises, and are conducted separately for state−owned and non-state-owned enterprises, and the results are shown as follows. As Table 4 shown, for non-SOEs, local government debt shows a significant positive effect on financing constraints, i.e., a 1 unit increase in local government debt pressure is associated with a 0.152 unit increase in financing constraints. However, for state-owned enterprises, the increase in local government debt did not put significant pressure on corporate financing. The special nature of SOEs makes them less affected by the credit crowding out effect when local government debt increases due to the state credit backing on the one hand, and on the other hand, local governments expand debt for infrastructure activities and government-enterprise business, SOEs have better future development expectations, which increases market confidence in enterprises, thus mitigating the positive effect of local government debt.

Table 4. Impact of local government debt on financing constraint (ww) heterogeneity.

	SOE	Non-SOE	SOE	Non-SOE
debt	0.065	0.156***	0.053	0.152***
	(0.98)	(2.65)	(0.81)	(2.60)
Size			−0.043***	−0.038***
			(−9.06)	(−6.71)
Lev			0.145***	0.209***
			(4.64)	(6.81)
Cf			−0.986***	−0.512***
			(−13.00)	(−6.81)
Big4			0.009	0.074**
			(0.46)	(2.53)
Mfee			0.146*	0.247***
			(1.86)	(3.73)
Cons.	−0.860***	−0.823***	0.062	−0.089
	(−139.91)	(−141.40)	(0.60)	(−0.74)

As Table 5 shows, for state-owned enterprises, local government debt shows a significant positive effect on stock price returns, i.e., a 1-unit increase in local government debt pressure is associated with a 0.003-unit increase in average weekly stock price returns. However, for non-SOEs, this positive effect is not significant. Since the SOEs mentioned above have smaller credit squeeze and better future development expectations, the expansion of local government debt leads to an increase in share price returns for SOEs, while there is no significant effect for non-SOEs. It proves that H3 is correct under the analysis of heterogeneity between SOEs and non-SOEs.

Regardless of the nature of the firm, an increase in financing constraints exposes the firm to the risk of lower share price returns. The increase in financing constraints affects the firm's capital chain and future growth potential, thus negatively affecting the share price (see Table 6). The negative effect is not affected by the nature of the enterprise. Although the coefficient of financing constraint of SOEs is not significant after adding control variables, this negative effect still has a high degree of confidence.

4.4 Robustness Analysis

To ensure the reliability of the model conclusions, this paper conducts robustness tests by adjusting the sample years to 2010–2020, and the regression results are shown in

Table 5. Impact of local government debt on stock price return (ret) heterogeneity.

	SOE	Non-SOE	SOE	Non-SOE
debt	0.003*	0.001	0.003**	0.001
	(1.96)	(0.95)	(2.04)	(1.28)
Size			−0.001***	−0.001***
			(−11.84)	(−10.66)
Lev			0.004***	0.003***
			(6.87)	(5.84)
Cf			0.015***	0.016***
			(10.08)	(12.18)
Big4			0.000	−0.000
			(0.42)	(−0.02)
Mfee			−0.002	0.008***
			(−1.44)	(6.84)
Cons.	0.004***	0.005***	0.026***	0.026***
	(33.73)	(42.00)	(12.89)	(11.67)

Table 6. Impact of financing constraints on stock price return (ret) heterogeneity.

	SOE	Non-SOE	SOE	Non-SOE
ww	−0.00003**	−0.00004*	−0.00002	−0.00004*
	(−2.26)	(−1.83)	(−1.59)	(−1.86)
Size			−0.00112***	−0.00114***
			(−12.53)	(−10.52)
Lev			0.00304***	0.00079
			(4.99)	(1.28)
Cf			0.01484***	0.01946***
			(9.98)	(12.87)
Big4			0.00041	0.00082
			(1.07)	(1.47)
Mfee			−0.00269*	0.00469***
			(−1.76)	(3.48)
Cons.	0.00390***	0.00494***	0.02697***	0.02813***
	(37.13)	(46.03)	(13.83)	(12.23)

Table 7. The regression results still maintain a good significance and the conclusions are more robust.

Table 7. Robustness results.

	ww	ww	ret	ret	ret	ret
debt	0.120***	0.108**	0.002**	0.002**		
	(2.72)	(2.47)	(1.98)	(2.36)		
ww					−0.00004***	−0.00003**
					(−2.95)	(−2.38)
Size		−0.042***		−0.001***		−0.00114***
		(−11.68)		(−15.86)		(−16.56)
Lev		0.177***		0.003***		0.00149***
		(8.27)		(8.69)		(3.49)
Cf		−0.744***		0.016***		0.01695***
		(−13.96)		(15.74)		(15.98)
Big4		0.025		0.000		0.00047
		(1.55)		(0.41)		(1.50)
Mfee		0.206***		0.004***		0.00194*
		(4.08)		(4.91)		(1.92)
Cons.	−0.841***	0.020	0.004***	0.026***	0.00445***	0.02804***
	(−199.05)	(0.26)	(53.83)	(17.46)	(59.17)	(18.99)

5 Conclusion

Through the analysis for the results, it is found that the results are consistent with the hypotheses and the hypotheses are fully verified. As a result, the following recommendations are made.

Listed companies should: (1) Non-state-owned enterprises should pay attention to the specific situation of local government debt, fully consider the impact on their own development, and selectively and purposefully adjust their corporate financing channels to find the most suitable financing path for them. For example, when the increase of local government debt leads to the strain of institutional problems, internal financing may be more suitable to cope with the decrease of financing opportunities. (2) Adjusting the financing structure to take full advantage of infrastructure crowding caused by local government debt in order to mitigate the negative impact of financing constraints on firms and thus improve financing efficiency. (3) Adjust dividend policies according to financing constraints, hold cash reasonably, and reduce cash dividend payouts to improve share price yields, while also paying attention to investors' interests.

The regulators should: (1) pay attention to the external financing of enterprises, especially to provide guarantees for non-state enterprises that lack state credit backing to have a fair financing environment. Firstly, diversify financing channels for SMEs and appropriately reduce financing access requirements to effectively solve the financing dilemma of enterprises; secondly, pay attention to improving the crowding-in effect of infrastructure construction and provide more and better financing opportunities for infrastructure construction. (2) Manage local government debts reasonably and pay attention to the fluctuation of corporate dividend policy in order to improve the stability of dividend policy and protect investors' interests.

References

1. Ren, X., Xie, J.: Local government debt risk, interest rate liberalization and corporate financing capacity. Finan. Account. Commun. **06**, 66–71 (2022)
2. Shu, Q., Gao, H.: Dividend, cash-cash flow sensitivity and corporate financing constraints. J. Chengdu Univ. Technol. (Soc. Sci. Ed.) **24**(02), 43–47 (2016)
3. Wen, W., Zhang, Q.: Cash dividends, controlling shareholders and stock price crash risk. Account. Friend **03**, 69–76 (2020)
4. Hu, Y., Fan, J.: The impact of local government debt on corporate financing: based on the perspective of "infrastructure crowding-in effect" and "credit crowding-out effect." Jianghai Acad. J. **05**, 86–92 (2019)
5. Chen, J., Zhao, H., Xu, Y.: Local government debt and corporate financing structure. J. Guizhou Univ. Finan. Econ. **03**, 45–52 (2021)
6. Wang, R., Wang, J.: Infrastructure and Chinese economic growth: a VAR-based study. World Econ. **03**, 13–21 (2007)
7. Li, L.: An empirical analysis of China's stock price index and economic growth. Times Finan. **10**, 23–25 (2009)
8. Hong, Y., Qin, Y., Wang, Q.: Performance assessment, impact mechanism and optimal governance of local government debt size. J. Public Manag. **18**(3), 87–99 (2021)
9. Yang, H., Zhuo, W., Shao, L., et al.: Mean-variance analysis of wholesale price contracts with a capital-constrained retailer: trade credit financing vs. bank credit financing. Eur. J. Oper. Res. **294**(2), 522–533 (2021)
10. Lin, J. Y.: State-owned enterprise reform in China: The new structural economics perspective. Structural Change and Economic Dynamics. Advance online publication (2021)

Sustainable Supply Chains: A Comprehensive Analyse of Drivers and Practices

Qichao Gong[1], Yuxi Wang[2(✉)], and Yuli Zhu[3]

[1] College of Civil Engineering and Architecture, Shandong University of Science and Technology, Qingdao 266590, China
[2] School of Management, Harbin University of Commerce, Harbin 150028, China
wangyx@s.hrbcu.edu.cn
[3] College of Quality and Standardization, Qingdao University, Qingdao 266000, China

Abstract. With the increasing prominence of resources, environment, and social issues, sustainable development has taken root in people's hearts, and sustainable supply chain management has come into being. Many domestic and foreign scholars have researched sustainable supply chain management in recent years, but there are still problems and shortcomings in its practical application in enterprises. This paper firstly reviews the literature on sustainable supply chain management (SSCM), summarizes the basic motivations for studying sustainable supply chains, and analyses the environmental, social responsibility, and corporate benefits of the practical results through the successful cases of some enterprises. At the same time, this paper points out the problems of the current domestic research. It puts forward suggestions in the context of the times, aiming to provide an implementation path and expand the research direction for the relevant domestic research.

Keywords: SSCM · Motivation · Practice Results · Recommendations

1 Introduction

With the rapid development of the social economy and continuous exploitation of resources, the current situation of environmental pollution has become more serious. In the prevention and control process, problems have emerged, and the environment has become a core element that restricts and affects social and economic development. With the advent of globalization, the concept of sustainable development was introduced. In the past two decades, with the growing awareness of the concept of sustainability among all stakeholders, companies have been paying more and more attention to the sustainable management of their supply chains. Traditional supply chain management (SCM) is mainly human centered. It focuses more on economic considerations, whereas sustainable supply chain management (SSMC) combines three dimensions: environmental, economic, and social, which can improve the competitiveness of enterprises more comprehensively and achieve long-term and sustainable development. Research on sustainable supply chains has been carried out for many years at home and abroad.

Q. Gong, Y. Wang and Y. Zhu—These authors contributed equally.

Still, due to different research perspectives, there needs to be a more systematic overview and summary of sustainable supply chains in China. Therefore, this paper adopts a literature research approach. First, sort out the existing literature and then analyze the factors driving sustainable supply chains and the practical achievements according to different perspectives and dimensions. Secondly, it summarizes the problems of research and application in the field of SSCM in China and makes recommendations. Finally, the shortcomings of this paper are elaborated on, and the article is summarized.

2 Literature Review

The idea of sustainable supply chains can be traced back to 1994, which was proposed by Drumwrigt. He believed that companies should be socially responsible in their production and development, pursuing their economic benefits and focusing on social benefits [1]. Seuring et al. defined sustainable supply chains as "the management of logistics, information, and financial flows and the cooperation between companies in the supply chain while considering the three aspects of the sustainable economic environment and social customer and stakeholder demand objectives." This is also the more widely accepted definition [2]. The sustainable supply chain can be defined as the effective management of information flow, capital flow, logistics, and cooperation among enterprises in the supply chain based on the concept of sustainable development, maintaining a dynamic balance among the three dimensions of society, economy, and environment, to achieve long-term and benign development of the enterprise [3]. According to Zhu et al., the research on sustainable supply chains has gradually expanded to the macro-level circular economy and the micro-level global supply chains. In recent years has paid particular attention to the impact of social and environmental changes and new technologies on sustainable supply chains. Through the search and analysis of relevant literature, we decided to explore the driving factors and practical outcomes of sustainable supply chains from social, economic, and environmental perspectives based on existing research and applications and to make relevant recommendations.

3 Sustainable Supply Chain Drivers and Results in Practice

3.1 Motivation Analysis

At the end of the 20th century, scholars began to study sustainable supply chain management as stakeholders' awareness of sustainable development grew [4]. By searching the database literature, we can find that multiple factors have contributed to promoting sustainable supply chains.

External Drivers. Firstly, in terms of environment and resources, the rapid development of global productivity in the middle and late 20th century has led to the continuous deterioration of the worldwide environment and the overconsumption of resources, which has become a globalization challenge, as well as a key factor affecting and constraining socio-economic development. As a result, theoretical research into sustainable supply chain management (SSCM) has emerged [4]. More and more enterprises are adopting sustainable supply chain management models to adapt to the globalized business environment and circumvent the possible green barriers in international trade. Building green supply chains and sustainable management models has become a trend. Since the Asian financial crisis in 2008, the new crown epidemic crisis in late 2019, and the Russia-Ukraine war in 2022, this series of economic, environmental, and social issues have continuously impacted the global supply chain. It has therefore become particularly important to examine how supply chains can maintain stability, resilience, and performance reliability in a changing environment.

Secondly, in terms of policies and laws, and regulations, the concept of "sustainable development" was first used by the United Nations General Assembly in March 1980, and humanity has since chosen the path of sustainable development. The Chinese government has also introduced relevant laws and regulations to implement the new concept of ecological civilization. In May 2015, the State Council officially issued 'Made in China 2025', which was approved by the Premier of the State Council. This document includes the "comprehensive implementation of green manufacturing" as one of the important tasks to achieve the manufacturing power strategy. The paper proposes building a green supply chain to promote various industries' sustainable and healthy development [5]. In addition, the influence of international policies has encouraged the concept of sustainable development to be instilled into the business community, which has promoted the emergence of the SSCM management model.

As consumers become more aware of environmental protection, the popularity of sustainability is influencing their purchasing choices. More and more consumers are inclined to buy green-related products, and this change in demand profoundly affects the output and production of upstream products. As a result, the choice of the SSCM management model has become an urgent issue that companies must face.

Endogenous Dynamic Factors. In the 1980s, many companies devoted considerable resources and energy to reducing production costs. But now, many companies have reached the limits of cost reduction and are struggling to reduce production costs further. At the same time, the government's call for sustainable development is growing stronger, the public's awareness of environmental protection is also increasing, and enterprises are entrusted with greater social responsibilities. The purpose of enterprise transformation is to gain a better brand reputation and win the favor of consumers. To realize the transformation from a circulation economy to a circular economy, the concept of a sustainable supply chain should be introduced to improve ecological efficiency and the controllability of risk management [6]. Globalization, information technology, and the need for superior service performance drive supply chain management toward lifecycle and competitive advantage maintenance sustainability.

3.2 Practical Achievements

The practice of a sustainable supply chain refers to the practical activities that an enterprise that integrates the concept of sustainable development to achieve the goals of economic, environmental, and social performance in production, sales, storage, information exchange, and so on related to inner-enterprise and supply chain [7]. Through the analysis of the cases of modern enterprises and the combination of SSCM and emerging technologies, the supply chain management mode under the concept of sustainability plays an important role in environmental protection, enterprise management level, social responsibility, and other aspects.

Level of Environmental Protection. Environmental protection is the foundation of a sustainable supply chain. Enterprises realize the importance of developing based on the environment and gradually explore the construction and implementation of green supply chains. For example, as the American retail industry giant, Walmart has always adopted a low-cost strategy to occupy the consumer market. However, as the importance of the sustainable concept is gradually recognized, enterprises begin to rectify and transform their supply chain management and establish a green supply chain management system. Walmart put forward the "Environmental 360" plan on February 1, 2007, which formulated green environmental protection rules covering product packaging, transportation logistics, upstream supplier procurement standards, store design management in consumer markets, etc. This management mode enables enterprises to reduce resource energy consumption and material cost while meeting the requirements of long-term green consumption concept and enhancing their core competitiveness and customer-oriented awareness and ability of supply chain [8]. Another example is Lenovo, which has built a green supply chain system by constructing green production, supplier management, logistics, recycling, packaging, and information disclosure (display) platforms. They have achieved carbon dioxide reduction targets, promoted, and improved fuel efficiency in Asian cargo shipments, and reduced air pollution (source from Lenovo's official website).

Level of Social Responsibility. More and more companies have begun to pay attention to constructing sustainable supply chains to realize social responsibility. As a well-known sports brand in Germany, Adidas adopts strict supplier social responsibility supervision, integrates sustainable development into corporate management performance indicators, and evaluates suppliers' social responsibility performance through compliance key performance indicators (C-KPIs) and environmental key performance indicators (E-KPIs). It has been recognized as a leading brand in corporate social responsibility at home and abroad [9]. Adidas has taken a series of measures, including improving product research and development capabilities and internal regulatory standards, to ensure strict compliance with social commitments and become an example of active social responsibility practice in the industry. At the same time, Huawei has increased its investment in human rights, environmental protection, and social aspects while increasing sales revenue and expanding the market to achieve sustainable company development. First, in the face of the oppression of American policies, it continues to implement the radical talent strategy and fully reflects the Wolf culture of the team. While stimulating production innovation, it also realizes the management of internal personnel and talent retention through encouraging policies. It strives to break through technical barriers, which is conducive to the sustainable development of the enterprise [10]. In addition, Huawei has permanently attached importance to its corporate image in the international community, implemented ethical procurement, developed a sound and meticulous sustainable supply chain management system, and attached great importance to sustainable development within the enterprise [10]. For Starbucks, its sustainable supply chain program focuses on three aspects, including supporting farmers and helping them adopt eco-friendly farming practices; Distribute coffee beans in a fair-trade manner to safeguard farmers' economic interests; at the same time, promoting recyclable materials and energy-efficient technologies to reduce dependence on natural resources. These measures are aimed at achieving the goals of sustainable development.

Level of Enterprise Strategy. Promoting integrity, transparency, and fair conduct in the supply chain ensures that all suppliers, customers, and partners comply with relevant regulations and industry standards. For example, the leisure sports brand Patagonia focuses on implementing high environmental, social, and Labour rights policies throughout its supply chain, requiring all suppliers to meet its stringent standards and manage processes such as procurement, production, and transportation in a fair, transparent, and accountable manner. Yili combines the concept of sustainable supply chain management with OPM's working capital strategy, provides technical assistance upstream of the supply chain, cooperates with authoritative international institutions to build a sustainable quality management system, ensures production output and quality acceptance in the middle stream, and establishes cooperative partnerships with leading enterprises and the consumer market in the downstream to accurately analyze consumer demand and realize product informatization. The enterprise strives to achieve efficient management through upstream and downstream cooperation and management while ensuring economic benefits and maintaining stable capital flow [11].

They are Enabling Innovative Technology. Innovation is the driving force for the development of enterprises and the main driving force for the further development of sustainable supply chains. Companies can drive sustainable supply chains by developing new products and services and improving supply chain costs, efficiency, flexibility, reliability, and collaboration.

The application of innovation and technology is the key to the development of a sustainable supply chain. With the intersection of Industry 4.0 and sustainable supply chains, technologies such as blockchain and big data analytics will provide real-time tracking and analysis, as well as end-to-end visibility, including to the most distant suppliers at the bottom, helping to eliminate redundancy and bottlenecks and ultimately reduce resource consumption and carbon emissions.

Blockchain technology is a decentralized database that is both open and transparent. Blockchain is also immutable, where data cannot be modified or deleted. It is a kind of infrastructure that solves the credit problem, based on which all social activities will be trusted [12]. Applying blockchain to sustainable supply chain management, building and relying on this platform can achieve the goal of sustainable supply chain management. The technical feasibility of blockchain is mainly manifested in the following aspects: multi-center, reliability, trustworthiness, openness, high efficiency, and security. Blockchain technology enables open collaboration between the upstream and downstream of the supply chain while ensuring transaction security and trust, which is of great help to the sustainable development of the supply chain [13]. Blockchain technology is mainly applied in three areas of supply chain management: information flow, logistics, and cash flow. The product traceability system is the most representative among blockchain applications in the information flow field. One product with one code is realized by combining Internet technology, the Internet of Things, and automatic identification technology. The tracking information of the whole process, from product production to transportation to sales, is recorded. This system mainly applies to clothing and various practical products to help enterprises achieve product traceability [13]. For example, in November 2019, Volvo cooperated with two battery material suppliers in China and South Korea, as well as several blockchain technology companies in China, to ensure that the precious metal in the cobalt material for power batteries is traceable, making Volvo the world's first automaker to use blockchain technology to trace cobalt material for power batteries.

3.3 Some Problems in Related Research and Application in China

The sustainable supply chain management level in Chinese enterprises is at the initial stage, which needs to be improved in both theoretical research and practical application. In addition, there needs to be more in-depth research based on the actual situation to promote the further development of sustainable supply chain management in enterprises.

To be specific, the main problems existing in sustainable supply chain management in China are as follows:

Enterprises lack strategic cooperation and professional talents for the integrity and coordination of sustainable supply chains. The staff turnover of enterprise management is frequent, the degree of informatization is not high, and the efficiency of information transfer between units is not high, thus increasing the market risk. In addition, because enterprises consider different interests, selecting evaluation indicators for sustainable suppliers is subjective, and there is a lack of a unified index evaluation system [14].

The research on the coordinated development of the environment and economy has been relatively complete. However, after adding social responsibility, stakeholders need to assume full social responsibility by considering the environment and maximizing benefits, which hinders the combination of sustainable development and supply chain [15]. The lack of coordination between enterprises for environmental management and the unable to ensure the ecological attributes of supply chain management; According to the theoretical research, the cost invested by enterprises in the green supply chain may not generate the same amount or surplus economic return after operation [16].In addition, since the evaluation indexes of environment, economy, and society are independent, the comprehensive evaluation of them needs to be carried out under a unified framework, so it is still challenging to realize the coordination of multi-objectives of economy, environment, and society [17].

3.4 Suggestions

Based on the study of existing business cases and technology-enabling cases, this paper makes the following suggestions to help enterprises achieve sustainable management:

Develop strict sustainability standards and monitor suppliers to ensure compliance. Work closely with suppliers to develop sustainable sourcing strategies and products to ensure the sustainability of the entire supply chain.

Improve the internal impetus of enterprises and mobilize the enthusiasm for green development. Especially for small and medium-sized enterprises need to consider how to save the investment of sustainable management mode, reduce investment costs, and retain skilled talents.

Senior leaders must have good values and a strong focus on sustainable management. Establish and strengthen communication and engagement mechanisms with all stakeholders in the supply chain, including employees, suppliers, customers, communities, and governments. Work with governments, non-governmental organizations, industry associations, and other stakeholders to share best practices and promote the meaning and value of sustainable supply chains.

To achieve sustainability goals by building a digital supply chain network and using environmentally friendly materials and manufacturing processes. With the development of technology and the widespread use of CHAT GPT, the new generation of AI enabling sustainable supply chain management is becoming more practical.

Pay attention to the implementation of corporate social responsibility and public image maintenance. Comprehensively implement the concept and system of sustainable development, carry out the common technology research and development and sharing mechanism, establish the supplier social evaluation and credit rating system, integrate into the international production capacity cooperation, and improve the reputation and popularity of the enterprise.

4 Conclusion

This paper adopts the theoretical research method, mainly analyzes the factors that promote sustainable supply chains and practical results and gives corresponding suggestions. Hence, the research method is relatively simple. In addition, although this paper analyzes the field of the sustainable supply chain from the perspectives of the internal and external environment of organizations, enterprise management, social responsibility, innovation, etc., it still needs some improvement and further improvement.

Faced with global resource depletion and environmental deterioration, the government and the public are increasingly demanding low-carbon environmental protection, which has greatly changed the competitive environment of enterprises and the role of enterprises in society. Enterprises should not only pursue their economic interests but also consciously undertake more social responsibilities. Combining sustainable development concepts and supply chains has become an inevitable trend. As research on sustainable supply chains continues to deepen, more companies are integrating sustainability into their supply chain management practices. By reviewing the existing literature on sustainable supply chain management and analyzing the research results of domestic and foreign scholars on sustainable supply chains in different dimensions, this paper summarizes the motivation and practical results of promoting a sustainable supply chain. It suggests that future supply chain management contributes to sustainable development.

References

1. Drumwright, M.E.: Socially responsible organizational buying: environmental concern as a noneconomic buying criterion. J. Mark. **58**(3), 1–19 (1994)

2. Stefan, S., Martin, M.: From a literature review to a conceptual framework for the sustainable supply chain management. J. Clean. Prod. **16**(15), 1699–1710 (2018)
3. Zhu, Q., Yu, F.: Research on sustainable supply chain management under dynamic environment. Supply Chain Manag. **1**(12), 32–47 (2020)
4. Du, W.: Overview of foreign research status of sustainable supply chain. China Commer. Trade **23**, 156–157 (2014)
5. Yu, Y.: Research on Green Supply Chain Innovation Path and Strategy of Ningbo Manufacturing Industry Under the Background of "Made in China 2025." Zhejiang Wanli University, Ningbo (2019)
6. Winkle, R.: Closed-loop production systems-a sustainable supply chain approach. J. Manuf. Sci. Technol. **4**, 243–246 (2011)
7. Zhao, J.: Research on the Influence Mechanism of Information Technology on Sustainable Supply Chain Practice. Zhongnan University of Economics and Law, Wuhan (2020)
8. Zhang, Q.: Walmart's green supply chain management. Mark. Weekly **02**, 29–30 (2011)
9. Li, L., Liu, Y., Wang, H.: Promoting the transformation and upgrading of traditional industries with sustainable supply chain innovation. Macroecon. Manag. **11**, 44–50+56 (2020)
10. Liu, R.: Development history and enlightenment of Huawei sustainable supply chain. Finan. Account. Monthly **17**, 143–149 (2017)
11. Lan, S., Qin, X.: An analysis of Yili's OPM Strategy from the perspective of Supply chain Management. Time Finan. **15**, 331–332 (2018)
12. Zhang, X.: Optimization of supply chain management mode based on blockchain. China Circ. Econ. **32**(08), 42–50 (2018)
13. Ge, L., Xu, J., Wang, Z., Zhang, G., Yan, L., Hu, Z.: Research status and challenges of Blockchain application in the supply chain. Comput. Appl. (2023)
14. Yang, D.: Research on Supplier Evaluation and Selection Based on Sustainable Supply Chain Management. Hebei University of Technology, Tianjin (2021)
15. Craig, R., Dale, S., Thomas, Y.: Toward the theory of the supply chain. J. Supply Chain Manag. **51**(2), 89–97 (2015)
16. Scheinin: Extraction of green supply chain management theory problems. J. Nat. Bus. **49**(7), 1653–5051 (2007)
17. Liu, J., Feng, Y., Zhu, Q.: Research trends and prospects of sustainable operations management. Syst. Eng. Theory Pract. **40**(08), 1996–2020 (2020)

Innovating Online Operational Models for Independent Hotels: Assessing the Feasibility of a "Regional Independent Hotel Network Alliance" in Yunnan

Qijing Li[✉]

Stanfort Academy, London Metropolitan University, Singapore 248922, Singapore
cian_lqj@mail.sdufe.edu.cn

Abstract. This research ascertained the efficacy of establishing a hotel alliance online strategy, namely, "Regional Independent Hotel Online Alliance (RIHOA)", for a group of independent hotels in Yunnan province. RIHOA is intended to help these independent hotels to compete with member hotels of Online Travel Agency (OTAs). This research adopted qualitative analysis. In-depth semi-structured interviews were conducted using a sample of 15 key hotel executives selected from a group of independent hotels in Yunnan. Thematic analysis was employed to generate key codes and categories. This research offered qualitative insight for establishing a hotel alliance to make up for the massive gap in capital and technology compared with OTAs and develop an independent online distribution channel to help a group of independent hotels secure market share in Yunnan.

Keywords: RIHOA · Yunnan · Independent hotels

1 Introduction

"RIHOA" was intended to establish a purposive linkage among a group of independent hotels in Yunnan with intended collaborations involving information exchange, co-development of promotion campaign or vacant room sharing, and offering collective services in the form of a common online marketing channel, online booking, and pickup or Chauffeur-driven service. In other words, this alliance entails a process of convergence of interests.

The significance of this study can be explained using the following two reasons. Firstly, the research study was motivated by the Chinese government's plan for the development of the tourism industry, the opportunity for establishing the linkage and cyberization among hotel enterprises, and the potential for introducing RCEP in the hotel industry of Yunnan Province in the next ten years starting from the year 2020 [1]. These motivations were the primer for this research journey, especially for promoting B&R tourism in China [2].

Secondly, several research studies have explicated the limitations of independent hotels' technology and capital, resulting in a negative revenue return when each independent hotel pursues its online direct marketing channels. Besides, the commission charge posed by OTAs was high, which would reduce the profit margin of an independent hotel if it joined OTAs [3]. Therefore, establishing RIHOA helped independent hotels in Yunnan secure market share and increase profit margins via an economical direct marketing channel compared with the OTA approach.

Thirdly, the "Hotel + OTA" type of hotel operation model is a typical independent hotel service supply chain model. Its primary forms of existence are the net price wholesale and commission agency models [4]. Many studies have been conducted to compare and analyze this model in depth, but no new form has been created for the direct marketing channel of independent hotels.

China's hotel industry had entered a period of transition from the old normal to the new normal. By the year 2020, the structure of China's hotel industry has undergone three levels of differentiation, namely, high-end international brands, mid-range domestic chain brands, and independent hotels. This research focused on independent hotels in Yunnan. The "tourism boom" after the Covid-19 epidemic has prompted the quest for online marketing and innovative business models to revitalize the hotel industry.

Yunnan is located on the southwestern border of China. It has 10 national and nearly 20 provincial-level ports, constituting a tourist hub for travelers from China to Southeast Asia and South Asia and vice versa. At the same time, it is an essential province for China's "Belt and Road (B&R)" initiative that offers superior geographical conditions for the development of Yunnan's tourism industry [5]. The nicknames "Animal Kingdom", "Plant Kingdom," and "Non-Ferrous Metal Kingdom" made Yunnan a natural heritage site that includes scenic views of Dali, Lijiang, and Shangri-La. It also offers great archeological finds of completed sauropod dinosaur fossils in Lufeng. These diverse natural resources increased the attractiveness of tourism in Yunnan. Yunnan owned 25 Chinese ethnic minorities, whose total population accounted for more than 30% of the total population of Yunnan Province [2]. Ethnic diversity has created diverse and distinctive ethnic festivals in Yunnan, such as the torch festival of the Yi people, the water splashing festival of the Dai people, and the twin festival of the Hani people. And many of these ethnic groups have national languages and cultural products. These rare and diverse cultural resources in Yunnan have created Yunnan's unique position in the tourism industry.

The natural and cultural heritage of Yunnan has fueled its hotel industry. Since 2008, the flow of tourists in Yunnan has shown a growth trend, which has induced the expansion of the hotel industry in Yunnan [5]. However, the existing hotels in Yunnan have faced complex business problems such as the isolation mode of hotel operation and management, the low degree of marketing investment, the unbalanced distribution of investment funds, the backward management model, and the difficulty of introducing international brands [6].

Independent hotels emerged as a "light investment" form in the Yunnan hotel industry. The lower investment costs resulted in lower entry barriers. Therefore, independent hotels accounted for a large proportion of the Yunnan hotel industry in terms of numbers compared to other mid-to-high-end hotels. Tourists' quest for personalized and authentic requirements, internet celebrity homestays, and low prices have become the main drivers for stimulating the growth of independent hotels in Yunnan [6].

In addition, existing literature analyzed independent hotels' development in the Internet economy era. They pointed out that independent hotels relied too much on OTAs, so their bargaining power was seriously challenged. They suggested considering the establishment of an independent hotel alliance with a business strategy [7]. As such, the notion of RIHOA put forward in this research study was prompted by this induction.

2 Literature Review

RIHOA is distinguished from third-party service agencies (OTAs) for the avoidance of paying commissions for the same online transaction. RIHOA's online direct marketing system is a one-time investment. Independent hotel operators funded it at one time. It can be perceived as a marketing transformation for independent hotels. Compared with the business model of chain hotels, independent hotels in this study were limited to those small-scale hotels owned or operated solely by an enterprise, an organization, or an individual, and its' room scale was usually from 10 to 100 rooms.

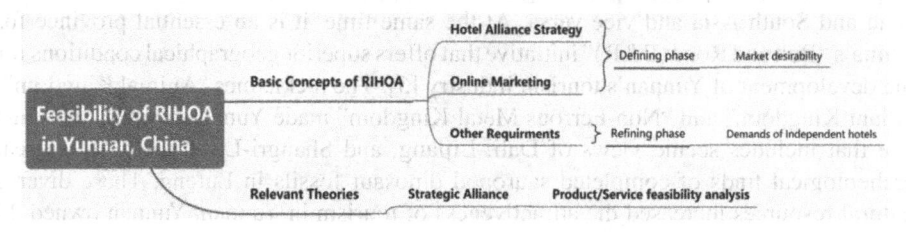

Fig. 1. Conceptual Framework for RIHOA

As depicted in Fig. 1, to ensure the feasibility of RIHOA in Yunnan, this study referred to "Product/Service feasibility analysis" to conduct market analysis. They were explicitly presented as defining phase-oriented to explore market desirability and refining phase-oriented to examine the actual demands of independent hotels. In addition, the related theories of the strategic alliance were used as the basis for perfecting and establishing RIHOA. "Strategic alliance is a form of cooperation in which two or more partners share knowledge, technology, and resources, ultimately benefiting all partners" [8]. This was not limited to large companies; small companies could learn and improve through "sharing".

3 Methodology

3.1 Research Method

RIHOA was currently in the stage of exploration and start-up in Yunnan. Most independent hotels still relied on OTAs for online marketing, and there needed to be marketing models established for individual businesses based on the reality in Yunnan. Therefore, this research adopted qualitative research, and the in-depth understanding of research questions was conducted with 15 semi-structured interviews.

In addition, concept testing and inductive thematic analysis served as the main qualitative research tools for this research. Replaced simple communication with concept testing to help potential customers better understand the RIHOA and absorb feedback; inductive thematic analysis was designed as a data-oriented induction and refinement [9, 10]. These research methods contributed to RIHOA modeling and revealed the constantly reflexive dialogue processing in the researcher's interviews. In addition, due to time constraints, this research study utilized the cross-sectional time-zone mode.

The Reliability, Validity, and Generalizability of this research were designed with the following methods to ensure the effectiveness of semi-structured interviews. And the researcher provided practical explanations in Table 1.

3.2 Data Collection

This study established the conceptual description, which contained RIHOA's Business Concept, Target Market, Specificity, Services, Operational implementation, Management team, Manager qualification, Specific management regulations, and the reasons for establishing RIHOA.

Non-probabilistic sampling was adopted as the sampling method of this study. The reason was that non-probabilistic sampling methods were applicable for those in the initial research stage, and it was convenient for researchers to collect samples [11]. Table 2 recorded all the essential information of the 15 participants.

In-depth and semi-structured interviews obtained initial data and information related to the research content for this qualitative research. Before the interview, all the interviewees were stakeholders of independent hotels in Yunnan identified by the researcher through actual screening beforehand. Each interviewee was asked to read the "RIHOA Concept Statement" beforehand to ensure a preliminary understanding of the purpose of the research and the content of the interview. And a 30-min interview was conducted through WeChat voice and video calls, which were recorded and transcribed through iFlytek APP. The researcher also recorded the specific content of each interview in the form of notes. In addition, for protecting the interviewees' privacy, all participants were anonymously written on each data item, and presented in the form of letters and numbers.

Inductive themes analyzed the acquired data, and the interpretation of the data was reflected in a phased form (Table 3). "The Data Interpretation Processing" was adapted from the various phases of thematic analysis designed by Braun & Clarke [9].

4 Data Analysis

4.1 Coding Process

In the initial coding stage, the author determined the semantic content and potential features of these 74 data extracts and obtained 90 corresponding data values as illustrated in Table 4.

The potential theme is the process of integrating and summarizing the code that has been identified. This process combines the highly similar and relevant codes obtained from data extracts to form each basic theme [12]. The author determined those potential

Table 1. The Analysis of Reliability, Validity, and Generalisability.

Items	Qualitative Research Methods	Values
Reliability	Semi-structured interviews:15 Concept Testing	15 participants were selected from three tourist areas in Yunnan, and they are independent hotel operators from Dali, Lijiang and Kunming. This lifted the barriers of relative geographical restrictions and ensured the objectivity of the interview RIHOA was explained in detail through "RIHOA's Concept Statement Diagram" instead of the simple narrative form. It ensured that all participants had a clear understanding before accepting the interview, thereby enhancing the reliability of the research
Validity	Inductive Thematic Analysis: it applied when the identified themes had a close connection with collected data, and the analysis was oriented by data itself(Walters, 2016) Adhere to the principle of theme formation	Through the "Inductive Thematic Processing" analysis and interpretation of the data, the effectiveness of the process was ensured by coding and thematic refining When refining themes, the researcher always adhered to the principle that more than half of similar codes could form a potential theme, that is, when a fact existed in 50% or more of the data items, it had the objective conditions to form a potential theme. This enhanced the effectiveness of data acquisition
Generalizability	This research carried out new insights into the construction of RIHOA in Yunnan through the logical induction of the RIHOA model and consideration of the feasibility analysis	A RIHOA can help independent hotels in Yunnan increase profitability and improve recognition. It also contributed feasible possibilities for the marketing and survival of independent hotels in local and other regions

themes with a support rate of more than 50%, and finally obtained 42 effective potential basic themes.

The basic themes were logically arranged into coherent groups, and were condensed into higher-level themes with common similarities. And the resulting organic theme was defined as an organizational theme [12]. As stated in Table 5, the author logically arranged the 42 effective basic themes obtained and ultimately formed the 8 organization themes.

Table 2. Demographic Profile of Interviewees (N = 15).

Variable	Items	Count
Gender	Male	8
	Female	7
	Others	0
Areas	Dali	5
	Lijiang	5
	Kunming	5
Position	Owner	12
	Manager	3
Work Experience	< 5 years	6
	9 years	8
	≥ 10 years	1
Room Scale	< 10 rooms	2
	10–20 rooms	9
	≥ 20 rooms	4

Table 3. The Data Interpretation Processing

Phase	Description of the process
Familiarizing texts with collected data	Transcribing data (if necessary), reading and re-reading the data, and noting down initial ideas
Generating initial codes	Coding specific features of initial data in a systematic fashion across the whole databases, collating data relevant to each code
Searching and defining for potential themes	Collating codes into potential themes, gathering all initial data relevant to each potential theme; and generating clear definitions and names for each theme
Integrating potential themes	Concentrate the common similarities of each potential theme, and integrate a higher-level logical organization theme
Producing the report	Perform a final analysis on the vivid examples and content of the integrated themes and excerpts. Turn back to the research questions and literature, and form an academic report. Completed the chapters of "Data Analysis" and "Discussion"

Table 4. Part of the Coding process.

Data extracts	The code obtained
O1: Basically, through OTAs such as Ctrip, Meituan and Airbnb, we started doing it when the market environment was good. We can accumulate part of our own resources, but basically there is no situation of directly communicating with customers, generally recommended by old customers or repeat customers	1: Mainly through Ctrip, Meituan and Airbnb ushered in the online marketing; 2: Direct marketing: old customers' recommendations; 3: When the market environment is positive, the independent hotel has accumulated customer resources

Table 5. Part of the Formation of Themes

Organization Themes	≥50%	Basic Themes	The Codes integrated
The current marketing channels of independent hotels in Yunnan	A: √	A: Mainly Online Marketing Channels Ctrip	O1–1: Mainly through Ctrip, Meituan and Airbnb ushered in the online marketing;
			O4–2: Online marketing: Ctrip and Qunar
	B1: √ B2: √	B1: Lack of direct marketing channels B2: Merchants are very passive in online direct sales	O1–2: Direct marketing: old customers' recommendations and Wechat Moments promotions;
			O4–1: Businesses generally receive self-driving trips and tour groups
			O5–1: In the off-season of travel, there will be more profits from self-coming visitors
			O4–3: Some guests will check the information of independent hotels on OTAs, and then decide whether to check in after actually getting to know the room type in the store

According to the thematic map, as shown in Fig. 2, the author clarified the relationship between the eight organization themes and related to each organization theme, the parent number of the effective basic themes were listed.

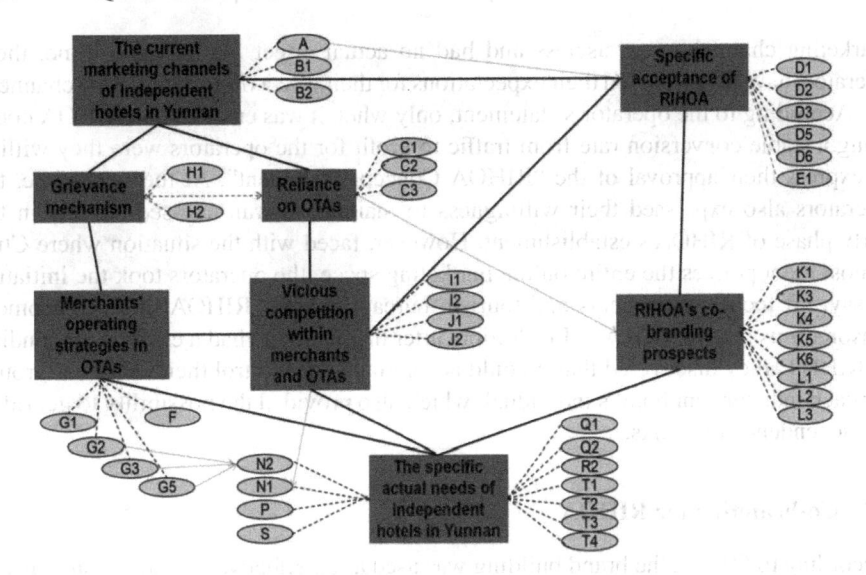

Fig. 2. Thematic Map

The logical relationships among the eight organization themes in the thematic map were: To confirm the acceptance of RIHOA by each business, first of all, it was necessary to objectively understand the current marketing channels of independent hotels in Yunnan; Secondly, with OTAs occupying the dominant position in the online marketing channels with absolute advantage, the grievance mechanism of OTAs and the dependence of merchants on OTAs were analyzed, and OTAs' contempt for merchants was found in the analyzing process; Finally, during the analysis process, the merchants actively talked about their operating strategies on OTAs, the situation of entering OTAs and vicious internal competition, which led to the expectations of the merchants on RIHOA. Thus, the research further confirmed the merchant's considerations and expectations of RIHOA's co-branding. After learning from the actual marketing situation of the merchants in OTAs, comprehensively considering that RIHOA can bring actual operation solutions to the merchants and obtain the merchants' demands for employee training, intelligent services, and equipment maintenance.

5 Discussion

5.1 Online Marketing for RIHOA

According to the basic themes obtained, the leading marketing channels of independent hotels in Yunnan rely on OTAs, such as Ctrip, Meituan, Airbnb, and Qunar APPs, which are indirect marketing channels for online marketing. The operators stated that the current tracks for direct communication with customers had been extremely passively restricted to self-driving tours, old customers, and the promotion of WeChat Moments. For homestays in tourist areas, these direct marketing channels would bring a small amount of income during the off-season; for independent hotels in cities, these direct marketing channels were useless and had no actual effect. At the same time, these operators have all expressed their expectations for their direct online marketing channels.

According to the operator's statement, only when it was ensured that RIHOA could bring a stable conversion rate from traffic to profit for the operators were they willing to express their approval of the "RIHOA Concept Statement". At the same time, the operators also expressed their willingness to maintain a wait-and-see attitude in the early phase of RIHOA's establishment. However, faced with the situation where Ctrip almost monopolizes the entire online marketing space, the operators took the initiative to say: "If local governments and tourism bureaus support RIHOA, it will become a reason for us to join RIHOA." In addition, after the operators had a clear understanding of RIHOA, they discovered that it could accumulate and control their customer groups for each independent hotel's individual, which also provided the possibility to get rid of the dependence on OTAs.

5.2 Co-branding for RIHOA

According to O1–21, the brand building was used as an effective way to expand visibility to obtain more profits. The brand building was recognized during the 15 interviews in three regions in Yunnan. The "hodgepodge" type of co-branding brought new customers to individuals, and it was also the key to achieving long-term contact between an independent hotel and regular customers. But the operators proposed:

Divide according to the service methods provided to customers by independent hotels in urban areas and tourist areas, namely, city-specialization and tourist area lifestyle. Under this premise, RIHOA subdivided each independent hotel and ultimately obtained a "hodgepodge" co-branding camp.

In fact, due to the lack of capital and technology, individual independent hotels cannot form a co-brand with a competitive advantage. Operators require RIHOA to stand on the standpoint of businesses in different regions, share essential resources, and expect RIHOA to replace the theme of "commercialization" with the concept of "home" as the content of the co-branding.

Consider other possibilities that can form a competitive advantage. For example, formulating standards for entering co-branding, etc.

5.3 Demands for Possible Services

B&B operators in the tourist area said that they almost had no staffs, and as for how to provide guests with a leisurely, comfortable, and warm service, all were done by themselves, so there was no need for staff training; A few operators with more than 20 rooms considered it advisable to provide regular staff training. For independent hotel operators in the cities, they insisted that staff training was necessary, which could improve the quality of services and enhance their capabilities. In this way, it was also possible to prepare candidate managers for opening a branch.

Operators in the tourist area described "wooden rooms" and "long-term use of equipment". Therefore, independent hotel operators expect RIHOA to provide a professional engineering team considering maintenance costs. When interviewing independent hotels with a room size of more than 20 rooms, the operators questioned the maintenance staff's unfamiliarity with the specific hotel furnishings and pipeline locations. They, therefore, were unable to provide effective maintenance services by RIHOA. And a hotel of this size usually had its engineering department, which was why RIHOA's equipment maintenance service was denied.

According to the compelling basic themes Q1 and Q2 provided by the participants, dividing the independent hotels with the scopes of the cities and the tourist area, the former insisted on the attitude of active introduction, while the latter expressed opposition. The reason is that, taking Lijiang as an example, the rise of homestays here is due to tourists' demands for a "lifestyle" travel accommodation experience, so independent hotels here are dominated by providing customers with a "home" concept butler service; This has led to many people-to-person contact behaviors, and these behaviors made artificial intelligence services impossible to complete in Lijiang. At the same time, the characteristic of cities is that they are developing fast and need to be constantly exposed to new information, such as artificial intelligence services.

According to O1–36, "which is also a manifestation of preventing missed orders and saving time and effort." among independent hotel operations with less than 20 rooms, most people cannot obtain a real-time room status monitoring system with mature technology due to the disadvantages of capital and technology. This caused issues with guest room management and connection to the online marketing system for independent hotel operators.

6 Conclusion

In the definition phase, the data-oriented results involved in the Hotel Alliance online strategy are positive responses to the acceptance of the establishment of RIHOA in Yunnan; It is also the guarantee for implementing RIHOA's actual operation in Yunnan. In the refining phase, the author revealed the demands for these four aspects of services from independent hotels in Yunnan. And considering the attributions and differences between urban areas and tourist areas, the results of this research study carried out solutions applicable to local conditions. Thus, the preliminary establishment model for implementing RIHOA in Yunnan has been completed.

This research uses an inducement method to explore the scope of a specific event in a particular context. Therefore, this study only applies to special situational conditions and cannot be inferred beyond the sample size. In addition, this research has absorbed the author's personal value orientation, so the research conclusion has certain limitations.

According to the interviews and data analysis results, the market has affirmed the feasibility of establishing RIHOA. And the research followed the data-oriented principle to refine the possibility of further strengthening RIHOA's services for independent hotels in Yunnan and obtaining profits.

The application of RIHOA in the future should be developed based on the region as a specific "point" and the country as a whole "face". Only in this way can the mutual promotion and exchange of independent hotels among multiple regions be realized, and a broader contribution can be made to the development of the tourism industry in China.

References

1. Chinadaily Homepage. https://www.chinadaily.com.cn/a/202012/11/WS5fd2b403a31024ad0ba9b224.html. Accessed 11 Feb 2023
2. Duan, Y.: Research on the development of Yunnan tourism industry under the background of 'One Belt One Road.' Technol. Econ. Guide **26**(34), 91–94 (2018)
3. Li, G., Wang, J.: Research on the development strategy of individual hotels in the era of big data. Tour. Overview **16**, 77 (2018)
4. Du, X., Wang, Y., Ding, Y.: Research on the typical operation mode of 'hotel + OTA' type tourism service supply chain. Mark. Week **05**, 1–3+44 (2022)
5. Zhang, Y., He, J.: Study on the relationships among hotel alliance network relationship diversity resource integration process and hotels performance. Tour. Tribune **34**(2), 83–93 (2019)
6. Chen, M., Han, Z., Yin, J., Tang, X.: Research on crisis management of China's hotel industry under the new coronary pneumonia epidemic. Ind. Econ. **1053**(26), 57–58 (2020)
7. Liu, Q.: Research on the innovation of hotel and OTA competition and cooperation in the "Internet +" Era'. Tour. Overview **20**, 80–81 (2018)
8. Trott, P.: Innovation Management and New Product Development. Machinery Industry Press, Beijing (2020)
9. Barringer, R.B., Ireland, D.R.: Entrepreneurship: Successfully Launching New Ventures. Machinery Industry Press, Beijing (2017)
10. Braun, V., Clarke, V.: Using thematic analysis in psychology. Qual. Res. Psychol. **3**(2), 77–101 (2006)
11. Lin, Q.: Research on the application of non-probability sampling methods in the context of big data. Chin. Foreign Entrepre. **27**, 228 (2019)
12. Walters, T.: Research note using thematic analysis in tourism research. Tour. Anal. **21**, 107–116 (2016)

Supply Chain Management in the Era of "Internet+": Case Analysis of Agricultural Product Supply Chain

Huimin Liu[1], Yangmeng Liu[2(✉)], and Siyan Yi[3]

[1] School of Business, Shaoguan University, Shaoguan 512005, China
[2] College of Business Administration, Guangdong University of Finance, Guangzhou 510000, China
201526131@m.gduf.edu.cn
[3] School of Civil Engineering and Geomatics, Southwest Petroleum University, Chengdu 610000, China

Abstract. In the era of "Internet+", people are influenced by many factors, such as big data and transboundary thinking. Their demand has become more diverse, and the competition among enterprises is escalating. Therefore, supply chain management (SCM) has become the key to occupying the market. To satisfy consumers' demand and realize enterprise profit, the transformation and optimization of supply chain management is a way worth exploring. Supply chain management aims to achieve the lowest cost while achieving the best operation. The transformation of modern supply chain management requires digitalization, intellectualization by internet technology, and big data planning to adapt to the rapid changes in the global economy. Nowadays, the "Internet+" industry has become a hot development direction. The two complement each other and gradually form a preliminary Internet social ecology.

Keywords: Internet+ · Transformation · Agricultural Product Supply Chain

1 Introduction

With the development of the modern internet, Internet ecology has become a key factor in global terms. Global economic integration and the booming Internet economy promote enterprises to turn to information, intelligence, and digital. The transformation of supply chain management is imminent because the competition between enterprises has intensified. It is an important way to make enterprises master time-sensitive internal information and external resources by establishing a modern supply chain management model. Innovation and transformation of supply chain management mean enterprises can access external details more rapidly and accurately analyze the market demand simultaneously to improve the efficiency of enterprise management and promote enterprise reform and transformation.

H. Liu, Y. Liu and S. Yi—These authors contributed equally.

Based on the background of the Internet, the concept of intelligent supply chain management was created. By transforming supply chain management into intellectual and digital, enterprises can establish an interconnected supply chain management ecology to promote the optimization of supply chain management further. Transformation supply chain management can maximize the operational efficiency of enterprises and enhance their competitiveness.

An intelligent supply chain takes modern logistics and supply chain management as the center, combines it with the Internet of Things, cloud computing, big data, and other technical applications, follow the ideas and principles of intra-function and inter-function business process engineering, divides the business scope clearly, and defines the process boundary precisely. On the premise of strengthening the flexibility of the supply chain, by optimizing the existing management process and business process, we can continuously reduce the operating cost of enterprises, improve the efficiency and quality of enterprises, and provide support for intelligent decision-making of enterprises.

An intelligent supply chain, which achieves the digitalization of business, evaluates the supply chain process by collecting and analyzing data in a timely and accurate manner, making business management more convenient and accurate. By accurately forecasting the market, analyzing the collected data, forecasting customer needs, and market development can reduce the influence of the Bullwhip effect. At the same time, using AI, human-less technology, and Blockchain technology improves transparency and visualization of the supply chain, thus reducing procurement costs.

Based on the understanding of enterprise supply chain, combined with the Internet, this study has comprehensively analyzed how to transform supply chain management in the era of "Internet+". Based on the disadvantages of traditional supply chain management, this study has elaborated on the advantages and direction of supply chain transformation in detail. This study used the supply chain management of an agricultural products enterprise as an example and analyzed its basis、pattern, and economic value. This study has specific reference significance for optimizing supply chain management in agriculture and other enterprises.

2 Literature Review

It is a significant development trend for enterprises' supply chain management to contribute to digital platforms using Internet technology such as big data and digital management tools. Digital supply chain replaces traditional management with digital interconnection technology [1]. In the process of implementing supply chain transformation, it should ensure that the main framework of the supply chain pattern, business operation pattern, and product output model is consistent, rely on big data to build a comprehensive and coordinated core link of the supply chain, including tendering and bidding, inventory distribution and other aspects [2]. Wang analyzed the operational functions of traditional and big data supply chains and put forward relevant suggestions [3]. However, there needs to be more analysis of actual supply chain-related cases in their research. Zhang summarized the disadvantages of the traditional supply chain and the advantages of the intelligent supply chain and explored the transforming principle of a traditional supply chain to an intelligent supply chain [4]. Zhao proved its importance by analyzing the significance of intelligent supply chain transformation of agricultural products and key issues in the construction and operation process and considering the framework of the latest intelligent supply chain system of agricultural products in various aspects [5]. Future research should focus on practical cases while analyzing the intelligent supply chain, especially for the supply chain models of different industries.

A famous British logistician, Professor Martin Christopher, defined a supply chain as "A network of upstream and downstream business organizations involved in the processes and activities that deliver a product or service to the final consumer" [6]. Downey pointed out that the supply chain of agricultural products is a vertical chain from top to bottom; it covers the production of agricultural products and the processing and marketing processes [7]. Wang claimed that the relationship between agricultural supply chain and industry chain he thinks agricultural supply chain and industry chain constitute a complete industry chain in the macro research, which is called the agricultural industry chain, and the upper, middle, and downstream links of agricultural products are called the agrarian supply chain [8]. Chen summarized the goal of supply chain management as "6R"; that is, the right products needed by customers are delivered to the right place at the right time, with the right quality, and in the right state, and the total cost is minimized [9]. Duan pointed the rapid development of Internet technology provides opportunities for supply chain cost reduction and service improvement [10]. In the background of "Internet+", scientific agricultural production has been promoted, and experts can guide farmers to carry out scientific planting remotely through the Internet [11]. Yang aimed at the problems such as weak storage and management ability, theft, tampering, deletion, and information inconsistency of information in the supply chain of agricultural products [12]. Hong proposed that applicated blockchain in the application path of "three products and one standard" high-quality agricultural products e-commerce field [13]. Jiang studied the blockchain mathematical shared farm represented by the "taste of kindness". They believe combining blockchain technology with the agricultural supply chain can revolutionize it [14].

3 The Problem of Traditional SCM

Backward management thinking is not compatible with the technology. Most of the enterprise's supply chain management still uses ERP systems, disconnected from digital management in the Internet context and lacking intelligent control. The main contradiction facing China's business management is the disconnect between traditional supply chain management thinking and the ever-changing Internet technology. From the current perspective, if a company wants to grow in the long term, it must change its supply chain management model.

The communication and collaboration between various departments in the supply chain management model need to be closer, failing to achieve information sharing, and the supply chain information level needs to be fixed. Due to the lack of a digital platform, information cannot be shared among departments or enterprises, resulting in information lag, making enterprises inefficient or top management unable to make the right decision in time. In addition, the lack of information, such as resource procurement, can also lead to increased operating costs for businesses. However, due to the backwardness of

China's Internet-related technology, the enterprise supply chain management model cannot be further optimized and improved. But with the development of Internet technology, Chinese enterprises will gradually build up an information-sharing platform. Therefore, enterprise supply chain management optimization will likely stagnate before the only Chinese Internet information technology breakthrough.

On the supply side, traditional supply chain management needs to be updated. Most of the current supply chains adopt the mode of production-based sales on the supply side and mass production for a single species. Under the influence of the bullwhip effect, the difference in information transmission increases. It is challenging to match supply and demand, which indirectly restricts the development of customer personalization. This leads directly to high costs, long production cycles, low efficiency, disconnected sales and production, and slow supply chain response.

4 The Advantages of an Intelligent Supply Chain

4.1 Digital Platform

A digital management platform can be constructed using Internet technologies such as big data technology and digital management tools to improve supply chain management efficiency in enterprises. Digital supply chain management links the various links of the traditional supply chain through Internet technology while building a digital platform for information sharing to improve the science and efficiency of enterprise management, reduce economic losses, and form good risk management measures. The digital platform can accelerate the speed and security of high-level corporate decision-making while improving the interface between various departments within the enterprise to form an efficient cycle. In addition, modern Internet technology can overturn the traditional supply chain management model, realize platform-based management, reduce enterprise management costs, and guarantee continuous optimization of the enterprise supply chain. The digital platform ensures the timely transmission of information, enabling all enterprise parties to receive information in time to make correct decisions. In the process of implementation, it is necessary to ensure the coordination of the main framework of the supply chain model, the business operation model, and the output model of each form of the enterprise and to build a comprehensive and coordinated supply chain core links based on big data, such as bidding and bidding and inventory allocation.

4.2 Service Platform

In transforming the supply chain model, user thinking is one of the important components of Internet thinking. To realize the transformation to a service-oriented supply chain, the traditional supply chain model must be combined with the Internet, using big data technology to segment customers and realize refined data management to optimize and upgrade the service platform and better meet customer needs. People's demand for products is more diversified, so product customization has been widely discussed.

However, combining the traditional supply chain model with the Internet takes work. Implementing this combination can quickly put the customer's trust in the company to the ground. Therefore, business managers should personally and strictly control the supply chain transformation process and improve each supply chain link while guaranteeing customer privacy and timely delivery of high-quality products. Customer feedback can be collected in time to improve the shortcomings of the supply chain service model so that the transformed supply chain can meet the richer and more diversified customer needs, efficiently allocate market resources, reduce costs and improve the efficiency of business operations. In the transformation process, it is necessary to discard the redundant information in the supply chain in time to adapt to the continuous progress of the supply chain service management model under digitalization.

4.3 Transformation of Different Companies or Industries

For companies supported by big data, the intelligent supply chain can use the company's information system to integrate and optimize logistics resources, improve the transparency of the logistics process, and provide intelligent solutions to the problems encountered by customers and carriers in logistics. Taking Robinson Global Forwarding Ltd. as an example, the company has used big data technology to establish two systems to share the transportation status with customers and visualize the transportation process. In addition, through the platform derived from the system, the company has accumulated an extensive database of customers and transporters, which facilitates the company's business development in other areas. For companies that rely on smart technology innovation, the intelligent supply chain can help them eliminate rising labor costs, reduce manual links and promote the development of unmanned technology. Take New Stone as an example, the company, the originator of uncrewed logistics vehicles, has saved time while reducing costs through unmanned vehicle technology, which has greatly improved the efficiency of end-of-line delivery.

The intelligent supply chain is significant in promoting structural reform on the supply side. Building an information platform can promote coordinated supply chain management, accelerate the transformation and improvement of the manufacturing industry; improve the operational efficiency of intelligent storage of supply chain and transportation connection, promote the development of the distribution industry; promote the upstream and downstream linkage of agricultural and industrial products, solve the problem of regional overcapacity, and help the rapid transformation and development of agriculture.

5 Case Study

With the rapid development of e-commerce, consumers are paying more and more attention to shopping methods and the speed of goods circulation. The traditional supply chain system for agricultural products can no longer meet the needs of consumers. In the ever-changing market, we need to reform and innovate the supply chain system through the Internet+ to build a more complete, reliable, and efficient modern agricultural products supply chain system. The agricultural product supply chain is an integral part of our market system, and maintaining its sustainable development is of great significance to the order of social production and life. The agricultural product supply chain has become a research focus and is part of the national project to support strong towns in the agricultural industry. Therefore, taking Shaoguan Supply and Marketing Cooperative Society as an example, this paper introduces the background of the society through literature research and relevant research practices and focuses on analyzing and extrapolating the transformation ideas and models under the Internet+ model to provide suggestions for promoting the development of the agricultural supply chain management field in China.

5.1 Foundations for Transforming Agri-Products Business Supply Chains

Coordinating supply chain relationships, capital, logistics, production, and marketing conditions are the basis for supply chain transformation in agricultural product enterprises. To this end, the Shaoguan Supply and Marketing Cooperative has built an agricultural social service system, supporting innovation in operation, organization, and services. Through online platforms on the internet, the cooperative has been able to transform its cooperation in multiple fields, such as the "Guangdong Agricultural Services" APP platform built by the Guangdong Provincial Department of Agriculture and Rural Development, which realizes the "Internet+ agricultural machinery and agricultural technology" strategy. In terms of logistics, the Internet is also initially involved. Based on various aspects such as service, cooperation, and logistics, the supply and marketing cooperatives can establish an e-commerce platform in the context of the Internet+ era to create distinctive brands and thus facilitate the transformation of the supply chain of Shaoguan's agricultural product enterprises.

5.2 Transformation Models for Agri-Product Business Supply Chains

The use of "Internet+" to establish an intelligent agricultural machinery service platform and realize the integration of agricultural services. With the rapid development of the Internet+, consumer behavior has changed, facilitating the development of online and offline agriculture. This development has reduced the price differential between raw material markets and distributors, broken time and space constraints, and made online agricultural shops an essential sales channel, adding value to the agricultural supply chain. Through the Internet+ Agriculture platform, new agricultural operators are provided high-quality data on rice pests and fertilizer ratios, which can be analyzed and compared to predict the extent of problems and fertilizer ratios. Grid points and probing instruments are used in the rice fields to present crop growth in the form of data, which is then linked to thousands of agricultural operators through the internet to establish service centers and service outlets to help farmers. The supply and marketing agency plays the role of a comprehensive platform to help farmers, using the part of "Internet+" intelligent online management to link individual agricultural enterprises together and provide one-stop industry chain services in seedling breeding, fertilization, harvesting, storage, and acquisition so that new agrarian business entities have unified guidance and management.

With the power of "Internet+", establish an e-commerce platform and create a distinctive brand. With the rapid development of the Internet, e-commerce platforms have become one of the key sales channels for agricultural product enterprises in small areas. Agricultural products enterprises can use the shared resources and infrastructure the platform provides to expand their sales at a low cost. Shaoguan Supply and Marketing Society can rely on the characteristics of local resources and unite with the supply and marketing societies in each district to create a Shaoguan flavor brand through equity participation. In addition, agricultural products can be processed into easily portable and ready-to-eat products, and brand awareness can be strengthened to create an e-commerce platform for Shaoguan's special agricultural products by taking advantage of the rapid spread of the modern internet. The internet space has effectively opened the door to selling Shaoguan's special products, providing new ideas for developing the "three rural areas" of the supply and marketing cooperatives. With the gradual maturity of Shaoguan's special agricultural products e-commerce platform, it can also be connected to China's supply and marketing e-commerce "supply and marketing cloud warehouse" operating platform to expand the brand influence further and enhance the brand effect. Finally, it is also possible to gradually build a procurement platform in northern Guangdong and connect it to the Guangdong-Hong Kong-Macao Greater Bay Area's direct supply and distribution system to further promote the compelling connection between agricultural product enterprises and the markets in Guangdong, Hong Kong, and Macao.

5.3 Management Insight

Supply chain management is a complex and critical task involving coordination between multiple segments, including production, logistics, and distribution. The role of government is crucial in supply chain reform and development. Supply and marketing agencies should work to create infrastructure and build a whole set of logistics platforms for agricultural products from output to sale so that buyers and sellers can be familiar with the transportation of goods and ensure the quality and safety of agricultural products. Secondly, with the rapid development of the Internet, agricultural product enterprises have also ushered in a reasonable development period. Through the Internet platform, enterprises can better disseminate and sell their products, enhance their visibility, and promote the development of local agricultural product enterprises. Finally, an information exchange platform between agricultural products and buyers and sellers should be built to reduce information differences and the bullwhip effect and to realize the integration of supply chain information. At this point, supply and marketing societies should play the role of public information technology and actively promote the development of e-commerce, tracking every link of agricultural products in real-time, achieving effective control and management, improving consumers' buying experience, and making producers more trustful of the integrated management and sales platform of supply and marketing societies.

6 Conclusion

With the advent of the Internet era, the supply chain management model is facing new challenges. Yet, modern supply chain management will also be based on Internet technology, which will closely integrate all aspects of the enterprise, significantly improve enterprise management efficiency, achieve information sharing, reduce operating costs, and efficiently allocate resources. With the help of this platform, the transformation of agricultural production enterprises will inject strong momentum into the development of China's agriculture.

References

1. Zhang, H.: Exploring the innovation path of enterprise supply chain management mode in the background of the Internet economy. Bus. Exhib. Econ. **7**, 94–96 (2022)
2. Zhang, S.: Explorations of the transformation of modern supply chain management under the Internet thinking. In: Small and Medium-Sized Enterprise Management and Technology, pp. 138–140 (2022)
3. Wang, H., Liu, S., Zhao, Y.: Comparative analysis of big and traditional data supply chains. Value Eng. **36**(26), 112–113 (2017)
4. Zhang, W.: The role of big data in the process of supply chain wisdom. Logist. Eng. Manag. **42**(04), 89–92 (2022)
5. Zhao, Z., Zhang, L.: Construction and operation mode of the intelligent supply chain of agricultural products in the era of new technology. Bus. Econ. Res. **11**, 132–135 (2019)
6. Cao, Y.: Research on Supply Chain Management of Agricultural Products in China. Jiangnan University, Wuxi (2009)
7. Downey, D.: The challenges of food and agro-product supply chains. In: Proceedings of the 2nd International Conference on Chain Management in Agribusiness and the Food Industry, The Netherlands, pp. 3–11(1996)
8. Wang, Y., Li, T.: Agricultural supply chain management of international grain merchants and its inspiration to China-Cargill in the United States as an example. China Dev. Watch **02**, 60–62 (2013)
9. Chen, G.: Supply chain management. China Soft Sci. **10**, 3–5 (1999)
10. Duan, Q., Xu, X., Liu, X.: Accelerating internet adoption in China's fresh produce supply chain: a VEG-NET approach. N. Z. J. Agric. Res. **50**(5), 1299–1305 (2007)
11. Zou, Y.: "Internet+" informatization development of agricultural supply chain. Sci. Technol. Innov. Herald **11**, 154–155 (2019)
12. Yang, C., Sun, Z.: Design of agricultural products supply chain data management system based on blockchain technology. J. Agric. Big Data **2**(2), 74–83 (2020)
13. Hong, T.: Research on blockchain application in agricultural products e-commerce in China. China Mark. **39**, 65–68 (2016)
14. Jiang, X., Wang, X.: The application and challenges of blockchain technology in the supply chain of an agricultural products-an example of good food taste. Rural Econ. Technol. **17**, 147–148 (2018)

An Empirical Study on the Causes of Default of US Dollar Debt in the China's Property Based on Z-score Model

Yijing Wang(✉)

School of Economics and Management, Zhejiang Sci-Tech University, Hangzhou 310018, China
2020333503010@mails.zstu.edu.cn

Abstract. The Chinese real estate industry heavily relies on U.S. dollar debt as a critical tool for financing. However, since 2018, frequent and substantial defaults on Chinese real estate dollar bonds have raised financial market risks. This paper examines the case of Sunac China to analyze the reasons behind the default of Chinese real estate dollar bonds using the Z-score model. The study finds that a combination of internal and external factors caused the default, with internal factors dominating during the risk accumulation phase before 2020, and external factors becoming prominent after 2020. Internal factors include high leverage ratios, weakened solvency, and reduced profitability. These factors led to financial distress for Sunac China, making it difficult to meet its debt obligations. External factors include the COVID-19 pandemic, a sharp decline in market demand, and regulatory policies aimed at controlling the real estate market's speculation. These factors, combined with the internal factors, triggered the default of Sunac China. The findings have implications for risk management and governance policies in the industry. Prudent debt management policies should be adopted to control the risks associated with U.S. dollar debt, such as limiting excessive borrowing and enhancing financial transparency. Regulatory policies aimed at controlling speculation need to be balanced with the need for sustainable growth in the real estate market. Overall, this paper provides valuable insights into the intrinsic causes of stabilizing the Chinese real estate industry, which can inform policies to mitigate financial risks and promote sustainable development.

Keywords: Chinese Real Estate Industry · US Dollar Debt · Sunac China

1 Introduction

High investment risks, long development cycles, and large capital requirements characterize real estate enterprises. Bond financing is one of the vital financing tools for real estate enterprises. US dollar bonds of real estate enterprises refer to US dollar-denominated bonds issued by Chinese real estate enterprises (or their overseas listed branches) in the offshore market. When the domestic financing environment was tightened, and the real estate market was on the upside, it was once a "trend" for real

© The Author(s), under exclusive license to Springer Nature Singapore Pte Ltd. 2024
X. Li et al. (Eds.): ICEMGD 2023, AEPS, pp. 1102–1111, 2024.
https://doi.org/10.1007/978-981-97-0523-8_104

estate enterprises to issue USD bonds offshore to solve the liquidity problem [1]. However, since 2021, several real estate enterprises have announced defaults on their USD-denominated bonds, causing widespread concern in the market. 2022 saw a peak in the maturity of real estate enterprises' USD-denominated bonds, with a total of 60.69 billion RMB. Frequent and large-scale bond defaults affect the credit ratings of defaulting enterprises and make their financing more challenging. They also aggravate market instability, disrupt the regular operation of China's bond market, and impede the long-term healthy development of China's financial needs.

Sunac China Holdings Limited (now referred to as "Sunac China") is one of the well-known companies in China's real estate industry. Since its establishment in 2003, the company has focused on real estate as its core business. Today, it has become a leader in the real estate industry. The company's prominent businesses are real estate development and post-property services. According to the research report of the top 100 real estate companies released by CMI Institute in March 2021, Sunac China is ranked fifth in China. It is the veritable head of the real estate industry in China. However, on May 12, 2022, Sunac China announced that it would not pay the interest on the four US dollar bonds due in April, declaring a default.

This paper introduces the Z-score model to analyze the financial situation and risk exposure of Sunac China. The Z-score model was proposed by scholar Edward Altman in 1968, a data model with solid professionalism and authority. The Z-score model can be used to assess and predict the current financial status of enterprises and the risk of future bond defaults and then analyze the mechanism of the factors influencing their defaults. Even as a leading real estate company with over 100 billion dollars in revenue, Sunac China has defaulted on its US dollar bonds. Based on the Z-Score model, this paper analyzes the operating conditions in recent years and explores the reasons for its default. It is crucial to re-examine the development of China's Chinese real estate industry and prevent future default risk of real estate companies.

2 Literature Review

Scholars in China and abroad have studied the factors influencing bond defaults, mainly from internal and external factors. Nippani and Smith found that macroeconomic factors significantly correlate with bond default rates. When there is a downward trend in the macro economy, the default rate of U.S. Treasury bonds rises significantly [2]. Agrawal and Maheshwari studied the different performances of two types of Indian firms in response to macroeconomic changes using logistic and multivariate discriminant approaches with the presence or absence of default as a variable. The study proves that stock market volatility and inflation will affect the probability of default on corporate bonds [3]. Wang et al. argued that the macroeconomic downturn and the industry slump have led to frequent bond defaults in China [4]. Wang found that stock market volatility and gross domestic product significantly impact the occurrence of default events in housing firms using ten-year data from 327 listed companies in China [5].

Internal company influences include company shareholding structure, management education level, corporate leverage, company financial position, and governance. Qiu and Zhang developed an econometric model and found that the higher the shareholding of the first shareholder, the higher the probability of credit default. In addition, the higher the education level of the company's management, the lower the company's credit risk [6]. Rose et al. used 28 corporate financial indicators and found that deteriorating economic conditions would significantly affect corporate bond defaults. When a firm's capital chain is under pressure, it is prone to trigger bond defaults [7]. Gatti et al. suggest that gearing is also one of the internal influences on default. A firm's gearing ratio is positively correlated with the default rate [8]. In analyzing the relationship between a firm's cash flow position and bond defaults, Douglas found that the likelihood of bond defaults occurring is relatively higher when cash flow volatility is higher [9]. In addition, deficiencies in corporate governance structure and aggressive strategic decisions cause bond defaults. Luo and Liang argues that business decisions play an essential role in the sound development of a firm. If a company makes mistakes in its business strategy, it can expose the company to a financial crisis [10]. Zhao et al. analyze the data of listed companies with substantial bond defaults from 2015–2019 based on a Probit regression model, thus finding the magnitude of bond default risk is positively related to the equity pledge rate of significant shareholders [11]. Miao summarized the factors influencing bond default into four aspects: institutional environment, firm characteristics, industry characteristics, and macroeconomic characteristics. As a result, the process of bond default is summarized as external environment-firm decision-making behavior-financial characteristics-bond default [12].

3 Hypotheses Development

The immediate trigger for bond default is the deterioration of the company's financial position, which leads to the inability of the company to pay the interest on the bonds. The factors influencing financial risk come from both internal and external dimensions.

The corporate governance structure, management, and financing decisions from the internal environment will impact the company's finances. For example, Chen and Sun argue that the internal governance structure of the company has a significant impact on the financial situation, which is mainly influenced by factors such as equity concentration and the proportion of independent directors; in addition, the level of management governance and financing decisions will affect the capital structure of the company, which in turn will affect the financial situation of the company [13]. From the external environment, macroeconomic cycles and policy adjustments can also cause corporate financial risks. In a macroeconomic upswing, the overall financial risk of the firm will be reduced. For example, Lu found that the growth of real GDP plays a role in reducing the financial risk of firms. In addition, macro policy regulation will also affect how companies finance their businesses, affecting their financial risk [14]. Zhao points out that when macroeconomic regulation tightens, and real estate financing conditions are gradually tightened, firms may be forced to choose more costly financing methods, thus increasing their financial risk [15]. Therefore, hypothesis 1 is proposed in this paper.

Hypothesis 1: The causes of the default of Chinese real estate dollar bonds include internal factors such as corporate governance structure, management characteristics, and financing decisions, as well as external factors such as macroeconomic cycles and policy regulation.

At the same time, the default of bonds is a dynamic process, and there is a "risk germination period - risk accumulation period - risk explosion period". The factors leading to the change will also vary at different stages. Because all the existing Chinese real estate bonds defaulted after 2018, a period of macroeconomic downturn and real estate policy regulation, the external environment is more of a catalyst than a dominant factor for risk budding and accumulation. Therefore, this paper proposes hypothesis 2.

Hypothesis 2: Chinese real estate dollar debt default is a dynamic process in which internal factors are the leading cause during the initial risk budding and accumulation stage. In contrast, external factors cause the risk outbreak.

4 The Causes of Bond Default of Sunac China Based on the Z-Score Model

4.1 Z-Score Model Analysis

To evaluate the bond default risk of Sunac China, this paper uses the Z-score model, which can quantitatively measure the financial soundness of the company, and calculates the Z-score by considering five financial indicators, including asset utilization efficiency, profitability, asset and liability size, financial structure and debt servicing capacity, and calculates the Z-score by weighting the average. The Z-score model has the following expressions.

$$Z = 1.2X_1 1.4X_2 + 3.3X_3 + 0.6X_4 + 1.0X_5 \tag{1}$$

where X_1 = net working capital/total assets = (current assets and current liabilities)/total assets; X_2 = Retained earnings/total assets = (undistributed earnings + surplus)/total assets; X_3 = EBITDA/Total Assets = (Total Profit + Finance Costs)/Total Assets; X_4 = Owner's equity/total liabilities = (share price per share * number of shares)/total liabilities; and X_5 = Operating Income/Total Assets.

In general, the lower the Z-score, the worse the business and financial situation of the company and the greater the risk of default. In particular, 1.81 is the warning line for Z-score. When the Z-value is lower than 1.81, it indicates that the firm has greater financial risk. Conversely, if the Z-value exceeds 1.81, it suggests that the firm's financial status is better than that of firms facing more significant risks. Although there is still a particular risk of default and bankruptcy, the probability does not reach a severe level. This paper selects the required values of total assets, total liabilities, operating income, and current assets of Sunac China from 2010 to June 2021 (as shown in Table 1) and calculate the Z-values of Sunac China from 2010 to June 2021 according to the weighted average formula of Z-score model (as shown in Table 2).

Figure 1 shows that in 2010, Sunac China's Z-score performed better and was always above the alert line. However, during the period from 2010–2019, the company's Z-score keeps decreasing. This is mainly influenced by internal factors such as the company's continuous financing for expansion overlaid with corporate governance and management after its IPO. Although the company's Z-score rebounded in 2017 due to massive land purchases and diversification, it is still below the warning line of 1.81. This indicates that since 2010, Sunac China has been in a phase of budding and accumulating risks - the

Table 1. Financial data of Sunac China's operating segments (in ¥ million)

Yr	Assets	Liabilities	Revenue	Current Assets	Current Liabilities	Retained Earnings	EBIT	Equity
10	15,750	11,086	6,660	13,973	6,118	4,405	2,597	4,664
11	33,614	26,207	10,609	30,863	14,628	6,792	3,528	7,406
12	70,934	58,940	20,848	64,832	44,294	9,229	4,685	11,994
13	97,355	79,144	30,887	87,590	51,789	13,320	5,684	18,211
14	112,362	91,380	25,096	97,467	64,949	12,368	4,902	20,983
15	115,509	96,089	23,113	93,725	64,495	14,610	4,564	19,420
16	293,183	257,772	35,661	252,698	168,594	16,201	4,409	35,411
17	623,102	562,464	66,614	499,601	385,708	26,775	15,359	60,638
18	716,660	643,553	126,245	553,238	471,253	42,198	28,664	73,107
19	960,649	846,555	171,974	724,680	620,881	65,180	42,546	114,094
20	1,108,405	930,575	233,048	834,939	683,915	97,201	57,535	177,830
21	1,205,453	997,122	97,266	910,258	754,961	108,507	17,610	208,331

Table 2. Sunac China Development Z-Value (2010- Jun. 2021).

	2010	2011	2012	2013	2014	2015
Z-Value	2.2091	1.6937	1.1632	1.2805	1.0523	0.982
X1	0.4988	0.483	0.2895	0.3677	0.2894	0.2531
X2	0.2797	0.2021	0.1301	0.1368	0.143	0.162
X3	0 1649	0 1050	0 0660	0 0584	0 0436	0 0395
X4	0.4207	0.2826	0.2035	0.2301	0.2296	0.2021
X5	0.4228	0.3156	0.2939	0.3173	0.2233	0.2001
	2016	2017	2018	2019	2020	2021.06
Z -Value	0.7073	0.5697	0.6237	0.656	0.8177	0.5574
X1	0.2869	0.1828	0.1144	0.1081	0.1363	0.1288
X2	0.0782	0.0697	0.0788	0.0861	0.113	0.1062
X3	0 0150	0 0246	0 0400	0 0443	0 0519	0 0146
X4	0.1374	0.1078	0.1136	0.1348	0.1911	0.2089
X5	0.1216	0.1069	0.1762	0.179	0.2103	0.0807

Z-score is low but remains relatively stable. However, after 2019, the company's Z-value is at a new downward trend point, mainly due to external factors - the three red lines policy, the Covid-19 pandemic, etc. Therefore, the different dominant characteristics of the two phases - internal and external factors - are extracted and summarized in the following section.

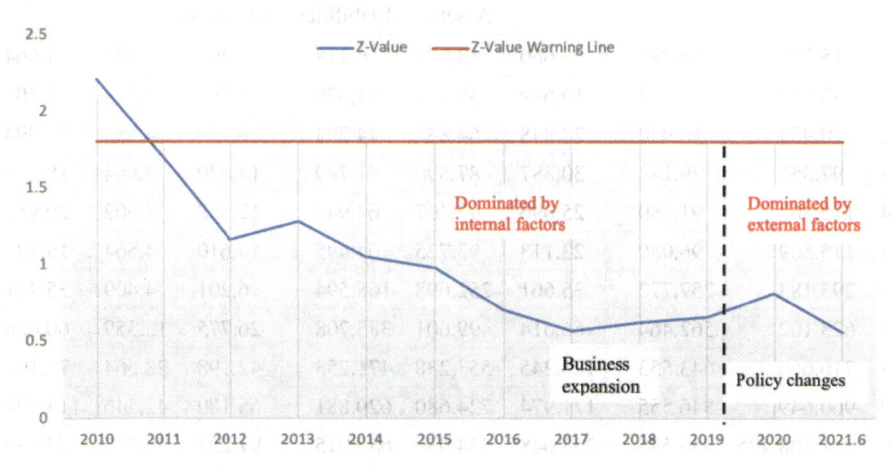

Fig. 1. Z-score of Sunac China from 2010 to 2021.

4.2 Internal Factors

In the early stage of company development, the level of company risk exposure is dominated by internal factors.

Firstly, at the corporate governance level, Sunac China mainly needs capital structure and operational strategy problems. Although the high leverage model is the structural model adopted by most real estate companies, Sunac China is overly dependent on it. As of 2020, its financing costs and the net debt ratio are among the highest of all major real estate companies in China. Although its leverage level has been reduced, as seen in Sunac China's interim results announcement published in FY2021. However, judging from the trend of its share price, it has not risen but shows a continuous downward trend, which indicates that its capital structure model still needs to be revised. In terms of operational strategies, one of the main characteristics of Sunac China compared to other real estate companies is that it has persistently adopted expansion strategies since its IPO. Although these expansion strategies have broadened its operating business to a certain extent, such as through large-scale mergers and acquisitions, which have enabled it to have more cash flow and thus, its Z-value did not decline during 2017–2019 and even showed a rebounding trend. However, there are specific problems with its expansion strategy. For example, Sunac China needed to grasp the process of expansion operations, resulting in excessive cost wastage on relevant projects and the subsequent failure to keep up with sales and funding, which in turn led to its profitability needing to be increased to support its expansion strategy. These indicate that, despite the advantages of Sunac China's operation strategy, its counter-cyclical way of bottoming out on mergers and acquisitions laid hidden dangers for its further development and future planning, accumulated risks, was not conducive to corporate governance, and eventually led to the strain and deterioration of the company's financial situation, which in turn prevented it from repaying the bonds as scheduled.

Secondly, at the management level, Sunac China has the problem that the actual controller of the company is a gambler and has a personal nature that is difficult to change. The shareholding structure of Sunac China shows that the management of Sunac China's shareholding structure consists of three parties: Sun Hongbin and Tianjin Target Investment Consulting Co. Among them, Sun Hongbin is the actual controller of the company. Therefore, the development of Sunac China has the problem of "one share is too big." Although this is conducive to the creation of decision-making power and the improvement of decision-making efficiency, it also faces the problem of concentration of power in one person and the need for control among the management. This leads to no scientific and transparent decision-making. Under Sun Hongbin's control, it is evident that Sunac China is too aggressive. The continuous M&A expansion since 2010, especially the massive land purchase in 2017, made the debt high, which increased the scale superficially but made the financial risk and bankruptcy risk accumulate, eventually leading to the default of USD debt.

In addition, Sunac China needed better financing decisions at the corporate decision-making level, which led to inadequate financing and put the company in a cut-off capital crisis. Since the outbreak of Covid-19 in 2020, economic development in various countries has been curbed. During this period, the United States mitigated the economic problems caused by the Covid-19 pandemic by issuing large amounts of dollars to boost demand and consumption. Other countries moved to sell dollars in response to the dollar's depreciation, considering the significant increase in dollars. Against the above background, it was unwise for Sunac China to decide to use US dollar debt for debt financing. Moreover, due to the change in the international situation, the credit rating of Sunac China was downgraded, which led to a downward trend in investors' confidence in it and a shift in risk appetite, which in turn led to difficulties in financing for Sunac China.

4.3 External Factors

In the later stage of the company's development, the extent of the company's risk exposure was dominated by external factors.

First, the macroeconomic downturn increased the risk of default on Chinese property bonds. The emergence of an unbalanced economic structure, a severely aging population structure, declining economic vitality, and regional economic imbalances in China has led to a downward macroeconomic trend in recent years, which has increased the systematic risk of Chinese real estate companies.

According to Fig. 2, China's GDP growth rate year-over-year reached a high point in 2012. Since 2012, China's GDP growth rate has slowed due to its large base. With systemic risks such as the Covid-19 outbreak, GDP growth dropped to a new low of less than 3% year-over-year in 2020. Despite a rebound in 2021, the negative impact of the Covid-19 pandemic and other economic factors must be addressed. This decreases national consumption and aggregate demand, negatively impacting Sunac China's sales revenue. At the same time, Sunac China faces higher financing and production costs due

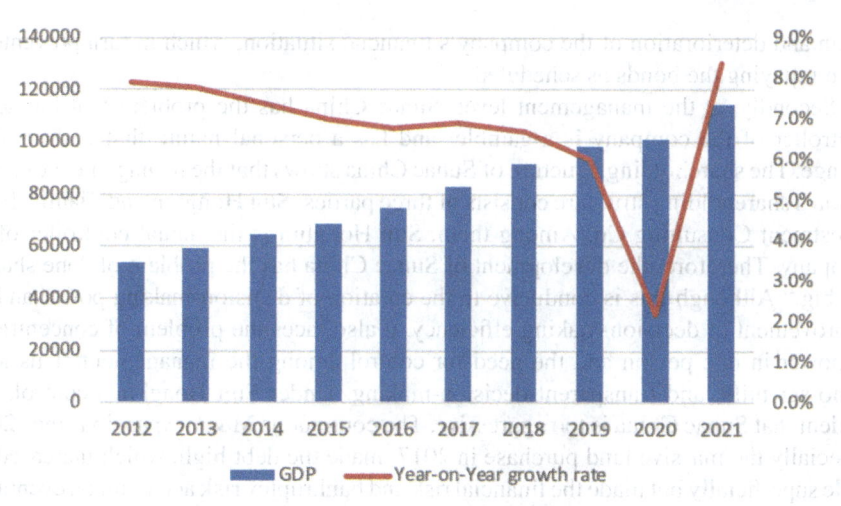

Fig. 2. Change in China's GDP and its year-on-year growth rate, 2012–2021 (¥billion).

to the "deleveraging" policy, thus tightening its financial position, one of the primary reasons for the downward trend of its Z-value again.

Secondly, the economy shrank, and the market was depressed due to the recurrence of the Covid-19 pandemic. 2020 saw the impact of the Covid-19 pandemic drastically, affecting all industries nationwide. Although Sunac China Group actively sought to operate and expand other aspects of its business, its core business remained in the real estate industry. The Covid-19 pandemic had a negative impact on the macro economy, the US dollar debt market, Sunac China's internal governance, and the company's management operating model. It accumulated through the impact of these factors, and eventually, under the uncertain environment of the capital market, Sunac China saw the outbreak of default.

Third, the financial environment changed, and problems such as credit risk were exposed. The economic climate is in a state of constant change. However, the mere appearance of the changing financial climate is not enough to cause the default of Sunac China. From a deeper perspective, this default results from the accumulation of financial risks and default risks in the early stage of the company's development overlaid with changes in the external economic environment. The changing financial climate has led to a decrease in the risk appetite of some investors for real estate companies. For Sunac China, in 2022, in addition to the vast internal liquidity pressure problem, the decline of external credit rating will more directly lead to the financial deterioration of Sunac China, thus prompting a material default of Sunac China to trigger the crossover clause.

Fourth, introducing and implementing the three red lines policy and deleveraging increase the burden on enterprises. The three-red-line policy was officially introduced in 2020, a massive challenge for real estate companies, especially those with high-leverage models. Among them, Sunac China is a typical high-leverage enterprise. Therefore, the new downward trend of Sunac China's Z-value in 2020 is, to a certain extent, due to the constraints of the three red-line policies. Under the impact of the three red line policies,

Sunac China needs to improve its low-cost financing ability and capital turnover. However, according to the data, at the peak of Sunac's massive land purchase, its weighted average financing cost remained high, and its net debt ratio was once close to 200%, which was against the provisions of the three red lines policy. In the context of "de-capacity" and "deleveraging," Sunac failed to reduce its financing cost and increased its debt. This further worsened the operating condition of Sunac China in all aspects and improved the economic burden of transformation and upgrading of the company.

5 Conclusion

The default of Sunac China's US dollar debt is the result of both internal and external factors, including capital structure problems, inappropriate operation strategies, macroeconomic downturn, increased risk of default on Chinese real estate bonds, outbreak of the Covid-19 pandemic, changes in the economic environment, credit risk, and the implementation of the three red lines policy. The factors that played a significant role in different stages and periods differed, eventually leading to the bond default problem of Sunac China. To prevent future default incidents, policy recommendations include maintaining high sensitivity to environmental changes and adjusting development strategies in advance, reasonably laying out business operation strategies and broadening business sales channels, strengthening corporate risk control and consciously controlling the leverage ratio, and enriching innovative financing models and optimizing internal checks and balances. These measures aim to help companies like Sunac China to anticipate potential financial and bankruptcy risks, respond to external environmental changes, improve sales performance, control investment strategy risks, and expand financing channels. In conclusion, the default of Sunac China's US dollar debt highlights the importance of corporate governance, risk control, and strategic planning in the real estate industry. By addressing the internal and external factors that contributed to the default, companies can better prepare for potential risks and improve their overall financial stability.

References

1. Li, J., Dong, Y., He, C.: More debt, more investment? Spatial differentiation of debt-investment behavior of real estate enterprises under housing financialization. Econ. Manag. (8), 171–189 (2020)
2. Nippani, S., Smith, S.D.: The increasing default risk of US Treasury securities due to the financial crisis. J. Bank. Finan. **34**(10), 2472–2480 (2010)
3. Agrawal, K., Maheshwari, Y.: Default risk modelling using macroeconomic variables. J. Indian Bus. Res. **6**(4), 270–285 (2014)
4. Wang, H., Huang, B., Yao, L.: Analysis of default and investor protection issues in China's bond market. New Finan. (10), 54–56 (2016)
5. Wang, X., Hou, S., Shen, J.: Default clustering of the nonfinancial sector and systemic risk: evidence from China. Econ. Model. (96), 196–208 (2021)
6. Qiu, R., Zhang, J.: Empirical study on the influence factors of credit default risk of china's small and medium-sized listed companies: based on the panel data of 273 small and medium-sized listed companies in Shenzhen for 5 years. Seeker (4), 28–30 (2010)

7. Rose, P.S., Andrews, W.T., Giroux, G.A.: Predicting business failure: a macroeconomic perspective. J. Acc. Audit. Financ. **6**(1), 20–31 (1982)
8. Gatti, D.D., Gallegati, M., Greenwald, B., Russo, A., Stiglitz, J.E.: The financial accelerator in an evolving credit network. J. Econ. Dyn. Control **34**(9), 1627–1650 (2010)
9. Douglas, A.V., Huang, A.G., Vetzal, K.R.: Cash flow volatility and corporate bond yield spreads. Rev. Quant. Finan. Account. (46), 417–458 (2016)
10. Luo, X., Liang, C.: Characteristics, trends, financing features, and risk disposal mechanisms of corporate bond defaults in China. Finan. Dev. Res. (04), 44–53 (2020)
11. Zhao, Y., Shang, Y., Zhao, J.: Controlling shareholder equity pledge, risk-bearing level, and bond default risk. J. Nanjing Audit Univ. (01), 80–88 (2022)
12. Miao, X.: The formation of bond defaults: a comprehensive framework from the perspective of literature. Finan. Commun. (06), 124–129 (2018)
13. Chen, L., Sun, J.: Corporate governance and financial distress: Evidence from the Shanghai stock market. J. Southeast Univ. (Phil. Soc. Sci. Ed.) (05), 28–31+126 (2005)
14. Lu, Y.: An empirical analysis of the impact of macroeconomic factors on the risk of corporate financial distress. Macroeconomics (05), 53–58 (2013)
15. Zhao, D., Zhu, W., Wang, Z.: Macroeconomic regulation and capital structure adjustment of real estate listed companies. Finan. Res. (10), 78–92 (2008)

The Influence of Key Opinion Leaders on High-End Beauty Brands in the Age of Self-media

Xilin Liu[1], Haonan Qian[2(✉)], and Haoyun Wen[3]

[1] School of Journalism and Media, Southwest University, Chongqing, China
[2] School of Humanities and Media, Ningbo University, Ningbo, China
206002760@nbu.edu.cn
[3] Faculty of International Tourism and Management, City University of Macau, Macau, China

Abstract. As social marketing continues to thrive, as well as the bright prospect of the beauty industry, KOL marketing gets considerable attention. Several organizations rely on KOL to attract customers and build brand image, which gained remarkable success. KOL is a popular topic emerging in recent years, and previous studies concentrate on its generalized characteristics and effects. This study identified the influence of KOL on high-end cosmetics and emphasized the importance of KOL. Through questionnaire distribution and quantitative analysis, the results showed that the impact of KOL on premium beauty brands is positive. And customers' purchase intention is highly linked with KOL because of their expertise, trustworthiness, and intimacy. KOL is influential in promoting cosmetic sales even better than the official account. The study's findings help businesses identify which aspects of high-end cosmetic companies should be emphasized in social media marketing to influence consumers' purchase intentions.

Keywords: Luxury Beauty Brands · Beauty Industry · Social Media Marking

1 Introduction

Due to the development of technology, as well as the impact of COVID-19, online shopping is getting popular. People prefer to use a mobile phone or website rather than visit a brick-and-mortar store. Furthermore, as social media become pervasive and ubiquitous, it promotes interactivity among people. Meanwhile, Key Opinion Leader (KOL) springs up in different areas, significantly influencing public perceptions, attitudes, and consumption habits.

According to China Digital Marketing Trends Report 2022, KOL promotion became advertisers' top choice for social marketing, with short-form video and official account operations close behind. The KOL plays a prominent role in self-media marketing, creating an immense volume of customers and assignable value. So, more organizations rely on KOL to interact with potential customers and make a profit.

Although Chinese consumers' average monthly cosmetic consumption level is low, the consumption potential is considerable and worthy of high-end cosmetic brands to explore. According to the 2023 China Digital Marketing Trends Report, KOL marketing is firmly on top of the 2023 social media marketing priorities. KOL can assist premium beauty brands in attracting prospective customers and helping them retain existing ones as their prices continue to rise. Moreover, the purpose of KOL investment by high-end cosmetic brands is not only the sales of products but also the deepening of brand image and the construction of scenarios.

The beauty and cosmetics industry's online trend is apparent. Nowadays, the KOL economy is in full swing, and a wide range of high-end beauty brands enter the fray to compete for traffic, whether foreign or local brands. According to the research report, TikTok and Little Red Book are KOL's most representative platforms for beauty sales. The former has a large number of active people and the latter that most users are women. Moreover, both have good user stickiness. Currently, the specialization of KOL marketing content in the high-end beauty industry is evident, and KOL is gradually developing into vertical fields to help brands achieve maximum traffic monetization. Finally, the KOL marketing model and self-media reach a mutually beneficial symbiosis.

Social media influencers (SMI) can be defined as online key opinion leaders (KOL) [1]. The broad characteristics and implications of KOL marketing are prominently highlighted in much of the literature. Expertise, authenticity, and intimacy are critical to constructing a successful influencer image [2]. The expertise of KOL may not necessarily come from formal schooling or training but rather from their experience and passion for the relevant topic [3]. Influencers are considered authentic, genuine individuals (Lee & Eastin, 2021), and their strong bonds with followers (Lou, 2021) can also influence customers' purchase intentions [4, 5]. Furthermore, more than any other feature, KOL credibility has a more profound effect on purchase intention [6].

The mutual relationship between KOL, customers, and brands in influencer marketing has been discussed [7]. According to industry surveys, many marketers have used influencers to promote their businesses and commodities [8]. Brand marketers are switching from traditional celebrities to KOL for brand endorsement due to the substantial impact KOLs have had on social media marketing [9]. A series of recent studies have indicated the importance of KOL marketing strategy in different ways. For example, demonstrate the effect of KOL from a social identity perspective [10].

The rapid use of social media platforms has altered consumer behavior and how luxury brands interact with their followers. The study's findings support that digital marketing significantly moderates consumer behavior connected to luxury brands [11]. Moreover, KOL is an excellent way of digital marketing. It was reported in the literature that consumer intention to purchase high-end beauty products is positively driven by social media WOM [12]. However, KOL is conducive to the establishment of a brand reputation.

The prior study also covered how KOL efficacy affected the perception of the brand [13]. Past research identified several important considerations about Chinese consumers' purchase intention of high-end cosmetics, such as word-of-mouth [14]. Each of them can be deeply linked with KOL. Moreover, a study also analyzed the phenomenon and effect of KOL marketing in the Chinese fashion industry [15].

This paper focuses on the efficiency and importance of KOL, combined with the characteristics of high-end beauty brands, to explore the role and significance of KOL in the future development of the high-end beauty industry.

2 Method

2.1 Survey Method

The items used questionnaire stars for data collection. A self-reported questionnaire including single-choice, multiple-choice, and a 5-point scale ranging from strongly disagree (1) to agree (5) powerfully was used to measure each construct.

Investigate the six factors consumers utilize to purchase products: the motivations, platforms, sources of Information, product categories, and channels. The three constructs comprising KOL qualities are familiarity, trustworthiness, and competence. Three operationalized items from Gefen, Magnini, Honeycutt, Cross, and Ohanian are carried by each build, such as 'I often search for KOL's recommendations to help me make beauty decisions; prefer to buy beauty products or brands recommended by KOL [16–18]. KOL's sharing helps me to learn more about the brands or knowledge of beauty products.' According to Aqueveque, three factors determine KOL efficacy for high-end beauty brands: I find KOLs' sharing more beneficial than the Information on the official account.' The impact of social influence on premium beauty brands is adopted from Aqueveque [19]. There are two items, 'Information you will refer to when you buy cosmetics: recommendations from friends, KOL recommendations, counter clerks, advertisements', measuring this construct. To study whether the promotion of high-end beauty brands has significant advantages compared to other categories of beauty brands, there are two items: prefer to buy which type of products KOL recommends.

2.2 Literature Research Method

Collect information and data according to academic literature. Indirect, non-invasive investigation to avoid reactive errors in research results Beyond time and space constraints, it is an efficient, accessible, and safe research method.

2.3 Quantitative Analysis Method

Quantitative analysis based on the collected data to reveal the influence of KOL on beauty products more precisely. The items used SPSS for data analysis. Reliability statistics, component matrix, common factor variance, total variance interpretation, and correlation analysis were performed on the data. Total variance calculation: Suppose there are 5 agrees for the test items: $x_1, x_2, ..., x_5$. The square of the difference between each group of data and their mean x is $(x_1 - x), (x_2 - x)...(x_n - x)$, ... Then we use their mean. The formula for calculating the total variance is shown below:

$$S^2 = \frac{1}{n}\left[(x_1 - x)^2 + (x_2 - x)^2 + ... + (x_n - x)^2\right] \quad (1)$$

To calculate the variance of this set of data, which is the size of the variations in the data. After being distilled:

$$S^2 = \frac{\sum_i^n = (x_i - x)^2}{n} \qquad (2)$$

where x is the data's mean. Additionally, respondents are questioned about their gender, age, educational background, monthly income, and prior use of skincare products.

3 Experiment Result and Analysis

3.1 Data Description

Most of the survey data included in this article came from responses to online surveys. The questionnaire adopted a non-random arbitrary sampling method by arbitrarily inviting people around Chongqing, Macau, and Shanghai to complete the questionnaire. Of 401 people, 331 accepted the invitation to answer a questionnaire. The response rate was 82.5%. The survey was conducted in March 2023, and a diverse group of individuals from various ages, professions, and educational levels was included in our sample.

Moreover, 331 data on the content of the study were collected by designing single-, multiple-, and quantitative questions. The content of the questionnaire aims to understand the influence and perception of different people on KOL on beauty products and to study the range and degree of influence. The results were also processed and analyzed according to spss27, and the data related to the survey's reliability, validity, total variance interpretation, and correlation were derived.

3.2 Data Preprocessing

In the survey of this paper, due to the use of online questionnaires for arbitrary sampling, the results may be biased and contradictory because the people who fill in the questionnaires do not know KOL, do not buy beauty, and fail to fill in carefully. For example, the age is "under 18," but the education level is "master or above," and the occupation is "student." Still, the education level is "elementary school or below," the answers are not logical such as contradictory or too different in the quantitative questions. The questionnaire is completed in more than 10 s.

The total number of missing and incorrect questionnaires was 14, accounting for 4.2% of the original questionnaire, and the reliability was .852 after spss27. We eliminated the 14 out and inaccurate questionnaires. We collected five additional questionnaires by invalidating the answers and inviting other people to answer again, so the total number of questionnaires increased from 326 to 331, and the reliability was .912 after spss27. .912, which meets the academic requirements.

3.3 Experiment Result and Analysis

Descriptive Analysis. Of the quantitative questions, they scored out of five.

'KOL's sharing can help me learn more about the brand or knowledge of beauty products.' The average score is 4.07, with 4 and 5 grades accounting for 78.2% of the total number of respondents, indicating that the respondents are more recognized for KOLs knowledge and brand promotion degree.

'Sharing by KOLs on social media platforms is more helpful to me than content from official brand accounts'. The average score is 4.05, indicating that most respondents think the content shared by KOL accounts will be more helpful than official self-publishing accounts.

The average score of 'KOL's sharing content affects my willingness to buy high-end beauty products is 3.85, which shows a lower score than the first two questions, proving that relatively speaking, the content shared by KOL has a lower influence on respondents' willingness to buy.

'I often search for KOL's recommendations to help me make a purchase decision on beauty products scored 3.76 on average, indicating that respondents actively search for KOLs less frequently and more passively accept the publicity and promotion of beauty KOLs on self-media platforms.

The average score of 'I usually have a positive attitude towards beauty products recommended by my favorite KOL' is 3.61, the lowest score among all quantitative questions. 41.1% of the respondents have no certain opinion or less, which shows that respondents, even if their favorite KOL recommends beauty products, may need to follow it more carefully. KOL's recommendation mainly plays a reference role.

'I am more inclined to buy beauty products or brands recommended by KOL' scored 3.73 on average, with the intermediate values of "not necessarily" and "rather agree" accounting for 75.6% of the total respondents. The extreme bias is less.

'Compared with the official flagship store, KOL's recommended purchase method is more affordable. The average score is 3.71, among which 4.8% of the respondents "strongly disagree," which is the scale with the most choices among the eight scales. Sixteen respondents believe that the price of KOL's products is more favorable than the official flagship store. Sixteen respondents believe that the price of KOL products is more favorable than the official flagship store.

'More detailed introduction of products by KOL compared to the official flagship store's average score of 3.8 indicates that respondents are more willing to learn about the products from KOL's recommendation than the official flagship store.

In general, the average score of each scale is higher than 3.6, and the percentage of option four also takes the first place among all scales, reflecting that most consumers have an agreeable attitude towards the relevant topics. Consumers' familiarity with KOL, its credibility and professionalism of KOL itself, and the increase of direct and indirect benefits to the brand after KOL releases promotional content tend to be positive attitudes in users' perceptions. Meanwhile, the factor variance values extracted from the factor variance table are high, showing that the extracted factors can better describe the eight indicators.

Correlation Analysis. First, this paper tests the reliability of the data using Cronbach's alpha. Also, this paper uses a value of 0.8 as a benchmark for evaluating the scale's reliability. Table 1 and Table 2 can obtain Cronbach's alpha over 0.9 for all cases, which indicates that the structure was measured reliably and without random error.

Table 1. Case Processing Summary.

Case Processing Summary		Number of cases	%
Case	Effective	331	100.0
	Exclusiona	0	.0
	Total	331	100.0

a. Based on the column deletion of all variables in the procedure

Table 2. Reliability statistics.

Reliability statistics	
Cronbach Alpha	Number of items
.912	8

According to the Pearson correlation analysis, the Pearson correlation between [positive attitude toward KOL] and [more inclined to buy products recommended by KOL] was the highest, at .825**, and the higher the user's favorability toward KOL, the more inclined to buy products recommended by KOL; the Pearson correlation between [think KOL's sharing is more helpful] and [think KOL's products are more affordable] was the lowest, at .330**. The Pearson correlation between [think KOL's sharing is more helpful] and [think KOL's products are more affordable] is the lowest, at .330**, and the correlation between the knowledge and professionalism of KOL's shared content and the price of KOL's promoted products is not significant. The rest of the data are between .330** and .825**, and all of them have significant correlation at the 0.01 level (two-tailed), and all of them are positively correlated. 25 of them have Pearson correlation coefficients greater than 0.4, indicating a strong relationship.

4 Discussion

Although this work is of great significance, this research has some limitations and provides a chance for the future. Firstly, most of study was based on a review of previous relevant studies and cross-sectional data collected from social media users under 35 years old. Therefore, there may be some limitations to the generalizability of the analysis. Future studies may consider using a longitudinal study design and comparing across age groups with different beauty brands to enhance generalizability.

Second, this research only focuses on the positive impact of KOL on high-end beauty brands while ignoring the negative impact. In some cases, KOL will adversely expand the purchase intention. Future studies could consider both advantages and disadvantages of KOL, allowing for a complete understanding of KOL.

Thirdly, because the study was limited to the population within China, it failed to cover beauty product consumers worldwide comprehensively. Moreover, more beauty products are purchased by customers worldwide, and the influence power of KOLs can vary in different regions. The influence of different countries' regions, cultures, and religions needs to be fully considered in future research to improve the breadth of the study.

Fourthly, this paper finds that high-end beauty brand KOLs emphasize promoting product culture and corporate image. In contrast, the KOLs of low-end beauty brands tend to carry more product promotions and low-price shopping activities. In future analysis, we can compare more high-end and low-end beauty products KOLs to improve the study's comprehensiveness.

Finally, many consumers today are passive recipients of KOL marketing promotions. This also shows that the attractiveness of KOL to consumers in the beauty product field still needs to be improved. If merchant can actively attract consumers to accept KOL marketing, it will be more beneficial to the sales and promotion of beauty products.

5 Conclusion

With the development of the online era and self-media KOLs are becoming more and more common, but fewer studies have evaluated the impact of KOLs on high-end beauty brands. This study then analyzed this issue to assess how KOLs influence high-end beauty brands and moderate them through awareness and social influence. Although our current study is limited to high-end beauty products, it can also be extended to other consumables promoted by KOLs. KOLs might better promote lifestyle products such as skin care, cosmetics, sports, food service, and fashion. Professional services and information products, such as financial, medical, consulting, and educational products, may be more appropriate for the specialized industry experts for promotion. The results of this study indicate that KOL has a positive impact on high-end beauty products. Beauty companies of all premium brands should strengthen their enterprise information systems to collect KOL's influence data on social media, further enhance the use of KOL promotion to expand the influence and benefits of KOLs and increase product sales.

References

1. Casaló, L.V., Flavián, C., Ibáñez-Sánchez, S.: Influencers on Instagram: antecedents and consequences of opinion leadership. J. Bus. Res. **117**, 510–519 (2020)
2. Hudders, L., De Jans, S., De Veirman, M.: The commercialization of social media stars: a literature review and conceptual framework on the strategic use of social media influencers. Int. J. Advert. **40**(3), 327–375 (2021)
3. Al-Emadi, F.A., Ben Yahia, I.: Ordinary celebrities related criteria to harvest fame and influence on social media. J. Res. Interact. Mark. **14**(2), 195–213 (2020)
4. Lee, J.A., Eastin, M.S.: Perceived authenticity of social media influencers: scale development and validation. J. Res. Interact. Mark. **15**(4), 822–841 (2021)
5. Lou, C.: Social media influencers and followers: theorization of a transparasocial relation and explication of its implications for influencer advertising. J. Advert. **51**, 1–18 (2021)
6. Ao, L., Bansal, R., Pruthi, N., Khaskheli, M.B.: Impact of social media influencers on customer engagement and purchase intention: a meta-analysis. Sustainability **15**, 2744 (2023)

7. Caruelle, D.: Influencer marketing: a triadically interactive relationship between influencers, followers, and brands. In: Wang, C.L. (ed.) The Palgrave Handbook of Interactive Marketing. Palgrave Macmillan, Cham (2023)
8. Mediakix. What are micro-influencers: definitions, trends & advantages (2019). [WWW document]. Mediakix
9. Ye, G., Hudders, L., De Jans, S., De Veirman, M.: The value of influencer marketing for business: a bibliometric analysis and managerial implications. J. Advert. **50**(2), 160–178 (2021)
10. Farivar, S., Wang, F.: Effective influencer marketing: a social identity perspective. J. Retail. Cons. Serv. **67**, 103026 (2022). ISSN 0969–6989,
11. Khan, S.A., Shamsi, I.R.A., Ghila, T.H., Anjam, M.: When luxury goes digital: does digital marketing moderate multi-level luxury values and consumer luxury brand-related behavior? Cogent Bus. Manag. **9**(1), 2135221 (2022)
12. Park, J., Hyun, H., Thavisay, T.: A study of antecedents and outcomes of social media WOM towards luxury brand purchase intention. J. Retail. Cons. Serv. **58**, 102272 (2021)
13. Xiong, L., Cho, V., Law, K.M.Y., Lam, L.: A study of KOL effectiveness on brand image of skincare products. Enterpr. Info. Syst. **15**(10), 1483–1500 (2021)
14. Gilitwala, B., Nag, A.K.: Factors influencing youngsters' consumption behavior on high-end cosmetics in China. J. Asian Finan. Econ. Bus. **8**, 443–450 (2021)
15. Zou, Y., Peng, F.: Key opinion leaders' influences in the chinese fashion market. In: Kalbaska, N., Sádaba, T., Cominelli, F., Cantoni, L. (eds.) FACTUM 2019, pp. 118–132. Springer, Cham (2019). https://doi.org/10.1007/978-3-030-15436-3_11
16. Gefen, D.: E-commerce: The Role of Familiarity and Trust. Omega **28**(6), 725–737 (2000)
17. Magnini, V.P., Honeycutt, E.D., Cross, A.M.: Understanding the use of celebrity endorsers for hospitality firms. J. Vacat. Mark. **14**(1), 57–69 (2008)
18. Ohanian, R.: Construction and validation of a scale to measure celebrity endorsers' perceived expertise, trustworthiness, and attractiveness. Journal of Advertising **19**(3), 39–52 (1990)
19. Aqueveque, C.: Extrinsic cues and perceived risk: the influence of consumption situation. J. Cons. Market. **23**(5), 237–247 (2006)

Supply Chain Risk Management Process: Case Study of the Chinese Aviation Industry in COVID-19

Jiangjia Xu[✉]

College of Social Science, Michigan State University, East Lansing 48824, USA
xujiangj@msu.edu

Abstract. As production shifts from a single conventional process to a multifaceted supply chain model, the importance of supply chain risk management is gradually emerging. The topic of supply chain risk management is explored in this essay. The literature review found that scholars categorize risk management processes differently and need uniform standards. Therefore, we propose a more precise and thorough method of risk management. Risk identification, risk analysis, risk control, and risk monitoring are the four steps in SCRM, it goes into great depth about every step's characteristics and backs up its viability and efficacy with actual instances. The study aims to provide managers with a more scientific and systematic risk management process and a reference for research in related fields.

Keywords: SCRM · Aviation Industry · COVID-19

1 Introduction

Early on, production was comprised of a single product flow from a supplier of raw materials through a manufacturer to a market. Today, shorter product life cycles and increased demand have led to a complex supply chain. Due to cost concerns of cost and competitive advantages, corporations are using international and outsourcing methods. The number of supply chain components increases as a result of this action. It also means the increase of uncontrollable factors, such as the loss of control in the transportation process, the loss of business information, the uncertainty of delivery time, language and cultural differences, and so on. Therefore, many scholars have summarized the supply chain risks, but there needs to be a unified caliber. For example, Ou Tang and S. Nurmaya Musa indicates that risk can be classified into four dimensions, source, make, deliver, and supply chain scope. However, in the article 'Global Strategy: an organizing framework', Ghoshal divides risks into four categories: macroeconomic, policy, competitive, and resource risks [1]. Ou Tang, S. Nurmaya Musa, and Ghoshal classified the risk into different dimensions, which means that the difference is reflected in each step of SCRM [2]. Therefore, this study will develop a more precise and comprehensive supply chain risk management method in this article.

Risk will be defined in this article along with a supply chain risk management technique. A case study built on the suggested technique will then be addressed. The results and conclusions will then be compiled.

2 Literature Review

Supply Chain Risk Management (SCRM) is a multifaceted concept. As a result, different people define SCRM in different ways. Risk is defined by Lowrance as a measure of the likelihood and seriousness of negative outcomes [3, 4]. According to Rowe, risk is the potential for an event or activity to have unanticipated negative effects [4, 5]. According to Moore, the meaning of phrases like "critical risk" and "limited risk" rely often on the effects that the risk's presence would have on the company's financial status [4, 6]. Therefore, the risk is the anticipated result of an unknown occurrence, i.e., and uncertain events cause risks to exist [7].

Effective supply chain risk management could substantially help enterprises. Therefore, the risk management process is an essential topic in the supply chain risk management literature. Many scholars have put forward different views on the risk management process, and some scholars tend to put some low-dimension management processes into high dimensions. Fan and Stevenson's division of risk management process is very concise. The four steps of risk management are identifying risks, evaluating risks, controlling risks, and monitoring risks [8]. Tummala and Schoenherr have slightly different classification methods. They separated SCRM into three phases: the first phase included recognizing risks, measurement of risk, and risk evaluation. The second stage entails the evaluation, rating, acceptance, and planning of risks as well as the study of the Hazard Totem Pole analysis. The control and monitoring of risks are classified into the third stage [9].

The two groups of academics share a surprising amount in common. The identification of risks, evaluation of risks, control of risks, and monitoring of risks are the four main phases that they all include. But Tummala and Schoenherr's risk management method needs to be revised. Firstly, risk acceptance and risk mitigation both belong to risk treatment. Second, according to Tummala and Schoenherr, risk measuring and assessment involve determining how likely a risk will materialize and the degree of that risk's threat. It can be summarized by the term risk evaluation.

3 Supply Chain Risk Management (SCRM)

The SCRM was designed based on the literature research. A thorough risk management procedure is claimed to require four components: risk recognition, risk evaluation, control of risks, and monitoring of risks. Scholars can then build on this framework and tailor their research methodology accordingly.

3.1 Risk Identification

Using checklists of risk is a useful tool for identifying risks. Risk checklists are inventories of prevalent threats in our environment, and they could originate from previous experience or market research [10]. Risks can be identified as internal risks and external risks. From this perspective, risk can be classified into eight types.

Financial risk. This risk frequently emerges as a result of market volatility, losses, and adjustments in the value of stocks, interest rates, and exchange rates for foreign currencies.

Informational risk. Information risk is a threat posed by an undisclosed third party with the intent to steal sensitive data or impair a business's operations [7].

Operation risk. Operational risk is the potential that a circumstance may adversely affect the company's ability to produce goods and services internally, the pace at which the business produces its products, and its profitability [7].

Supply risk. Supply risk is the potential for an incoming supply-related event to occur that could lead to supplier or supply failures in the marketplace, thereby rendering it difficult for the organization to satisfy the demand from consumers within anticipated price ranges [11].

Macroeconomic risk. Economic shifts in prices, exchange, wage, and interest rates.

Climate risk. Risks caused by natural disasters.

Policy risk. Risks arising from changes in national policies.

Demand risk. It is an unwelcome event, primarily brought on by changes in customer demand. Prediction gets more incorrect if volatility is extremely high, and the bullwhip impact is the most unfavorable result of this danger due to forecast inaccuracy [10].

3.2 Risk Analysis

Identify risks based on known risk activities. Once the classification is complete, it can begin the risk analysis. The steps of risk analysis depend on the analysis method used by the researcher. Here this study will use the Two-dimensional diagram for risk assessment. The Two-dimensional diagram is composed of the severity of the risk and the possibility of risk.

$$R = P \times S \qquad (1)$$

R stands for the risk assessment value. P is the risk's chance of happening. S stands for the risk seriousness index.

Therefore, it first needs to evaluate the severity of the risk and the possibility of risk, respectively. Severity and Probability were each rated as low as 1 and high as 3. After the severity and probability score are known, the risk evaluation value can be derived, which can be used to make a two-dimensional diagram.

The full risk evaluation value is 9 out of 9. A risk evaluation value between 1 and 3 is considered low risk, and a risk evaluation value between 4 and 6 is regarded as medium risk. A risk evaluation value of 7 to 9 is high risk.

Severity of risk. The description of the Severity of the risk is shown in Table 1.

Table 1. The description of the Severity of the risk.

Rating	Description	Definition
3	High Severity	Catastrophic impact on company
2	Moderate Severity	Tolerable negative impact on company
1	Low Severity	Negligible negative impact on company

Probability of risk. The description of the Probability of risk is shown in Table 2.

Table 2. The description of the Probability of risk.

Rating	Description	Definition
3	High	Every week
2	Medium	Every month
1	Low	Every year

Two-dimensional Diagram. The description of the Two-dimensional Diagramis shown in Table 3.

Table 3. The description of the Two-dimensional Diagramis.

Probability\Severity	1 (Low Severity)	2 (Moderate Severity)	3 (High Severity)
1 (Low Probability)	Low threat risk	Low threat risk	Medium threat risk
2 (Medium Probability)	Low threat risk	Medium threat risk	High threat risk
3 (High Probability)	Medium threat risk	High threat risk	High threat risk

3.3 Risk Control

The steps risk executives take to prevent or reduce the potential of risk-related occurrences happening or to mitigate the harm brought on by the appearance of risks are referred to as risk control. Risk transfer, risk mitigation, risk acceptance, risk sharing, and risk avoidance are the five fundamental approaches to risk management.

Risk acceptance. The type of financial risk management technology known as a risk acceptance approach is brought on by the enterprise's loss from a risk accident. Its main objective is to accept the inherent risk of the business as well as the certain financial risk associated with production and management and to take the required control measures to lessen the degree of risk or the likelihood of unfavorable outcomes.

Risk avoidance. When considering the likelihood of risk loss, risk avoidance refers to taking the initiative to forego or modify a certain action in order to avoid the risks associated with it.

Risk transfer. The term "risk transfer" describes the entire or partial transfer of risk and the potential loss to other people or organizations. Risk management emphasizing protection through risk transfer is the most popular and efficient.

Risk sharing. Risk sharing means that an enterprise transfers some risks to another enterprise or all risks to another enterprise.

Risk mitigation. Risk mitigation refers to the methodology of risk control to reduce the risk loss frequency or impact degree.

The table of risk control is a strategy selection table based on the risk evaluation value. In Table 4, supply chain managers can match the risk control strategy with the risk evaluation result by using the table of risk control.

Table 4. The risk evaluation result.

Risk acceptance	Risk transfer/Mitigation/sharing	Risk avoidance
Low risk	Medium risk	High risk
Low priority	High priority	

The Table 5 is the template for summarizing the result after the process of risk identification, risk analysis and risk control for each risk event.

Table 5. The template for summarizing the result after risk identification, analysis and control.

	Evaluation and assessment	Evaluation value (S*P = R)	Risk event	Risk type	Strategy
High priority	High risk	3*3 = 9	Event A	Information risk	Risk avoidance
	High risk	3*3 = 9	Event B	Demand risk	Risk avoidance
	High risk	3*3 = 9	Event C	Supply risk	Risk transfer
	Medium risk	2*3 = 6	Event D	Information risk	Risk mitigation
	Medium risk	3*2 = 6	Event E	Policy risk	Risk sharing
	Medium risk	2*3 = 6	Event F	Financial risk	Risk transfer
Low priority	Low risk	1*3 = 3	Event G	Macroeconomic risk	Risk mitigation
	Low risk	3*1 = 3	Event H	Climate risk	Risk acceptance
	Low risk	3*1 = 3	Event I	Operation risk	Risk acceptance

3.4 Risk Monitoring

The continuing practice of controlling risk is known as risk monitoring. It is the procedure for monitoring and evaluating the degree of risk inside a business or organization. Risk monitoring involves regularly detecting and managing new risks while also assessing the effectiveness of risk management. The outcomes of the risk monitoring process may be utilized to upgrade outdated systems and assist create new tactics that may be successful.

The goal of risk monitoring is to keep track of dangers that arise and the efficiency of the organization's reaction. By monitoring risks, it is possible to ascertain if the right methods are being used, whether new hazards may be found and whether earlier presumptions about these risks are still true. Due to the dynamic nature of hazards, monitoring is essential. Therefore, risk monitoring is a cyclic process from risk identification to risk control.

4 Case Study: The Impact of COVID-19 on the Chinese Aviation Industry

4.1 Risk Identification

The risks associated with the COVID-19 outbreak in the Chinese aviation industry were identified, including financial risks, supply chain risks, operational risks, and policy risks. These risks were categorized into internal and external risks, and a risk checklist was used to aid in the identification process. Table 6 displays the analysis' findings.

Table 6. Risk Identification of Chinese Aviation Industry.

Source of risk	Risk events	Type of risk	Risk Encoding
Internal risk	Quarantine spending	Operational Risk	Risk event A
External risk	Reduced demand for planes due to reduced travel	Demand risk/Policy risk	Risk event B
	Customer order cancellations	Demand risk	Risk event C
	Reduced productivity due to COVID-19	Supply risk	Risk event D
	Policy restrictions on travel cause delays in the delivery of materials or products	Supply risk/Policy risk	Risk event E
	Restriction of international trade cause Supplier shutdown/Supplier unavailable	Supply risk	Risk event F

4.2 Risk Analysis

They assess the risks using the Two-dimensional Diagram and record the scores using a risk control template. The results of the analysis about severity of risk, probability of risk, and two-dimensional diagram are shown in Tables 7, 8 and 9.

Table 7. The results of the analysis about severity of risk of Chinese Aviation Industry.

Rating	Description	Definition
3	High Severity	Catastrophic impact on company
2	Moderate Severity	Tolerable negative impact on company
1	Low Severity	Negligible negative impact on company

Table 8. The results of the analysis about probability of risk of Chinese Aviation Industry.

Rating	Description	Definition
3	High	Every week
2	Medium	Every month
1	Low	Every year

Table 9. The results of the analysis about two-dimensional diagram of Chinese Aviation Industry.

Probability\Severity	1 (Low Severity)	2 (Moderate Severity)	3 (High Severity)
1 (Low Probability)	Low threat risk	Low threat risk	Medium threat risk
2 (Medium Probability)	Low threat risk	Medium threat risk	High threat risk
3 (High Probability)	Medium threat risk	High threat risk	High threat risk

4.3 Risk Control

Using the Table of risk control to sort risks, select control methods and record the results in a template of risk control. The results of the analysis are shown in Table 10.

Table 10. The results of Risk Control.

		Evaluation and assessment	Evaluation value((S*P = R)	Risk event	Risk type	Strategy	Detailed risk control strategy
High Priority		High threat risk	3*3 = 6	Event F	Supply risk	Risk mitigation	Search for local suppliers instead
		High threat risk	3*3 = 9	Event B	Demand risk/Policy risk	Risk mitigation	Reduce sales price
		Medium threat risk	3*2 = 6	Event C	Demand risk	Risk mitigation	Reduce sales price
		Medium threat risk	2*3 = 6	Event D	Supply risk	Risk mitigation	Production automation
Low Priority		Medium threat risk	2*3 = 6	Event E	Supply risk/Policy risk	Risk mitigation	Change the mode of transport
		Medium threat risk	2*3 = 9	Event A	Operation risk	Risk mitigation	Layoff/wage cuts

5 Conclusion

This study proposes a novel risk management process incorporating a risk assessment method into the conventional risk identification, control, and monitoring steps. As shown in Fig. 1, an analysis template was developed and applied to a real-world case study to demonstrate its effectiveness. The proposed risk management process is summarized as a figure, referred to as the risk management overview.

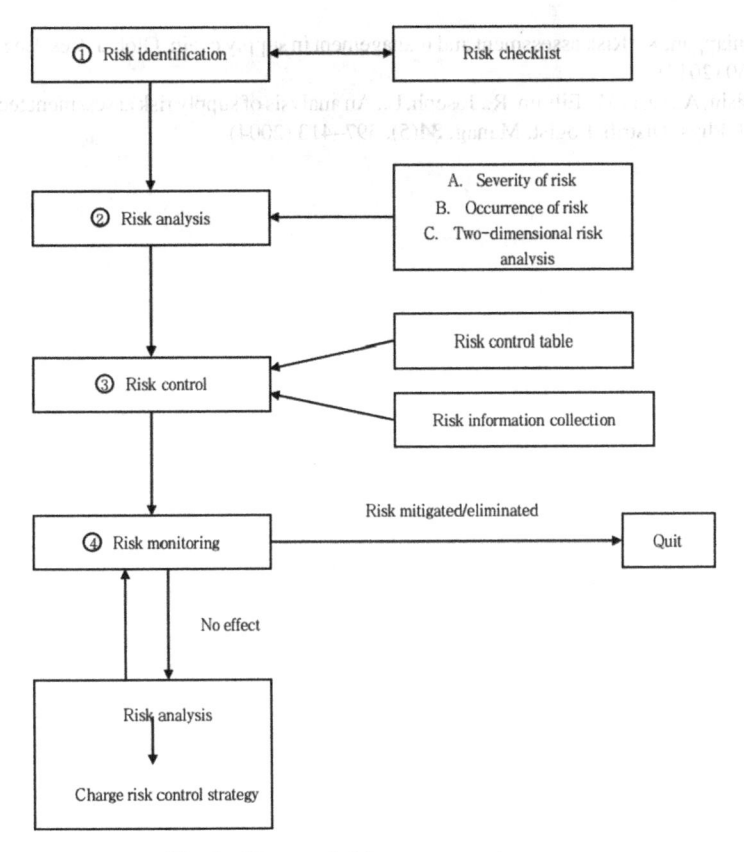

Fig. 1. The novel risk management process.

References

1. Ghoshal, S.: Global strategy: an organizing framework. Strateg. Manag. J. **8**(5), 425–440 (1987)
2. Tang, O., Nurmaya, S.: Identifying risk issues and research advancements in supply chain risk management. Int. J. Prod. Econ. **133**(1), 25–34 (2011)
3. Lowrance, W.: The nature of risk. In: Schwing, R.C., Albers, W.A. (eds.) How Safe is Safe Enough?, Plenum Press, New York (1980)
4. Khan, O., Bernard. B.: Risk and supply chain management: creating a research agenda. The international journal of logistics management, (2007)
5. Rowe, W.: Risk assessment: approaches and methods. In: Conrad, J. (ed.) Society, Technology and Risk Assessment. Academic Press, London (1980)
6. Moore, P.G.: The Business of Risk. Cambridge University Press, Cambridge (1983)
7. Manuj, I., Mentzer, J.T.: Global supply chain risk management strategies. Int. J. Phys. Distrib. Logist. Manag. **38**, 192–223 (2008)
8. Fan, Y., Mark, S.: A review of supply chain risk management: definition, theory, and research agenda. Int. J. Phys. Distrib. Logist. Manag. **48**, 205–230 (2018)
9. Tummala, R., Tobias, S.: Assessing and managing risks using the supply chain risk management process. Supply Chain Manag. Int. J. **16**(6), 474–483 (2011)

10. Palaniappan, K.: Risk assessment and management in supply chain. Glob. J. Res. Eng. **14**(G2), 19–30 (2014)
11. Zsidisin, A., Lisa, M., Ellram, R., Joseph, L.: An analysis of supply risk assessment techniques. Int. J. Phys. Distrib. Logist. Manag. **34**(5), 397–413 (2004)

The Marketing Value of User-Generated Content in the Mobile Industry

Le Han[1], Zhuoer Wei[2(✉)], and Shuyan Zhang[3]

[1] School of International Studies, Hangzhou Normal University, Hangzhou, China
hanle@stu.hznu.edu.cn
[2] Faculty of Humanities and Arts, Macau University of Science and Technology, Macau, China
2009853ja111006@student.must.edu.mo
[3] Department of Media and Communication, Xi'an Jiaotong-Liverpool University, Suzhou, China
Shuyan.zhang20@student.xjtlu.edu.cn

Abstract. With smartphones' popularity and the mobile Internet's rapid development, User Generated Content (UGC) has become a popular marketing tool. UGC refers to the content ordinary consumers actively create and share, such as user comments, order displays, short videos, pictures, etc. The emergence of UGC breaks the boundary between enterprises and consumers in traditional marketing, making consumers the participants and promoters of brand marketing. UGC increasingly affects customers' choices. For example, many potential customers may buy digital products according to the posts about evaluating specific products online. This study adopts a combination of quantitative and qualitative research methods. Using the Questionnaire survey and Text sentiment analysis methods, the study analyzes the marketing value of UGC for four smartphone brands: Apple, Huawei, Xiaomi, and Samsung. The study discovered the advantages and limitations of UGC's dissemination effects.

Keywords: UGC · bandwagon effect · cognitive dissonance · marketing value · sentiment analysis

1 Introduction

With the rapid development of the internet, user-generated content has received a great deal of attention. Now people can create content through social networking websites, review-sharing websites, and image and video-sharing platforms [1]. With the websites, users are more allowed to take part in the discussion of public events and express opinions about different things. Also, the content which the users create can spread widely. At the same time, a large amount of user-generated content causes different reactions among people who browse specific websites. The theories included in the study are the bandwagon effect, polarization effect, cognitive bias, and cognitive dissonance.

From the branding perspective, researching consumers' cognition and acceptance of the mobile phone brand UGC will help to understand consumers' attitudes and opinions on UGC. Thus, it can provide a reference for brands to formulate marketing strategies that can better meet the needs of consumers. Moreover, the disclosure of UGC's marketing value helps to explore its application and successful cases in brand marketing to enhance brand fame and awareness further and increase brand sales [2]. At the same time, to improve brand reputation and loyalty, it is also essential to study UGC's impact on consumers' purchase intention and their word-of-mouth communication.

From the perspective of the common interests of consumers and brands, collecting user reviews under the brand's product page and doing sentiment analysis will help companies and enterprises better understand consumers' behavior and psychological activities when they participate in brand marketing. At the same time, it will further improve marketing effectiveness and efficiency to improve the service level of the brand and thus achieve a mutually beneficial situation for the brand and the consumers [3, 4]. At the theoretical level, the research can provide empirical data and theoretical support for the strategy, purpose, effect, and other aspects of UGC marketing and provide reference and learning materials for the development and innovation of UGC marketing [5].

The primary significance of this paper is to deeply explore the marketing value of user-generated content in the mobile phone industry. By discovering the value of UGC, corresponding marketing strategies will be made to use the potential functions of the contents. To have a further study in terms of the digital market and the strategies in this field, four brands should be considered in the essay. The research objects named Apple, Samsung, Xiaomi, and Huawei in this study are four brands that occupy a vital position in the Chinese mobile phone market. An in-depth analysis of these brands' application of user-generated content may provide companies with valuable marketing experience and references for other brands to adopt UGC in marketing.

Considering today's increasingly fierce market competition, strategies corresponding to the modern market should be conducted to catch up with the newest trend. In addition, new ways of promoting brand influence have become vital in occupying a leading position in the competition. The study will delve into the impact of user-generated content on brand awareness, purchase intention, and word-of-mouth communication. Through the results of this study, we can better understand the contribution of user-generated content to brand influence, provide more scientific marketing strategies for enterprises and further improve the market competitiveness of enterprises. To explore the effectiveness of UGC in influencing audiences, this paper first proposes two hypotheses:

H1: Users' acceptance of mobile phone brand-related UGC positively correlates with the degree of change in their attitude towards mobile phone brands.

H2: The intensity of a user's brand loyalty for a mobile phone brand is directly proportional to the frequency of UGCs associated with that mobile phone brand.

A questionnaire survey and analysis will be used to test the hypotheses. The paper then conducts sentiment analysis on UGC texts related to phone brands' reviews on shopping platforms based on the results of the hypothesis testing. The aim is to understand further how brands can utilize UGC for marketing purposes.

2 Related Work

2.1 Bandwagon Effect

The bandwagon effect describes a phenomenon in which a person tends to show a stronger endorsement of one thing that the person thinks is more popular in society [6]. It can commonly happen on the internet now. Previous relevant opinions can be easily passed to people who have similar ideas. According to snowballing effects, these ideas then become stronger on the websites. It can lead to strong community-driven consensus [7]. Nowadays, the bandwagon effect has been used in terms of business strategies. By using this theory, brands can build up their ideal images. Because of the great value of the application of the bandwagon effect on the websites, companies treat it as a vital part of to study of the relationship between customer and brand and the engagement of customers [8]. At the same time, it also tightly connects with brand loyalty topics.

2.2 Polarization Effect

Another theory that will be used is the polarization effect. Polarization means that people in one group usually have similar ideas and support the same values. They conform to some specific rules within the group [9]. When an individual joins a group and feels the existence of pressure which other group members bring, the individual will stop expressing themselves straightly. Instead, they will first observe if the idea corresponds with others' opinions. If the ideas are contradicted, though the individual may disagree with other views, they will choose not to express opposition. The main reason for the phenomenon is people's desire to be acknowledged by groups [9]. Because many websites are designed to help find friends, users in some specific groups easily have similar value systems, which can produce similar thoughts. As a result, polarization can now easily occur on the websites such as Facebook [10]. This explains why people's opinions on the Internet gradually move from a balanced position to an extreme one [11].

2.3 Cognitive Bias

Consumers have a psychological phenomenon of cognitive bias towards UGC of mobile phone brands. In cognitive theory, bias is people's inability to process and integrate information. Thus, when users spontaneously express their views in the UGC communication mode, they often help tagged language show personal emotional tendencies. Automatic attentional and interpretational tendencies are examples of cognitive biases. Attentional biases have been discovered in various diseases, from addiction disorders to depression and anxiety disorders. They relate to the individual's preference for allocating attention to or away from stimuli that are emotionally salient to them. The cognitive framework and thinking mode are formed by people in this process. And they will directly or indirectly affect the degree of positivity or negativity of the user-generated content they produce. These natural processes would also cause people with anxiety disorders to pay attention to signals connected to threats, people with depression to cues related to negative information, and those with addiction disorders to pay attention to cues associated to substances [12]. Cognitive bias is closely connected with human decision-making because people learn and develop predictable thinking patterns [13]. The aspect of cognitive bias in response to minority and majority influence is where beneficiaries routinely deal with a persuasive message detached from social conflict and attitudinal differences [14]. Therefore, UGC will also affect the impression of mobile phone brand consumers on each mobile phone brand and their purchase desire.

2.4 Cognitive Dissonance

Another psychological phenomenon of consumers is cognitive dissonance. A person with two contradictory beliefs will feel the pressure of cognitive dissonance, an aversive motivational condition. To relieve this pressure, the person may try changing one of the two "dissonant" beliefs, among other things. Festinger's theory of cognitive dissonance is based on this premise [15]. Like many psychological theories, the theory of cognitive dissonance makes an effort to illustrate the functional relationships between present stimuli and reactions by postulating some fictitious physiological process, in this case, an implied process of the arousal and decrease of dissonance [16]. While making a regular purchase, more involved buyers experience less cognitive dissonance than less involved buyers. Notably, while highly involved customers experience less cognitive dissonance, doing so presents greater challenges. Another conclusion is that higher levels of cognitive dissonance are linked to more planned and less impulsive purchasing behavior [17]. One of the main reasons for dissonance was a consumer's belief, which stopped them from making an intelligent choice and led to feelings of regret [18]. In his 2012 study, Chou examined the relationship between pre-purchase consumers' internal beliefs about an online store and the product's online reviews and how these perceptions impacted the choice to buy. The research came to the conclusion that a consumer's cognitive dissonance rose as the gap between his or her subjective opinions about an online retailer and online reviews of the retailer grew larger [19].

3 Methods

The method is divided in two parts: questionnaire survey and text sentiment analysis.

3.1 Questionnaire Survey

The research objects are existing users of APPLE, HUAWEI, Xiaomi, and SAMSUNG. The questionnaire is divided into two parts. The first part is to collect basic demographic information, including age, educational background, occupation, and family economic status. The second is the study of question scale measurement, including the use of mobile phone brands, UGC acceptance, publication behavior, and the change of attitude towards mobile phone brands.

Questionnaires were distributed offline directly to college students in China's Guangdong, Jiangsu, and Zhejiang provinces. The survey lasted for three days, and 101 questionnaires were received. After excluding invalid questionnaires, 87 valid questionnaires were obtained.

SPSS 26.0 was used to verify the model. Through Cronbach's α coefficient test, it was found that Cronbach's α coefficient of the variable was 0.757, higher than the threshold value of 0.7. Thus, it firmly proves that the questionnaire has good reliability. Then the factor analysis in the dimensionality reduction module was used to analyze the validity of the questionnaire. The measured KMO value was 0.863, more significant than the threshold value of 0.6. Thus, it firmly proved that the validity of the questionnaire was good.

3.2 Text Sentiment Analysis

To further understand the impact of mobile phone brand UGC on mobile marketing, it is necessary to understand which UGCs users are most interested. Therefore, the study extracted 1500 recent reviews each from iPhone 14, iPhone 14 Pro Max, HUAWEI mates 50, HUAWEI mate50 xs2, Xiaomi 13, Xiaomi MIX Fold2, SAMSUNG Galaxy S23, SAMSUNG Galaxy Z Fold4 on the JD online shopping platform (before March 23, 2023). That is 3000 reviews for each brand for keyword screening and sentiment analysis. ATLAS.ti 23 was used for text sentiment analysis based on general rule methods. In the study, S first analyzed the sentiment of each sentence of the 3000 reviews from each of the four brands. It mainly divides the text sentiment into negative, neutral, and positive and encodes and counts the sentiment of each comment.

4 Experimental Results and Analysis

4.1 Questionnaire Survey

H1: Users' acceptance of mobile phone brand-related UGC is positively correlated with the change degree of their attitude towards mobile phone brands.

In the verification of this hypothesis, the relevant index Q13 in the questionnaire (the frequency of my contact with user-produced content related to mobile phone brands on the Internet) is multiplied with the four items of Apple, Huawei, Xiaomi and Samsung in Q14 (in my opinion, the popularity evaluation of mobile phone brands on the Internet), and they are compiled into four new variables: APPLE reviews quality, HUAWEI reviews quality, Xiaomi reviews quality, SAMSUNG reviews quality; Apple reviews quality, Huawei reviews quality, Xiaomi reviews quality, Samsung reviews quality. These four new variables and Q16 (user-produced content related to mobile phone brands on the Internet has changed my attitude towards this brand) are tested for relevance according to brand differentiation. It is analyzed and tested through bivariate correlation analysis. The results are shown in Tables 1, 2, 3 and 4.

By analyzing Pearson correlation values, a strong positive correlation exists between users' acceptance degree of UGC related to the four mobile phone brands and their attitude change degree to mobile phone brands. The correlation is significant. So H1 is proven.

Based on demonstrating H1, it further explores whether there is an obvious linear regression relationship (functional relationship) between the two variables. Taking brand SAMSUNG as an example, SAMSUNG attitudes change set as Dependent Variable

Table 1. Correlation test of Apple reviews quality with Apple attitudes change.

		APPLE reviews quality	APPLE attitudes change
APPLE reviews quality	Person Correlation	1	.402**
	Sig.(2-tailed)		.000
	N	87	87

**. Correlation is significant at the 0.01 level (2-tailed).

Table 2. Correlation test of HUAWEI reviews quality with HUAWEI attitudes change.

		HUAWEI reviews quality	HUAWEI attitudes change
HUAWEI reviews quality	Person Correlation	1	.385**
	Sig.(2-tailed)		.000
	N	87	87

**. Correlation is significant at the 0.01 level (2-tailed).

Table 3. Correlation test of Xiaomi reviews quality with Xiaomi attitudes change.

		Xiaomi reviews quality	Xiaomi attitudes change
Xiaomi reviews quality	Person Correlation	1	.398**
	Sig.(2-tailed)		.000
	N	87	87

**. Correlation is significant at the 0.01 level (2-tailed).

Table 4. Correlation test of Samsung reviews quality with Samsung attitudes change.

		SAMSUNG reviews quality	SAMSUNG attitudes change
SAMSUNG reviews quality	Person Correlation	1	.439**
	Sig.(2-tailed)		.000
	N	87	87

**. Correlation is significant at the 0.01 level (2-tailed).

X. SAMSUNG reviews quality was set as Independent variable Y. Coefficient a was analyzed first, as shown in Table 5.

Table 5. Coefficient a analysis of Samsung reviews quality and Samsung attitudes change.

Model	Unstandardized Coefficients		Standardized Coefficients		
	B	Std. Error	Beta	t	Sig.
(Constant)	2.036	.050		40.695	.000
SAMSUNG reviews quality	.081	.018	.439	4.502	.000

[a]Dependent Variable: SAMSUNG reviews quality

A simple linear regression model can be obtained:

$$Y = 0.81X + 2.036 \tag{1}$$

Its significance value was less than 0.01, indicating extremely significant statistical significance. SAMSUNG attitudes change, and SAMSUNG review quality has an extremely significant linear relationship.

H2: The intensity of a user's love for a mobile phone brand is directly proportional to the frequency of UGCs associated with that mobile phone brand.

In the verification of this hypothesis, the correlation test is conducted on the four variables of Apple, Huawei, Xiaomi, and Samsung, respectively, in the relevant index Q9 (my fondness for mobile phone brands) and Q15 (the frequency of mobile phone related information published on the Internet) in the questionnaire. It is analyzed and tested through bivariate correlation analysis. The results are shown in Tables 6, 7, 8 and 9.

Table 6. Apple reviews frequency and apple love degree correlation test.

		APPLE reviews frequency	APPLE love degree
APPLE reviews frequency	Person Correlation	1	.044
	Sig.(2-tailed)		.686
	N	87	87

Through the Pearson correlation value analysis, it can be seen that there is no correlation between the intensity of users' love for a mobile phone brand and the frequency of UGC related to the published mobile phone brand. So H2 cannot be demonstrated.

It can be found from the demonstration results of H1 and H2 that users' acceptance of UGC related to mobile phone brands can significantly change their impression of the brand. Moreover, positive UGC acceptance brings a positive impression change, and negative UGC acceptance brings a negative impression change. However, the degree of affection for the mobile phone brand does not affect the frequency of UGC releases of the mobile phone brand.

Table 7. Correlation test of HUAWEI reviews frequency with HUAWEI love degree.

		HUAWEI reviews frequency	HUAWEI love degree
HUAWEI reviews frequency	Person Correlation	1	.126
	Sig.(2-tailed)		.244
	N	87	87

Table 8. Correlation test of Xiaomi reviews frequency with Xiaomi love degree.

		Xiaomi reviews frequency	Xiaomi love degree
Xiaomi reviews frequency	Person Correlation	1	.001
	Sig.(2-tailed)		.992
	N	87	87

Table 9. Correlation test of Samsung reviews frequency with Samsung love degree.

		SAMSUNG reviews frequency	SAMSUNG love degree
SAMSUNG reviews frequency	Person Correlation	1	.107
	Sig.(2-tailed)		.323
	N	87	87

4.2 Text Sentiment Analysis

ATLAS.ti 23 was used for text sentiment analysis based on general rule methods. In the study, S first analyzed the sentiment of each sentence of the 3000 reviews from each of the four brands. It mainly divides the text sentiment into negative, neutral, and positive and encodes and counts the sentiment of each comment. The results are shown in Table 10:

Table 10. Shopping review sentiment analysis by Apple, HUAWEI, Xiaomi & SAMSUNG.

	APPLE	HUAWEI	Xiaomi	SAMSUNG
Negative	847	591	743	538
Neutral	1365	975	1185	1071
Positive	5956	3781	4247	4886
Total	8168	5347	6175	6495

UCG Comparison Between Brands. Even in the review area of a single brand, there is no shortage of reviews of other brands. In order to analyze the sentiment of consumers of mobile phone brands in the UGC that compares their purchase brand to other brands, first encode sentences that mention the other three mobile phone brands in all reviews. Then distinguish other brands directly from other brands and buy brands. If the bytes about APPLE or iPhone appear in the comment area of Huawei mobile phones, "Apple phones do a good job of taking pictures" are encoded as "Comments on APPLE" and "better than Apple in taking photos" is encoded as "Comparison with APPLE." Because both express opposite meanings. However, both are classified as positive emotions.

Then the coding is cross-analyzed. For instance, in the coding "Comments on APPLE" and "Comparison with APPLE" and the three brand sentiments of HUAWEI, Xiaomi, and SAMSUNG, a total of nine types of codes are cross-analyzed. Furthermore, Table 11 is obtained:

Table 11. Apple sentiment analysis that appears in shopping reviews from other brands (complex).

	HUAWEI: Negative	HUAWEI: Neutral	HUAWEI: Positive	Xiaomi: Negative	Xiaomi: Neutral	Xiaomi: Positive	SAMSUNG: Negative	SAMSUNG: Neutral	SAMSUNG: Positive
comments on APPLE	29	19	45	19	15	62	10	26	61
Comparison with APPLE	6	5	13	1	8	16	2	4	23

Then simplify the table by calculation, through the formula:

$$Positive(A) = Comments(A)\&Positive - Comparison(A)\&Positive + Comparison(A)\&Negative$$

$$Negative(A) = Comparison(A)\&Positive + Comments(A)\&Negative - Comparison(A)\&Negative$$

$$Neutral(A) = Comments(A)\&Neutra$$

Can obtain the following simplified Table 12:

Table 12. Apple sentiment analysis that appears in shopping reviews from other brands.

	HUAWEI	Xiaomi	SAMSUNG	Total
Negative	36	34	31	101
Neutral	19	15	26	60
Positive	38	47	40	125
Total	93	96	97	286

Using the same steps, the evaluation sentiment of the other three brands in other review areas can be obtained, as shown in Tables 13, 14 and 15 below:

Table 13. HUAWEI sentiment analysis that appears in shopping reviews from other brands.

	APPLE	Xiaomi	SAMSUNG	Total
Negative	9	17	14	40
Neutral	6	8	2	16
Positive	18	25	17	60
Total	33	50	33	116

Table 14. Xiaomi sentiment analysis that appears in shopping reviews from other brands.

	APPLE	HUAWEI	SAMSUNG	Total
Negative	1	5	3	9
Neutral	2	2	0	4
Positive	6	7	7	20
Total	9	14	10	33

Table 15. Samsung sentiment analysis that appears in shopping reviews from other brands.

	APPLE	HUAWEI	Xiaomi	Total
Negative	5	5	10	20
Neutral	1	3	12	16
Positive	5	5	16	26
Total	11	13	38	62

From Tables 12, 13, 14 and 15, it is easy to find that APPLE is mentioned most frequently in the shopping reviews of other mobile phones. The mentions (286 times) exceed the sum of the other three mobile phones (211 times). The ratio of negative to positive reviews for Apple is the highest (0.81), surpassing HUAWEI (0.67), Xiaomi (0.45), and Samsung (0.77). In the scale, the results obtained from Q16 (user-produced content related to mobile phone brand on the Internet changes my attitude towards this brand) show that when users receive online UGC content related to mobile phones, their attitude towards APPLE is the most positive (2.32/3). It is higher than HUAWEI (2.17), Xiaomi (2.06/3), and Samsung (2.06/3).

It shows that users post UGCs from brands they prefer or think are better. In this context, bad reviews are more of a sign of cognitive dissonance than a negative effect.

Even the users' negative comments on APPLE mostly aim to highlight the excellence of the mobile phones they buy. They compare their mobile phones with APPLE because APPLE is the best among the remaining three brands, although they are unwilling to admit it. Therefore, APPLE is used too much as a comparison, which can show that APPLE is excellent. Even though there are so many Apple-related UGCs in the comments section of other brands, it is natural that users are more and more impressed with APPLE.

Key Factor Exploration. The product page comment area is more about the evaluation of the product. This study explores which mobile phone elements are mentioned most often in the comment area. It can be found that among the four brands, the photograph is the element that accounts for the first proportion. Through text comparison, it was found that the number of times that taking photos appeared in Xiaomi comments (802 times). It is much higher than that of Apple (413 times), HUAWEI (478 times), and SAMSUNG (502 times). Moreover, almost all of them were positive (760/802).

To explore the reasons for this, further analyze the reasons why Xiaomi-related UGC content is large and mostly positive, continue to search for the elements that appear together with "taking photos," and find that Leica only appears in the Xiaomi comment area, and the frequency is quite high (336/802). Almost all UGC about Leica is positive content (330/336). Xiaomi chose Leica for the mobile phone camera module and received much praise. Although most users only know that Leica is a professional camera brand and know nothing about everything else about this brand. However, it was enough for them to praise Xiaomi's UGC for being more professional, so they were happy to mention Leica in the comments. Users who read more reviews do not need to know what Leica does because of the herd effect. Xiaomi agreed because of the powerful camera and the powerful camera taking pictures. This is a smart example of using UGC marketing.

5 Discussion

One of the limitations of the sentiment analysis is that the analysis was based on the content available on one platform, JD.com. Other e-commerce platforms and social media channels may have different patterns of user-generated content and customer perceptions. Therefore, the results of this study may not be generalizable to all customer segments and may not represent the entire population of Xiaomi, Apple, Huawei, and Samsung customers.

Moreover, the questionnaire survey did not consider the demographic characteristics of the users who posted the comments. Different demographic groups may have different preferences and perceptions, and their comments may not represent the overall customer base. Future studies may consider analyzing the content based on demographic factors such as age, gender, and location to gain more insight into customer preferences and perceptions.

Future studies may consider analyzing the UGC on social media platforms to gain a more comprehensive understanding of the customer perceptions and preferences. Social media platforms such as Twitter, Facebook, and Instagram may provide more diverse and representative samples of customer perceptions than e-commerce platforms.

6 Conclusion

Overall, the methods used in this study provide valuable insights into user attitudes toward smartphone brands and how UGC affects these attitudes. The study findings have important implications for marketers and can help them develop more effective strategies for promoting smartphone brands. The research results show that UGC significantly affects changing users' impressions of mobile phone brands. Therefore, improving brand awareness and loyalty is feasible by guiding mobile phone users to post UGC about their use of mobile phone brands. Further research shows that users' liking for mobile phone brands is unrelated to the frequency of their UGC postings. Therefore, mobile phone brands need to guide users' UGC postings in choosing marketing strategies.

The findings suggest that Xiaomi has successfully leveraged UGC marketing to promote its camera features, and the collaboration with Leica has been a key factor in achieving this. The positive perception of the camera features has contributed significantly to the overall positive perception of Xiaomi among its customers. This is an excellent example of how UGC can be used to create a positive brand image and promote product features effectively. The research results show that UGC significantly affects changing users' impressions of mobile phone brands. Therefore, improving brand awareness and loyalty is feasible by guiding mobile phone users to post UGC about their use of mobile phone brands. Further research shows that users' liking for mobile phone brands is unrelated to the frequency of their UGC postings. Therefore, mobile phone brands need to guide users' UGC postings in choosing marketing strategies. This is demonstrated in case studies of effective marketing methods. Overall, effective methods of using UGC for brand marketing include: 1) Sponsoring digital opinion leaders in the field to publish brand-related UGC. 2) Improving the quality of one's own mobile phone to gain public recognition, which in turn leads to unconscious UGC postings related to the brand, such as Apple being used more often for comparison with other brands. 3)Enhancing certain aspects of the product or collaborating with other brands to create a stunt and attract users to post relevant UGC, triggering a bandwagon effect, such as the collaboration between Xiaomi and Leica, which significantly increased UGC related to Xiaomi's excellent camera performance.

References

1. Hooper, M.W.: User-generated content. Salem Press Encyclopedia (2020)
2. Daugherty, T., Eastin, M.S., Bright, L.: Exploring consumer motivations for creating user-generated content. J. Interact. Advert. 8(2), 16–25 (2008)
3. Timoshenko, A., Hauser, J.R.: Identifying customer needs from user-generated content. Mark. Sci. 38(1), 1–20 (2019)
4. Ransbotham, S., Kane, G.C., Lurie, N.H.: Network characteristics and the value of collaborative user-generated content. Mark. Sci. 31(3), 387–405 (2012)
5. Van Dijck, J.: Users like you? Theorizing agency in user-generated content. Media Cult. Soc. 31(1), 41–58 (2009)
6. Knyazev, N., Oosterhuis, H.: The bandwagon effect: not just another bias. In: Proceedings of the 2022 ACM SIGIR International Conference on Theory of Information Retrieval, pp. 243–253 (2022)

7. Anantharaman, R., Prashar, S., Vijay, T.S.: Uncovering the role of consumer trust and bandwagon effect influencing purchase intention: an empirical investigation in social commerce platforms. J. Strat. Mark. **31**, 1–21 (2022)
8. Anantharaman, R., Prashar, S., Tata, S.V.: Examining the influence of customer-brand relationship constructs and bandwagon effect on brand loyalty. Benchmark. Int. J. **30**, 361–381 (2022)
9. Gould, M., Walker, K.: Group Polarization. Salem Press Encyclopedia (2021)
10. Boyd, K.: Group epistemology and structural factors in online group polarization. Episteme **20**(1), 57–72 (2023)
11. Dai, J., Zhu, J., Wang, G.: Opinion influence maximization problem in online social networks based on group polarization effect. Inf. Sci. **609**, 195–214 (2022)
12. Zhang, M., Ying, J., Song, G., Fung, D.S., Smith, H.: Mobile phone cognitive bias modification research platform for substance use disorders: protocol for a feasibility study. JMIR Res. Protocols **7**(6), e9740 (2018)
13. Phillips-Wren, G., Power, D.J., Mora, M.: Cognitive bias, decision styles, and risk attitudes in decision making and DSS. J. Decis. Syst. **28**(2), 63–66 (2019)
14. Erb, H.P., Bohner, G., Schmilzle, K., Rank, S.: Beyond conflict and discrepancy: cognitive bias in minority and majority influence. Pers. Soc. Psychol. Bull. **24**(6), 620–633 (1998)
15. Gawronski, B.: Back to the future of dissonance theory: cognitive consistency as a core motive. Soc. Cogn. **30**(6), 652–668 (2012)
16. Bem, D.J.: Self-perception: an alternative interpretation of cognitive dissonance phenomena. Psychol. Rev. **74**(3), 183 (1967)
17. George, B.P., Edward, M.: Cognitive dissonance and purchase involvement in the consumer behavior context. IUP J. Mark. Manag. **8**(3/4), 7 (2009)
18. Zafar, B.: Can subjective expectations data be used in choice models?-Evidence on cognitive biases. J. Appl. Economet. **26**(3), 520–544 (2011)
19. Bolia, B., Jha, S., Jha, M.K.: Cognitive dissonance: a review of causes and marketing implications. Res. World **7**(2), 63 (2016)

Direct Carbon Emissions, Indirect Carbon Emissions, and International Trade: An Analysis of OECD Member Countries

Yirong Xi[✉]

King's College London Strand, London WC2R 2LS, UK
xyrgang@163.com

Abstract. This paper takes OECD member countries as the research object, and through the calculation of direct carbon emissions and indirect carbon emissions for each country, it discusses in depth the issue of carbon emissions transfer caused by international trade. The study found that global carbon emissions increased from 1995 to 2019, while those of OECD countries decreased. This paper analyzes the possibility that the reason for this phenomenon may be related to the relatively clean industrial structure of the countries within the organization. Over the past two decades, carbon intensity has declined across OECD countries, but there are significant differences between countries. The foreign trade volume of all OECD countries is on the rise, and the United States is the largest import and export country in the organization. Within the OECD, there is no significant transfer of carbon from developed to developing countries. Instead, the United States and Germany emit more carbon directly than indirectly. The study in this paper reveals the real carbon footprint behind the trade between OECD countries and provides indicators such as carbon intensity and transfer for similar studies, which can provide inspiration for policymakers to deal with global climate change.

Keywords: Carbon Transfer · Carbon Intensity · OECD · International Trade

1 Introduction

With the deepening of the international division of labor under the global production network and the advancement of the process of global trade liberalization, production and consumption are separated to a certain extent on a global scale. Products made in one country can be used in other parts of the world, but the damage to the environment from the use of natural resources and pollution is mostly done during production and stays in the country that made the product. In other words, the production link is spread across different countries based on the principle of making the best use of resources. This leads to the cross-border geographical segmentation of production and consumption activities, which also causes the regional transfer of carbon emissions. At the same time, in the context of global climate governance, some international powers have put forward carbon-peaking and carbon neutrality goals. These goals can only be achieved through the cooperation of different countries. However, how to make a fair energy conservation and emission reduction policy has been controversial because each country may have direct and indirect carbon emissions. In such a complex context, the direction, production, and consumption of carbon emissions need to be analyzed concretely. On this basis, this paper explores the carbon footprint of OECD member countries, hoping to provide some basis for policymaking to help achieve carbon peaking and carbon neutrality goals.

This paper looks at how international trade affects the transfer of carbon between 38 OECD countries. As an example, the paper looks at OECD countries. Firstly, this paper analyzes the global carbon emission and industrial structure and finds that the overall carbon emission of the OECD shows a downward trend, which is inconsistent with the global total carbon emission. Through further analysis of the industrial structure, this paper finds that this is because the economies of OECD countries are highly specialized and the industrial structure is mainly technical industry and service industry. On this basis, the paper calculates the carbon emission intensity of OECD countries, and the calculation results show that the carbon emission intensity of OECD countries has shown a decreasing trend in the past two decades. In this paper, carbon emission intensity is combined with international trade to calculate the carbon transfer situation of OECD countries. The United States and Germany are the two countries with the highest direct carbon emissions among OECD member countries. Considering the key role of carbon emissions in global climate change, the study in this paper is of great significance for global emission reduction. The research in this paper provides a reference for rational policy formulation in energy conservation and emission reduction.

The rest of this paper will be divided according to the following structure: In the second section, relevant literature is reviewed and summarized. In Sect. 3, the industrial structure and carbon emissions are analyzed, and the index of carbon emission intensity is constructed. In Sect. 4, the transfer of carbon emissions between OECD countries is calculated. Finally, the thesis is summarized in the fifth section.

2 Literature Review

A large number of literature studies have shown that carbon emissions can be transferred between countries through international trade. As for the direction of transfer, existing literature mainly points out the following two types: one is from the perspective of national development level: carbon emissions transfer from developed countries to developing countries through trade, and developed countries should be responsible for this type of carbon emissions, that is, to provide technical assistance in environmental protection for developing countries [1–5]. Another direction is that, from the perspective of national resource endowment, environmentally intensive and resource-intensive countries are more vulnerable to environmental harm in international trade [6–10]. Existing literature on carbon emission transfer based on international trade mainly focuses on specific carbon transfers between two countries, and China, as a typical developing country, is often taken as the main research object in this field. As a result, the research countries for relevant literature are too concentrated, and the research perspective is limited.

Later, some scholars discussed the intrinsic relationship between carbon emissions and industrial structure. As for the impact of primary, secondary, and tertiary industries on carbon emission intensity, some scholars have shown that the secondary industry is the main factor affecting regional or national carbon emission intensity, while the impact of the tertiary and primary industries on carbon emission intensity decreases successively [11–13]. In terms of how to reduce carbon emissions from the perspective of adjusting the industrial structure, scholars proposed that the country should optimize industrial structure and reduce carbon emissions through multi-industry and multi-sector cooperation [14, 15, 17]. Most of the existing studies on industrial structure and carbon emissions focus on a certain country and study the situation of different regions and provinces within that country. There are few articles comparing carbon emission intensity and industrial structure among countries. Therefore, there is still room for improvement in this research.

Based on the existing research, the marginal contribution of this paper is reflected in the following aspects: First, this paper selects the OECD, an economic organization that includes countries with different levels of development, as the research object and studies the carbon emission transfer between member countries by relying on bilateral trade between countries rather than solely studying the carbon emission transfer between two countries. Second, this paper uses the GDP and carbon emissions of OECD member countries to construct the index of carbon emission intensity. It does not simply compare the absolute value of carbon emissions among countries but also analyzes the reasons for differences in the carbon emission intensity of specific countries in combination with industrial structure.

3 Carbon Emissions and Industrial Structure

Carbon emissions are a hot issue in the world. OECD, as a typical economic cooperation organization, is confronted with serious environmental problems while its economy is growing rapidly. Studying the carbon emissions of OECD countries has important theoretical and practical significance for understanding the overall trend of global carbon emissions, exploring the influencing factors of carbon emissions, and formulating countermeasures. Meanwhile, as an important part of economic development, industrial structure is closely related to carbon emissions. In this section, the carbon emission of OECD countries will be statistically described and their industrial structure analyzed, and the carbon emission intensity index will be constructed to understand the carbon emission situation and industrial structure characteristics of OECD countries so as to provide a reference for the mitigation of carbon emission and the realization of sustainable development.

The data sources for this paper include three parts: The first is the OECD database. The comprehensive database, maintained by OECD, includes a wealth of statistical data on the economic, social, and environmental aspects of OECD countries. In this study, we will obtain carbon emission data and GDP data of OECD countries from the OECD database for calculations and analysis. The second is UN Comtrade, an international trade data exchange platform under the responsibility of the United Nations Statistics Division, which provides international trade data on a global scale. This paper will obtain the import and export data of OECD countries from this platform so as to analyze the bilateral trade within countries. The third is Statista data. This paper will obtain global carbon emissions, industrial structure, and other relevant data for OECD countries from this database so as to further study the relationship between direct carbon emissions, indirect carbon emissions, and international trade.

3.1 Descriptive Statistical Analysis of Global and OECD Carbon Emissions

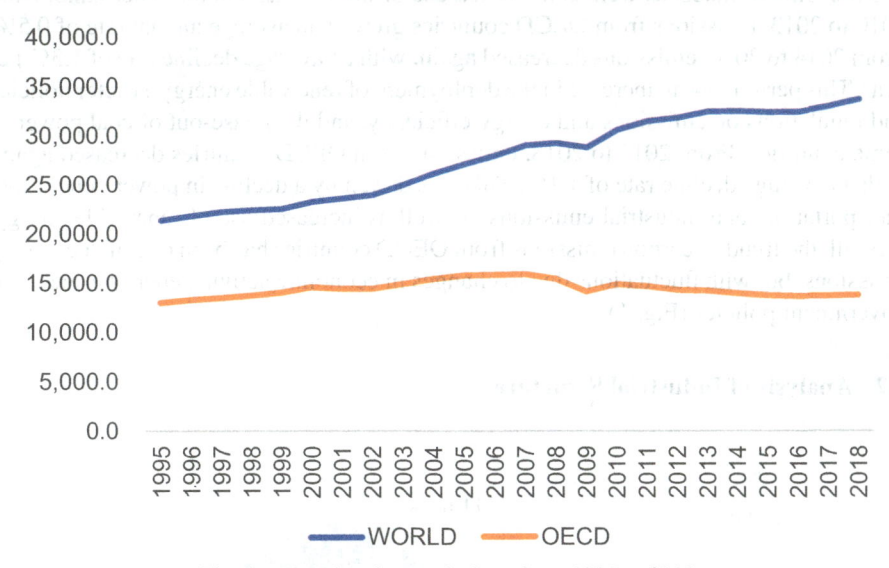

Fig. 1. Global carbon emissions from 1995 to 2019.

The chart above shows the overall trend of global carbon emissions between 1995 and 2018, as well as the carbon emissions of OECD member countries. First of all, global carbon emissions and the total carbon emissions of OECD member countries show an increasing opposite trend, and the gap is widening. While global carbon emission trends are rising, total carbon emissions in OECD countries are falling. In 2018, global carbon emissions totaled approximately 33,635 Mt, up 57.4% from 21,367 Mt in 1995; carbon emissions in OECD member countries peaked in 2007 at 15,856 Mt and then declined; by 2018, this value was 13,754 Mt, a decrease of 13.2% from 2007. At the same time, the gap between the two widened from 8,351 Mt in 1995 to 19,881 Mt in 2018. Secondly, both of them increased significantly from 1995 to 2007. From 1995 to 2007, global carbon emissions grew at an average annual rate of 1.3%. Emissions growth accelerated from 2000 to 2007, averaging 2.4% per year. A major contributor to this increase was China's rapid industrialization and urbanization. From 1995 to 2007, emissions from OECD countries grew at an average annual rate of 0.7%. However, emissions growth slowed down in the early 2000s, with an average annual rate of 0.3% from 2000 to 2007. Finally, the two showed different trends after the volatility of 2008 and 2009. In 2008, the global financial crisis led to a decrease in economic activity, which led to a decrease in emissions. In 2009, global carbon emissions and those of OECD countries fell by a further 1.4% and 4.5%, respectively. Then, on the one hand, from 2010 to

2013, global emissions grew at an average annual rate of 2.2%. From 2014 to 2016, emissions leveled off, with an average growth rate of 0.5% per year. This period saw an increase in the deployment of renewable energy but also a slowdown in the pace of emissions reductions in developed countries and a lack of progress in reducing emissions in developing countries. From 2017 to 2018, emissions grew again, with an average growth rate of 1.6%. This was driven by a rebound in coal consumption in China, India, and the United States, as well as increased use of oil and gas. On the other hand, from 2010 to 2013, emissions from OECD countries grew at an average annual rate of 0.5%. From 2014 to 2016, emissions decreased again, with an average decline rate of 1.3% per year. This period saw an increase in the deployment of renewable energy, stricter policies and regulations on emissions and energy efficiency, and the phase-out of coal power in some countries. From 2017 to 2018, emissions from OECD countries decreased again, with an average decline rate of 1.1%. This was driven by a decline in power generation, transportation, and industrial emissions, as well as increased use of renewable energy. Overall, the trend of carbon emissions from OECD countries has been one of decreasing emissions, but with fluctuations due to changes in economic activity, energy prices, and government policies (Fig. 1).

3.2 Analysis of Industrial Structure

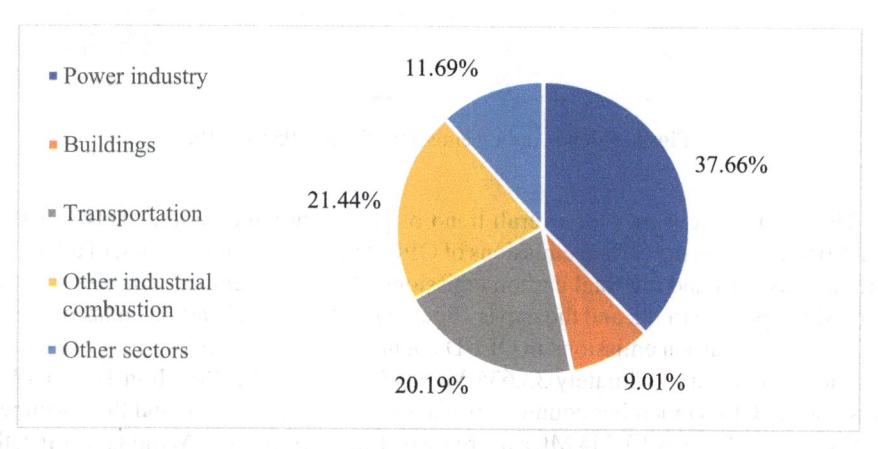

Fig. 2. Global carbon emissions in 2021, by segment.

First of all, it is undeniable that carbon emissions are closely related to industrial structure because many industries are major sources of carbon emissions. For example, the power generation, transportation, and heavy manufacturing industries are responsible for a significant portion of global carbon emissions. These industries tend to be energy-intensive and rely on fossil fuels, such as coal, oil, and natural gas, as their primary energy source. As a result, changes in the structure of these industries, such as transitioning to cleaner energy or implementing more efficient production methods, can significantly reduce carbon emissions. Secondly, the industrial structure of OECD countries is characterized by a high degree of economic specialization and a strong focus on technology and services. The energy-intensive industries such as power generation, transportation, and heavy manufacturing are responsible for a significant portion of these countries' carbon emissions. For example, the power generation sector in the United States is the largest source of carbon emissions, followed by transportation and industry. In Europe, the transportation sector is the largest emitter of CO_2, mainly due to the high number of vehicles in circulation (Fig. 2).

3.3 Carbon Emission Intensity Analysis

In order to investigate the relationship between carbon emissions and economic development in OECD countries, the carbon emission data and GDP data of each country were used to construct the following index of carbon intensity (CI):

$$CI_i = \frac{CE_i}{GDP_i}$$

This measure measures the amount of carbon emissions needed to produce a unit of GDP, and the results are shown in Table 1.

First of all, the carbon intensity of OECD countries has shown a weakening trend over the past three decades, with the average carbon intensity of all OECD countries declining by 0.30. Among them, Estonia has the largest reduction in carbon emission intensity, which is 0.85, which is related to its industrial structure transformation. On the one hand, Estonia's shift from traditional manufacturing to services has helped reduce carbon emissions. On the other hand, while reducing fossil fuels and phasing out old coal power plants, Estonia has increased the use of renewable energy, especially wind energy and biomass energy, which has significantly reduced carbon intensity. Second, the countries with the strongest and weakest carbon emissions are essentially the same. In 1998 and 2008, Estonia consistently ranked first in carbon intensity at 1.15 and 0.52, respectively. By 2018, Estonia had decreased its carbon intensity and was in second place, followed by Australia with 0.31 carbon intensity. Colombia's carbon emission intensity was the lowest in 1998, 2008, and 2018, which were 0.28, 0.16, and 0.12, respectively, which was related to its industrial structure. The country is dominated by services and agriculture, with a relatively small share of industry. Compared with other member states, Colombia does not have large-scale heavy or heavy chemical industries, nor does it have large-scale energy-intensive, high-emission production and manufacturing. On the contrary, Colombia is rich in hydroelectric power, a clean energy source that emits less carbon than fossil fuels, which has played a positive role in reducing the country's carbon intensity. Finally, there are obvious differences in carbon emission intensity among OECD countries. Estonia's carbon intensity in 1998, for example, was 1.15, while France's was just 0.33. This is mainly due to differences in the industrial structures of different countries. Some countries rely heavily on industries with relatively high carbon emissions, such as heavy industry and energy, while others focus on light industry and services. The differences in industrial structures between different countries lead to differences in carbon emission intensity. Therefore, the policy formulation of energy conservation and emission reduction needs to be combined with the characteristics of various industries.

Table 1. Three-year carbon intensity of OECD member countries.

country	1998	2008	2018	country	1998	2008	2018
AUS: Australia	0.67	0.49	0.31	JPN: Japan	0.43	0.33	0.25
AUT: Austria	0.40	0.28	0.17	KOR: Korea	0.44	0.36	0.27
BEL: Belgium	0.53	0.36	0.21	LVA: Latvia	0.62	0.32	0.18
CAN: Canada	0.55	0.42	0.29	LTU: Lithuania	0.68	0.30	0.17
CHL: Chile	0.42	0.28	0.20	LUX: Luxembourg	0.57	0.31	0.18
COL: Colombia	0.28	0.16	0.12	MEX: Mexico	0.37	0.29	0.17
CRI: Costa Rica	0.32	0.22	0.13	NLD: Netherlands	0.44	0.26	0.17
CZE: Czech Republic	0.65	0.37	0.21	NZL: New Zealand	0.43	0.36	0.23
DNK: Denmark	0.53	0.34	0.17	NOR: Norway	0.45	0.25	0.20
EST: Estonia	1.15	0.52	0.30	POL: Poland	0.76	0.44	0.24
FIN: Finland	0.52	0.33	0.22	PRT: Portugal	0.38	0.25	0.15
FRA: France	0.33	0.24	0.14	SVK: Slovak Republic	0.63	0.33	0.20
DEU: Germany	0.49	0.31	0.19	SVN: Slovenia	0.53	0.35	0.19
GRC: Greece	0.49	0.43	0.23	ESP: Spain	0.35	0.26	0.15
HUN: Hungary	0.52	0.30	0.16	SWE: Sweden	0.36	0.22	0.13
ISL: Iceland	0.48	0.29	0.21	CHE: Switzerland	0.36	0.23	0.15
IRL: Ireland	0.46	0.33	0.12	TUR: Türkiye	0.36	0.29	0.17
ISR: Israel	0.49	0.41	0.25	GBR: United Kingdom	0.48	0.31	0.17
ITA: Italy	0.35	0.28	0.16	USA: United States	0.67	0.43	0.28

4 Carbon Emissions and International Trade

4.1 Analysis of International Trade in OECD Countries

We collated OECD countries' import and export volumes over the past 20 years, as well as data for 2002, 2012, and 2013. We got the following table:

According to Table 2, the import and export trade of OECD countries mainly presents the following characteristics: First, on the whole, the import and export trade volume of OECD countries shows an upward trend, but the growth rate of each country is different. In terms of exports, Germany will show the fastest growth, increasing by 165% from $61.501 billion to $163.56 billion in 2021 compared to 2002. The second fastest-growing country is the US, with exports up 135% in 2021 from 2002. In terms of imports, the two fastest-growing countries remained Germany and the US, with growth rates of 190 percent and 144 percent, respectively. Second, the ranking of import and export volumes among OECD countries is relatively stable. In terms of the volume of imports. In 2002, the three countries with the largest import volume were the United States, Germany, and Britain; in 2012, they were the United States, Germany, and Japan; and in 2021, the United States, Germany, and Japan will remain the top three countries, while the United

Table 2. Overall trade in OECD countries.

	In total						Within the organization	
	Import			Export			Import	Export
	2002	2012	2021	2002	2012	2021	2018	2018
Australia	73.03	250.47	261.59	64.98	256.24	342.04	1037.28	910.11
Austria	72.80	169.66	218.97	73.11	158.82	201.65	1490.35	1407.55
Belgium	198.10	318.43	393.66	215.80	305.14	386.35	3130.17	2629.13
Canada	222.44	462.37	489.39	252.58	454.10	501.46	3828.80	3994.18
Chile	15.38	80.00	92.19	17.42	78.28	94.68	356.38	340.61
Colombia	12.69	58.09	61.10	11.90	60.27	41.39	295.33	235.21
Costa Rica	6.89	18.36	18.43	4.95	11.25	14.35	98.33	78.14
Czechia	48.23	139.73	212.48	44.26	156.42	227.17	1374.02	1771.74
Denmark	49.29	91.33	121.78	55.67	106.10	125.02	840.31	754.60
Estonia	5.86	20.07	24.15	4.34	18.16	22.28	155.63	138.72
Finland	33.44	76.09	86.26	44.52	72.97	81.50	570.31	552.61
France	303.83	666.68	714.84	304.89	558.46	585.15	5096.83	4129.19
Germany	490.45	1161.25	1424.67	616.00	1410.15	1635.60	8998.24	11454.23
Greece	31.30	62.50	77.29	10.33	35.15	47.24	340.09	204.89
Hungary	37.61	94.30	139.13	34.34	102.83	141.16	877.40	994.60
Iceland	2.27	4.77	7.84	2.23	5.06	5.97	60.45	49.68
Ireland	52.04	72.22	122.76	88.83	120.21	196.00	781.51	1398.11
Israel	33.11	73.11	92.16	29.51	63.14	60.16	453.68	393.50
Italy	238.78	489.10	568.20	252.24	501.53	615.91	3259.27	3863.40
Japan	337.61	886.03	772.28	416.73	798.62	757.07	2478.13	3258.57
Latvia	3.36	16.08	23.09	1.90	12.69	19.46	2019.69	1999.38
Lithuania	7.71	32.24	44.48	5.48	29.65	40.70	155.88	119.58
Luxembourg	11.53	24.29	25.54	8.59	13.73	16.25	230.55	229.16
Mexico	168.65	370.75	506.57	160.75	370.71	494.60	238.48	132.38
Netherlands	194.12	500.61	623.37	219.82	552.50	696.87	3450.18	4109.81
New Zealand	15.04	38.24	49.88	14.38	37.31	73.37	3838.62	4755.38
Norway	34.85	87.31	99.19	59.62	160.95	161.69	230.68	182.72
Poland	54.27	191.43	335.45	40.25	179.60	317.83	734.69	1123.62
Portugal	40.03	72.51	98.34	25.83	58.14	75.24	2075.07	2212.40

(*continued*)

Table 2. (*continued*)

	In total						Within the organization	
	Import			Export			Import	Export
	2002	2012	2021	2002	2012	2021	2018	2018
Rep. of Korea	152.12	519.58	615.01	162.47	547.85	644.41	672.17	612.33
Slovakia	16.63	76.37	105.14	14.48	79.95	104.73	671.01	813.16
Slovenia	10.93	28.38	49.07	10.36	27.08	46.69	297.99	260.29
Sweden	67.12	164.55	187.12	82.98	172.44	189.85	2567.77	2542.88
Switzerland	98.88	295.06	323.36	101.27	312.26	379.77	1301.49	1311.37
Turkey	51.55	236.55	271.43	36.06	152.46	225.21	1129.71	996.02
United Kingdom	372.06	689.14	688.24	286.00	481.23	470.55	4917.97	3438.30
USA	1200.10	2334.68	2932.98	693.07	1544.93	1753.14	14440.83	11097.76

Kingdom, which ranked third in 2002, will only rank fifth in terms of import volume. In 2002, the countries with the smallest volume of imports were Iceland, Latvia, and Estonia, and in 2021, this rank changed to Iceland, Costa Rica, and Latvia. In terms of export volume. The top three countries in terms of export volume in 2002, 2012, and 2013 were the United States, Germany, and Japan. Exports from Latvia, Iceland, Estonia, and Costa Rica have remained low. Third, the U.S. trades most closely with OECD countries. In terms of import trade, the United States is far ahead in trade volume within the OECD. The rest of the OECD members export to the United States. The country with the lowest amount of imports in 2018 was Iceland, which imported just $6.045 billion. In terms of export trade, Germany and the United States exported more, while Iceland exported the least.

4.2 Carbon Transfer Between OECD Countries

In order to better demonstrate the carbon emission transfer among OECD countries accompanied by trade, this paper constructs the carbon transfer index using carbon emission intensity and export trade among OECD countries, as follows:

$$\text{Carbon Transfer}_{ij} = Trade_{ij} * CI_i$$

where Carbon Transfer$_{ij}$ represents the implied carbon emissions of a product exported from country i to country j, $Trade_{ij}$ represents the volume of trade exported from country i to country j, and CI_i represents the carbon emission intensity of country i. The results of carbon transfer in 2018 are shown in Fig. 3. The vertical axis represents product exporting countries, namely carbon emitting countries, and the horizontal axis represents product importing countries. Therefore, we stipulate that the carbon emissions produced by each

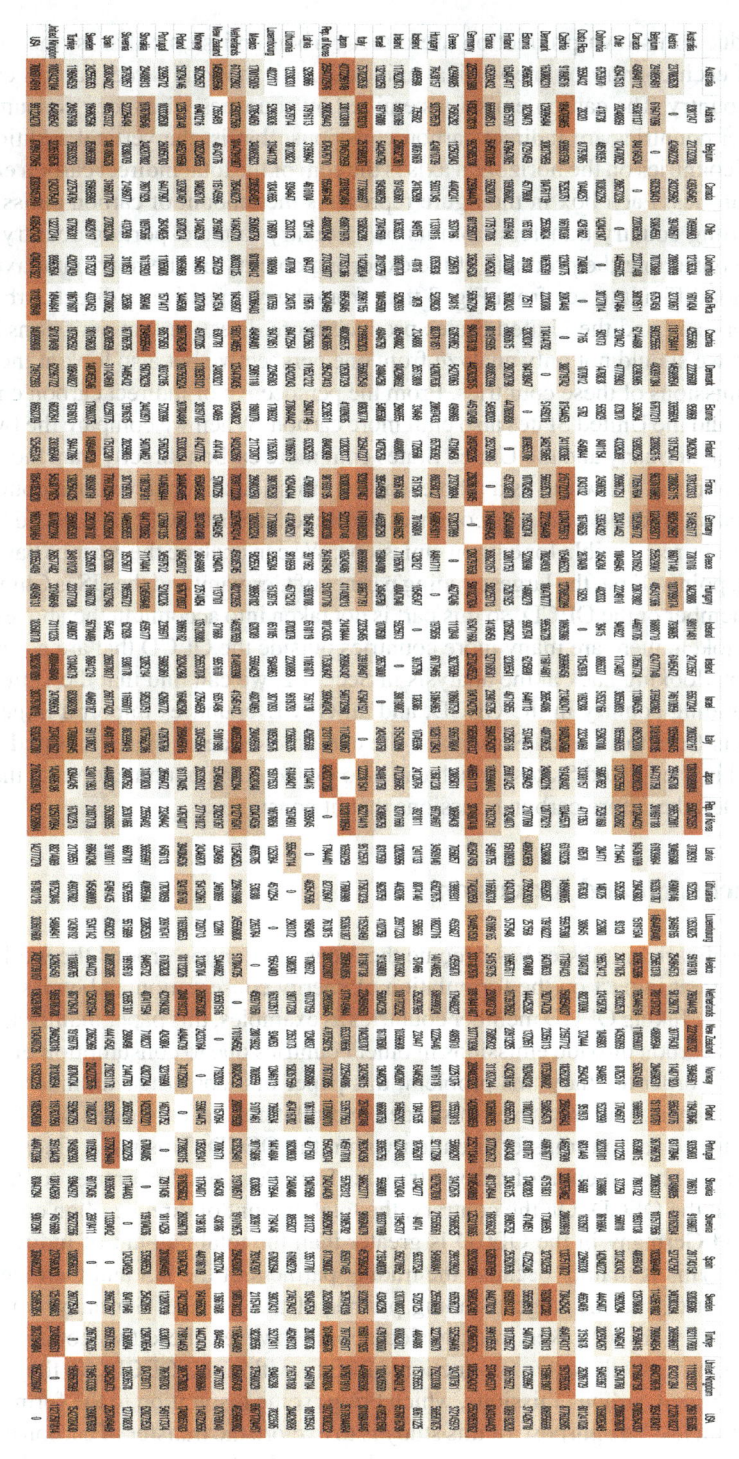

Fig. 3. Carbon transfers between OECD countries in 2018.

country due to its own production are direct carbon emissions; that is, the horizontal values of each country on the vertical axis add up to the total direct carbon emissions of each country. The carbon emissions emitted by countries when they consume goods from other countries are indirect carbon emissions; that is, the vertical addition of the values of countries on the horizontal axis is the sum of the total indirect carbon emissions of all countries. Each box in the figure represents the amount of carbon emissions that the importing country transfers from its own country to the exporting country through trade by consuming the products of the exporting country on the horizontal axis.

It is not difficult to see from Fig. 3 that, from the perspective of direct carbon emissions, Germany and the United States produce more direct carbon emissions in trade. However, we should not only analyze from one perspective but also look at the indirect carbon emissions of these countries. From the perspective of indirect carbon emissions, Germany and the United States also emit more carbon. When we compare the two totals, we find that Germany and the United States emit more carbon directly than they do indirectly. Looking at the world as a whole, carbon emissions from developed countries are usually transferred to developing countries. However, in the OECD, the US and Germany are the parties responsible for carbon emissions. We can analyze the reasons based on the following points: First, the largest trading partner of Germany and the US is China, which is not a member of the OECD, so this part is not taken into account in the above data; By the same token, there are many more countries outside the OECD that are not included. In addition, looking back at the analysis in Sect. 4.2, we can find that the United States is a big trading country in the OECD, and all OECD countries import a large number of products from the United States, and the carbon dioxide of these imported products is emitted in the United States, which can also explain the phenomenon that the United States undertakes more carbon emissions than it consumes.

5 Conclusion and Extension

The issue of carbon transfer has become the focus of attention around the world, which has had a great impact on the formulation of energy conservation and emission reduction policies. Taking OECD member countries as examples, this paper mainly studies the problem of carbon dioxide emissions in other countries due to consumption of imported products. In order to study this problem, this paper first constructs an index of carbon emission intensity and then uses this index and bilateral trade among OECD countries to calculate the carbon transfer situation within the OECD. This paper finds that there is no obvious phenomenon of carbon transfer from developed countries to developing countries in the OECD. On the contrary, the total amount of direct carbon emissions of the US and Germany in the OECD is greater than the total amount of indirect carbon emissions. This is mainly because the trading partners of the US and Germany are all over the world, and the largest trading partner of the US and Germany is not in the OECD, so they are not taken into consideration. However, these two countries are big trading countries with strong production capacity within the OECD, so they will produce more direct carbon emissions, which brings some inspiration to the formulation of relevant policies. The purpose of this study is to explore the transfer of carbon emissions between OECD countries and construct relevant indicators to provide a reference for policymakers, as well as to help reveal the true carbon footprint of trade. This study can provide inspiration for the global emission reduction work and provide ideas and methods for the research of similar problems.

Based on the above situation, we can provide some suggestions for the international formulation of energy conservation and emission reduction policies. First, when formulating relevant policies, we should not only consider the direct carbon dioxide emission caused by a country's consumption of its own products but also the indirect carbon emission caused by other countries' consumption of its products. Second, policies should not only be made based on the absolute value of national carbon emissions but should also be made after analyzing the national industrial structure and considering the contribution of the products produced by the country to the world. Third, the formulation of energy conservation and emission reduction policies also needs to consider the intensity of national carbon emissions. Looking back at Table 1, the table of carbon emission intensity of OECD countries, we can find that as a large producer, the US is at the middle level in the OECD, and there is still room for decline.

The research in this paper proves that the situation in a small region is not necessarily the same as the global situation. We should analyze the situation on a case-by-case basis, take into account the characteristics of each economic organization before making policies within this scope, strive to formulate more equitable policies for energy conservation and emission reduction, and encourage all countries to strive for this. While studying carbon transfers between OECD countries can provide valuable insights into the global carbon cycle and its impact on climate change, there are still some drawbacks to consider. One potential problem is that this study only looks at emissions from OECD countries and ignores emissions from non-OECD countries. As a result, the analysis does not fully reflect the true scale of global carbon emissions, which are concentrated in developing countries. This can lead to misunderstandings in readers' understanding of the distribution of carbon emissions and lead to misleading policy decisions. In addition, when selecting data for analysis within an organization, this study only selected data a few years apart for comparison without taking into account the continuity of the data, thus ignoring the special circumstances that may exist in consecutive years.

References

1. Copeland, B.R., Taylor, M.S.: North-South trade and the environment. Q. J. Econ. **109**(3), 755–787 (1994)
2. Yu, H., Wang, L.: A study of carbon emissions transfer from China-US commodity trade. J. Nat. Res. **24**(10), 1837–1846 (2009)
3. Yan, Y., Zhao, Z., Wang, L.: Implicit carbon in China-Europe trade and policy implications: An empirical study based on the input-output model. Finan. Trade Stud. **23**(02), 76–82 (2012)
4. Gong, T.: Research on the Environmental Effects of Global Value Chain Embedding from a Network Perspective. Zhongnan University of Economics and Law (2020)
5. Yu, J., Tong, G.: Deconstruction of global carbon transfer networks and analysis of influencing factors. China Popul.-Res. Environ. **30**(08), 21–30 (2020)
6. Pethig, R.: Pollution, welfare, and environmental policy in the theory of comparative advantage. J. Environ. Ecol. Manag. **2**(3), 160–169 (1976)
7. Chichilnisky, G.: North-South trade and the global environment. Am. Econ. Rev. **84**(4), 851–874 (1994)

8. Copelandb, R., Taylor, M.S.: Trade and the environment: a partial review. Am. J. Agric. Econ. **77**(3), 765–771 (1995)
9. Antweiler, W., Copeland, B.R., Taylor, M.S.: Is free trade good for the environment? Am. Econ. Rev. **91**(4), 877–908 (2001)
10. Li, Y.: Study on the Impact of China-Japan Trade on Carbon Emission Transfer. Hunan University, Changsha (2012)
11. Li, J., Zhou, H.: Analysis of the correlation between carbon emission intensity and industrial structure in China. China Popul. Res. Environ. **22**(01), 7–14 (2012)
12. Wang, Q., Li, W.: Study on the relationship between industrial structure and carbon emissions–based on panel data of 286 cities in China. Anhui Agric. Sci. **41**(20), 8748–8751 (2013)
13. Yuan, L., Xi, Q., Sun, T., Li, G.: The impact of industrial structure on regional carbon emissions–an empirical analysis based on multi-country data. Geogr. Res. **35**(01), 82–94 (2016)
14. Wang, L., Wang, Z.: The impact of industrial structure optimization on carbon emissions–based on the spatial econometric model. Sci. Technol. Ind. **19**(11), 9–15 (2019)
15. Lu, F., Pang, Z.: An empirical analysis of carbon emission transfer between China and major countries in the world. Stat. Decis. Mak. **37**(03), 94–97 (2021)
16. Chen, X.: Carbon transfer in China's international economy-an empirical study based on total volume, intensity and impact factors. J. Yangzhou Univ. (Humanit. Soc. Sci. Ed.) **26**(04), 13–29 (2022)
17. Yu, J., Xiao, R., Ma, R., Zhang, W.: Hot spots and trends of "carbon neutral" research in international trade. J. Nat. Res. **37**(05), 1303–1320 (2022)

To What Extent Can We Use Google Trends to Predict Inflation Statistically?

Minrui Huang[1] and David Tai Li[2(✉)]

[1] School of Economics, The University of Sydney, Sydney 2000, Australia
mhua8355@uni.sydney.edu.au
[2] King's College, Auckland 1640, New Zealand
dl386652@kings.net.nz

Abstract. Inflation is a direct expression of the increase in the Consumer Price Index, which can strongly impact the general living standard. Therefore, a method that can predict the future inflation rate is significant to improve the stability of the economy internationally. Unlike the previous attempts at predicting future inflation, in this paper, data from Google Trends is used, whose data source is reliable and fast. By comparing our results with the real historical inflation data, we found that OLS and AR models both show similar results. While using both a fixed method and a method with rolling coefficients, a better result is obtained compared to the AR(2) model. However, estimating through Google Trend data has its own weakness in long-term prediction, as it has more decreasing accuracy.

Keywords: Inflation · Statistics · OLS · AR

1 Introduction

Inflation, an important economic index, is of great interest to researchers. It can be calculated by the growth rate of the Consumer Price Index (CPI), which is the change in price for particular goods and services that certain people buy [1]. Thus, inflation of past periods can be found. However, for acts like policy-making and investing, knowing inflation in the future would be vital. Therefore, "how and how much can we predict inflation" becomes a frequently asked question. To answer this, data from various related areas were used: GDP, productivity, and the price of food and fuels are all variables that are considered effective for such prediction [2].

In recent studies, Internet data has become a new focus. Nowadays, almost every aspect of the economy is tightly connected to the Internet, which reflects the movements and decisions of individuals and institutions. Specifically, Google can be considered reasonably as the representative of data on the Internet. So, it is fair to ask whether data from Google can be beneficial for forecasting inflation.

Therefore, the purpose of this study is to ascertain whether Data from Google Trends, an index developed by Google that shows the frequency in the searches of words, can help to forecast inflation, and to what degree it can improve the predictability of a model statistically. In this study, the USA will be the central focus: data on the CPI growth rate in the US and related popular keywords will be gathered and selected, while AR and OLS models will be applied for analysing the improvement of estimating from Google Trends data.

2 Literature Review

The use of data from Google Trends has been well-established in the academic realm for making predictions. The following section reviews multiple related studies with the aim of forecasting through Google Trends.

It is imperative to first investigate effective methods to obtain high-quality time series data. Some suggest that the optimal method to do this via Google Trends is to construct the time series data by reversing Google's use of standardisation.

To execute this idea, researchers developed the *Index of Prices Searched Online* (IPSO), which represents the average amount of money that people are willing to pay for a product by creating distributions based on Google's search volume indices (SVI).

Benefits of using this method include the ability to compare multiple SVIs with each other (Google only allows at most 5 comparisons), a reduction the RMSPE value by 30% when forecasting inflation and overcoming potential pitfalls such as random spikes in the data or indices with a value of 0.

The results from this study seem to be promising: the authors concluded that Google Trends can be a good method for estimating inflation. Although the results of the Granger-causality analysis only provide slim support for their conclusion, the null hypothesis that there is no relationship between inflation and Google Trends' data was rejected at any significance level that is conventional (this is supported by their RMSPE value). However, such a study was not ultimately perfect, as it had to rely on the assumption that before people purchase on the internet, they search for information of the products' prices, thus disregarding those who do not look for such information [3].

Like the previous researchers, others also invented an index, but by adding the search volumes (up to 100) of each of the keywords. However, the authors only selected 3 keywords to analyse: inflation, price rise, and fuel prices, meaning that more keywords were potentially not accounted for.

To verify that it is possible to estimate inflation from Google Trends, the authors simply wanted their estimations to be unbiased and efficient. Ultimately, they were able to attain the desired outcome using a simple regression model [4].

However, other models, such as ARIMA and MIDAS, can also be successfully used to predict inflation. However, two assumptions, that the daily inflation rate be constant, and the annual rate of change of inflation be linear, were made by this group of researchers [5].

3 Methodology

3.1 OLS

Let there be a dependent variable y and independent variables $x_1, x_2..., x_p$, then there is a linear regression model

$$y = \beta_0 + \beta_1 x_1 + \beta_2 x_2 + \cdots + \beta_p x_p + \epsilon \tag{1}$$

If n sets of independent variables $(x_{i1}, x_{i2}..., x_{ip})$ where $(i = 1, 2, ..., m)$ is obtained, the model can thus be

$$y = \beta_0 + \beta_1 x_{i1} + \beta_2 x_{i2} + \ldots \beta_p x_{ip} \qquad (2)$$

When expressed in matrix form, usually the assumptions of linearity, homoscedasticity, independence of errors, and independence of variables are made for the multiple linear regression (MLR). To obtain unknown coefficients in a MLR, one can adopt ordinary least squares (OLS), which finds a balanced situation where the sum of squares of derivatives reach the minimum, satisfying

$$Q\left(\widehat{\beta_0}, \widehat{\beta_1}, \ldots \widehat{\beta_p}\right) = \min_{\beta_0, \beta_1, \ldots \beta_p} (y_1 - \beta_0 - \beta_1 x_{i1} - \beta_2 x_{i2} - \cdots - \beta_p x_{ip}) \qquad (3)$$

By partial differentiation, it is possible to deduce that

$$\begin{cases} \frac{\partial Q}{\partial \beta_0} = -2\sum_{i=1}^{n}(y_i - \beta_0 - \beta_1 x_{i1} - \cdots - \beta_p x_{ip}) = 0 | \beta = \widehat{\beta_0} \\ \frac{\partial Q}{\partial \beta_1} = -2\sum_{i=1}^{n}(y_i - \beta_0 - \beta_1 x_{i1} - \cdots - \beta_p x_{ip}) = 0 | \beta = \widehat{\beta_1} \\ \vdots \\ \frac{\partial Q}{\partial \beta_p} = -2\sum_{i=1}^{n}(y_i - \beta_0 - \beta_1 x_{i1} - \cdots - \beta_p x_{ip}) = 0 | \beta = \widehat{\beta_p} \end{cases} \qquad (4)$$

3.2 AR

The general AR(p) model is given by Wold's decomposition theorem. Any weakly stationary process Yt with mean zero can be expressed as the sum of two uncorrelated processes Xt and Zt. Thus, under the assumption that Zt equals 1,

$$Y t = \epsilon t + \sum_j X \epsilon t - j \qquad (5)$$

Therefore, when we have an AR model

$$Y_t = \phi_1 x_1 - \phi_2 x_2 - \ldots \phi_p x_p \qquad (6)$$

Also, it can be shown that an AR(p) model is stationary if all the roots of this equation have absolute values greater than one. Thus, assuming stationary and zero means, a recursive relationship arises:

$$\rho(k) = \phi_1 \rho(k-1) + \phi_2 \rho(k-2) + \ldots \phi_p \rho(k-p) \qquad (7)$$

4 Exploratory Data Analysis

4.1 Data Acquisition

The monthly growth rate of CPI of all consumer items in the US (in %) can represent the 'inflation rate' [6]. To maximise the number of observations for model building, data between January 2004 to November 2022 were selected. Then, data for inflation is selected in the same time frame and on a monthly basis.

Two approaches are used to select keywords that may be used to predict inflation in the preliminary stage: manual selection of potential keywords, and extraction from literature. (22 potential keywords were extracted from the literature) [7]. For some keywords added, other keywords or phrases associated with them were also included. Finally, a random forest variable selection algorithm is used to trim down this set of keywords or phrases. Our 80 keywords are the following: rate of inflation, auto loan, salary, what is inflation, loan calculator auto, wage, inflation is, auto loan calculator, wheat, supply chain, loan calculator car, the inflation rate is the, inflation rate, car auto loan calculator, commodity price, what is inflation rate, inflation ac, Fed, what is the inflation rate, cheap store, Federal reserve, what is the rate of inflation, gold price, copper price, interest rate, rice, silver price, what is unemployment rate, sugar, cheaper, what is interest, meat, what is interest rate, expensive, gas price, what is the interest rate, pork, what is the federal reserve, what is an interest rate, combustible, what is federal reserve, annual interest rate, cost, what is money, interest rates, diesel, federal reserve bank, rate of return, food, how to make money, mortgage, how to make money with money, gas, mortgage interest rates, gasoline, make money online, mortgage calculator, inflation, mortgage rates, how to make money with no money, mortgage rates, income, how can i make money, payment calculator, corn, how to make more money, propane, payment, how to get more money, payment calculator car, bread, need to make more money, car payment, price, make more money, car loan calculator, prices, cheap airlines, loan calculator, mortgage payment calculator, cheap flights, cheap. Having acquired the keywords, an established method of random forest variable selection process is carried out 20 times, whereby those which appeared more than once would make up the output of this algorithm [8]. Ultimately, 15 keywords remain, which include income, loan calculator, gasoline, payment calculator, inflation, gas, gas price, price, cheap store, corn, diesel, commodity price, make money online, cheap airlines, and mortgage.

4.2 Exploratory Data Analysis and Data Pre-processing

A key requirement for any time series analysis is that the variables of concern are stationary. In this case, the result of an Augmented Dickey-Fuller (ADF) test supports that the acquired variables of concern are stationary: a p-value of less than 0.01 is obtained with a Dickey-Fuller statistic of -5.8315. Therefore, CPI monthly growth rate is used in subsequent model-building processes as it is stationary.

To ensure that each keyword is stationary, logarithm (base 10) transformation is applied to the raw data in the form below:

$$KeywordFinal_t = log_{10}(Keyword_t) - log_{10}(Keyword_{t-1}) \qquad (8)$$

where $t \in$ February 2004, March 2004,..., November 2022 and $Keyword_T$ indicates the normalised popularity level of a keyword or phrase at time T.

Now, the results obtained by running the same three tests (ADF, PP, KPSS) suggest that the data is now reasonably stationary, as shown in Table 1. Therefore, in the subsequent sections, models are built and tested using the transformed data. This means that our entire data set of concern ranges from February (instead of January) 2004 to November 2022 ($n = 226$).

Table 1. Results from three tests for stationarity on data post-transformation.

	Keyword	ADF P value	Paris Perron P value	KPSS Level
1	income	0.01	0.01	0.01
2	loan calculator	0.01	0.01	0.02
3	gasoline	0.01	0.01	0.02
4	inflation	0.01	0.01	0.17
5	payment calculator	0.01	0.01	0.02
6	gas	0.01	0.01	0.01
7	gas price	0.01	0.01	0.02
8	price	0.01	0.01	0.04
9	cheap store	0.01	0.01	0.17
10	corn	0.01	0.01	0.01
11	diesel	0.01	0.01	0.02
12	commodity price	0.01	0.01	0.01
13	make money online	0.01	0.01	0.13
14	cheap airlines	0.01	0.01	0.03
15	mortgage	0.01	0.01	0.03

KPSS significance level: 10%: 347, 5%: 0.463, 2.5%: 0.574, 1%: 0.739

Lastly, to assess the performance of our model in the context of predicting future monthly CPI growth, our data is split into a training (February 2004 to December 2021) and a test set (January 2022 to November 2022). All subsequent models are first fitted with training data before being tested on the test set.

5 Model Building

First, a pure AR model is created based on the data in consideration with the results of another paper [9]. However, while exploring the AR model, both Maximum Likelihood Estimation and Ordinary Least-Squares seem to be similar in estimating the growth rate in CPI. Thus, we will be building models from both the extension of AR and OLS methods.

5.1 AR Model

Since the data is of a time series structure, the sample of CPI growth rate is strongly correlated with past periods. Therefore, a basic AR(p) model is built, where we choose $p = 1, 2, 3, 4$ for different models to estimate the best number of lag terms for *CPI*. By comparing the AIC, RMSE, adjusted R-squared in same data set for different models, as shown in Table 2, as well as ANOVA, AR(2) seems the most effective and was thus chosen as the basic model.

$$CPI_t = \lambda_1 CPI_{t-1} + \lambda_2 CPI_{t-2} + \epsilon \qquad (9)$$

Table 2. Model comparison.

	AIC	RMSE	Adj R^2
AR(1)	148.4235	0.3385546	0.3916
AR(2)	142.523	0.3328845	0.4075
AR(3)	143.2916	0.3324212	0.403

5.2 ARDL Model

To improve the effectiveness of the model, the index from Google Trends were added in the form of distributed lags. The ARDL model will be as follows:

$$CPI_t = \alpha + \lambda_1 CPI_{t-1} + \lambda_2 CPI_{t-2} + \sum_{i=1}^{n} \beta_i X_{i,t-1} + \sum_{i=1}^{k} \theta_i Z_{i}, t-2 + \epsilon \qquad (10)$$

where CPI_t is the growth rate of CPI in period t, $X_{i,t-1}$ is popularity growth rate of a word in period $t-1$, $Z_{i,t-2}$ is a popularity growth rate of a word in period $t-2$.

5.2.1 Variable Selection

Though 15 words were selected by Random Forest process, adding all of them is not suitable, as if $n = k = 15$, there would be a total 35 variables, which might cause over-fitting.

Therefore, Stepwise Algorithm is used for further selecting our variables [10]. In this case, with a pure AR(2) model as the base, both forward and backward methods are used to find the best model with smallest AIC score.

As result, variables *payment calculator, gas, gas price, price, diesel, commodity price, make money online* and *cheap airlines* are removed. The F-test also shows there were no joint significance for these variables while the *adj* R^2 of the restricted model has increased.

Furthermore, based on the best outcome above, the ANOVA test was also applied to remove variables which are not of high significance [11]. Here, the $period_{t-1}$ terms of *inflation* and $period_{t-2}$ terms of *income, gasoline, cheap store* and *mortgage*, are removed, for they were not significant at a 10% level and do not have joint significance with other variables. It is accepted from a statistical view, that with a restricted model, AIC decreases by 6.5% and *adj* R^2 increased by 0.0057.

5.2.2 Model Diagnosis

Based on the selection above, our ARDL model is formed as follow:

$$CPI_t = \alpha + \lambda_1 CPI_{t-1} + \lambda_2 CPI_{t-2} + \sum_{i=1}^{6} \beta_i X_{i,t-1} + \sum_{i=1}^{3} \theta i Z i, t-2 + \epsilon \quad (11)$$

where $X_{1,t-1}$ is $income_{t-1}$, $X_{2,t-1}$ is $loancalculator_{t-1}$, $X_{3,t-1}$ is $gasoline_{t-1}$, $X_{4,t-1}$ is $cheapstore_{t-1}$, $X_{5,t-1}$ is $corn_{t-1}$ and $X_{6,t-1}$ is $mortgage_{t-1}$, $Z_{1,t-2}$ is $loancalculator_{t-2}$, $Z_{2,t-2}$ is $inflation_{t-2}$ and $Z_{3,t-2}$ is $corn_{t-2}$.

Through the result of a Durbin-Watson Test (2.0006), the residuals of the fitted value of ARDL model is shown to be mostly normally distributed. In addition, in the training set, the model achieves an *AIC* value of 85.74669, *RMSE* of 0.287 and *adj.* R^2 of 0.464 (Table 3). Compared to the basic AR(2) model, the *adjR*^{2} improved for 14%, while both *AIC* and *RMSE* values reduced significantly (for more than 10%). All coefficients except the 1 period lag of *gasoline* is at least significant at 10% level. Furthermore, the only exception also has a joint significance with other variables at 5% significant level.

Table 3. Fitted result of ARDL model.

	Dependent variable
	cpi
L(cpi, 1)	0.563***
	(0.068)
L(cpi, 2)	− 0.121*
	(0.068)
L(income, 1)	− 0.575*
	(0.293)
L(loan calculator, 1)	2.157***
	(0.647)
L(gasoline, 1)	0.408
	(0.253)
L(cheap store, 1)	0.874*
	(0.454)
L(corn, 1)	− 1.083***
	(0.291)
L(mortgage, 1)	− 1.183**
	(0.457)
L(loan calculator, 2)	2.097***
	(0.534)
L(inflation, 2)	− 0.651*
	(0.349)

(continued)

Table 3. (*continued*)

	Dependent variable
	cpi
L(corn, 2)	− 1.113***
	(0.290)
Constant	0.110***
	(0.023)
Observations	213
R^2	0.492
Adjusted R^2	0.464
Residual Std. Error	0.287 (df = 201)
F Statistic	17.703*** (df = 11; 201)

Note: *p < 0.1; **p < 0.05; ***p < 0.01

5.2.3 Forecasting Ability

To test the forecasting ability of our model, the ARDL model is used for an one-step-ahead forecast for every month in the test set, which re-estimates the coefficients each time with newest data before forecast period. Then, we use the predicted value to calculate RMSE as a criterion of the forecasting ability compared to basic AR(2) model.

As Fig. 1 shows, for the first several periods, the ARDL model can capture the change of growth rate of CPI, but in latter periods, the accuracy consistently decreases. In fact, until April 2022, the *RMSE* of ARDL model is 0.3658105, 0.1914101 or 34% lower than AR(2) model. But if we extend the period to 2022 November, the *RMSE* increases to 0.5632205, which is not different with the *RMSE* of the AR(2) model at three decimal places.

5.3 OLS Model

AR(2) Using OLS. In Sect. 5.1, AR(2) was determined to be the best-performing AR model. Building on this finding, we estimated coefficients in an AR(2) framework using OLS. An intercept is included here to provide greater flexibility with regard to the model specification. This model will serve as the standard estimation CPI monthly growth rate, whose performance will be compared to other models.

As shown in Table 4, the results of measures of goodness-of-fit and the Durbin-Watson statistic (DW) of the model suggest that the model is unlikely to suffer from auto-correlation.

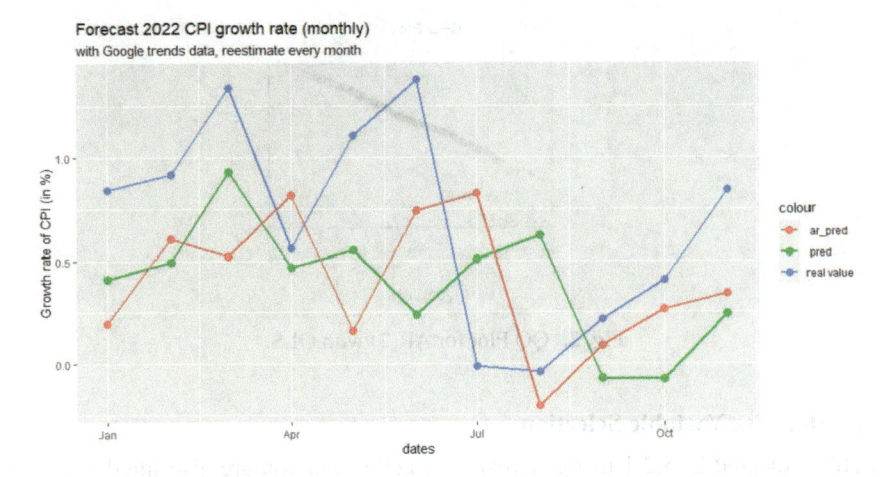

Fig. 1. Forecasting CPI using AR.

Table 4. AR(2) with OLS.

	CPI_t
(Intercept)	0.11***
	(0.03)
CPI_{t-1}	0.67***
	(0.07)
CPI_{t-2}	−0.26***
	(0.07)
R^2	0.33
Adj. R^2	0.33
Num. Obs.	213
AIC	125.50
BIC	138.95
DW	2.01

***$p < 0.001$; **$p < 0.01$; *$p < 0.05$
'CPI' indicates the CPI monthly growth rate

When examining the Q-Q Plot for this model (Fig. 2), we find that observations such as those in October and November of 2008 may be potential outliers, which may potentially cause the simple AR(2) model as well as all subsequent models estimated using OLS to deviate substantially from the true relationship between CPI monthly growth rate and our explanatory variables.

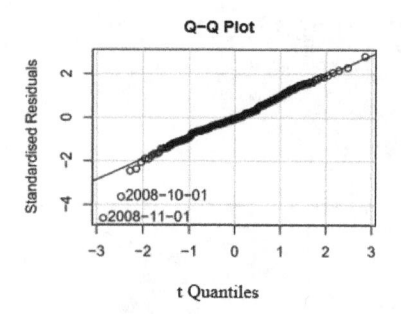

Fig. 2. QQ Plot for AR(2) with OLS.

5.3.1 Stepwise Variable Selection

Variables selected in 5.2.1 using stepwise variable selection are also fitted to an OLS framework, whose results are shown in Table 5. Regarding in-sample performance, by including variables selected from this approach, the goodness of fit clearly improves across all measures when compared to the AR(2) model. Once again, autocorrelation seems not to be of particular concern with the DW-statistic close to 2. However, the previous two potential outliers appear to persist under this model also (Fig. 3).

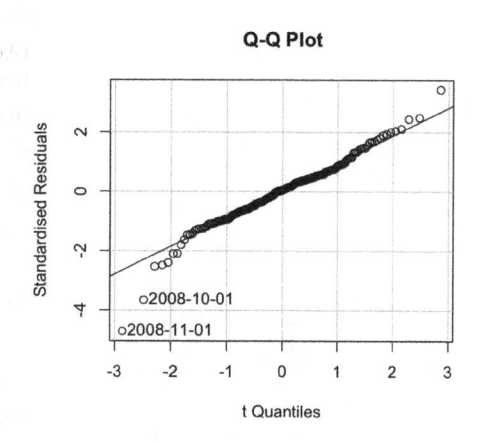

Fig. 3. QQ Plot for Stepwise regression selected variables with OLS.

5.3.2 Best Subset Variable Selection Technique

A significant drawback of the stepwise variable selection approach is its failure to incorporate the performance of all 2^p models into consideration, where p is the total number of variables available. The technique of best subset variable selection tackles this problem by finding the best OLS model (one with the lowest RSS) containing k variables, where $k = 1, 2, ..., p$ [12]. Among the set of selected models with a different number of variables, we then filter out the best model by assessing their respective BIC value for the purpose of exploring as many different avenues in constructing the forecasting models as possible. The model with the least BIC value is found to be the model containing 7 variables, $loancalculator_{t-1}$, $loancalculator_{t-2}$, $cheapstore_{t-1}$, $corn_{t-2}$, $corn_{t-1}$, $mortgage_{t-1}$, $CPIgrowthrate_{t-1}$, as shown in Table 6. Again, all measures of fit demonstrate an improvement as compared to the base AR(2) model, suggesting a better in-sample fit performance on the training data. However, concern over potential outliers still persists under this model.

Table 5. Stepwise variables selected with OLS

	CPI_t
(Intercept)	0.11***
	(0.02)
$income_{t-1}$	− 0.58
	(0.29)
loan calculator$_{t-1}$	2.16**
	(0.65)
loan calculator$_{t-2}$	2.10***
	(0.53)
$gasoline_{t-1}$	0.41
	(0.25)
$inflation_{t-2}$	− 0.65
	(0.35)
cheap store$_{t-1}$	0.87
	(0.45)
$corn_{t-1}$	− 1.08***
	(0.29)
$corn_{t-2}$	− 1.11***
	(0.29)
$mortgage_{t-1}$	− 1.18*
	(0.46)
CPI_{t-1}	0.56***
	(0.07)
CPI_{t-2}	− 0.12
	(0.07)
R^2	0.49
Adj. R^2	0.46
Num. Obs.	213
AIC	85.75
BIC	129.44
DW	2.01

***$p < 0.001$; **$p < 0.01$; *$p < 0.05$
'CPI' indicates the CPI monthly growth rate

Table 6. Best subset variable selection with OLS.

	CPI_t
(Intercept)	0.09***
	(0.02)
loan calculator$_{t-2}$	2.23***
	(0.54)
loan calculator$_{t-1}$	2.34***
	(0.65)
cheap store$_{t-1}$	1.08*
	(0.44)
corn$_{t-2}$	−1.09***
	(0.27)
corn$_{t-1}$	−1.09***
	(0.28)
mortgage$_{t-1}$	−1.19**
	(0.46)
CPI_{t-1}	0.52***
	(0.06)
R^2	0.46
Adj. R^2	0.44
Num. Obs.	213
AIC	90.85
BIC	121.10
DW	1.89

***$p < 0.001$; **$p < 0.01$; *$p < 0.05$
'CPI' indicates the CPI monthly growth rate

5.4 Forecasting Performance

5.4.1 Comparison between Forecasting Techniques

As mentioned in Sect. 5.2.3, one of the two methods used to evaluate our model's performance in the test sample is more of a 'rolling approach'. However, the model constructed in Sect. 5.3 is further evaluated by calculating the RMSE based on one step ahead predicted CPI growth rate for each of the 11 months in the test set. From the results, one can conclude that the latter approach, where no coefficient re-estimation takes place using data from the test set, provides more observations to evaluate the out-of-sample predictive performance of a single model.

In addition, the short-term performance (the first four months of 2022), as well as the performance for the first eleven months of 2022, are both evaluated, as shown in Table 7 and Table 8.

Table 7. RMSE on test set (January to November 2022), fixed and rolling coefficients.

	Estimation techniques	RMSE (rolling estimates)	RMSE(fixed stimates)
1	Least Trimmed Square (LTS, Best subset)	0.45	0.45
2	OLS (Best subset)	0.46	0.46
3	Elastic net	0.51	0.51
4	OLS (Stepwise)	0.51	0.51
5	Least Quantile Square (LQS, Stepwise)	0.52	0.61
6	Least Quantile Square (LQS, Best subset)	0.56	0.45
7	Least Median Squares (LMS, Stepwise)	0.56	0.62
8	Least Trimmed Squares (LTS, Stepwise)	0.56	0.55
9	AR(2) - with intercept (OLS)	0.56	0.56
10	AR(2) – with no intercept (OLS)	0.57	0.58
11	Least Median Square (LMS, Best subset)	0.59	0.44

In assessing the general performance of all the forecasting techniques outlined above, as shown in Fig. 4 and Table 7, one can conclude that based upon fixed coefficient estimates obtained from the training set, variables selected by the best subset approach using BIC do far better than the rest of the methods, which have a mean RMSE value of 0.450. Forecasting techniques using variables selected from stepwise regression in particular, which have an average RMSE value of 0.572, do not appear to improve on the general AR(2) model estimated using OLS at all, which, when an intercept term is included, has an RMSE value of 0.562.

However, when the coefficient estimates are re-estimated every month, models using variables selected from the best subset approach perform significantly worse (Fig. 5), as their mean RMSE value increases from 0.450 to 0.516 (only marginally better than the best performing AR(2) model with a RMSE value of 0.564), which potentially signals the presence of over-fitting.

A similar conclusion can be reached when examining the short-term forecasting performance of our models, as shown in Fig. 6, Fig. 7 and Table 8). However, in this case, forecasting techniques involving stepwise regression perform significantly worse than those containing variables from the best subset approach for both methods.

Table 8. RMSE on test set (January to April 2022).

	Estimation techniques	RMSE (rolling estimates)	RMSE (fixed estimates)
1	OLS (Best subset)	0.25	0.25
2	Least Median Square (LMS, Best subset)	0.25	0.34
3	Least Quantile Square (LQS, Best subset)	0.26	0.34
4	Least Trimmed Square (LTS, Best subset)	0.26	0.28
5	OLS (Stepwise)	0.34	0.34
6	Least Trimmed Squares (LTS, Stepwise)	0.36	0.50
7	Elastic net	0.37	0.37
8	Least Quantile Square (LQS, Stepwise)	0.42	0.51
9	Least Median Squares (LMS, Stepwise)	0.43	0.57
10	AR(2) - with intercept (OLS)	0.56	0.56
11	AR(2) – with no intercept (OLS)	0.58	0.57

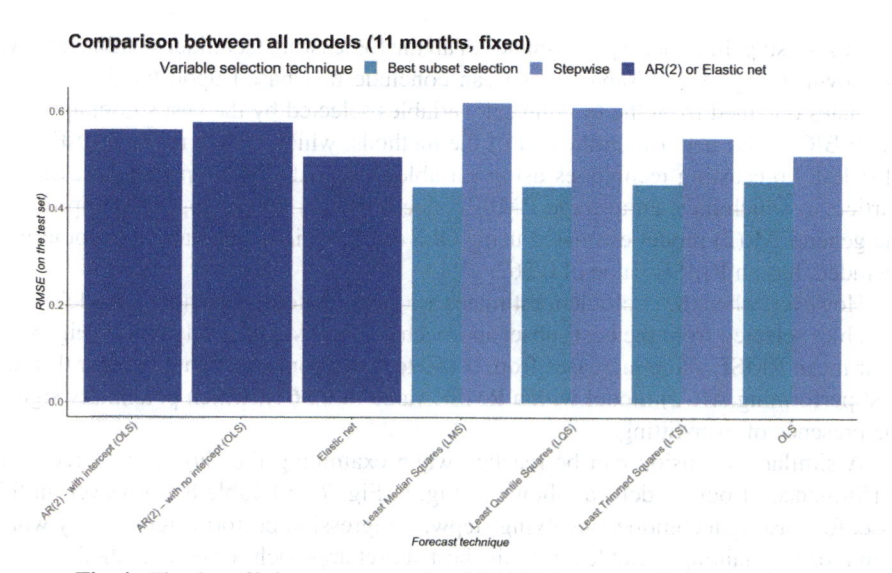

Fig. 4. Fixed coefficients, one step ahead RMSE, January to November 2022.

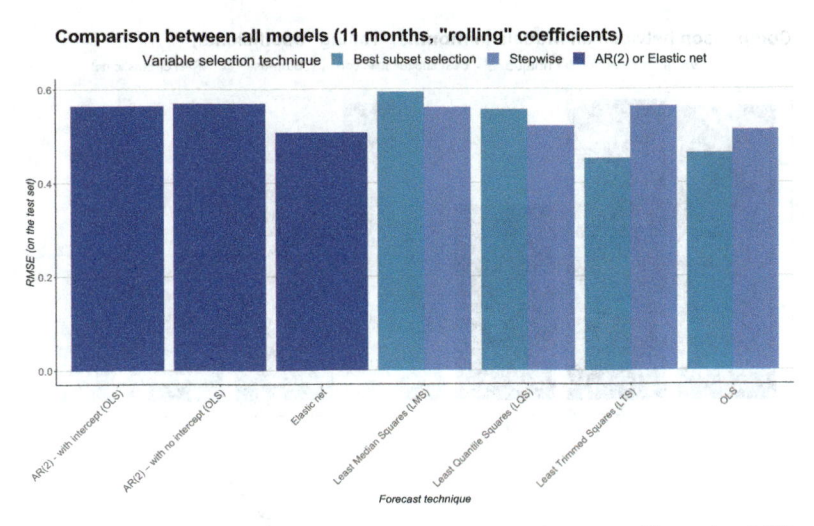

Fig. 5. 'Rolling' coefficients, one step ahead RMSE, January to November 2022.

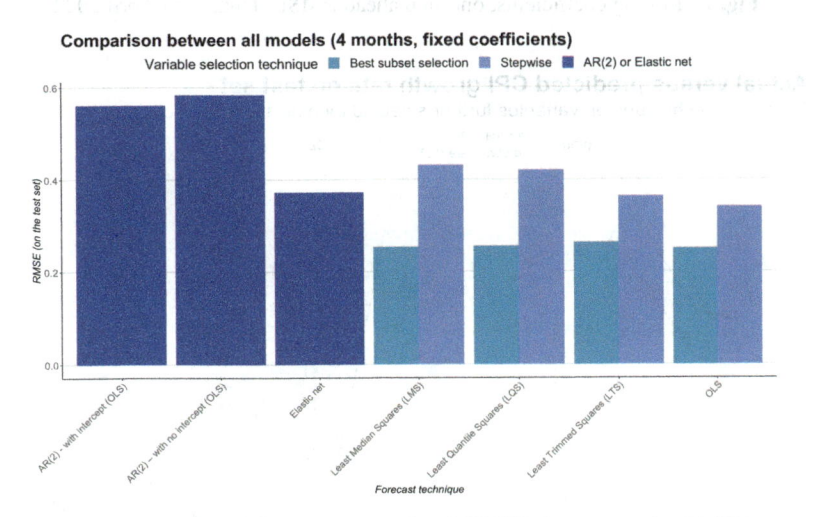

Fig. 6. Fixed coefficients, one step ahead RMSE, January to April 2022.

5.4.2 Fitted Versus Actual Trend

By incorporating Google Trends data, some of our models arguably perform very well during the first four months of 2022, before declining significantly when predictions of CPI growth rate in latter months are included (Fig. 8 and Fig. 9). Thus, a potential advantage of forecasting the growth rate of CPI using Google Trends may therefore be the capture of signals such as those related to consumer sentiment and inflationary expectations.

However, a significant drawback of modeling using Google Trends data is that the predicted CPI monthly growth rate from the models appears to decline at a much earlier point in time. This may explain the decline in the forecasting ability of the models using Google Trends' data after the first quarter, and may also indicate that if Google Trends

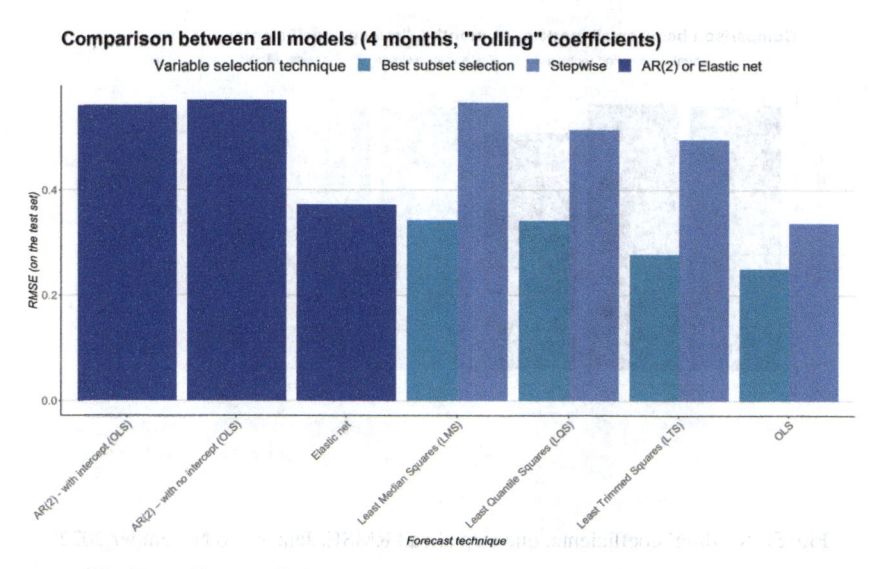

Comparison between all models (4 months, "rolling" coefficients)

Fig. 7. Rolling coefficients, one step ahead RMSE, January to April 2022.

Actual versus predicted CPI growth rate on test set
Estimation techniques on variables further selected by best subset selection

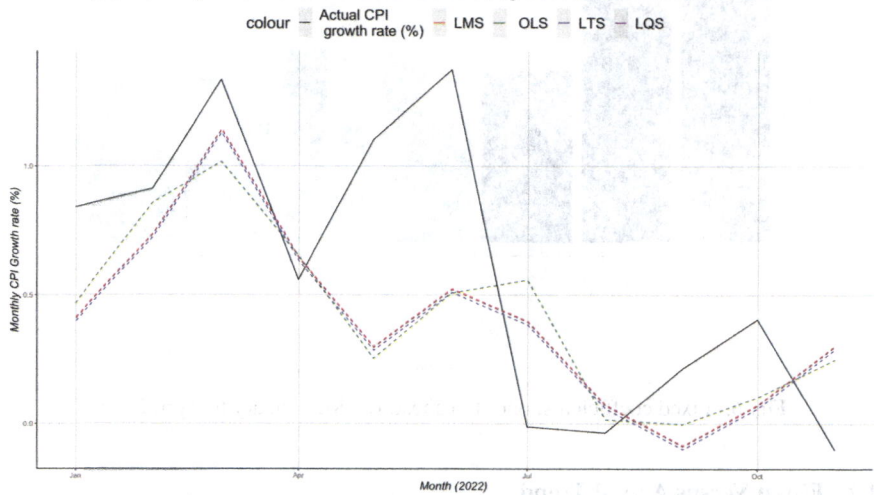

Fig. 8. Predicted versus actual CPI monthly growth rate, January to November 2022.

were indeed a valid proxy for public interest in inflation, it may suddenly increase (but my subside quickly) when a sudden change is expected to, or have occurred in the inflation environment. This means that one may not be able to consistently predict inflation in the long term from Google Trends. Thus, the inclusion of other data may be needed to best forecast using Google Trends.

Actual versus predicted CPI growth rate ("rolling" coefficients)
Four best performing models (lowest RMSE for the whole test set)

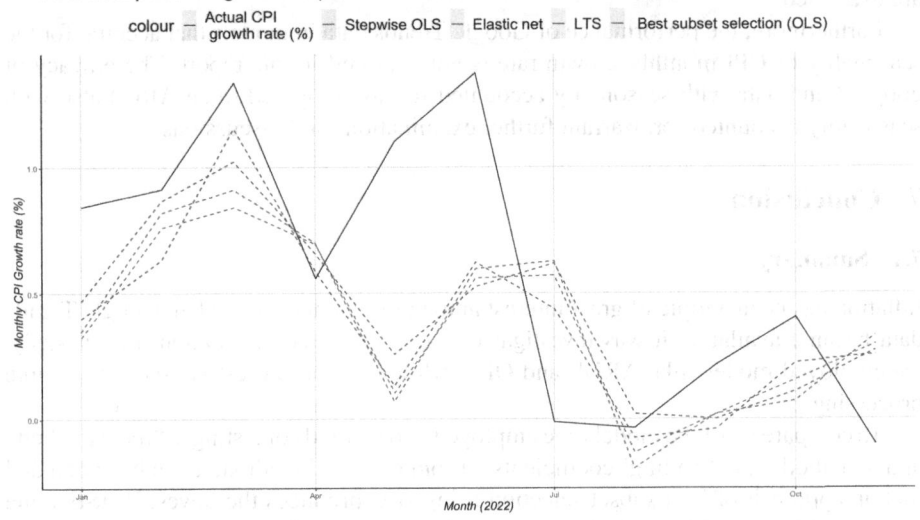

Fig. 9. Predicted versus actual CPI monthly growth rate, January to November 2022 with "rolling" coefficients.

6 Limitation and Discussion

6.1 Intrinsic Limitations of Our Dataset

An obvious limitation that exists intrinsically in the data is a small dataset, due to Google Trends' data only becoming available after January 2004. It is also worth noting that the test set is chosen as January to November 2022 in an attempt to maximise the number of observations in the training set and to select a test set that covers observations with the greatest temporal proximity to when this analysis is conducted. However, 2022, especially during the first quarter, arguably has a significantly different underlying inflation dynamic and macroeconomic environment than the past. As a result, the forecasting techniques in this report should be further evaluated when inflation is tamed in the US.

6.2 Limitations in Methodology and Data Collection

Due to potential fluctuations in the index based on the time at which the index associated with each keyword (phrases) is extracted, ideally, the data from Google Trends should be collected in several different dates, before an average technique is applied to the data [7]. However, due to the time scope of the project, data are only obtained once.

In addition, several issues exist in the random forest variable selection process. Firstly, variable importance is obtained through all the observations, rather than solely from the training data. This may potentially have led to data leakage in our preliminary variable selection process. Also, Variable importance of a keyword variable at time t with regards to the CPI growth rate at time t is used, which may lead to a different set of variables being obtained than if the variable importance of lagged keyword variables are examined.

Furthermore, the performance of Google Trends data in models that account for the seasonality of CPI monthly growth rate is not explored in this report. The efficacy of google trend data with seasonality accounted for, as compared to an AR(2) also with seasonality accounted for, warrant further examinations and discussions.

7 Conclusion

7.1 Summary

Inflation has been a topic of great interest among researchers, and when Google Trends data became available, it was investigated if it could forecast inflation. In our study, we employed models like ARDL and OLS, while Random Forest is used for variable processing.

To compare all of the models, we employed two methods of testing, a "fixed method" and a method with "'rolling' coefficients". From our fixed method, it can be concluded that an approach of best subset selection using BIC produces the lowest RMSE value across multiple models, with their mean value being 0.450, but best subset selection performs worse in the 'rolling' method, as its mean RMSE increases to 0.516. However, the worse-performing stepwise technique displays the opposite with a better outcome in the 'rolling' method. Overall, all of our models perform no worse, or even better than a standard AR(2) model in all of our tests.

It is reasonable to conclude that Google Trends data is an effective estimator of inflation, especially in the short term, for on the whole, its RMSE value is lower than when this data was not used in estimating (the ARDL model has a RMSE value of 0.366 until April 2022, 0.191 or 34% lower than AR(2) model). However, it does seem that Google Trends data quickly fails to accurately estimate consistently in the long term, thus becoming less effective, for this decline in accuracy happens sooner than an AR(2) model.

7.2 Future Work

Future studies are expected to use a more pleasant dataset from Google, and account for the effects of major events such as the Russo-Ukrainian War. Furthermore, future research on the topic should examine whether our aforementioned issues with Random Forest are truly problematic, and more accurately select the keywords not only through a larger sample of potential words but also using a superior model. Another potential area of concern would be whether other data could be used to complement Google Trends in estimating inflation.

Acknowledgements. Minrui Huang and David Tai Li contributed equally to this work and should be considered co-first authors. Work on sections on "Exploratory Data Analysis", "OLS Model", "Forecasting Performance", and "limitation and discussion" as well as the results obtained in said sections should be accredited to Zihan Zhou. A part of the writing of sections on "Literature Review" and "Methodology" should be accredited to Junchen Guo.

References

1. OECD. Inflation (CPI) (indicator) (2023). https://doi.org/10.1787/eee82e6e-en
2. Pasaogullari, M., Meyer, B.: Simple ways to forecast inflation: what works best?. Econ. Commentary (2010-17) (2010)
3. Bleher, J., Dimpfl, T.: Knitting multi-annual high-frequency google trends to predict inflation and consumption. Econom. Stat. **24**, 1–26 (2022). https://www.sciencedirect.com/science/article/pii/S2452306221001210
4. Bicchal, M., Durai, S.R.S.: Rationality of inflation expectations: an interpretation of google trends data. Macroecon. Financ. Emerg. Mark. Econ. **12**(3), 229–239 (2019). https://doi.org/10.1080/17520843.2019.1599980
5. Yanzhao, G.: Prediction of real rates, inflation risk premium and inflation expectation based on arima model. China Acad. J. (5), 75 (2018)
6. Federal Reserve Bank of St. Louis. Organization for Economic Co-operation and Development, Consumer Price Index: Total All Items for the United States (CPALTT01USM657N) | FRED | St. Louis Fed (2023). https://fred.stlouisfed.org/series/CPALTT01USM657N
7. Seabold, S., Coppola, A.: Nowcasting prices using google trends: an application to Central America. World Bank Policy Research Working Paper, no. 7398 (2015)
8. Genuer, R., Poggi, J.-M., Tuleau-Malot, C.: VSURF: an R package for variable selection using random forests. R J. **7**(2), 19 (2015). https://hal.science/hal-01251924
9. Marcellino, M., Stock, J.H., Watson, M.W.: A comparison of direct and iterated multistep are methods for forecasting macroeconomic time series. J. Econom. **135**(1–2), 499–526 (2006)
10. Ripley, B.D.: Modern Applied Statistics with S. Springer, New York (2002). https://doi.org/10.1007/978-0-387-21706-2
11. Chambers, J.M., Hastie, T.J.: Statistical Models in S. Wadsworth & Brooks/Cole, Pacific Grove (1992)
12. James, G., Witten, D., Hastie, T., Tibshirani, R.: An Introduction to Statistical Learning, vol. 112. Springer, Cham (2013). https://doi.org/10.1007/978-1-4614-7138-7

A Literature Review on the Model of EGARCH-MIDAS, LMM, GBM for Stock Market Prediction

Yingtong Wang[✉]

College of Business, Beijing Technology and Business University, Beijing 100048, China
wangyingtong2002@126.com

Abstract. The stock market prediction has been an active research area in finance and eco-nomics for decades. In recent years, mathematical models have often been used by various experts and scholars for stock market forecasting because of their ability to take into account complex relationships and patterns in the data. This paper summarizes several common mathematical models for stock market prediction, including the Exponential Generalized Autoregressive Conditional Heteroskedasticity - Mixed Data Sampling Model (EGARCH-MIDAS), The Local Linearization Method Model (LMM), and The Geometric Brownian Motion Model (GBM). This paper will discuss the theoretical basis, modeling methods, ad-vantages, and limitations of each model, as well as their application scope and evaluation analysis.

Keywords: Stock Market Prediction · EGARCH-MIDAS Model · LMM Model · GBM Model

1 Introduction

As the stock market continues to fluctuate and risks increasing in the stock market, there is a growing demand for stock market forecasting. However, different mathematical models have their applicability and limitations in different situations, so how to choose the appropriate mathematical model to predict the stock market is an important research topic. In this paper, various mathematical models to predict stock market trends and volatility proposed by previous researchers have been discussed and analyzed specifically [1–4].

In past studies, many scholars have tried to use fundamental analysis, technical analysis, macroeconomic analysis, and machine learning to predict the stock market. However, all these methods have different flaws and limitations. For example:

1) Fundamental analysis only considers a few factors and cannot account for all the complex interactions of factors.
2) Technical analysis relies too heavily on historical data and overlooks changes in market risk.

3) Macroeconomic analysis only considers some macroeconomic indicators and cannot fully reflect the market's complexity.
4) Machine learning methods can handle large amounts of data but struggle with feature selection and model interpretation.

In order to solve these problems, researchers have proposed many new mathemat-ical models to predict the stock market in recent years. For example, the Exponential Generalized Autoregressive Conditional Heteroskedasticity - Mixed Data Sampling Model (EGARCH-MIDAS) can combine the EGARCH model and the MIDAS model to predict The Local Linearization Method Model (LMM) is a model that takes into account company fundamentals, macroeconomic data and market sentiment to predict stock returns more accurately. The Geometric Brownian Motion Model (GBM) is a stochastic process-based model that can describe the random walk behavior of stock prices.

Although all these models have certain advantages and applicability, they also have some limitations. Therefore, when selecting and applying mathematical models to forecast the stock market, the advantages, disadvantages and applicability of different models need to be taken into account. For example, the EGARCH-MIDAS model will be applied to various types of stock markets; the LMM model is suitable for quantitative analysis of various factors; the GBM model is suitable for short-term forecasting and high-frequency trading situations [3, 5–7].

Apparently, research on stock market forecasting requires continuous exploration and innovation, and this paper will help readers to choose the appropriate mathemat-ical model to forecast the stock market needs to consider the applicability and limita-tions of different models in order to achieve the best forecasting results.

2 EGARCH-MIDAS Model, LMM Model and GBM Model

The EGARCH-MIDAS model, LMM model and the GBM model are chosen for this thesis firstly because they are both common mathematical models used to forecast the stock market and secondly because they are complementary to each other. Their specific methods and applications are different.

EGARCH-MIDAS model and LMM model are both models used to deal with time series data, but the EGARCH-MIDAS model is suitable for predicting continuous time series variables such as stock prices and volatilities, especially for forecasting tasks with longer time horizons, such as medium and long-term forecasting; while LMM model is suitable for predicting time series variables such as stock prices and returns, especially suitable for forecasting tasks with shorter time horizons, such as short-term forecasting.

The GBM model is a stochastic process model that can be used to model the stochastic volatility of stock prices. It uses Geometric Brownian Motion (GBM) as the underlying model, assuming that the logarithm of stock prices follows Brownian motion. In this model, the volatility of stock prices is determined by a combination of the stock's return and the volatility of the stochastic wandering. The GBM model is commonly used for long-term forecasting, predicting the long-term trend and range of volatility of stock prices.

Although the specific methods and applications of these three models differ, they are all mathematical models used to forecast the stock market and share a common goal: to improve the accuracy and reliability of stock market forecasts.

2.1 EGARCH-MIDAS

Principle and Definition. The EGARCH-MIDAS model combines two models, the EGARCH model and the MIDAS model. The EGARCH model is a GARCH model and they are both derivations of the ARCH model. The EGARCH model is often used to model time series with time-varying volatility, especially in finance. The other model, the MIDAS model, is a mixed-frequency time series model that will use both high and low-frequency data to predict variables. The EGARCH-MIDAS model has been used to predict continuous time series variables, such as stock prices and volatility [9].

The theoretical basis of the EGARCH-MIDAS model lies in the concept of conditional heteroscedasticity. It assumes that the volatility of stock prices is not constant over time, but rather depends on historical volatility and other factors. The model combines high-frequency and low-frequency data to capture the complex relationship between stock prices and volatility.

The modeling method of the EGARCH-MIDAS model is based on the Maximum Likelihood Estimation (MLE) method. The model arguments are measured by minimizing the negative log-likelihood function. The model parameters can be estimated using various algorithms, such as the Quasi-Newton method or the Newton-Raphson method [1].

$$r_t = \alpha_0 + \alpha_1 \epsilon_{t-1}^2 + \beta_1 r_{t-1} + \sum_{j=1}^{p} \theta_j y_{t-j} + u_t \tag{1}$$

where denotes stock returns, denotes the error term of stock returns, denotes macroeconomic variables, and denotes the high-frequency noise term.

Advantages and Disadvantages. The EGARCH-MIDAS model has several advantages for stock market forecasting. Firstly, it fully takes into account the heteroskedasticity in financial time series and the relationship between high-frequency and low-frequency data. By doing so, the model can improve the accuracy and reliability of stock market forecasting. Secondly, the theoretical basis and modeling methods of the EGARCH-MIDAS model are more mature, and the model has been widely applied and studied. However, the EGARCH-MIDAS model has some limitations as well. Firstly, numerous of parameters need to be estimated in the model, which requires more data and computational resources. Secondly, the model is based on certain assumptions, such as time series data satisfying a normal distribution, which may not always match the actual situation [1–4].

Applications, Extension and Evaluation
Application. The EGARCH-MIDAS model is suitable for predicting continuous time series variables, and is particularly suitable for forecasting tasks with long time horizons, such as medium- and long-term forecasting [9].

EGARCH-MIDAS is a popular model for predicting stock market volatility. This model has been applied in many different scenarios to assess its effectiveness and usefulness.

One example of the EGARCH-MIDAS model's application is a study by C.W. Yang, M.J. Hwang, B.N. Huang (2002). This paper uses the model to analyze and forecast oil price volatility and determines that the EGARCH-MIDAS model outperforms other models in terms of forecasting accuracy.

Extension. There are many extensions of the EGARCH-MIDAS model, and the EGARCH-MIDAS-X model is chosen here as an example.

The EGARCH-MIDAS-X model is an extension of the EGARCH-MIDAS model, which adds exogenous variables to the EGARCH-MIDAS model to better capture other factors that affect stock prices and volatility [9].

$$r_t = \alpha_0 + \alpha_1 \epsilon_{t-1}^2 + \beta_1 r_{t-1} + \sum_{j=1}^{P} \theta_j y_{t-j} + \sum_{k=1}^{K} \gamma_k x_{t,k} + u_t \qquad (2)$$

where $x_{t,k}$ denotes the kth exogenous variable and γ_k denotes the effect of exogenous variables on stock returns.

Evaluation. Regarding the evaluation method of the EGARCH-MIDAS model, it is usually performed using techniques such as cross-validation. The dataset is often divided into a training set and a test set according to a specific ratio. The training set will build the model, while the test set will test the prediction accuracy of the model. Also, some statistical metrics can measure the prediction accuracy of the model. Such as mean squared error, and mean absolute error.

2.2 LMM

Principle and Definition. The LMM model is a local linearization method model, which is a type of time series model that uses local linearization to approximate the nonlinear function of the data. The LMM model has been used to predict stock prices and returns.

The theoretical basis of the LMM model is based on the Taylor expansion of the nonlinear function of the data. The model linearizes the nonlinear function around the current observation point, using a weighted least squares estimator to estimate the model parameters.

The modelling method of the LMM model is based on the Kalman filter. The model parameters are estimated using the recursive Kalman filter algorithm, which is a type of state-space model algorithm.

The advantages of the LMM model are that it can capture the nonlinear relationship between stock prices and returns and that it is computationally efficient. However, the model may not be able to capture long-term trends in the data and may be sensitive to the choice of the model parameters [10, 11].

$$y_t = f(x_t) + \varepsilon_t \qquad (3)$$

where denotes the stock price or return, denotes time or other relevant factors, denotes a nonlinear function, and denotes the error term.

Advantages and Disadvantages. The Local Linearization Method (LMM) model has the advantage of integrating company fundamentals, macroeconomic data, and market sentiment, resulting in more accurate stock return predictions, particularly in long-term forecasting. However, the LMM model has certain limitations, such as its inability to fully consider all factors and reflect the market's complexity. Furthermore, it requires extensive data processing and pre-processing due to its high data requirements, and model parameter adjustment requires a high level of expertise.

Applications, Extension and Evaluation

Applications. The LMM model is mainly applicable to long-term investors and fund managers and can predict stock returns over the medium to long term. It also requires the selection of stable stocks or indices.

A study used the LMM model to predict the return of the U.S. Standard & Poor's 500 Index and showed that the model predicts returns more accurately and captures the long-term trend of the index. The researchers also compared the LMM model with other commonly used stock forecasting models and showed that the LMM model performed better in long-term forecasting. The study also mentioned that LMM models require a lot of data pre-processing, otherwise, the forecasting results may be inaccurate.

Another study used the LMM model to forecast the returns of Chinese stock market indices and the results showed that the model has high forecasting accuracy and is able to capture the long-term trends of the market. Also, the researchers used other commonly used stock forecasting models for comparison, and the results showed that the LMM model outperformed the other models. The study further analyzed the prediction error of the LMM model and found that its error distribution is approximately normal and has good stability.

Extension. The GARCH-LMM model is an extension of the LMM model, which adds a GARCH process to the LMM model to better capture the volatility of time series data.

The mathematical equation of the GARCH-LMM model is as follows [10]:

$$\sigma_t^2 = \alpha_0 + \sum_{i=1}^{p} \alpha_i \varepsilon_{t-i}^2 + \sum_{j=1}^{q} \beta_j \sigma_{t-j}^2 \qquad (4)$$

where σ_t^2 denotes the variance of the time series data, α_0 denotes the baseline level of variance, α_1 and β_j denote the coefficients of ARCH effect and GARCH effect, respectively.

Evaluation. In addition, some studies have also optimized and adjusted the parameters of the LMM model to further improve its prediction accuracy. For example, one study improved the ability of the LMM model to fit macroeconomic data by adjusting the model parameters, thus improving prediction accuracy. Another study further improved the forecasting effectiveness of the LMM model by optimizing the model using a Bayesian approach.

2.3 GBM

Principle and Definition. The GBM model is a stochastic process model that presumes that stock prices comply with a geometric Brownian motion. The GBM model has been used to simulate stock prices and to predict long-term trends in the stock market [12–14].

The GBM model is based on the random walk theory. The model would assume that stock prices conform to geometric Brownian motion, in other words, that the logarithmic returns on stock prices follow a normal distribution.

The modeling method of the GBM model is based on the Monte Carlo simulation method. The model simulates the stock price trajectories based on the assumed parameters, such as the stock price drift and volatility. The model can be calibrated to the historical stock price data [12–14].

$$S_t = S_{t-1} exp\left\{\left(\mu - \frac{\sigma^2}{2}\right)\Delta t + \sigma\sqrt{\Delta t}\epsilon_t\right\} \quad (5)$$

$$d\ln S_t = \left(\mu - \frac{\sigma^2}{2}\right)dt + \sigma dW_t \quad (6)$$

where S_t denotes the stock price, μ denotes the growth rate of the stock price, σ denotes the volatility of the stock price, ϵ_t denotes the standard normally distributed random variable, Δt denotes the time interval, and W_t denotes standard Brownian motion.

Here the parameters are set to do a bit of graphing, setting $\mu = 1$, $dt = 0.1$, and σ in the range of values (0.8, 2) in steps of 0.2

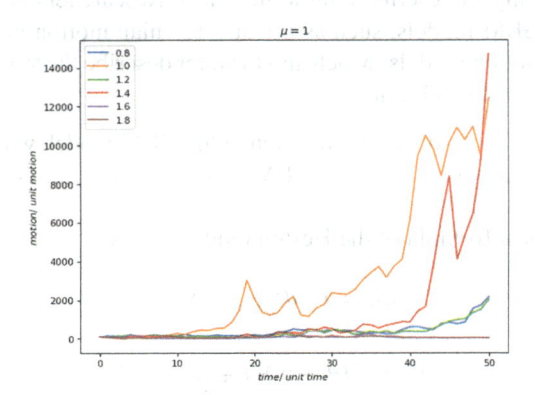

Fig. 1. Realizations of Geometric Brownian motion with different variances.

Figure 1 shows the graph of the underlying Brownian motion based on the above equation, after assuming the parameters. When the independent variable time is in the range of 0–50, the area of the range of motion is the largest when sigma takes the value of 1. When sigma takes the values of 1.6 and 1.8, the line of motion is flatter. When sigma takes the value of 1.4, the volatility is the largest.

Advantages and Disadvantages. The Geometric Brownian Motion (GBM) model has several advantages, including the ability to capture stochastic fluctuations in stock prices and simulate trends in stock price changes, its simplicity to understand, implement, and calculate, its applicability for short-term forecasting and high-frequency trading, and its suitability for markets with liquidity. However, the GBM model also has some disadvantages. First, because it assumes that the stochastic fluctuations in stock price changes are unbounded, resulting in a failure to truly reflect the actual situation of the stock market; second, the model ignores the impact of external factors on stock prices, such as macroeconomic and policy factors, which can lead to unsatisfactory forecasting results in some cases. As well, the model, like most academic models, cannot anticipate extreme situations, such as financial crises and other abnormal fluctuations, in advance.

Applications, Extension and Evaluation
Applications

1) Short-term forecasting and high-frequency trading;
2) High market liquidity situations;
3) For situations where stock prices are changing more smoothly;
4) Suitable for simpler stock markets, not for complex markets.

GBM models have been widely used in stock price forecasting, for example, in trading decisions, risk management, option pricing and hedging strategies. Several studies have shown that GBM models can provide effective short-term forecasting results [12–14].

However, GBM models also have some problems, such as sensitivity to parameter selection and inability to describe long-term trends. Researchers have proposed many ways to improve GBM models, such as fractal Brownian motion models and multiple fractal Brownian motion models, which aim to better describe the stochastic fluctuations and long-term trends of stock prices.

Extension. The Heston model is an extension of the GBM model, which adds stochastic changes in stock price volatility to the GBM model to better simulate the dynamics of actual stock prices.

The mathematical formula of the Heston model is as follows [12–14]:

$$dS_t = rS_t dt + \sqrt{v_t} S_t dW_1 \qquad (7)$$

$$dv_t = k(\theta - v_t)dt + \sigma \sqrt{v_t} dW_2 \qquad (8)$$

$$dW_{1,t} dW_{2,t} = \rho dt \qquad (9)$$

where S_t represents the stock price, v_t represents volatility, r represents the risk-free rate, k represents the rate of return of volatility to the mean, θ represents the long-term mean of volatility, σ represents the volatility of volatility, $W_{1,t}$ and $W_{2,t}$ are standard Brownian motion, and ρ represents the correlation coefficient between the stock price and volatility.

Table 1. Comparison of EGARCH-MIDAS model, LMM model and GBM model.

Model	Advantages	Disadvantages	Applicable Scenarios
GBM	Can capture stochastic fluctuations in stock prices and simulate trends in stock price changes; Simple to understand, easy to implement and calculate; Can be used for short-term forecasting and high-frequency trading; Suitable for markets with liquidity	Assumes that the stochastic fluctuations in stock price changes are unbounded and do not truly reflect the actual situation in the stock market; GBM model does not take into account the impact of external factors on stock prices, such as macroeconomic and policy factors, leading to its less-than-satisfactory forecasting in some cases; Inability to handle extreme situations, such as financial crisis and other abnormal fluctuations	Short-term forecasting and high-frequency trading, markets with liquidity
EGARCH-MIDAS	Fully takes into account the heteroskedasticity in financial time series and the relationship between high or low-frequency data, which can improve the accuracy and reliability of stock market forecasting; Theoretical basis and modeling methods are more mature and widely applied and studied	Numerous arguments need to be estimated in the EGARCH-MIDAS model, so more data and computational resources are required; The model is based on certain assumptions, such as time series data satisfying a normal distribution, which may not always match the actual situation	Stock market forecasting with both high-frequency and low-frequency data
LMM	Integrates company fundamentals, macroeconomic data, and market sentiment, resulting in more accurate stock return predictions, especially in long-term forecasting	Limited consideration of factors, unable to fully reflect the market's complexity; High data requirements, necessitating extensive data processing and pre-processing, and requires a high level of expertise in parameter adjustment	Long-term forecasting, selecting more stable stocks or indices

Evaluation. For evaluation analysis, researchers usually use metrics for instance mean square error (MSE), mean absolute error (MAE) and mean absolute percentage error (MAPE) to assess the forecasting of GBM and compare them with other models, such as ARIMA models, GARCH models, etc. [14].

Table 1 provides a cross-sectional comparison of the three different mathematical models. The charts show that the different models each have advantages and disadvantages and are suitable for different ranges. In general, GBM is suitable for short-term forecasting and requires a large amount of data to train and optimize the model; LMM is suitable for long-term forecasting and is suitable for stocks with low vola-tility; EGARCH-MIDAS is suitable for medium- and long-term forecasting and is best when both high-frequency and low-frequency data are available.

3 Conclusion

In conclusion, this paper has discussed three common mathematical models for stock market prediction: the EGARCH-MIDAS model, the LMM model, and the GBM model.

The EGARCH-MIDAS model is suitable for capturing the long-term and short-term volatility patterns in time series data. This makes it particularly useful in finan-cial markets, where long-term trends and short-term fluctuations can significantly impact investment decisions. The model's ability to capture nonlinear and asymmet-ric volatility makes it well-suited for modeling the behavior of financial markets, especially during periods of uncertainty.

The LMM model is useful for analyzing the relationships between different finan-cial assets, such as stocks and bonds. It is particularly effective in capturing the common factors that drive asset prices and their volatility, which makes it useful for portfolio management and asset allocation. The model's ability to estimate time-varying correla-tions between different assets also makes it well-suited for analyzing the co-movements of different financial markets.

The GBM model is a simple and widely-used model that can be used for short-term forecasting and high-frequency trading. It is particularly useful in liquid markets, where price changes occur frequently and the impact of external factors is minimal. However, its assumptions of unbounded stochastic fluctuations and inability to han-dle extreme situations limit its usefulness in modeling financial markets over longer time horizons or during periods of market stress.

Looking to the future, it is likely that advancements in technology and data analy-sis will lead to the development of even more sophisticated models that can better capture the complexities of the financial markets. Additionally, as global events and economic factors continue to impact the markets, there will be a need for models that can accurately incorporate external factors into their predictions.

Finally, the success of any mathematical model in predicting market trends will depend on its ability to adapt and evolve along with the markets themselves. It is likely that we will continue to see new models developed and refined in the years to come, as researchers and analysts strive to better understand and predict the behav-ior of the financial markets.

References

1. Harvey, A.C.: Dynamic Models for Volatility and Heavy Tails: With Applications to Financial and Economic Time Series, vol. 1. Cambridge University Press, Cambridge (2013)
2. Engle, R.F., Kroner, K.F.: Multivariate simultaneous generalized ARCH. Economet. Theor. 11(1), 122–150 (1995)
3. Islam, M.R., Nguyen, N.: Comparison of financial models for stock price prediction. J. Risk Financ. Manage. 13(8), 181 (2020). https://doi.org/10.3390/jrfm13080181
4. Engle, R.F., Rangel, J.G.: The spline GARCH model for low-frequency volatility and its global macroeconomic causes. Rev. Financ. Stud. 21(3), 1187–1222 (2008). https://doi.org/10.1093/rfs/hhn015
5. Liu, L., Ma, F., Zeng, Q., Zhang, Y.: Forecasting the aggregate stock market volatility in a data-rich world. Appl. Econ. 52(32), 3448–3463 (2020)

6. Wang, L., Ma, F., Liu, J., Yang, L.: Forecasting stock price volatility: new evidence from the GARCH-MIDAS model. Int. J. Forecast. **36**(2), 684–694 (2020). https://doi.org/10.1016/j.ijforecast.2019.08.005. ISSN 0169-2070
7. Yang, C.W., Hwang, M.J., Huang, B.N.: An analysis of factors affecting price volatility of the US oil market. Energy Econ. **24**(2), 107–119 (2002). https://doi.org/10.1016/S0140-9883(01)00092-5. ISSN 0140-9883
8. Chen, W., Ma, F., Wei, Y., Liu, J.: Forecasting oil price volatility using high-frequency data: new evidence. Int. Rev. Econ. Financ. **66**, 1–12 (2020). https://doi.org/10.1016/j.iref.2019.10.014. ISSN 1059-0560
9. Castiglianc, F.: Forecasting price increments using an artificial neural network. Adv. Complex Syst. (2001)
10. Neslihanoglu, S., Bekiros, S., McColl, J., et al.: Multivariate time-varying parameter modelling for stock markets. Empir. Econ. **61**, 947–972 (2021). https://doi.org/10.1007/s00181-020-01896-2
11. Ahangar, R.G., Mahmood, Y., Hassan, P.: The comparison of methods artificial neural network with linear regression using specific variables for prediction stock price in Tehran stock exchange. Int. J. Comput. Sci. Inf. Secur. (2010)
12. Lee, S.-W., Hansen, B.E.: Asymptotic theory for the GARCH(1,1) quasi-maximum likelihood estimator. econometric theory 10, 29–52. Bollerslev, T., Chou, R.Y. & Kroner, K.F. (1992) ARCH modeling in finance: A review of the theory and empirical evidence. J. Econom. **52**, 5–59 (1994)
13. Neslihanoglu, S.: Linearity extensions of the market model: a case of the top 10 cryptocurrency prices during the pre-COVID-19 and COVID-19 periods. Financ Innov **7**, 38 (2021). https://doi.org/10.1186/s40854-021-00247-zVB
14. Experimental and Data-driven approach of investigating the effect of parameters on the fluid flow characteristic of nanosilica enhanced two phase flow in pipeline. AEJ – Alex. Eng. J. **61**(2) (2021). https://doi.org/10.1016/j.aej.2021.06.017. LicenseCC BY-NC-ND 4.0

The Impact of Changes in Sales Prices of Non-durable Goods on Consumers' Purchase Intentions When Using Online Shopping Platforms

Zehao Xu[✉]

Department of Social Science, University of Southampton, Southampton SO17 1BJ, UK
greyyyxu777@gmail.com

Abstract. Online shopping platforms have gradually taken over as consumers' preferred means of purchasing because of the fast-paced development of electronics and technology in the twenty-first century. Price is one of the main benefits of online platforms over traditional retail stores. This is particularly true for the trendy clothing products that are currently the millennial generation's favorites because they can be purchased online for less money. Therefore, the purpose of this article is to examine how pricing changes for non-durable commodities affect customers' desire to use online shopping platforms. In order to examine the relationship between price fluctuation and consumers' propensity to purchase, this article will use dynamic pricing strategies, which are widely used in the travel industry. An analysis is also done on the effect that pricing discrimination has on consumer purchasing intentions on online shopping platforms. This study only synthesizes and summarizes the literature on dynamic pricing fluctuation and price discrimination in the form of a literature review. The findings show that non-durable goods, such as trendy items, are sold on today's online shopping platforms using a resale business model. As a result, these non-durable goods are also subject to price changes, which has increased consumers' willingness to purchase non-durable goods.

Keywords: Price discrimination · Dynamic pricing strategy · Online shopping · Purchase intentions

1 Introduction

With the rapid development of modern electronic technology, new retail business patterns represented by online shopping platforms are gradually changing the traditional way of consumption and physical shops are slowly closing [1]. Online platforms are more convenient for customers than traditional stores [2]. The Internet retail business in the United States may have generated close to $300 billion in sales as of 2014, according to data from Lee et al. [3]. By 2024, $476 billion is the estimated value [4]. It can be concluded that consumers currently prefer shopping online over traditional retail outlets all around the world. However, these online platforms are not immune to price changes;

for instance, on Black Friday or Boxing Day, multiple platforms provide customers with discounts or coupons, enabling them to purchase things for cheap prices. Many people think that pricing is one of the most significant variables influencing a customer's purchasing choice because the price of a product changes over time [5]. Discounts on the price of items may improve consumers' tendency to buy a variety of goods, claim [6]. Furthermore, it was discovered that buyer intention was negatively correlated with an item's selling price, such as the lower the consumer's purchasing intention, the higher the selling price of the item [7]. Konuk summarizes a conclusion based on previous research that price is a purposeful marketing component that affects consumers' purchasing intentions [8]. Because consumers are affected by price, it is common for consumers to explore various online platforms to compare the selling prices of their desired products to determine which website offers the best offer. Price is typically the main determinant of whether customers will continue to stick around and have further opportunities to make a purchase [9]. In order to enhance sales and encourage consumers' purchase intentions, sellers can benefit from consumers' sensitivity to different prices of similar goods by employing dynamic pricing strategies to create an appropriate price [10]. Dynamic pricing is a revenue management strategy that constantly modifies rates in accordance with demand as well as supply dynamics [11]. It can be done by modifying pricing in response to shifts in customer demand and based on variables like product inventories and price comparisons with rivals [12]. It is currently typical in the hotel business for hotels to temporarily raise the price of rooms in response to increases in customer demand and temporarily lower rates in response to slumps in demand [13]. This paper classifies products into two categories, durable and non-durable goods, and focuses on the impact of changes in the selling price of non-durable goods on consumers' purchase intentions. Some researchers define nondurable goods as those that have a useful life of fewer than three years [14]. For example, products made of paper and cardboard, and products such as clothing and footwear.

This paper reviews previous research. Firstly, the paper analyses previous research. Through reading studies on pricing strategies, we have developed a basic understanding of the current prices of goods in both shops and online platforms. This study also examines the Sobel oligopoly model with regular sales, which is employed in many price discrimination studies. It is a typical early model that serves as an effective framework and theoretical foundation for this research. It also investigates different levels of pricing discrimination theories. Finally, the article summarizes the key flaws of past research and evaluates previous researchers' results on price changes.

2 Theoretical Framework and Literature Review

There are two sources of relevant literature. One focuses on dynamic pricing strategies for products, and the other studies price discrimination at different levels.

2.1 Dynamic Pricing Strategies

Considering dynamic price changes, Abrate et al. state that there are various main literature streams in which dynamic pricing strategies have been researched, including

i) intertemporal price discrimination [15]. This implies that sellers typically alter their prices over time in order to charge various prices to target customers with various levels of willingness to pay, ii) price fairness, which focuses on the relationship between commodity prices and their prices change, and iii) inventory control, which is a behavior that guarantees that a store's inventory is the proper amount of supply. A review of each point follows.

Intertemporal Price Discrimination. Pricing consumers differently for identical items is referred to as price discrimination, which is a sort of pricing disparity. When a store or business charges various prices for identical products with the same marginal cost, this is known as price discrimination [16]. Although price discrimination primarily happens in monopolistic markets, Dana's theoretical economics literature illustrates that price discrimination by sellers in competitive marketplaces is also possible in order to get benefits [17]. Due to the presence of this theory, we are able to apply the mechanism of price discrimination to online trading platforms where a broad variety of commodities are offered. As previously mentioned, customers would compare some of these non-monopoly items in keeping with the characteristics of a competitive market. Additionally, there are two different types of pricing discrimination recognized by modern economics. Intertemporal price discrimination and behavior-based price discrimination are two examples of this form of pricing discrimination [18, 19]. Therefore, when a good's price varies depending on when it is purchased but is the same for all consumers at the beginning of the period, intertemporal price discrimination has taken place. To demonstrate how prices vary over time, several studies on price discrimination have emphasized intertemporal price discrimination.

Sobel proposes a model of the relationship between sales and time in which he makes the assumption that a new consumer group enters the market at regular intervals and that they are equally eager to make a one-time purchase of a non-resaleable product, either right away or later [20]. A buyer who makes an immediate purchase is one who is willing to pay the item's full price, but a buyer who makes a delayed purchase may not be as anxious about the item because they are waiting for the seller to lower the price before making a purchase. Conlisk's previous model demonstrated that a market is a monopoly when there is only one seller in it and that the monopolist will typically sell to consumers at varied levels of price decrease over time [21]. The model from Sobel now expands on this by demonstrating that even if there are many sellers on the market, there is still an incentive for sellers to keep selling and that this strategy is appealing to customers who continue to pay cheap prices, increasing their willingness to purchase [20].

In conclusion, the literature on intertemporal price discrimination above shows that a strategy of altering prices over time (dynamic price change) is one that could increase consumers' willingness to purchase while also increasing sellers' profitability.

Price Fairness. Consumers' perception of whether the price of the product they would like to purchase is fair and reasonable is referred to as price fairness [22]. According to Malc et al., consumers' opinions of sellers and their propensity to make purchases are influenced by how fair the price is in relation to whether they are satisfied with the product [23]. In order to summarize the unique relationship between price fairness and consumers' propensity to buy, I am going to analyze the concept of price fairness.

Xia et al. stated that during the consuming process, consumers' perceptions of pricing fairness might not be rational but rather emotional [22]. For instance, when a consumer notices that another consumer spends less than he does for an identical commodity, price fairness may be weakened. Other circumstances, such as the use of coupons by other customers or the reasons for the storage of the items that I will cover next, could also be to blame for the sudden price difference.

Narasimhan proposed a 'coupon' model, which is an interesting model where he first assumes that there is only one company and one coupon product and that the coupons are cents off coupons, i.e., whatever the price of the item purchased by the consumer in the same purchase, the use of the coupon enables the total price to be a fixed amount is subtracted from the total price, resulting in a price discount [24]. In this case, consumers can choose coupons by themselves according to the savings associated with using coupons and the opportunity cost of using them, because in the view of Narasimhan, each consumer has a varied level of price elasticity, therefore those who use coupons are more price-elastic, which makes it difficult to estimate the change in consumer demand as a result of price discounts. A larger discount rate may immediately reduce the purchase of consumers with high reservation prices, as they will define the item as a "bargain" and reduce willingness to buy, according to Reimers et al., which found that the proper use of coupons will increase consumers' purchase intention and demand during product promotions (such as Black Friday) [25]. Therefore, when the dynamic pricing strategy is in an unfair price state (excessive discount), it has a negative impact on the purchase intentions of consumers with high reservation prices, as they will lower their valuation of the product before purchasing it and wait for the time when commodity prices continue to decline.

Any price fairness model's central tenet is that consumers, either expressly or implicitly, have some sort of reference price they can use to determine whether a price is reasonable. Fairness is not an absolute context, to put it plainly. Consumers establish benchmarks or reference prices in a variety of ways, including remembering past transactions, examining prices offered by rivals, learning the seller's costs, or examining prices paid by other customers [26]. In conclusion, an extensive quantity of literature on price fairness contends that dynamic price changes might reduce customers' propensity to purchase if they cause them to believe that prices are unjust. On the other hand, if consumers believe that prices are reasonable, this may enhance their propensity to buy.

Inventory Control. "Inventory control" is defined as all models and processes for selling the exact number of each item at any given time, which means that sellers limit the number of items available during the sales process, such as airplane seats, remaining hotel rooms, and inventory of durable goods, to ensure that items are available until the end of the booking window [27]. A flash sale strategy is discussed and examined by Dilme et al. [28]. He begins by defining a market in which a seller has a fixed number of similar items in his inventory that must all be sold by a certain date. This monopoly seller determines the price and whether to give some goods to customers in that market through a low-priced flash sale at each time period. Additionally, this flash sale model takes into account two different customer types: the arriving (high-value) buyer and a fixed group of (low-value) shoppers. When a buyer comes, he has the right to check the current price and the amount of storage still available before deciding whether or not to purchase an item. Dilme et al. claim that this sales model works by attracting cumulative buyers, consumers who purchase the product, and some of the cumulative buyers' desire to buy if they decide not to purchase [28]. Dilme et al. also describe a Markov equilibrium in which only publicly available information—the calendar time and the number of products the seller still has in stock—influences the actions of participating consumers [28]. Sellers are unable to make commitments in this equilibrium, so they conduct flash sales right before the deadline to clear their remaining stock. Before the deadline, buyers who are thinking ahead speculate that there might be a flash sale in the future, so they postpone their purchase in the hopes that they will have the chance to purchase the item they want at a lower price. However, there is a chance that someone else will purchase the object if you wait for a flash sale.

In conclusion, the literature on inventory control indicates that dynamic price changes generate revenue for sellers and can lead to lower prices for goods in order to attract lower-value consumers to make purchases.

Other Factors. In addition to the above factors, they can change consumers' sensitivity to price, thus further allowing price to influence consumers' intention to shop. There are also the following factors that can make a difference in the relationship between consumers' intentions to make a purchase and the price.

Trust in Online Shopping. A successful online shopping website, according to Liu et al., is one that attracts prospective customers and gives them the impression that it is reputable and trustworthy [29]. According to Ha et al., a crucial assumption in the growth of online purchases is the ability to make customers trust and enjoy the shopping experience [30]. They contend that customers are more likely to buy services or goods from online retailers when there is trust between them and the platforms. Bilgihan hypothesized a situation [31]. He contends that consumers who believe a brand are more likely to use that brand's website, whether it be for a simple return visit or to actually make a purchase, which, in turn, somewhat increases their intention to do so. Additionally, he makes the argument that customers are more likely to maintain their relationship with a company if they believe that the website's service provider is reliable.

Loyalty to the Website or Brand. Rose et al. made a research on the effects of online purchasing platforms on enhancing customer loyalty to a store or brand and customers' repeated purchases from the same store [32]. According to their study, online shopping platforms need to maintain a compelling online customer experience over time if they want to develop customer loyalty in an online setting. Before the above, Serra et al. contends that brand loyalty is expressed by the number of customers who consistently purchase a brand because they perceive its superior quality [33]. In this situation, whether or not the price of the brand's products is reduced is not the primary concern of these customers. As defined by Ahmad et al., loyalty is also the intention or propensity of consumers to purchase products from the same brand or retailer because they are persuaded that the value of the items they receive from that source is higher than the value of alternatives [34]. Value in this context primarily refers to the pleasure and utility that customers experience. In other words, price is no longer the only standard by which these customers decide whether or not to purchase a product, nor is it the primary variable influencing their likelihood to buy the brand.

2.2 Price Discrimination

Pigou advocated categorizing traditional kinds of pricing discrimination as follows: i) first-degree price discrimination ii) second-degree price discrimination iii) third-degree price discrimination [35]. This article provides background information on the three types of price discrimination mentioned above and analyses it.

First-Degree Price Discrimination. According to Pigou, imposing first-tier pricing is a harsh pricing technique in which the merchant tailors the price for each consumer in order to ensure that each user pays the highest price he or she is willing to pay for the commodity, so capturing the full consumer surplus [35]. Full price discrimination was costly to operate and difficult to achieve entirely in most areas in the old economy since each consumer's demand curve was different and merchants had trouble achieving the greatest price that consumers were prepared to pay [35]. Currently, with the advancement of information technology and the popularity of internet applications [1], online shopping platforms allow merchants to practice price discrimination because online consumers are independent, mutually closed individuals and different bids for the same goods are difficult to detect. Stole discovered that in a sales model similar to an online platform, the seller, as a monopolist, is able to capture all consumer surplus and each consumer's marginal buy is based on marginal cost once the seller has control of the monopoly [36]. In a market with first-degree price discrimination, each customer obtains the best offer that is reasonable and ideal for them, and their motivation to shop is unaffected by price.

Second-Degree Price Discrimination. The literature on secondary pricing discrimination is not very extensive. Secondary price discrimination, also known as non-linear pricing, is when prices vary depending on how much of a good is purchased by the customer but not based on how they behave or other variables [35]. Each customer in this scenario is subject to the same price schedule, where the cost is determined by the number of units purchased.

Third-Degree Price Discrimination. Pigou defined third-degree price discrimination as a tactic where various buyers are charged different prices, yet each buyer is required to pay a set sum for each unit of the commodity [35]. He decides to set a consistent price since he believes the merchant has no knowledge of the consumer and can only see the market as a whole. In monopolistic markets, three-level price discrimination is fairly common. According to Stole, the best price for three-level price discrimination in monopolistic markets can be obtained by individually applying the well-known inverse pricing elasticity rule to each market [36]. Beyond this, Robinson was the first to establish the case for monopoly, arguing that the shape of the demand curve for consumers determines whether aggregate output increases when monopolistic price discrimination exists [37]. In conclusion, when a monopolistic market experiences three degrees of price discrimination, the seller's, or monopolist's, revenue in that market is positively correlated with both the quantity desired by customers at that price as well as the product's price. This indicates that the fairness of the price of the commodity in the monopoly market is related to the consumer's inclination to shop.

Research Gap. It is certain that many scholars have made significant contributions to the field of research on dynamic price changes as well as price discrimination. Sobel's price discrimination model, a remarkable price model that examines pricing dynamics at the arrival of a new buyer in each period, has served as a solid model basis for subsequent studies on the dynamic aspects of pricing [20]. The importance of this research lies in the fact that price models can be used to forecast fair prices more accurately for goods, increasing consumer propensity for buying while also enhancing profitability for retailers. The models that are the current basis of the study are based on durable goods as the type of commodity, which can allow the models to ignore the impact of the quality of the goods on the consumer as well as the price. However, there are limitations to most of the content and concepts of the relationship between most price models and commodity price changes. This means that the model and subsequent studies do not adequately cover the realities of shopping, which leads to challenges in this study in examining price changes and consumption intentions of consumers (millennials) who are interested in new age trends in non-durable goods such as clothes and sneakers. A new consumption model called collaborative consumption has evolved because of today's advances in information technology [38]. Consumers now recognize collaborative consumption as a viable alternative to purchasing from brick-and-mortar stores, thanks largely to the use of digital technology. The internet has powered resale brands, giving rise to the digital second-hand market. Price research centered on non-durable goods is therefore essential, and this is where this study has decided to focus, seeking to fill a gap in the field of price research on non-durable goods by examining the impact of price changes on non-durable goods on online platforms on consumers' propensity to shop.

3 Discussion

This study looks at how online platforms are growing, how prices for non-durable goods are changing, how they affect brand-loyal and product-trusted customers, and how they further affect consumers' buying intentions. Such studies are uncommon in the body of literature currently in existence, so this research aims to fill the gap in the field.

Current studies have explored common marketing strategies in online markets while concentrating on dynamic price changes and price discrimination models. It has been discovered that the online marketplace for shopping has a positive effect on consumers who have low reserve prices and prefer fair prices as well as their tendency to shop for a single brand. Online shopping platforms are a practical choice for customers with loyalty and low reservation prices who anticipate obtaining price equity, according to experts in the field [2, 23, 34]. These platforms can also have a positive effect. However, since durable products are more characterized by price changes, current research has focused on these items [20]. However, in modern society, this is not an unquestioned truth. For instance, rising labor costs in China, rising raw material costs, and inflation have caused a general increase in prices over time, increasing the cost of sports shoes among non-durable products [39]. And today, as the internet is further optimized, it has given many companies the motivation to resell, spawning a digital secondary market [40]. According to Slaton et al., online purchasing platforms with these fashion brands can now successfully attract this consumer group by implementing a resale business model [41]. This is because Gen Z and millennial consumers are drawn to fashionable and trendy brands. These products are considered non-durable goods because they are fashionable and trendy and are among the most well-liked items among consumers today, but there hasn't been a lot of study on non-durable goods in the past. However, when combined with the previously mentioned research references, we can conclude that some non-durable commodities are likewise consistent with the above literature conclusions for durable goods. That is, if prices are gradually reduced, they become more appealing to consumers with low reservation prices, and many online platforms must also adhere to the principle of price fairness and refrain from raising or lowering prices excessively, as perceived price unfairness can significantly alter consumers' willingness to pay [42]. Additionally, loyal customers do not experience price discrimination, price fairness, or stock management restrictions when buying non-durable sneaker labels like Nike, Adidas, Puma, and others.

First-degree price discrimination has been seen as an impossibility in terms of price discrimination and is only rational from an academic standpoint [43]. However, Steppe contends that contemporary technology does make it easier for covert discriminatory pricing strategies to be used on a wider range of customers [43]. When shopping online on a personal computer or smartphone, pricing may change significantly from those in brick-and-mortar stores, where prices are often fixed at the same level for all customers. The 'coupon' model from Narasimhan is cited in this essay [24]. Numerous assessments of conventional price discrimination contend that the introduction of coupons into clearly defined markets is always advantageous for monopolists [44]. This well-organized market can be compared to the digital second-hand market [40], an online marketplace that divides products into groups based on their purpose, cost, and scarcity. Using coupons alters the buying environment by encouraging customers to make impulsive purchases in addition to lowering the price at which some consumers pay for goods. The inclusion of coupons may, however, boost consumers' willingness to purchase, particularly in markets where the products are clearly categorized [45].

4 Conclusion

This paper is the result of research on the impact of price changes of non-durable goods on consumers' willingness to use online shopping platforms. Specifically, this study focuses on investigating some representative non-durable goods markets and the overall situation of online shopping platforms and tries to explore the factors that affect consumers' use of online platforms to make purchases. This study adopts the form of a literature review and analyzes dynamic price changes and price discrimination models. And through further study of the past literature, several important discoveries have been formed.

4.1 Key Summary and Conclusions

This research began with a review and analysis of dynamic pricing techniques for goods.

According to the findings of the review of prior studies, practical dynamic pricing techniques for items can influence consumers' inclinations to make purchases positively. Additionally, modern customers have more purchasing options and a better awareness of the perceived justice of product prices thanks to advancements in information technology. Today's consumers have a new way of purchasing with online platforms, which might lessen or completely ignore the consideration of waiting time as a limitation while shopping, in contrast to prior studies indicating inter-period pricing disparity in the literature.

According to the analysis, when implemented properly, inter-period price discrimination and inventory control for the product can successfully help consumers, particularly those with low reservation prices, boost their intentions to buy. Second, while dynamic pricing can have a good impact on consumers' intentions to buy, the impact differs from one consumer to the next, requiring merchants to make a decision on how to apply this tactic appropriately. Dynamic pricing has a primarily positive effect on the price of durable products. This has been verified by earlier studies.

This study also studies non-durable items to assess whether these factors influence consumers' propensity to buy. According to the literature, non-durable items have historically been more responsive to price changes than durable goods because they lack the features of price changes. This method has a restriction. Today's online marketplace, on the other hand, has given rise to a digital resale market, in which online shopping platforms can successfully attract the purchasing tendency of a set of customers interested in such goods by adopting a resale business model for the selling of non-durable goods such as trendy goods.

To summarize, customers' propensity to purchase non-durable goods has increased since the rise of online shopping platforms in the twenty-first century. However, a variety of hurdles to acquiring non-durable items continue to exist, which may be caused by variables such as the shopping environment, the life cycle of non-durable goods, and the good or bad material of non-durable goods. This also implies that the non-durable goods strategy for selling on online shopping platforms will need to be maintained and developed in the future.

4.2 Limitations

There are also some limitations to this study. The paper focuses on consumers' sensitivity to fairness in the price of goods and the importance of changes in the price of goods, but this is sometimes not necessary to increase purchase intentions, ignoring the fact that consumers are influenced by their own subjective level factors such as their motivation to shop online, utilitarian, and hedonistic values [46]. Also, there is no standardization of the timing of the establishment of online shopping platforms and whether or not these platforms engage in advertising and other practices to raise awareness, thus making the conclusions subject to many confounding factors.

4.3 Suggestions for Future Work

Firstly, future non-durable product research should not be restricted to representative items but should instead choose a wide variety of non-durable goods for data tracking and gathering, making the findings more generalized for a more thorough analysis. Second, when looking into online shopping platforms, platforms that have been around for a comparable amount of time can be selected in order to avoid interfering with new user benefits brought on by the creation of new websites on consumers' propensity to shop, as this is a component of price changes for goods made by websites to draw in customers.

References

1. Glueck, J.: E-commerce is affecting brick and mortar retail, but not in the way you think (2017). https://www.forbes.com/sites/quora/2017/11/27/e-commerce-is-affecting-brick-and-mortar-retail-but-not-in-the-way-you-think. Accessed 25 Mar 2023
2. Rita, P., Oliveira, T., Farisa, A.: The impact of e-service quality and customer satisfaction on customer behavior in online shopping. Heliyon **5**(10), E02690 (2019). https://doi.org/10.1016/j.heliyon.2019.e02690
3. Lee, R.J., Sener, I.N., Mokhtarian, P.L., Handy, S.L.: Relationships between the online and in-store shopping frequency of Davis, California residents. Transp. Res. Part A: Policy Pract. **100**, 40–52 (2017)
4. Statista. Retail e-commerce sales in the United States from 2017 to 2024 (2020). https://www.statista.com/statistics/272391/us-retail-e-commerce-sales-forecast/. Accessed 26 Mar 2023
5. Pathak, G., Yadav, R.: Determinants of consumers' green purchase behavior in a developing nation: applying and extending the theory of planned behavior. Ecol. Econ. **134**, 114–122 (2017). https://doi.org/10.1016/j.ecolecon.2016.12.019
6. Palazon, M., Delgado, E.: The moderating role of price consciousness on the effectiveness of price discounts and premium promotions. J. Prod. Brand Manage. **18**(4), 306–312 (2009)
7. Kukar-Kinney, M., Ridgway, N.M., Monroe, K.B.: The role of price in the behavior and purchase decisions of compulsive buyers. J. Retail. **88**(1), 63–71 (2012). https://doi.org/10.1016/j.jretai.2011.02.004
8. Konuk, F.A.: The effects of price consciousness and sale proneness on purchase intention towards expiration date-based priced perishable foods. Br. Food J. **117**(2), 793–804 (2015)
9. Chi, B.C., Henry, C., Wen, C.H.: Pricing and promotion strategies of an online shop based on customer segmentation and multiple objective decision making. Expert Syst. Appl. **38**(12), 14585–14591 (2011). https://doi.org/10.1016/j.eswa.2011.05.024
10. Sahay, A.: How to reap higher profits with dynamic pricing. MIT Sloan Manage. Rev. (2007)
11. McGuire, K.A.: Hotel Pricing in a social World: Driving Value in the Digital Economy. Wiley, Hoboken (2015)
12. Melis, G., Piga, C.A.: Are all online hotel prices created dynamic? An empirical assessment. Int. J. Hospit. Manage. **67**, 163–173 (2017)
13. Viglia, G., Mauri, A., Carricano, M.: The exploration of hotel reference prices under dynamic pricing scenarios and different forms of competition. Int. J. Hosp. Manag. **52**, 46–55 (2016)
14. United States Environmental Protection Agency. Nondurable Goods: Product-Specific Data (2022). https://www.epa.gov/facts-and-figures-about-materials-waste-and-recycling/nondurable-goods-product-specific-data. Accessed 27 Mar 2023
15. Abrate, G., Nicolau, J.L., Viglia, G.: The impact of dynamic price variability on revenue maximization. Tour. Manage. **74**, 224–233 (2019). https://doi.org/10.1016/j.tourman.2019.03.013
16. Armstrong, M.: Recent developments in the economics of price discrimination. In: Advances in Economics and Econometrics: Theory and Applications: Ninth World Congress, vol. 2, pp. 97–141 (2006). https://discovery.ucl.ac.uk/id/eprint/14558
17. Dana, J.D., Jr.: Advance-purchase discounts and price discrimination in competitive markets. J. Polit. Econ. **106**(2), 395–422 (1998)
18. Stokey, N.L.: Intertemporal price discrimination. Q. J. Econ. **93**(3), 355–371 (1979)

19. Villas-Boas, J.M.: Dynamic competition with customer recognition. Rand J. Econ. 604–631 (1999)
20. Sobel, J.: The timing of sales. Rev. Econ. Stud. **51**(3), 353–368 (1984)
21. Conlisk, J., Gerstner, E., Sobel, J.: Cyclic pricing by a durable goods monopolist. Q. J. Econ. **99** (1984)
22. Xia, L., Monroe, K.B.: Is a good deal always fair? Examining the concepts of transaction value and price fairness. J. Econ. Psychol. **31**(6), 884–894 (2010)
23. Malc, D., Mumel, D., Pisnik, A.: Exploring price fairness perceptions and their influence on consumer behavior. J. Bu. Res. **69**(9), 3693–3697 (2016). https://doi.org/10.1016/j.jbusres.2016.03.031
24. Narasimhan, C.: A price discrimination theory of coupons. Mark. Sci. **3**(2), 128–147 (1984). https://doi.org/10.1287/mksc.3.2.128
25. Reimers, I., Xie, C.: Do coupons expand or cannibalize revenue? Evidence from an e-Market. Manage. Sci. **65**(1), 286–300 (2019)
26. Briesch, R.A., Krishnamurthi, L., Mazumdar, T., Raj, S.P.: A comparative analysis of reference price models. J. Consum. Res. **24**(2), 202–214 (1997)
27. Weatherford, L.R., Bodily, S.E.: A taxonomy and research overview of perishable-asset revenue management: yield management, overbooking, and pricing. Oper. Res. **40**(5), 831–844 (1992)
28. Dilme, F., Fei, L.: Revenue management without commitment: dynamic pricing and periodic flash sales. Rev. Econ. Stud. **86**(5), 1999–2034 (2019)
29. Liu, C., Arnett, K.P.: Exploring the factors associated with Web site success in the context of electronic commerce. Inf. Manage. **38**(1), 23–33 (2000)
30. Ha, S., Stoel, L.: Consumer e-shopping acceptance: antecedents in a technology acceptance model. J. Bus. Res. **62**(5), 565–571 (2009)
31. Bilgihan, A.: Gen Y customer loyalty in online shopping: an integrated model of trust, user experience and branding. Comput. Hum. Behav. **61**, 103–113 (2016). https://doi.org/10.1016/j.chb.2016.03.014
32. Rose, S., Clark, M., Samouel, P., Hair, N.: Online customer experience in e-retailing: an empirical model of antecedents and outcomes. J. Retail. **88**(2), 308–322 (2012)
33. Serra, E.M., González, J.A.V.: Consistencia entre categorías de productos, congruencia entre imágenes y valoración de las extensiones de marca. Rev. Eur. Dirección Econ. Empresa **6**(3), 79–92 (1997)
34. Ahmad, S., Pachauri, S., Creutzig, F.: Synergies and trade-offs between energy-efficient urbanization and health. Environ. Res. Lett. **12**(11), 114017 (2017)
35. Pigou, A.C.: The Economics of Welfare, 1st edn. Macmillan, London (1920)
36. Stole, L.A.: Price discrimination and competition. Handb. Ind. Organ. **3**, 2221–2299 (2007). https://doi.org/10.1016/S1573-448X(06)03034-2
37. Robinson, J.: The Economics of Imperfect Competition. Springer, Heidelberg (1969). https://doi.org/10.1007/978-1-349-15320-6
38. John, N.A.: Sharing, collaborative consumption and web 2.0. In: Media@ LSE Electronic Working Paper, vol. 26, no. 1, pp.1–19 (2013)
39. Elder, B.: Why sneakers are getting more expensive than ever. Complex (2015). https://www.complex.com/sneakers/2015/03/why-sneakers-are-more-expensive/
40. Hufford, J.: How recommerce is changing the fashion industry (2020). https://www.nchannel.com/blog/fashion-recommerce-resale
41. Slaton, K., Pookulangara, S.: Collaborative consumption: an investigation into the secondary sneaker market. Int. J. Consum. Stud. **46**(3), 763–780 (2021). https://doi.org/10.1111/ijcs.12725
42. Ajzen, I., Rosenthal, L.H., Brown, T.C.: Effects of perceived fairness on willingness to pay. J. Appl. Soc. Psychol. **30**(12), 2439–2450 (2000)

43. Steppe, R.: Online price discrimination and personal data: a general data protection regulation perspective. Comput. Law Secur. Rev. **33**(6), 768–785 (2017). https://doi.org/10.1016/j.clsr.2017.05.008
44. Anderson, E.T., Simester, D.I.: Price discrimination as an adverse signal: why an offer to spread payments may hurt demand. Mark. Sci. **20**(3), 315–327 (2001). https://doi.org/10.1287/mksc.20.3.315.9763
45. Sen, S., Johnson, E.J.: Mere-possession effects without possession in consumer choice. J. Consum. Res. **24**(1), 105–117 (1997)
46. Pappas, I.O., Kourouthanassis, P.E., Giannakos, M.N., Lekakos, G.: The interplay of online shopping motivations and experiential factors on personalized e-commerce: a complexity theory approach. Telem. Inform. **34**(5), 730–742 (2017). https://doi.org/10.1016/j.tele.2016.08.021

Analyzing Problems and Strategies of International Organizations in Global Governance and Cooperation – Taking UNDP as an Example

Haosen Xu(✉)

School of International Studies, Zhejiang University, Hangzhou 310058, Zhejiang, China
3210106069@zju.edu.cn

Abstract. The role of international organizations in global governance and cooperation has become more prominent since the middle of the last century. However, the problems and limitations of international organizations in dealing with a wide range of global issues cannot be ignored. The purpose of this article is to analyze specific cases, using the United Nations Development Programme (UNDP) as an example, and to find the problems arising from international organizations at the bureaucratic, financial, and international cooperation aspects, while giving appropriate recommendations. This article analyzes the different problems mentioned above arising from the UNDP in different cases by using theories related to international organizations such as game theory, realism theory, constructivist theory and neoliberal theory. In addition, international organizations can improve their effectiveness and role in global governance by engaging more with civil society and private enterprises and by innovating their own working models.

Keywords: UNDP · Realism Theory · Game Theory · Constructivist and Neoliberal Theory

1 Introduction

Since the conclusion of World War II, international organizations have played a crucial role in global governance and cooperation. These organizations, including the United Nations (UN) and its various agencies, were established in response to the need for international collaboration on issues such as human rights, economic development, and peace and security. With the emergence of new challenges, such as terrorism, climate change, and global health crises, international organizations have expanded their functions and number to address them. However, despite their success in promoting cooperation among nations, international organizations still face significant obstacles. To increase their impact in helping countries achieve the Millennium Development Goals, including poverty reduction, the United Nations Sustainable Development develops policies and procedures that enable member agencies to work together to analyze country issues, plan support strategies, implement support programs, monitor results and advocate for change. As a key agency of the United Nations and an important part of the international community, the UNDP's strategies and issues reflect the current state of many international organizations [1].

As the world becomes increasingly interconnected, the role of international organizations in global governance and cooperation has become more important than ever. These organizations are tasked with addressing a wide range of global issues, including poverty, inequality, conflict, environmental degradation, and public health. They play a key role in coordinating international efforts and mobilizing resources to address these challenges.

However, international organizations face a number of significant challenges in carrying out their work. These challenges include lack of resources, limited authority, and the need to balance the interests of different member states [2]. In addition, they must navigate complex political and social dynamics, including the rise of populism and nationalism in many countries, which can undermine support for international cooperation. Despite these challenges, a number of new models have emerged in the work of international organizations that are seeking to address these issues. These paradigms include greater engagement with civil society and the private sector, the use of new technologies, and a focus on more inclusive and participatory approaches to governance. By embracing these new paradigms and adapting to the changing global landscape, international organizations can continue to play a critical role in fostering global cooperation and addressing the world's most pressing challenges.

This paper, therefore, will showcase UNDP's governance strategies and issues through an analysis of three case studies on gender issues, poverty governance, and the Sustainable Development Goals (SDGs), and thus present the issues and new models of global governance and cooperation of international organizations, explore the reasons for their limitations, and suggest new ways to address these challenges.

The paper is organized as follows: Sect. 2 deals with cases on gender topics, Sect. 3 with examples on poverty governance, followed by Sect. 4 with an analysis of cases on sustainable development, and concluding with conclusions in Sect. 5.

2 UNDP's Strategies in Gender Equality in Afghanistan

In 2015, the United Nations adopted the Sustainable Development Goals (SDGs) to address global challenges, including poverty, inequality, and climate change. Goal 5 of the SDGs aims to achieve gender equality and empower all women and girls [3]. However, gender inequality remains a significant issue in many countries, including Afghanistan, where women and girls face discrimination, violence, and limited access to education, healthcare, and political participation.

To address these issues, UNDP launched a project in Afghanistan starting in 2010 aimed at promoting gender equality by empowering women and girls and addressing the root causes of gender-based discrimination. The project had several components, including education and vocational training for women and girls, supporting their political participation and decision-making, addressing gender-based violence, and promoting gender-sensitive policies and practices [4].

The UNDP collaborated with local partners such as government agencies, civil society organizations, and community leaders to execute the initiative. The project also involved men and boys in supporting gender equality and confronting negative gender stereotypes.

The project had a significant impact on the lives of women and girls in Afghanistan, with over 28,000 women and girls receiving vocational training and education, more than 500 women participating in political processes and decision-making, and the adoption of several gender-sensitive policies and laws, including the Elimination of Violence Against Women law and the National Action Plan for Women. The project also raised awareness of gender-based violence and provided support to over 6,000 survivors, increasing access to justice and services [5].

The UNDP project in Afghanistan illustrates the importance of a multi-sectoral, rights-based approach to promoting gender equality. The project demonstrated that gender inequality is not just a women's issue, but a societal issue that requires the engagement of all stakeholders. The project also highlights the need for sustained investment and commitment to gender equality programming and the importance of monitoring and evaluating interventions to ensure accountability and learning. Despite the challenges faced in implementing the project, the UNDP was able to adapt its approach and build trust and partnerships with local actors to achieve its objectives.

2.1 Analysis on UNDP's Strategy Using Game Theory

Game theory can be applied to the UNDP's efforts to promote gender equality in Afghanistan by considering the interaction between various actors and their incentives. In this case, the key actors are the UNDP, the Afghan government, civil society organizations, and community leaders. Each actor has its own goals and incentives, which may be aligned or in conflict with each other.

The UNDP's goal is to promote gender equality in Afghanistan, but it also needs the support of other actors to achieve this goal. The Afghan government has the power to enact policies and laws that promote gender equality, but may be hesitant to do so due to cultural or political reasons. Civil society organizations and community leaders may be more willing to support gender equality, but may have limited resources and reach [6].

One way to analyze this situation is through a coordination game, in which each actor's best strategy is to coordinate their actions with the others in order to achieve the best outcome for everyone. In this game, the best outcome is achieved when all actors work together to promote gender equality and empower women and girls in Afghanistan.

However, there may be incentives for some actors to defect from this strategy. For example, the Afghan government may be more concerned with maintaining its own power and legitimacy than with promoting gender equality, and may resist efforts to change the status quo. Civil society organizations may have limited resources and capacity to carry out their activities, and may prioritize other issues over gender equality. Community leaders may also resist efforts to change traditional gender roles and norms.

To overcome these challenges, the UNDP may need to use a combination of incentives and persuasion to encourage all actors to cooperate and work towards the common goal of promoting gender equality. This may involve providing financial or other resources to support the activities of civil society organizations and community leaders, and working with the Afghan government to build support for gender-sensitive policies and laws. The UNDP may also need to use communication strategies to raise awareness about the importance of gender equality and to challenge harmful gender norms and practices.

In this case, to improve bureaucratic efficiency, the UNDP should enhance internal communication and coordination among its staff members, especially those working in different countries. This can be done by implementing regular team meetings, developing standardized procedures for different departments, and introducing digital tools for collaboration.

Overall, the UNDP's project in Afghanistan appears to be effective in promoting gender equality and empowering women and girls. The project's multi-sectoral approach and focus on addressing the root causes of gender-based discrimination have led to positive outcomes, such as increased participation of women in politics and decision-making, and improved economic opportunities for women and girls. However, the effectiveness of the project may vary depending on the local context, and it may be difficult to achieve universality in promoting gender equality due to the complex and deeply ingrained nature of gender inequality.

3 UNDP's Strategies in Poverty Issues in Bangladesh

The UNDP aims to foster sustainable development and equity in Bangladesh, with a special emphasis on diminishing poverty and enhancing access to fundamental amenities like healthcare and education. Bangladesh is amongst the most underprivileged nations globally, with more than one-fifth of its inhabitants surviving below the poverty level [7].

UNDP aims to promote inclusive growth and sustainable development in Bangladesh, with a particular focus on reducing poverty and improving access to basic services, including healthcare and education. However, international cooperation has been a significant challenge for the UNDP in Bangladesh, as many developed countries prioritize their own economic interests over promoting development in poor countries like Bangladesh. To overcome this, the UNDP has worked closely with the Bangladeshi government to implement a range of programs and initiatives aimed at reducing poverty, improving access to basic services, and promoting sustainable development. The UNDP also seeks to build support for its mission among the international community through advocacy and partnership building.

However, a lack of cooperation among various stakeholders in Bangladesh, including government agencies, civil society organizations, and the private sector, has hindered progress towards achieving the Sustainable Development Goals (SDGs) [8]. To address this, the UNDP has adopted a strategy of promoting multi-stakeholder partnerships and collaboration to foster greater cooperation and coordination. The UNDP works closely with the government of Bangladesh to implement various programs and initiatives, while also establishing partnerships with civil society organizations and the private sector to leverage their expertise and resources. The UNDP also facilitates regular consultations and meetings with stakeholders to promote dialogue and consensus-building towards achieving common goals.

Despite these efforts, there are still challenges to effective cooperation and coordination due to divergent priorities among stakeholders. To address this issue, the UNDP has developed various tools and resources to help stakeholders align their priorities and develop common goals. The UNDP's mission in Bangladesh provides an important example of how international cooperation can impact efforts to reduce poverty and promote sustainable development. While there are challenges to overcome, the UNDP's strategy of working closely with the Bangladeshi government and building support among the international community has helped to make progress towards its mission [9].

3.1 Analysis on UNDP's Strategy Using Realism Theory

Realism in international relations theory suggests that states act in their own self-interest and prioritize their own national security above all else. This theory can also be applied to international organizations such as the UNDP, which must balance the interests of multiple countries while still working to achieve its goals.

In the case of the UNDP mission in Bangladesh, realism could impact the mission in several ways. For example, some countries may not want to contribute resources or support the mission if they do not see a direct benefit to their own national interests. Additionally, some countries may try to influence the mission to align with their own foreign policy agenda, which could undermine the effectiveness of the UNDP's work [10].

To address these challenges, the UNDP must navigate the complex political landscape of international relations while remaining committed to its mission of reducing poverty in Bangladesh. One strategy the UNDP can use is to build coalitions with countries that have a stake in the success of the mission. By working with these countries and demonstrating the benefits of the UNDP's work, the organization can secure the support it needs to carry out its mission effectively.

Another strategy is to remain transparent and accountable in its work. By demonstrating that its actions are motivated by a genuine commitment to reducing poverty, rather than political interests or hidden agendas, the UNDP can build trust and credibility with its partners and stakeholders.

Besides, to avoid over-reliance on a few key donors, the UNDP should actively seek to diversify its funding sources. This can be achieved by exploring partnerships with private enterprises, philanthropic organizations, and civil society groups, as well as pursuing innovative financing mechanisms such as social impact bonds.

Overall, the UNDP's mission in Bangladesh highlights the challenges of working in a complex and politically charged environment. By using a combination of strategic partnerships and transparent, accountable practices, the UNDP can navigate these challenges and achieve its goal of reducing poverty in the region.

4 UNDP's Strategies in Sustainable Development Goals in Yemen

The UNDP has been working to address the challenges faced by Yemen, which is currently experiencing one of the worst humanitarian crises in the world. The protracted conflict in Yemen has led to widespread displacement, food insecurity, and a collapsed health system, with more than 80% of the population requiring humanitarian assistance, and millions at risk of famine. The UNDP's efforts in Yemen have focused on supporting conflict prevention and peacebuilding, strengthening governance and the rule of law, and supporting economic recovery and resilience, all of which align with the goals of SDGs 16 and 17. Specifically, the UNDP has worked with local communities to promote peace and prevent conflict through community dialogue and mediation, as well as by supporting the integration of conflict-sensitive approaches into development planning. Additionally, the UNDP has worked with the Yemeni government and civil society organizations to strengthen governance and the rule of law, including by supporting electoral processes and promoting human rights and access to justice. Finally, the UNDP has implemented programs aimed at supporting economic recovery and building resilience among Yemeni communities, including through the provision of emergency cash transfers and support for small and medium-sized enterprises [11].

The impact of the UNDP's work in Yemen has been significant, with over one million vulnerable Yemenis receiving emergency cash transfers to alleviate the immediate impacts of the conflict and the humanitarian crisis. The UNDP has also supported over 50 community dialogues and peace initiatives, which have helped to prevent and resolve conflicts in several Yemeni communities. Furthermore, the UNDP has trained over 4,000 government officials, civil society representatives, and journalists on human rights, access to justice, and conflict prevention.

Despite these successes, the UNDP's response in Yemen has been challenging due to a lack of funding, limited access to conflict-affected areas, and bureaucratic hurdles. To address these challenges, the UNDP has built partnerships with other UN agencies, international organizations, and NGOs to pool resources and maximize impact. The UNDP has also worked closely with the Yemeni government and local partners to ensure that programs are aligned with local priorities and needs. Furthermore, the UNDP has adapted its approach to the challenging operating environment in Yemen, including by using remote communication technologies to engage with communities in conflict-affected areas.

However, despite these efforts, funding remains a major challenge for the UNDP's work in Yemen, with the organization only receiving $42 million out of the $173 million it appealed for in 2020 [12]. This limited funding has restricted the scope and impact of the UNDP's interventions. Additionally, the UNDP has faced challenges in cooperating with the Yemeni government, particularly due to the country's political instability and ongoing conflict. Finally, bureaucracy within the UN system has also hindered the UNDP's ability to respond effectively to the crisis in Yemen, particularly in terms of timely procurement and deployment of resources. Overall, the UNDP's work in Yemen provides a concrete example of how the organization is working to achieve the SDGs in a challenging operating environment, and highlights the importance of partnerships, cultural sensitivity, and flexibility in achieving sustainable development in conflict-affected areas.

4.1 Analysis on UNDP's Strategy Using Constructivist and Neoliberalism Theory

According to constructivist theory, international organizations such as UNDP are not neutral actors, but rather social constructions created by shared ideas and values of the member states that support them. The UNDP's work in Yemen reflects the importance placed on promoting peaceful and inclusive societies and building partnerships for sustainable development, which are key principles of the SDGs. The UNDP has focused on supporting conflict prevention and peacebuilding, strengthening governance and the rule of law, and supporting economic recovery and resilience, all of which align with the goals of SDG 16 and 17.

Moreover, constructivists argue that actors in international relations are not solely driven by material interests but also by ideational factors such as norms, identities, and culture. The UNDP's efforts to work closely with the Yemeni government and local partners to ensure that programs are aligned with local priorities and needs demonstrate a commitment to cultural sensitivity and recognition of local norms and values. This approach is crucial for the success of the UNDP's interventions in Yemen as it creates a sense of ownership and buy-in among local communities, which increases the likelihood of sustainability and effectiveness.

Neoliberalism, focuses on the role of market mechanisms in promoting efficiency, competition, and economic growth. The UNDP's work in Yemen reflects a mix of market-oriented and state-led interventions. The support of small and medium-sized enterprises and the provision of emergency cash transfers demonstrate a focus on market mechanisms and the private sector, while working with the Yemeni government and civil society organizations to strengthen governance and the rule of law reflects a more state-led approach.

To enhance cooperation with other countries and regional organizations, the UNDP should seek to build stronger partnerships at both the national and regional levels. This can be done by identifying key stakeholders and developing tailored strategies for each country, as well as engaging with regional organizations such as the African Union, the Association of Southeast Asian Nations (ASEAN), and the Economic Community of West African States (ECOWAS) [13].

Overall, the UNDP's work in Yemen has had a significant impact on the ground, but the effectiveness and universality of its interventions are limited by funding constraints, political instability, and bureaucratic hurdles. The UNDP's efforts to build partnerships with other UN agencies, international organizations, and NGOs to pool resources and maximize impact reflect a neoliberal approach that emphasizes efficiency and effectiveness through cooperation and coordination. However, the challenges in cooperating with the Yemeni government and the bureaucratic hurdles within the UN system demonstrate the limitations of this approach in a context of political instability and conflict. Furthermore, the lack of funding highlights the tension between market mechanisms and the need for state-led interventions to address humanitarian crises.

5 Conclusion

In conclusion, this article aimed to analyze the problems and limitations of international organizations, with a specific focus on the UNDP. By using theories such as game theory, realism theory, constructivist theory, and neoliberal theory, the article was able to identify problems at the bureaucratic, financial, and international cooperation levels. This paper also provided recommendations and strategies for improving the effectiveness of the UNDP and other international organizations.

One of the key strategies suggested was for international organizations to engage more with civil society and private enterprises, as this could help to address some of the limitations they face. It is also recommended that international organizations innovate their working models to better adapt to the changing global landscape.

However, the limitations of our analysis should be acknowledged. While the article focused on the UNDP, the problems and limitations of international organizations are complex and multifaceted, and cannot be fully addressed in one article. In addition, the use and analysis of data in this article is still insufficient, and further research is needed to increase the use and design of data models and to further analyze the problems of international organizations such as UNDP in the process of global governance through more specific analysis.

Moving forward, future studies should continue to explore the problems and limitations of international organizations, and seek to identify new strategies and solutions for improving their effectiveness and role in global governance. By doing so, International Organizations can work towards a more collaborative and effective global system for addressing the pressing challenges facing our world today.

References

1. Qu, S., Tan, Q.: Analysis of efficiency evaluation models of international organizations. In: International Monetary Institute (eds.) IMI Research Information, 2016 Compilation, pp. 1716–1721 (2016)
2. Tang, B.: Dual roles of UNDP and the coordination of UN development system. Int. Rev. (04),83–97 (2016)
3. Ahmed, F.B., Shahidzai S.S.: Final evaluation of enhancing gender equality and mainstreaming in Afghanistan (EGEMA) (2019)
4. UNDP Afghanistan: Pitfalls and Promise Minerals Extraction in Afghanistan: Afghanistan Human Development Report 2020. Published by UNDP Afghanistan Country Office (2020)
5. Wang, M.: A study on the management of international multilateral development assistance projects: the case of the United Nations development programme (UNDP) assistance to China. University of International Business and Economics (2010)
6. Castillejos-Aragón, M.: A Need for Change: Why Do Women in the Judiciary Matter? Konrad Adenauer Stiftung (2021)
7. Roy, D., Datta, S.K.: Analysis of achievement of selected MDGs: a comparative study between India and Bangladesh. Bangladesh Dev. Stud. **43**(1/2), 79–108 (2020)
8. Urban Partnerships for Poverty Reduction Project: Urban Poverty Reduction in Bangladesh: The UPPR Experience, Documentation of UPPR Learning and Good Practices (Abridged Version), Published by United Nations Development Program (UNDP) [Urban Partnerships for Poverty Reduction Project] (2016)
9. United Nations Development Programme Evaluation Office: Country Evaluation: Assessment of Development Results – Bangladesh, Published by United Nations Development Programme Evaluation Office (2005)
10. Lempert, D.: Testing the global community's sustainable development goals (SDGs) against professional standards and international law. Consilience **18**, 111–175 (2017)
11. United Nations Yemen: United Nations Yemen Sustainable Development Cooperation Framework 2022–2024, United Nations Yemen (2022)

12. The Guardian: 'Not perfect, but it is effective': UN from the point of view of its staff. https://www.theguardian.com/world. Accessed 25 Apr 2023
13. Olsen, S.H., Elder, M.: Upgrading the United Nations environment programme: a phased approach. Institute for Global Environmental Strategies (2012)

Implementation of Monte-Carlo Simulations in Economy and Finance

Jintian Zhang[✉]

Department of Mathematics and Applied Mathematics, Shandong University (Weihai),
Wenhuaxi Road 180, Weihai 264209, Shandong, China
202000820226@mail.sdu.edu.cn

Abstract. As a matter of fact, Stochastic processes are widely happened in the daily life, where a typical approach to simulate the process by calculating the mean value is achieved through Monte Carlo simulation. Monte Carlo simulation arose from the research requirements of the Manhattan Project in the United States. Because this method is closely related to probability, its name is derived from Monte Carlo, a gambling city in Monaco. This paper investigates the methods and ideas embodied in the use of Monte Carlo simulation in finance and economics. According to the analysis in this study, Monte Carlo simulation is used in three practical cases of real estate project investment, barrier option, and highway construction to obtain prediction results and feasibility suggestions based on a series of indicators. This research aims to help people understand Monte Carlo simulation and the thinking mode of probability science it embodies, then promote the optimization of Monte Carlo simulation method itself. Overall, these results shed light on guiding further exploration of implementations for Monte Carlo simulations.

Keywords: Monte Carlo Simulation · Real Estate Project Investment · Barrier Option · Expressway Construction · Example of Calculation

1 Introduction

Monte Carlo simulation, also known as computer stochastic simulation method, is a calculation method based on "random numbers". This method was born in the "Manhattan Project" of the United States in the 1940s. During the Second World War, in order to simulate the random diffusion of neutrons of fissile materials in the atomic bomb development project, American mathematicians Ulam and von Neumann, who are known as the father of computer, invented a statistical method. It was named Monte Carlo Simulation because Monte Carlo is a city in the tiny European country of Monaco, which was a very famous gambling city at that time. Since the essence of gambling is to calculate probabilities, and Monte Carlo simulation is a method based on probabilities, the method is named after the gambling city. Since Monte Carlo simulation is based on probability, it belongs to non-deterministic algorithm, and its counterpart is deterministic algorithm.

The basic idea of Monte Carlo method has been discovered and used for a long time. Algorithms similar to Monte Carlo methods existed before Monte Carlo methods were invented. As early as the 17th century, it was known that the "frequency" of an event was used to determine the "probability" of an event. The origins of the Monte Carlo method can be traced back to the 18th century, Buffon's famous needle drop experiment used to calculate π was the Monte Carlo simulation. In 1777, the French mathematician Buffon proposed to use the method of needle experiment to calculate π, a total of 2212 needles, 704 times intersecting a straight line, $2212 \div 704 \approx 3.142$, the resulting number is the approximate value of π, later he wrote the experiment into his paper [1]. This is considered to be the origin of the Monte Carlo method. Mathematicians have known about statistical sampling for a long time, However, before the advent of computers, the cost of random number generation was high, so this method was not practical. With the rapid development of computer technology in the second half of the 20th century, the stochastic simulation technology soon entered the practical stage. In the case of deep learning, it is also very obvious that computing forces push algorithms. The Monte Carlo method often offers hope for problems that are impossible or impossible to solve with deterministic algorithms.

This article focuses on finance and economics. Finance has uncertainty, which is often referred to as risk. In the eyes of holders of financial assets, this risk is the possibility and degree of loss. On the other hand, in investment, it is the relationship between cost and profit. The central idea of Monte Carlo method is the theorem of large numbers. When using this method, one needs to set the process of data generation of things, and combine random sampling to simulate the probability distribution of the development of things, so as to further analyze financial and economic events. With the development of computer technology, Monte Carlo simulation has gained rapid popularity in the last 10 years. In modern Monte Carlo simulation, it is no longer necessary to do experiments by hand, but with the help of the high-speed operation ability of the computer, which makes the process of time-consuming and laborious experiment become fast and easy. It is not only used to solve many complex scientific problems, but also is often used by project managers in the financial field. With the help of computer technology, Monte Carlo simulation has realized two advantages, i.e., simplicity and quickness, which is the technical basis for Monte Carlo method to be applied in modern project management.

In order to solve the problems in the field of financial economy, people often need to rely on computers to analyze and forecast financial and economic events. Monte Carlo simulation is a very effective method to analyze random events by simulating numerical experiments. This paper firstly introduces the history and current status of Monte Carlo simulation, then elaborates the operation principle of Monte Carlo simulation, and introduces the application of Monte Carlo simulation in the financial and economic fields through three examples, finally summarizes the research results and prospects of this paper.

2 Basic Descriptions of Monte Carlo Simulation

Monte Carlo method is a computational method that extracts a large number of random samples from the population through computer simulation. Its basic principle is: According to the problems of financial analysis, engineering technology and mathematical calculation, a probability model conforming to the actual situation is constructed, and then the process described in the model is simulated, the simulation results can be used as the approximate solution of the problem to be solved. The Monte Carlo method regards the integral to be calculated as the expectation of a random variable $g(r)$, which obeys some distribution density function $f(r)$, and then uses the method of random sampling experiment to calculate the integral:

$$\langle g \rangle = \int g(r) \cdot f(r) dr \qquad (1)$$

By some sampling, N sample values $r_1, r_2, \ldots, r_N$ are obtained (that is, N subsamples $r_1, r_2, \ldots, r_N$ are extracted from the distribution density function $f(r)$, and the corresponding arithmetic mean of N random variable $g(r_1), g(r_2), \ldots, g(r_N)$ is calculated [2]:

$$g_N = \frac{1}{N} \sum_{i=1}^{N} g(r_i) \qquad (2)$$

This value can be used as an approximate estimate of the integral. Convergence and error are two key points in Monte Carlo calculation [3–5]. The arithmetic means in random samples $X_1, X_2, \ldots, X_N$ is:

$$\overline{X} = \frac{1}{N} \sum_{i=1}^{N} X_i \qquad (3)$$

The Law of large numbers tells us that if $X_1, X_2, \ldots, X_N$ are independently and identically distributed and have a finite expectation, then one has:

$$P\left(\lim_{N \to \infty} \overline{X_N} = E(X) \right) = 1 \qquad (4)$$

The error of Monte Carlo method can be explained by the Central limit theorem. When the random variable $X_1, X_2, \ldots, X_N$ are independently and identically distributed, then:

$$\lim_{N \to \infty} P\left(\frac{\sqrt{N}}{\sigma} |\overline{X_N} - E(X)| < x \right) = \frac{1}{\sqrt{2\pi}} \int_{-x}^{x} e^{\frac{-t^2}{2}} dt \qquad (5)$$

The Eq. (5) is valid if:

$$0 \neq \sigma^2 = \int (x - E(X))^2 f(X) dx < \infty \qquad (6)$$

That means that the variance σ^2 a is non-zero and finite. Where $f(x)$ is the density function of x distribution [4]. When N is large enough in Eq. (5), the following equation is given:

$$P\left(|\overline{X_N} - E(X)| < \frac{\lambda_\alpha \sigma}{\sqrt{N}} \right) \approx \frac{2}{\sqrt{2\pi}} \int_{0}^{\lambda_\alpha} e^{\frac{-t^2}{2}} dt = 1 - \alpha \qquad (7)$$

Here, α is the significant level and λ_α is the normal deviate. At the confidence level of $1 - \alpha$ the following inequality holds:

$$|\overline{X_N} - E(X)| < \frac{\lambda_\alpha \sigma}{\sqrt{N}} \quad (8)$$

The probability that inequation is tenable can be approximated as $1 - \alpha$. When α is infinitely small, the approximation is infinitely close to the true value. According to the formula, the order of convergence rate of random sample error is $o\left(\frac{1}{\sqrt{N}}\right)$. It is known that ε, $\sqrt{N}$ and σ are the three values that affect the error of Monte Carlo method on the premise that α is determined. Therefore, the error can be reduced and the calculation accuracy can be improved by increasing the number of samples N or decreasing the variance σ^2 [2].

3 The State-of-Art Applications

3.1 Real Estate Investment

In a real estate development project as an example, the project area is 56659.1 m², volume rate is 2.04, a total construction area is 159536 m², including the floor plan should the building area is 115341 m², developing residential construction area is 103992 m², Commercial and service facilities construction area is 8379 m², the community housing construction area is 2970 m² underground building area is 44195 m², had 962 underground parking Spaces. The project is scheduled to start in September 2021, complete and deliver in September 2024, get the sales license in April 2022, and sell out by the end of 2023. The land cost is expected to be 1,014.73 million yuan, which will be paid by the end of 2021. The construction cost is 728.82 million yuan, and the construction period is 4 years. Project capital source: self-owned capital investment of 1,105.28 million yuan, bank loan of 66 million yuan, the annual interest rate of the loan is 6.175%, the rest of the capital source is sales fund recovery. Based on the economic data of Wind database, this paper selects the investment net interest rate index of the top 30 domestic listed real estate companies in terms of sales amount in 2020. According to the cash flow six main risk factors affecting the project economic benefit are screened out, namely, sales income, land cost, construction investment, sales cost, management cost and financial cost. Inputting the probability distribution function of each economic variable and the financial model, NPV and IRR were used as prediction objects, the discount rate of NPV simulation analysis was set to 10%, and then Monte Carlo simulation was carried out, and the number of simulation was set to 3000 times, and the first 5% value in the NPV simulation distribution was extracted, By calculating the average of its measuring CVaR values under the confidence level of 95%.

Figure 1 is the project's NPV simulated distribution and cumulative probability distribution. The results showed that NPV minimum value is 38.6407 million yuan, the maximum value is 268.7833 million yuan, the standard deviation is 5323.11, kurtosis is $2.57 < 3$, the slant degree is 0.0472; Under the confidence level of 95%, VaR is 33.4858 million yuan, CVaR is 119.4343 million yuan. Moreover, NPV simulation of the distribution and normal distribution of skewness is similar, the average is 119.4343

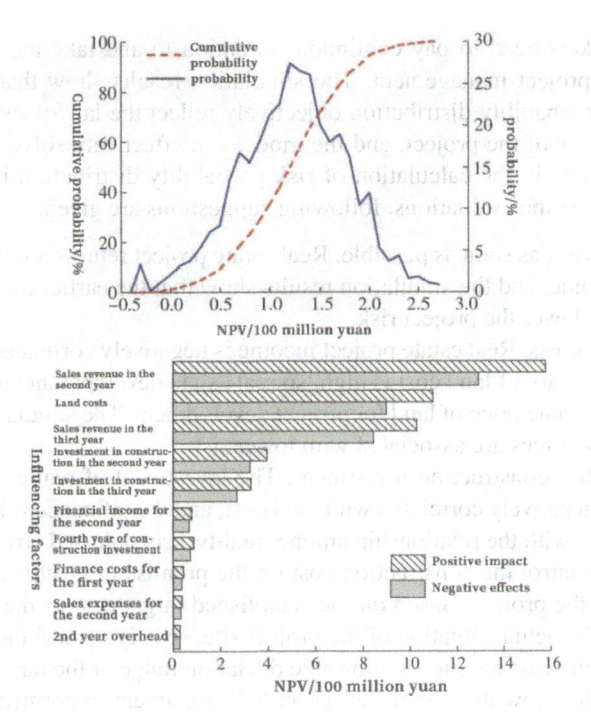

Fig. 1. NPV simulated distribution and cumulative probability distribution (left panel) with sensitive analysis (right panel).

million yuan, is greater than zero, and NPV the cumulative probability distribution that NPV is greater than zero can reach 98.48%, indicates that the project has good earnings expectations, with a strong ability to resist risks. IRR simulation results have similar distribution rules with Fig. 1, the minimum return rate is 7%, the maximum is 35%, the standard deviation is 0.05, the kurtosis is 2.54 < 3, the skewness is 0.1548, and the standard deviation rate of IRR is 0.2414. The probability that IRR is not lower than the average return rate of real estate investment (10%) is 99.17%. In addition, the IRR R is greater than 10% of the benchmark return rate, indicating that the project has good return expectation and strong risk resistance. According to the analysis results of NPV and IRR, −10%, −5%, 5% and 10% are selected as the degree of change of economic variables, and the sensitivity analysis of the simulation results of NPV and IRR is carried out. When the degree of influence is ranked quantitatively, the two have the same rule, as shown in the right panel of Fig. 2. The results show that real estate project returns are positively related to sales revenue, but negatively related to land fees, construction investment, and financial fees. At the same time, sales revenue, land fee and construction investment in the first three years have a great impact on project NPV and IRR, among which sales revenue in the second year is the most sensitive, followed by land fee, sales revenue in the third year and construction investment in the second year. To sum up, sales revenue, land fees and construction investment are the most important sensitive risk factors affecting NPV and IRR, which are also the risk factors that policy makers need to pay continuous attention to and take measures to control in subsequent project management. The simulation results show that the calculation results of risk probability distribution objectively reflect the law of risk distribution in the whole process of the project, and the model can effectively solve the weakness of strong subjectivity in the calculation of risk probability distribution in the traditional method. Based on the evaluations, following suggestions are given:

- Implement sales as soon as possible. Real estate project returns are positively related to sales revenue, and the simulation results show that the earlier the sales revenue is realized, the lower the project risk.
- Reduce land costs. Real estate project income is negatively correlated with land cost, and the sensitivity of land cost is high, so real estate development enterprises should choose reasonable price of land for project development. The simulation results show that lower land fees are associated with lower risk.
- Strictly control construction investment. The investment of real estate project construction is negatively correlated with land cost, and the influence is large; Therefore, when dealing with the relationship among quality, schedule and cost, enterprises can reasonably control the construction cost on the premise of ensuring the quality and schedule of the project. Based on the established target cost as the guidance, combined with the actual situation of the project site, strictly control the design change, and control the cost within the allowable deviation range of the target cost. The simulation results show that the lower the initial investment in construction, the lower the risk.
- Reasonable financing to control financial expenses, sales expenses, and administrative expenses. The financial cost of real estate projects is negatively related to the land cost, so a reasonable financing plan should be formulated to reduce the financing cost and improve the project profit [6].

3.2 Barrier Option

The term "barrier option" refers to an option whose efficacy is constrained. Its goal is to keep investors' gains and losses within a specific range. Knock-out options and knock-in options are the two groups into which barrier options typically fall. Barrier options are not necessarily more profitable than other options; however, because of their reduced premium, people tend to favor them. Monte Carlo method is also widely used in financial pricing, and its basic steps are as follows;

- Step 1: Build the probability model.
- Step 2: Sample values are obtained by random sampling.
- Step 3: Determine and select the statistics.
- Step 4: Estimate the statistics.

According to the basic Monte Carlo theory, the simulation using the conventional Monte Carlo technique has a big error and a sluggish convergence pace. As a result, the Moro algorithm must be used to randomize the Halton sequence, Faure sequence, Sobol sequence, etc., and then create quasi-random numbers to substitute the original random numbers for modeling. These random numbers have a more consistent distribution, are less volatile, have a quicker convergence speed, and have a smaller inaccuracy. The

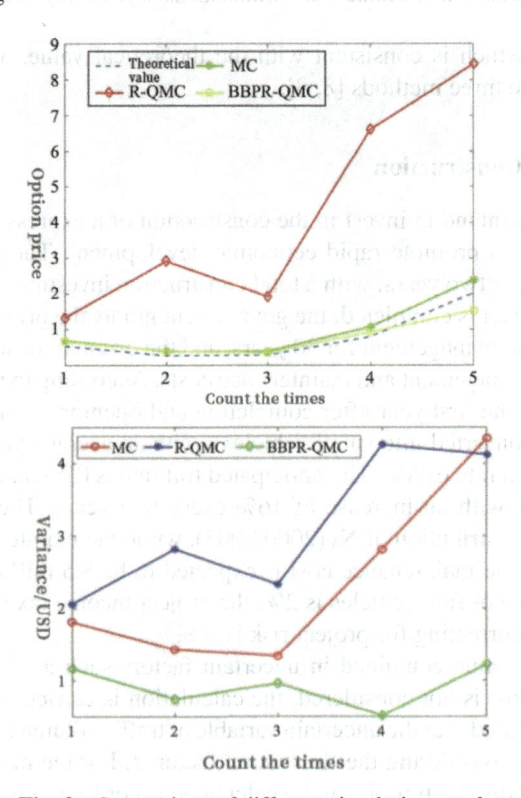

Fig. 2. Comparison of different simulation results.

Monte Carlo technique is used to price a barrier option, which needs a sample route, as a typical option with weak reliance on path. The Euler approximation method is the most used discretization path method, and the Brownian bridge method is used to create paths to minimize inaccuracy in the discretization process. This gives rise to the BBPR-QMC technique. Assuming that stock prices obey geometric Brownian motion, consider the price of a knock-down call option and use the classical Monte Carlo simulation to simulate the knock-down call option price.

For comparison, the example in literature [7] is selected: the initial price of the stock is $50, the risk-free interest rate is 0.1, the time is 5 months, and the standard deviation of the annual volatility of the stock is 0.4. Under different barrier values and option strike prices, the MC method, the R-QMC method and the BBPR-QMC method in this paper are used to simulate the price of the down-knock call option, and the simulation variance is calculated. The left panel of Fig. 2 compares the option prices of the three methods with the theoretical value of the option, and the right panel compares the variances of the three methods. R-OMC method introduces quasi-random sequence but increases the error. The variance of MC method is smaller than that of R-QMC method. The BBPR-QMC method fills the sample path through the method of Brownian bridge and random number, and can effectively control the sample variance, so as to obtain a better estimation result, which is consistent with the theoretical value, and has the highest accuracy among the three methods [8, 9].

3.3 Expressway Construction

Two cities A and B intend to invest in the construction of a expressway connecting the two cities in order to promote rapid economic development. The project's estimated construction period is two years, with a total construction investment of 5,307.8 million yuan. After the project is completed, the government grants the original owner the right of toll collection and management for 30 years, and the original owner is responsible for the expressway's management and maintenance costs. According to the project plan, the total traffic flow in the first year after completion and opening is anticipated to be 695 million vehicles (converted into small vehicles), with an average yearly growth rate of 7% and a fluctuation rate of 8%. The anticipated toll rate is 0.5 yuan per vehicle (based on small vehicles), with an increase of 16% every five years. The management cost reflects the normal distribution of N\ (2000,7002), while the maintenance cost grows at a 3% annual rate. The maintenance cost is expected to be 8.5 million yuan in the first year. The percentage of free vehicles is 2%, the project income tax rate is 25%, and the discount rate after correcting for project risk is 9%.

If the potential value contained in uncertain factors such as future traffic volume and management cost is not considered, the calculation is carried out according to the traditional *NPV* method. For the uncertain variable of traffic volume Q, the annual growth rate is 7%, without considering the fluctuation factor σ. For the management cost that follows the normal distribution, it can be calculated according to the mean value of 20 million yuan, and the market value of the project can be obtained by substituting it into the following formula:

$$NV(t) = [Q(t)a(1-c) - G(t) - W(t)](1 - r_1) \tag{9}$$

$Q(t)$ is the annual traffic volume of this section of expressway in year t; a is the expected prevailing rate; c is the percentage of free vehicles in the passing vehicles to the total passing vehicles; $G(t)$ is the annual management cost after the completion and operation of the highway; $W(t)$ is the annual maintenance fee after the completion and operation of the highway; r_1 is the income tax rate and is a certain value (the income tax rate will generally not change every year after completion)

$$V = \frac{-K + \sum_{t=1}^{T} NV(t)}{(1+r)^{t+2}} \tag{10}$$

K is the initial investment of the expressway project; T is the franchise period of the project; r is the risk-adjusted discount rate of the project. According to the basic idea of Monte Carlo simulation, and with the help of the reduction method of the variance of dual variables, according to the following formula,

$$C = \frac{1}{N} \sum_i \left(\frac{\widehat{C_i + \overline{C_i}}}{2} \right) \tag{11}$$

$$NV(t) = [Q(t)a(1-c) - G(t) - W(t)](1-r_1) \qquad (12)$$

The traffic volume Q follows geometric Brownian motion

$$dQ = \mu Q dt + \sigma Q \varepsilon \sqrt{dt} \qquad (13)$$

For geometric Brownian motion, the recursive form of the traffic volume Q in discrete time is shown below

$$Q(t) = Q(t-1) exp\left[\left(\frac{\mu - \sigma^2}{2}\right)\Delta t + \sigma \varepsilon_t \sqrt{\Delta t}\right] \qquad (14)$$

If the value of traffic depends on $Q(t)$, then the above formula can be used to give the value of $Q(t)$ after "one step", which will save calculation time

$$Q(t) = Q(1) exp\left[\left(\frac{\mu - \sigma^2}{2}\right)t + \sigma \varepsilon \sqrt{t}\right] \qquad (15)$$

$Q(1)$ is the traffic volume in the first year; μ is the annual growth rate of traffic volume, σ is the fluctuation rate of traffic volume, and μ and σ are assumed to be constant. ε is a random, fluctuating term that follows the normal distribution $N(0, 1)$.

$$V = \frac{-K + \sum_{t=1}^{T} NV(t)}{(1+r)^{t+2}} \qquad (16)$$

MATLAB software programming is used to simulate the relevant data of the expressway construction project. Through 40 000 random number inputs, Simulate and calculate the market value of the project, and output the simulation results of the market value of the project. When the Monte Carlo simulation method is used to evaluate the value of highway projects, the simulation results tend to be stable with the increase of simulation times, that is, the simulation results converge. The following Fig. 3 depicts the intuitive convergence process.

The more intuitive simulation results in the project value convergence process diagram show that the majority of the project's market value is concentrated in the interval [216 862, 217 332], with a probability of 95% in this interval. The results in this interval converge to *RMB* 2,170.97 million, which is the project's market value. The calculation results show that the project value calculated after accounting for project uncertainty factors is significantly higher than the project value calculated using the traditional *NPV* method. When the number of simulations increases from 1000 to 3000, both the simulation results using the reduction method of variance of dual variables and those without the method converge quickly, and the simulation results then stabilise in a specific interval as the number of simulations increases. However, after about 25 000 simulation times, the simulation results using the reduction method of variance of dual variables tend to be stable, whereas the simulation results without the reduction method of variance of dual variables still fluctuate around the mean, and the magnitude is greater than that using the simulation results of variance of dual variables. Moreover, the standard deviation of the simulated outcomes obtained using this method is substantially lower than the

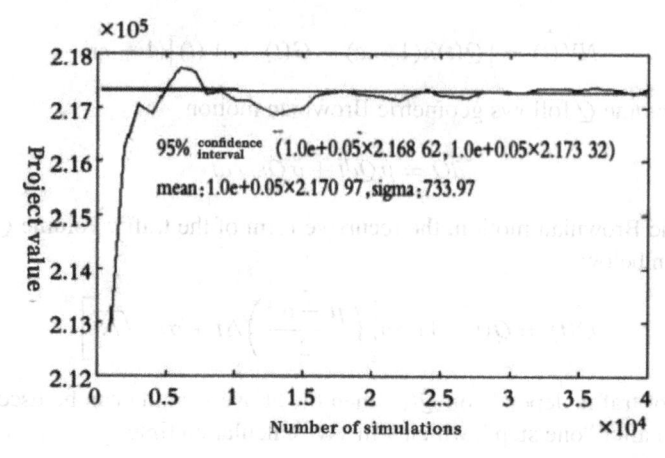

Fig. 3. Simulation results.

standard deviation of the results acquired without employing this method. When Monte Carlo simulation for project value is performed, the variance reduction technology of dual variables can cause the simulation results to quickly converge and tend to be stable in the case of few simulation times, thus reducing simulation times and saving calculation cost. Meanwhile, reducing variation in the simulation process helps to improve simulation accuracy. This increases the realism of the project value simulation findings [10].

4 Limitations

Through the basic principle of Monte Carlo simulation and its application in the field of economics and finance, its research scope is limited to the problem of randomness. Thereby, for deterministic problems, one still needs to use statistical methods to transform them into stochastic problems, which reflects the limitations of Monte Carlo simulation in the application of objects. Secondly, from the simulation results of Monte Carlo method, although researchers can take some methods to reduce the error of their simulation, such as BBPR-QMC method used in the study of the application of Monte Carlo simulation in barrier options, the error of the result is probability error, which cannot be eliminated. Researchers can only reduce the error by taking a series of measures so as to get a more accurate result for research and prediction. In addition, the initial needle throwing experiment reflects that Monte Carlo simulation always requires a large number of calculation steps, which leads to a huge amount of computation in operation. Finally, this paper only studies the application of Monte Carlo simulation in the field of finance. At present, Monte Carlo method is widely used in financial engineering, macroeconomics, biomedicine, computational physics (such as particle transport calculation, quantum thermodynamics calculation, aerodynamic calculation, nuclear engineering), computer science and engineering (non-deterministic calculation) and other fields.

The classical Monte Carlo method has the disadvantage of large errors and slow convergence speed, which will affect the accuracy of the simulation. However, research into optimizing Monte Carlo simulations has made significant strides in recent years. The quasi Monte Carlo (QMC) method is generated based on the development of random sequences such as the Halton sequence, the Faure sequence, and the Sobol sequence. For the discretization error problem, the pseudo-random number in the Monte Carlo method is replaced by a Faure sequence, and the randomization quasi Monte Carlo (R-QMC) method is obtained using the Moro algorithm. The Brownian bridge path randomization quasi Monte Carlo (BBPR-QMC) is presented in conjunction with the technique of path generation by Brownian bridge. Numerical experiments show that the BBPR-QMC method and the R-QMC method are more efficient than the classical Monte Carlo method, with lower fluctuation variance and higher simulation accuracy. In terms of the field of application of Monte Carlo simulation, it is very possible that Monte Carlo simulation will be applied to the research and development of artificial intelligence in the future. Perhaps it can transform something in human society into a random problem, give a better answer or solution through big data simulation, and give some feasible suggestions for the event. If this were to happen, it would be a huge leap for Monte Carlo simulation and a boost for the career of artificial intelligence.

5 Conclusion

In summary, this study describes the process of using Monte Carlo simulation in real estate investment projects, barrier alternatives, and highway building by examining its application in finance and economics. Computer technology optimizes the Monte Carlo modelling technique during the process. The Monte Carlo simulation analysis provides more accurate anticipated results and feasibility recommendations in many aspects for the aforementioned financial and economic issues. Although Monte Carlo simulation has limitations such as limited study subjects, unavoidable errors, and a large quantity of calculation, it has great growth potential and may be used in the field of AI in the future. To sum up, the purpose of this article is to help people comprehend Monte Carlo simulation from the viewpoint of financial economics. In addition, when people face problems in various fields, Monte Carlo simulation method and the thinking mode of probability and statistics behind it can be used as the best method to study and solve problems.

References

1. Binder, K., Heermann, D.W.: Monte Carlo Simulation Methods in Statistical Physics. Peking University Press (1994)
2. Yao, L.H.: Investigation and simulation of radiation protection of fixed industrial X and γ inspection equipment by Monte-Carlo method. Xinjiang University (2016)
3. Huang, Z.F.: MCNP program Instruction. Data from Nuclear Power Software Center, NPSC 0105, pp. 1–20 (1986)
4. Rubinstein, R.: Simulation and the Monte Carlo Method, pp. 32–41. New York (1981)
5. Briesmeister, J.F.: MCNP4C General Monte Carlo N-particle transport code, pp. 1–28. Los Alamos National Laboratory, LA-13709-M (2000)
6. Zhou, Z.G., Huo, Z.G., She, Y.B., et al.: Risk assessment of real estate project investment based on Monte Carlo. J. Yangzhou Univ. (Nat. Sci. Edn.) **24**(06), 1–7 (2021)

7. Pelsser, A.: Efficient Methods for Valuing Interest Rate Derivatives. Springer, New York (2000). https://doi.org/10.1007/978-1-4471-3888-4
8. Huang, H., Yang, X., Yang, X.: Barrier option pricing an efficient Monte Carlo method. J. Chin. Sci. Pap. Online Boutique Pap. **14**(4), 440–446 (2021)
9. Huang, H.: Two types of option pricing model of Monte Carlo simulation. North China Electric Power University, Beijing (2022)
10. Wang, J., Qi, C.: Application of Monte Carlo simulation method in highway project value evaluation. Account. Monthly **553**(21), 52–54 (2010)

InstaCart Analysis: Use PCA with K-Means to Segment Grocery Customers

Chenyu Lang[✉]

University of British Columbia, Vancouver, BC, Canada
`emma0203@student.ubc.ca`

Abstract. Researching customer classification can effectively help businesses predict future buying trends and help customers have a better purchase experience. The study can be applied to major retail enterprises to help them improve the payment conversion rate and order rate at the same cost. This paper uses InstaCart as the subject of the study and analyses its customer orders for three years. The classification results of the study to describe each clusters' characteristics and help enterprises maintain the best level of inventory supply. The study is based on the Gold Award python notebook of participant Andrea Sindico. Principal Component Analysis is a machine learning approach in various applications. This paper aims to use PCA to find new dimensions and to cluster the customers by their purchase behaviour. After analysis, this study only keep the top 6 key component and chooses two best-selling of the six aisles (PC1 and PC4). The study resulting in four different clusters for customer segmentation, and different clusters have their unique characteristics for customers' future orders.

Keywords: Data Science · Machine Learning · K-means · Principal Component Analysis · Customer · Segmentation · Grocery

1 Introduction

Have you ever seen thousands of products but needed help deciding what to buy? People are unique individuals, and each individual has different shopping habits. The effective use of customer segmentation management can help companies to create more value more efficiently and at the same cost. Customer classification management can formulate different marketing strategies according to customers' different demand characteristics, consumption behavior, expectations, reputation, etc. Customer spending behaviour is a reflection of the customer's consumer psychology, which allows companies to develop more targeted marketing programmes and resource management. Targeting enhancements to different customer characteristics maximises customer value and the return on business investment. An effective customer segmentation approach can significantly increase a company's sales and build a sustainable and scalable e-commerce business.

Within the last decade, there have been many studies showing that many offline enterprises is trying to use customer segmentation by various variables. According to Gil-Saura and Ruiz-Molina, they analyses customers by cost conversion rate, logistics services, shop quality, attitude, trust, commitment and other factors, and identifies the two most influential customer segmentation characteristics for retail businesses [1]. Yılmaz Benk et al. use Customer lifetime value (CLV) as a metric for multi-category e-commerce retailers, and segment customers their valuable for the retailers [2].

As technology continues to evolve, online shopping has partially replaced experiential shopping in physical shops, they have also started to use specific customer segments to drive sales. Pauwels et al. has concluded that while online shopping provides customers with information on products and prices, online transaction rates depend heavily on matching product and customer categories [3].

Some other companies have even begun to use customer classification as a prediction system. According to Gulfraz et al. proposed that online customers' shopping experience (OCSE) is a important factor to strongly predict online impulsive buying behaviour [4]. Besides, Magesh et al. use Artificial Neural Network (ANN) algorithm to determine whether customers will buy again online [5]. The proposed model strongly predicted that 84.6 percent of e-shoppers as either repeat purchases or will not repeat purchases.

In order to divide customers into different groups according to their behaviors, there are various types of machine learning can be chosen. In last few decades, the most common machine learning algorithm used for customer classification problems is the k-means clustering algorithm. According to Christy et al. efficiently segment customers with similar behaviour based on the RFM value (Recency, Frequency and Monetary), and extend to the cluster using K-means and Fuzzy C-Means algorithms [6]. Bilgihan et al. also help company develops marketing strategies that are specific to an individual segment to retain customers [7].

There is also a rich literature on customer analysis by using principal component analysis. The use of PCA has been successful in the telecommunications and apparel industries. Alkhayrat et al. used PCA to reduce the dimension, applied K-means clustering and performed telecom customer segmentation [8]. They also shows the Silhouette score results after PCA. Bandyopadhyay et al. also used PCA to combine product variables (clothing brand, size, price) and effectively segmented customers by using the K-Means clustering algorithm [9]. They successfully built an online recommendation system for their customer. The system not only helps customers to meet their purchase requirements, but also helps companies to manage their supply chains and develop strategies.

However, the existing studies do not explain the detailed classification process and do not focus on companies in the grocery industry. Therefore, this research will be conducted using Instacart company as an example for the grocery industry. The main purpose is to enrich the customer analysis research of the grocery industry and apply our research to the whole industry. The research will help companies to better capture user characteristics and help them to increase their online sales through effectively conversion click rates. The detailed segmentation model will help other companies to provide a good case study and help them to build a long-term stable and growing online sales platform.

2 Data and Method

2.1 Data Source

InstaCart is a retail company with online services that provides grocery delivery and pick-up services in the United States and Canada. The InstaCart grocery shop has a wide range of products for customers, but too much choice can lead to confusion, ending with no purchase.

InstaCart is looking for a more effective way to increase order conversion rates through Kaggle competitions. By predicting customer shopping behaviour, the business hopes to help confused customers find targeted items and keep stock levels at a good level over time. Segmenting customers is meaningful, and this research is not only valid for InstaCart, but also for other businesses facing similar situations.

Users on Kaggles find and publish datasets, use the data science environment to explore and build models, and join competitions to solve challenges. InstaCart asked Kaggle users to published data on customer orders to guess which products will be in customer's next order. InstaCart provides data from more than 200,000 users. Multiple orders per customer are provided for research into customer purchase behaviour analysis, and result in over 3 million orders. The dataset also provides user's purchase behaviour and sequence.

This paper is based on Andrea Sindico's python notebook, which won the gold medal in this competition [10]. Sindico aims to use PCA to reduce the dimension and "predict" possible future purchases depending on different clusters. Like previous research, Andrea Sindico tried to apply PCA for the InstaCart grocery application. The python notebook aims to create a product prediction system based on the order of transactions, shopping cart additions and orders for online shopping. The system helps shoppers to get more targeted product recommendations, thus increasing product sales and improving the customer's online shopping experience.

2.2 Data Exploration and Filter

In total, InstaCart company provided six CSV files. Raw data need to Explore and cleaned before data analysis. As there are thousands of items, the dataset uses the aisles numbers of the items to represent the product categories. An aisle is a long narrow gap between rows of shelves in a supermarket. 143 Aisle IDs are used to identify the products, and each aisle is given a descriptive name. 21 product departments is treated the same way, with its own ID and department summary. There are some null values when exploring the raw data. Aisle 100 and department 21 were eliminated to ensure the accuracy of the data analysis that followed, results in 142 aisles and 20 sections overall (see Table 1. & 2.).

Table 1. Raw data for 142 aisle (only first 10 aisles was shown due to limited space).

Aisle_id	Example
1	prepared soups salads
2	specialty cheeses
3	energy granola bars
4	instant foods
5	marinades meat preparation
6	other
7	packaged meat
8	bakery desserts
9	pasta sauce
10	kitchen supplies
...	...

Table 2. Raw data for 20 department (only 10 department was shown due to limited space).

Department_id	Department
1	frozen
2	other
3	bakery
4	produce
5	alcohol
6	international
7	beverages
8	pets
9	dry goods pasta
10	bulk
...	...

Following the consolidation of 49688 products, information on each product is summarized on the same line. Such information includes the product number, the product name, the aisle number and the department number to which it belongs (see see Table 3.).

After processing the information about the product, move forward to user information. The *user_id* code serves to identify users. In addition to the encoding, the dataset provides additional information about the user's purchases, such as *order_dow*, *order_hour_of_day*, and *days_since_prior_order* (see Table 4.). Aimed to describe the future purchases of users based on their previous shopping habits, InstaCart provides a

Table 3. Integrated 49688 products' data (only first 20 products was shown).

Product_id	Product_name	Aisle_id	Department_id
1	Chocolate Sandwich Cookies	61	19
2	All-Seasons Salt	104	13
3	Robust Golden Unsweetened Oolong Tea	94	7
4	Smart Ones Classic Favorites Mini Rigatoni With Vodka Cream Sauce	38	1
5	Green Chile Anytime Sauce	5	13
6	Dry Nose Oil	11	11
7	Pure Coconut Water With Orange	98	7
8	Cut Russet Potatoes Steam N' Mash	116	1
9	Light Strawberry Blueberry Yogurt	120	16
10	Sparkling Orange Juice & Prickly Pear Beverage	115	7
11	Peach Mango Juice	31	7
12	Chocolate Fudge Layer Cake	119	1
13	Saline Nasal Mist	11	11
14	Fresh Scent Dishwasher Cleaner	74	17
15	Overnight Diapers Size 6	56	18
16	Mint Chocolate Flavored Syrup	103	19
17	Rendered Duck Fat	35	12
18	Pizza for One Suprema Frozen Pizza	79	1
19	Gluten Free Quinoa Three Cheese & Mushroom Blend	63	9
20	Pomegranate Cranberry & Aloe Vera Enrich Drink	98	7
...	...	...	...

combination of 4–100 order records for each user. For constructing the segmentation, each user's orders were divided into n-1 previous orders and 1 training order, or n-1 previous orders and 1 test order. The data on the user's behavioral habits also includes the order in which products were added to the shopping cart and the order in which they were purchased.

There is some null value in the variable *days since previous order*. Order number 1 shows null value twice in the raw dateset (see Table 4.). After retrieving the data for this variable, the highest value of the data was 30. It is improbable that all users have made a second purchase on the thirtieth day of the interval, and I hypothesize that the data for this variable will always show 30 if the day length is equal to or more than one month. Those null values may appear because the user has not purchased for over a month, and the data collection tool entered an invalid value in error rather than replacing it with 30. For further analysis in the future, all null values have been replaced with 30.

Table 4. Variables about customer behavior (only first 15 order' id was shown).

Order_id	User_id	Eval_set	Order_number	Order_dow	Order_hour_of_day	Days_since_prior_order
2539329	1	prior	1	2	8	
2398795	1	prior	2	3	7	15
473747	1	prior	3	3	12	21
2254736	1	prior	4	4	7	29
431534	1	prior	5	4	15	28
3367565	1	prior	6	2	7	19
550135	1	prior	7	1	9	20
3108588	1	prior	8	1	14	14
2295261	1	prior	9	1	16	0
2550362	1	prior	10	4	8	30
1187899	1	train	11	4	8	14
2168274	2	prior	1	2	11	
1501582	2	prior	2	5	10	10
1901567	2	prior	3	1	10	3
738281	2	prior	4	2	10	8
...	...	...	...	...	...	...

Following the data-cleaning process, all data and variables were integrated, resulting in 14 variables. The 14 variables led to a complex high dimensionality, which made it extremely challenging to segment customers. Hence, principal component analysis (PCA) was used to reformat the data into smaller-dimensional (only keep top 6 principal component) while attempting to keep the majority of the information intact (Table 5).

Table 5. Variables after data filtering [10].

Order_id	Product_id	Add_to_cart_order	Record	Product_name	Aisle_id	Department_id	User_id	Eval_set	Order_number	Order_dow
2	33120	1	1	Organic Egg Whites	86	16	202279	Prior	3	5
26	33121	5	0	Organic Egg Whites	87	17	153404	Prior	2	0
120	33122	13	0	Organic Egg Whites	88	18	23750	Prior	11	6
327	33123	5	1	Organic Egg Whites	89	19	58707	Prior	21	6
390	33124	28	1	Organic Egg Whites	90	20	66654	Prior	48	0
537	33125	2	1	Organic Egg Whites	91	21	180135	Prior	15	2

(*continued*)

Table 5. (*continued*)

Order_id	Product_id	Add_to_cart_order	Record	Product_name	Aisle_id	Department_id	User_id	Eval_set	Order_number	Order_dow
582	33126	7	1	Organic Egg Whites	92	22	193223	Prior	6	2
608	33127	5	1	Organic Egg Whites	93	23	91030	Prior	11	3
623	33128	1	1	Organic Egg Whites	94	24	37804	Prior	63	3
689	33129	4	1	Organic Egg Whites	95	25	108932	Prior	16	1
...	...	...	...	...	...	...	...	...	...	...

3 Clustering

3.1 Clustering Customers

With thousands of products in the dataset, relying on 142 aisles makes it more efficient for future data analysis. In 142 aisle types, fresh fruit and fresh vegetables are the best-selling items. Each user_id was substituted with the cluster to which they belong, to find clusters for customers (Tables 6 and 7).

Table 6. Aisle types sales top 10 ranking [10].

Aisle types	Numbers
fresh fruits	33755
fresh vegetables	31004
packaged vegetables fruits	16319
yogurt	13477
packaged cheese	9133
milk	8254
water seltzer sparkling water	7634
chips pretzels	6581
soy lactosefree	5965
bread	5457

Although products have been replaced by their aisles, there were still too many features to analyze. The principal component analysis enabled the clustering to be made less complicated by creating new dimensions. With PCA, the same number of variables were obtained as before, but the new variables diagonalized the covariance matrix. The new variables are formed from the original variables and attempt to capture most of their characteristics. In the process of PCA, the original data is projected onto the new basis vector (PC). Thus, the negative values obtained are not in the original space but the new

Table 7. User's aisle purchase type [10].

User_id	Aisle							
	Air fresheners candles	Asian foods	Baby food formula	Baking supplies decor	...	Beauty	Spreads	Tea
13	0	0	0	0		0	0	0
23	0	0	0	1		0	0	1
27	0	0	0	0		1	0	0
36	0	0	0	0		0	0	0
42	0	0	0	0		0	0	0
66	0	0	0	1		0	0	0
67	0	0	0	0		0	0	0
70	0	0	0	0		0	0	0
71	0	0	0	1		0	2	0
...	...	...	...	...	...	...	...	...

coordinate system. After calculating all the PCs, the original data has been rewritten and recorded in terms of the PCs. For K-Means clustering, the two best-selling of the six principal component (PC1 and PC4) have been chosen for the principal component analysis (Table 8).

Table 8. PCA (n_components = 6) [10].

	0	1	2	3	4	5
0	−0.286251	1.005868	−1.030293	-0.898912	−0.587639	−0.998674
1	−1.972748	−0.487659	−0.120542	0.213114	0.045948	−0.181976
2	−1.168974	1.284089	3.228124	0.594040	−0.648839	−1.091874
3	−1.433967	1.250081	3.261985	1.237734	−0.353569	−0.346436
4	−2.070709	−0.422148	−0.101553	0.278172	0.005972	−0.097313

Following the completion of dimensionality reduction, information compression, and data de-noising through the effective application of principal component analysis (PCA), the number of clusters was decided to be 4. A PCA biplot displays both the principal component scores (represented by dots) and the variables (vectors). The greater the distance between these vectors and the origin of a PC, the greater their influence on that PC. After randomly creating the center points of four clusters, each sample belongs to the cluster with the shortest distance. Afterwards, potential clustering for the customers has been successfully identified.

After using PCA to complete dimensionality reduction, information compression, and data de-noising, four have been chosen as the number of clusters. A PCA biplot displays both the loadings of variables (vectors) and the PC scores of samples (dots). These vectors have a more significant impact on a PC the further they are from the PC's point of origin. After randomly creating the center points of four clusters, each sample belongs to the cluster with the shortest distance. Following that, four potential clusters for the customers have been successfully identified (Table 9 and Fig. 1).

Table 9. PC1 and PC4 (25831, 2) [10].

	4	1
0	−0.587639	1.005868
1	0.045948	−0.487659
2	−0.648839	1.284089
3	−0.353569	1.250081
4	0.005972	−0.422148

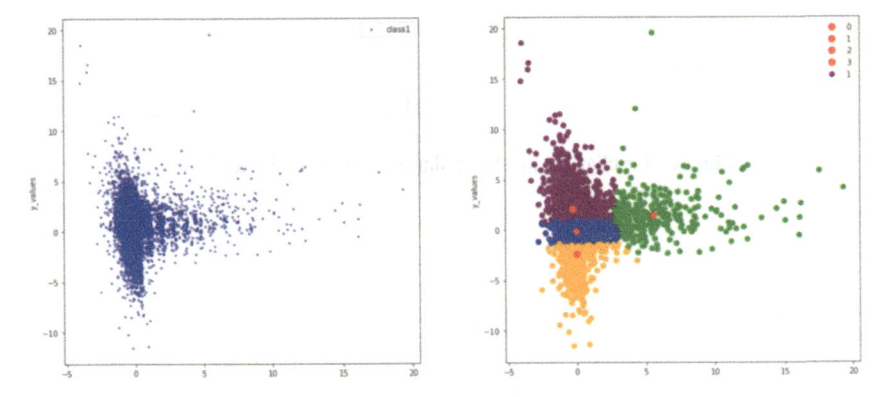

Fig. 1. PCA biplot, KMeans (n_clusters = 4) [10].

3.2 Top Goods in Four Clusters

Based on the four clusters, Python generated data for the product aisle in each cluster. The top ten product aisle sales for each cluster are reported in these bar charts. Data has been evaluated to see if clusters differed in number and proportion, or if one cluster had items not found in other clusters (Figs. 2, 3, 4 and 5).

```
aisle
fresh vegetables              4.620428
fresh fruits                  1.163216
packaged vegetables fruits    0.922015
packaged cheese               0.423395
fresh herbs                   0.421670
soy lactosefree               0.288475
yogurt                        0.287095
frozen produce                0.282264
milk                          0.279848
canned jarred vegetables      0.261560
dtype: float64
```

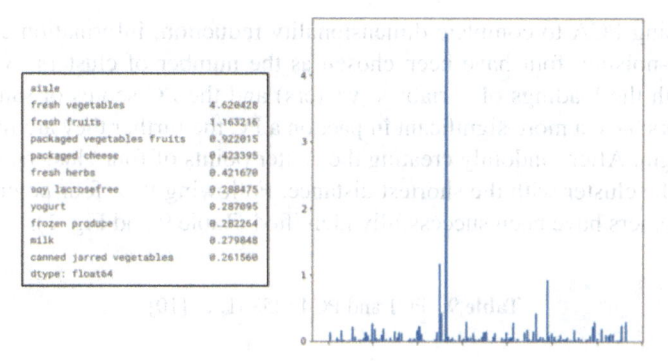

Fig. 2. Bar chat for most popular aisle type in cluster 0 [10].

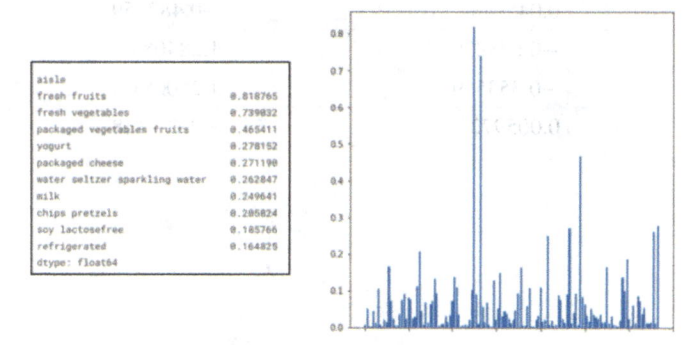

```
aisle
fresh fruits                     0.818765
fresh vegetables                 0.739832
packaged vegetables fruits       0.465411
yogurt                           0.278152
packaged cheese                  0.271190
water seltzer sparkling water    0.262847
milk                             0.249641
chips pretzels                   0.205824
soy lactosefree                  0.185766
refrigerated                     0.164825
dtype: float64
```

Fig. 3. Bar chat for most popular aisle type in cluster 1 [10].

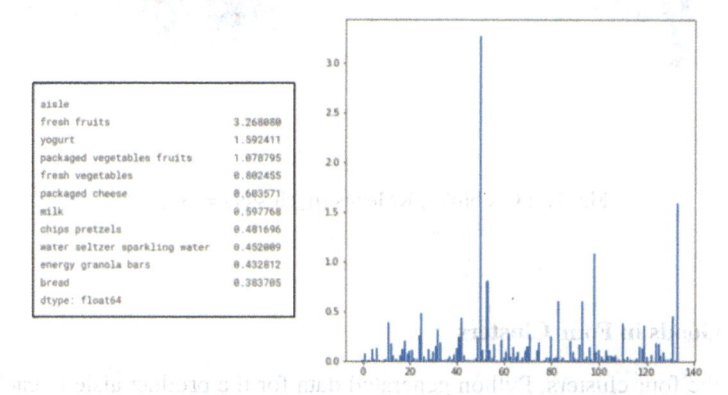

```
aisle
fresh fruits                     3.268080
yogurt                           1.592411
packaged vegetables fruits       1.078795
fresh vegetables                 0.802455
packaged cheese                  0.683571
milk                             0.597768
chips pretzels                   0.481696
water seltzer sparkling water    0.452009
energy granola bars              0.432812
bread                            0.383705
dtype: float64
```

Fig. 4. Bar chat for most popular aisle type in cluster 2 [10].

For further conducting data analysis, the eight most popular product aisles have been specified based on the absolute data and percentages of each aisle in each of the four clusters. People who belonged to Cluster 0 bought significantly more 'fresh vegetables' than those who belonged to any of the other clusters; people who belonged to Cluster 2

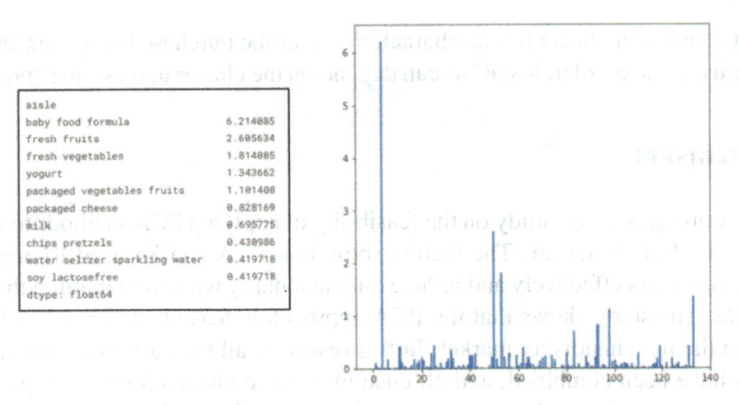

aisle	
baby food formula	6.214885
fresh fruits	2.605634
fresh vegetables	1.814885
yogurt	1.343662
packaged vegetables fruits	1.101408
packaged cheese	0.828169
milk	0.695775
chips pretzels	0.430986
water seltzer sparkling water	0.419718
soy lactosefree	0.419718
dtype: float64	

Fig. 5. Bar chat for most popular aisle type in cluster 3 [10].

bought significantly more 'fresh fruit'; and people who belonged to Cluster 3 bought a lot of 'baby food formula', which was not even listed in the top 8 highest selling products (Table 10).

Table 10. Percentage of top aisle type in each cluster (Andrea, 2017).

	Fresh fruits	Fresh vegetables	Packaged vegetables fruits	Yogurt	Packaged cheese	Milk	Water seltzer sparkling water	Chips pretzels
0	14.313617	56.855335	11.345590	3.532759	5.209970	−0.998674	3.443591	2.314127
1	24.879949	22.457101	14.142517	8.452265	8.240707	−0.181976	7.585883	6.254407
2	36.816033	9.039932	12.152987	17.939046	6.799437	−1.091874	6.734058	5.426474
3	28.201220	19.634146	11.920732	14.542683	8.963415	−0.346436	7.530488	4.664634

4 Segment Analysis

After successfully classifying customers into clusters using PCA with K-Means, it illustrates that customers belonging to cluster 0 were more likely to purchase fresh vegetables (56.86%), fresh fruits (14.31%), and packaged vegetables fruits (11.35%) in the following order. Customers from cluster 1 were more likely to purchase fresh fruits (24.87%), fresh vegetables (22.46%), and packaged vegetables fruits (14.14%) in the following order. Customers in cluster 2 were more likely to purchase fresh fruits (36.81%), yogurt (17.94%), and packaged vegetable fruits (12.15%) in the following order. Customers belonging to cluster 3 were more likely to purchase baby food formula (67.23%), fresh fruits (28.20%), and fresh vegetable fruits (19.63%) in the following order.

According to the above analysis, it shows two best-selling of the six aisles (PC1 and PC4) was chosen for the principal component analysis. Resulting in 4 clusters of customers, and each cluster has its characteristics of the purchase behaviour. In order to guess the user's next order, InstaCart can depend on the cluster to make the "prediction".

5 Conclusion

This paper presents a case study on the feasibility of applying PCA methods to customer analysis based on InstaCart. The results show that PCA can be used to analyse and segment customers effectively and reduce dimensionality while maintaining the validity of the data. The study shows that the PCA approach is feasible and can be effectively applied to the merchandising market. In this research, all the customer's buying habits variables have been combined, and all customers were clustered into four groups. For future recommendation and improvement, choose an odd number for clustering to prevent the situation from the same distance from the sample to every cluster. The variable "*days since_ prior_order*" is also a variable of interest for segmenting customers, as order frequency also affects product type and order value. A customer who buys something fresh every day and buys a week's supply of food once a week through InstaCart are two apparent clusters of customers.

The research successfully describe the customer's future purchasing tendencies, which can further improve into a recommended system which suggests corresponding aisles products for customers more effectively. In addition, establishing a recommendation system could significantly boost transaction conversion rates. A successful prediction system can also help retailers maintain optimal stock levels. Prediction systems can help companies build sustainable, profitable, and scalable e-commerce businesses.

However, this paper also has some limitation. The principal component analysis is a simple way to rewrite complex raw data into a two-dimensional data set while retaining most information. All the information contents have been summarized, and the clustering of customers has been done based on that. Even though this is a safe and easy way to make linear regression, it still contains disadvantages. The biggest weakness of this machine learning algorithm is the difficulties in explaining the new dimensions (PCs). Due to the combination of variables and original data projected onto new basis vectors, it's hard to explain the causal relationship or correlation between variables. It should be further explored in future search.

References

1. Gil-Saura, I., Ruiz-Molina, M.E.: Retail customer segmentation based on relational benefits. J. Relationsh. Mark. **8**(3), 253–266 (2009)
2. Yılmaz Benk, G., Badur, B., Mardikyan, S.: A new 360° framework to predict customer lifetime value for multi-category e-commerce companies using a multi-output deep neural network and explainable artificial intelligence. Information **13**(8), 373 (2022)
3. Pauwels, K., Leeflang, P.S.H., Teerling, M.L., Huizingh, K.R.E.: Does online information drive offline revenues? J. Retail. **87**(1), 1–17 (2011)
4. Gulfraz, M.B., Sufyan, M., Mustak, M., Salminen, J., Srivastava, D.K.: Understanding the impact of online customers' shopping experience on online impulsive buying. J. Retail. Consum. Serv. **68**, 103000 (2022)

5. Magesh, K.R., Pradeep, E., Vakayil, S.: Predicting the dynamics of customer repurchase in internet shopping-an artificial neural network (ANN) approach. Acad. Mark. Stud. J. **26**(2) (2022)
6. Christy, A.J., Umamakeswari, A., Priyatharsini, L., Neyaa, A.: RFM ranking–an effective approach to customer segmentation. J. King Saud Univ. - Comput. Inf. Sci. **33**(10) (2018)
7. Bilgihan, A., Kandampully, J., Zhang, T. (Christina).: Towards a unified customer experience in online shopping environments. Int. J. Qual. Serv. Sci. **8**(1), 102–119 (2016)
8. Alkhayrat, M., Aljnidi, M., Aljoumaa, K.: A comparative dimensionality reduction study in telecom customer segmentation using deep learning and PCA. J. Big Data **7**(1) (2020)
9. Bandyopadhyay, S., Thakur, S.S., Mandal, J.K.: Product recommendation for e-commerce business by applying principal component analysis (PCA) and K-means clustering: Benefit for the society. Innov. Syst. Softw. Eng. **17**(1) (2021)
10. Andrea, S.: Customer Segments with PCA. Kaggle Homepage (2017). http://www.kaggle.com/code/asindico/customer-segments-with-pca. Accessed 10 Mar 2023

Research on the Influencing Factors of Housing Prices Based on Multiple Regression: Taking Chongqing as an Example

Yijia Qi(✉)

School of Public Finance and Taxation, Southwestern University of Finance and Economics, Chengdu 611130, China

42003051@smail.swufe.edu.cn

Abstract. With the continuous growth of China's overall economy and the improvement of people's quality of life, housing prices in China are also constantly increasing. Housing prices are closely related to individual family decision-making and the national economy and have always been a hot issue in the whole society. Chongqing is the fourth municipality reporting directly to the Chinese central government. And also the economic and political center of the Southwest region. For the entire real estate market, the analysis of the factors that affect housing prices in Chongqing is of great importance. Based on relevant information from the real estate sector in Chongqing, China, from 2000 to 2021, this paper takes the average room rate of commercial housing in Chongqing as the dependent variable, and selects eight factors, including consumer price index and population, as independent variables. Two main components are selected by analyzing the main components and a multiple regression model is developed. Research shows, among the eight variables, GDP, per capita disposable income, average wage per job, and per capita consumption expenditure of urban residents have significant impacts on average room rate.

Keywords: House Price · Spss · Principal Component Analysis · Multiple Linear Regression

1 Introduction

1.1 Background

Chongqing is located in the southwestern China, upstream of the Yangtze River. It extends over 82,400 square kilometers and has a permanent population of 32.13 million. It is the economic and political center of the southwestern region of China. In 1997, Chongqing was established as the fourth municipality directly under the Chinese central government. In the past 20 years, housing prices in Chongqing have increased by more than six times, and Fig. 1 shows the specific growth trend.

The housing sector is a mainstay of China's domestic economy, and the fluctuation of housing prices has become an important factor affecting the operation of the Chinese

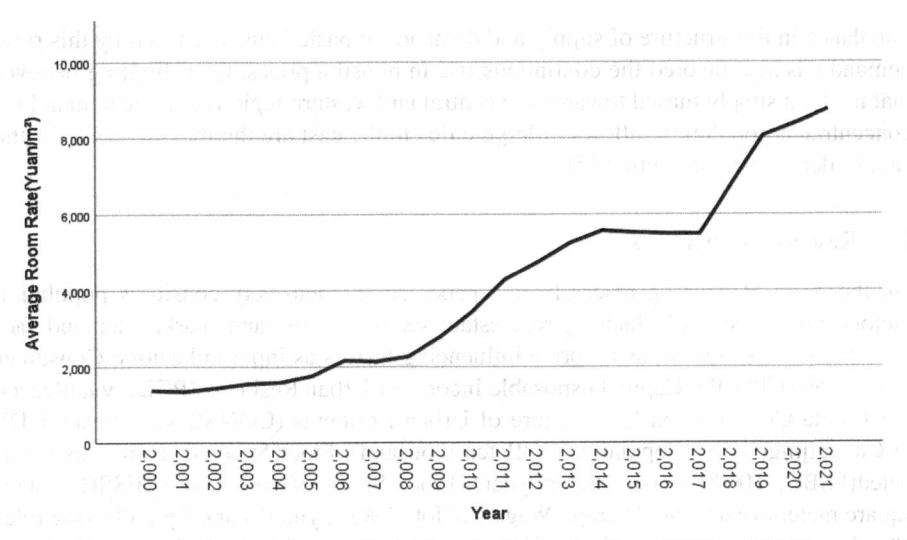

Fig. 1. The Growth Trend of Average Room Rate in Chongqing from 2000 to 2021(Photo credit: Original).

economy. In the past thirty years, the urbanization of China has expanded rapidly, with a large amount of funding coming from the real estate market [1]. In 2016, China's housing prices surged again, and the huge fluctuations in housing prices have attracted widespread attention from all sectors of society. Many complex factors have a joint effect on housing price fluctuations. The research on the influencing factors of housing prices will help to summarize the formation rules of housing prices, guide the healthy and orderly development of the real estate, and prevent the generation of foam.

1.2 Literature Review

Many researchers have investigated the causes and factors that influence changes in housing prices. Pasharde believes that gross domestic product is the best indicator to measure the local economic situation, reflects the local economy and market scale, and affects the supply and demand of housing [2]. Määättänen N believes that per capita disposable income reflects residents' consumption ability when purchasing houses, and is a guarantee of housing demand [3]. Xue Jianpu stressed that income is a major factor driving up housing prices, but its truly prominent driving force is short-term [4]. The research results of Fan Yunqi show that population growth is not a factor driving the rise of housing prices, income factors may not have an initial effect on housing prices, and land costs have an impact on housing prices [5]. Zhou Ermin pointed out that there is a positive relationship between housing prices and residents' per capita disposable income [6]. The increase in disposable income will enhance residents' ability to pay for housing, promote their pursuit of a better living environment, and stimulate the market demand for improved housing. At the same time, the increase in disposable income has also prompted some high-income individuals to choose to invest in housing. The increase in urban population has led to a direct demand for commodity housing by residents, and the imbalance in the structure of supply and demand for basic housing caused by this rigid demand has also favored the continuous rise in housing prices. Qian Jingjing believes that the land supply biased towards the central and western regions and the demand for concentrated population inflows to large cities in the east are the main reasons for the supply-demand contradiction [7].

1.3 Research Objectives

On the basis of existing research, this paper comprehensively considers population factors, macroeconomic factors, real estate sector factors, and market demand factors, and selects eight housing price influencing factors as input indicators: Consumer Price Index(CPI), Per Capita Disposable Income of Urban Residents(PCDI, yuan/year), Per Capita Consumption Expenditure of Urban Residents (CONSP, yuan/year), GDP in Chongqing(GDP), Population(POP, ten thousand), Floor Space of Buildings Competed(FSBC, 10000 square meters/year), Floor Space of sold houses(FSSH, 10000 square meters/year), and Average Wage per Job(AWPJ, yuan/year). By collecting relevant data on the real estate sector in Chongqing, China from 2000 to 2021, SPSS 26.0 was used to analyze these influencing factors, identify the main influencing factors, establish a regression model and analyze the factors influencing changes in housing prices in order to examine the reasons for the increase in housing prices.

2 Methodology

2.1 Source of Data

The variables in the economic field are interdependent and interdependent. In order to identify the factors influencing housing prices, a large amount of data must be available, and determine the factors that affect housing prices based on four aspects: population, macroeconomics, real estate industry, and market demand. This paper collects the data of CPI, PCDI, CONSP, GDP, POP, and AWPJ from the Chongqing Statistical Yearbook, and the data of completed area (FSBC) and sales area of commercial housing (FSSH) in Chongqing from the China Real Estate Yearbook. Considering the issue of missing data, this article collected 22 years of data from 2000 to 2021, qualitatively exploring the relationship between the above variables and housing prices, and analyzing the degree of correlation.

2.2 Principal Component Analysis

Principal Component Analysis (PCA) is a statistical method used for dimensionality reduction of data. Transforming potentially related variables into linearly independent variables through orthogonal transformation, that is, transforming a large number of original variables into several principal components This method integrates complex multiple sets of data variable indicators into a few comprehensive indicators through data dimensionality reduction, which does not only reduce the number of indicators that need to be compared, ensures data consistency, but also ensures the degree of interpretation of the data [8].

PCA combines multiple indicators and certain correlations to form a new set of comprehensive independent indicators [9]. It is an optimal transformation in the sense of the lowest mean square, intended to eliminate the correlation between the random input vectors and to highlight the characteristics implicit in the original data [10]. It can efficiently identify the main parts of the data, reduce the dimensionality of existing complex data, and remove redundancy from the entire data (Table 1).

Table 1. Data on the Average Room Rate and it is Influencing Factors in Chongqing from 2000 to 2021.

TIME	ARR	GDP	CPI	PCDI	CONSP	POP	FSBC	FSSH	AWPJ
2000	1377	1822.1	96.7	6176	5472	3091.09	3083.72	579.96	8020
2001	1351	2014.6	101.7	6572	5725	3097.91	4341.38	746.05	9523
2002	1443	2279.8	99.6	7238	6360	3113.83	4711.06	1381.09	10960
2003	1556	2615.58	100.6	8094	7118	3130.10	5958.8	1316.83	12440
2004	1596	3059.5	103.7	9221	7973	3144.23	5559.8	1329.32	14357
2005	1766	3448.4	100.8	10244	8623	3169.16	6384.62	2017.66	16630
2006	2167	3900.3	102.4	11569	9399	3198.87	5309.27	2228.46	19215
2007	2135	4770.7	104.7	13715	10876	3235.32	2253.14	3553.07	23098
2008	2269	5899.5	105.6	15708	12269	3257.05	2368.22	2877.92	26985
2009	2785	6651.2	98.4	17191	13507	3275.61	2907.05	4002.89	30965
2010	3442	8065.3	103.2	19099	14755	3303.45	2626.59	4314.39	35326
2011	4281	10161.2	105.2	20249	14974	3329.81	3424.33	4533.5	40042
2012	4734	11595.4	102.6	22968	16573	3343.44	3990.63	4522.4	45392
2013	5244	13027.6	102.7	23058	19049	3358.42	3804.36	4817.56	51015
2014	5569	14623.8	101.8	25147	20509	3375.20	3717.78	5100.39	56852
2015	5519	16040.5	101.3	27239	19742	3371.84	4630.29	5381.37	62091
2016	5489	18023.0	101.8	29610	21031	3392.11	4421.3	6257.15	67386
2017	5485	20066.3	101.0	32193	22759	3386.82	5055.73	6711	73272
2018	6792	21588.8	102.0	34889	24154	3403.64	4083.45	6536.25	81764
2019	8068	23605.8	102.7	37939	25785	3416.29	5069.17	6104.68	89714
2020	8402	25041.4	102.3	40006	26464	3412.71	3774.33	6143.47	98380

3 Empirical Analysis

3.1 Correlations

To ensure the accuracy of regression results and avoid errors caused by serious multicollinearity, it is necessary to first carry out a correlation test on the data.

In correlation testing, the closer the number in the table is to 1, the stronger the correlation between the two variables. It is generally assumed that when the correlation coefficients between variables are lower than 0.3, the effect obtained by applying principal component analysis is not ideal [11]. Table 2 shows that the correlation coefficient between the variables is greater than 0.8, indicating that the method of PCA is adequate.

To eliminate the errors caused by the correlation, this article adopts principal components analysis in order to create the main components from all influencing factors.

Table 2. Correlation coefficient matrix of independent variables.

	GDP	CPI	PCDI	CONSP	POP	FSBC	FSSH	AWPJ
GDP	1.000	0.062	0.994	0.987	0.911	−0.002	0.919	0.998
CPI	0.062	1.000	0.113	0.124	0.262	−0.211	0.198	0.076
PCDI	0.994	0.113	1.000	0.994	0.938	−0.062	0.940	0.997
CONSP	0.987	0.124	0.994	1.000	0.957	−0.079	0.952	0.990
POP	0.911	0.262	0.938	0.957	1.000	−0.184	0.984	0.916
FSBC	−0.002	−0.211	−0.062	−0.079	−0.184	1.000	−0.156	−0.025
FSSH	0.919	0.198	0.940	0.952	0.984	−0.156	1.000	0.919
AWPJ	0.998	0.076	0.997	0.990	0.916	−0.025	0.919	1.000

3.2 KMO and Bartlett's Test

Before applying principal component analysis, it is necessary to perform KMO and Bartlett's spherical tests on the raw data. The Bartlett Spherical Test is a test based on the correlation matrix. The initial premise of the test is that the correlation matrix should be an identity matrix. If this initial assumption is not rejected, this means that the original variables are independent of each other, so this data set is not suitable for the analysis of the main components. If the correlation matrix of the original data is an identity matrix, and the original variables are not related to each other, then the principal component analysis is performed, and the principal components obtained are the original variables themselves, which is obviously not suitable for principal component analysis.

The purpose of the KMO (Kaiser Meyer Olkin Sampling Sufficiency Measure) test is to compare the sizes of simple correlation coefficients and partial correlation coefficients between initial variables. If the KMO value is close to 1, it indicates that the bias coefficient is very small, and then principal component analysis can be performed [12].

In real analysis, the KMO is more efficient when the value exceeds 0.7. When the KMO statistic is less than 0.5, PCA is unsuited for application. When the result of SPSS test show that Sig. is less than 0.05, this is an indication that the standard is being met. The data is distributed in a spherical shape, and each variable is to some extent independent of the other.

As shown in Table 3, the KOM value is equal to 0.815, indicating a certain correlation between indicators. The Bartlett sphere test result is 413.276, and the sig. value is 0.000, which shows that each index is related. After the two tests, it can be considered that the data set in this article is suitable for the PCA method.

Table 3. KMO and Bartlett's test result.

KMO and Bartlett's Test		
Kaiser-Meyer-Olkin Measure of Sampling Adequacy		0.815
Bartlett's Test of Sphericity	Approx. Chi-Square	413.276
	df	28
	Sig.	0.000

3.3 Principal Component Analysis

Principal Components. In PCA, the number of principal components selected is generally determined through the Total Variance Explained table, and the variance interpretation rate is the core basis for determining the number of principal components. The higher the rate at which the cumulative variance is interpreted, the more representative the principal component is of the original variable. When the cumulative variance interpretation rate reaches 80%, it indicates that the original variable has been well-dimensionally reduced [13]. SPSS 26.0 was used to extract the original data using principal component analysis, and the total variance interpretation results are shown in Table 4.

Table 4. Total Variance explained.

Component	Initial Eigenvalues			Extraction Sums of Squared Loadings		
	Total	% of Variance	Cumulative %	Total	% of Variance	Cumulative %
1	5.833	72.916	72.916	5.833	72.916	72.916
2	1.231	15.393	88.309	1.231	15.393	88.309
3	0.788	9.853	98.162			
4	0.124	1.554	99.716			
5	0.016	0.201	99.917			
6	0.003	0.041	99.959			
7	0.003	0.035	99.993			
8	0.001	0.007	100.000			

Extraction Method: Principal Component Analysis

The initial eigenvalues of the first and second components are 5.833 and 1.231, with explained variance percentages of 72.916% and 15.393%, and cumulative explained variance percentages reaching 88.309%. This indicates that these two components can comprehensively express the explanatory variables of various influencing factors, and the degree of data loss is very small, with a high level of representativeness. Therefore, these two components are extracted as the main components to reflect the influencing factors of housing prices in Chongqing.

A scree plot is a scatter plot that describes the changes in principal component variance based on the order of eigenvalues in the correlation matrix. The shape of the scree plot should theoretically resemble a cliff. Starting from the first principal component, the curve rapidly descends, then the descent becomes gentle and finally becomes an approximate straight line. Obviously, the more obvious the curvature of the scree plot, the more like a cliff, and the more suitable for PCA. On the contrary, the scree plot approximates a straight line from the beginning, indicating that principal component analysis is not suitable.

The transition point and steepness of the scree plot (Fig. 2) reflect the expression level of the two components, assisted in explaining that two principal components should be selected with principal components 1 and 2 denoted as y1 and y2, respectively.

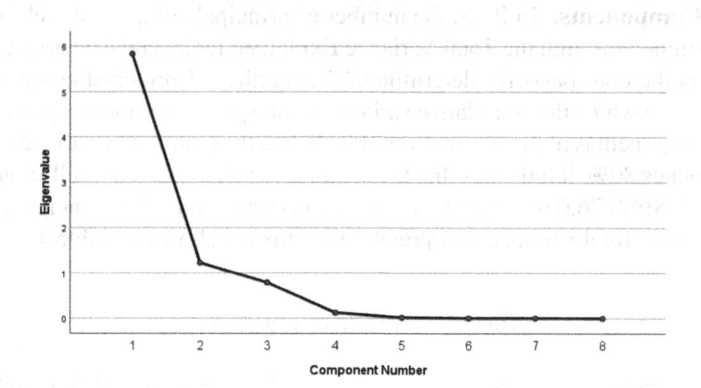

Fig. 2. Scree plot (photo credit: Original).

Calculate the Principal Component Coefficient. After selecting the two principal components, the component matrix in Table 5 can be obtained. The numerical values in the component matrix represent the relationship between the original variables and the two principal components. The closer the absolute value is to 1, the closer it is to the principal component during clustering. Table 5 shows that Component 1 has a significant impact on the first six variables, while Component 2 has a significant impact on the last two variables.

After obtaining the above matrix, the score coefficients of each component can be calculated and summarized into the component score coefficient matrix in Table 6.

Based on the principal component coefficients, the linear combination of y1 and y2 is obtained:

$$y2 = 0.05 \times CONSP + 0.069 \times PCDI + 0.114 \times AWPJ$$

Table 5. Component Matrix

	Component 1	Component 2
CONSP	0.996	0.055
PCDI	0.992	0.077
AWPJ	0.983	0.126
GDP	0.980	0.149
POP	0.972	−0.124
FSSH	0.971	−0.065
FSBC	−0.110	0.774
CPI	0.174	−0.753

Extraction Method: Principal Component Analysis

Table 6. Component score coefficient matrix

	1	2
CONSP	0.412	0.050
PCDI	0.411	0.069
AWPJ	0.407	0.114
GDP	0.406	0.134
POP	0.402	−0.112
FSSH	0.402	−0.059
FSBC	−0.046	0.698
CPI	0.072	−0.679

$$+ 0.134 \times GDP - 0.112 \times POP - 0.059 \times FSSH$$
$$+ 0.698 \times FSBC - 0.679 \times CPI \tag{1}$$

3.4 Multiple Linear Regression

Following the analysis of the main components, a multiple linear regression model was developed to perform linear regression analysis on y1, y2, and ARR. The regression equation was obtained as follows:

$$ARR = 4101.455 + 990.125 y1 + 235.505 y2 \tag{2}$$

In the above equation, ARR represents the value of standardized housing prices in Chongqing. According to Table 7, the t-statistic corresponding to the parameters is greater than 1.96, and the determinable coefficient R^2 is 0.958, indicating that the model is fit for purpose, has high data reliability, and has significant significance. Principal components y1 and y2 are important influencing factors of housing prices in Chongqing. The regression equation of ARR regarding the original variable can be obtained:

$$ARR = 4101.455 + 419.707 \times CONSP + 423.191 \times PCDI \\ + 429.83 \times AWPJ + 433.55 \times GDP + 371.65 \times POP \\ + 384.14 \times FSSH + 118.84 \times FSBC - 88.62 \times CPI \tag{3}$$

According to the regression: Among the eight variables, GDP, per capita disposable income, the average wage per job, and per capita consumption expenditure of urban residents have significant impacts on ARR.

Table 7. Regression coefficient table.

Coefficients[a]								
Model		Unstandardized Coefficients		Standardized Coefficients	t	Sig.	Collinearity Statistics	
		B	Std. Error	Beta			Tolerance	VIF
1	(Constant)	4101.455	107.548		38.136	0.000		
	y1	990.125	45.585	0.975	21.720	0.000	1.000	1.000
	y2	235.505	99.073	0.107	2.377	0.028	1.000	1.000

a. Dependent Variable: ARR

3.5 Effect Analysis

According to Fig. 3, the scattered points are located near the diagonal, and the histogram in Fig. 4 is relatively close to the normal distribution, we can know that the regression residual follows the normal distribution. According to Table 7, the VIF values of y1 and y2 are less than 5, indicating that there is no multi-linearity among the independent variables.

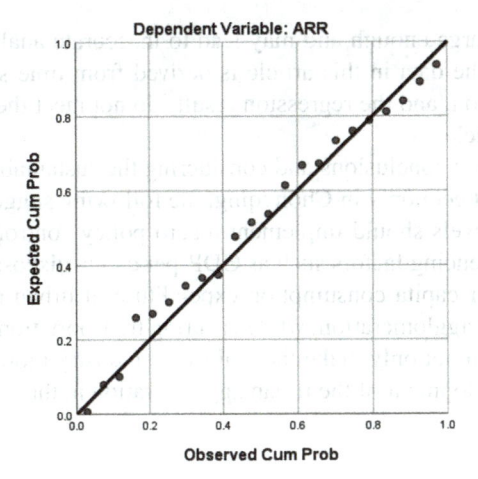

Fig. 3. Normal P-P Plot of Regression Standardized Residual (Photo credit: Original).

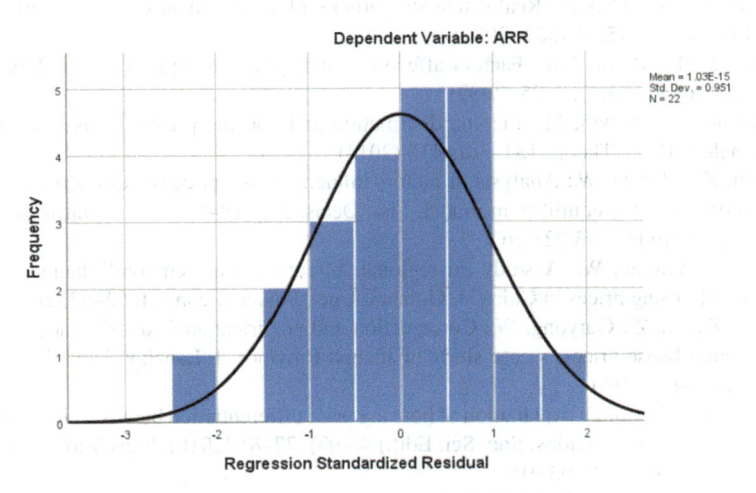

Fig. 4. Histogram (Photo credit: Original).

4 Conclusion

This article selects 8 factors that may affect housing prices in Chongqing through literature analysis. Because there is multicollinearity among explanatory variables, this paper combines eight explanatory variables into two main components through principal component analysis and uses spss to conduct multiple linear regression. Finally, the regression equation is established. It is determined that GDP, per capita disposable income, average wage per job, and per capita consumption expenditure of urban residents are the most influential variables among the eight variables.

However, there are also shortcomings in the research process of this paper. As this article mainly selects the influencing factors on housing prices from a macro perspective, the data source is the Chongqing Statistical Yearbook, which means that the scale of the original data is not large enough and may lead to inaccurate analysis results. Besides, due to the fact that the data in this article is derived from time series, there is a case of sequence correlation, and the regression results do not meet the DW test, which is a deficiency of this article.

Based on the above conclusions and considering the sustainable and healthy development of the market economy in Chongqing, the following suggestions are proposed: governments at all levels should implement macro policy control to ensure the stable development of influencing factors such as GDP, per capita disposable income, average wage per job and per capita consumption expenditure of urban residents. Expanding the Chongqing urban agglomeration, while ensuring transportation, education, and economic conditions, can not only make the real estate industry more prosperous but also drive the further development of the urban agglomeration in the southwest region.

References

1. Cai, Z., Liu, Q., Cao, S.: Real estate supports rapid development of China's urbanization. Land Use Policy **95**, 104582 (2020)
2. Pashardes, P., Savva, C.S.: Factors affecting house prices in Cyprus: 1988–2008. Cyprus Econ. Policy Rev. **3**(1), 3–25 (2009)
3. Määttänen, N., Terviö, M.: Income distribution and housing prices: an assignment model approach. J. Econ. Theory **151**, 381–410 (2014)
4. Jianpu, X., Weihua, W.: Analysis of factors influencing the price of commercial housing in China based on the equilibrium model. Stat. Decis. **22**, 118–121 (2013). https://doi.org/10.13546/j.cnki.tjyjc.2013.22.026
5. Yunqi, F., Yiming, W.: A study on regional differences and temporal changes in factors affecting housing prices in China. J. Guizhou Univ. Financ. Econ. **01**, 62–67 (2014)
6. Ermin, Z., Jin, Z., Guiyong, W.: Construction and empirical analysis of a model of factors influencing house prices: a case study of Jiangxi Province. J. Lanzhou Univ. Financ. Econ. **32**(04), 34–43 (2016)
7. Jingjing, Q.: Economic explanation of housing price differentiation between cities in China. J. Henan Norm. Univ. (Philos. Soc. Sci. Edit.) **43**(03), 77–81 (2016). https://doi.org/10.16366/j.cnki-1000-2359.2016.03.018
8. Hasan, B.M.S., Abdulazeez, A.M.: A review of principal component analysis algorithm for dimensionality reduction. J. Soft Comput. Data Min. **2**(1), 20–30 (2021)
9. Kherif, F., Latypova, A.: Principal component analysis. Machine Learning. Academic Press, pp. 209–225 (2020)
10. Kwitt, R., Meerwald, P., Uhl, A.: Lightweight detection of additive watermarking in the DWT-domain. IEEE Trans. Image Process. **20**(2), 474–484 (2010)
11. Akoglu, H.: User's guide to correlation coefficients. Turk. J. Emerg. Med. **18**(3), 91–93 (2018)
12. Krishnan, V.: Constructing an area-based socioeconomic index: a principal components analysis approach. Edmonton, Alberta: Early Child Development Mapping Project (2010)
13. Alemzero, D.A., Sun, H., Mohsin, M., et al.: Assessing energy security in Africa based on multi-dimensional approach of principal composite analysis. Environ. Sci. Pollut. Res.Pollut. Res. **28**, 2158–2171 (2021)

Game Analysis of Cross-Border Entry of Enterprises into New Markets: Case Study of Bytedance

Feiyue Lei[1(✉)] and Lu Meng[2]

[1] Department of Business Administration, Applied Economics, Beijing Normal University-Hong Kong Baptist University United International College, Zhuhai 519000, China
r130001040@mail.uic.edu.cn

[2] Business School, Macau University of Science and Technology, Macau 999078, China

Abstract. China's takeaway market has been growing rapidly since the beginning of its development. Nowadays, it has formed a double oligopoly market pattern of Meituan Takeout and ELEME Takeout. Recently, Bytedance announced its intention to enter the Chinese takeaway market has attracted widespread attention. Bytedance today is flush with cash and can compete well with the big incumbents. Its every move is closely watched, and it is even considered a threat to other delivery players, which could change the landscape of the delivery market in the future. Taking Bytedance's cross-border entry into the takeaway industry as an example, based on the actions of Bytedance and existing enterprises in the takeaway industry at the moment of cross-border entry, this paper uses evolutionary game theory to establish an evolutionary game model, and introduces the conversion of available resources in the original industry of Bytedance in the game process to explore the influence of different resource conversions on the evolution results of the double development of the game. Furthermore, it is concluded how the resource conversion rate of the original industry affects the enterprises' cross-border entry into the new market, so as to provide theoretical support for the decision of enterprises' cross-border entry in reality.

Keywords: Evolutionary Gaming · Takeaway Market · Bytedance · Cross-border Entry

1 Introduction

China's takeaway industry is an industry with high growth rate, large scale and good development prospects. Data shows that from 2011 to 2019, the market size of the online takeaway industry grew from 21.68 billion yuan to 577.93 billion yuan, with an eight-year compound growth rate of 50.74%. The COVID-19 outbreak in 2020 led to further rapid development of the online takeaway industry, with the market size growing to $664.62 billion, representing a year-on-year growth of 15% and accounting for 16.8% of the

---

F. Le and L. Meng—These authors contributed equally.

© The Author(s), under exclusive license to Springer Nature Singapore Pte Ltd. 2024
X. Li et al. (Eds.): ICEMGD 2023, AEPS, pp. 1242–1251, 2024.
https://doi.org/10.1007/978-981-97-0523-8_116

overall food and beverage industry [1]. According to Statista, the total revenue of Chinese food and beverage takeaway services was approximately RMB 1 trillion (US$139 billion) in 2022. This market size could increase to $200 billion per year within five years. This would put China on top of the global take-out market and would reach more than twice the size of the U.S. market [2]. China's once-competitive takeaway industry has now consolidated into a duopoly. According to industry researcher ChinaIRN, Meituan now holds 69% of the market share, while Alibaba's ELEME has 26%. The combined share of the two amounts to 95% [2].

Recently, the news of Byted ance's intention to enter the Chinese take-out market has once again attracted widespread attention from the community. This is yet another cross-border expansion of the tech giant. Beijing Douyin Information Service Co., LTD., or Bytedance for short, is a multinational Internet technology company located in Beijing, China. Founded in March 2012, it owns products such as Toutiao, Douyin (and its overseas version TikTok), Watermelon Video, etc. Bytedance's products and services are available in 150 countries and regions and 75 languages worldwide. And have been ranked at the top of the overall app store rankings in more than 40 countries and regions [3]. As of the third quarter of 2019, Toutiao had 303 million monthly active users (MAU), Douyin has 486 million monthly active users. And still maintain a high growth rate [4]. Today Bytedance is a well-deserved giant in the Internet industry.

Presently, Bytedance has significant financial resources and strategic positioning to rival established market players. This trajectory mirrors the trajectory previously undertaken by numerous Chinese companies that experienced rapid growth, leveraging the influx of new funding to venture into entirely disparate fields [2]. Back in 2018, Douyin set up a POI team to try to make a push into the group buying business through seeding videos. After that, the platform has developed "online booking", "group purchase discount" and other businesses, wanting to share the market of local life. In 2021, Douyin also tested the "heartbeat takeaway", which was also seen as a sign of its real large-scale entry into the takeaway industry, and once invited brands such as KFC and HEYTEA to join, but eventually it failed. Its official cooperation with ELEME in August 2022, namely the small program as a carrier to provide Douyin users with online ordering and instant delivery of local life services, opened a new way to play in the take-out industry. In recent months, Douyin has launched a pilot service for group food purchases in Beijing, Shanghai and Chengdu [5]. A spokeswoman for Bytedance recently said the company will expand its takeaway service to more cities based on the results of the pilot service [2]. As a national app with more than 600 million daily users, Douyin's every move is getting a lot of attention and is even considered a threat to other takeaway players, which may be able to change the takeaway market structure in the future [5].

In recent years, cross-border entry and issues related to the takeaway industry have received attention from scholars, and research results related to this have been conducted. There are two main aspects of research related to this paper. One is the research on cross-border entry and cross-border competition of enterprises. Based on previous studies, Pi Shenglei proposed that in cross-border competition, firms need to build basic competitive advantages such as terminal market contact or resource dominance [6]. Taking the classic cross-border competition case (DIDI takeaway and Meituan taxi) around 2017 as an example, Zhu Sijia studied the competitive strategies used by the two in conducting cross-border competition as huge economic subsidy and competition for traffic and related resources [7]. As well as the reasons for cross-border competition as maturity in established fields and user stickiness becoming low in the face of benefits. Wenlei Xie proposed that the characteristics of cross-border expansion of digital giants include using capital advantages to adopt low-price competition to seize the market, and competing with the original advantages such as traffic, data, and algorithms [8]. Second is related studies about the Chinese take-out industry. Guo Haiyan conducted a study on customer loyalty cultivation strategies in the take-out industry and concluded that campus take-out targeting student groups, who are younger, have lower spending power, are easily attracted by preferential subsidies and other means, and are easier to market penetration with low loyalty [9]. Big data sharing also helps a lot to cultivate customer loyalty. In his study, Chen Xinyang outlined the current situation of the take-out market, comparing and analyzing the basic situation of Meituan and ELEME as well as the game analysis between them and between them and food service outlets [10]. Suggestions are provided for how the up-and-coming takeaway platforms can penetrate the market (targeting the most receptive user groups such as young people, etc.). He also suggests that big data improves the possibility of profitability in the takeaway market. Cao Shuxiao provides an in-depth analysis of the development status, development prospects and current problems of the bilateral platform Meituan Takeaway [11]. Jin Rong pointed out in his study that the State Administration of Market Supervision conducted an anti-monopoly investigation as well as administrative punishment against Meituan [12].

In summary, scholars have done a lot of research and analysis on cross-border competition and the take-out industry and have achieved many results. However, few studies have adopted the evolutionary game approach to explore which factors influence the ease of entry of a firm into another industry and its decision. Based on the previous studies, this study takes Bytedance's entry into the take-out industry as an example, takes the actions of Bytedance and the original companies in the take-out industry at the moment of entry, uses evolutionary game theory, establishes an evolutionary game model, and introduces the conversion of available resources in Bytedance's original industry in the game process to explore the impact of different resource transformation level on the evolutionary outcome of the game, and further conclude how the factor affects the cross-border entry of enterprises into new markets, so as to provide theoretical support for the decision of cross-border entry of enterprises in reality.

2 Game Model Construction

2.1 Problem Description and Basic Assumptions

Problem Description. Recently, ByteDance plans to enter the takeout market across the border and compete with existing companies in the takeout market across industries.

For the original enterprises in the take-out market, if they do not prevent the entry of new enterprises, their original market share will shrink and their income will be reduced. If they choose to prevent the entry of new enterprises, the usual means of competition in this industry are huge economic subsidies and traffic competition (publicity and marketing), which will cause the existing enterprises to incur new costs.

For Bytedance, to enter a new market, it needs to build a network platform, contact merchants, cooperate with mobile payment terminals, and conduct marketing and other preparatory work, which will incur additional costs. Entering new markets and increasing the number of users will increase its revenue. Due to cross-border entry and the particularity of Bytedance's original business, the user portrait of Bytedance in the original industry has a high degree of compatibility with the mainstream user group in the takeout market, which can greatly reduce its marketing and publicity costs.

Basic Assumptions. Make assumptions according to the evolutionary game theory and the actual situation.

Hypothesis 1: Bytedance and all existing entities in take-out industries are bounded rationality,

Hypothesis 2: For Bytedance, the strategy set is entering and not entering. Let the probability of Bytedance choosing to enter at time is, then the probability of choosing not to enter is. When the existing enterprises in the takeout industry choose the non-preventing strategy, the increased income of Bytedance entering the takeout market is, and the cost need to be paid is. Due to the conversion of resources provided by the original industry, the cost saved by Bytedance is. When the existing enterprises in the takeout industry choose the preventing strategy, the new income of Bytedance entering the takeout market will decrease, while the prevent effect of existing enterprises in the takeout market will decrease due to the differentiation strategy implemented by Bytedance.

Hypothesis 3: For the existing enterprises in the takeout industry, the strategies are not preventing and preventing. Let the probability of the existing enterprises choosing not preventing at time is, the probability of choosing preventing is. When the existing enterprises choose the non-preventing strategy, the revenue loss caused by Bytedance entering the takeout market is equal to the new revenue of Bytedance, and the cost of preventing Bytedance from entering the market is.

2.2 Return Matrix and Dynamic Replication Equation

Based on the above assumptions, the strategy combination and income matrix of both sides of the game can be obtained, as shown in Table 1.

Table 1. Strategy combination and payoff matrix of both sides of the game.

Game-agent		Existing enterprises in take-out industry	
		Not Preventing	Preventing
Bytedance	Entering	$R_1 - (C_1 - \beta), -R_1$	$R_1 - (\alpha - \gamma) - (C_1 - \beta),$ $-[R_1 - (\alpha - \gamma)] - C_2$
	Not Entering	0, 0	$0, -C_2$

In the income matrix in Table 1, existing enterprises in Bytedance and food delivery industry are constantly changing their strategies in the game process in order to obtain greater profits. According to evolutionary game theory, when the expected return of a selected strategy is higher than the average expected return of the game system, the strategy will spread in the system.

Replication Dynamic Equation of Bytedance. Set the expected return E_{11} of ByteDance entering the market, and the expected return E_{12} that does not enter the market and the average expected income $\bar{E}_x$ can be obtained:

$$E_{11} = y[R_1 - (C_1 - \beta)] + (1 - y)[R_1 - (a - r) - (C_1 - \beta)]$$
$$= R_1 + (a - r)(y - 1) - C_1 + \beta \tag{1}$$

$$E_{12} = y \times 0 + (1 - y) \times 0 = 0 \tag{2}$$

$$\bar{E}_x = xE_{11} + (1 - x)E_{12} \tag{3}$$

Further obtain the dynamic replication equation of ByteDance entering the market.

$$dx/dt = F(x) = x(E_{11} - \bar{E}_x) = x(1 - x)(E_{11} - E_{12}) \tag{4}$$

Replication Dynamic Equation of Existing Enterprises in the Take-out Industry. Set the takeaway platform monopoly market already exists in the expected income E_{21} that enterprises do not stop, and the expected income E_{22} and the average expected income $\bar{E}_y$ can be obtained:

$$E_{21} = x(-R_1 + \lambda R_0) + (1 - x)\{-[R1 - (a - r)] - C2\}$$
$$= -R1 + (a - r)(1 - x) + xC2 \tag{5}$$

$$E22 = x \times 0 + (1 - x)(-C2) = C2(x - 1) \tag{6}$$

$$\bar{E} = yE21 + (1 - y)E22 \tag{7}$$

Further obtain the dynamic replication equation that does not stop the existing enterprises in the takeaway platform monopoly market.

$$dy/dt = F(y) = y(E21 - \bar{E}y) = y(1 - y)(E21 - E22) \tag{8}$$

3 Evolutionary Game Model Analysis

3.1 Evolutionary Game Evolutionary Stability Strategy Solution

In the above-mentioned game model, the probability of ByteDance entering at t time is x(t), and the probability of existing enterprises not rejecting in the takeaway monopoly market is y(t). Both probabilities are related to t, and x(t), y(t) ∈ [0,1]. Make F(x) = 0, F(y) = 0. At this time, the selection rate of the strategy no longer changes. You can get 4 pure strategy solutions (0, 0), (0,1), (1,0), (1,1) and a mixed strategy solution (x*, y*) in the evolution process.

According to the dynamic replication equation of the two main bodies, the corresponding Jacobian matrix can be obtained:

$$J = \begin{bmatrix} \partial F(x)/\partial x & \partial F(x)/\partial y \\ \partial F(y)/\partial x & \partial F(y)/\partial y \end{bmatrix} = \begin{bmatrix} a_{11} & a_{12} \\ a_{21} & a_{22} \end{bmatrix} \quad (9)$$

And $\det J = a_{11}a_{22} - a_{12}a_{21} > 0$, $\mathrm{tr}J = a_{11} + a_{22} < 0$.

a_{11}, a_{12} are the partial derivatives of the replication dynamic equation $F(x)$ to x and y respectively.

a_{21}, a_{22} are the partial derivatives of the replication dynamic equation $F(y)$ to x and y respectively.

$$a_{11} = (1 - 2x)[\,R1 + (a - r)(y - 1) - C1 + \beta] \quad (10)$$

$$a_{12} = x(1 - x)(\,R1 - C1 + \beta) \quad (11)$$

$$a_{21} = y(1 - y)(-R1 + C2) \quad (12)$$

$$a_{22} = (1 - 2y)[-R1 + (a - r)(1 - x) + C2] \quad (13)$$

3.2 Equilibrium Point Evolution Stability Analysis

According to the Lyapunov stability theory, the Jacobian matrix can be used to determine the stability of some points in the evolutionary system. For a specific point, when all the eigenvalues in the corresponding Jacobian matrix are negative, that is, the determinant of the Jacobian matrix should be greater than 0 and less than 0. That is, when $\det J > 0$ and $\mathrm{tr}J < 0$, this point can be determined as an evolutionary stabilization strategy (ESS). The stability analysis of the five local equilibrium points is shown in the Table 2.

Table 2. Equilibrium point.

Equilibrium point	detJ	trJ
(0,0)	$(R_1 - a + r - C_1 + \beta)(-R_1 + a - r + C_2)$	$C_2 - C_1 + \beta$
(1,0)	$-(R_1 - a + r - C_1 + \beta)(-R_1 + C_2)$	$-2R_1 + a - r + C_1 + C_2 - \beta$
(0,1)	$-(R_1 - C_1 + \beta)(-R_1 + a - r + C_2)$	$2R_1 - a + r - C_1 - C_2 + \beta$
(1,1)	$(R_1 - C_1 + \beta)(-R_1 + C_2)$	$C_1 - C_2 - \beta$
(x*,y*)	+	0

The equilibrium point (x*, y*) is used as a mixed strategy solution, and the trace of its corresponding rows is always 0, so the point is a saddle point and cannot become ESS. Among them, this time, we mainly analyze the impact of the successful conversion (β) of the original resources on ByteDance, (0, 0), (1, 0), (0, 1) and (1, 1). The impact on the entry of ByteDance into the takeaway market can be seen. The following is the main analysis.

Case 1: When $\beta > C_1 + a - R_1 - r, C_2 > R_1 - a + r$, the system is stable at (0, 0). At this time, the conversion of ByteDance to the original resources is higher than the cost of entering the takeaway market. At the same time, the cost of preventing ByteDance from entering the market is relatively high, which is not enough to prevent ByteDance from entering the takeaway market. Here, ByteDance finally chooses to enter the market, and the market does not prevent ByteDance from entering. The evolutionary phase diagram is shown in Fig. 1.

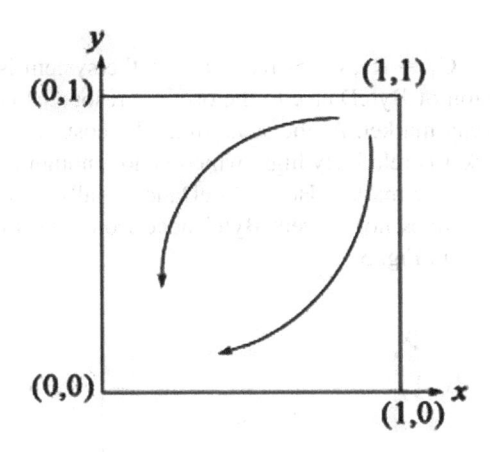

Fig. 1. A figure for the market enters the evolutionary system.

Case 2: When $\beta < C_1 + a - R_1 - r, C_2 > R_1$, the system reaches stability at (1, 0). At this time, the conversion of ByteDance to the original resources is lower than the cost of entering the takeaway market. At the same time, the cost of preventing ByteDance from entering the market is relatively low, which is enough to prevent ByteDance from entering the takeaway market. Here, ByteDance finally chose not to enter the market, and the market prevented ByteDance from entering. The evolutionary phase diagram is shown in Fig. 2.

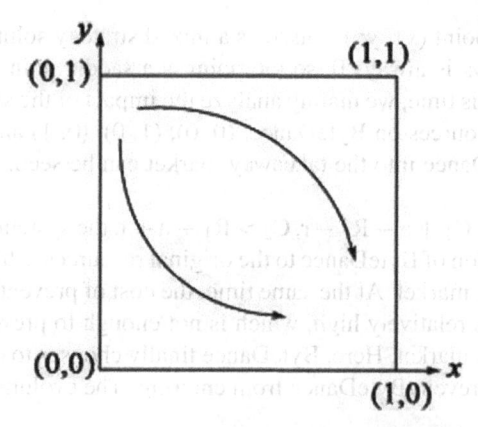

Fig. 2. A figure for the market enters the evolutionary system.

Case 3: When $\beta < C_1 - R_1$, $C_2 > R_1 - a + r$, the system is stable at (0, 1). At this time, the conversion of ByteDance to the original resources is lower than the cost of entering the takeaway market. At the same time, the cost of preventing ByteDance from entering the market is relatively high, which is not enough to prevent ByteDance from entering the takeaway market. Here, ByteDance finally chooses not to enter the market, and the market does not prevent ByteDance from entering. The evolutionary phase diagram is shown in Fig. 3.

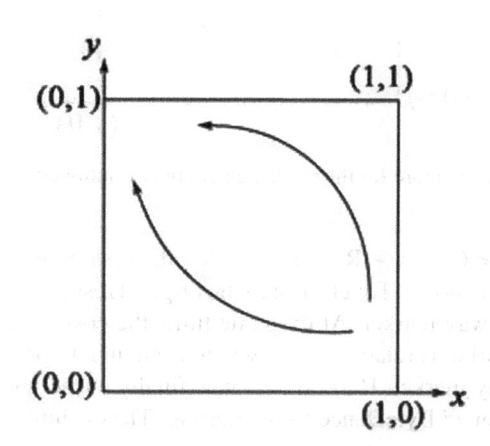

Fig. 3. A figure for the market enters the evolutionary system.

Case 4: When $\beta > C_1 - R_1$, $C_2 > R_1$, the system reaches stability at (1, 1). At this time, the conversion of ByteDance to the original resources is higher than the cost of entering the takeaway market. At the same time, the cost of preventing ByteDance from entering the market is relatively low, which is enough to prevent ByteDance from entering the takeaway market. Here, ByteDance finally chooses to enter the market, and the market prevents ByteDance from entering. The evolutionary phase diagram is shown in Fig. 4.

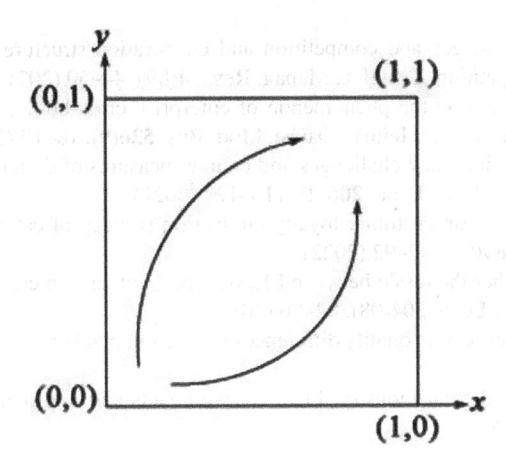

Fig. 4. A figure for the market enters the evolutionary system.

4 Conclusion

The article establishes an evolutionary game model between ByteDance and the takeaway market, which does enter or not enter, and block or not stop. Then studies the impact of cost savings on the game results caused by the resource conversion provided by the original industry of ByteDance. The following conclusion is obtained: ByteDance action is the original one brought by cross-industry market entry Resource conversion can help it enter the takeaway market to a certain extent. The greater the possibility of conversion of the original resources, the more successful the strategy of ByteDance will be. When entering a monopoly market, cross-border enterprises need to pay more attention to the transformation of resources in the original industry, so as to make it more helpful. When the resource conversion rate is the highest, the lower the cost of entering the new market.

The article only considers the impact of resource transformation on cross-industry entry, and other aspects such as government policy assistance can be considered in future research.

References

1. Qianzhan Industry Research Institute (n.d.). https://bg.qianzhan.com/report/detail/300/211223-4098960b.html. Accessed 23 Dec 2021
2. Brown, T.: Bytedance is set to enter China's food delivery market, challenging Meituan and ElEME. Wall Street J. (2023)
3. Steven. 2022 ByteDance Research Report - OFweek Artificial Intelligence Network [Internet]. https://m.ofweek.com/ai/2022-10/ART-201713-8110-30576187, https://hot.cnbeta.com.tw/articles/movie/1346461.htm
4. Geng, S.: Bytedance depth research report. Hua'chuang Securities (2020). 1.12
5. cnBeta (n.d.). Tiktok delivery card on the "entry" [Internet]. https://hot.cnbeta.com.tw/articles/movie/1346461.htm. Accessed 26 Feb 2023/2/26

6. Pi, S.L.: The advantages and competition and cooperation structure of enterprises under cross-border competition. Tsinghua Manag. Rev. **94**(09), 44–50 (2021)
7. Zhu, S.J.: Discussion on the phenomenon of enterprise cross-border competition – a case study of Didi Takeout and Meituan Dache. Mod. Bus. **526**(9), 18–19 (2019)
8. Xie, W.L.: Competition law challenges and countermeasures of digital giants' cross-border expansion. J. Hubei Univ. Econ. **20**(02), 116–124 (2022)
9. Guo, H.Y.: Research on customer loyalty cultivation strategy of catering takeout industry. Manag. Manag. **584**(06), 90–92 (2022)
10. Chen, X.Y.: Whether the tussle between ElEME and Meituan can create opportunities for a new platform. Bus. Econ. **504**(08), 82–86 (2018)
11. Cao, S.X.: Consider service quality differences of take-out platform pricing strategy research. Donghua university (2021)
12. Jin, R.: Depth of take-out industry: Enabling merchants and improving efficiency. Hua'an Securities. (2022).8

Research on the Effectiveness of Clarifying Rumors by Listed Companies in the Pharmaceutical Industry – Taking the Market Reaction of Ling Pharmaceutical as an Example

Chuhan Wang[1(✉)], Beining Xu[2], and Qianwen Zhang[3]

[1] Tianyou College, East China Jiao Tong University, Nanchang 330013, China
1811031138@mail.sit.edu.cn

[2] Accounting College, Wuhan Textile University, Wuhan 430200, China

[3] International Business Management College, Sichuan International Studies University, Chongqing 400031, China

Abstract. The stock market is the information market, and issuing clarification announcements is an important way for listed companies to respond to rumors and reports in the market media. This study will study the impact of the company's clarification announcement on the short-term market response from the perspective of media rumors. Swedish media published a media rumor report on Yiling Pharmaceutical Company, Yiling Pharmaceutical Company immediately issued a relevant clarification announcement. This paper uses the event research method to study the stock price changes before and after the emergence of rumors and before and after the issuance of the clarification announcement by Yiling Pharmaceutical, so as to explore the effectiveness of the clarification announcement. This article collects the stock price data of Yiling Pharmaceutical between September 2019 and May 2020 and the 2020 quarterly report of Yiling Pharmaceutical, and analyzes the short-term market reaction of listed companies in the 7 trading days before and after and the long-term market reaction in 2020. The results show that the role of the clarification announcement on the market is not effective in the long term, and even in the short term, it may not bring about a large recovery in the stock price through the response to the event, but it can more play a role in alleviating the large change in the stock price in response to the rumored event and stabilizing the market.

Keywords: Media Rumors · Clarification Announcements · Market Reactions

1 Introduction

This paper adopts the event study method as the main research method, and takes Shijiazhuang Yiling Pharmaceutical Co., Ltd. as the research object. Using the stock abnormal return rate (AR) and the cumulative abnormal return rate (CAR), this paper studies the

---

C. Wang, B. Xu and Q. Zhang—These authors contributed equally.

© The Author(s), under exclusive license to Springer Nature Singapore Pte Ltd. 2024
X. Li et al. (Eds.): ICEMGD 2023, AEPS, pp. 1252–1264, 2024.
https://doi.org/10.1007/978-981-97-0523-8_117

impact of the clarification announcement on the market reaction under the influence of rumors by responding to the event process of the Swedish media with the clarification announcement of Ling Pharmaceutical.

1.1 Research Background

In recent years, the phenomenon of media rumors and corporate clarification announcements in the securities market has aroused widespread attention and discussion among market participants, reflecting the problems of information quality and supervision by relevant laws and regulations in information disclosure of listed companies. The Administrative Measures for Information Disclosure of Listed Companies have been deliberated and adopted by the 3rd Committee Meeting of the China Securities Regulatory Commission in 2021 on March 4, 2021, and are hereby promulgated and will come into force on May 1, 2021. It stipulates that for the disclosure of relevant matters in a timely manner in the event of major event leaks, market rumors, abnormal securities transactions, etc., the Shenzhen Stock Exchange and the Shanghai Stock Exchange have also formulated more standardized provisions for clarification statements. Therefore, the research on media rumor reporting and clarifying announcements has important theoretical and practical significance.

With the continuous improvement of material civilization and spiritual civilization and the continuous development of science and technology, people can keep abreast of the latest news released by the media anytime and anywhere, and pay attention to the development of enterprises. Therefore, relevant media coverage has a crucial impact on the long-term development of enterprises. The prosperity of the capital market has brought huge profits to the investment participants in the market, and at the same time, a large number of investors have begun to realize the significance of both media releases and corporate clarification announcements. People usually think of the capital market as a market for information transactions, and the relevant information is effectively discounted by the trading price of stocks, and the events and clarification announcements reported by media rumors often have a crucial impact on the ups and downs of the company's stock price.

In the traditional paper media era, mainly because the media carrier limits the speed and scope of information dissemination, but with the advent of the Internet information age, information dissemination is no longer restricted by the carrier, rumor reports in the stock market can be summarized by "flying all over the sky", not only limited to financial media, but also a variety of other self-media, such as "Weibo" and "WeChat". Similarly, the quality of clarification announcements issued by listed companies is uneven. The company may also issue a clarification announcement for the following two reasons: first, when it will adversely affect the enterprise or damage the image of the enterprise, the company will tend to issue a clarification announcement to clarify the facts; The other is that under the current supervision, failure to issue a clarification statement will be punished, and listed companies need to issue clarification announcements on relevant matters in a timely manner under this pressure. When the relevant regulatory authorities issue that the regulatory regime is the same as the interests pursued by the enterprise, the company will release more complete and true information when issuing a clarification announcement.

The Chinese government has been paying close attention to the healthy development of the media and promoting the authenticity and timeliness of media coverage of events. With the rapid development of the Internet, the impact of events reported by the media will also increase. Therefore, the work of the news media should uphold the state's commanding role in the work of the news media. The content and reasons of media reports are different, so the operating effects of listed companies are also different. Finally, the speed of response of listed companies and the different attitude of clarifying the media coverage of events will have a great impact on the company's future operating results.

This paper adopts the event study method as the main research method, and takes Shijiazhuang Yiling Pharmaceutical Co., Ltd.as the research object. Using the stock abnormal return rate (AR) and the cumulative abnormal return rate (CAR), this paper studies the impact of the clarification announcement on the market reaction under the influence of rumors by responding to the event process of the Swedish media with the clarification announcement of Ling Pharmaceutical.

1.2 Research Significance

The research of this paper has certain theoretical and practical significance. The theoretical significance lies in:

(1) Eling Pharmaceutical's media coverage and clarification announcement is equivalent to two parts of one event. Through this study, it is possible to compare the two events that will have different effects on the market.
(2) At present, few people in the academic circles at home and abroad have studied media rumors, clarification announcements and market reaction research. In particular, there are very few studies on negative news and market reactions, and generally mainstream academia studies the impact of positive news on market reactions. Therefore, the study of negative news and market reaction can be slightly filled.
(3) The cumbersome process of media rumor reporting and company clarification can be perfectly presented in the case study method, and the results analyzed through the case study method can provide some reference significance for other enterprises. Since media coverage and company clarification is a more complex process, each media report and company clarification is a relatively complete and unique event. It is hoped that the analysis of the case of Yiling Pharmaceutical Co., Ltd. can provide better reference significance to other enterprises.

The practical significance of this study lies in:

(1) For Yiling Pharmaceutical, through the analysis of its data, it is found that the media rumor reports and the company's clarification announcement will have a certain impact on the market reaction. Therefore, it is recommended that Yiling Pharmaceutical should clarify this media rumor as soon as possible when it appears next time, and the market should not be directly in a negative mood.
(2) Through the analysis of the case of Yiling Pharmaceutical, it can also be reflected that the market's report on media rumors will be reflected in the stock price in time, and the company's clarification announcement will also be reflected in the company's stock price in time.

(3) Through the analysis of data, it can be concluded that the negative rumor reports of the media have a negative effect on the market, while the company's clarification announcement will have a positive effect on the market, and the company's attitude of clarifying the announcement will also affect the market reaction. That is to say, when the media publishes rumors, the company should clarify it as soon as possible and in a good manner.

1.3 Innovations and Difficulties

The innovations of this paper are as follows:

First, the case study is media rumor reporting, and it is a study of negative media rumor reporting in companies, which has been rarely studied in domestic and foreign academia before.

Second, in the past, academic circles at home and abroad generally conducted specific research on a certain event, for example, either for the research on the market reaction of media rumors and reports, or the research on the market reaction of the company's clarification announcement. It is rare to combine media rumor reports with company clarification announcements.

The difficulty of this paper is: Based on the global environment of the new coronavirus pneumonia epidemic, Yiling Pharmaceutical Co., Ltd. was affected by the epidemic, and there were many abnormal fluctuations in stock trading. When analyzing the market reaction research caused by the clarification announcement, the case selected in this paper cannot be separated from the direct impact of the environment.

2 Literature Review

2.1 The Causes of Rumors

Zheng Yifan studied the causes of rumors and found that uncertainty is one of the most basic characteristics of the securities market. When investors face uncertainty, rumors will spread [1]. The 'unconfirmed' rumor brings abnormal fluctuations to the securities market, disrupts investors' reasonable judgment and rational decision-making, and has a negative impact on the stability of the securities market.

Peng Qing explained the relationship between trust and rumors through research. Trust is inversely proportional to the generation of rumors [2]. When the public's trust level in the company decreases, the probability of rumors will increase significantly. Corporate rumors have a significant impact on stock prices. Positive rumors cause significantly positive stock abnormal returns and cumulative abnormal returns. Negative rumors cause significantly negative stock abnormal returns and cumulative abnormal returns.

Frederick Davis Research has found that insiders' net purchases have increased in the year prior to the first announcement of a takeover rumor, especially when the rumor article is accurate (leading to a takeover announcement) or informative (providing a good reason for the rumor's release) [3].

2.2 The Effect and Influence of Clarification Announcement

Gao found that a shorter clarification delay can improve the clarification effect by studying the timeliness of clarification announcements [4]. The possible reason is that the rapid release of clarification announcements reflects the attitude of listed companies to rumor denial, which makes market investors less confident in the rumor content and helps the recovery of stock prices.

By taking source honesty as a research variable, Fang found that source honesty has a moderating effect on the relationship between clarification wording and clarification announcement effectiveness [5]. The higher the source honesty, the better the clarification effect. The clarification effect is best in the case of high source honesty and strong denial; in the case of low source honesty and weak denial, the clarification effect is the worst.

Zhang studied the internal and external characteristics of the clarification announcement and found that in the internal characteristics of the clarification announcement, information quality and information quantity may have an impact on the clarification effect [6]. In the external characteristics of the clarification announcement, the timeliness of clarification and the regulatory environment will have an impact on the clarification effect, and the direct effect of corporate reputation on the clarification effect is not significant.

Qin studied the content of the clarification announcement, and found that both good and bad rumor stocks showed relatively abnormal returns [7]. The abnormal fluctuations caused by good rumors are greater than the abnormal fluctuations caused by bad rumors. The recovery of the stock's abnormal return rate is faster than that of good rumors.

He studied the impact of clarification attitude on market reaction [8]. When the clarification announcement acknowledges the rumor content, significant stock price changes in the same direction as the rumor impact can be found within a few days of the announcement. When denying the content of rumors, clarifying the day of the announcement does not bring negative changes to the stock price, and it cannot completely offset the impact of rumors for a long time after the release.

Jun et al. found that digitized rumor information affects the abnormal returns of related stocks, and this effect can be quantified and measured by the emotional polarity of rumor clarification. Lastly, the company's network clarification behavior, including information disclosure frequency, response time, wording, etc., has a limited impact on abnormal returns [9].

Liu et al. found that overnight announcements can facilitate price discovery as eye-catching events. However, investors' attention may be distracted by other companies' overnight announcements, which dilutes the enhanced effect of overnight announcements on price discovery [10].

Kumar et al. found that companies should wait until the market recovers before issuing clarification announcements during the pressure of the pandemic, because even events with a positive impact can lead to a negative market reaction during the pressure of the pandemic [11]. The results show that the impact of all corporate announcements on stock returns is not consistent. Although bonus announcements, dividend-free and pre-split events led to positive significant abnormal returns on the event day, rights issuance and stock split announcements failed to affect stock returns.

2.3 Comment

The research on the impact of clarification announcements on stock prices is a problem that cannot be ignored in the development of the market. Based on the rumors that the company will have a positive or negative impact, domestic and foreign scholars have found that the content and attitude of clarification announcements will have different effects on stock prices. However, in the case of the outbreak of the COVID-19 epidemic, the economic market has been greatly affected. In the process of collecting literature, the author also found that the pharmaceutical industry has a strong momentum of development in the context of the epidemic, and its clarification announcement is representative. The research significance, and the academic community has less research on the impact of rumors brought by foreign media on the release of clarification announcements by domestic companies, and the fluctuation of stock prices after the release of external clarification, which provides some space and possibility for the writing of this article. This paper plans to expand and study this issue accordingly.

3 Case Analysis

3.1 Basic Information of Yiling Pharmaceutical

Introduction of Yiling Pharmaceutical. Shijiazhuang Yiling Pharmaceutical Co., Ltd., a national key high-tech enterprise, is a pharmaceutical enterprise that promotes the industrialization of traditional Chinese medicine with the innovation of traditional Chinese medicine and uses modern high-tech to develop traditional Chinese medicine, western medicine and biological medicine. Create a unique operation model of "theory-clinical-scientific research-industry-teaching". Research and development of more than 10 patented new drugs such as Tongxinluo capsules for the treatment of coronary heart disease and cerebral infarction, Jiansong Yangxin capsules for both fast and slow treatment of arrhythmias, Qianqiangxin capsules for the treatment of chronic heart failure, Lianhua Qingwen capsules for the treatment of colds and anti-flu, etc., the company has built production bases in many places, created a perfect production layout, ensured product supply, introduced advanced equipment and pharmaceutical processes at home and abroad, created a comprehensive quality control system that meets international standards, established a strong marketing network and academic marketing team, formed scientific and technological traditional Chinese medicine, The three major business sectors of chemical and biological drugs and health industry continue to grow in their influence in the pharmaceutical industry. (ticker code 002603). The company is in the pharmaceutical manufacturing industry, the main products include Tongxinluo capsules, Jiansong Yangxin capsules, Lianhua Qingwen capsules, Qianqiang Xin capsules, etc.).

Company Operating Conditions of Yiling Pharmaceutical. As shown in Table 1, it can be seen that the number of products sold by Yiling Pharmaceutical in 2021 is still greater than in 2020, indicating that its main products such as Lianhua Qingwen capsules are still in the sales advantage. And as shown in Table 2, it is obvious that the company's operating income and operating profit in 2021 are much better than in 2020, indicating that the company's operating conditions in 2021 are significantly better than those in 2020, and the operating conditions in 2020 are far more than those in 2019.

Table 1. Sales of the Company's products.

Products Sold	Capsules (10,000 capsules)	Granules (10,000 bags)	Tablets (10,000 tablets)
Sales volume in 2020	1,463,731	72,961	522,517
Number of sales in 2021	1,481,703	69,618	401,667

Source: Oriental Fortune Network

Table 2. Company operating situation (billion yuan).

Time Operating	Income Operating	Profit	Net profit attributable to the parent company
2019	58.52	6.030	6.065
2020	87.82	14.38	12.19
2021	101.2	15.69	13.44

Source: Oriental Fortune Network

3.2 Case Overview of Yiling Pharmaceutical

Overview of Yiling Pharmaceutical's Media Reports. Recently, Swedish media said that the Swedish customs laboratory tested the anti-new crown traditional Chinese medicine Lianhua Qingwen advocated by China, claiming that its ingredients were "only menthol".

The Swedish Medicines Agency said there is currently a large number of current products in circulation in Europe. The Swedish Drug Administration and Customs Agency described Lianhua Qingwen as a drug that "cannot be transported from countries outside the Schengen Area without permission" and detained it at the border.

Dan Larhammar, a Swedish professor of molecular cell biology, claims that Lianhua contains about 13 herbs, "but in fact the ingredient is only menthol."

Yiling Pharmaceutical Clarified the Overview of The Announcement.

(1) The company's Lianhua Qingwen products have not been registered as drugs in the European country reported by the relevant media, nor have they been exported and sold to that country, and the company does not currently know the specific situation of the country's customs restrictions on import and the source of the drugs tested by the media.
(2) In addition, the "Lianhua Qingwen only contains menthol" mentioned in relevant media reports is seriously inconsistent with the facts.

Lianhua Qingwen is a large compound Chinese patent medicine for colds and anti-flu made from a combination of 13 flavors of Chinese medicine, and menthol is one of the medicinal components. Since the launch of Lianhua Qingwen products, the company has carried out in-depth research on its material basis, content determination and quality control. It was found that Lianhua Qingwen products can be isolated and identified with a variety of compounds. At the same time, after the US FDA carried out the phase II clinical trial, with reference to the recommendations of the US FDA, a fingerprinting method was established for 15 ingredients, and a systematic quality control system from intermediate to finished product was established, so the information reported in the media "only menthol" was inaccurate.

(3) In 2012, the company's Lianhua Qingwen products passed the legal registration (registration number: 80033781) of the natural health products regulations of the Ministry of Health of North America reported by the media, and officially entered the country's market to carry out compliant sales, and has never been refused entry by the country.

(4) Lianhua Qingwen products do not contain aristolochic acid. The problem of "the drug is rich in aristolochic acid" said by the media is mainly aimed at the medicinal herb Houttuynia contained in Lianhua Qingwei. Based on pharmacological studies, no carcinogenicity and nephrotoxicity of aristolochilactam II contained in houttuynia have been reported.

(5) Lianhua Qingwen has been on the market for 17 years, and systematic toxicological studies have shown that Lianhua Qingwen has good safety and no genotoxicity and nephrotoxicity. No hepatic and renal toxicity was found in the Lianhua Qingwen test group (the research paper was published in Chinese Journal of Pharmaceutical Evaluation and Analysis, 2013-13-(8): 676-681).

In addition, the company has established a sound pharmacovigilance management system, has been conducting post-marketing risk monitoring of drugs, and has not found any adverse reactions such as carcinogenicity and nephrotoxicity after monitoring.

4 Research Methods and Case Selection

4.1 Data Source

The sample data are from the relevant individual stock data of Yiling Pharmaceutical from September 1, 2019 to May 20, 2020 provided by Juchao Information, as well as the relevant market data of the CSI 300 Medical and Health Index from September 1,2019 to May 20,2020.

4.2 Determination of the Test Time Interval

On May 8,2020, Sweden issued the relevant information banning the import of Lianhua Qingwen drug, and claimed that "the drug ingredient of Lianhua Qingwen is only menthol"; and then on May 11,2020, Yiling Pharmaceutical issued a notice to clarify that the matter is seriously inconsistent with the facts. Therefore, in this paper, May 11,2020 of Ling Pharmaceutical is selected as the event date "t", and the event window period selects the seven trading days (t-7, t+7) before and after the announcement, that is, from April 27 to May 20 as the event window. The reason why the event window was selected seven trading days before and after was that relevant rumors had been generated and spread before the media released the ban on imported drugs. However, due to the background of the epidemic, the long event window period may have little correlation between the relevant individual stock data obtained and this case.

4.3 Selection of Samples and Data

This paper uses the event research method to measure the effect of issuing the announcement to clarify the rumors, and uses the effective market hypothesis to calculate the expected and abnormal return rates based on the market model, namely

$$AR_{i,t} = R_{i,t} - (\alpha + \beta R_{m,t}) \quad (1)$$

Which "R_{it}" to ridge pharmaceutical current stock actual yield, "α_i "said excess yield, "β_i" said market risk, "R_{mt}" said the CSI 300 medical health index market yield, and by"$\alpha_i + \beta_i\ R_{mt}$ "calculated to ridge pharmaceutical expected yield "R'_{it}", actual yield R_{it} and expected yield R'_{it} difference is abnormal yield "AR_i", by summing the abnormal yield "AR_{it} "can draw cumulative abnormal yield "CAR". The formula can be expressed as follows:

$$CAR_i(t_{-7}, t_7) = \sum_{t=t-7}^{t_7} AR_{i,t} \quad (2)$$

4.4 Data Processing

Determine the Event Window and the Estimation Window. Securities name event window Period Estimation window is shown in Table 3:

Table 3. Selection period of the event study method.

Securities Name	Event Window Period	Estimation Window
002603-SZE Yiling Pharmaceutical	27th April, 2020 —— 20th May, 2020	1st September, 2019 —— 24th April, 2020

Calculate the Cumulative Excess Yield Rate. According to the data provided by Juchao Information, and with the help of excel software, the paper establishes the regression equation between the return rate of individual stocks and the rate of return of the market, and obtains the scatter plot, as shown in Fig. 1.

Thus, the regression equation is given for y = 0.6097x + 0.0069.

According to the regression equation obtained above, the expected rate of return can be calculated, and the expected rate of return can be compared with the actual rate of return rate of this period to obtain the abnormal rate of return Table 4. According to Table 4, the abnormal yield trend chart and cumulative abnormal yield trend chart can be obtained, as shown in Fig. 2.

4.5 Short-Term Market Reaction Evaluation

As shown in Fig. 2, on the whole, the stock price of Yiling Pharmaceutical fluctuated greatly during the event period, both rising and falling. The day before the clarification

$$y = 0.6097x + 0.0069$$
$$R^2 = 0.0566$$

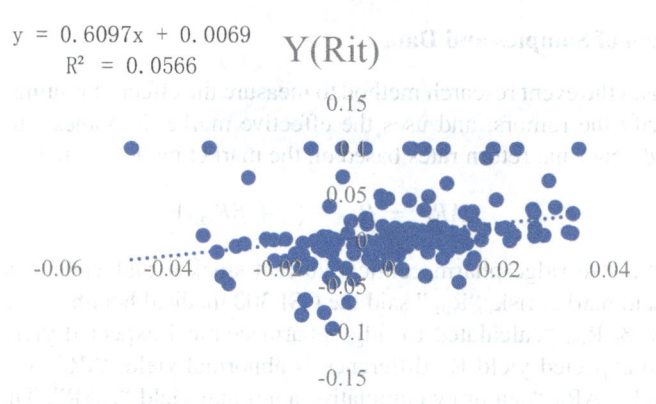

Fig. 1. Scatter chart of Yiling pharmaceutical company.

Table 4. Cumulative abnormal return rate of Yiling pharmaceutical company.

Trade Date	t	Expected Return	AR	CAR	Trade Date	t	Expected Return	AR	CAR
2020/4/27	−7	1.8910%	−7.3039%	−7.3039%	2020/5/12	1	1.5274%	−3.0351%	−1.9432%
2020/4/28	−6	0.8377%	−6.0045%	−13.3084%	2020/5/13	2	1.5411%	−4.1317%	−6.0749%
2020/4/29	−5	-0.1134%	−1.3349%	−14.6433%	2020/5/14	3	0.6203%	−3.9143%	−9.9892%
2020/4/30	−4	0.3707%	0.3291%	−14.3142%	2020/5/15	4	0.0265%	0.8485%	−9.1406%
2020/5/6	−3	2.0157%	7.9913%	−6.3230%	2020/5/18	5	1.7932%	−6.6569%	−15.7976%
2020/5/7	−2	0.7079%	5.7672%	−0.5558%	2020/5/19	6	1.1207%	−1.8045%	−17.6020%
2020/5/8	−1	1.1776%	−4.9154%	−5.4712%	2020/5/20	7	−0.0299%	−2.9209%	−20.5230%
2020/5/11	0	−0.2764%	6.5630%	1.0918%					

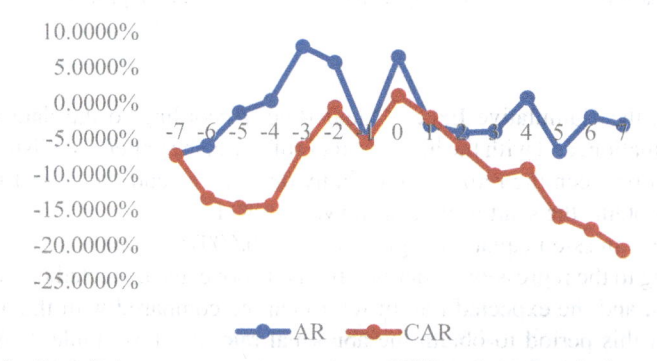

Fig. 2. Cumulative excess return rate chart of Yiling pharmaceutical company.

was the day of the rumor. In the days of the cumulative abnormal rate, the cumulative abnormal rate has reached nearly-15%. In the case of No. But within a few days after the announcement, from t = 1 to t = 3 within a few days, excess yield and excess yield has not been rising, excess yield even at around 5%, its trend slowed obviously, after the announcement 4 days, shares are no longer affected by the clarification announcement, d began to hold normal fluctuations, and the cumulative excess yield all the way down. It shows that the clarification announcement can only play a short-term effect on the recovery of the stock price of Yiling Pharmaceutical, and can alleviate the stock price fluctuation to some extent. In the long run, the release of a clarification announcement can not change the changes brought by the general environment of the listed company.

It can be seen that the clarification announcement issued by Yiling Pharmaceutical has indeed played a positive role in responding to the rumors and stabilizing the market, but its effect is not significant.

4.6 Long-Term Market Response Evaluation

As shown in Table 5, the overall profit and profit of Yiling Pharmaceutical industry still show an upward trend in the whole year. The event day appeared in the middle of 2020, which can be seen from the mid-year report that the basic earnings per share and net assets per share still showed an upward trend, but the net assets per share increased less in the medium term, indicating that the impact of the received rumors was strong. Even if the clarification announcement was issued, there was still a certain negative impact. However, from the return on investment assets and net profit growth trend, the growth ratio has not changed much. It shows that in the long term, the clarification of negative rumors does not change most of the long-term financial indicators, but also shows that the clarification announcement will not bring a big reaction to the long-term market, nor can it change the impact of the environment on listed companies.

Table 5. Table of Yiling Pharmaceutical Company.

	First Quarter 2020	Second Quarter 2020	Third Quarter 2020
Basic earnings per share (RMB)	0.3700	0.4275	0.6082
Net assets per share (RMB)	6.9643	6.9955	7.2438
Total operating revenue (RMB)	2.334billion	4.487billion	6.447billion
Gross profit (RMB)	1.515billion	2.790billion	4.077billion
Return on input capital	5.34%	8.53%	11.86%
Single quarter total operating income year-on-year	50.56%	50.13%	43.84%

(continued)

Table 5. (*continued*)

	First Quarter 2020	Second Quarter 2020	Third Quarter 2020
Single quarter total operating income chain ratio	57.88%	−7.73%	−8.95%
Net profit	437.6million	713.3million	1015million

5 Conclusion

5.1 Results

This article to Shijiazhuang ridge pharmaceutical co., LTD., as a research object, through the event study, using the stock abnormal yield (AR) and cumulative abnormal yield (CAR) description to ridge pharmaceutical issued the clarification announcement response to negative rumors on the impact of the stock market, and evaluate the clarification of short-term market before and after the reaction. According to the trend chart can be concluded, although the cumulative abnormal yield in the final negative, but the trend of abnormal yields in the event in the future, especially in the announcement on the same day, abnormal yield value rose significantly and above 0%, the cumulative yield above 0%, on the day in this period the market for even spend blast clarification of the event is more important.

5.2 Research Implications

Through the study of Yiling Pharmaceutical in response to negative rumors, The following enlightenment can be obtained: First, clarify that the release of the announcement is timely, Listed companies' timely and accurate response to the rumors to minimize the negative impact, The second trading day of the negative news release on May 8,2020, That is, on May 11,2020, Yiling Pharmaceutical company issued a clarification notice to clarify this; next, The clarification content must be true, effective and persuasive, It is better to have relevant documents or scientific research data as a factual basis, Yiling Pharmaceutical demonstrated the systematic toxicology studies in this clarification response, Established a system quality control system from intermediate to finished product, And citing a large amount of pharmacological literature as a basis, So the clarification can be justified, Strong response to the rumors; in addition, Clarification announcement to clarify the information in the rumor, And should not avoid serious matters, Response to every message whenever possible.

Through data, clarify the announcement is not long-term effective effect on capital markets, which has no significant influence on its financial index data, even in the short term can not necessarily through the response to events and share price rebound, but its more can have the effect of stable market, clarification before and after the stock price volatility. Generally speaking, it is essential to clarify negative rumors by issuing clarification announcements, and high-quality clarification announcements can play a positive and effective role to some extent.

References

1. Zheng, Y.S.: Uncertainty and market rumors. Xiamen University (2019)
2. Peng, Q.: Economic consequences and coping mechanisms of market rumors: an empirical study from the perspective of trust. Southwest University of Finance and Economics (2019)
3. Davis, F., Khadivar, H., Pukthuanthong, K., Walker, T.J.: Insider trading in rumored takeover targets. Eur. Financ. Manag. **27**(3), 490–527 (2020)
4. Gao, J.: Empirical study on rumor and its clarification and investor market reaction. Inner Mongolia University (2021)
5. Fang, W.: Refutation degree and clarification effect of M & A rumors: the moderating effect of source honesty. Nanjing University (2012)
6. Zhang, N.: To clarify the influencing factors of the effectiveness of the announcement and the moderating effect of the degree of negative rumors. Nanjing University (2011)
7. Qin, Y.: Empirical study on the impact of clarification announcement of listed companies on stock volatility. Tianjin University of Finance and Economics (2021)
8. He, J.: Market reaction research on the clarification of stock market rumors in China. Zhejiang University (2015)
9. Wang, J., et al.: Effect of digitalized rumor clarification on stock markets. Emerg. Mark. Financ. Trade **55**(2), 450–474 (2019)
10. Liu, C., Han, L., Chu, G.: The effect of overnight corporate announcements on price discovery. Financ. Res. Lett. **53** (2023)
11. Mahmoudi, N., Docherty, P., Melia, A.: Firm-level investor sentiment and corporate announcement returns. J. Bank. Financ. **144** (2022)

The Relationship Between ESG Performance and Financial Constraints and Its Impact on Firm Value

Shengyang Qu(✉)

School of Economics and Management, Yunnan Normal University, Kunming 650000, China
1811581116@mail.sit.edu.cn

Abstract. Based on the data of China's A-share market from 2015 to 2020, this project examines the relationship between environmental protection performance and financing restrictions at the corporate level, and discusses the mechanism of financing restrictions on corporate valuation. Empirical analysis shows that the enterprises with better environmental protection performance have fewer financing restrictions, and the enterprises with better environmental protection performance have fewer financing restrictions. In addition, there is a significant positive relationship between environmental protection performance and enterprise value, that is, the higher the environmental protection performance, the higher the enterprise value. The study found that the impact of environmental governance performance on companies is mainly determined by financing restrictions, that is to say, environmental governance performance can improve the value of companies by reducing financing restrictions. Industrial attributes, property rights and other factors will also have a certain impact on the impact between the two, among which, high pollution industries, state-owned enterprises and other factors have a greater impact on the two. Finally, the results obtained through empirical analysis have a certain guiding significance for the business decisions of relevant departments and enterprises.

Keywords: ESG performance · Financial Constraints · Enterprise Value

1 Introduction

Environment, society and governance are key points in CSR research, and it is also a main index to measure whether CSR can achieve sustainable development. In modern society, the shortage of funds is a very common problem, which will have a great impact on the financial situation of the company, which will have a certain impact on the growth and value of the company. This project takes the ESG performance of listed companies in China as the research object, systematically studies the internal relationship between ESG performance and corporate financial constraints, reveals the mechanism of corporate financial constraints on corporate financial management, and provides a scientific basis for improving the company's financial management level. The interaction between environmental governance performance, financing constraints and corporate value has become a hot issue in academic circles. Previous literatures mostly focus on the impact of environmental governance performance on corporate value, and believe that environmental governance performance has a significant positive impact on corporate value. Today, when the concept of environmental governance is increasingly rooted in the hearts of the people, scholars pay more and more attention to the relationship between environmental governance performance and financing constraints. However, due to the particularity of the subjects and the limitations of research methods, the existing related research still needs to be discussed at a deeper level. Based on the data of China's A-share market from 2015 to 2020, we will use the method of multivariate regression analysis to study the action mechanism of Chinese enterprise environmental protection policy on enterprise environmental protection behavior from the micro level, and reveal its mechanism. The main innovations include: (1) Using financing restrictions as intermediate variables to explore the mechanism between environmental governance performance and corporate value. (2) From the point of view of the influence of enterprise attributes, equity attributes and other factors on environmental governance performance, this paper discusses the interaction mechanism between environmental governance performance and financing restrictions. Using Wind and WIND databases and multiple linear regression analysis, this paper makes an empirical analysis on the performance of China's A-share market from 2015 to 2020.

2 Theoretical Analysis and Hypothesis Formulation

2.1 Hypotheses on the Interaction Among ESG Performance, Financing Constraints and Firm Value

ESG (Environment, Social, Governance) performance refers to the performance of enterprises in environmental, social, corporate governance and other aspects. Environment includes the enterprise's environmental protection measures and the protection of the ecological environment; Society includes enterprises' care for employees and consumers, social responsibility and public welfare activities, etc. Corporate governance includes corporate management structure, internal control, transparency and compliance, etc. [1]. As an important manifestation of corporate social responsibility, ESG performance is closely related to the long-term operation, social reputation and sustainable development of enterprises.

According to the ESG rating standard, ESG standard refers to the sustainable development index and regional sustainable development index, so the sustainable development index can be linked to financing constraints and enterprise value. Enterprises with good ESG performance enjoy a good reputation and brand image among investors and consumers, which in turn improves market competitiveness and promotes enterprise growth and profitability [2]. His paper proposes the following research hypotheses:

H1: There is a positive relationship between ESG performance and firm value
H2: Excellent ESG performance can reduce financing constraints

2.2 Theoretical Link Between ESG Performance and Financial Constraints

There is an interactive relationship between ESG performance and financial constraints. On the one hand, enterprises with good ESG performance can gain more social recognition and investor trust, which makes it easier to obtain financing, and the financing cost is relatively low. On the other hand, the impact of financing constraints on ESG performance is also significant. Financial constraints may lead to the lack of financial support for enterprises [3], which in turn affects their investment and performance in environmental, social, corporate governance and other aspects.

2.3 Influence Mechanism Between ESG Performance and Corporate Value

There is also a significant positive correlation between ESG performance and enterprise value [4]. Companies with good ESG performance enjoy a good reputation and brand image among investors and consumers, which in turn improves market competitiveness and promotes corporate growth and profitability. Some studies have shown that enterprises with good ESG performance have superior stock performance and performance in the long run, and investors are more inclined to choose these enterprises for investment.

First of all, enterprises with good ESG performance can reduce their operational risks and avoid financial risks caused by some potential environmental and social problems. For example, the practice of environmental protection and social responsibility can reduce the risk of environmental and social events, thus reducing legal proceedings and other negative impacts on enterprises. By practicing ESG management, these companies are able to better control operational risks, protect their corporate brand, and improve their reputation and social trust.

Secondly, enterprises with good ESG performance can also obtain better financing opportunities and financing costs [5]. As ESG investment attracts more and more attention from the capital market, investors and financial institutions pay more and more attention to the ESG performance of enterprises, so enterprises with good ESG performance can more easily obtain financing support, and the financing cost is relatively low. For example, enterprises with good ESG performance can attract more ESG investment, obtain more financial support such as socially responsible investment and green bonds, and at the same time can more easily obtain financing support from banks and other financial institutions [6, 7]. Finally, companies with good ESG performance are able to attract more consumers and employees. As consumers and employees pay more attention to environmental, social and governance, it is easier for companies with good ESG performance to attract and retain good employees and consumers, thus increasing their market share and profitability. In addition, companies with good ESG performance are also able to attract more consumers to choose their products and services through their excellent corporate image and brand image. Therefore, enterprises with good ESG performance can enhance the value of enterprises, promote their long-term sustainable development, obtain more market opportunities and financing support, and attract more consumers and employees.

3 Empirical Test and Results

3.1 Variable Selection and Data Description

The research object for this paper is Chinese A-share listed firms from 2015 to 2020. Data sources for this paper include the Wind database and company annual reports. This student chooses the comprehensive score of the ESG rating as the measuring index of ESG performance in accordance with the above-described ESG rating methodology. Financial restrictions are measured using the debt to equity ratio (DER) and interest coverage ratio (ICR), which, respectively, indicate the debt to shareholders' equity ratio and interest coverage multiple. Corporate value is calculated using the market value to total assets (MVE/TA) ratio. Business size (LnTA), profitability (ROA), growth (coefficient of variation of ROA), financial leverage (Leverage), stock liquidity (ST), industry (Industry), and ownership type (Ownership) are examples of control variables.

3.2 Empirical Model Setting

In order to test the promotion effect of ESG performance on enterprise value, this paper takes enterprise value (MVE/TA) as the explained variable and ESG performance as the explanatory variable, and establishes Model (1) to test H1:

$$(MVE/TA) = \beta_0 + \beta_1 ESG + \beta_2 LnTA + \beta_3 ROA + \beta_4 ROAvariablecoefficient + \beta_5 Leverage + \beta_6 ST + \beta_7 Ownership + Industry_b \quad (1)$$

For the impact of ESG performance on financial constraints, this paper takes financial constraints as the explained variable and ESG performance as the explanatory variable, and establishes Model (2) to verify H2:

$$DER/ICR = \beta_0 + \beta_1 ESg + \beta_2 \ln TA + \beta_3 ROA + \beta_4 ROA \ variablecoefficient + \beta_5 QLeverage + B + \beta_6 ST + \beta_7 ownership + Industry \quad (2)$$

The descriptive statistical analysis of the variables is shown in Table 1.

As can be seen from the table, the mean ESG score is 53.98 points, the standard deviation is 12.34 points, and the range of variation is relatively small. The average value of DER was 96.31%, and the standard deviation was 120.56%, indicating a large range of variation. The mean value of ICR was 4.41, the standard deviation was 5.72, and the range of variation was relatively large. The mean value of MVE/TA was 1.73, the standard deviation was 1.49, and the range of variation was also relatively small. The mean and standard deviation of LnTA, ROA, coefficient of variation of ROA, financial leverage and ST were 10.17 and 0.70, 0.05 and 0.02, 0.06 and 0.01, 1.08 and 0.66, 0.18 and 0.39, respectively, with relatively small range of variation. The results of correlation analysis among variables are shown Table 2. It can be seen from the correlation coefficient matrix that ESG is significantly correlated with DER, ICR, ROA, financial leverage, ST and other variables. In particular, the correlation coefficient between ESG and DER is -0.154, and the correlation coefficient between ESG and ICR is -0.195, both of which show significant negative correlation.

Table 1. Descriptive statistical analysis of variables

Variables	Average	Standard deviation	Minimum	Maximum
ESG score	53.98	12.34	18.33	87.42
DER	96.31	120.56	84.78	1265.09
ICR	4.41	5.72	0.12	109.38
MVE/TA	1.73	1.49	0.06	22.96
LnTA	7.73	1.39	3.40	11.86
ROA	0.05	0.08	1.01	0.64
Coefficient of variation in ROA	0.67	0.36	0.00	2.93
Financial leverage	2.13	1.58	0.00	9.71
ST	1.29	0.42	0.00	2.00

Table 2. Results of correlation analysis among variables

Variables	ESG	DER	ICR	MVE/TA	LnTA	ROA	ROA coefficient of variation	Financial leverage	ST
ESG	1	0.154	0.195	0.079	0.112	0.308	0.234	0.205	0.052
DER	0.154	1	0.253	0.043	0.104	0.021	0.138	0.628	0.218
ICR	0.195	0.253	1	0.019	0.023	0.074	0.071	0.073	0.03
MVE/TA	0.079	0.043	0.019	1	0.642	0.073	0.014	0.011	0.052
LnTA	0.112	0.104	0.023	0.642	1	0.074	0.041	0.208	0.067
ROA	0.308	0.021	0.074	0.073	0.074	1	0.214	0.291	0.014
Coefficient of variation in ROA	0.234	0.138	0.071	0.014	0.041	0.214	1	0.167	0

3.3 Analysis of Empirical Results

This paper uses multiple regression model to conduct empirical research on the relationship among ESG performance, financing constraints and enterprise value, and obtains the following empirical results (see Table 3):

(1) There is an important positive correlation between ESG performance and company value.

　　The multiple regression results show that the higher the ESG score is, the greater the enterprise value is, indicating that the enterprises with good ESG performance have more competitive advantages in the market competition, which can improve the profit level and market share of enterprises, and then improve the enterprise value.

Table 3. Empirical Results

Variable	(1) MVE/TA	(2) MVE/TA	(3) MVE/TA
ESG	0.3250*** (11.1884)		1.0154*** (3.3236)
DER		−1.0079*** (−21.3782)	−0.8941*** (−15.6218)
DERxESG			−0.1914** (−2.3991)
ROA	0.1217*** (14.2595)	0.1018*** (12.3986)	0.0983*** (12.1591)
Coefficient of variation in ROA	0.0004 (0.9541)	0.0001 (0.3962)	0.0002 (0.5643)
LnTA	−0.0811*** (−10.7503)	−0.0735*** (−10.1956)	−0.0722*** (−10.1873)
conS	8.3754*** (41.2645)	12.3702*** (45.4407)	12.0087*** (40.3734)
year	CONTROL	CONTROL	CONTROL
Ind	CONTROL	CONTROL	CONTROL
N	3304	3304	3304
adj.R^2	0.4854	0.5312	0.5469
F	98.3796	117.9804	118.2473

Note: The values in parentheses are t values

Specifically, when the variables such as industry characteristics, ownership nature, enterprise size and growth are controlled, the enterprise value (MVE/TA) increases by 0.18 percentage points for every percentage point increase in ESG score, and the result is significant ($t = 3.217$, $p < 0.01$).

(2) There is a significant negative correlation between ESG performance and financial constraints.

Multiple regression results show that firms with higher ESG scores have lower financial constraints, indicating that firms with good ESG performance enjoy better reputation and reputation in the financing market, and can more easily obtain external financial support to alleviate financial constraints. Specifically, when the variables such as industry characteristics, ownership nature, enterprise size and growth are controlled, the financial constraints index decreases by 0.13 percentage points for every percentage point increase in ESG score, and the result is significant ($t = -4.233$, $p < 0.001$).

In summary, the empirical results of this paper show that there is a significant positive correlation between ESG performance and firm value, and the influence of financial constraints on this relationship is not significant. This The conclusion not only supports the feasibility of the ESG investment strategy in theory, but also provides a reference to businesses to implement ESG management in practice.

This study also finds that financing constraints, ownership structure and industry characteristics have different impacts on the relationship between ESG performance and firm value [8]. This finding suggests that the government and regulators should give more consideration to the special circumstances and practical difficulties of soes when encouraging them to implement ESG management, and provide more policy support for them.. The results show that the impact of financial indicators on the relationship is more significant [9]. This finding shows that among investors and market participants, financial indicators are still the main indicators to evaluate corporate value and performance, and ESG factors, although valued, need to further improve their recognition and influence in the market. In summary, the research of this paper has certain theoretical value and practical significance, and provides some reference and guidance for relevant stakeholders in corporate ESG management. However, this study still has some limitations. First of all, this study uses cross-sectional panel data, which cannot reflect the causal relationship between ESG performance and enterprise value [10]. In the future, longitudinal data or experimental data can be considered for further research. Secondly, the variables controlled in this study are limited, and other factors that may affect the relationship between ESG performance and enterprise value, such as corporate governance and employee satisfaction, are not considered. Future research can further explore the impact of these factors on the relationship between ESG performance and enterprise value.

4 Conclusion

4.1 Research Conclusions

This project intends to explore the internal relationship between environmental governance performance and corporate valuation from the three dimensions of environmental governance performance, financing constraints and corporate valuation, and test the impact of industrial characteristics and corporate ownership structure. Through the statistical analysis of China's stock market from 2015 to 2020, we have come to the following conclusions:

First, the performance of environmental governance has a significant positive impact on the market value of the company. Specifically, every time the ESG score goes up, the company's market value increases by 0.58 yuan. This shows that if a company can pay attention to environmental protection, and can make a good performance, then the company can create more value for the company.

Second, the intermediary effect of financing constraints between environmental governance performance and corporate valuation is not obvious. This shows that under the financing restrictions, the performance of environmental governance will still play an important role in the value of the company.

Third, industrial characteristics have obvious intermediary effects among ESG performance, financing constraints and corporate valuation. In particular, when the industry has a high degree of development, ESG performance will have a greater impact on the value of the company.

4.2 Policy Suggestions and Management Implications

The research results of this paper provide the following suggestions for enterprise ESG management and policy making:

Firstly, enterprises should strengthen the attention and management of ESG issues, and continuously improve ESG performance, so as to achieve long-term sustainable development and value maximization.

Secondly, the government should strengthen the guidance and supervision of ESG management in enterprises, and promote the wide application of ESG concepts in enterprises.

Third, the government should establish a relevant ESG policy system to promote the continuous improvement of enterprise ESG performance and maximize the relationship between ESG performance and enterprise value.

4.3 Research Limitations and Prospects

The limitations of this survey are as follows:

First of all, as the research object of this subject is only China's A-share market, whether the conclusion of this topic is of universal significance still needs to be discussed in depth.

Secondly, this paper only discusses the internal relationship between environmental governance performance and corporate governance performance, shareholders' rights and interests and corporate value from three aspects: environmental governance performance, financing constraints and corporate value. While ignoring the effect of environmental governance performance on corporate governance performance, shareholders' rights and interests and corporate social responsibility.

Third, we only examine the interaction between environmental governance performance, financing constraints and corporate valuation from the perspectives of industrial attributes and equity attributes, while ignoring other possible intermediary variables such as company size, that is, the relationship between environmental governance performance and corporate valuation. In the future, we may explore more regulatory factors.

At the same time, it is pointed out that there are shortcomings in the current environmental protection assessment and financial assessment, and more comprehensive and accurate environmental protection assessment and financial assessment can be further studied in the future.

Therefore, on this basis, this paper further discusses the interaction among environmental governance performance, financing constraints and corporate value. In the future, this topic will improve the experimental results through the analysis of the experimental results, and analyze the experimental results. In this regard, business operators and regulators should pay attention to and monitor the performance of ESG, and build a corresponding evaluation and monitoring system to promote the sustainable development of enterprises.

References

1. Wang, N., Li, Y.: Research on ESG performance and corporate investment efficiency: impact effect and mechanism test. J. Financ. Financ. **200**(06), 23–31 (2022)
2. Wang, N., Li, Y.: The impact and mechanism of ESG performance on corporate investment efficiency: an analysis based on the data of Chinese A-share listed companies from 2011 to 2020. Res. Financ. Account. **558**(12), 30–39 (2022)
3. Chen, L., Yu, H., et al.: ESG performance, financing constraints and enterprise performance. Friends Account. **694**(22), 24–30 (2022)
4. Long, H., Ouyang, J.J.: The impact of ESG performance on the dynamic adjustment of capital structure of domestic enterprises. South China Financ. **556**(12), 33–44 (2022)
5. Li, Z., Shao, Y., Li, Z., et al.: ESG information disclosure, media supervision and corporate financing constraints. Sci. Decis. **300**(07), 1–26 (2022)
6. Li, Q.: ESG investment, financing constraints, and the enterprise value. Southwest university of finance and economics (2021)
7. Yu, H.: ESG performance, financing constraints, and the enterprise performance. Fujian normal university (2021)
8. Chen, L., Fan, J.: ESG performance and corporate High quality development: financial constraints and analysts' attention. Anhui university business school (2023)
9. Hao, Y.T., Zhang, Y.H.: ESG performance, financing constraints and high-quality innovation of coal enterprises under the "dual carbon" target. Nanjing University of Information Science and Technology (2023)
10. Li, J., Yang, Z., Yi, J.: Does ESG performance help reduce the cost of Corporate Debt financing? - Microscopic evidence from listed companies. Hubei economic accounting institute, school of Chinese Academy of Social Sciences industrial economy research institute, institute of politics and public administration, Wuhan university (2023)

A Study on the Relationship Between ESG Performance and Stock Returns – Take A-share Listed Company Stocks as the Example

Liqi Dong[1(✉)], Shifeng Deng[2], and Qian Gao[3]

[1] Business School, The University of Melbourne, Grattan Street, Parkville, VIC 3010, Australia
liqid@student.unimelb.edu.au

[2] School of Management, Huazhong University of Science and Technology, Wuhan 430074, China

[3] School of International Education, Shandong University of Finance and Economics, Jinan 250014, China

Abstract. With the transition of the global economy to sustainable development, ESG investment has received wide attention and recognition from the capital market. However, the relationship between ESG and stock returns has not yet reached a consistent conclusion. Therefore, this paper examines the relationship between ESG performance and stock returns using data from A-share listed companies from 2009–2021 as the research sample. The findings show that ESG performance of A-share listed companies in the last 13 years has a negative relationship with stock return, among which the performance of E has the weakest degree of negative impact on stock returns. Through further analysis, it is found that the performance of ESG in carbon-intensive industries has a weaker degree of negative impact on stock return compared to low-carbon industries. This finding still holds after the robustness test. Therefore, for the high-carbon industry, actively improving ESG performance can help it achieve sustainable development.

Keywords: ESG performance · stock return · high-carbon industries · sustainable development

1 Introduction

On September 22, 2020, at the 75th United Nations General Assembly, China made clear for the first time that it is striving to peak CO_2 emissions by 2030 and working towards carbon neutrality by 2060. It is a long-term policy signal for a low-carbon transition of its economy that has attracted widespread international attention. This is a challenging and daunting task, with policymakers, investors and businesses focusing on environmental, social and corporate governance (ESG) issues. Good ESG performance will help improve the environment, enhance corporate governance and maintain social stability and development, reflecting the significance of active corporate social responsibility.

L. Dong, S. Deng and Q. Gao—These authors contributed equally.

ESG is a core framework and assessment system that focuses on corporate environmental, social and governance responsibilities, which is a systematic methodology to promote the implementation of low-carbon transition and sustainable development. It has been deepened by various international organizations and investment institutions. According to a Bloomberg Intelligence survey, global ESG investment is expected to reach $50 trillion in 2025. In China, the capital market is gradually understanding and accepting the ESG investment concept, which is highly compatible with China's sustainable development strategy of 'innovation, coordination, green, openness and sharing' and is a reflection of the sustainable development concept at the micro level and a path for enterprises. It is a reflection of the concept of sustainable development at the micro level and a path for enterprises to achieve sustainable development.

This paper uses the data of A-share listed companies from 2009–2021 as the research sample, and investigates the relationship between ESG performance and stock returns through empirical analysis. It is found that stock returns of Chinese A-shares (2009–2021) have an overall negative relationship with ESG performance, and the negative relationship between ESG performance and stock returns of high-carbon industries is weaker compared to non-high-carbon industries. This indicates that there is a conflict of interest between corporate investment in environmental, social and corporate governance and shareholders' interest (stock returns) over a short period of time, with a weaker degree of negative relationship in the high-carbon sector than in the low-carbon sector. In the long run, good ESG performance in high-carbon industries will help improve the environment, enhance corporate governance and maintain stable social development, reflecting the significance of companies actively practicing social responsibility and in line with the concept of sustainable development.

2 Literature Review and Hypothesizes

2.1 Literature Review

Relevant Studies on Corporate ESG Performance. Zhou et al. showed that investors in the Chinese A-share market have a significant preference for ESG responsibility [1]; Xu suggested that ESG information disclosure of firms in China's manufacturing industry can help improve corporate value [2].

Relevant Studies on the Relationship Between ESG Performance and Stock Returns. According to the information asymmetry theory, good ESG practices can increase the information transparency of a company by communicating its business strategy to market investors through environmental, social, and corporate governance [3, 4]. Takahashi and Yamada showed that mutual fund firms with ESG-based investments outperformed other firms [5]. Zhang et al. found that ESG performance has a significant impact on stock returns [6].

Some scholars have also made arguments from principal-agent theory; Qiao studied that the preference of the management to maximize company profits and financial and non-financial indicators will lead to shareholders' stock returns being affected [7]. Feng found that overall ESG performance is negatively related to stock returns [8]. Yang et al. found that, for Chinese companies, the level of corporate carbon information disclosure has a negative relationship with stock returns [9, 10].

Summary of Literature Review. There is no uniform conclusion on the relationship between ESG performance and stock returns. In addition, the majority of studies correlate ESG performance with the stock returns of overall A-share market, while there is a lack of studies that distinguish A-share listed companies by the level of carbon emission. On this basis, this paper will explore the impact of ESG performance on stock returns in high- and low- carbon industries respectively. The industry classification method of this paper adopts the differentiation method of Yan and Chen. Specifically, the high-carbon industries include the secondary industry in the National Economic Classification and the transportation, storage and postal industry in the tertiary industry, and the rest are non-high-carbon industries.

2.2 Research Hypothesis

ESG performance of listed companies will have a direct impact on the capital market. Specifically, good ESG performance will lead to higher stock returns. Taking the stock data of A-share market from 2009–2021 as the sample, the hypotheses are proposed as followings:

H1-1: ESG performance has a positive relationship with stock returns of A-share listed companies.

On the other hand, the improved ESG rating will reduce corporate risk. However, it also represents that the company invests more cost in ESG, which is borne by shareholders and in turn leads to a decrease in shareholder return. Therefore, the hypothesis is proposed as the following:

H1-2: ESG performance has a negative relationship with stock returns of A-share listed companies.

In addition, Garcia et al. report that in emerging countries, companies belonging to carbon-sensitive industries perform better in terms of corporate sustainability and social responsibility performance compared to companies belonging to low-carbon industries [11]. This leads to the hypothesis H2 of this paper:

H2-1: Stock returns are higher for the same ESG performance in high-carbon sectors compared to non-high-carbon sectors.
H2-2: Stock returns are lower for the same ESG performance in high-carbon sectors compared to non-high-carbon sectors.

3 Research Design

3.1 Data Source

After excluding ST, *ST and missing data years, the final sample is 627 enterprises listed in the A-share market from 2009–2021.

The ESG rating scores of A-shares are provided by Sino-Securities Index, which has 3 first tier indicators, 16 s tier indicators, 44 third tier indicators, over 70 fourth tier indicators and over 300 underlying data indicators to assess the ESG performance. The stock and accounting data are provided by CSMAR and Wind databases, which are annual data.

3.2 Variable Definition and Model Design

The multiple linear regression models used in this paper are constructed as follows:

$$\text{Model 1.1 RET}_{i,t} = \alpha_1 + \beta_1 \text{ESG}_{i,t-1} + \sum_{m=2}^{6} \beta_m \text{Control}_{i,t} + \varepsilon_{i,t}$$

$$\text{Model 1.2 RET}_{i,t} = \alpha_1 + \beta_1 E_{i,t-1} + \sum_{m=2}^{6} \beta_m \text{Control}_{i,t} + \varepsilon_{i,t}$$

$$\text{Model 1.3 RET}_{i,t} = \alpha_1 + \beta_1 S_{i,t-1} + \sum_{m=2}^{6} \beta_m \text{Control}_{i,t} + \varepsilon_{i,t}$$

$$\text{Model 1.4 RET}_{i,t} = \alpha_1 + \beta_1 G_{i,t-1} + \sum_{m=2}^{6} \beta_m \text{Control}_{i,t} + \varepsilon_{i,t}$$

where i is the number of firms ($i = 1, 2,...,n$), and is the random disturbance term.

Table 1 shows the variable definition. The explanatory variable is the annual stock return (RET). A higher value indicates a higher stock return.

The core explanatory variables are ESG performance (ESG) and the individual E/S/G scores. The better the ESG performance of the company, the higher the score. One-year lagging is used for the ESG performance score to eliminate endogeneity [12].

This study included firm size, leverage, investment situation, stock volatility and sales as control variables to control for the effect of individual differences such as firm size on stock returns [12–14].

Firm size is expressed as the natural logarithm of its market capitalization; the larger the firm, the better the investment prospects are likely to be. Leverage is expressed as the firm's gearing ratio. A lower gearing ratio indicates a sound financial policy. Investment situation is expressed as the capital expenditures divided by book value of assets. A lower capital expenditure rate indicates a lower risk of the company. Stock volatility is expressed as the standard deviation of returns based on stock returns over the past 12 months, with lower volatility indicating a stable stock price for a long-term investment. Sales are expressed as sales per share. A higher sales per share indicates a better revenue profile of the company, which is suitable for long-term investment.

4 Result Analysis

4.1 Descriptive Statistics

Table 2 displays the descriptive statistics for the primary variables, with a total of 8,151 observations after excluding missing data. The mean value of stock return is positive, indicating that the overall stock return performs well during the sample period. The mean value of ESG composite score is 74.33, but the maximum and minimum value are 89.30 and 47.41 respectively, indicating that the ESG practice varies widely among selected Chinese A-share listed enterprises.

Table 1. Variable explanation.

	Variable	Variable symbol	Explanation
Explained variable	Stock return	RET	Annual stock return
Explanatory variable	ESG performance	ESG	Sino-Securities Index composite ESG scoring
	E performance	E	Sino-Securities Index individual E scoring
	S performance	S	Sino-Securities Index individual S scoring
	G performance	G	Sino-Securities Index individual G scoring
Control variable	Firm size	LN (Market Cap)	The natural logarithm of enterprise's market capitalization
	Leverage	Leverage	Gearing ratio
	Investment situation	Invest	Capital expenditures to book value of assets
	Stock volatility	Volatility	The standard deviation of returns based on stock returns over the past 12 months
	Sales	Sales	Sales per share

Table 2. Descriptive statistics.

Variable	Obs	Mean	Std. dev	Min	Max
RET	8,151	0.8017	2684	−0.9494	1533.46
ESG	8,151	74.33	4.974	47.41	89.30
E	8,151	60.83	0.0862	34.44	95.16
S	8,151	74.67	0.1232	4.88	100
G	8,151	80.76	0.0621	43.68	96.13
LN (Market Cap)	8,151	22.93	1.073	20.49	28.58
Leverage	8,151	2.421	7.227	−0.710	374.8
Invest	8,151	0.0467	0.0460	4.55e−06	0.477
Volatility	8,151	42.48	39.97	10.44	2726
Sales	8,151	9.088	13.48	0.00265	264.4

The mean value of leverage is 2.4212, which indicates that the majority of the enterprise's capital structure is with high risk. However, the investment situation varies widely among companies. The mean of volatility is 42.48, indicating that Chinese stock market is volatile. The mean value of sales per share is 9.088, the minimum and maximum value are 0.00265 and 264.4 respectively, showing that the number of stock offerings varies greatly between companies when sales are certain.

4.2 Correlation Test

Table 3. Correlation test.

	RET	ESG	LN (Market Cap)	Leverage	Invest	Volatility	Sales
RET	1						
ESG	−0.023**	1					
LN (Market Cap)	0.005	0.269***	1				
Leverage	−0.003	−0.044***	−0.031***	1			
Invest	−0.012	−0.013	0.045***	0.043***	1		
Volatility	0.514***	−0.041***	−0.011	0.005	−0.013	1	
Sales	−0.011	0.088***	0.205***	−0.016	−0.061***	−0.038***	1

* $p < 0.1$, ** $p < 0.05$, *** $p < 0.01$

Table 3 displays the correlation coefficients. The results indicate that the correlation coefficient of stock returns is related to the composite ESG score. In addition, the ESG composite score is correlated with the company's market capitalization, integrated leverage, stock volatility and sales per share. The correlation analysis shows that there is no multicollinearity, which will not harm the regression result.

4.3 Regression Result

Table 4 presents the results. The ESG composite score and the respective scores of the three pillars are negatively correlated with stock returns at the 1% level. One-point improved in E, S and G score is associated with a 0.037%, 9.056% and 4.567% decrease of the stock returns separately. Furthermore, in model 1.1, the stock return and market capitalization are significantly positive correlated, with a coefficient of 29.53 at the 1% level of significance. It indicates that the expansion of a company's market capitalization affects positively on the stock return. The coefficient of volatility is positive at 1% significance level, indicating that the increase of stock volatility has a contribution to the increase in stock return. However, the coefficient of combined leverage is negative at 5% significance level, indicating that a high level of debt is not conducive to higher stock returns. In addition, model 1.1 has a better fit than models 1.2–1.4. The regression results support hypothesis H1-2 that ESG performance and shareholder returns are negatively correlated in the sample.

Table 4. Regression analysis.

	Model 1.1	Model 1.2	Model 1.3	Model 1.4
	Full sample	Full sample	Full sample	Full sample
ESG	−0.00287***			
	(0.08362)			
E		−0.00037***		
		(0.00824)		
S			−0.09056***	
			(2.40334)	
G				−0.04567***
				(0.69915)
LN (Market Cap)	29.53339***	−3.1e+01	−1.5e+01	−3.2e+01
	(4.92042)	(62.94223)	(67.23733)	(61.85058)
Leverage	−0.05994**	−0.47650	−0.52604*	−0.37851
	(0.02488)	(0.27640)	(0.27098)	(0.25524)
Invest	−3.8e+01	5.7e+02	5.9e+02*	5.5e+02
	(29.31593)	(3.2e+02)	(3.3e+02)	(3.5e+02)
Volatility	1.30295***	36.65001***	36.61802***	36.66589***
	(0.22931)	(1.49782)	(1.48152)	(1.48061)
Sales	0.09992	0.74382	0.87172	0.67720
	(0.07325)	(0.75327)	(0.72910)	(0.70770)
_cons	−7.1e+02***	−1.1e+03	−8.1e+02	−1.5e+03
	(1.1e+02)	(1.3e+03)	(1.3e+03)	(1.3e+03)
Time-fixed effect	Under control	Under control	Under control	Under control
Individual-fixed effect	Under control	Under control	Under control	Under control
N	7524	8151	8151	8151
R2	0.4242	0.2669	0.2668	0.2667

* $p < 0.1$, ** $p < 0.05$, *** $p < 0.01$

Based on the industry classification method in 2.1.2, the sample companies are divided into low-carbon sector companies (Model 2) and high-carbon sector companies (Model 3). Table 5 displays the results of the regression. The ESG composite scores of both low-carbon and high-carbon industries are negatively correlated with stock returns, with regression coefficients of −0.0483 and −0.0269 respectively. When other variables unchanged, stock returns decrease by 4.83% and 2.69% for each one-point increase in the ESG composite scores of non-high-carbon and high-carbon industries respectively. The regression results show that for high-carbon industries, stock returns have a weaker negative relationship with ESG performance.

Table 5. Regression results by industry.

	Model 2	Model 3
	Low-carbon industry	High-carbon industry
ESG	−0.0483**	−0.0269*
	(0.21811)	(0.13659)
LN (Market Cap)	27.34043***	30.09954***
	(6.05903)	(4.65467)
Leverage	0.11997*	−0.11597***
	(0.06369)	(0.01872)
Invest	8.30556	−5.5e+01
	(11.07683)	(36.53891)
Volatility	1.06813***	1.37047***
	(0.23623)	(0.24603)
Sales	0.02479	0.23545
	(0.01486)	(0.18537)
_cons	0.00000	0.00000
	(0.00000)	(0.00000)
Time-fixed effect	Under control	Under control
Individual-fixed effect	Under control	Under control
N	2064	5460
R2	0.4291	0.4625

* $p < 0.1$, ** $p < 0.05$, *** $p < 0.01$

The results prove that, for the A-share market, there is a short-term inconsistency between the social responsibility presented by ESG performance and shareholders' interests (stock returns). While the enterprises' social responsibility and sustainable development are not immediately reflected in the stock price and may even harm shareholders' interests in the short term. However, especially in high-carbon industries, the investment in environment (E) has almost no impact on shareholders' interests.

4.4 Robustness Test

The robustness test was conducted by using the method of replacing variables. Specifically, the explanatory variables ESG and E/S/G performance and the dependent variable have been replaced respectively (see Table 6).

The new ESG performance was reassigned to 1 for C, CC and CCC, 2 for B, BB and BBB, and 3 for A, AA and AAA, based on the results of Sino-Securities Index ESG scoring. The test results of replaced-ESG-performance model are consistent with the original model.

The stock holding period return (HPY) is used to represent stock returns. The results of new models are consistent with the previous empirical results (see Table 7).

Table 6. Robustness test _replaced ESG performance.

	Model 4	Model 5	Model 6
Ranking(taking C level as the baseline)	Full sample	Low-carbon industry	High-carbon industry
B	−2.3e+02**	−7.6e+02*	−5.2e+01*
	(89.72548)	(3.5e+02)	(42.66203)
A	−2.2e+02**	−7.6e+02**	−4.1e+01**
	(89.39260)	(3.6e+02)	(68.75046)
LN (Market Cap)	−2.3e+01	3.1e+02	−3.2e+02***
	(63.94671)	(1.8e+02)	(40.00038)
Leverage	−0.63935**	−0.44551	−0.19340
	(0.23457)	(0.49380)	(0.56537)
Invest	5.5e+02	1.6e+02	1.4e+03**
	(3.2e+02)	(1.7e+02)	(5.9e+02)
Volatility	36.61721***	23.42281***	74.55005***
	(1.48484)	(0.79003)	(6.45422)
Sales	0.70777	1.48804***	−1.42130
	(0.76849)	(0.47539)	(1.48452)
_cons	−1.1e+03	−7.1e+03*	3.2e+03**
	(1.4e+03)	(3.8e+03)	(1.2e+03)
Time-fixed effect	Under control	Under control	Under control
Individual-fixed effect	Under control	Under control	Under control
N	7524	2064	5460
R2	0.4803	0.4979	0.5025

* $p < 0.1$, ** $p < 0.05$, *** $p < 0.01$

Table 7. Robustness test _replaced stock returns.

	Model 7	Model 8	Model 9
	Full sample	Low-carbon industry	High-carbon industry
ESG	−0.0091***	−0.0159***	−0.0078***
	(0.02399)	(0.01987)	(0.00940)
LN (Market Cap)	5.05978***	3.63763***	5.47990***
	(0.43289)	(0.19658)	(0.60123)
Leverage	−0.07639***	−0.06814**	−0.07674***
	(0.01732)	(0.02347)	(0.01998)
Invest	5.30196***	−4.79063***	8.49294***
	(0.68376)	(1.12053)	(1.12936)
Volatility	−0.01202	−0.05712**	−0.00007
	(0.01564)	(0.02172)	(0.01397)
Sales	0.05829***	0.02963***	0.11692***
	(0.01129)	(0.00936)	(0.01612)
_cons	−1.0e+02***	0.00000	0.00000
	(8.26077)	(0.00000)	(0.00000)
Time-fixed effect	Under control	Under control	Under control
Individual-fixed effect	Under control	Under control	Under control
N	7524	2064	5460
R2	0.4879	0.4932	0.4769

* $p < 0.1$, ** $p < 0.05$, *** $p < 0.01$

5 Conclusion

First, there is a negative relationship between overall ESG performance and stock returns in the A-share market;
Second, by comparing the degree of influence of E/S/G on stock returns, it is found that E has the weakest negative influence on stock returns;
Third, with the same ESG performance, stock returns are higher for high-carbon sectors than low-carbon sectors.

The above findings still hold after the robustness tests.

This study has important implications for investors, company managers, and national policy makers.

Firstly, for all companies, positive ESG performance is a good way for them to communicate with investors, especially when companies actively invest in environmental management. It brings positive corporate externalities and conveys the concept of practicing green development to investors and the whole society, which is the way to achieve sustainable development in the long run.

Secondly, for high-carbon industries, it is important to actively improve ESG performance, including reducing environmental pollution, establishing a good social image, and strengthening internal corporate governance. It can help the company gain investors' favor and market recognition.

Thirdly, compared with the ESG performance of developed countries, the A-share market has a late start in ESG disclosure. The government and regulators should give full play to the supervision and regulation functions in the process of ESG disclosure. The government should build a complete ESG data collection system and an efficient ESG reporting system, and smooth the communication mechanism with stakeholders to achieve the sound development of the A-share market.

References

1. Feng, G., Long, H., Wang, H., Chang, C.: Environmental, social and governance, corporate social responsibility, and stock returns: what are the short- and long-Run relationships? Corporate Soc. Responsib. Environ. Manag. **29**(5) (2022)
2. Garcia, A.S., Mendes-Da-Silva, W., Orsato, R.J.: Sensitive industries produce better ESG performance: evidence from emerging markets. J. Clean. Prod. **150**, 135–147 (2017)
3. Limkriangkrai, M., Koh, S., Durand, R.B.: Environmental, social, and governance (ESG) profiles, stock returns, and financial policy: Australian evidence. Int. Rev. Financ. **17**(3), 461 (2017)
4. Naeem, N., Cankaya, S., Bildik, R.: Does ESG performance affect the financial performance of environmentally sensitive industries? A comparison between emerging and developed markets. Borsa Istanbul Rev. **22**, S128–S140 (2022)
5. Ni, Y., Sun, Y.: Environmental, social, and governance premium in Chinese stock markets. Glob. Financ. J. **55** (2023)
6. Pedersen, L.H., Fitzgibbons, S., Pomorski, L.: Responsible investing: the ESG-efficient frontier. J. Financ. Econ. **142**(2), 572–597 (2021)
7. Takahashi, H., Yamada, K.: When the Japanese stock market meets COVID-19: impact of ownership, China and US exposure, and ESG channels. Int. Rev. Financ. Anal. **74** (2021)
8. Qiao, Y.: A study on financial governance of listed companies based on principal-agent theory. Chin. Foreign Corporate Cult. (10), 32–33 (2021)
9. Xu, G., Zhuo, Y., Zhang, Y., Zhang, J.: Does ESG information disclosure increase corporate value? Financ. Account. Newsl. (04), 33–37 (2022)
10. Yan, H., Chen, B.: Climate change, environmental regulation and the value of corporate carbon emissions disclosure. Financ. Res. (06), 142–158 (2017)
11. Yang, L.: Carbon information disclosure quality, institutional investors and stock returns. China Inst. Fiscal Sci. (2020)
12. Zhang, Z., Liu, W.: Study on the impact of a company's ESG performance on its stock returns. China Price **406**(02), 84–86 (2023)
13. Zhao, T., Xiao, X., Zhang, B.: The dynamic effect of corporate social responsibility on capital allocation efficiency: an empirical study based on corporate governance perspective. J. Shanxi Univ. Financ. Econ. (11), 66–80 (2018)
14. Zhou, F., Pan, W., Fu, H.: ESG responsibility performance of listed companies and institutional investors' shareholding preference-empirical evidence from Chinese A-share listed companies. Sci. Decis. Mak. (11), 15–41 (2020)

Digital Transformation in the New Energy Industry for Sustainable Development: A Grounded Theory Analysis

Ming Liu(✉)

School of Professional Studies, New York University, New York, USA
ml6625@nyu.edu

Abstract. China is accelerating the development of new energy sources due to growing environmental concerns and the need to reduce dependence on imported energy sources. Digital transformation can help industries improve efficiency and reduce costs. By introducing digital technologies and business models, the industry can make better use of data resources and information flows to digitise, smarten and network production and operations, further improving the efficiency of resource utilization and decision-making in enterprises. This study uses grounded theory, researches Frontline workers, the Public, Users, Experts, and scholars, and analyzes that internal factors, external factors, and innovation are the three most important factors to ensure. The analysis concluded that internal factors, external factors, and innovation are the three most important factors to ensure the digital transformation of the new energy industry to sustainability. A four-level indicator system for the digital transformation of new energy sustainability was developed.

Keywords: Digital Transformation · New Energy Industry · Sustainable Development · Grounded Theory

1 Introduction

Digital transformation is revolutionizing industries worldwide; the new energy industry is no exception. Adopting digital technologies such as smart grids, artificial intelligence, and the Internet of Things is transforming the industry by improving efficiency, reducing costs, and promoting sustainability [1].

This study analyzes the impact of digital transformation on the new energy industry, including the factors driving this transformation. The insights from this study provide valuable information for new energy industry participants seeking to drive digital transformation and promote sustainable development. The study identifies three key factors - internal, external, and innovation - crucial for the digital transformation of the new energy industry toward sustainability. Management, efficiency, and benefits are critical internal factors that digitization can improve. In contrast, external factors such as markets, consumers, and the environment are crucial in driving digital transformation. Technological and industrial innovations, such as smart grids and zero-carbon power plants, are also crucial for driving digital transformation and promoting sustainability in the industry.

2 Literature Review

Digitalization in the Energy Industry Kapitonov identified that the digital economy had influenced the energy industry's modernization [2]. The author highlighted that the energy industry is characterized by high capital investments, which require a long payback period, and digital technologies have become an essential tool for the industry to remain competitive. Ren et al. investigated the impact of internet development on China's energy consumption and found that digitalization has contributed to the increase in energy consumption [3].

Sustainability Implications of Digitalization The sustainability implications of digitalization in the energy industry have been extensively studied. Santarius and Wagner conducted a systematic literature analysis of ICT for sustainability research and identified that digitalization could contribute to sustainability but has significant adverse effects [4]. Loseva conducted a comparative study of energy digitalization trends in several Island States, including the UK, Japan, Indonesia, and Cyprus, and concluded that digitalization positively impacts energy efficiency and contributes to sustainable energy development [5].

Risk Management in Digitalized Energy Networks Integrating digital technologies in the energy industry has also brought new risks that need to be managed. Seyfried identified that digitalization had influenced business process management in the energy industry, and new risks have emerged, such as cyber-attacks and data breaches [6]. Häckel et al. assessed IT availability risks in smart factory networks and proposed a framework for evaluating and managing these risks. The authors highlighted that the increasing complexity of digitalized energy networks increases the need for risk management strategies [7].

Legal and Social Implications of Digitalization Bekezhanov et al. identified the legal significance of digitalizing environmental information in ensuring environmental safety [8]. The authors concluded that digitalization could help address environmental challenges by providing accurate and timely information to stakeholders. Fors discussed the implications of digitalization on society and highlighted that digitalization has both positive and negative effects on human interaction and communication [9]. Matyushok et al. reviewed modern trends in the global economy in technological transformation conditions and identified that digitalization significantly impacts economic growth and development [10].

3 Methodology

Grounded theory is a qualitative research method. The grounded interpretative theory is considered the most scientific research method in qualitative research, which uses qualitative methods in research design and data collection and quantitative methods in data analysis. The coding process is divided into initial, intermediate, and advanced coding, and the findings are drawn through theoretical sampling. This study extracts the Inevitable Link between Digital Transformation and The Sustainable Development of the New Energy Industry through the grounded theory.

3.1 Data Collection

Interviews are the most dominant data collection method of grounded theory. Most existing literature studies have no relevance to the digital transformation of the new energy industry, which leads to the need for more literature. It is difficult and unscientific to extract the evaluation indexes of the digital transformation policy of the new energy industry directly from the existing literature by literature or textual data analysis, so this paper chooses to collect data by questionnaire survey method. The textual information is only used as a supplementary data source for this study.

Sample Collection. Questionnaires provide a structured approach to data collection, with standardized questions designed to elicit specific information. This can ensure that relevant data is systematically captured, reducing the risk of missing essential insights and enhancing the rigor and reliability of the findings. Based on the above principles, the questionnaire samples selected for this study are as follows.

Front-line workers: Front-line workers are the specific users of digital transformation technologies in the new energy industry, so the questionnaire is sent to front-line workers first.

The Public: The public is the beneficiary and experience of digital transformation in the new energy industry, so the questionnaire is sent to the public (including groups and individuals);

Users: The primary users of digital transformation in the new energy industry are enterprises, and questionnaires are sent to enterprise representatives as interviewees.

Experts and scholars: The digital transformation of the new energy industry is related to multiple fields, so the questionnaire was sent to experts and professors in environmental and public policy.

Sample Size. Many studies in the literature have found that the sample size of most studies is between 20 and 30. The sample size was determined according to the theoretical saturation principle, i.e., the sample was drawn until the new sample no longer provided further information and was finally decided to be 20 (15 as the initial coding sample and 5 for the theoretical saturation test). The distribution of samples is shown in Table 1.

The sample selection of this study was combined with the stratified sampling method. China contains seven administrative regions: northeast, north, east, south, central, northwest, and southwest, each of which has a different level of economic, environmental, and social development and a further understanding and attitude toward digital transformation of the new energy industry. To ensure the sample's scientific credibility and the breadth and depth of data, based on the above four types of sample distribution, this study uses a stratified sampling method to draw questionnaire samples from the seven regions according to a certain proportion.

Questionnaire and Data Collection. Data collection was conducted through a questionnaire. Some broad, open-ended questions were pre-designed, and then the questions were focused on triggering a detailed discussion of the issues. The interviewers recorded the data in the form of text, and the questionnaire collection time of this study was two weeks in total, collating and obtaining 19,842 words of textual material.

Table 1. Distribution of study sample.

Number	Sample	Category	Size
1	Front-line Workers	Operations& maintenance staff	4
		Project Manager	2
2	Public	Individual	3
		Group	1
3	Users	New energy Industries	4
		IT companies	1
4	Experts& Scholars	Public Administration Experts	3
		Environment Scholars	2
		Total	20

3.2 Data Analysis

Open Coding. Open coding is the first collation of the original data by coding and naming the relevant literature and interview data line by line and sentence by sentence, conceptualizing the original coding, and reflecting the content of the data with relevant concepts. Finally, regroup the initial concepts to make further categorization, and eliminate some invalid samples in the data, such as vague and unclear responses and topics unrelated to this study. In the conceptualization process, the original text's original sentences were used as the object of concept mining as much as possible. In the categorization process, the initial concepts that appeared less than twice or were inconsistent were eliminated, and the remaining initial concepts were integrated and sorted out. Fifteen open coding interview samples were selected, covering four categories: "front-line workers", "public", "users", and "experts and scholars". The remaining five samples were used for the saturation test, covering the above four categories. Table 2 is an example of initial coding in this paper.

Axial Coding. Based on the above principles, 385 original data statements were obtained, and 116 initial concepts and 8 categorized concepts were obtained by initial coding. Table 3 shows the axial coding analysis.

Selective Coding. Selective coding is used to refine and reflect on the eight advanced concepts and find the correlation between them so that the categories of different categories can be clustered together. The original data can be re-arranged to make the analysis more coherent. The eight categories were grouped into five main categories by deep refinement and high abstraction of the concepts. The concepts were grouped into 4 main categories, as shown in Table 4.

Saturation Test. A saturation test was used to determine when to terminate the coding of the sampled data for analysis, which was considered "saturated" only when the sampled data would no longer generate new theories and could no longer reveal new properties

Table 2. Example of open coding categorization.

Original questionnaire data	Coding terminology		
	Initial coding	Intermediate coding	Advanced coding
Through digital transformation, the new energy industry integrates traditional production and operation processes into the information system platform, which can significantly improve enterprise productivity and operational efficiency, reduce resource consumption and cost expenditure	Improving production efficiency	Efficiency	Internal factors

Table 3. Results of axial coding analysis.

Number	Categories (Number of times)	Property (Number of times)
1	Management(20)	Scientific Decision Making(8), Talent Training(1), Strengthen supply chain management(1), Fault warning(3), Real-time monitoring(2), Optimize business model(2), Ensure stable equipment operation(3)
2	Efficiency(18)	Improving production efficiency(17), Optimization of production processes(1)
3	Benefits(12)	Cost saving(6), Enterprise Value(2), Enhance market competitiveness(1), Enhancing energy security(3)
4	Markets(3)	Business model change(1), Gain policy support(2)
5	Consumers(3)	Meet customers' requirements(1), Enhance customer experience(2)
6	Sustainability(26)	Improve the energy mix(8), Promoting sustainable social development(4), Environmental Protection(14)
7	Technology innovation(30)	5G(4), Smart Grid(4), GIS(1), AI(5), Big data(8), BIM(1), IoT(11)
8	Industrial innovation(4)	Zero Carbon Power Plants(1), Unmanned new energy stations(3)

Table 4. Selective coding analyst.

Number	Core categories	Categories
1	Internal factors	Management, Efficiency, Benefits
2	External factors	Markets, Consumers
3	Environment factors	Sustainability
4	Innovation	Technology innovation, Industrial innovation

in the core categories. The remaining five interview samples and the additional text data coding analysis. The results align with the abovementioned relationships, and no new types or concepts were created.

4 Discussion

4.1 Indicator Composition Factors

The study of the correlation between core categories and categories shows that internal factors, external factors, and innovation effects constitute essential factors in the digital transformation of the new energy industry.

Internal Factors. Three key internal factors that have significantly impacted the digitization of the new energy industry are management, efficiency, and benefits. As all types of operations in the new energy industry become increasingly complex, effective management practices are necessary to ensure that projects are completed on time, within budget, and with high quality. Digitization can streamline management practices by providing real-time data analysis and insights that help managers make more informed decisions. For example, digital tools can help managers track the performance of renewable energy assets, optimize energy production, and identify potential risks or problems before they become significant issues. The increasing competition puts pressure on the industry to reduce costs and improve efficiency, and digitization can help achieve these goals. For example, companies can optimize their operations, reduce downtime, and maximize energy production by automating specific processes and leveraging predictive analytics. Digital tools can also help companies identify opportunities to improve efficiency by analyzing energy consumption patterns, identifying waste areas, and implementing strategies to reduce energy use. Benefits are also a key factor driving digitization in the new energy industry. The numerous benefits of digitization include increased productivity, improved safety, reduced costs, and enhanced sustainability. For example, by implementing digital tools such as BIM, companies can improve energy distribution and reduce the need for costly and environmentally damaging infrastructure. In addition, digitization can help companies optimize their use of renewable energy, reducing their carbon footprint and contributing to a more sustainable future.

External Factors. The digitization of the new energy industry is influenced by a variety of external factors, most notably the market, consumers, and the environment, which can affect the adoption and diffusion of new energy technologies and digital innovations, highlighting the need for a holistic and multidisciplinary approach to the digital transformation of new energy. The market plays a crucial role in digitizing the new energy sector. The emergence of new business models, such as energy service companies (ESCOs) and peer-to-peer energy trading platforms, is changing the energy market landscape. These new players leverage digital technologies like blockchain and artificial intelligence to create more efficient and decentralized energy systems. In addition, market incentives, such as subsidies and feed-in tariffs, can accelerate the deployment of new energy technologies and spur innovation. Consumers are another key external factor influencing the digitization of the new energy sector. Growing awareness of environmental issues, rising electricity prices, and the desire for energy independence drive consumers to seek new energy solutions. Digital technologies, such as smart meters and home automation systems, enable consumers to monitor and control their energy consumption, reduce their carbon footprint, and save money on energy bills. The environment is also an important external factor influencing the digitization of the new energy sector. The transition to renewable energy sources, such as solar and wind, is driven by the need to reduce greenhouse gas emissions and mitigate climate change. Digital technologies can be crucial in integrating and optimizing renewable energy sources into the grid, making energy systems more resilient and sustainable.

Innovation. Technological and industrial innovations have significantly impacted the digitization of the new energy industry. Companies that embrace these innovations will be better positioned to meet the changing needs of consumers and remain competitive in a rapidly evolving market. Technology and innovation drive the new energy industry toward a more efficient, sustainable, and economic future. One of the keyways technology and industrial innovation drive digitalization in the new energy industry is by developing smart grids. Smart grids are intelligent, self-regulating electricity networks designed to optimize electricity generation, transmission, and distribution. They use sensors, meters, and communication networks to collect and analyze data, allowing for more efficient and effective management of energy resources. In addition to intelligent grids, Zero-carbon power plants, such as those that use renewable energy sources like wind and solar, are also transforming the new energy industry. They provide a sustainable source of clean energy, reducing carbon emissions and promoting environmental sustainability. Uncrewed new energy stations are being used to automate the management and maintenance of energy systems. They use advanced sensors, IoT devices, and artificial intelligence algorithms to monitor energy production, distribution, and consumption, reducing the need for human intervention and improving system efficiency.

4.2 The Inevitable Link Between Digital Transformation and the Sustainable Development of the New Energy Industry

The core factor association relationship model elaborates the path and mechanism of the interaction between the main and core factors. We find that internal factors, external factors, and innovation are the three most important factors to guarantee the digital transformation of the new energy industry to achieve sustainable development of the new energy industry, so it is also reasonable to take them as the core constituents of the inevitable link between digital transformation and the sustainable development of the new energy industry, thus forming A four-level indicator system of digital transformation for sustainable development of new energy is formed. Among them, the first level of indicators corresponds to the three core categories of selective decoding, the second level corresponds to the four main categories of spindle decoding, and the third level corresponds to the 14 categories of open. Table 5 shows the four-level index system of digital transformation for sustainable development of new energy, which is integrated from the root theory.

Table 5. The four-level index system of digital transformation for sustainable development of new energy industries.

Tier1 indicators	Tier 2 indicators	Tier 3 indicators	Tier 4 indicators
Internal factors	Internal factors	Management	Scientific Decision Making
			Talent Training
			Strengthen supply chain management
			Fault warning
			Real-time monitoring
			Optimize business model
			Ensure stable equipment operation
		Efficiency	Improving production efficiency
			Optimization of production processes
		Benefits	Cost saving
			Enterprise Value
			Enhance market competitiveness
			Enhancing energy security
External factors	External factors	Markets	Business model change
			Gain policy support
		Consumers	Meet customers' requirements
			Enhance customer experience

(*continued*)

Table 5. (continued)

Tier1 indicators	Tier 2 indicators	Tier 3 indicators	Tier 4 indicators
	Environment factors	Sustainability	Improve the energy mix
			Promoting sustainable social development
			Environmental Protection
Innovation	Technology Innovation	Technology innovation	5G
			Smart Grid
			GIS
			AI
			Big data
			BIM
			IoT
	Industrial innovation	Industrial innovation	Zero Carbon Power Plants
			Unmanned new energy stations

5 Conclusion

The analysis highlights the importance of internal factors, external factors, and innovation in driving digital transformation in the new energy sector. Effective management practices and efficiency are key internal factors that digitization can improve. External factors such as markets, consumers, and the environment also play a key role in adopting and diffusing new energy technologies and digital innovation. Technological and industrial innovations such as smart grids and zero-carbon power plants drive the new energy industry towards a more efficient, sustainable, and economic future. The analysis reveals that internal factors, external factors, and innovation are the three most important factors to ensure the digital transformation of the new energy industry toward sustainability. A four-tier system of indicators for digital transformation for new energy sustainability is developed.

The insights from this study provide helpful information for participants who wish to drive the digital transformation of the new energy industry and achieve sustainable growth in the new energy sector. However, this study also has some limitations. First, grounded theory, as a qualitative research method, is primarily a qualitative analysis rather than a quantitative statistic and is inherently subjective; the researcher's preconceptions or biases and the competent selection of data in the analysis process can impact the results. Second, the limited sample size may lead to an incomplete analysis, and additional indicator components need to be considered. Finally, this paper needs to provide an in-depth discussion of the specific paths of action between the main and core factors, the strength of the relationships, the intrinsic correlation mechanisms between the dimensions, and the weights of each indicator factor, which is the next step.

References

1. Turovets, J., Proskuryakova, L., Starodubtseva, A., Bianco, V.: Green digitalization in the electric power industry. Foresight STI Gov. **15**(3), 35–51 (2021)
2. Kapitonov, I.A., Voloshin, V.I., Filosofova, T.G., Syrtsov, D.N.: Digitalization of the energy industry as a direction for ensuring the growth of energy efficiency and the energy security of the state. Public Policy Adm. **19**(2), 191–204 (2020)
3. Ren, S., Hao, Y., Xu, L., Wu, H., Ba, N.: Digitalization and energy: how do internet development affect China's energy consumption? Energy Econ. **98**, 1 (2021)
4. Santarius, T., Wagner, J.: Digitalization and sustainability: a systematic literature analysis of ICT for sustainability research. GAIA-Ecol. Perspect. Sci. Soc. Suppl. Special Issue: Sustain. Digitalization **32**, 21–32 (2023)
5. Loseva, O.V., Karpova, S.V., Rasteryaev, K.O., Sokolova, E.S., Makar, S.V., Kharchilava, K.P.: Sustainable energy in island states: comparative analysis of new trends in energy digitalization and the experience of the UK, Japan, Indonesia, and Cyprus. Int. J. Energy Econ. Policy **10**(6), 722–731 (2020)
6. Seyfried, J.: Business Process Management in the Digital Age: Advancements in Data, Networks, and Opportunities. Universitaet Bayreuth (2019)
7. Häckel, B., Hänsch, F., Hertel, M., Übelhör, J.: Assessing IT availability risks in smart factory networks. Bus. Res. **12**(2), 523–558 (2019)
8. Bekezhanov, D., Rzabay, A., Nesipbaev, O., Kopbassarova, F., Halibiyati, H.: Legal significance of digitalizing environmental information in ensuring environmental safety. J. Environ. Manag. Tourism **13**(3), 656–664 (2022)
9. Fors, A.C.: The beauty of the beast: the matter of meaning in digitalization. AI & Soc. **25**(1), 27–33 (2010)
10. Matyushok, V., Krasavina, V., Berezin, A., Sendra García, J.: The global economy in technological transformation conditions: a review of modern trends: znanstveno-strucni casopis. Ekonomska Istrazivanja **34**(1), 1471–1497 (2021)

Causality Between Board Features and Corporate Innovation Level: Empirical Evidence from Listed Companies in China

Zicheng Bu(✉)

Antai College of Economics and Management, Shanghai Jiao Tong University, Shanghai 200030, China
pkbb4019@sjtu.edu.cn

Abstract. Under the condition of global economic recession after the pandemic of Covid-19, companies are seeking growth opportunities. Corporate innovation is an essential driver for the companies' competitiveness. The paper takes the advantage of fixed effect linear regression model to analyze board features' impact on firm innovation level. The model is based on the CSMAR database, a comprehensive research-oriented database focusing on China's Finance and Economy to obtain the latest 10-year (2012–2022) annual firm-level R&D and individual-level board member characteristics data. The empirical result shows that a board with a larger proportion of independent directors, a larger board size, a higher financial background rate, larger average age, and a higher average degree tends to be innovation-centric. Furthermore, this paper dives deeper into the determinants of board gender diversity, which is an essential explanatory variable for company innovation. The result indicates that a board with a female chairman, a high oversea background rate, and a low multi-subject rate is often correlated with high gender diversity.

Keywords: Board Features · Firm Innovation Level · Empirical Research

1 Introduction

Corporate innovation is and will always be an essential driver for companies' competitiveness, especially in today's situation where the global economy is in an overall recession. China's strategy for innovation-driven development will create opportunities for corporations with the capability of innovation to thrive better in the country. Investment in the R&D process not only ensures the company survives in the highly competitive market but also fulfills companies' future potential growth. Among all the factors which may pose an influence on R&D spending, the board decision is undeniably the decisive one.

In recent years, many research papers have researched the board characteristics' impact on the firms' performance. These researches aim to provide strong guidance for a well-designed and high-efficiency innovative board composition by analyzing innovative companies' board feature like Google or Apple. These researches mainly focus

© The Author(s), under exclusive license to Springer Nature Singapore Pte Ltd. 2024
X. Li et al. (Eds.): ICEMGD 2023, AEPS, pp. 1295–1302, 2024.
https://doi.org/10.1007/978-981-97-0523-8_121

on two aspects of the board features: the composition feature and the board member background feature. From the perspective of board composition features, the research is mainly conducted around board size, and the independent director ratio. Yoo and Sung conducted research on large companies in the Korean market from 1998 to 2005, the result of the empirical testing showed that the ratio of independent directors is negatively related to innovation-related investment. However, when the target company is in rapid growth, the negative impact can be mitigated [1]. Prencipa revealed that the board size is in a relationship of an inverted "U" with efficiency. The medium size is conducive to innovation activities. Besides, the research paper also pointed out that the independent ratio poses a tiny effect on the overall innovation level and financial performance [2]. Blibech and Berraies, however, proved that the board size is not significantly related to performance as well as innovation spending [3]. From the perspective of board member background feature, the education background, academic background, financial background, and career background. Drees and Heugens found that when making an influenced strategic decision, the background of members of the board contributes to the acquisition of outside resources [4]. Chen's research uncovered the capital of the board, including the educational background, the industry background, and the independent director, is positively related to corporate innovation [5]. Francis argued that the academic background of board members is helpful for making professional solutions [6]. Ghosh took advantage of the data on all the listed companies in the manufacturing industry in India, for the first time came up with the argument that the financial relationship between the board members may promote or decline the innovation based on the companies' Debt to Asset Ratio [7]. Belkacemi found that education background diversity and career diversity are positively related to corporate innovation [8]. An et al. found evidence to suggest that firms with diverse boards engage in more exploratory innovations and develop new technology in unfamiliar areas [9].

The research on board's feature's impact on firm innovation is meaningful and the consequences have been applied in many countries. However, in China, there has been no comprehensive analysis of onboard features in recent years. Given the above evidence of how the board features may affect the corporate innovation level, in this paper, aspects of board characteristics are included to manage to explain the innovation level, including age, gender diversity, degree, oversea background, multi-subjects background, industry background, academic background, and financial background. Next, the paper is going to dive deeper to examine the determinants of corporate board gender diversity, which is a popular factor contributing to firm innovation. The study by Griffin, Li, and Xu examined the relationship between board gender diversity and corporate innovation and found that gender-diverse boards acquire more patents and novel patents as well as a higher innovative efficiency [10]. This paper contributes to the literature in the following ways. First, by using China Stock Market & Accounting Research Database, up to 700 thousand observation in individual level in recent 10 years is included. The large sample size contributes to the reliability and generalizability of the result. Besides, in this passage, many robustness checks are conducted including adding non-linear-form independent variables, which largely makes the model fit to the real world better. In the end, the paper focuses on discrepancies between industries' features and controls for the fixed effect on years and industries to rule out potential exogeneity.

The paper proceeds as follows: Sect. 2 introduces the data selection and model building, Sect. 3 delivers the empirical results and Sect. 4 includes the conclusion and if possible, future research topics.

2 Methodology

2.1 Data Selection

The analysis is based on the CSMAR database, which is short for China Stock Market & Accounting Research Database. CSMAR is a comprehensive research-oriented database focusing on China's Finance and Economy. From CSMAR, the researchers obtained the latest 10-year (from 2012 to 2022) annual firm-level variables including RD Person, RD Person Ratio (the proportion of R&D person in the total employees), RD SpendSum, Number of Patents as well as industry name and industry code based on the "Guidelines for Industry Classification of Listed Companies" launched by China Securities Regulatory Commission (CSRC) in 2012. Besides, some individual-level variables are also covered in the research focusing on characteristics of the listed firm's figures. The characteristics contain the name, gender, age, service position, service position ID, degree, career background, oversea background, academic background, and financial background.

In the final step, to build a form-level model, the firm-level data set and individual-level data set are merged together, therefore some individual-level variables are transformed into firm-level variables such as gender-diversity rate (the ratio of female board members), average age, average degree, oversea background rate, academic background rate, multi-subjects rate, financial background rate. Besides, in order to measure innovation efficiency, this paper conducts two variables evaluate innovation efficiency, the first version is the R&D investment divided by patents, and the second one uses R&D investment divided by R&D person.

Next in the data cleaning section, companies without patents, R&D spending, or R&D person (R&D person ratio) are dropped. Considering the sample size would be too small to form panel data, the companies with missing data in some years between 2012 and 2022 are preserved. The final firm-level sample comprises 5885 firm-year observations and 105780 individual-level observations over the period of 2012–2022.

2.2 Modelling

This research employs the following linear model with a fixed effect on year and industry, as follows.

$$y_{it} = \alpha_{it} + X_{it} + F_{it} + \mu_{it} \tag{1}$$

$$g_{it} = \beta_{it} + W_{it} + F_{it} + v_{it} \tag{2}$$

In regression (1), this model is constructed to find the board features' impact on the firm innovation level. y_{it} is a dependent variable as an indicator of innovation input or innovation efficiency. X_{it} is a vector of firm-level board characteristics. F_{it} is the fixed effect of industry and year to mitigate the exogenous impact on the regression model. The key independent variables are characteristics of boards including Female Rate, Oversea Rate, Academic Background Rate, Multi-Subjects Rate, Financial Background Rate, Independent Director Rate, average age, average degree, and board size. To capture the innovation investment level, Patents, R&D spending, and R&D person, R&D person ratio are introduced to be dependent variables. To capture the efficiency of innovation, R&D spending per patent and R&D spending per person is also introduced.

In regression (2), the model intended to explain the determinants of board gender diversity. g_{it} is the dependent variable "gender diversity" measured by the female board member fraction. W_{it} comprises many dependent variables including Female Chairman (if the chairman of the board is female, this variable equals 1, else it equals 0), Oversea Rate, Academic Background Rate, Multi-Subjects Rate, Financial Background Rate, average age, average degree, and board size. F_{it} is the fixed effect of industry and year to mitigate the exogenous impact on the regression model.

3 Empirical Results

3.1 Descriptive Statistics

Table 1 reports firm-level descriptive statistics for the dependent and independent variables. Here, in order to illustrate the degree, 1–6 represents educational background from secondary school to MBA/EMBA: 1 = Secondary school and below, 2 = Junior college, 3 = Bachelor's degree, 4 = Master's degree, 5 = Ph.D. degree, 6 = Other (degree announced in other forms, such as an honorary doctorate, correspondence course, etc.), 7 = MBA/EMBA. The reason not to use the categorical variable is that the model is intended to link the correlation between educational background and the company's innovation level/ gender diversity. From Table 1, on average, each of the listed companies has a board with an average size of 18, an average age of 48.8, an average degree between junior college and bachelor's degree, a female rate of 21%, independent director rate of 17%, oversea background rate of 9%, academic background of 23%, multi-subject background of 72.7% and financial background rate of 7.7%.

3.2 Regression Results

In Table 2, the columns are the empirical results with explained variables including log R&D spending, log patents number, log R&D person, log efficiency measured by patents and R&D person, and R&D person ratio. With only board characteristics included as explanatory variables, the R-square of each model is around 0.2, which displays a certain degree of validity in explaining the firm innovation level and innovation efficiency. In all models, the fixed effect of year and industry is included.

In columns (1)(2)(3)(6), whose explained variables are all about R&D spending and person, female rate, independent director rate, financial rate, board average age, board average degree and constant are all significant at 1% level. In columns (1)(2)(3), the board size is significant under a 1% significance level. In column (1)(6) oversea background

Table 1. Descriptive statistics.

Variable	Obs	Mean	Std. dev.	Min	Max
rdspendsum	5,884	2.03E+08	9.68E+08	13692.75	2.48E+10
Patents	5,884	322.6114	1124.469	1	4.05E+04
Rdperson	5,884	1198.492	50922.18	2	3903909
rdpersonratio	5,884	1.88E−01	1.36E−01	0.0011	9.30E−01
efficiency(patent)	5,884	1201072	6733357	25.64185	3.97E+08
efficiency(person)	5,884	355797.2	302063	12.11621	6486533
Age	5,884	48.82473	3.266668	0	59.61905
Degree	5,884	2.645884	1.201773	0	5.083333
femalerate	5,884	0.2101635	0.116515	0	0.7058824
inddirrate	5,884	0.1771036	0.039386	0	0.4210526
oversearate	5,884	0.0995433	0.1314773	0	1
acaderate	5,884	0.2323208	0.1384507	0	1
Multirate	5,884	0.7268342	0.1349992	0.2	1
Finrate	5,884	0.0776742	0.0792267	0	1
size	5,884	17.97417	4.631189	9	53

rate is significant and in column (2), the multi-subject rate is significant under a 5% significance level. In column(3)(4), which provides measures of innovation efficiency, the oversea background, board size, average age and constant are all significant under 1% significance level.

The female rate is negatively correlated to the R&D spending and R&D person number, which indicates the conservatism of female board members in innovation decisions. In other words, female board members are more sensitive to risk exposure and therefore tend to be conservative in making a decision related to future uncertainty. In some cases, they give up innovation opportunities because of their risk aversion tendency. From this perspective, they pose a negative effect on the firm innovation level. The independent director rate is positively correlated to R&D spending. As part of external supervision, independent directors are responsible for the companies' continuing operation and thus are less likely to be manipulated by some major shareholders of listed companies. Independent directors are usually professional in some areas so they are able to predict the cost and benefit rationally and make reasonable decisions on innovation instead of just pursuing short-term profits. The board size is positively correlated to the innovation level, indicating that the larger board size contributes to curbing short-sighted behavior and increasing spending on corporate innovation. The financial background rate is positively correlated to R&D spending, which means that financial background promotes innovation spending.

The average age is positively correlated with innovation, and the experienced board member with come to realize the importance of innovation in corporate competence.

The average degree is positively correlated with innovation level. Educated boards tend to be aware of the necessity of innovation and spend more on R&D. In terms of innovation efficiency, oversea background rate, the board size, and board average age are all positively correlated with innovation efficiency under 1% efficiency level. Overseas experience, larger boards, and more related experience are conducive to improving innovation efficiency. From the coefficients of year fixed effect, the average innovation level and innovation efficiency are both growing steadily year by year.

Table 2. Regressive results of model (1).

Var.	(1)	(2)	(3)	(4)	(5)	(6)
	lnrdspendsum	lnpatents	lnrdperson	lneffpatent	lneffperson	rdpersonratio
femalerate	−0.719***	−0.819***	−0.762***	0.0994	0.043	−0.0418***
	(0.1320)	(0.1280)	(0.1160)	(0.1280)	(0.0728)	(0.0134)
inddirrate	3.547***	3.268***	3.391***	0.279	0.156	−0.229***
	(0.5970)	(0.6260)	(0.5110)	(0.6490)	(0.3460)	(0.0643)
oversearate	0.501***	−0.117	0.0708	0.618***	0.431***	0.0633***
	(0.13100)	(0.12100)	(0.10600)	(0.13100)	(0.07220)	(0.01500)
multirate	0.151	0.296**	0.146	−0.145	0.00478	0.0236*
	(0.1170)	(0.1160)	(0.1040)	(0.1090)	(0.0684)	(0.0127)
finrate	0.691***	0.667***	0.365**	0.024	0.326***	−0.0924***
	(0.2070)	(0.1990)	(0.1820)	(0.1910)	(0.1130)	(0.0228)
size	0.0945***	0.0616***	0.0824***	0.0329***	0.0121***	−0.000769
	(0.0057)	(0.0057)	(0.0047)	(0.0054)	(0.0034)	(0.0006)
age	0.0662***	0.0415***	0.0557***	0.0247***	0.0105***	−0.00301***
	(0.0055)	(0.0049)	(0.0049)	(0.0049)	(0.0028)	(0.0006)
degree	0.0776***	0.0495***	0.0678***	0.0281**	0.00986	0.00968***
	(0.0147)	(0.0141)	(0.0130)	(0.0128)	(0.0088)	(0.0016)
Constant	10.37***	−1.961***	−1.02	12.34***	11.39***	0.284***
	0.0000	0.0000	(1.0000)	(1.0000)	0.0000	0.0000
Obs.	5,884	5,884	5,884	5,884	5,884	5,884
R-squared	0.189	0.161	0.17	0.134	0.092	0.2
Fixed Effect	yes	yes	yes	yes	yes	yes

Note: Standard errors in parentheses; ***p < 0.01, **p < 0.05, *p < 0.1

In Table 3, the columns are the empirical results with explained variable female rate as an indicator of gender diversity. In column (2)(3), the fixed effect of year and industry is included. In column (1)(2)(3), oversea background rate, multi-subject rate, board size, board average age are all significant at 1% level. Compared with column (1)(2), column

(3) adds female chairman into the explanatory variable list to analyze whether female board chairman in a board is a determinant of gender diversity. The female chairman is a binary dummy variable, 1 means chairman is female, 0 means chairman is male. From column (3), the empirical result shows that it exert obvious impact on board gender diversity under 1% significant level.

Oversea background rate is positively correlated with gender diversity, a board comprising a larger proportion of members with oversea background are more gender diversified. Oversea experience narrow the gap in abilities between genders. Multi-subject rate is negatively correlated to gender diversity. A key reason is that some originally women-friendly position are taken by men with multi-ability. Board size and board average age are also negatively correlated to the gender diversity in board but their coefficients are smaller and therefore are less influential. From the coefficients of year fixed effect, the gender diversified trend is conspicuous with an increasing coefficients of year fixed effect.

Table 3. Regressive results of model (2).

Var.	(1)	(2)	(3)
	femalerate	femalerate	femalerate
oversearate	0.0896***	0.0809***	0.0817***
	(0.0114)	(0.0135)	(0.0136)
multirate	−0.0825***	−0.0914***	−0.0906***
	(0.0113)	(0.0118)	(0.0117)
finrate	−0.0171	−0.0384*	−0.0430**
	(0.0188)	(0.0198)	(0.0196)
size	−0.0031***	−0.0028***	−0.0027***
	(0.0003)	(0.0003)	(0.0003)
age	−0.0063***	−0.0062***	−0.0060***
	(0.0005)	(0.0006)	(0.0006)
degree	−0.0031**	4.12E−05	−0.0005
	(0.0012)	(0.0013)	(0.0013)
femalechairman			1.131***
			(0.1180)
Constant	0.6337***	0.538***	0.528***
	(0.0231)	(0.0639)	(0.0638)
Observations	5,884	5,884	5,884
R−squared	0.0749	0.0930	0.1100
Fixed Effect	no	yes	yes

Note: Standard errors in parentheses; ***p < 0.01, **p < 0.05, *p < 0.1

4 Conclusion

The model in Table 2 reveals the correlation between board features and firm innovation level as well as innovation efficiency. The empirical result shows that a board with a larger proportion of independent directors, a larger board size, higher financial background rate, larger average age and higher average degree tends to be innovation-centric. As the time goes on, listed companies' innovation level and innovation efficiency are all comprehensively improving. Furthermore, in Table 3, the model focuses on the determinants of board gender diversity. A board with female chairman, high oversea background rate, low multi-subject rate is often correlated with high gender diversity.

This paper analyzes the correlation between board features and firm innovation level as well as innovation efficiency using 10-year annual listed companies' data in China. Among all explanatory variables, comprehensive aspects of board features are included. The features are divided into two categories: the composition feature and the board member background feature according to researches before. Moreover, this paper dives deeper to analyze the determinants of board gender diversity, providing reliable guidance to gender diversified and innovation-centric board.

On account of the data availability, some data is missing which may lead to bias in the regression. Besides, in the future, the potential behind board features and firm innovation should be discussed to make the result presented in this paper more persuasive. Finally, some exogenous shock is needed to conduct a causal relationship analysis.

References

1. Yoo, T., Sung, T.: How outside directors facilitate corporate R&D investment? Evidence from large Korean firms. J. Bus. Res. **68**(6), 1251–1260 (2015)
2. Prencipe, A.: Board composition and innovation in university spin-offs: evidence from the Italian context. J. Technol. Manag. Innov. **11**(3), 33–39 (2016)
3. Blibech, N., Berraies, S.: The impact of CEO' duality and board's size and independence on firms' innovation and financial performance. E3 J. Bus. Manag. Econ. (2018)
4. Drees, J.M., Heugens, P.P.: Synthesizing and extending resource dependence theory. J. Manag. **39**(6), 1666–1698 (2013)
5. Chen, H.: Board capital, CEO power and R&D investment in electronics firms. Corporate Gov.: Int. Rev. **22**(5), 422–436 (2014)
6. Francis, B.B., Hasan, I., Wu, Q.: Professors in the boardroom and their impact on corporate governance and firm performance. Financ. Manag. **44**(3), 547–581 (2015)
7. Ghosh, S.: Banker on board and innovative activity. J. Bus. Res. **69**(10), 4205–4214 (2016)
8. Belkacemi, R., Bouzinab, K., Papadopoulos, A.: A cognitive approach to diversity: investigating the impact of board of directors' educational and functional heterogeneity on innovation performance. Int. J. Bus. Manag. **16**(2), 1–20 (2021)
9. An, H., Chen, C.R., Wu, Q., Zhang, T.: Corporate innovation: do diverse boards help? J. Financ. Quant. Anal. **56**(1), 155–182 (2021)
10. Griffin, D., Li, K., Xu, T.: Board gender diversity and corporate innovation: international evidence. J. Financ. Quant. Anal. **56**(1), 123–154 (2021)

Analysis of the Impact of Digital Inclusive Finance on Farmers' Income Growth - An Empirical Analysis Based on 31 Provinces in China

Yuhan Sun(✉)

School of Economics, Zhongnan University of Economics and Law, Wuhan 430073, Hubei, China
1811581132@mail.sit.edu.cn

Abstract. Digital inclusive finance can alleviate financial hardship in rural areas and is an essential way for finance to consolidate the achievements of poverty eradication, promote rural revitalization, and facilitate the attainment of shared prosperity. This paper selects panel data from 31 provinces in China between 2016 and 2020 and investigates the impact of digitally inclusive finance on the total income of farm households and their various income sources. The results indicate that, first, digital inclusive finance has a significant impact on agricultural households' total income. Second, digital inclusive finance has a boosting effect on farmers' wage income, production and business income, property income and transfer income. The impact on transfer income is the most significant. Thirdly, the effects of digital inclusive finance on different sources of regions differ between eastern, central and western regions. The paper concludes with policy recommendations for the development of digitally inclusive finance to increase the income of Chinese farmers in various regions.

Keywords: Digital Inclusive Finance · Farmers' Income Growth · Income Structure

1 Introduction

Since China's victory in the battle against poverty, the focus of the "three rural areas" has shifted to the comprehensive promotion of rural redevelopment. The main goal of rural redevelopment is to boost farmers' income levels, and having access to adequate and efficient financial services is a key step in this process. Under the traditional financial model, financial services in rural areas are characterized by high costs and insufficient supply due to the constraints of cost and service radius [1]. Unlike the traditional model, digital finance combines Internet technology with traditional financial structures. A new way for farmers to increase their income through various channels is made possible by the use of digital technology. This effectively increases the coverage and penetration of financial services [2].

Three primary areas have been the focus of current research on how digital inclusion affects revenue-raising. First, the impact on income levels. Most scholars, such as Song, believe that the development of inclusive digital finance has greatly contributed to boosting income levels of locals [3]. Li, Feng and Xie concluded that digital inclusive finance has outstripped the limitations of traditional financial services and led to an increase in the incomes of rural communities [4]. However, the positive impact is disputed by some academics. He, Zhang and Wan pointed out that lack of financial knowledge brought about by digital inclusive finance may cause a "digital divide" for those with limited income, preventing them from utilizing online financial management and other digitally accessible financial services to increase income [5]. Second, the effect on the disparity between rural and urban incomes. The majority of academics concur that the expansion of digitally inclusive finance could significantly reduce the income disparity between rural and urban regions. However, some researches have shown that digital inclusive finance has an inverse effect on income gap. For example, in their analysis of the combined effects of digital inclusive finance and new urbanization, Wang and Li discovered that farmers were not greatly impacted by digital inclusive finance, and that it only significantly contributed to the income rise of urban inhabitants [6]. Third, the effect on income growth channels. Through an empirical analysis, Liu, Zhang and Chen concluded that digital inclusive finance eased credit constraints and facilitated the improvement of total factor productivity and entrepreneurial activities, thus raising income levels [7]. Fang and Xu concluded through empirical analysis that digital inclusive finance supports income development through a number of important pathways, including economic expansion and greater employment opportunities [8]. Additionally, according to some researchers, expanding knowledge channels and enhancing investment channels are additional ways that digital inclusive finance might have an income-generating impact.

Overall, current researches about the effect of digital inclusive finance on the income development of farmers are generally positive, but more has to be done to understand its more subtle channel effects and its influences on farmers' income structures. To further investigate the subtle impact of digital inclusive finance on the income growth of rural farmers, this paper employs a full-sample fixed-effects model based on panel data from 31 provinces in mainland China between 2016 and 2020. The purpose of this paper is to extend the existing research in this area by analyzing, from the perspective of income structure, the impact of digital inclusive finance on the various revenue streams of farmers.

2 Status Quo, Theoretical Framework and Assumptions

2.1 Status Quo

China's government has always attached great importance to increasing farmers' income and rural development, and by 2020, China's poverty eradication efforts have been successful, with all rural poor people meeting the current poverty standard being completely lifted out of it and rural residents' disposable income per capita rising from RMB 7,393.92 in 2011 to RMB 17,131.47 in 2020 [9], an increase of 2.32 times, resulting in a significant improvement in farmers' living standards. However, the current internal and external economic environment is facing continuous downward pressure, and the income disparity between rural dwellers in various locations is still rather wide. In this context, how to prevent farmers from returning to poverty and maintain income growth has become one of the priorities of the "Three Rural Issues".

China has aggressively increased the use of digital information technology, adopted a number of rules, and plans to use digital technology to assist inclusive financing for agriculture since the idea of digital inclusive finance was announced in 2016.In order to narrow the disparity between urban and rural financial services and to expand access to formal financial services in rural places, it is necessary to, it was suggested in the No, 1 Document of the Central Government for 2021 to "Develop inclusive digital finance in rural communities". Additionally, this would continually encouraging rural resurgence, attaining shared development, and fostering economic prosperity. The People's Bank of China published its Opinions on the Key Work of Financial Support for the Comprehensive Promotion of Rural Revitalization in 2022 in which it emphasized the importance of advancing financial technology to support rural revitalization and create digital inclusive finance in rural areas. Currently, The growing adoption of digital inclusive finance in rural areas has had a substantial impact on agricultural production and rural development.

2.2 Research Assumption and Theoretical Foundation

Digital Inclusive Finance's Effect on Farmers' Income. Inclusive finance, with the original aim of increasing the income of disadvantaged groups and addressing poverty and inequality, is seen as an important mechanism to alleviate rural poverty, but the practice of inclusive finance in China's rural areas is plagued by high costs, low efficiency and imbalanced services. Digital inclusive finance, in contrast to traditional inclusive finance, organically merges digital technology with inclusive finance, focusing on big data and information interconnection technology to successfully widen the types and extent of financial services while lowering their cost and threshold. This promotes the integration of rural land, labor, and other production components into the process of rural rehabilitation and addresses the real issue [10]. Through this process, digital inclusive financing supports economic growth, the growth of rural industries, and higher farm incomes. As a result, the following is offered as Assumption 1.

Assumption 1: Digital Inclusive Finance can boost farmers' incomes.

Pathways Leading to the Significance of Digital Inclusive Finance in Farmers' Income Growth. Farmers' income can be broken down into four categories, depending on the source of income: wage income, production and business income, property income and transfer income.

The primary source of income for producers is wage income. The expansion of digital inclusive finance, which has improved the financial climate in rural areas, has attracted a significant number of social capitalists to invest and establish businesses there. At the same time, the chain services with a systemic concept, such as "finance + trading market + family market", actively supported by digital inclusive finance in to serve the rural real economy, have better met the financial needs of rural areas and increased farmers' non-farm employment opportunities through the "trickle-down effect" [11]. As a result, the following is offered as Assumption 2.

Assumption 2: Digital Inclusive Finance can boost farmers' wage incomes.

Digital inclusive finance uses big data and cloud computing to improve the convenience of payment systems and the availability of credit resources, reduce the transaction costs of agricultural economic development, and give rural "long-tail groups" access to the digital financial services they need for production and business. Also, the expansion of digital inclusive banking in rural areas has placed traditional financial institutions in some competition with one another, forcing financial institutions to improve their service quality, which helps break down service boundaries and alleviate financial exclusion in farmers' business and production processes. All this contributes to a rise in farmers' income. Therefore, As a result, the following is offered as Assumption 3.

Assumption 3: Digital Inclusive Finance can boost farmers' production and business incomes.

Digitally inclusive finance offers an extensive range of asset management services, including bonds, funds, stock purchases and savings deposits, to rural areas through online services, which helps farmers to allocate their assets according to their preferences, greatly expanding the channels and possibilities for farmers' property income, thus helping to increase their property income. As a result, the following is offered as Assumption 4.

Assumption 4: Digital Inclusive Finance can boost farmers' property incomes.

The convenient payment channels under the digital inclusive finance system can help the government to quickly and on time disburse the full amount of funds for farmers such as low income insurance, medical insurance and old age security to farmers. Digital inclusive finance also provides a convenient channel for social and private organizations' projects to help farmers, helping to increase their transfer income. As a result, the following is offered as Assumption 5.

Assumption 5: Digital Inclusive Finance can boost farmers' transfer incomes.

3 Materials and Methods

3.1 Variable Choice

Explained Variables: Farm Household Income (lgY). This paper measures the income level of farm households in terms of the logarithm of their total income per capita [12]. Total income is further divided into wage income (lgNcgx), production and business income (lgNccjys), property income (lgNccc) and transfer income (lgNczy) based on the source of the income. Among them, wage income includes the basic salary, bonus, performance and other labour remuneration income earned by local workers and those working outside, and is determined by the ratio of the overall income earned by farmers from their labour activities to the total number of farmers. Production and management income is measured as the ratio of the total income earned from farming, animal husbandry, fishing, forestry and sideline operations to the total population of the farming family. Property income is measured as the ratio of the total income earned from movable and immovable property to the total population of the farming family. Transfer income consists mainly of financial subsidies from the government, including compensation, pensions, unemployment benefits, etc., and is measured as the ratio of the total transfer income received by the farmer through society, the state and other households to the total population of the farming family.

Core Explanatory Variable: Digital Inclusive Finance (lgDIFI). The Peking University's Digital Inclusive Finance Index, which utilizes data from 31 Chinese provinces between 2016 and 2020, provides an accurate depiction of the current condition and progress of digital inclusive finance [13]. The logarithm of index is thus used in the empirical investigation in this paper.

Control Variables. (1) Economic development stage (lgGDP), which is calculated using the logarithm of GDP per capita. (2) Industrial structure (IS), calculated by value of primary sector growth in rural areas as a share of regional GDP. (3) Level of fixed asset investment (INV) is determined by ratio of the amount of the investment in rural fixed assets to the total population living in rural areas. (4) Consumption levels of rural dwellers (lgCONS), which is calculated using the logarithm of per-capita consumption expenditure of rural residents.

3.2 Data Sources and Processing

The Digital Inclusive Finance Index at Peking University is the primary data source for the main explanatory elements. The control variables and explained variables are derived from the China Rural Statistical Yearbook and the China Urban Statistical Yearbook from 2016–2020. The research subjects of this paper are selected as 31 provinces in China excluding Taiwan, Hong Kong and Macao [14]. This paper categorizes China into eastern, central, and western regions based on the China Statistical Yearbook of 2020. Twelve administrative provinces, including Guizhou, Yunnan, Sichuan, Chongqing, Tibet, Qinghai, Ningxia, Shaanxi, Gansu, Guangxi, Xinjiang, and Inner Mongolia, make up the western area. Eight administrative provinces make up the central region: Heilongjiang, Anhui, Shanxi, Jilin, Jiangxi, Hubei, Henan, and Hunan. Eleven administrative provinces make up the central region: Liaoning, Beijing, Zhejiang, Jiangsu, Tianjin, Hebei, Shanghai, Guangdong, Fujian, Shandong and Hainan. Table 1 displays the descriptive statistical results for the major variables.

3.3 Econometric Model

The primary focus of this essay is how farm people' income structures will be impacted by digital inclusive finance. Prior to building the generic panel data analysis model below, it analyze the effects of inclusive digital finance overall on farm households' income.

$$lgY_{it} = a_{it} + a_1 DIFI_{it} + \sum_{j=2}^{8} \alpha_j Control_{it} + \varepsilon_{it} \quad (1)$$

where lgY_{it} represents the level of farmer's income, a_{it} is the constant term, $DIFI_{it}$ denotes the core explanatory variable, a_1 denotes the effect of digital inclusive finance

Table 1. Descriptive statistics results.

Variable	Number of Observations	Mean	Std. Dev.	Min	Max
lgY	155	4.162	0.137	3.873	4.543
lgNcgx	155	3.744	0.249	3.327	4.33
lgNcjys	155	3.694	0.157	3.138	3.961
lgNccc	155	2.526	0.289	1.827	3.492
lgNczy	155	3.45	0.146	3.104	4.029
lgDIFI	155	2.462	0.072	2.302	2.635
lgGDP	155	4.77	0.17	4.438	5.217
IS	155	9.21	5.142	0.3	25.1
INV	155	0.169	0.081	0.002	0.382
lgCONS	155	4.058	0.121	3.757	4.351

development, $Control_{it}$ denotes the control variables, ε_{it} represents the stochastic disturbance.

According to the national statistical approach, the four primary types of income that make up the income gap among farm households in each province are wage income, production and business income, transfer income and property income and digital inclusive finance has varying effects on each category of income. In order to better understand this internal heterogeneity, from which the subsequent model is derived, this paper examines the distinctive effects of digital inclusive finance on these four kinds of income separately.

$$lgNcgx_{it} = \beta_{it} + \beta_1 DIFI_{it} + \sum_{j=2}^{8} \beta_j Control_{it} + \varepsilon_{it} \quad (2)$$

$$lgNcjys_{it} = \chi_{it} + \chi_1 DIFI_{it} + \sum_{j=2}^{8} \chi_j Control_{it} + \varepsilon_{it} \quad (3)$$

$$lgNccc_{it} = \gamma_{it} + \gamma_1 DIFI_{it} + \sum_{j=2}^{8} \gamma_j Control_{it} + \varepsilon_{it} \quad (4)$$

$$lgNczy_{it} = \lambda_{it} + \lambda_1 DIFI_{it} + \sum_{j=2}^{8} \lambda_j Control_{it} + \varepsilon_{it} \quad (5)$$

where β_{it}, χ_{it}, γ_{it}, λ_{it} are the constant terms, β_1, χ_1, γ_1, λ_1 are coefficients of core explanatory variables, β_j, χ_j, γ_j, λ_j are coefficients of the control variables.

4 Empirical Results and Robustness Test

4.1 Panel Data Model Regression Analysis

This paper uses the Hausman test, F-test and BP-LM test in deciding to employ the panel data fixed-effects model for regression analysis. Table 2 displays the outcomes for the complete sample following the fixed effects test for Models 1 through 5. Model 1's R-squared is 0.942, which shows that the model is significant. The regression coefficient of digital inclusion finance on total farm household income demonstrates a significant positive relationship between digital inclusion finance and farm household income. Among the control variables, GDP per capita and the amount of fixed asset investment by rural residents both have a positive influence on farm household income, while the share of primary industry in rural regions has a negative effect on farm household income.

Table 2. Regression results of the fixed effects model (full example).

	1	2	3	4	5
lgDIFI	0.740***	0.773**	0.553**	0.850*	1.041*
	(0.0501)	(0.0804)	(0.0768)	(0.175)	(0.124)
lgGDP	0.130**	0.153	0.0797**	0.438**	0.223*
	(0.0642)	(0.141)	(0.0995)	(0.318)	(0.136)
IS	−0.00199*	−0.0023**	−0.00129*	−0.0009	−0.0057***
	(0.0896)	(0.000106)	(0.000121)	(0.000147)	(0.00103)
INV	0.0180**	0.0441**	0.142	0.119**	0.119**
	(0.0369)	(0.0893)	(0.195)	(0.233)	(0.160)
lgCONS	0.0157	0.000980*	0.0449*	0.0290	0.00192
	(0.0142)	(0.0249)	(0.0340)	(0.0555)	(0.0484)
R-squared	0.942	0.836	0.795	0.747	0.832

The R-squared of Models 2 to 5 were 0.836, 0.795, 0.747 and 0.832 respectively, with high and significant explanatory strengths for each model. Further examination of the model coefficients reveals that farmers' wage income, production and business income, transfer income and property income all significantly increase due to the adoption of inclusive digital finance. The boosting effect on transfer income is the most significant, followed by the boosting effect on wage income and productive income, and the weakest boosting effect on property income. The reasons for this result may be due to the fact that farmers' access to government recurrent transfers is not sufficiently well understood under the traditional financial model, which greatly limits their access to transfer income; on the other hand, it is also influenced by the attributes of the income structure itself, such as the fact that property income mainly depends on the volume of movable and immovable property in the farmers' own names, and many areas are not covered by digital inclusive finance.

4.2 Endogeneity Test

This paper adds instrumental variables to test the model in order to circumvent the endogeneity issue. Drawing on the method of Zhang [15], the endogeneity test is performed on the logarithmic values of the lagged digital financial inclusion index, and the regression results are displayed in Table 3. Tables 2 and 3 can be compared to show that from Model 1 to Model 5, the signs of the explanatory factors are consistent and significant, and the signs of the control variables are likewise substantially consistent. As a result, the model passes the endogeneity test, demonstrating general reliability and validity of the empirical results. The results of the analysis performed above on how digital inclusion finance affects the income of various sorts of farm households are thus accurate.

Table 3. Results from regression with the addition of instrumental factors (full example).

	1	2	3	4	5
lnDIFI	0.641***	0.427*	0.699**	0.817*	0.769*
	(0.0301)	(0.334)	(0.251)	(0.196)	(0.223)
lnGDP	0.241**	0.177	0.0081**	0.438**	0.113*
	(0.021)	(0.231)	(0.0524)	(0.608)	(0.026)
IS	−0.023	−0.0018*	−0.0031***	−0.61	−0.00694**
	(0.057)	(0.0623)	(0.0045)	(0.00163)	(0.0303)
INV	0.0245*	0.0601***	0.0362	0.009**	0.0789
	(0.0577)	(0.012)	(0.289)	(0.469)	(0.210)
CONS	0.0237**	0.00850	0.0861*	0.0371	0.0229*
	(0.062)	(0.0448)	(0.0640)	(0.344)	(0.684)
R-squared	0.701	0.649	0.814	0.857	0.791

5 Further Discussion: Heterogeneity Analysis

This research divides the entire sample into three groups according to the eastern, central, and western areas of China and investigates regional disparities in the impact of digital inclusive finance on the composition of farm households in each of these three regions by performing regional heterogeneity analysis. Table 4 displays the heterogeneity test results.

The main explanatory variable's regression coefficients of 0.711, 0.734, and 0.805, respectively, indicate that the adoption of digital finance has a significant impact on the rate of income growth among farm households in the eastern, central, and western regions. Compared to eastern and central regions, western region is most positively affected by digital inclusive finance.

In Terms of Wage Income. Digital inclusive finance's effects on farmers' revenue varies greatly between regions, with the western region being the most affected by digital inclusion, followed by central region eastern region, respectively. This may be due to the fact that more farmers in the western region work outside the region and are therefore more affected by digital inclusion. In terms of production and business income, farmers in the eastern region are most affected by digital inclusion. This might be the case due to the eastern region's stronger industrial structure, where it is more probable that the advancement of digital inclusive finance can boost farmers' production and business income through the transfer of the industrial structure.In terms of property income, the impact of digital financial inclusion on income growth is most pronounced in the central

Table 4. Sub-regional heterogeneity results.

Explained variables	Region	Variables				
		lnDIFI	lnGDP	IS	INV	lgCONS
Farmers' income	nationwide	0.740*** (0.0501)	0.130** (0.0642)	−0.00199** (0.0896)	0.0180** (0.0369)	0.0157 (0.0142)
	eastern region	0.711* (0.040)	0.121** (0.0554)	−0.0045 (0.0463)	0.0171** (0.0775)	0.0168 (0.005)
	central region	0.734*** (0.032)	0.128* (0.0760)	−0.0008* (0.0954)	0.0162** (0.112)	0.0152 (0.0911)
	western region	0.805** (0.089)	0.139** (0.0717)	−0.0017** (0.0992)	0.0199 (0.002)	0.0151* (0.0446)
Wage income	nationwide	0.773** (0.0804)	0.153 (0.141)	−0.0023** (0.000106)	0.0441** (0.0893)	0.000980* (0.0249)
	eastern region	0.723* (0.012)	0.132** (0.253)	−0.0047** (0.000082)	0.0374* (0.0478)	0.000910 (0.0136)
	central region	0.759** (0.084)	0.147 (0.027)	−0.0033** (0.000987)	0.0509 (0.0965)	0.000880* (0.0542)
	western region	0.827*** (0.075)	0.166 (0.741)	−0.0019 (0.000750)	0.0876** (0.0912)	0.00108* (0.0811)
Production and business income	nationwide	0.553*** (0.0768)	0.0797** (0.0995)	−0.00129* (0.000121)	0.142 (0.195)	0.0449* (0.0340)
	eastern region	0.644*** (0.0890)	0.0876 (0.0889)	0.00020** (0.000677)	0.301 (0.182)	0.0527* (0.0229)
	central region	0.409* (0.233)	0.0553** (0.0654)	−0.00432 (0.0011)	0.198*** (0.191)	0.0401 (0.0621)
	western region	0.398* (0.0112)	0.0401 (0.0900)	−0.00517* (0.000009)	0.101** (0.219)	0.0338 (0.0394)
Property income	nationwide	0.850* (0.175)	0.438* (0.318)	−0.0009*** (0.000147)	0.119** (0.233)	0.0290 (0.0555)
	eastern region	0.732* (0.135)	0.378 (0.078)	−0.0018** (0.00013)	0.089** (0.032)	0.0217 (0.0812)
	central region	0.899** (0.405)	0.499** (0.519)	−0.0005* (0.000278)	0.129 (0.887)	0.0453** (0.0093)
	western region	0.516 (0.205)	0.384*** (0.265)	0.0006** (0.000356)	0.113* (0.109)	0.0171 (0.0976)
Transfer income	nationwide	1.041* (0.124)	0.223* (0.136)	−0.0057*** (0.00103)	0.119* (0.160)	0.00192 (0.0484)

(*continued*)

Table 4. (continued)

Explained variables	Region	Variables				
		lnDIFI	lnGDP	IS	INV	lgCONS
Transfer income	eastern region	0.911* (0.109)	0.179 (0.115)	−0.0084* (0.0006)	0.101** (0.155)	0.00156** (0.0287)
	central region	0.998 (0.114)	0.198** (0.158)	−0.0061 (0.00453)	0.117* (0.143)	0.00201 (0.0629)
	western region	1.109** (0.178)	0.277 (0.207)	−0.0032** (0.00090)	0.138* (0.291)	0.00224 (0.0557)

region, whereas it is less pronounced in the western region. This may be due to the fact that the penetration of internet technology is not high in the underdeveloped western regions and the level of financial literacy of local farmers is not high, so they are currently unable to use digital financial platforms to activate financial assets through wealth management and other means to conclude transactions, thus increasing their property income. In terms of transfer income, the boosting effect on the transfer income of farmers in the western region is more significant than that in eastern and central regions, probably because western region is now the least developed, and the state will be more inclined to the western region when spending on financial support for agriculture, which will help farmers in the western region to achieve more transfer income.

6 Conclusion

This study uses the income structure as a starting point to evaluate the impact of digitally inclusive finance on the total income of farm households and their various income sources from 2016 to 2020, utilizing panel data from all 31 Chinese provinces.

The study finds that: First, the whole sample data show that the overall income of farm households was significantly increased by digital inclusive financing. Second, digital inclusive finance increased farmers' wage income, production and business income, transfer income and property income from a variety of sources of income. Transfer income experienced the most impact, followed by wage income, production and business income, while property income experienced the least impact. Thirdly, according to regional sample data, the eastern region saw the greatest boosting impact of digital inclusive finance on production and business income, the central region saw the greatest positive impact on property income, while the western region saw the greatest effect on farmers' wage and transfer income and also the greatest impact on overall income growth.

Following policy proposals are offered to further leverage the income-enhancing effect of this type of financing and to advance the achievement of the goal of common prosperity.

Enhance Pomotion of Digital Inclusive Finance to MSMEs to Create More Jobs. By utilizing the Internet, mobile payment, big data and other technologies, financial institutions of all kinds should be encouraged to offer credit and other financial services to more MSMEs. This will encourage the continued growth of MSMEs, which will in turn encourage an increase in farmers' non-farm employment and raise their wage income.

The Government Needs to do More to Support the Growth of a Rural Area's Inclusive Digital Banking Ecosystem. On the one hand, it should continue to increase financial support for the construction of "digital countryside", establish a basic data service platform related to agriculture, and enhance the data availability and convenience of supply and demand subjects. On the other hand, financial subsidies for digital inclusive finance should be strengthened, including supporting financial enterprises to conduct businesses related to agriculture, in order to boost the income of farmers and attract additional funding to the rural revitalization strategy.

Highlighting the Value of Digital Inclusive Finance in Boosting Farmers' Property Revenue and Enhancing Their Financial Literacy. Digital inclusive finance's potential to boost property income has not yet been fully realized. This may be because there are minimum requirements for using digital financial goods, and whether farmers can efficiently use digital financial services to boost their property revenue greatly depends on their level of financial literacy. Therefore, financial institutions and grassroots governments should vigorously promote relevant knowledge and make extensive use of relevant digital channels such as the WeChat public platform to enhance farmers' financial literacy and promote the increase of property income through digital financial platforms.

Dependable Administrative Framework for Digital Inclusive Finance. Organizations in the government's financial sector should coordinate and plan the organizational structure for digital inclusive finance, distribute financial resources to rural areas in different provinces in a sensible manner, and encourage the flow of digital inclusive finance resources from developed eastern regions to rural areas in less developed central and western regions.

References

1. Xiquan, P.: Innovative mechanisms for digital inclusive finance to help alleviate poverty with precision. Contemp. Econ. Manag. **40**(10), 93–97 (2018)
2. Yiping, H., Zhuo, H.: China's digital finance development: now and the future. Economics **17**(04), 1489–1502 (2018)
3. Xiaoling S.: Does "Internet+" financial inclusion affect the balanced growth of urban and rural incomes?–empirical analysis based on inter-provincial panel data in China. Res. Financ. Issues (07), 50–56 (2017)
4. Muchen, L., Sixian, F., Xing, X.: A study on the heterogeneous impact of digital inclusive finance on the urban-rural income gap. J. Nanjing Agric. Univ. **20**(03), 132–145 (2020)
5. Zongyue, H., Xun, Z., Guanghua, W.: Digital finance, the digital divide and multidimensional poverty. Stat. Stud. **37**(10), 79–89 (2020)
6. Yongjing, W., Hui, L.: Digital inclusive finance, new urbanisation and the urban-rural income gap. Stat. Decis. Mak. **37**(06), 157–161 (2021)
7. National Statistical Office. http://www.stats.gov.cn/
8. Guanfu, F., Jiayi, X.: Does digital financial inclusion promote employment for residents - evidence from the China Household Tracking Survey. Res. Financ. Econ. **35**(02), 75–86 (2020)

9. Xinyi, L., Wei, Z., XiaoZhi, C.: A study on the differential impact of digital inclusive finance on farm household income in different regions - based on the perspective of digital foundation and urbanization. Agric. Modernization Study **43**(06), 984–994 (2022)
10. Meihua, Z., Mengjie, C.: Poverty reduction effects and spatial heterogeneity of digital inclusive finance - an empirical analysis based on inter-provincial panel data. **22**(04), 7–12 (2020)
11. Xiaohua, W.: The evolutionary logic of the income structure of Chinese farmers and the measurement of its income increasing effect. J. Southwestern Univ. **45**(05) (2019)
12. Caixia, Y., Xia, X., Zhili, H.: Analysis of the impact of urbanisation on the income structure of farmers. Urban Dev. Stud **17**(10), 26–30 (2010)
13. Cailan, L., Yinxing, H.: Analysis of rural financial development and farmers' income structure in Jiangsu Province. Bus. Res. (06), 181–187 (2013)
14. Guo, F., Wang, J., Wang, F., Kong, T., Zhang, X., Cheng, Z.: Measuring China's digital financial inclusion: index compilation and spatial characteristics. China Econ. Q. **19**, 1401–1418 (2020)
15. Haiyan, Z.: A heterogeneous study of the impact of digital inclusive finance on the income structure of farming households. Stat. Decis. Mak. **37**(24), 152–156 (2021)

The Energy Consumption and Economic Growth

Yiguo Huang[1(✉)], Yizhen Zhang[2], and Heyu Cai[3]

[1] University of California San Diego, Thurgood Marshall, San Diego 92093, USA
`1007207052zxc@gmail.com`
[2] Alfred Lerner College of Business and Economics, University of Delaware, Newark 19711, USA
`yzyz@udel.edu`
[3] Rutgers Business School, Rutgers, NB 08854, USA
`hc866@rutgers.edu`

Abstract. Throughout human history, energy has played a critical role in society's development. Many people believe that energy consumption has a close relationship with economic growth. We created a simple regression model to verify this assumption. We also compared fossil and renewable energy to see if there is a different impact on high-income compared fossil and renewable energy to see if there is a different impact on high-income and low-income countries. As a result, we found that energy consumption doesn't have a strong relationship with high-income countries, and it has a negative relationship with low-income countries. Due to this finding, we conclude that energy consumption does not typically represent economic growth as people used to believe, and it should not be seen as a symbol that indicates a country's development.

Keywords: Energy Consumption · Economic Growth · High-Income · Low-Income

1 Introduction

Economic boosts always associate with energy consumption. Since the innovation of the steamer released in the first industrial revolution, humans have started to use energy to serve their society. Human power was rapidly replaced by steam. Boats roar on the ocean, trains rage on the trail, and clouds float in the sky. Humans advanced to a new level, and the economy also launched. Then it's the second. Oil was discovered. Cars get rid of trails, and thus coach starts fading from people's eyes. Electricity connected people together. The night no longer means darkness. Not more limited to sunlight, commerce no longer needs to sleep with the moon. People keep draining resources from the earth and using them as the basement of the economy. And now, traditional energy, such as coal, oil, and gas, is challenged by renewable energy. Human again stands in front of another boosting.

However, is it true about energy consumption pushes the economy? This question seems to have been clarified. Many people have indicated that there is a bi-directional causal relationship between energy consumption and economic growth [1, 2]. They believe that energy consumption does help people to enhance their economic growth and this relationship has stood for a long time. On the other hand, there are people who argue that this relationship has a limit as a threshold, and it doesn't hold for every economic status [3]. Regarding this distinction, this paper is trying to examine the relationship between energy consumption and economic growth through the data after 2000 and find the impact difference of fossil and renewable energy between high-income countries and low-income countries.

2 Literature Review

Many studies have investigated the relationship between economic growth and energy consumption. In most cases, the energy feeds the flourishing human society. For example, a study reveals that energy consumption spurs economic growth in Tanzania [4]. Another study of Turkey also concludes that a high level of coal consumption leads to a high level of real GDP. The consumption of coal is the key factor in people's well-being in Turkey [5]. On the other hand, exporting energy also becomes a major commercial activity for countries that store ample resources, since other countries may have problems with energy scarcity. Energy trade becomes a key factor for these rich countries' economies. A study concludes that traditional energy has a stable market, reasonable prices, stable income, safe supply, and fair returns for investors. The development of oil and natural gas energy can meet the growing demand for energy [6]. For example, another research indicates that countries with poor economic development need to utilize traditional energy to meet basic thermal and electricity needs. The export of traditional energy can promote the development of international trade and bring benefits to countries with abundant natural resources [7].

Besides these traditional fossil fuels, renewable new energy also plays a huge role in economic expansion. More and more countries start to consider replacing fuel energy with renewable energy to balance economic growth. A case study of Brazil suggests that expanding renewable energy would not only enhance economic growth but also retard the deterioration of the environment at the same time [8] Another investigation also proves that the influence of renewable energy consumption or its share of the total energy mix on economic growth is positive and statistically significant [9]. What's more, using renewable energy also helps people to solve a major problem due to the usage of transitional energy-environmental costs. There is no doubt that the concern about the environment, when people are using traditional energy, prohibits their economic growth. However, using renewable energy doesn't cause these kinds of plights. One study suggests that renewable energy provides a stable energy foundation for a country. A country that can master the utilization of renewable energy can overcome the economic problems caused by purchasing non-renewable energy, thereby promoting national economic development and redistribution [10]. However, although countries advocate the use of clean and renewable energy, according to data, the utilization of non-renewable energy is still increasing year by year [11]. It means there is still a long way for people to move away from fossil fuels to new energy, but people are confident about the potential for renewable energy and seek for the change to have a greater market.

Lots of research have argued the association between economic growth and energy consumption, but rare of them have compared the economic impact of fossil energy consumption and renewable energy consumption. Due to this research gap, we made a hypothesis that energy consumption has a positive impact on the economy, and it is different by type of energy to discuss their impact on the economy of high-income and low-income countries.

3 Methodology

3.1 Research Method

This study tries to identify the relationship between energy consumption and economic growth. Finding this relationship can help people better understand how energy affects the economy throughout the world and thus help people better predict the near future of economic growth. This study also tried to figure out how different types of energy work in the economy thus assisting the policy maker to make a better decision on which types of energy should be used in their countries to have a greater profit. Moreover, this study made a comparison between high-income countries and low-income countries, hoping to determine the role which energy consumption played in their society and how these consumptions impact their economic growth.

3.2 Model Constructure

To estimate the relationship, we created a simple model that helps us to examine the assumptions.

$$GDP = \beta_0 + \beta_1 Fossil + \beta_2 Renew + \beta_3 Pop + \beta_4 Inflation + \varepsilon \qquad (1)$$

In this model (1), Gross Domestic Product (GDP) is our dependent variable while Fossil and Renew are our core independent variables. Considering different inflation might be critical for countries economies, we add it as a control variable, since the higher it is, the lower GDP will be [12]. Moreover, the population also expresses a huge effect on energy consumption and energy consumption contributes to economic growth [13]. Thus, we also put population as one of our control variables. $\beta 0$ in the model is an intercept; $\beta 1 - \beta 4$ are the coefficients of Fossil, Renew, Pop, and Inflation, respectively. ε is the error term that represents the variables that could not be included in the models.

3.3 Data Collection

Data is collected through World Bank databases. This database collected the data from each country's report on either a calendar year basis (CY) or fiscal year basis (FY). Each country has been assigned a different income level. For example, the United Kingdom, France, Korea, and the United States are included as high-income countries, and Uganda, Zambia, Rwanda, and Mozambique are included as low-income countries. We use the GDP per capita to help indicate the GDP growth for each level of countries and use the energy consumption of total energy usage as an indicator of each level of countries'

Table 1. Operationalization and expected sign.

Variables	Description	Measurement
Dependent:		
GDP	GDP per capita	current US$
Independent Variables:		
Fossil	fossil energy consumption	% of total energy consumption
Renew	Renewable energy consumption	% of total energy consumption
Pop	Population	Millions
Inf	Inflation rate	Annual %

energy consumption. To compare the impact difference between different types of energies, we separate the energy consumption by fossil energy and renewable energy, thus helping to determine the roles played on economic growth by each category of energy. We collected data from 1990 to 2015 to help provide a better understanding of the relationship between energy consumption and economic growth in the modern world and make a more accurate prediction of the near future. Table 1 displays the names of the variables, measurements, and expected signs in the operational process.

3.4 Analysis

Table 2. Basic regression results for high-income countries.

Explanatory Variables	Intercept	Fossil	Renew	Pop	Inflation
Coefficients	−217843.198	877.381	906.916	147.263	1260.404
Standard Error	62311.261	747.316	670.089	15.668	366.648
P-value	0.002	0.254	0.190	0.000	0.002
R^2	0.971				

Table 3. Basic regression results for low-income countries.

Explanatory Variables	Intercept	Fossil	Renew	Pop	Inflation
Coefficients	3484.636	−15.408	−49.777	2.194	0.095
Standard Error	629.893	4.075	7.425	0.248	2.230
P-value	0.000	0.001	0.000	0.000	0.966
R^2	0.890				

This article uses a basic regression model to find the coefficient between each variable and GDP growth. Table 2 shows the results of energy consumption's impact on economic growth in high-income countries. The results show that the coefficient of fossil energy consumption is 877.381, and it is insignificant at the 5% significance level; the coefficient of renewable energy consumption is 906.916, but it is also insignificant at the 5% significance level. That is, even though the more energy consumption is, the greater economic growth will be, those two don't have a strong relationship. This might be due to energy consumption affecting other factors thus boosting the economic growth.

Table 3 shows the results of energy consumption's impact on economic growth for low-income countries. The results show that the coefficient of fossil energy consumption is negative 15.408, and it is significant at the 5% significance level; the coefficient of renewable energy consumption is negative 49.777, and it is also significant at the 5% significance level. This means energy consumption has the opposite impact on low-income consumers' economic growth. The more energy they consume, the worse their countries' economy will be. It is a surprise finding that energy consumption doesn't work as people believe before, and in some cases, it can be harmful to the economy.

4 Finding

4.1 Impact on High-Income Countries

Based on our study, we find that energy consumption has a positive nut not the significant relationship with high-income countries' GDP growth. It means energy consumption doesn't have a direct impact on high-income countries' economic growth, thus we reject the hypothesis that energy consumption pushes economic growth on high-income countries. However, there is a positive relationship between those. According to this finding and combined with our literature review, we believe even though energy consumption doesn't have a direct impact on economic growth, it stimulates growth through some intermedia such as industry, and technology. Moreover, renewable energy pushes the economy even further, since it helps to save environmental cost and creates more job positions.

Starting from the industrial age, countries like the United Kingdom, France, and German used a lot of energy in their countries' growth. Several industries were built and thousands of people influx into these industries spending their strength and sweat contributing to the rise of their countries. All these efforts create a great stage for these high-income countries, which remain today. However, behind these flourishing prosperities are tons of energy such as oil, coal, and gas. These resources were the blood of these achievements. Before the Industrial Revolution, societies relied on the annual cycle of photosynthesis in plants for their source of heat and mechanical energy. As a result, there was a finite amount of energy accessible each year, which forced economic expansion to be limited. Energy use soared during the Industrial Revolution, and output followed behind [14]. Without these liquid golds, cars won't run, boats won't sail, and all the industries won't run. Only when this kind of blood flows in society, these symbols of prosperity can be active as they are breathing.

Technology is another factor to determine the relationship between energy consumption and economic growth. Countries with a greater technology tend to consume more energy to build their countries since they can use them more efficiently. Data from the world bank shows a dramatic distinction. Countries with a higher technology level, such as United State and Canada, are consuming eight times more fossil energy than countries with limited natural resources, such as Mozambique. The difference in energy-using efficiency also indicates a dip gap between these countries. As a low-income country, Mozambique needs 363.7 kg of oil equivalent per $1000 while high-income countries such as United States only need 116.5 kg. The same amount of currency with triple times difference in consumption of energy. Even though it has changed a lot since 1990, which is 5 times. It still expresses an unbalanced stage. This explains why the economic growth of these countries is so different.

What's more, renewable energy also plays an important role in high-income countries' economic growth. As a new section of resources, renewable energy also plays an important role in economic growth. By replacing traditional energy, renewable maintains the energy consumption needs with a cut-off of environmental costs which are mostly due to fossil energy's combustion. A study about China indicates that as more and more energy consumption is needed for developing countries, CO_2 emissions also soar in the same way. Greenhouse effects and other related problem starts to retard the progress of development [15]. However, by switching to renewable energy, people can find a way to cross this plight and thus save numbers of the budget which is used to solve this question. A comparative analysis of non-renewable and renewable energy consumption proves that non-renewable energy consumption increases CO_2 emissions, whereas renewable energy consumption decreases CO_2 emissions [16]. These studies show that to significantly reduce non-renewable energy use and mitigate climate change, policymakers should concentrate on developing as well as clean energy development. It's also a method of saving money.

Moreover, investigating renewable energy also create thousands of work position. Ranging from manufacturing, and engineering to environmental research. According to an article, in 2016, the number of persons employed by the renewable energy industry, both directly and indirectly, was 9.8 million, a rise of 1.1% from 2015. The number of jobs in the renewable energy sector, excluding major hydropower, climbed by 2.8% in 2016 to 8.3 million [17]. One example is electric cars. Starting with Tesla, more and more auto manufacturers begin their exploration of electric cars. Traditional fuel cars fade away. These explorations create a lot of open job positions. The last boost like this is computer science. These newly created jobs push economic growth to the next level, especially for high-income countries that have more technology and resources to spend on innovation.

Concluding all the above, we believe energy consumption doesn't have a direct impact on economic growth. Thus for high-income countries we reject the hypothesis that energy consumption will affect economic growth. However, it does have something to do with economic growth through some intermedia factors such as industrial level, population, and technology. Moreover, renewable energy usage avoids the government's environmental cost and creates a lot of new job opportunities thus boosting economic growth even further. Considering these, we think that even though those two do not have a direct relationship, energy consumption can still be seen as a variable when people predict economic growth.

4.2 Impact on Low-Income Countries

To analyze the relationship between carbon emissions and economic growth in low-income countries, it is first necessary to analyze the main sources of carbon emissions in low-income countries. After understanding the main sources of carbon emissions, we can analyze their main contributions to economic growth, thereby understanding the relationship between carbon emissions and economic growth.

By observing and comparing the total carbon emissions of high-income and low-income countries, we can conclude that the total carbon emissions of low-income countries are much smaller than those of high-income countries. However, low-income countries often lack modern energy and rely heavily on traditional energy fuels. This has led to a serious upward trend in the total carbon emissions of low-income countries. These traditional fuels often have low combustion efficiency, leading to high levels of carbon emissions. However, the main sources and reasons for carbon emissions in low-income countries are not limited to energy consumption patterns. There are several other major sources of carbon emissions in low-income countries.

As mentioned earlier, the lack of renewable energy is one of the main reasons for carbon emissions in low-income countries. People in these countries heavily rely on traditional fuels for basic electricity, which emit a large amount of carbon dioxide when burned for power generation.

Industrial Activities and Changes in Land Use. Low-income countries are in a stage of urgent need for economic development. Industrial development is one of the best ways for these low-income countries to improve their economic levels. The proportion of industrial development in low-income countries using nonrenewable energy is much higher than the proportion using renewable energy. This has led to low-income countries having to consume a large amount of traditional energy if they want to accelerate development. This makes it difficult for low-income countries to cope with increasingly strict environmental and carbon emission standards. If emissions are reduced, low-income countries cannot accelerate economic development; If we accelerate economic development, we cannot achieve emission reduction.

For the sake of economic development, low-income countries are gradually not satisfied with using land for basic agriculture but are increasing investment and developing urbanization. This will result in fewer and fewer natural lands being able to absorb carbon dioxide from the atmosphere, as well as in high-income countries.

Transportation. Transportation is another important source of carbon emissions for low-income countries. Although residents of low-income countries mostly use zero-emission honest transportation, in many low-income countries, their public transportation, such as buses, trains, and so on, may use older and more polluting engines. Meanwhile, in high-income countries, industrial transportation mainly relies on efficient and low-carbon public transportation. However, in low-income countries, industrial transportation and cargo transportation mainly rely on private transportation vehicles with high emissions, such as trucks and trucks. This strengthens the carbon emissions that low-income countries rely on for industrial development.

Current Situation on Economic Growth and Energy Use. Governments in low-income countries actively respond to global environmental policies. However, the economic development of low-income countries also relies on the use of traditional energy. Low-income countries need more economic and energy support to develop their own renewable energy systems. And these economic and energy support are based on the use of traditional energy. Many high-income countries have also relied on traditional energy for economic growth and the construction of new energy sources in the past few decades "Growing RE is one part of the solution. But given existing fossil fuel plants in developing regions (especially new ones) aren't going away any time soon, we need to make them cleaner, more efficient, and flexible" [18]. In this article, it is mentioned that low-income countries cannot urgently pursue renewable energy and zero emissions. Because building renewable energy systems and zero emissions requires an economic and industrial foundation, which low-income countries do not have. The most feasible solution for low-income countries is to achieve efficient energy use in industrial production. Low-income countries are among the vulnerable groups in this global environmental action Sub-Saharan Africa is where most people lacking modern energy services live. "Giving 250 million homes electricity connectivity, with 35 kWh/month usage (enough for a TV, refrigerator, and fan), even entirely from coal, would only be 0.25% of global emissions" [19]. Residents of low-income countries have low energy use, but high-income countries also need to understand that if low-income countries cannot reduce most of their carbon emissions in a short period of time.

In summary, the economic development of low-income countries at the current stage relies on the use of energy, especially traditional energy. Low-income countries need to increase their efforts in industrial construction, which is one of the most effective ways for low-income countries to significantly increase their economic level. Industrial development cannot be separated from the transportation industry. In low-income countries, transportation is not efficient and energy efficient. So, the carbon emissions generated by transportation cannot be ignored. Since most industrial development in low-income countries currently relies on traditional energy sources, such as coal, for energy supply, transforming low-income countries into high-income countries requires traditional energy to contribute to industrial development. At the same time as economic growth, land urbanization is also an active project faced by governments in various low-income countries. Land urbanization reduces vegetation and increases energy consumption. From these three most obvious parts, low-income countries cannot increase their economic development without traditional energy.

How low-income countries can reduce carbon emissions while growing their economies is currently the biggest issue. The industrial development of low-income countries can gradually be transformed into efficient and energy-saving forms. Although this still relies on traditional fuels. But this will reduce the use of traditional fuels and the total amount of carbon dioxide emissions. Based on achieving this step, continuous research on the utilization of renewable energy is a stable, green, and development plan. This includes improving the combustion efficiency of factory machinery and adding more industrial transportation vehicles with lower emissions. Based on industrial development, low-income countries need to utilize a portion of funds to establish infrastructure for renewable and clean energy. For example, solar power stations, hydroelectric and wind power stations, and so on. This will help low-income countries establish sustainable economic models while gradually reducing carbon emissions.

4.3 Relationship Between Energy Consumption and Economic Growth

The main purpose of this short essay is to critically evaluate the relationship between energy consumption and economic growth based on the reviews of previous academic studies and empirical research. Evidence will be collected to justify the key viewpoints that compare the relationship between high-income and low-income countries.

The link between energy consumption and economic growth has been a subject of discussion, which is generally supported by two main approaches as key theoretical foundations. On one hand, the neoclassical growth model views energy as an intermediary input in the production and manufacturing process. The restrictions on energy supply would not negatively impact economic growth, because technological change and other physical inputs can be utilized to generate renewable energy resources efficiently [20]. On the other hand, the ecological economic theory considers energy consumption as a critical input and the primary source of value since other factors, such as labor and capital cannot work without energy [21].

During the past decades, both the academic and real worlds attached importance to identifying the direction of causality between energy consumption and economic growth because the results could guide and shape the policies to facilitate sustainable growth. Empirical studies and experiments have been conducted across countries to evaluate and measure the detailed effects. However, these studies have produced varying and sometimes contradictory results. Differently, other research found no evidence of causality between energy consumption and GDP, which implies the lack of policy stability shown by the early results [22]. Other studies have demonstrated causal relationships that run in both directions, depending on the country and time involved. It is a noticeable fact that most empirical studies focus on the national economy in high-income countries, where public awareness of environmental protection has become increasingly strong to facilitate corporate social responsibility and policies pursuing sustainable growth [23]. The marginal benefits of economic growth no longer outweighed the marginal costs of sacrificing the environment. Under such circumstances, the quick development and widespread low-carbon economy have accelerated the transition into sustainable energy [24]. Under such circumstances, consumption of traditional energy and economic development have been gradually decoupling in the developed economy, as the market demands have been switching to more sustainable goods and services, which forces radical innovation and responsible business practices.

Differently, empirical results show that many developing economies, especially countries in Eastern and Southeastern Asia, have still struggled with the balance between economic growth and environmental protection [25]. Lack of advanced technology and an extremely large population base become two main obstacles that prevent the widespread use of clean and renewable energy sources [26].

Different from the fact that energy consumption has switched to more sustainable and renewable ways in high-income countries as discussed above, this essay argues that the consumption of traditional energy is still closely linked to the national economy in low-income countries.

First, pillars of the national economy in low-income countries are usually energy-intensive industries like manufacturing, which consumes abundant, affordable energy to produce goods for export and increase GDP. The report demonstrated that over 57% of Indian GDP is created based on the consumption of fossil fuel, while the data in Malaysia and Vietnam are 62% and 59%, respectively [27].

5 Conclusion

This article aims to find out the relationship between energy consumption and economic growth. Through a simple regression model with 30 years of data from 1990, we find that for high-income countries energy consumption has an insignificant positive relationship with economic growth which means people shouldn't use energy consumption as a main predictor of economic growth.

Through the analysis of low-income countries, we can draw conclusions. In low-income countries, the use of energy can seriously affect economic development, especially traditional energy. The industrial and urbanization development of low-income countries cannot be separated from traditional energy. At the same time, developing renewable energy requires industrial infrastructure and technological support for low-income countries. It is obvious that low-income countries do not fully meet these two conditions. The best approach for low-income countries now is to develop their economy while making the use of traditional energy more efficient and reducing the carbon emissions caused by using traditional energy.

It is the type of energy source that causes the different situations in high-income and low-income countries. In most high-income countries where a low-carbon economy has been promoted by public awareness and government policies, the consumption of traditional energy and national economic development are decoupling, as most business entities switch to clean and renewable energy to reduce their carbon footprint. However, in low-income countries, the traditional industrial structure, and the lack of investment in new energy have made such consumption not affordable in the short run.

References

1. Belke, A., Dobnik, F., Dreger, C.: Energy consumption and economic growth: new insights into the cointegration relationship. Energy Econ. **33**(5), 782–789 (2011). https://www.sciencedirect.com/science/article/pii/S0140988311000417
2. Bildirici, M.E., Bakirtas, T.: The relationship among oil, natural gas and coal consumption and economic growth in BRICTS (Brazil, Russian, India, China, Turkey and South Africa) countries. Energy **65**, 134–144 (2014). https://www.sciencedirect.com/science/article/pii/S0360544213010633
3. Tran, B.-L., Chen, C.-C., Tseng, W.-C.: Causality between energy consumption and economic growth in the presence of GDP threshold effect: evidence from OECD countries. Energy **251**, 123902 (2022). https://www.sciencedirect.com/science/article/pii/S0360544222008052
4. Odhiambo, N.M.: Energy consumption and economic growth nexus in Tanzania: an ARDL bounds testing approach. Energy Policy **37**(2), 617–622 (2009). https://www.sciencedirect.com/science/article/abs/pii/S0301421508005442

5. Narayan, P.K., Liu, R., Westerlund, J.: A GARCH model for testing market efficiency. J. Int. Financ. Mark. Inst. Money **41**, 121–138 (2016). https://www.sciencedirect.com/science/article/pii/S1042443115001213?via%3Dihub
6. Aktaş, C.: Causal relationship between coal consumption and economic growth in Turkey. Ünye İktisadi ve İdari Bilimler Fakültesi Dergisi **1**(2), 78–83 (2017). https://dergipark.org.tr/en/pub/uiibfd/issue/35259/360049
7. Pickard, S., Scott, A.: FAQ 2: Oil and gas, poverty and economic development (no date) ODI. https://odi.org/en/about/our-work/climate-and-sustainability/faq-2-oil-and-gas-poverty-and-economic-development/. Accessed 25 Apr 2023
8. Rahman, M.: Oil and gas: the engine of the world economy. Presentation as OPEC Secretary General at the Tenth International Financial and Economic Forum, Vienna, Austria (2004). https://www.opec.org/opec_web/en/900.htm
9. Barro, R.J.: Inflation and economic growth, NBER (1995). https://www.nber.org/papers/w5326. Accessed 4 May 2023
10. Shaari, M.S., Rahim, H.A., Rashid, I.M.A.: Relationship among population, energy consumption and economic growth in Malaysia. Int. J. Soc. Sci. **13**(1) (2013). https://web.archive.org/web/20180421075647id_/http://tijoss.com/TIJOSS%2013th%20Volume/shahidan%20shari.pdf
11. Pao, H.-T., Fu, H.-C.: Renewable energy, non-renewable energy and economic growth in Brazil. Renew. Sustain. Energy Rev. **25**, 381–392 (2013). https://www.sciencedirect.com/science/article/pii/S1364032113002906
12. Inglesi-Lotz, R.: The impact of renewable energy consumption to economic growth: a panel data application. Energy Econ. **53**, 58–63 (2016). https://www.sciencedirect.com/science/article/pii/S0140988315000171
13. Zhe, L., et al.: The positive influences of renewable energy consumption on financial development and economic growth. Sage Open **11**(3), 21582440211040133 (2021). https://journals.sagepub.com/doi/10.1177/21582440211040133
14. Ivanovski, K., Hailemariam, A., Smyth, R.: The effect of renewable and non-renewable energy consumption on economic growth: non-parametric evidence. J. Cleaner Prod. **286**, 124956 (2021). https://www.sciencedirect.com/science/article/abs/pii/S0959652620350009
15. Suck, A.: Renewable energy policy in the United Kingdom and in Germany. SSRN 349900 (2002). https://papers.ssrn.com/sol3/papers.cfm?abstract_id=349900
16. Wang, S., et al.: The relationship between economic growth, energy consumption, and CO_2 emissions: empirical evidence from China. Sci. Total Environ. **542**, 360–371 (2016). https://www.sciencedirect.com/science/article/pii/S0048969715308433
17. Shafiei, S., Salim, R.A.: Non-renewable and renewable energy consumption and CO_2 emissions in OECD countries: a comparative analysis. Energy Policy **66**, 547–556 (2014). https://www.sciencedirect.com/science/article/pii/S0301421513010872
18. Ferroukhi, R., et al.: Renewable energy and jobs: annual review 2015. Int. Renew. Energy Agency (IRENA) (2017). https://www.voced.edu.au/content/ngv:77403
19. Tongia, R.: It is unfair to push poor countries to reach zero carbon emissions too early (2022). https://www.brookings.edu/blog/planetpolicy/2022/10/26/it-is-unfair-to-push-poor-countries-to-reach-zero-carbon-emissions-too-early/
20. Adhikari, D., Chen, Y.: Energy consumption and economic growth: a panel cointegration analysis for developing countries. Rev. Econ. Financ. **3**(2), 68–80 (2012). https://www.researchgate.net/profile/Dipa-Adhikari-2/publication/291128778_Energy_consumption_and_economic_growth_A_panel_cointegration_analysis_for_developing_countries/links/5e5fdaea299bf1bdb8540a4a/Energy-consumption-and-economic-growth-A-panel-cointegration-analysis-for-developing-countries.pdf

21. Bartleet, M., Gounder, R.: Energy consumption and economic growth in New Zealand: results of trivariate and multivariate models. Energy Policy **38**(7), 3508–3517 (2010). https://www.sciencedirect.com/science/article/abs/pii/S0301421510001060
22. Ismail, N.H.M., et al.: Carbon dioxide (CO_2) emission, energy consumption and economic growth: evidence from selected Southeast Asia countries. J. Emerg. Econ. Islamic Res. **8**(2), 1–12 (2020). https://myjms.mohe.gov.my/index.php/JEEIR/article/view/8937
23. Jamel, L., Derbali, A.: Do energy consumption and economic growth lead to environmental degradation? Evidence from Asian economies. Cogent Econ. Financ. **4**(1), 1170653 (2016). https://www.tandfonline.com/doi/full/10.1080/23322039.2016.1170653
24. Shi, C.: Decoupling analysis and peak prediction of carbon emission based on decoupling theory. Sustain. Comput. Inform. Syst. **28**, 100424 (2020). https://www.sciencedirect.com/science/article/abs/pii/S2210537920301517
25. Shuai, C., et al.: A three-step strategy for decoupling economic growth from carbon emission: empirical evidences from 133 countries. Sci. Total Environ. **646**, 524–543 (2019). https://www.sciencedirect.com/science/article/abs/pii/S0048969718325269
26. Stern, D.I.: Economic growth and energy. Encyclopedia Energy **2**(00147), 35–51 (2004). http://www.sterndavidi.com/Publications/Growth.pdf
27. Tariq, G., et al.: Energy consumption and economic growth: evidence from four developing countries. Am. J. Multidisciplinary Res. 7(1) (2018). http://www.onlinejournal.org.uk/index.php/ajmur/article/view/320

Research on the Merger and Acquisition Performance and Brand Management of Cross-Border LBO—Take Qumei Home's Acquisition of Norwegian Ekornes Company as an Example

Runbang Liu(✉)

School of Accountancy, Southwestern University of Finance and Economics, Chengdu, China
lrbang2002@163.com

Abstract. With the rapid development of China's economic globalization and the implementation of "going out", "Belt and Road" and "Made in China 2025", Chinese enterprises begin to seek the transformation and upgrading of product structure, improve product layout and technological innovation, and strive to expand overseas market, expand market share, improve the competitiveness and international influence. In recent years, more and more enterprises begin to try to achieve rapid development through cross-border merger and acquisition activities. However, many studies point out that the overall success rate of cross-border M&A of Chinese enterprises is relatively low, and the profitability is not ideal. In this context, this paper will use the case that Qumei Home acquired Norway Ekornes ASA company in 2018 as the analysis object. First, PEST analysis was used to macroscopically analyze the development of status and trend, and the situation of M&A in the furniture industry. Meanwhile, from the micro level, this paper will elaborate and analyze the process of this M&A case. Next, this paper analyzes the merger and acquisition motivation of Qumei Home from internal factors and external factors; then, this paper selects 3 listed companies in the furniture industry as the benchmarking enterprises, and uses the method of financial index analysis to analyze and demonstrate the impact of this M&A on Qumei's financial performance and corporate value from horizontal and vertical aspects. Finally, this paper uses the method of brand matrix analysis to analyze and discuss the brand matrix change and brand management after the M&A.

Based on the above research process, the following research conclusions are drawn: First, mergers and acquisitions have become the trend of the domestic furniture industry. Also, cross-border mergers and acquisitions can promote enterprises to expand the market and pursue international development. The motivation of Qumei Home's cross-border merger and acquisition also lies in this. Second, Qumei Home's acquisition of Norwegian Ekornes company has both positive and negative impact on Qumei's financial performance. And the negative impact on the solvency and profitability is more obvious. Third, Qumei Home's acquisition of Norwegian Ekornes company has little negative impact on Qumei's stock market value and investment value in the furniture industry, and the value is still in a relatively medium and balanced position.

© The Author(s), under exclusive license to Springer Nature Singapore Pte Ltd. 2024
X. Li et al. (Eds.): ICEMGD 2023, AEPS, pp. 1327–1360, 2024.
https://doi.org/10.1007/978-981-97-0523-8_124

Fourth, Qumei Home's acquisition of Norwegian Ekornes company enriched the brand matrix of Qumei Home. In addition, Qumei Home has played a better role in brand management and brand synergy, so that after the M&A, the brand has achieved mutual empowerment and joint development.

This paper holds that enterprises need to broaden financing channels, innovate payment methods and enhance their integration ability when carrying out cross-border mergers and acquisitions. At the same time, after M&A, enterprises should also focus on the possible influence on performance and brand, and prevent financial risks and so on.

Keywords: Qumei Home · Cross-border M&A · M&A motivation · M&A performance · Brand management

1 Introduction

1.1 Research Background

M&A activities are a common means for enterprises to achieve rapid expansion and transformation. Cross-border mergers and acquisitions can broaden the expansion of enterprises to the international stage, which also can help enterprises draw on international experiences and technology for enterprise transformation. The International Monetary Fund defines cross-border merger and acquisition as the acquisition of the control of a foreign enterprise through the merger or acquisition of a certain proportion of the equity, so as to obtain the lasting production and operation interests of the foreign enterprise. Through cross-border mergers and acquisitions, enterprises can effectively reduce the barriers to entering new regions and new industries, and quickly gain competitive advantages in technology and so on.

In recent years, with the proposal of the strategic goal of "Made in China 2025", China's outbound investment activities have become an important development force in the cross-border M&A market. From 2016 to 2021, the number of cross-border mergers and acquisitions in China has increased from 11,407 cases to 12,790 cases, and the amount of cross-border M&A has always remained at a high level [1]. By 2022, Chinese enterprises have a history of cross-border mergers and acquisitions for more than 40 years. More enterprises have gradually joined the market wave of cross-border mergers and acquisitions.

At the same time, from the perspective of the industry, furniture products, which are the fourth most important consumer goods, make the furniture industry occupy an important position in the national economy. The "Belt and Road" development strategy implemented in China brings opportunities for China's traditional manufacturing industry. And the furniture industry, as the main force of China's traditional manufacturing industry, is also constantly trying to enter the international market [2]. In addition, the introduction of Industry 4.0, and major changes in consumer demand, put forward higher requirements for the process, quality and design of household products. Driven by the current situation of the industry, furniture enterprises adopt cross-border M&A activities to seek the road of development and transformation.

In September 2018, Qumei Home, a listed furniture enterprise known as "the first stock of Chinese furniture enterprises", acquired the Norwegian furniture brand Ekornes ASA, which is known as "national treasure", at a high price of nearly 4 billion yuan with a total asset of only 2 billion yuan, setting the largest overseas merger and acquisition case in the furniture industry. Qumei Home's cross-border merger and acquisition behavior, which is like "a snake swallows an elephant", triggered hot discussions and mixed views in society. The reason and the performance of Qumei Home's cross-border M&A need to be studied urgently. Therefore, this paper selects Qumei Home's acquisition of Norwegian Ekornes company as the research object, analyzes the behavior of the case, and explores the impact of cross-border LBO on corporate performance and brand management.

1.2 Study Significance

The furniture industry plays an important role in the national economy, but there are fewer cross-border M&A cases in the furniture industry compared with other industries, and there are few theoretical studies and case studies on the furniture industry. In the current situation of the transformation of the furniture industry, many furniture enterprises have begun to achieve international development through cross-border mergers and acquisitions. Therefore, this paper selects Qumei Home's acquisition of Norwegian Ekornes ASA as the research object to analyze the M&A cases and draw conclusions and enlightenment, which has certain significance for cross-border M&A of enterprises.

Theoretical Significance. Domestic and foreign research activities on cross-border mergers and acquisitions were carried out early, so the research literature is abundant. But most of them are conducted in some popular fields and industries, with relatively few studies on the traditional furniture industry. This M&A activity is the largest merger and acquisition activity in the domestic furniture industry at present, and it is a M&A activity like a snake swallows an elephant, which has a strong theoretical research significance. But scholars have relatively little research on this type of cross-border M&A. Therefore, this paper selects Qumei Home's acquisition of Ekornes as the research object, which is helpful to enrich the theoretical research of furniture industry's M&A.

In addition, most of scholars' studies on M&A cases focus on M&A motivation and M&A performance, so there are few studies on M&A cases combined with brand management. Therefore, this paper studies the motivation, performance and brand management of M&A cases, enriches the theoretical dimensions of M&A case study, and is conducive to a more comprehensive and in-depth theoretical analysis of M&A cases.

Practical Significance. In this paper, Qumei Home's acquisition of Ekornes is selected as the research object. This case is the largest M&A case in the domestic furniture industry at present, which is difficult and has high risk. Therefore, in such a realistic background, the study of this case can provide M&A experience for other enterprises, especially the weak M&A parties, and provide reference for more enterprises to go international stage in the future. At the same time, the furniture industry, as one of the important industries in the transformation and upgrading of China's traditional manufacturing industry, supports the development of the national economic level. Exploring the cross-border M&A case can provide reference for cross-border mergers and acquisitions in the future and promote the development of the traditional manufacturing industry.

1.3 The Innovation Points of This Paper

First, the case selected in this paper is typical and representative. The case selected in this paper is in the furniture industry. And furniture is the fourth most important consumer goods outside real estate, automobile and food, which makes the furniture industry occupies an important position in the national economy. Therefore, the industry of the case is representative. In addition, the case in this paper is the largest merger and acquisition case in the furniture industry at present, and it is a "snake swallowing elephant" type case, which has aroused wide social attention, so this case event is representative and has research value.

Secondly, the case selected in this paper is scarce. From the perspective of the number of cases of the same type, the number of cross-border M&A cases accounts for a small proportion in the total number of M&A cases, while the cross-border M&A cases in the furniture industry are less compared with other industries. In addition, as a case of "snake swallowing elephant" in cross-border merger and acquisition cases in the furniture industry, the number of cases of the same type is less and this type is rarer. From the perspective of the number of studies of the same type, scholars have done little research on the "snake swallowing elephant" cross-border merger and acquisition cases. It can be seen that the merger and acquisition case in this paper is highly scarce, highly innovative, and have good research value.

Finally, the research dimensions and methods of this paper are diverse. Most of the scholars' studies on M&A cases focus on M&A motivation and M&A performance, and rarely analyze other dimensions of M&A cases. For the research cases, this paper adopts PEST analysis, financial index analysis and brand matrix analysis to deeply analyze the M&A cases from multiple dimensions such as acquisition motivation, acquisition performance and acquisition brand management. The diversity of dimensions and methods makes the analysis of the case more comprehensive, specific and in-depth, and also enhances the innovation and application value of this paper.

2 Literature Review

Chinese scholars have done a lot of research on the motivation, financial performance and brand management of cross-border mergers and acquisitions, which brings important reference value for Chinese enterprises to conduct cross-border mergers and acquisitions.

2.1 Research on the Motivation of Cross-Border M&A

Geng Huiting [3], based on the hybrid monetary policy rules, made the use of multiple Logit models to empirically test the differential impact of monetary policy uncertainty on the six driving factors of cross-border M&A. The results show that increasing monetary policy uncertainty will reduce Chinese enterprises choose to conduct the same industry skills upgrading overseas M&A motivation, industrial chain expanding overseas M&A motivation, pure profit seeking type overseas M&A motivation, natural resources seeking the relative probability of overseas M&A motivation, the Chinese enterprises will be more inclined to have preferential tax seeking type overseas M&A motivation.

Xiao Ming et al. [4] used the EEMD model to examine the relationship between the macroeconomic environment and cross-border mergers and acquisitions in two short-term and long-term time scales. The results show that in recent years, the sustained and rapid development of China's macro economy is the main reason for the long-term fluctuations of cross-border mergers and acquisitions, and the rising uncertainty of domestic economic policies will also promote it. The short-term fluctuations of the stock market and the adjustment of economic policies are the important factors driving the short-term fluctuations of cross-border M&A.

Wang Kui et al. [5] analyze through empirical analysis and use gravity model to show that Chinese enterprises' overseas M&As have the motivation of market seeking, resource seeking and strategic assets seeking. The motivation of state-owned enterprises is more obvious than non-state-owned enterprises. At the same time, Chinese enterprises tend to choose the target countries with higher system quality.

Zhao Rong [6] divided the motivation for cross-border mergers and acquisitions of Chinese enterprises into three categories. The first category is government motivation, including government policy incentives, support of merger and acquisition laws, and attraction of the host country; the second category is strategic motivation, including seeking technical support and brand development channels; and the third category is investment motivation, including strengthening the development ability of developing the market and dispersing some operational risks. The article finally believes that for Chinese enterprises, cross-border mergers and acquisitions is an important choice to become bigger and stronger.

Tang Xiaohua et al. [7] analyzed the drivers and trends of overseas mergers and acquisitions of Chinese manufacturing enterprises from the perspective of global value chain. The results show that the drivers of overseas M&A of Chinese manufacturing enterprises include technology acquisition, market expansion, diversification, brand acquisition and global value chain restructuring.

Liao Dongsheng et al. [8] analyzed the current situation and characteristics of cross-border mergers and acquisitions of Chinese manufacturing enterprises, and the six agents of overseas mergers and acquisitions of manufacturing enterprises are concluded, including bypassing trade barriers and realizing international operation strategy; obtaining economies of scale and improving the efficiency of resource allocation; acquiring manufacturer advantage and realizing operation synergies; acquiring core technology and forming competitive advantage; exploiting the international market.

2.2 Research on the Financial Performance of Cross-Border M&A

Based on the concept of resource basis and system theory, Wu Tianlan [9] tested the influence of resource correlation and system distance on the duration of merger and acquisition transactions, and combined with the theory of M&A motivation and social capital, and discussed the regulatory role of M&A market seeking motivation and M&A professional consultants. The results show that the longer the transaction lasts, the more time the enterprise can have to prepare for the subsequent integration work, the integration process is less likely to produce contradictions, and the positive effects generated in the later stage can offset the cost in the early stage, making the higher the merger and acquisition performance.

Liu Decai [10] and others took SF Holding cross-border acquisition of Kerry Logistics as an example to study the causes, results and preventive measures of financial risks in the process of cross-border mergers and acquisitions of listed companies. Finally, the paper believes that sufficient due diligence and audit, expanding financing channels, constructing reasonable financial organization structure, paying attention to the integration of financial resources and technical resources, information resources, cultural resources, management resources and human resources are effective measures to prevent financial risks.

Wang Dupeng [11] used dual difference and PSM-DID model to empirically study the overall and continuous impact of cross-border mergers and acquisitions on the performance of enterprises, and analyzed the impact of cross-border mergers and acquisitions of enterprises of different ownership on their own performance. The results of the study show that, The impact of cross-border M&A on Chinese corporate performance is positive, And the impact on the performance of private enterprises is significantly positive, However, the impact on the performance of state-owned enterprises is not significant.

Dai Jiangxiu [12] conducted a descriptive statistical analysis of the cross-border merger and acquisition performance of some listed automobile companies in China. First, the financial indicators such as inventory turnover ratio, asset-liability ratio and net sales interest rate were selected for KMO test, and then the factors with strong correlation were selected for factor analysis. The final results show that the overall cross-border merger and acquisition of China's automobile industry has a positive impact on enterprise performance, but the impact degree gradually decreases with the growth of time.

Huang Xiao et al. [13] took YTO Express's acquisition of Xianda as an example. This paper adopts the comprehensive evaluation method of financial indicators to construct the performance evaluation index system of merger and acquisition from six aspects: profitability, solvency, operation ability, growth ability, industry potential energy and development potential. The study found that in terms of financial dimension, the merger has brought different adverse effects on the profitability, solvency, operating capacity and growth ability of YTO Express, but its R&D investment, overseas income and market share have increased, and the potential and development potential of the industry have increased.

2.3 Research on Brand Management of Cross-Border M&A

Xu Guanghui further studied ANTA Sports of cross-border acquisition brand management. In 2016, anta sports started "single focus, brand, all channel" strategy. With the well-known FILA acquisition case in the market, Japanese high-end outdoor skiing brand Disant Descente, outdoor brand Kolon Sport and high-end children's sports brand Xiaoxiao Kingkow will expand the market space with multi-brand combination and improve the omni-channel operation efficiency to support the development of various brands. In 2019, Anta acquired Yamafen Amer Sports, and won the Archaeopteryx Arc'teryx,

Salomon Salomon, Wilsheng Wilson and other top brands in the segment, completing the cross-scene coverage from the mass to the high-end market. In 2020, Anta brand made revolutionary changes again, who accelerated the building of DTC operation mode, established a more streamlined channel structure, improved the efficiency of operation and management.

Lin Sijie et al. deeply studied Marriott International (MAR.O) cross-border M&A management. By the end of 2021, Marriott International has operated 7,989 hotels in 30 brands in 139 countries and regions, with more than 160 million members and a complete brand matrix, including full-service and limited service hotels of different levels such as Ritz-Carlton, Westin, Courtyard and so on. The development of Marriott has a strong reference significance for domestic hotel groups to achieve full coverage of brand matrix. At the same time, the author is also highly optimistic about the development path of "Marriott mode" with asset-light, high profit margin and internationalization with Chinese characteristics.

3 Related Theoretical Basis

3.1 Acquisition-Related Motivation Theory

The research of domestic and foreign scholars can be divided into two categories, the first explains the perspective of resource acquisition, enterprise strategy and company managers; the second is the external motivation, external environment, and try to explain the factors affecting the merger and acquisition from the external macro perspective.

Internal Motivation of Merger and Acquisition. The internal motivation of mergers and acquisitions at home and abroad mainly has the following theories. The first is the agency theory [14], which holds that mergers and acquisitions are an important measure to alleviate the agency problem of enterprise managers. Enterprises can pose an effective threat to the existing management through fair acquisition or agency competition and reduce the agency cost, so as to alleviate the agency problem. The second is the efficiency theory [15], which holds that mergers and acquisitions can promote enterprises to obtain synergies with other subjects, so as to help enterprises improve business performance, reduce business risks and enhance social benefits. Finally, there is the arrogant theory [16], which holds that corporate executives may overestimate the real value of the target enterprise and their actual ability [17], and still make M&A decisions despite the acquisition of low or even no profit, which ultimately leads to the damage of the interests of the shareholders of the acquisition enterprise.

External Motivation of M&A. According to relevant research on external drivers of M&A, mergers and acquisitions are closely related to external macroeconomic factors, capital market environment and technological progress. Zhang Feiyan [18] studied the impact of macroeconomic factors on China's M&A market, and believed that three factors: GDP growth, inflation rate and stock yield would have an important impact on China's M&A market. Liu Liya et al. [19] found that the productivity improvement played an important role in promoting both domestic M&A and cross-border M&A. Chen Zeyi et al. [20] found that the negative reports significantly improved the probability that the company would actively terminate the restructuring plan and the restructuring plan failed to pass the review of the Merger and Acquisition Committee, and thus increased the probability of restructuring failure.

3.2 M&A Performance Theory

The research on M&A performance can be divided into the following methods. The first is the financial index analysis method. Liu Chang et al. [21] studied the performance of listed companies through the financial index analysis method. The results show that although the performance impact of M&A of domestic enterprises has improved in the short term and the effect is not obvious, the M&A performance needs to be improved in the long term. The second is the event research method. Chi zhaomei and Qiao Tong [22] used the event research method to study the acquisition of Qibin Group in Malaysia as an example. The research results show that although in the short term, mergers and acquisitions have a weak positive impact on the enterprise, in the long term, the performance of mergers and acquisitions showed a downward trend. Finally, EVA index analysis method. Tang Hengshu et al. [23] analyzed the merger and acquisition events of Kweichow Moutai through EVA index analysis method. The results showed that the merger and acquisition performance of listed companies was more accurate than the traditional accounting indicators, but it could not completely replace the traditional financial indicators. Investors can make a reasonable collocation to make more effective investment decisions.

3.3 Brand Management Theory

Zhang Xian [24] combines brand management and marketing, and thinks in the new economic situation, enterprises should attach importance to brand management marketing strategy, update the marketing concept, innovate brand management marketing model, which will help to enhance enterprise competitive advantage, improve profit margins and establish a good image for the enterprise.

Wang Hui [25] takes the brand integration in overseas mergers and acquisitions of China's dominant local enterprises as the research object, and establishes a systematic strategic decision model of brand integration that is suitable for the actual situation of China's dominant local enterprises. The final conclusion is that brand integration should run through the overseas mergers and acquisitions, and enterprises should actively cultivate their own internationally renowned brands, conduct systematic research and evaluation of target brands, and formulate a perfect brand integration plan.

4 Introductions of Qumei Home's Acquisition of Norwegian Ekornes Company

4.1 Brand Management Theory

Furniture Industry Development Status and Trend. This paper adopts PEST analysis method to analyze the macro environment of the development of furniture manufacturing enterprises in China, and explore the development status and trend of furniture industry.

Macro environment refers to the non-enterprise subjective factors that can cause indirect influence on the development of enterprises, which can be summarized into four factors: politics, economy, society, technology, and is referred to as PEST.

Policy Environment (P)

"The 2018 Work Report of the Government of The State Council" proposed to "expand international cooperation on production capacity and drive Chinese manufacturing and Chinese services to go global". Qumei Home actively responds to the national "go global" strategy, actively builds the Qumei brand, integrates the global supply chain and market channels, and comprehensively enhances the international competitiveness of the enterprise. In 2019, a special plan was proposed to improve the manufacturing production capacity, and was committed to increase the design innovation of competitive traditional industries.

Through the above major policies to China's furniture industry in recent years, we can see that China attaches great importance to the green development, property rights protection, brand construction and various aspects of furniture industry, and China emphasizes the transformation, upgrading, industry innovation and foreign trade of furniture industry, which can promote "the made in China" "going out" and improve the international competitiveness of Chinese enterprises.

Economic Environment (E)

Key factors that make up the economic environment include gross domestic product, the level of household disposable income, interest rates level and fiscal and monetary policies, etc. In recent years, the per capita disposable income of Chinese residents has been rising, promoting the continuous improvement of residents' consumption level, which will increase the demand of Chinese residents for high-end furniture. In addition, in order to promote the domestic economic development, China has implemented a relatively loose monetary policy in recent years. This makes the financing cost of furniture enterprises decrease, and the sales volume and income of middle and high-end furniture products rise, which promotes the development of furniture enterprises. From 2013 to 2018, the per capita disposable income and per capita consumption expenditure of Chinese residents are shown in the Fig. 1 below.

Social Environment (S)

The social and cultural environment and residents' consumption habits also well influence and promote the development of the furniture industry. First of all, from the perspective of social consumption concept, with the rise of income in the economic environment, consumers have gradually produced a change in the concept of striving for saving to pursuing quality. In terms of living environment, consumers begin to improve the requirements of personalized living environment, environmental protection performance, overall collocation and other aspects; In furniture products, consumers pay more and more attention to the quality, design and beauty of products, and the demand for products gradually transfers to the high-end furniture. Secondly, with the rapid development of the Internet era and the popularity of e-commerce, online shopping has become a social trend today. This has prompted domestic furniture enterprises to build online channels and achieve both online and offline sales, which not only expands the market

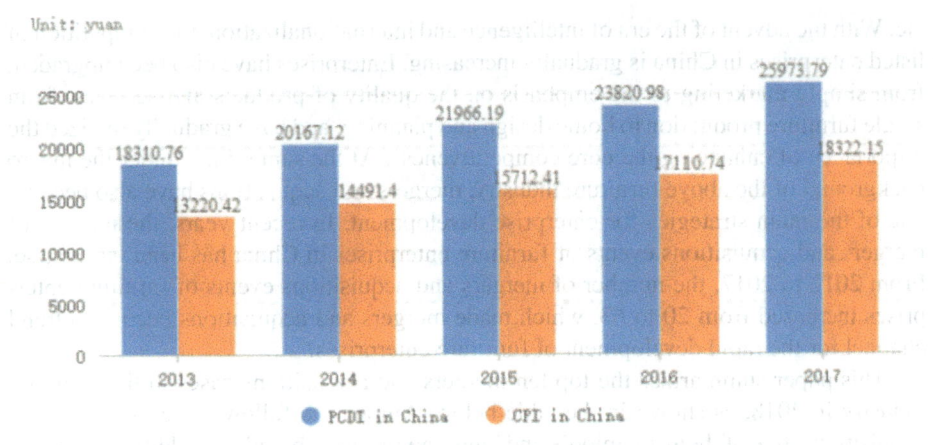

Fig. 1. PCDI and CPI in China from 2013 to 2017.

scope, but also expands the sales revenue. Finally, the social customs such as housewarming, purchase of a new house when marriage reflect the residents' concerns to buying a house, and buying a house will inevitably make the residents' demand for furniture products rise.

Technical Environment (T)
The development of science and technology has promoted the innovation and progress in the production and sales of furniture manufacturing industry. In terms of production, the proposal of Industry 4.0 makes furniture production gradually develop to the direction of automation, flexibility and intelligence. Moreover, in the era of artificial intelligence, mechanical automation production has gradually replaced human manual production, which not only reduces a lot of labor costs, but also improves the production capacity and efficiency of enterprises. In terms of sales, the application of big data can enable enterprises to collect massive information on customer demand, which can make them design and sell products more specifically. At the same time, 3D, VR and AR technologies have also well improved the scene experience of consumers, and have promoted the increase of consumption and sales volume.

According to the above PEST analysis, we can see that the four major factors of the macro environment emphasize the change of consumer demand and the importance of foreign investment and brand building. In order to comply with the national policy support and policy direction, and grasp the development opportunities under the macro environmental welfare, Chinese furniture enterprises strive for technological innovation, transformation, upgrading and seek international development. Merger and acquisition is a good way for enterprises to integrate brands, transform and upgrade, introduce advanced technology and go international. Therefore, merger and acquisition has become the development trend of China's furniture industry in recent years.

Listed Companies in Furniture Industry and Their Mergers and Acquisitions. China's influential listed companies in the furniture industry mainly include Oppein Home, Kuka Home, Markor Home, SOGAL, Shangpin Home, Qumei Home, etc. With, Markor Home, Sophia, Shangpin Home Products, Qumei furniture, etc. With the advent of the era of intelligence and internationalization, the competition of listed enterprises in China is gradually increasing. Enterprises have also been upgraded, from simple marketing to the emphasis on the quality of products and services, from single furniture production to home design and planning, and have gradually realized the importance of enhancing the core competitiveness. At the same time, under the macro background of the above furniture industry, mergers and acquisitions have also become one of the main strategies for enterprise development. In recent years, the number of mergers and acquisitions events of furniture enterprises in China has been on the rise. From 2012 to 2017, the number of mergers and acquisitions events of furniture enterprises increased from 20 to 63, which made mergers and acquisitions become a trend channel for the rapid development of furniture enterprises.

This paper summarizes the top ten mergers and acquisitions cases in the furniture industry in 2018, as shown in the table below. Among the following ten mergers and acquisitions, five of them are middle and high-end furniture brands. In addition, there are six mergers and acquisitions cases belonging to cross-border mergers and acquisitions, among which Qumei Home ranked first with 3.677 billion yuan. The top ten classic mergers and acquisitions in the furniture industry in 2018 show that the furniture enterprises attach great importance to the international development and actively adopt the merger and acquisition strategy to move forward to the high value-added field. Similarly, the Qumei Home analyzed in this article is no exception (Table 1).

4.2 Company Profiles of Both Parties to the Merger

Under the background of the macro environment and development trend of the furniture industry analyzed above, Qumei Home conforms to the development of The Times and adopted the decision of cross-border acquisition of Norwegian Ekornes company. The following introduces the basic situation of the two parties and the process of merger, and analyzes the motivation of Qumei Home.

Introduction to the Acquisition Party Qumei Home
Company Overview

Qumei furniture Group Co., Ltd. (hereinafter referred to as Qumei furniture) was established on April 10,1993, with a registered address of Shunyi District, Beijing. Qumei Home is a large furniture group integrating design, research and development, production and sales. Its products cover everything from hard installation, finished products, customization to soft decoration, and it is committed to providing users with one-stop home space solutions. At the same time, Qumei is also the first curved wood furniture manufacturer in China, which is in a leading position in China's furniture market. In April 2015, Qumei was listed in the Shanghai Stock Exchange (stock code: 603818). Qumei household thus also became the first listed furniture enterprises in Beijing.

Overview of the Company's Main Business
Qumei household is mainly engaged in the design, production and sales of middle and high-grade civil furniture and supporting household products, providing consumers with overall furniture solutions.

Table 1. Summary of the top ten mergers and acquisitions cases in the furniture industry in 2018.

Release time	Company	Company that is acquired	Attribute	Equity share	Acquisition amount
In May, 2018	Qumei Home	Ekornes ASA	Norwegian listed company	90.5%	3.68 billion yuan
In October, 2018	Kuka Home	SLEEMON	Mattress leading brand	No less than 23%	1.38 billion yuan
In January, 2018	Kuka Home	Natuzzi Natuzzi	Italian listed company	51%	65 million euros
In November, 2018	Kuka Home	Xibao home	Mattress export leader enterprises	51%	0.42 billion yuan
In March, 2018	Kuka Home	Nick Scali	Australian Furniture retailer	13.63%	A$77.3 million
In April, 2018	TUBAO	Nature home	Wood-type furniture products	18.39%	HK$ 418 million
In February, 2018	Kuka Home	Rolf Benz	High-end software furniture	99.92%	41.57 million euros
In July, 2018	Morris Home	Jennifer Convertibles Inc	American Furniture Chain	100%	$35 million
In March, 2018	Markor Home	Rowe Fine Furniture	high-end custom soft body furniture manufacturers	100%	$25 million
In September, 2018	SEAGULL	Yakeboluo	Main cabinets, bathroom cabinets and so on	55%	60.5 million yuan

In terms of product design and production, Qumei Home continues to promote the flexible and intelligent transformation of the factory production line, and continues to create a product system with both aesthetics and quality. At the same time, the company has always adhered to the original design, cooperation with excellent designers at home and abroad, combined with 30 years of lean manufacturing advantages, to provide consumers with environmental protection quality, original design products.

In terms of brand building, under the background of consumption upgrading and the market demand and consumption habits in new retail era, Qumei accelerates the integration of online and offline, determines the brand positioning of lifestyle content providers, establishes the new Qumei strategy centering around "new products, new models, new value", launches a comprehensive brand upgrade plan, and promotes the great upgrade of consumption experience.

In the first three years of the acquisition in 2018, the main business income of Qumei Home is classified by product as follows (Table 2):

Table 2. Income of Qumei Home from 2015 to 2017.

Product	Company		Company that is acquired		Attribute	
	amount of money	scale	amount of money	scale	amount of money	scale
Artificial board furniture	103,223.17	51.98%	79,848.58	48.33%	55,016.83	44.03%
Comprehensive furniture	33,091.54	16.66%	35,326.21	21.38%	31,133.43	24.92%
Solid wood furniture	30,311.07	15.26%	26,142.83	15.82%	22,435.12	17.95%
Home accessories	30,938.96	15.58%	22,767.25	13.78%	15,069.03	12.06%
Other main businesses	1,012.14	0.51%	1,140.58	0.69%	1,301.82	1.04%
Amount to	198,576.89	100.00%	165,225.45	100.00%	124,956.23	100.00%

Unit: ten thousand yuan

Company Profile of the Acquired Party Ekornes ASA
Company Overview

Ekornes is a global furniture manufacturing and sales company, which is a "national treasure" furniture enterprise in Norway, headquartered in Ikornnes. In 1934, the founder, Mr.Jens Ekornes founded the Ekornes brand and began to produce furniture and mattresses. In 1995, the company was listed on the Oslo Stock Exchange. As of the end of 2017, Ekornes had 21 sales companies, 9 factories, and 2,140 employees worldwide. Ekornes Mainly develops and makes furniture and mattresses, and sells its products through direct sales and retailers, including reclining armchairs, sofas, office chairs, home theater seats, fixed back sofas, tables, mattresses, accessories, etc. Its main brands include Stressless, IMG, Svane and Ekornes Contract.

Development Process of the Company
The development history of Ekornes is shown in the following Table 3:

4.3 Review of the Key Points of Merger and Acquisition Cases

Merger and Acquisition Plan

Table 3. Development history of Ekornes ASA.

Time	Major issue
1934	Founder Mr.Jens Ekornes founded Ekornes
1935–1938	Participate in the Alesund furniture exhibition; the first Svane mattress is listed
1947	Start to produce wooden structural parts for sofa beds and bed frames
1959	Start producing mattresses and furniture parts with foam and plastic
1966	Launch of the first living room furniture product range; Ekornes family acquisition of listed company Vik & Blindheim Møbelfabrikk AS
1970	Changing its sales strategy to focus on the Norwegian market has reduced the number of dealers from 1,200 to 200
1971	The first Stressless chair was available in the Norwegian market and brought about the rapid development of the Ekornes
1975	Brand sales revenue of more than NOK 100 million
1977	The company became the largest furniture manufacturer in the Scandinavian region
1980	Stressless Sales exceeded NOK 100 million; the United States became the largest export market
1983	Exports of over 100 million NOK 200
1984	The 50th anniversary of the establishment of the brand, the acquisition of Ulferts AB 75% equity, doubled the production capacity
1995	Shares of the company are listed on the Oslo Stock Exchange
1999	Stressless Won the best lounge chair award at the Birmingham Furniture Show
2003	Group sales revenues exceed NOK 2 billion
2008	Publish a whole new, interactive category of furniture; the founder dies
2010	The Shanghai World Expo
2014	purchase IMG

Transaction Method

On May 23,2018, Qumei furniture, Huatai Zijin and Ekornes ASA signed the Transaction Agreement. Qumei furniture intends to cooperate with Huatai Zijin to make a cash offer to purchase the shares of the underlying company of Ekornes ASA of the Oslo Stock Exchange through its overseas subsidiary Qumei Investment AS. This tender offer is an open voluntary cash tender offer, which intends to acquire at least 55.57% (fully diluted) of the outstanding shares of the target company and at most all the outstanding shares of the target company.

Transaction Target

The underlying assets of this tender offer shall be up to 100% of the shares of Ekornes ASA held by all the shareholders who intend to accept the tender offer.

Trading Structure

After obtaining the required regulatory approval, Qumei Home, Huatai Zijin set up a Norwegian company with European corporate structure as soon as possible. The offeror of this tender offer intends to be Qumei Investment AS. It is a company established and registered under Norwegian law, indirectly owned by Qumei furniture and Huatai Zijin.

Transaction Consideration

The consideration for this tender offer will be paid in cash at a tender offer price of NOK 139.00 per share. Assuming that all shareholders of the target company accept the offer, the transaction price is NOK 5,128,125,500, in accordance with China.

The People's Bank of China authorized the China Foreign Exchange Trade Center to publish it on May 22,2018 (i. e., the day before the board meeting). The central parity rate (the exchange rate is 100 / 126.21) is 406,31.7 million yuan.

Merger and Acquisition Process. Qumei Home and Huatai Zijin set up a Norwegian investment subsidiary QM Investment AS, cash to acquire Ekornes ASA equity. On August 29,2018, Qumei Home completed all the equity delivery. Important times and events in the M&A process are shown in the Table 4 below.

Table 4. M&A process.

Time	Event
On January 30,2018	The transaction was confirmed by the National Development and Reform Commission
On April 25,2018	Issue a major assets restructuring suspension announcement
On May 23,2018	The board of directors deliberated and adopted the "Proposal on the Company's Ekornes ASA and Major Asset Purchase Plan"
On May 24,2018	Publish the valuation report of the project to be acquired, the announcement of the material asset reorganization resolution of the board of directors and the board of Supervisors, and the material asset purchase report (draft)
On June 14,2018	Release of the Major asset purchase Report (revised)
On June 27,2018	The General Office of the National Development and Reform Commission issued the Filing Notice of Overseas Investment Projects (2018) No.423) to record this transaction
On July 6,2018	The Administrative Committee of Shanghai Free Trade Zone promulgated the Enterprise Overseas Investment Certificate (Overseas Investment Certificate No. N3109201800072) to put the transaction on record
On August 29,2018	Completion of the voluntary offer for delivery and settlement
On September 27,2018	Ekornes ASA All 36,892,989 shares were transferred to QM Investment AS, and Ekornes ASA was delisted

LBO Payment Method. This transaction is a cash acquisition, assuming that all shareholders of the target company accept the offer, the transaction price is NOK 5,128,125,500, in accordance with the 2018 published by the China Foreign Exchange Trade Center authorized by the People's Bank of China, the central parity rate of RMB (the exchange rate is 100 RMB to 126.21 NOK on May 22, (i. e. the day before the board meeting), a total of 406,31689 million RMB. Qumei Home holds 90.5% of the equity of the target company, and the consideration to pay for this transaction is about NOK 4,64,0953,600, based on the above exchange rate, is RMB 3,67,7167,900.The fund source of this transaction is the company's own funds, funds raised by non-public offering shares and funds raised by other ways permitted by laws and regulations.

The company's self-raised funds include its own funds, shareholder loans and bank loans, etc. In terms of funds raised by non-public offering of shares, the total amount of funds raised by the proposed non-public offering is not expected to exceed RMB 250,000 million (including RMB 250,000 million), and the net amount of raised funds after deducting issuance and related expenses shall be used to pay cash offers to all shareholders of Ekornes ASA, a listed company on the Oslo Stock Exchange. As shown in the following Fig. 2:

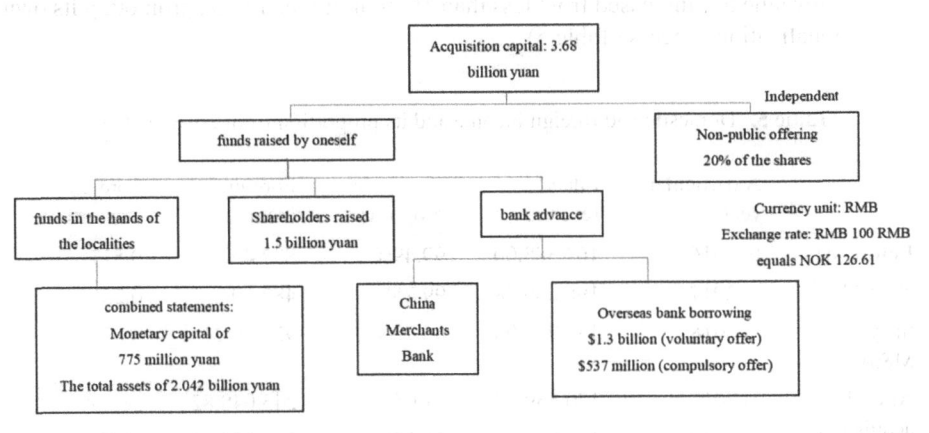

Fig. 2. Schematic diagram of the merger and acquisition payment method.

4.4 Analysis of M&A Motivations

External Influencing Factors

Macro-level Environmental Factors
According to the above analysis of the macro environment of the furniture industry by PEST analysis method, it can be seen that the four major factors of the macro environment reflect the importance of innovation and upgrading and international development. In order to cater to the general trend of macro environment development and consumption upgrading and transformation, Qumei Home has adopted the merger and acquisition decision.

The Current Situation of Mergers and Acquisitions

The fierce market competition in the industry of our country puts forward higher requirements for the comprehensive strength of enterprises. With the deepening of the implementation of China's "going out" strategy, many enterprises often take the form of overseas mergers and acquisitions, with the purpose of being mainly to expand the market, acquire and integrate advanced technology, advanced management experience and other advantageous resources, and at the same time to cater to the mainstream trend of high-end intelligent manufacturing, and enhance the comprehensive strength and core competitiveness of enterprises. Qumei household in the current situation of industry mergers and acquisitions at that time, adopted the merger and acquisition decision.

Internal Influencing Factors

Expand Overseas Markets

Before the implementation of cross-border mergers and acquisitions, its main business is concentrated in the domestic market, high-end market as well. But foreign markets are not involved. With the help of Ekornes's global brand effect and marketing channels, Qumei Home has successfully entered the international market, and the proportion of overseas revenue has increased from less than 1% to more than 50%, promoting its own internationalization process (Table 5).

Table 5. Domestic and foreign income and its proportion from 2016 to 2020

	A particular year	Inland revenue	Domestic proportion	Foreign income	Foreign proportion
Before the acquisition	In 2016	164,388.00	99.49%	837.45	0.51%
	In 2017	198,089.78	99.75%	487.10	0.25%
the year of M&A	In 2018	185,985.05	66.72%	92,796.21	33.28%
After the acquisition	In 2019	170,659.99	41.05%	245,048.82	58.95%
	In 2020	163,896,99	39.28%	253,322.89	60.72%

Unit: ten thousand yuan

Synergy Effect Drive

The synergistic effect drive of Qumei household merger and acquisition is mainly reflected in three aspects: first, the synergistic effect of operation, Qumei Home has enriched its brand portfolio and product portfolio through mergers and acquisitions, And to acquire advanced technical resources, Reduce the comprehensive cost of products and provide product quality; Second, the management of collaborative utility, Qumei furniture absorbs a lot of Internet marketing experience through mergers and acquisitions, Further enhance the online marketing ability of Qumei, Constantly improve the supply chain system, To realize the combination of online and offline collaboration mode, Give full play to the advantages of the global supply chain; Third, the financial synergy and utility, Promote the efficient interaction between the two parties through M & A, Promote resource sharing between the two parties, Improve the production and operation efficiency, Bring more considerable profit inflow.

5 Comprehensive Evaluation of M&A Performance

5.1 Selection of Benchmarking Enterprises

The case of Qumei Home acquiring the Norwegian Ekornes company took place in 2018. This paper selects the first two years of the acquisition event, namely 7 years from 2016 to 2022, as the time period, and vertically analyzes the performance changes of Qumei Home before and after the acquisition in this period. At the same time, to better prove the performance of the analysis range changes mainly caused by the acquisition case, and combined with the horizontal comparison data of Qumei Home acquisition comprehensive evaluation, this paper choose A-Zenith Furniture Co., Ltd. (hereinafter referred to as A-Zenith), Guangzhou Holike Creative Home Co.,Ltd. (hereinafter referred to as Holike), Zhe Jiang Ue Furniture Co.,ltd. (hereinafter referred to as Ue Furniture) as the enterprise comparative analysis, specific choice reason analysis is as follows.

Equivalent Industry Status. Qumei home and Yazhen home, Holaike, Ue Furniture belong to the furniture industry listed companies. The listing time of four companies is close in 2015–2016, meanwhile, in the 7-year period, the market value of four companies is relatively close, as follows. This shows that the market value of the four companies is comparable to the industry position, strong comparability is suitable for horizontal comparative analysis (Tables 6 and 7).

Table 6. Comparison of the listing time of the four major companies.

The name of firm	Time to market
Qu mei home	On April 22, 2015
A-Zenith	On December 15, 2016
Holike	On February 17, 2015
Ue Furniture	On January 23, 2015

Proper Variable Control. After consulting the 2018 annual report of Qumei furniture, it was found that Qumei furniture disclosed the merger of Ekornes ASA company in the column of "merger scope change" in the 2018 annual report as a business merger not under the same control, which belongs to the category of cross-border merger and acquisition. Further, by referring to three to the enterprise in 2016–2020 annual report found that in addition to the disposal of subsidiaries and other reasons of the merger scope changes (such as a new subsidiary, liquidation subsidiary, etc.) two situations, the vibration household in 2016–2020, good guest and yong art shares in 2016–2019 no other merger scope changes, namely no merger, reverse purchase, etc. Therefore, in the

Table 7. Market value comparison of the four major companies in the last trading day from 2016 to 2022.

Time	Qumei home	A-Zenith	Holike	Ue Furniture
2016.12.30	84.48	52.79	97.08	52.14
2017.12.29	70.49	27.96	94.99	35.96
2018.12.28	32.92	22.93	49.07	21.19
2019.12.31	40.85	15.34	50.59	37.15
2020.12.31	49.08	9.14	50.18	40.17
2021.12.31	82.36	13.69	38.16	37.36
2022.12.30	84.48	13.64	35.24	29.49

Unit: 100 million yuan

nearby years of the merger in Qumei Home in 2018, the performance of the three standard enterprises was not affected by the merger. Therefore, taking Yazhen furniture, Holleke and Ue Furniture as the three standard enterprises of Qumei furniture can well control the enterprise merger, the key variable affecting the performance. This also makes the comparative analysis results more reasonable and reliable to prove that the performance change of Qumei Home in the time range is mainly caused by the merger and acquisition case.

5.2 Performance Analysis of Mergers and Acquisitions

Financial Performance Analysis. In this paper, the influence of the financial performance of the financial indicators of the year from 2016 to 2021 and the financial indicators at the end of the third quarter of 2022 for the horizontal comparison. In the aspect of the horizontal comparison, the details are as follows:

Debt Solvency Analysis

In this paper, the current ratio and quick ratio are selected as the evaluation indicators of short-term solvency, the asset-liability ratio and the total profit before interest, tax, depreciation and amortization/liabilities are selected as the evaluation indexes of long-term solvency, and comprehensively analyze the changes of Qumei household solvency before and after the merger and acquisition (Table 8).

Table 8. Comparison table of the financial indicators of the solvency of the four major enterprises.

Current ratio	Qu mei home	A-Zenith	Holike	Ue Furniture
2016.12.31	2.76	5.14	2.15	1.89
2017.12.31	3.01	4.4	3.63	1.65

(continued)

Table 8. (*continued*)

Current ratio	Qu mei home	A-Zenith	Holike	Ue Furniture
2018.12.31	1.54	3.34	2.70	2.09
2019.12.31	0.72	2.81	3.17	1.93
2020.12.31	1.1	3.03	1.36	1.21
2021.12.31	0.92	2.46	1.36	1.14
2022.9.30	1.09	1.95	2.84	1.40
Quick ratio	Qu mei home	A-Zenith	Holike	Ue Furniture
2016.12.31	2.27	3.85	2.02	1.46
2017.12.31	2.55	3.02	3.51	1.10
2018.12.31	0.90	1.8	2.56	1.64
2019.12.31	0.47	1.47	2.94	1.48
2020.12.31	0.67	1.78	0.99	0.78
2021.12.31	0.46	1.16	0.94	0.73
2022.9.30	0.58	0.63	2.40	1.03
Asset-liability ratio	Qu mei home	A-Zenith	Holike	Ue Furniture
2016.12.31	21.98%	16.96%	26.29%	33.15%
2017.12.31	22.49%	17.47%	18.12%	39.18%
2018.12.31	77.73%	18.36%	19.72%	32.64%
2019.12.31	74.83%	21.71%	30.62%	34.51%
2020.12.31	66.04%	20.59%	44.88%	56.16%
2021.12.31	73.52%	29.96%	48.61%	54.75%
2022.9.30	71.13%	32.76%	32.12%	42.38%
Total EBITDA/Total liabilities	Qu mei home	A-Zenith	Holike	Ue Furniture
2016.12.31	0.86	0.69	1.06	0.53
2017.12.31	0.82	0.57	1.05	0.42
2018.12.31	0.08	−0.29	1.03	0.29
2019.12.31	0.11	−0.55	0.62	0.43
2020.12.31	0.13	0.39	0.27	0.33
2021.12.31	0.13	−0.12	0.09	0.18
2022.9.30	0.06	−0.25	0.25	0.21

In terms of short-term solvency, the current ratio and quick ratio of Qumei Home decreased significantly in 2018 in the year of acquisition, and neither of the two indicators recovered to the pre-merger level until 2022; horizontally, the current ratio and quick ratio of Qumei Home were at a higher level compared with the three standard companies. But after the merger and acquisition, both indicators are lagging behind the three standard enterprises. In addition, the two indicators of Hollywood company and Ue Furniture have been in a relatively stable state for a long time, while the two indicators of Qumei furniture have fluctuated and declined significantly after the merger. All this shows that the merger has a certain negative impact on the short-term solvency of Qumei Home, which is also related to the LBO payment method includes current assets such as monetary funds, bank loans and other current liabilities, which reduce current assets and increase current liabilities.

In terms of long-term solvency, the asset-liability ratio of Qumei Home increased significantly in 2018, decreased significantly, and the two indexes did not recover to the pre-merger level until 2022; Horizontally, the asset-liability ratio and combined EPS/liabilities before the merger were at a moderate level compared with the three standard enterprises. But after the merger and acquisition, the asset-liability ratio is obviously greater than the three standard enterprises. In addition, similar to the short-term solvency index, the stability of the asset-liability ratio of Qumei Home in the merger and acquisition year is significantly lower than that of the three standard enterprises. All this shows that the merger has had a certain negative impact on the long-term solvency of Qumei Home, which is also related to the LBO payment method including bank borrowing, shareholder borrowing and other liabilities, which increases the liabilities. But on the other hand, the obvious increase in the asset-liability ratio also shows that all parties are willing to lend money to Qumei Home, which makes its debt increase. This shows that the market position of Qumei household may have a certain promotion. Further, combined with the combined EBIT, TDA/liabilities, due to the COVID-19, the combined EBITDA/liabilities of the three standard companies all declined to a certain extent, and even appeared negative, which shows that the epidemic has hit the profits of the furniture industry hard. In such a time background, although Qumei Home has a huge debt after the acquisition in 2018, its profit before interest, tax, depreciation and amortization/liabilities still remain stable as far as possible, and there is no negative loss phenomenon. This shows that the profitability and comprehensive strength of Qumei furniture have been improved, which is enough to support its high debt and to survive and develop under the impact of the epidemic.

To sum up, through the analysis of the financial indicators of the solvency of the four major enterprises, it can be seen that Qumei furniture has had a certain negative impact on the acquisition of Norwegian Ekornes company's solvency. But at the same time, Qumei household has also played a better leverage role of debt, making its profitability has been enhanced, and enhance its comprehensive strength and market position.

Operation Capacity Analysis

This paper selects accounts receivable turnover, inventory turnover, current assets turnover and total asset turnover as the evaluation indicators of operating capacity, and comprehensively analyzes the changes of operating capacity before and after the acquisition (Table 9).

It can be found from the above financial index data that the receivables turnover of Qumei Household has decreased significantly after the merger, and the inventory

Table 9. Comparison table of the financial indicators of the operating capacity of the four major enterprises

Accounts receivable turnover rate	Qu mei home	A-Zenith	Holike	Ue Furniture
2016.12.31	56.27	19.43	367.33	8.77
2017.12.31	28.13	19.57	319.70	8.99
2018.12.31	11.15	13.71	198.04	8.13
2019.12.31	10.65	16.57	105.08	6.41
2020.12.31	10.88	13.06	23.87	6.44
2021.12.31	12.24	9.38	19.67	7.38
2022.9.30	9.67	6.88	8.35	8.32
Inventory turnover ratio	Qu mei home	A-Zenith	Holike	Ue Furniture
2016.12.31	6.34	1.14	19.59	9.33
2017.12.31	7.02	1.10	22.27	8.10
2018.12.31	4.06	0.77	20.57	8.26
2019.12.31	3.73	0.88	12.85	7.14
2020.12.31	3.20	0.81	3.62	5.22
2021.12.31	3.29	0.76	3.14	5.36
2022.9.30	2.88	0.60	3.37	5.92
Circulating assets turnover rate	Qu mei home	A-Zenith	Holike	Ue Furniture
2016.12.31	1.81	0.94	1.94	2.46
2017.12.31	1.87	0.73	1.50	2.83
2018.12.31	2.09	0.66	1.40	2.53
2019.12.31	2.52	0.81	1.38	2.00
2020.12.31	2.11	0.72	1.06	2.01
2021.12.31	2.28	0.66	1.37	2.26
2022.9.30	2.12	0.62	1.27	2.33
Turnover of total capital	Qu mei home	A-Zenith	Holike	Ue Furniture
2016.12.31	1.02	0.69	1.05	1.61
2017.12.31	1.08	0.55	0.91	1.80
2018.12.31	0.62	0.41	0.79	1.68
2019.12.31	0.57	0.42	0.68	1.34
2020.12.31	0.56	0.38	0.49	1.35
2021.12.31	0.66	0.33	0.63	1.45
2022.9.30	0.66	0.26	0.57	1.36

turnover and total assets turnover have also declined in a certain proportion, but the turnover of current assets is always relatively stable. Generally speaking, the turnover of

Qumei household is in the middle level of the industry; the downward trend of inventory turnover and total asset turnover is similar to that of the three standard companies. The current asset turnover of the four major enterprises is relatively stable, but the turnover of Qumei household decreases greatly.

Based on the above analysis, the merger did not have a significant impact on the overall operating capacity of Qumei Home. However, Qumei Home should pay attention to the change of its accounts receivable turnover rate, and pay attention to improving its utilization efficiency of accounts receivable. At the same time, the overall operating capacity of Qumei home does not occupy an advantage in the industry, Qumei home should pay attention to and enhance the operating capacity, improve the efficiency of the use of major assets, and ultimately improve its position in the industry.

Profitability Analysis

This paper selects the return on assets, return on equity, return on invested capital and operating net interest rate as the evaluation indicators of profitability, and comprehensively analyzes the changes of profitability before and after the acquisition of Qumei Home (Table 10).

Table 10. Comparison of financial indicators of the four major enterprises.

Asset remuneration rate	Qu mei home	A-Zenith	Holike	Ue Furniture
2016.12.31	0.14	0.11	0.21	0.15
2017.12.31	0.15	0.07	0.20	0.12
2018.12.31	0.02	−0.09	0.17	0.07
2019.12.31	0.04	−0.16	0.13	0.12
2020.12.31	0.05	0.03	0.08	0.13
2021.12.31	0.06	−0.08	0.01	0.07
2022.9.30	0.04	−0.08	0.10	0.10
Return on equity	Qu mei home	A-Zenith	Holike	Ue Furniture
2016.12.31	0.14	0.12	0.24	0.20
2017.12.31	0.16	0.07	0.22	0.15
2018.12.31	−0.03	−0.11	0.17	0.11
2019.12.31	0.05	−0.18	0.15	0.15
2020.12.31	0.05	0.02	0.10	0.18
2021.12.31	0.08	−0.11	0.00	0.13
2022.9.30	0.08	−0.12	0.14	0.18

(*continued*)

Table 10. (*continued*)

Capital input rate of return	Qu mei home	A-Zenith	Holike	Ue Furniture
2016.12.31	0.13	0.09	0.22	0.17
2017.12.31	0.15	0.07	0.17	0.17
2018.12.31	0.01	−0.12	0.16	0.08
2019.12.31	0.05	−0.19	0.11	0.14
2020.12.31	0.06	0.02	0.08	0.15
2021.12.31	0.06	−0.09	0.01	0.10
2022.9.30	0.04	−0.10	0.11	0.12
Net operating interest rate	Qu mei home	A-Zenith	Holike	Ue Furniture
2016.12.31	0.11	0.14	0.18	0.09
2017.12.31	0.12	0.11	0.19	0.05
2018.12.31	−0.02	−0.23	0.18	0.04
2019.12.31	0.02	−0.35	0.16	0.08
2020.12.31	0.03	0.04	0.12	0.07
2021.12.31	0.04	−0.25	0.00	0.04
2022.9.30	0.04	−0.44	0.19	0.09

According to the above profitability financial index data, it can be found that in terms of vertical comparison, the four profitability indicators of Qumei Home decreased significantly in the year of 2018, and even the return on equity and net operating interest rate decreased to negative value. However, after the acquisition, the four indicators are gradually increased; in terms of horizontal comparison, the four profitability indicators of Qumei Home are at the middle level of the industry before the acquisition. But after the merger and acquisition, in addition to the loss of Asia zhen home, most of the profitability indicators of Qumei home are significantly lower than the standard enterprises. All these show that the merger has hindered the profitability of Qumei Home in recent years. In addition, the decline in return on equity makes the dividend of shareholders decline, which may reduce shareholders' desire to invest, leading to a decline in the ability to raise funds. Therefore, Qumei household should pay attention to and enhance its profitability, should control the cost while expanding its income, so that the net profit can be increased. In addition, the four low profitability indicators are also related to their operating capacity, that is, the ability to use invested capital. Therefore, Qumei household should improve the improvement of profitability with the enhancement of operating capacity, improve the efficiency of capital utilization, management and control the cost. On the other hand, although the profitability index has decreased significantly after the merger and acquisition, the value has increased slightly year by year, which shows that Qumei Home has a certain development ability, and its profitability will be expected to further grow and gradually recover in the future.

Analysis of Development Ability

This paper selects the growth rate of total assets, sustainable growth rate, growth rate of net assets per share and net profit growth rate as the evaluation indicators of development ability, and comprehensively analyzes the changes of development ability before and after the acquisition (Table 11).

Table 11. Comparison of the development ability of four major enterprises.

Total asset growth rate	Qu mei home	A-Zenith	Holike	Ue Furniture
2016.12.31	0.19	0.69	0.35	0.18
2017.12.31	0.19	0.05	0.60	0.18
2018.12.31	2.46	−0.12	0.14	0.58
2019.12.31	0.06	−0.13	0.29	0.09
2020.12.31	0.00	0.01	0.39	0.68
2021.12.31	−0.01	0.02	0.06	0.01
2022.9.30	−0.03	−0.10	−0.19	−0.07
Sustainable growth rate	Qu mei home	A-Zenith	Holike	Ue Furniture
2016.12.31	0.12	0.07	0.18	0.11
2017.12.31	0.14	0.05	0.13	0.10
2018.12.31	−0.03	−0.11	0.13	−0.03
2019.12.31	0.05	−0.17	0.10	0.05
2020.12.31	0.05	0.00	0.09	0.13
2021.12.31	0.10	−0.10	−0.01	0.09
2022.9.30	0.08	−0.12	0.16	0.20
Net assets per share rate of rise	Qu mei home	A-Zenith	Holike	Ue Furniture
2016.12.31	0.13	0.57	0.20	0.14
2017.12.31	0.18	0.04	0.68	−0.58
2018.12.31	−0.02	−0.13	0.12	0.47
2019.12.31	0.20	−0.31	0.15	0.06
2020.12.31	0.13	0.03	0.10	0.12
2021.12.31	−0.22	−0.10	−0.01	0.04
2022.9.30	−0.01	−0.17	−0.03	0.20

(*continued*)

Table 11. (*continued*)

Net profit growth rate	Qu mei home	A-Zenith	Holike	Ue Furniture
2016.12.31	0.58	0.01	0.55	0.32
2017.12.31	0.33	−0.19	0.38	−0.16
2018.12.31	−1.23	−2.52	0.10	0.05
2019.12.31	2.72	−0.37	−0.07	0.75
2020.12.31	0.23	1.10	−0.24	0.27
2021.12.31	0.60	−6.45	−0.99	−0.23
2022.9.30	−0.19	−0.95	0.39	0.79

As can be seen from the above financial index data of development ability, in terms of vertical comparison, first of all, the total asset growth rate of Qumei Home acquisition in the year increased significantly, which should be caused by the substantial increase of assets after the acquisition. However, in the long run, the growth rate of total assets after Qumei Home acquisition slowed down significantly, which may also be due to the larger asset scale after the merger, resulting in the growth of total assets may be large, but the growth rate is obviously small. Secondly, the sustainable growth rate of Qumei Home decreased to negative in the year of merger and acquisition, but the sustainable growth rate gradually recovered and increased after the merger and acquisition. In addition, the growth rate of net assets per share of Qumei Home decreased to negative in the year of acquisition. Although it recovered positively in 2019, it continued to fall in the future. Finally, the net profit growth rate of Qumei Household decreased significantly in the year of merger and acquisition, and then showed an unstable change for a long time.

In terms of horizontal comparison, the total asset growth rate of Qumei furniture does not occupy an advantage over the three standard enterprises before the merger and acquisition, but the gap gradually increases after the merger and acquisition, and the growth rate is at a low level of the industry. In terms of sustainable growth rate, the sustainable growth rate of Qumei furniture before the acquisition is at a high level in the industry. Although the merger declined to negative in the year, the sustainable growth rate gradually recovered after its adjustment, making the sustainable growth rate still occupy an advantage in the industry. Finally, in terms of the growth rate of net assets per share and net profit growth rate, Qumei household industry status stability is poor, sometimes occupy an advantage, and sometimes at a disadvantage.

From the above analysis, it can be concluded that the sustainable growth rate of Qumei Home is in a high position in the industry, and mergers and acquisitions have not had a significant impact on its sustainable growth rate. However, the merger and acquisition event has a certain negative impact on the growth rate of total assets, net assets per share and net profit of Qumei Home, resulting in a significant decline in the growth rate of total assets, and the stability of the growth rate of net assets per share and net profit. Face these circumstances, qu Mei household should foster strengths and circumvent weaknesses. On the one hand, continue to develop the advantage of sustainable growth rate and keep it in the industry leader; on the other hand, we should integrate and manage the existing total assets, enhance the utilization efficiency of total assets and reasonable and appropriate asset expansion. This combination of the two will jointly promote the stable and sustained growth of the development capacity.

Based on all the above analysis of the financial performance of Qumei Home, it can be concluded that the acquisition of Norwegian Ekornes company has had both a positive impact and a negative impact on its financial performance. Qumei household should give full play to and enlarge the positive impact of mergers and acquisitions, while reducing and solving the negative impact caused by mergers and acquisitions, and promote the comprehensive and comprehensive development of its own financial performance.

Enterprise Value Analysis. As listed companies, the stock market value and investment value of Qumei furniture company and the three major standard enterprises are very important for the comprehensive strength and future development of the enterprise. Therefore, this paper chooses the price-to-book ratio and price-to-sales ratio as the evaluation index of enterprise stock market value and investment value to analyze the value change before and after the merger and acquisition (Table 12).

Table 12. Comparison of the value indicators of the four major enterprises.

Price-to-Sales ratio	Qu mei home	A-Zenith	Holike	Ue Furniture
2016.12.31	5.08	9.39	6.77	3.72
2017.12.31	3.36	4.88	5.10	1.95
2018.12.31	1.14	5.50	2.30	0.88
2019.12.31	0.95	4.12	2.27	1.52
2020.12.31	1.15	2.93	2.30	1.17
2021.12.31	1.62	4.96	1.13	0.80
2022.9.30	0.75	5.76	1.00	0.66
Price-to-Book ratio	Qu mei home	A-Zenith	Holike	Ue Furniture
2016.12.31	6.11	6.22	8.38	8.29
2017.12.31	4.32	3.15	4.61	5.34
2018.12.31	2.03	2.96	2.12	1.79
2019.12.31	2.10	2.38	1.97	2.98
2020.12.31	1.88	1.38	1.76	2.87
2021.12.31	4.07	2.29	1.36	2.56
2022.9.30	1.78	2.63	1.02	1.67

From the above data, it can be found that in terms of vertical comparison, the price-to-sales ratio and price-to-book ratio of Qumei furniture after the merger and acquisition have decreased significantly. However, the price-to-book ratio at the end of 2021 has increased. Combined with the data in the financial performance analysis, this may be caused by the negative growth of Qumei Household's net assets in 2021. In terms of horizontal comparison, the market sales ratio and book ratio before the acquisition are in the middle level of the industry. After the merger, the price-to-sales ratio of Qumei furniture dropped to the low level of the industry, while the price-to-book ratio decreased, but it was still at the middle level of the industry.

Based on the above analysis, it can be seen that the decline of the price-to-price ratio and price-to-sales ratio of TMC furniture may lead to the decline of its stock market value and the undervalued stock price, and thus the increase of its investment value. In addition, from the perspective of the industry level of the two indicators after the merger, the price-to-sales ratio is at a low level, which may indicate that the market value of Qumei Home is undervalued and the investment value is rising, but at the same time, it is necessary to be alert to the risk of low market value. On the other hand, the price-to-book ratio is at a medium level, indicating that the stock market value and investment value of Qumei furniture are relatively balanced, and the risk of the stock price being overvalued or undervalued is small. Therefore, in general, after the acquisition of Qumei furniture, its stock market value and investment value in the industry are still in a relatively medium and balanced position. However, in terms of value, the price-to-book ratio and price-to-book ratio did decrease significantly, so enterprises should be alert to the risk of low stock market value.

6 Research on Brand Management of Ekornes, Norway

6.1 Brand Matrix Analysis After Acquisition

Qumei Home and Ekornes company have strong synergy in market layout, business development, production research and development, supply chain management and other aspects. With the drive of synergistic effect, Qumei Home has adopted the decision of acquiring Ekornes.

From the perspective of brand, Qumei Home acquired Ekornes Company with its brand, and formed a more diversified brand matrix through integrated management, realizing the coordinated development of the brand. Qumei furniture brand, after more than 20 years of steady development, it has now become a leading domestic set of design, production, sales in one of the large-scale, standardized furniture group.

In terms of Ekornes, it founded in 1934, which is the largest furniture manufacturer in Norway and one of the most famous furniture brands in the European market. Ekornes has Stressless, IMG, Svana, Ekornes Contract and other brands. Stressless, IMG, Svana and Ekornes Contract constitute a brand matrix of different regions and different prices. Finally, the new brand matrix of Qumei Home formed by the two is in Fig. 3 as follows:

Among the brands of Ekornes, Stressless was founded in 1971, which is Ekornes's largest product segment. It is also a globally renowned comfort chair brand, known as "the most comfortable chair in the world"; The IMG brand was founded in 2006, Positioned as a "leading the market trend, high cost-effective" comfortable chair products, As a brother brand of Stressless, IMG can provide consumers with high quality, high comfort, high cost-effective comfortable chairs and supporting furniture products at a reasonable price; besides, The Svana brand was founded in 1937, Is a famous Norwegian furniture brand, The main product is mattresses. The brand's products are highly design and functional,

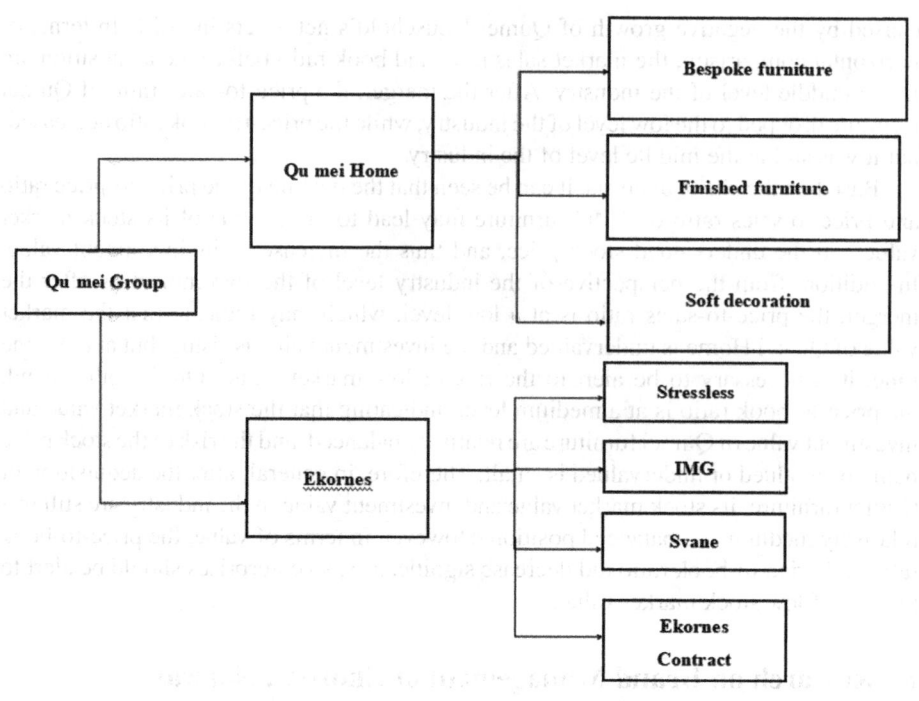

Fig. 3. Qumei furniture brand matrix chart.

the product market is distributed in Norway and other Nordic countries, Central European countries. Finally, Ekornes Contract, founded in 1989, produces lounge chairs with products targeted for maritime, hotel and office furniture markets.

After Qumei acquired Ekornes, these brands provided Qumei with a more diversified brand matrix. Stressless focuses on global high-end furniture brands, IMG's products have moderate prices, which can be used as an effective supplement to Stressless brand in the middle and high-end market. Mattress brand Svana and Ekornes Contract brands for hotels and other channels have realized the differentiated development of the brand. The rich product matrix helps the company to cover more consumer groups and consumer fields, and occupy a broader market space for Qumei.

6.2 Analysis of Brand Mutual Empowerment Brought About by M&A Transactions

Promote the Strategic Upgrading of Enterprises. Through the acquisition of Ekornes, Qumei Home has entered a new stage of development. On the basis of the strategy of "New Qumei", the company proposed "Qumei + Strategy" according to the market situation and the situation of the enterprise, cultivate the existing business of Qumei, build the Chinese market in depth of products, channels and Stressless brand Qumei and Ekornes, upgrade the global market, and explore the new retail mode of IMG brand in Chinese market as an opportunity to innovate development ideas.

"Qumei + Depth"

The addition of Norwegian Ekornes company and its brands makes the brand matrix of Qumei Home more diversified. All of these have put forward new requirements for Qumei's business development. "Qumei + depth" strategy is developed from three aspects: product, channel and operation management, which is through the continuous polishing and refinement of the business model and business process, comprehensively improves the quality of operation management and refinement level.

"Qumei + Width"

Qumei Home takes the opportunity of the acquisition of Ekornes, gives full play to the synergistic effect of Qumei + Ekornes in brand, products, channels, production capacity, supply chain and other links, enables the business of both sides, and further promotes the globalization of Qumei Group business. With the help of the domestic channel resources and market operation experience, the "Qumei + width" strategy optimizes the business model of Stressless China, and takes this as a starting point to promote the strategic upgrading of the global market. At the same time, Qumei will start the exploration of the new retail development model of IMG brand in the Chinese market, and take this opportunity to innovate the development ideas of the global market.

Promote the Internationalization and Development of the Brand. Qumei home acquired the Norwegian Ekornes company, let it form a global business layout. With the help of Ekornes's strong channel resources, supply chain resources, brand resources and production capacity, Qumei opened the international curtain.

Channel Globalization

After the acquisition of Ekornes, Qumei has more than 6,400 retail terminals around the world, successfully realizing the global channel layout. As of December 31,2018, Qumei has 1,036 stores in China, and Ekornes has 5,394 stores worldwide, of which Stressless has 3,271, IMG 171, and Svana 410. By the end of 2020, the total number of dealer stores of Ekornes's three major brands increased from 5,394 in 2018 to 6,942 at the end of 2020, an increase of 28.70%. By June 30,2022, Qumei Home has more than 200 large independent stores nationwide, and Ekornes AS company has more than 7,000 stores and 9 factories in the world.

Globalization of Supply Chains
Relying on the global factory layout, Ekornes has established a complete supply chain system in the world. Ekornes purchases all production raw materials uniformly. Benefiting from the strict SKU quantity control mechanism, focused product strategy and developed global supply chain system, Ekornes has always enjoyed the most advantageous raw material procurement cost in the comfortable chair industry.

Qumei supply chain system has been deeply cultivated in China for many years, and the purchase price of core raw materials such as plate and hardware is leading in the industry. China is a country full of steel, and the production cost of hardware materials is leading in the world. Ekornes purchases a large number of hardware products from China every year. In the future, Qumei will give full play to the advantages of supply chain globalization, and further optimize the procurement cost with the help of the supply chain resources of both sides.

Introduce Strong International Brands
After the acquisition of Ekornes, the company has formed a diversified matrix of Qumei series you + life hall, residence + life hall, B8 whole house customization, everything, Fanxi brand and Ekornes series Stressless, IMG and Svana brand. The current situation of multi-brand and multi-channel parallel development has enhanced the company's ability to attract investment and channel public relations in key markets and problem markets. For the original dealers in Qumei system which obtain the management right of new brand, Stressless and IMG brands are expected to become the effective supplement of Qumei series brands, and enhance the ability of collaboration with single and customer unit price.

7 Research Conclusions and Enlightenment of Capital Operation

7.1 Study Conclusion

This paper studies the performance and brand management of cross-border LBO based in the acquisition of Ekornes of Norway in 2018. First of all, this paper analyzes the capital operation status quo, development trend and M&A situation of the furniture industry from the macro perspective, and reviews and analyzes the causes of M&A events from the micro perspective. Secondly, this paper selects 2016–2022 as the vertical time line, selects three listed companies in the furniture industry as the standard enterprises, and conducts financial analysis and enterprise value analysis of merger and acquisition events in a horizontal and vertical combination. Finally, this paper studies the brand management of Ekornes company in Norway, and analyzes the brand matrix and mutual brand empowerment after the acquisition. Finally, the research conclusions of this paper are as follows:

First, mergers and acquisitions have become the development trend of the residential industry in our country. Mergers and acquisitions may occur for brand integration, transformation and upgrading, technology introduction and so on. In addition, cross-border mergers and acquisitions can also promote enterprises to expand the market and move toward international development. Similarly, this is also the motivation of Qumei household cross-border mergers and acquisitions.

The Impact of Investor Sentiment on Stock Returns

Xinran Fu(✉)

Central University of Finance and Economics, Beijing 102206, China
xinxin040505@163.com

Abstract. This paper constructs investor sentiment index for individual stocks according to the unique characteristic of the Chinese stock market by employing panel data. Based on that, we apply panel regression to this index to investigate the impact of investor sentiment on stock returns in the stock market in China during the period from 2013 to 2022. Empirical evidence demonstrates that the influence of investors' sentiment is significantly positive. Further, we find that firms with small market value (small-cap stocks) tend to be more susceptible to investor sentiment than those with large market value (large-cap stocks). The results also show that there is a distinct difference in the impact of low investor sentiment and high level of investor sentiment on stock returns.

Keywords: Investor Sentiment · Stock Returns · Panel Regression Model

1 Introduction

The efficient market hypothesis [1] is challenged from the behavioral finance perspective by the finding of anomalies in the financial market as the hypothesis does not take into account investors' irrational behavior and heterogeneous in the stock market. The proposed DSSW model [2] explains the vital impact of noise traders on financial asset pricing and why noise traders can earn higher levels of expected returns. It is regarded as the beginning of the later research on investor sentiment. This study focuses on constructing the Chinese investor sentiment index based on the BW index [3] and using panel data to explore the delicate impact of investor sentiment on stock returns in the Chinese stock market.

Previous studies reveal that young and small stocks with high volatility are more sensitive to investor sentiment [3]. The Chinese equity market is mainly made up by small stocks and by retail investors who are often unsophisticated and prone to behavioral biases [4, 5]. In this case, investor sentiment is prone to play a vital part in the Chinese capital market. Therefore, it is of great importance to investigate the indispensable role of investor sentiment in the Chinese market.

Investor sentiment has been widely proved to have a strong power in predicting and determining stock prices. Some authors demonstrates that the overoptimism sentiment can predict post-IPO prices. In the long run, price reversal occurs as powerful investors, for instance, institutional investors, have the opportunity to choose between reselling

13. Huang, X., Wang, J., Lin, L.: Performance evaluation and influencing factors of cross-border mergers and acquisitions of logistics enterprises—take YTO Express M&A Shanda International as an example. Account. Account. Res. (09), 48–55 (2022)
14. Li, X., Tao, J.: Empirical analysis of executive compensation changes and merger and acquisition agency motivation—based on a comparative study on the governance structure of state-owned and private listed companies. China Soft Sci. (5), 122–128 (2011)
15. Li, Q., Tian, C., Tang, J., et al.: Company horizontal merger motivation: efficiency theory or market power theory—Case study from Huiyuan Juice and Coca-Cola. Account. Res. (5), 58–64 (2011)
16. Shefrin, H.: How the disposition effect and momentum impact investment professionals. Soc. Sci. Electron. Publ. **8**, 68–79 (2007)
17. Song, S., Dai, S.J.: Overconfidence, M&A type and M & A performance. Macroecon. Res. (2015)
18. Zhang, F., Wu, N.: Dynamic measurement analysis of China's M & A market—is based on a macroeconomic perspective. J. Guizhou Commer. Coll. **25**(03), 27–33 (2012)
19. Liu, L., He, Y., Yang, J.: Productivity and enterprise merger: analysis based on China's macro level. Econ. Res. (2016)
20. Chen, Z., Li, C., Wei, Z.: Does negative media coverage affect the success or failure of the merger—come from the empirical evidence of the material asset reorganization of listed companies. Nankai Manage. Rev. **20**(01), 96–107 (2017)
21. Liu, C., Han, A., Shen, X.: Acquisition performance evaluation of listed companies based on factor analysis method. Stat. Decis.-Making (2017)
22. Chi, Z., Qiao, T.: Take the acquisition of Qibin Group as an example. Friends Account. (20), 67–72 (2019)
23. Tang, H., Li, Q.: EVA, traditional accounting indicators and stock price performance of listed companies—based on a typical case study of Kweichow Moutai Company. Res. Financ. Dev. (03), 38–43 (2017)
24. Zhang, X., Zhao, L.: Analysis of the marketing strategy of enterprise brand management under the new economic situation. Time-Honored Brand Mark. (2022)
25. Wang, H.: Research on brand integration in overseas mergers and acquisitions of dominant local enterprises in China. Southeast University (2015)
26. Zhao, X.: Performance research in mergers and acquisitions—based on YTO express starm international. China Mark. (2022)

enterprise, so as to achieve the real success of the merger and acquisition. For Qumei furniture, the high cost of merger and acquisition makes it difficult for it to have sufficient funds for effective resource integration in the short term. Therefore, the positive effect of merger and acquisition on the financial performance and value performance of Qumei furniture is not obvious at present. Enterprises should carry out comprehensive resource integration and brand management after merger and acquisition, give full play to the positive role brought by merger and acquisition, and promote the future development of enterprises.

The limitation of this paper is that subject to the limitation of data availability, the article failed to collect the Norwegian Ekornes company profit data in recent years and after mergers and acquisitions of the company's profit in the household profit share data. So the article failed to more fully reflect the Ekornes company in the household international market share, the key role of financial performance. Future studies will collect data as widely as possible to capture more comprehensive analytical samples. In addition, more theories and methods of performance analysis and brand management analysis can be used for analysis, which should be improved later on.

References

1. Zeng, F.: Study on the motivation and performance of cross-border mergers and acquisitions of furniture enterprises. Zhongnan University of Economics and Law (2020)
2. Sun, Y.: Research on the performance of cross-border mergers and acquisitions of listed companies. Anhui University of Finance and Economics (2022)
3. Geng, H.: Study on the influence of monetary policy uncertainty on the difference of overseas merger and acquisition of Chinese enterprises. Southwestern University of Finance and Economics (2021). https://doi.org/10.27412/d.cnki.gxncu.2021.001630
4. Xiao, M., Guo, Y., Zhu, J.: Analysis of the macroeconomic drivers of cross-border M & A in China based on EEMD model. J. Northeastern Univ. (Nat. Sci. Edn.) **43**(04), 599–608 (2022)
5. Wang, K., Gao, T., Hu, F.: Analysis of the motivation and impact of overseas merger by Chinese enterprises—and American enterprises. Asia-Pac. Econ. **230**(01), 93–101 (2022). https://doi.org/10.16407/j.cnki.1000-6052.2022.01.014
6. Zhao, R.: The uses and influence of cross-border mergers and acquisitions of Chinese enterprises. Shangxun **209**(19), 89–90 (2020)
7. Tang, X., Gao, P.: Analysis of the causes and trends of overseas mergers and acquisitions of Chinese manufacturing enterprises from the perspective of global value chain. Econ. Issues Explor. **440**(03), 92–98 (2019)
8. Liao, D., Liu, X.: Research on overseas mergers and acquisitions of Chinese manufacturing enterprises. Friends Account. **554**(02), 44–47 (2017)
9. Wu, T.: Research on the performance of cross-border merger and acquisition of chinese listed enterprises. University of International Business and Economics (2020)
10. Liu, D., Liang, X., Chen, Y.: Research on financial Risk and Prevention of cross-border mergers and acquisitions of listed companies—take SF Holding's acquisition of Kerry Logistics as an example. Account. Commun. (14), 132–136 (2022)
11. Wang, D., Hong, M.: Research on the performance of cross-border mergers and acquisitions of Chinese enterprises—comparative analysis based on ownership. Invest. Res. **41**(06), 127–141 (2022)
12. Dai, J.: Research on cross-border M&A performance of China's automobile industry. Nanjing University of Posts and Telecommunications (2020)

Second, Qumei's acquisition of Ekornes has had both positive and negative impacts on its financial performance. Among them, the negative impact on the solvency and profitability is more obvious. Qumei household should give full play to and enlarge the positive impact of mergers and acquisitions, while reducing and solving the negative impact caused by mergers and acquisitions, and promote the development of its own financial performance.

Third, the acquisition of Ekornes company in Norway has little negative impacts on the company's stock market value and investment value in the industry, and it is still in a relatively medium and balanced position. However, due to the decline of enterprise value index after the acquisition, Qumei Home should be alert to the risk of low stock market value.

Fourth, Qumei home acquisition of Norwegian Ekornes company, enriched the brand matrix of Qumei home. In addition, Qumei Home has played a better role in brand management and brand synergy, so that the brand after the merger to achieve mutual empowerment and development.

7.2 Inspiration of Case Capital Operation

This paper studies the performance and brand management of The Norwegian Ekornes company, and draws the following enlightenment [26].

Expand Financing Channels. The capital sources of the acquisition include its own funds, shareholder loans, bank loans and non-public offering of shares, which has a relatively rich financing channel. Qumei furniture can further broaden the financing channels on this basis, such as issuing bonds, issuing convertible bonds, to enhance their own financing ability. This will help qumei household increase the amount of financing, conducive to expand their own scale thereby. In addition, the rich financing channels can well prevent the financing risk and debt repayment risk caused by the channel fracture caused by a single financing channel.

Innovative Payment Methods. The payment method for Qumei Home cross-border LBO is a cash acquisition, assuming that all shareholders of the target company accept the offer, the transaction price is NOK 5,128,125,500, in accordance with the 2018 published by the China Foreign Exchange Trade Center authorized by the People's Bank of China, the central parity rate of RMB (the exchange rate is 100 RMB to 126.21 NOK on May 22, (i. e. the day before the board meeting), a total of 406,31689 million RMB. Qumei Home holds 90.5% of the equity of the target company, and the consideration to pay for this transaction is about NOK 4,64,0953,600, based on the above exchange rate, is RMB 3,67,7167,900, about RMB 3.677 billion, all of which are paid in cash. Enterprises can innovate merger and acquisition payment methods according to their own operating conditions and financial status. 3, and can adopt various merger and acquisition payment methods to avoid the financial risks that may be caused by a single payment method.

Enhance the Enterprise Integration Ability. After the enterprise decides to adopt the merger and acquisition strategy, the completion of the merger and acquisition does not mean the successful end of the merger. The enterprise should also pay attention to the resource integration after the merger and enhance the integration ability of the

or keeping their shares when their counterparts are overoptimistic [6]. Studies validate the influence of investor sentiment on the US market and find that during low-sentiment periods, market's conditional variance exhibits a positive effect on the expected excess return of stock market. However, when market is being through high-sentiment periods, no influence could be observed [7]. Under a linearity assumption, some authors have examined the predictive content hypothesis of investor sentiment in the German stock market [8]. Their result shows that investor sentiment affects stock returns through a specific feedback process, but the predictive ability varies in different market situations. Based on that, scholars further find that within a nonlinear framework, investor sentiment also embodies a significant power in predicting stock returns [9]. In the global context, investor sentiment also has the ability to predict the trading volume and market returns, although different studies have different conclusions on the direction of the impact [10, 11]. Besides, investor sentiment can correct the mispricing it caused in the short run. There are several reasons for the mispricing lead by investor sentiment. Specifically, the limits-to-arbitrage biases investor sentiment towards overvaluation [12, 13], and unexpected demand could deviate the mood of investors to an abnormal level [14].

Based on that, many papers have attempted to study the cross-section effects investor sentiment has on different classes of stocks. For example, many studies show that investor sentiment exhibits a stronger influence on stocks with low market value [3, 15]. In addition, the reverse effect investor sentiment has towards the expected return of non-profit stocks or high-fluctuation-level stocks is more significant than others [3]. There is also evidence that some specific stock's return can be attributed to investor sentiment, for instance, non-profit stocks, stocks in distress, stocks with no dividend paying, and stocks with extreme growth [16]. Nevertheless, most of the leap in volatility attributes to the younger age of firms, rather than the firm's profitability, size, or the amount of tangible assets possessed by it, as none of them shows signs of unusual volatility [17]. Study focus on the impact of stock returns on retail trading patterns indicates that retail investors' mood and expectations have a remarkable influence on stock prices that are not highly held by institutions [18]. In terms of national culture worldwide, investor sentiment is varied to have a greater impact on monthly stock returns in countries with more herding behavior, overreaction and less efficient integrity or less regulators [19]. On the macro level, stock returns is proved to have a more intense reaction towards monetary news than other type of macro policy news [20].

Many scholars further conclude that the interrelation between investor sentiment and the returns of stocks depends on time, which means that the effects in short period and long period are different. Studies indicate that the influence is positive in short period but shows a negative pattern in long period [21, 22]. It is also empirically confirmed that short-term investment strategy is more profitable than long-term investment in the period of high investor sentiment, while long-term investment strategy seems to have no significant relationship with investor sentiment [13]. Through the study of American stock market, investor sentiment is not only correlated with stock market returns, but can also increase stock returns under extreme market conditions [23]. In terms of the overall market, some authors construct a daily investor sentiment indicator through high-frequency data to represent investor sentiment in the American stock market. The research results indicate that overall market returns is highly correlated with investor sentiment [24]. Furthermore, time-series empirical results support that during periods of high investor sentiment, individual equity returns can move more synchronized with the overall market [25].

There have been some studies based on panel data to investigate how investors' mood exhibits influence on stock returns worldwide [14, 26, 27]. Nevertheless, as one of the emerging economies, literature with regard to China is relatively rare. Among previous studies on the capital market in China, investor sentiment volatility exerts a stronger impact on the returns of particular types of stocks. For example, low market value stocks, low-profit stocks and penny stocks [28]. In line with the situation worldwide, there is also an asymmetrical and reversed nonlinear effect of investor sentiment in China [22]. Meanwhile, optimistic environment greatly contributes to excess stock returns [29]. However, most of the studies with regard to the Chinese stock market are based on the variable autoregressive model (VAR), and are mainly about the impact of overall investor sentiment and the whole market's returns. Only a few papers use panel data of each listed stock to verify the influence of investor sentiment on stock returns. In this study, we progressively construct an investor sentiment index for the Chinese stock market by applying the data of each company to study the intricate cross-section influence investor sentiment makes on equity returns in China in the hope of plug the lacuna in the literature.

The meaningful contributions this paper makes are summarized as follows. Firstly, this study employs and innovatively modifies the method of Baker and Wurgler [3] according to the unique characteristics of Chinese capital market and investors to structure a composite sentiment index for China. Such construction of investor sentiment effect on Chinese individual stocks is quite rare. The principal components we select to construct investor sentiment are through delicate consideration, and the regression results demonstrate that this index can well reflect the mood and expectations of traders in the stock market in China. Secondly, after confirming the causality of investor sentiment and stock earnings, this study further explores how investor sentiment affects stocks with disparate market values, as well as the distinct impact of different levels of investors' sentiment on equity returns. This provides new evidence for the cross-section effect that investor sentiment has on different classes of stocks.

The reminder structure of this paper is arranged as follows. We elaborate the model and data set we apply in this article in Sect. 2. We present the empirical results of our study in Sect. 3. Finally, we make a conclusion in Sect. 4.

2 Data and Empirical Model

2.1 Data

Our sample contains all listed stocks in the Chinese stock market with a span of 10 years from 2013 to 2022. The data we collect is available from the Wind and CSMAR database, and all of the data is yearly based.

Drawing on the previous literature and the principle of index selection, we derive our sentiment index for individual stocks by employing five principal components. Specifically, we use trading volume, turnover rate, price earnings ratio, new investor accounts, and consumer confidence index as indicators. Considering that the Chinese stock market adopts the approval system to issue shares, there tends to be a delay in public access to the company's application materials. Therefore, variables related with IPO are excluded in this paper.

Trading volume refers to the number of transactions made in a unit of time, and it is the best indicator of market activity [3]. A large trading volume indicates that there are a huge amount of investors, which leads to an active trading in the market and a relatively high level of investors' mood. In this article, we use the logarithm of trading volume so as to get a better series.

Turnover rate is based on the ratio of trading volume to total shares. It represents the frequency at which stocks exchange in the market. As a measurement of liquidity [30], turnover can serve as an index of sentiment: Irrational traders can increase liquidity only when they hold a positive attitude (optimistic) in a market with short-selling restrictions [31].

Price earning ratio is based on share price to average earnings per share, it can not only reflect investors' subjective judgement of future stock returns, but also provide visions for investors' decisions through the analysis of corporate profitability. Meanwhile, it represents the correlation between present stock price and the profit prospect of a company. Generally, the higher the P/E ratio is, the more willing investors are to buy the company's shares.

The bull markets are usually accompanied by simultaneous expansion of market participants, which can be described by number of new investor accounts. This indicator shows how attractive the market is to the investors. Many scholars apply this indicator to construct investor sentiment index in China [32, 33]. This is confirmed by the drastic fluctuation of stock market in China in 2015, with a huge amount of investors piling into the stock market and Shanghai Securities Composite Index soaring over 100% within six months synchronously.

The investor confidence index is compiled by the China Insurance Fund Corporation (CIFC) and ranges from 0 to 100. Its validity and applicability has been validated by a sufficient series of studies [34, 35]. The higher the exponent is, the more confidence investors are towards the capital market. The exponent goes over 50 means a relatively positive attitude, while under 50 means a pessimistic sentiment.

The stock price in the market and the expectations of investors are dependent on some macroeconomic conditions, for instance, the regime of the capital market, and these variables should be included in the model [36]. Therefore, in order to ensure the rigor of article, we choose consumer price index (CPI), money supply (calculated in million), and growth in industrial added value as control variables (Tables 1 and 2).

2.2 Empirical Model

Principal components analysis is first applied to construct the Chinese investor sentiment index. The final linear synthetic evaluation function is as follows:

$$SENT = G_1 Y_1 + G_2 Y_2 + \ldots + G_i Y_i \tag{1}$$

where $i = 1, \ldots N$, N indicates the number of principal components selected. SENT refers to the investor sentiment index in China. Y means selected principal component G_i represents the contribution rate of the ith predominant indicator.

Table 1. Descriptive statistics for underlying variables.

Variable	Mean	Std	Min	Max
R	0.126	0.567	−0.924	15.212
SENT	−14.023	0.805	−47.55	26.034
M2	1.890	0.483	1.110	2.660
GAV	6.681	2.081	2.900	9.700
CPI	103.232	4.715	100.901	119.932

Table 2. Correlation matrix for variables.

	R	SENT	M2	GAV	CPI
R	1				
SENT	0.446***	1			
M2	−0.191***	−0.195***	1		
GAV	0.086***	0.122***	−0.224***	1	
CPI	0.075***	0.077***	−0.469***	0.358***	1

In order to investigate how investor sentiment affects stock returns, we use panel data to analyze the linear panel fixed effect regression model. This method allows us to have a deeper insight into the heterogeneity of impact investor sentiment has on stock returns, which can be attributed to different corporate characteristics.

The regression model we employ is as follows:

$$R_{i,t} = c_i + \beta_1 SENT_t + \beta_2 ME_{i,t} + \gamma \varphi_t + \varepsilon_{i,t} \quad (2)$$

where i = 1, … N, N indicates the firms number. t = 1, …, T, T is the time number. $R_{i,t}$ denotes the return on company i's stock at period t. ME refers to market value. As for the control variables, we adapt the macroeconomic variables. To be specific, the consumer price index (CPI), growth in industrial added value (GAV) and money supply (M2). They are integrated and represented in φ_t. The parameter c_i takes in to account firms specific fixed effect. $\varepsilon_{i,t}$ is disturbance terms.

3 Empirical Results

In this section, we first construct a Chinese investor sentiment index and confirm its applicability to the stock market. Subsequently, we exploit this exponent to explore how investors' sentiment affect overall stock returns in detail. Furthermore, we categorize the data to explore how different levels of investor sentiment influence firms with distinct characteristics.

3.1 Construction of Investor Sentiment Index

The result from Table 3 shows that the spherical statistic is significant at the level of 1%. The KMO value is 0.652, which is in the interval suitable for principal component analysis (Table 4).

Table 3. KMO and Bartlett's test.

Kaiser-Meyer-Olkin Measure of Sampling Adequacy		0.652
Bartlett's test of Sphericity	Approx. Chi-Square	314.71
	df	15
	Sig.	0

Table 4. Total Variance explained.

Factor	Initial Eigenvalues		
	Total	% of Variance	Cumulative %
1	2.09551	40.298	40.298
2	1.50192	28.883	69.181
3	0.926434	17.816	86.997
4	0.676137	13.003	100

During the factor construction process, we extract two principal components in this paper according to the statistical criteria with the total of eigenvalues > 1. According to the variance contribution rate of each principal component factor divided by the cumulative contribution rate, the respective weights are obtained as follows:

$$G1 = 40.298 \div 69.191 = 0.583 \tag{3}$$

$$G2 = 28.883 \div 69.191 = 0.417 \tag{4}$$

Subsequently, we obtain the expression of investor sentiment index (SENT) on the basis of the calculation:

$$SENT = 0.583F_1 + 0.417F_2 \tag{5}$$

3.2 Panel Regression on the Impact of Investor Sentiment on Stock Returns

After the construction of investor sentiment of individual stocks, here we first conduct a fundamental panel regression on the investors' sentiment and equity returns in China. It is clear from Table 5 that there is a strong correlation between selected variables, and

Table 5. Panel Regression Results on investor sentiment and stock returns.

	R
SENT	0.378***
	(−85.04)
M2	0.542***
	(−5.52)
GAV	0.006***
	(−3.42)
CPI	0.003***
	(−3.84)
_cons	−0.266***
	(−3.18)
N	8549
r^2_a	0.114
F	1944.1

t statistics in parentheses. * $p < 0.1$, ** $p < 0.05$, *** $p < 0.01$.

the effect of investor sentiment is significantly positive. This result strongly supports the findings of previous studies [3, 14, 19].

Following that, we deepen our study by investigating how investor sentiment influence firms with distinct characteristics. To be specific, we use market value to categorize firms of different sizes and divide all firms into two groups. The large market value group is made up by the first 50% of stocks with higher market value, while the small market value group is composed of the last 50% of stocks with relatively lower market value. In Table 6, we find that small-cap (small market value) stocks tend to be influenced more by investor sentiment than large-cap (large market value) stocks. We deem that this is because stocks with large market value are more mature, so that they are less likely to be susceptible to the reasonless behaviors of noisy traders, as they are large in size and more capital is needed to make a change on the stock returns even though the investor sentiment is particularly high or low. This result is highly in line with the actual situation in the Chinese capital market considering that retail investors dominate the majority of the market [4, 5]. Such type of investors usually has limited amount of money available for investment to decide the trend of stocks in large size.

Meanwhile, we study the impact of different degree of investor sentiment to stock returns. We divide investor sentiment into two groups, known as low and high investor sentiment categories, representing whether investors are optimistic or negative about the stocks respectively. The grouping method is the same as mentioned before. It can be seen that the influence of low investor sentiment on stock returns differs from that of high sentiment. Investor sentiment tends to exhibit a more significant influence on stock returns when it is rather low. This is because negative emotions could lead to widespread panic among investors, thus affecting their decision-making to a greater extent.

Table 6. Panel Regression Results on groups divided by market value and sentiment level.

	(1)Large market value	(2)Small market value	(3)Low investor sentiment	(4)High investor sentiment
	R	R	R	R
SENT	0.320***	0.422***	0.102***	0.231***
	(−68.77)	(−54.73)	(35.60)	(16.05)
M2	0.005***	0.009***	0.007***	0.001
	(−4.53)	(−5.29)	(9.94)	(0.44)
GAV	0.0195***	−0.011***	0.001	−0.010***
	(−11.38)	(−3.96)	(0.89)	(−3.19)
CPI	0.005***	0.012***	0.005***	−0.002
	(−6.67)	(−8.28)	(3.67)	(−1.24)
_cons	−0.677***	−1.011***	−0.813***	0.678***
	(−7.89)	(−6.52)	(−5.98)	(4.33)
N	13986	14563	9275	10867
r2_a	0.149	0.007	−0.333	−0.388
F	1376.4	795.6	350.6	112.6

t statistics in parentheses. * $p < 0.1$, ** $p < 0.05$, *** $p < 0.01$.

4 Conclusion

There are only few empirical studies with regard to the panel regression on the impact of investor sentiment on stock returns in the stock market of China. This paper further demonstrates the cross-sectional effect of investors' sentiment on different classes of stocks in China. In the hope of investigating a more complex correlativity between the emotion of investors and stock returns, we employ panel regression models with yearly data from 2013 to 2022.

Specifically, we conduct a Chinese investor sentiment index for individual firms using five principal components based on panel data. It proves to be effective in reflecting the emotion of Chinese investors towards the stock market and has a strong power in explaining their behavior. We apply panel regression to this index to investigate how do investors' emotions and stock returns correlate with each other in the Chinese stock market. Meanwhile, in consideration of the effect of macro factors, we use macro variables as controlled variables to obtain a more accurate result. Our empirical result shows that the impact of investor sentiment on equity returns is significantly positive, providing new panel evidence from China to plug the lacuna in the literature.

Based on that, we investigate how different levels of investor sentiment influence firms with distinct characteristics by dividing the samples by market capitalization (market value) and the level of investor sentiment respectively. We find that small-cap stocks tend to be influenced more by investor sentiment than large-cap stocks. One possible explanation for this phenomenon is that large capitalization stocks are prone to be impervious to noisy traders' reasonless behaviors, and more capital is needed to form a trend for the stocks. Besides, our results reveal that the influence of low investor sentiment is different from that of high level of investor sentiment. It tends to have a more significant impact on stock earnings when it is low (negative) rather than high (positive). The explanation for this is that investors' negative expectations towards stock price are prone to lead to a widespread panic among investors, which could further implement a greater influence on their investment decisions.

We consider that the Chinese stock market is worth-studying as it has an unique financial environment and market supervision system and needs more academic attention. This paper expounds the delicate influence of investors' emotions on the returns of equity, and reveals the indispensable role of investor sentiment in the stock market in China. This study can also lay a foundation for future research on the worth-studying correlation between investor sentiment and stock returns.

References

1. Fama, E.F.: Efficient capital markets: a review of theory and empirical work. J. Financ. **25**(2), 383–417 (1970)
2. De Long, J., Shleifer, A., Summers, L., Waldmann, R.: Noise trader risk in financial markets. J. Polit. Econ. **98**(4), 703 (1990)
3. Baker, M., Wurgler, J.: Investor sentiment and the cross-section of stock returns. J. Financ. **61**(4), 1645–1680 (2006)
4. Lee, D.W., Liu, M.H.: Does more information in stock price lead to greater or smaller idiosyncratic return volatility? J. Bank. Financ. **35**(6), 1563–1580 (2011)
5. Li, X., Shen, D., Zhang, W.: Do Chinese internet stock message boards convey firm-specific information? Pac. Basin Financ. J. **49**, 1–14 (2018)
6. Cornelli, F., Goldreich, D., Ljungqvist, A.: Investor sentiment and pre-IPO markets. J. Financ. **61**(3), 1187–1216 (2006)
7. Yu, J., Yuan, Y.: Investor sentiment and the mean–variance relation. J. Financ. Econ. **100**(2), 367–381 (2011)
8. Lux, T.: Sentiment dynamics and stock returns: the case of the German stock market. Empirical Econ. **41**(3), 663–679 (2011)
9. Theologos, D.: Do investors' sentiment dynamics affect stock returns? Evidence from the US economy. Econ. Lett. **116**, 404–407 (2012)
10. Chiah, M., Hu, X.L., Zhong, A.: Photo sentiment and stock returns around the world. Financ. Res. Lett. **46**, 102417 (2022)
11. Wang, W.Z., Su, C., Duxbury, D.: Investor sentiment and stock returns: global evidence. J. Empir. Financ. **63**, 365–391 (2021)
12. Shleifer, A., Vishny, R.W.: The limits of arbitrage. J. Financ. **52**, 35–55 (1997)
13. Stambaugh, R., Yu, J., Yuan, Y.: The short of it: investor sentiment and anomalies. J. Financ. Econ. **104**(2), 288–302 (2012)
14. Brown, G.W., Cliff, M.T.: Investor sentiment and asset valuation. J. Bus. **78**(2), 405–440 (2005)
15. Yang H., Ryu D.: Investor sentiment, asset returns and firm characteristics: evidence from the Korean stock market. Invest. Anal. J. **46**(2), 1–16 (2017)
16. Zhou, G.: Measuring investor sentiment. Annu. Rev. Financ. Econ. **10**, 239–259 (2018)
17. Fink, J., Fink, K.E., Grullon, G., Weston, J.P.: What drove the increase in idiosyncratic volatility during the internet boom? J. Financ. Quant. Anal. **45**(5), 1253–1278 (2010)
18. Kumar, A., Lee, C.: Retail investor sentiment and return comovements. J. Financ. **61**(5), 2451–2486 (2006)

19. Schmeling, M.: Investor sentiment and stock returns: some international evidence. J. Empir. Financ. **16**(3), 394–408 (2009)
20. Kurov, A.: Investor sentiment and the stock market's reaction to monetary policy. J. Bank. Financ. **34**(1), 139–149 (2010)
21. Berger, D., Turtle, H.: Cross-sectional performance and investor sentiment in a multiple risk factor model. J. Bank. Financ. **36**(4), 1107–1121 (2015)
22. Ni, Z.X., Wang, D.Z., Xue, W.J.: Investor sentiment and its nonlinear effect on stock returns—new evidence from the Chinese stock market based on panel quantile regression model. Econ. Model. **50**(4), 266–274 (2015)
23. Li, H., Yu, G., Park, S.Y.: Asymmetric relationship between investor's sentiment and stock returns: Evidence from a quantile non-causality. Int. Rev. Financ. **17**(4), 617–626 (2017)
24. Sun, L., Najand, M., Shen, J.: Stock return predictability and investor sentiment: a high-frequency perspective. J. Bank. Financ. **73**, 147–164 (2016)
25. Morck, R., Yeung, B., Yu, W.: The information content of stock markets: why do emerging markets have synchronous price movements? J. Econ. Financ. **58**, 215–260 (2000)
26. Eyden, V.R., Gupta, R., Nielsen, J., Bouri, E.: Investor sentiment and multi-scale positive and negative stock market bubbles in a panel of G7 countries. J. Behav. Exp. Financ. **38**, 100804 (2023)
27. Plakandaras, V., Tiwari, A.K., Gupta, R., Ji, Q.: Spillover of sentiment in the European union: evidence from time-and frequency-domains. Int. Rev. Econ. Financ. **68**, 105–130 (2020)
28. Huang, D.L., Wen, F.H., Yang, X.G.: Investor sentiment indices and empirical evidence in Chinese stock market. Syst. Sci. Math. **1**, 1–13 (2009)
29. Jiang, Y.M., Wang, Z.M.: The relationship of investor sentiment and stock returns. Nankai Bus. Rev. **3**, 150–160 (2010)
30. Baker, M., Stein, J.: Market liquidity as a sentiment indicator. J. Financ. Markets **7**, 271–299 (2004)
31. Boubaker, S., Chourou, L., Saadi, S.: Does institutional investor horizon influence US corporate financing decisions. Int. Rev. Financ. Anal. **63**, 382–394 (2019)
32. Chen, H., Chong, T.T.L., She, Y.: A principal component approach to measuring investor sentiment in China. Quant. Financ. **14**, 573–579 (2014)
33. Han, X., Li, Y.: Can investor sentiment be a momentum time-series predictor? Evidence from China. J. Empir. Financ. **42**, 212–239 (2017)
34. Fisher, K.L., Statman, M.: Consumer confidence and stock returns. J. Portf. Manag. **30**(1), 115–127 (2003)
35. Song, Z., Gong, X., Zhang, C., Yu, C.: Investor sentiment based on scaled PCA method: a powerful predictor of realized volatility in the Chinese stock market. Int. Rev. Econ. Financ. **83**, 528–545 (2023)
36. Sotomayor, L.R., Cadenillas, A.: Explicit solutions of consumption-investment problems in financial markets with regime switching. Math Financ. **19**(2), 251–279 (2009)

9789819705221VOL02